WRITE NOW

Daniel Anderson

Prentice Hall

Boston   Columbus   Indianapolis   New York   San Francisco   Upper Saddle River
Amsterdam   Cape Town   Dubai   London   Madrid   Milan   Munich   Paris   Montreal   Toronto
Delhi   Mexico City   Sao Paulo   Sydney   Hong Kong   Seoul   Singapore   Taipei   Tokyo

Senior Editor: Brad Potthoff
Editorial Assistant: Nancy C. Lee
Senior Development Editor: Michael Greer
Senior Supplements Editor: Donna Campion
Senior Marketing Manager: Sandra McGuire
Senior Media Producer: Stefanie Liebman
Project Manager: Barbara Mack
Project Coordination, Text Design, and Electronic Page Makeup: PreMedia Global

Operations Specialist: Mary Ann Gloriande
Art Director, Cover: Pat Smythe
Cover Designer: Rachael Cronin
Cover Photos: (left) ©Randy Faris/Corbis; (top right) ©Anderson Ross/Blend Images/Corbis; (bottom right) ©Laura Doss/Corbis
Printer and Binder: Quad Graphics, Taunton
Cover Printer: Lehigh-Phoenix/Hagerstown

For permission to use copyrighted material, grateful acknowledgment is made to the copyright holders on pages 527–530, which are hereby made part of this copyright page.

Library of Congress Cataloging-in-Publication Data

Anderson, Daniel (Daniel Randolph)
  Write now / Daniel Anderson. —1st ed.
    p. cm.
  Includes index.
  ISBN 978-0-13-241547-7 (alk. paper)
  1. English language—Rhetoric.   2. Report writing.   I. Title.
  PE1408.A588 2011
  808'.042--dc22

                            2010050128

1 2 3 4 5 6 7 8 9 10—QGT—14 13 12 11

Prentice Hall
is an imprint of

www.pearsonhighered.com

ISBN-13: 978-0-13-241547-7
ISBN-10:   0-13-241547-X

Contents

iii

Note: Chapters E1 through E9 are additional chapters included in the Pearson eText. Log in to MyCompLab and click on "View eText" on your course home page to access these chapters and accompanying media resources.

PART 3   Research Strategies

PART 5 Visual and Design Strategies

Preface

If there's one thing I've discovered in my twenty-plus years of teaching, it's that learning requires motivation. It's possible to create some of that desire through the usual channels—grades, degrees, or the need to get a job. But it's also possible to spark an interest in learning that goes beyond these external rewards. When learning is driven by curiosity, by an eagerness to craft something meaningful, by a sense of enjoyment in the work, something special happens. The difficulty for teachers is creating environments where that kind of interest-driven learning can take place. *Write Now* is meant to provide one tool to help meet that challenge.

When it comes to writing, the most direct route to making learning more engaging is to provide authentic composing tasks. The less artificial a task, the more likely it is to prompt genuine interest and effort on the part of writers. To this end, *Write Now* is built around the model of flexible genres. The book and eText together include detailed coverage of eighteen genres ranging from personal forms like memoirs to academic staples like position arguments to less familiar compositions like photo essays.

To accommodate the project-based model, the book provides a framework that includes proven elements like rhetorical situations, writing strategies, critical thinking, research skills, and so on. But the framework extends these approaches by providing a flexible method of understanding what it means to read and write. The instruction in *Write Now* focuses on the idea of cultural networks and the process of zooming. The concept of a cultural network provides a contemporary context for writing projects. Any text exists within a network of people, ideas, and things. By exploring the relationships among these elements, readers and writers can make sense of and produce a wide range of texts.

To help students understand such networks, *Write Now* uses the concept of zooming. Zooming can be seen as a visual metaphor for critical thinking. We can zoom in to focus on elements of culture—looking at a person or analyzing a paragraph or sentence. And we can zoom out to examine the bigger picture—connecting a person to an idea or looking at the overall shape of an essay. In practice, zooming entails a continual shifting between focusing on details and connecting those details to larger concerns. By building zooming into the structure of the book, *Write Now* promotes this flexible way of thinking critically as part of the process of reading and writing.

Write Now provides fundamental knowledge of concepts like rhetorical situations and practice with skills like research. It gives detailed advice on how to read and write a range of genres. And it extends this framework by helping students ask questions and make decisions as they zoom in and out to consider elements of culture. To move fluidly in a world where people, ideas, and texts shape one another is a challenge. But a challenge is what makes learning interesting and engaging. I hope this book will help.

How This Book Is Organized

Write Now recognizes that students today often need to compose in forms that extend beyond the printed essay, but that they also need solid instruction in the fundamentals of rhetoric and the composing process. Combining a compact printed text with an innovative Pearson eText that includes the printed text plus additional project chapters and extensive media support, the *Write Now* package offers a flexible and engaging learning experience covering a broad range of writing projects, from academic research and argument to photo essays and multimedia presentations.

To take advantage of the video and other online resources, instructors may adopt the book packaged with access to the Pearson eText, or may opt for paperless delivery by adopting only the eText. Instructors who prefer not to use the media have the option of adopting the printed book alone.

- **Nine project-based chapters** in Part 2 provide the core writing forms and assignments of the text. **An additional nine project-based chapters in the Pearson e-Text** include media-based forms like audiovisual presentations, podcasts, and digital videos as well as traditional forms like business letters and timed essay examinations.
- **Seven concise strategy chapters** in Part 4 provide practical support for all facets of organizing and designing compositions in both print and media environments.
- **Core concerns of rhetoric and the composing process** are presented in Part 1, which provides the key terms, concepts, and strategies that students will use in their writing projects.
- **Research and documentation** are covered in the four chapters of Part 3, which include sample student research papers in the MLA and APA styles.
- **Visual rhetoric and document design** are the focus of Part 5, which includes numerous visuals and samples for discussion and analysis.

The Pedagogy and Apparatus of the Book

- **Learning Objectives**: Each chapter in the book begins with a feature, **Zoom In: Key Concepts and Learning Objectives**. Here, you will find learning objectives that reflect the content appearing in that chapter. Instructions at the end of every chapter suggest related supporting resources and assessment activities in MyCompLab. Discussions in the text that focus on specific learning objectives are identified by numbered icons in the margins so these discussions can be easily located.

- **Zoom In** and **Zoom Out** features offer a unique visual metaphor for the critical thinking process. "Zooming in" and "zooming out" discussions in each chapter help students recognize the importance of focus, perspective, and context. Zooming in to focus on details in a particular reading teaches students to attend to texts carefully and to pay attention to how they are constructed. Zooming out broadens their view to help them see how texts relate to larger cultural contexts, historical moments, and to other texts.

- **Examples first!** The structure and style of *Write Now* are built upon the assumption that students learn best when they are given concrete, specific examples *first*. Concepts are introduced and built "from the ground up," developed through scenarios and case studies, in a friendly, accessible style. The "rhetorical situation," for example, is introduced through a series of short readings about commerce and sustainability.

- **Know It, Plan It, Compose It, Revise It, Push It:** A consistent pedagogical sequence is built into every major project-based chapter. Built around professional and student samples, each core chapter provides students with a workable set of strategies and tools they can apply to their own writing, culminating in an option for extension into additional genres and mediums.

- **Student examples** for each major assignment demonstrate effective composition and creative possibilities.

- **Forty professional readings** in the text and **another eighteen** in the *Write Now* eText are chosen for student appeal and to demonstrate rhetorical principles at work. Readings include both popular and academic sources, ranging from magazine and newspaper essays to journal articles. Many are visual or include visual arguments or other illustrations. A number of the readings are concise and can be covered in-depth in a single class session.

Online Resources

Comprehensive Online Media for *Write Now* help students understand key concepts of rhetoric and composition and provide practical advice for composing in traditional and new modes.

WN

- **The *Write Now Pearson eText*** includes all of the printed text and nine additional assignment chapters, videos, extra readings and student examples as well as scholarly and practical information from authoritative online sources to create flexibility for an exceptionally robust, personalized writing course.
- **Instructional videos:** Accessed by way of marginal icons and links in the eText, nearly sixty brief (two- to three-minute) video mini-lessons present key topics and strategies in a highly engaging audiovisual style that captures student interest and helps reinforce key lessons in the text. These include videos and screencasts of several types:
    - **Animations:** Abstract concepts like rhetorical situations and cultural networks are presented in a series of clever visual animations that bring line drawings in the book to life, with audio narrations that extend and expand on the discussions in the text.
    - **Concept videos** explore the major ideas of rhetoric and composition, including topics like ethos, point of view, logical fallacies, and argumentation; complementing or foreshadowing instructor lectures, they are ideal for both traditional and online courses.
    - **How-to videos** teach practical aspects of creating both traditional and multimedia compositions, covering topics ranging from drafting to revising to making decisions about intellectual property to creating audio essays, saving time for instructors and students.
    - **Student-to-student videos:** A special series of videos produced and developed by the author with a team of undergraduate writing students offers a unique angle on student concerns like finding a topic, considering alternative perspectives, and peer review, in students' own voices.
- **Thirty resource links** connect to additional readings, audio and video materials, multimedia compositions, scholarly sites for further reading, and practical "how-to" resources for effective composition. Additional student sample papers supplement the samples in the book and provide a wider range of models for students to use in their writing and composing.

Additional Resources

MyCompLab is an eminently flexible application that empowers student writers and teachers by integrating a composing space and assessment tools with multimedia tutorials, services (such as online tutoring), and exercises for writing, grammar, and research. Students can use MyCompLab on their own, benefiting from self-paced diagnostics and a personal study plan that recommends the instruction and practice each student needs to improve his or her writing skills. Teachers can recommend it to students for self-study, use it to track student progress, or leverage the power of administrative features to be more effective and save time. The assignment builder and commenting tools, developed specifically for use in writing courses, bring instructors closer to their student writers, make managing assignments and evaluating papers more efficient, and put powerful assessment within reach. Students receive feedback linked directly to their own writing, which encourages critical thinking and revision and helps them to develop skills based on their individual needs. Learn more at www.my-complab.com.

A CourseSmart e Textbook

Write Now is also available as a CourseSmart e textbook. This is an exciting new choice for students, who can subscribe to the same content online and search the text, make notes online, print out reading assignments that incorporate lecture notes, and bookmark important passages for later review. For more information, or to subscribe to the CourseSmart e textbook, visit www.coursesmart.com.

Social Media Resources

Join us to create an online community around your course. For additional teaching tips and other resources and announcements, follow us on Twitter @iamdan and visit Pearson's Facebook fan page for this book (www.facebook.com/AndersonWriteNow).

The ***Write Now* Newsletter** will be e-mailed to registered adopters semi-annually detailing updates to the Resource Links. Instructors using *Write Now* are encouraged to join the community of users who send the author their exemplary student compositions to be considered as additional Resource Links.

The **Instructor's Manual** that accompanies this text is designed to be useful for new and experienced instructors alike. The Instructor's Manual briefly discusses the ins and outs of teaching the material in each chapter. Also provided are in-class exercises, homework assignments, discussion ideas for each reading selection, model paper assignments and syllabi, and strategies for integrating the e-book resources and MyCompLab into your course.

Acknowledgments

Thanks to the many professionals who have helped push this project to fruition. First, thanks to Brad Potthoff, who helped shape the project and has hung in there with me from start to finish. Thanks also to Paul Crockett for helping to conceptualize and make the project a possibility, and to Leah Jewell. And special thanks go to Joe Opiela for the strong support that has been key to making *Write Now* a reality. Thanks also to Sandra McGuire for all the work spreading the word about the project. Thanks go out as well to the many hands who have guided the development of the project: to Lindsay Bethoney and Cindy Bond for all the work with the manuscript; and to Sara Gordus for all the help with the e-book materials. And my deepest gratitude goes to those who have helped me closely with the creation of *Write Now*. Thanks to Leslie Taggart for helping shape the direction of the work. Deep thanks to Mary Gawlik for the dedication and care devoted to the project. And special thanks to Michael Greer for expert guidance, insightful advice, and work behind the scenes that I can't even begin to imagine. And thanks to Cynthia Anderson for endless help with research and with developing sample materials for the project. I feel honored to have joined all of you in a project that can only be celebrated as a true collaboration.

I would also like to acknowledge the many people who have shaped the pedagogy informing the book. First, to some of my own teachers: Michael Fischer and John Slatin, who taught me how to write and think; and special thanks to Erwin Schlaack, who taught me how to be in the world. I think of all of you often. Over the years I have also worked with many creative and inspiring students—far too many to list; you know who you are, and I am in your debt. And thanks to those students who have had a hand in the project, especially to Emily Evans and Sydney Stegall for help with e-book materials. Special thanks go to Ashley Hall and Jennifer Ware for their work as authors of media resources for the project.

Finally, a word of thanks to those closest to me: To Cindy, Peter, and Palmer for the joy and inspiration you bring to life everyday; to my mother, Lee, (who was my first teacher and who is always in my thoughts); and to my father, Roger, (who by now must realize how much I follow in his footsteps as a thinker and tinkerer). I offer this project to all of you as a token of my love and dedication.

The development of this project has been informed and improved by comments and editorial feedback from a remarkable group of teachers and scholars around the nation. I am grateful to the following for their reviews, insights, and constructive criticism:

James Allen, *College of DuPage*; Jeffrey Andelora, *Mesa Community College*; James Anderson, *Johnson & Wales University*; Edith M. Baker, *Bradley University*; Jessica Bannon, *University of Illinois at Urbana-Champaign*; Evelyn Beck, *Harrisburg Area Community College*; Josianne Bigham, *University of North Carolina–Charlotte*; Glenn Blalock, *Baylor University*; Mechel Camp, *Jackson State Community College*; Gary Christenson, *Elgin Community College*; Tami Comstock-Peavy, *Arapahoe Community College*; Jennifer P. Courtney, *University of North Carolina–Charlotte*; Mark Crane, *Utah Valley State College*; Avon Crismore, *Indiana University–Purdue University Fort Wayne*; Darren DeFrain, *Wichita State University*; Doug Downs, *Montana State University*; Chitralekha Duttagupta, *Utah Valley University*; Beverly D. Fatherree, *Hinds Community College*; Ellen Feig, *Bergen Community College*; Jean S. Filetti, *Christopher Newport University*; Marie A. Fitzwilliam, *College of Charleston*; Patrice Fleck, *Northern Virginia Community College*; Robert G. Ford, *Houston Community College*; Michael Fukuchi, *Barton College*; Kristin R.G. Glasser, *Delta College*; Valerie Gray, *Harrisburg Area Community College*; Gregory Dennis Hagan, *Madisonville Community College*; Ella Hairston, *Guilford Technical Community College*; Matthew Hartman, *Ball State University*; R. Evon Hawkins, *University of Southern Indiana*; Linda Collins Haynes, *Purdue University*; Daniel Hendel De La O, *San Jose State University*; Karen C. Holt, *Brigham Young University–Idaho*; Glenn Hutchinson, *University of North Carolina–Charlotte*; Matthew S.S. Johnson, *Southern Illinois University Edwardsville*; Sara Kaplan, *Del Mar College*; Jessica Fordham Kidd, *University of Alabama*; Bonnie Kyburz, *Utah Valley University*; Lindsay Lewan, *Arapahoe Community College*; Claire Lutkewitte, *Ball State University*; Rebecca McGeehan, *George Mason University*; Timothy F. McGinn, *NorthWest Arkansas Community College*; Darin A. Merrill, *Brigham Young University–Idaho*; Kelly Neil, *Guilford Technical Community College*; Denise Nemec, *NorthWest Arkansas Community College*; Julie J. Nichols, *Utah Valley University*; Shelley Harper Palmer, *Rowan-Cabarrus Community College*; David J. Ragsdale, *Kingwood College*; Nancy Schneider, *University of Maine at Augusta*; Su Senapati, *Abraham Baldwin Agricultural College*; Tracey Sherard, *College of the Canyons*; Susan Slavicz, *Florida State College at Jacksonville*; Andrew Scott, *Ball State University*; Terry Spaise, *UC Riverside*; Dean Swinford, *Fayetteville State University*; Anne Wilson Twite, *Eastern New Mexico University*; Kevin Waltman, *University of Alabama*; Jeana West, *Murray State College*; Carol Westcamp, *University of Arkansas at Ft. Smith;* and Debbie J. Williams, *Abilene Christian University*.

DANIEL ANDERSON

Writing in the Media Age

Understanding Rhetorical Situations, Genres, and Mediums

Zoom In   Key Concepts and Learning Objectives

After studying this chapter, you should be able to:

1.1 Focus on details (zoom in) and cultural contexts (zoom out) to analyze texts and create compositions of your own.

1.2 Identify the elements of rhetorical situations (speakers, audiences, and messages) and the way these elements influence one another.

1.3 Explore the cultural networks that shape rhetorical situations.

1.4 Make decisions about rhetorical strategies.

1.5 Understand how genres and mediums influence the way texts are shaped and circulated.

Y ou have probably used the magnifying glass or "zoom" tool that comes with most computer applications. If you were editing a picture, you might have magnified a portion of the image to examine a detail. Zooming is a nice metaphor because it can work in two ways. Think about a well-known image like one of Monet's paintings of water lilies. Zoom in and you see details that you might otherwise overlook—amazing dabs of color forming flower petals. Zoom out, and you will see dozens of flowers among lily pads in a serene pond scene. Zoom out more and you might see the painting affixed in a frame, surrounded by museum patrons in a Western city. This book is meant to help you learn to read and write skillfully: it guides you in practicing this kind of adjustment of focus, asking you to zoom in at times on details and to zoom back out to consider the larger picture.

As you practice adjusting your focus, you will need to constantly ask questions. If you were studying Monet's painting, you might zoom in to ask, *What do shapes, colors, and imagery in the painting tell us? What tools and materials did Monet use?* Or you might zoom out to ask, *How does placing a painting on a museum wall change the way viewers judge the piece? Who visits museums? What are contemporary attitudes toward art?* You could train your attention similarly on a museum brochure, a news piece on art funding, or an article on Impressionist landscape paintings. Zooming in and zooming out, asking questions as you go, helps you make sense of any text that you encounter.

Continuing this practice of adjusting your focus and asking questions, you will develop skills in making decisions as you write. To draft an essay on Impressionist landscapes, you would need to zoom out to consider big questions. *Are you writing for an academic assignment? What are the expectations? Should you produce a personal response, an evaluation, or an informational report? Who is your audience? What resources can you use? What have others said about your topic? How will you portray yourself in your composition?* And you will have to make choices as you explore each of these larger questions.

Of course, you will have to adjust your focus again, asking about particulars. Maybe you have decided to compose an argument in a photo essay; if so, you will need to zoom in again. *How best can you construct an argument? What claims might you make? What evidence can back up your points? What are the characteristics of photo essays? How will you incorporate images into your project? How will you cite your sources?* You can see that each of these questions calls for more decisions. Writing, just like careful reading, can be a complex undertaking. Still, if you keep in mind the basics—zoom in and out, ask questions, and make decisions—you can work through the challenges.

Keep in mind the basics—zoom in and out, ask questions, and make decisions

Your first big task is understanding how reading and writing take place within cultural networks and rhetorical situations.

Cultural networks are the linked collections of people, ideas, and things that make up our social world. Think about a video clip that has gone viral on the Internet—perhaps a clip of a movie preview that has been remixed with a new voiceover to create a spoof trailer (see Figure 1.1). Perhaps an author wants to comment on the latest blockbuster, so she creates the spoof and then submits the clip to YouTube. A blogger discovers the clip, notes its humor, and posts a link on her Web site. A blog reader follows the link, reads the clip as a critique of formulaic Hollywood films, and sends an e-mail to a friend, passing the clip along. All of these elements—people, ideas, and things—make up the larger contexts in which communication takes place.

These contexts are especially important when it comes to reading and writing texts. Texts (college essays, blog postings, video clips, magazine articles, etc.) all occupy a unique situation within a cultural network by virtue of their links to writers and readers. The people connected with texts ask questions and make decisions about writing and reading. *How should I organize this essay? With whom should I share this Web site? How should I revise this e-mail message?* These kinds of questions are central to the practice of communication. Historically, this study of communication and this process of making decisions about texts have been called rhetoric. When you create or encounter texts, you practice rhetoric by asking questions and making decisions about messages, readers, and writers. When we examine relationships between texts, readers, and writers, we explore rhetorical situations.

When you create or encounter texts, you practice rhetoric by asking questions and making decisions about messages, readers, and writers

FIGURE 1.1
Elements in a cultural network.

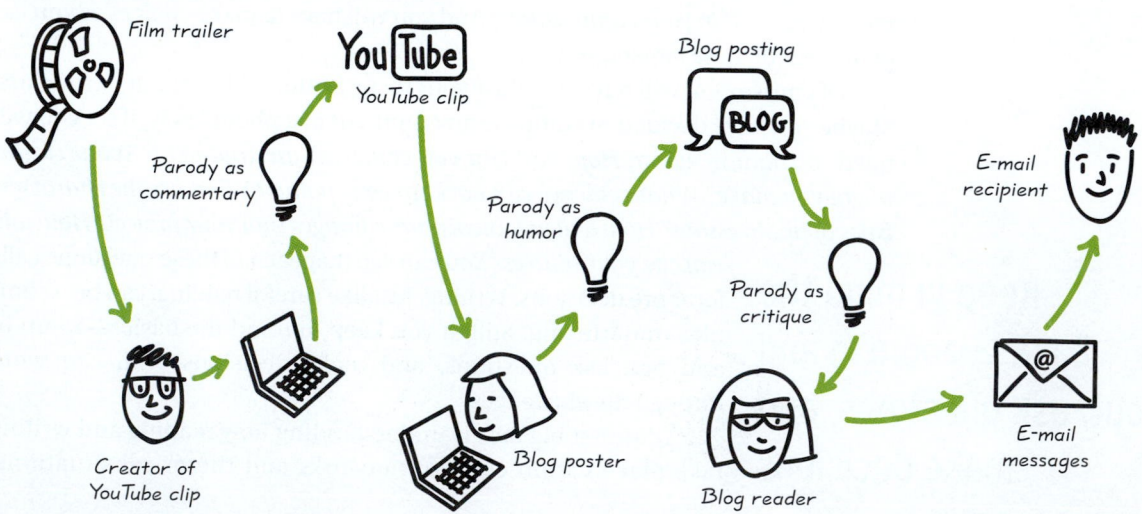

Film trailer

YouTube clip

Blog posting

E-mail recipient

Parody as commentary

Parody as humor

Parody as critique

E-mail messages

Creator of YouTube clip

Blog poster

Blog reader

Learning
Objective 1.1

Figure 1.2 demonstrates the ways we can zoom in to focus on a rhetorical situation. A rhetorical situation represents any act of communication in which a message is exchanged between a writer and a reader. If we want to understand a text, we need to examine the creator of the message—the speaker. We can also think about the purposes a speaker might have in creating a message—in our example, perhaps to make a point about parody and humor. We can also explore recipients of the message—the audience. And we can look at the ways an audience interprets or receives a message—in our example, perhaps recognizing a cultural critique. Understanding that speakers create messages for audiences is the key to learning to read and write in rhetorical situations.

In fact, learning to evaluate rhetorical situations and cultural networks will make you a more critical reader of messages. When you listen to a speech or read a text, you can explore the context and ask questions about the decisions and strategies the speaker or author uses. *What tools were used to create the text? What people were involved? Why did the writer choose this genre or medium? What might be her purpose? What assumptions does she make about her readers? Why pick this example or that word?* Every choice begs a question, and you will zoom in and out as you explore them. This process is rhetorical analysis.

In this chapter, you will learn about rhetorical situations. Every kind of message—from essays to speeches to status updates to résumés to a point made in a

VIDEO
1. Understanding
Cultural Networks

FIGURE 1.2
Zooming in to focus on
a rhetorical situation.

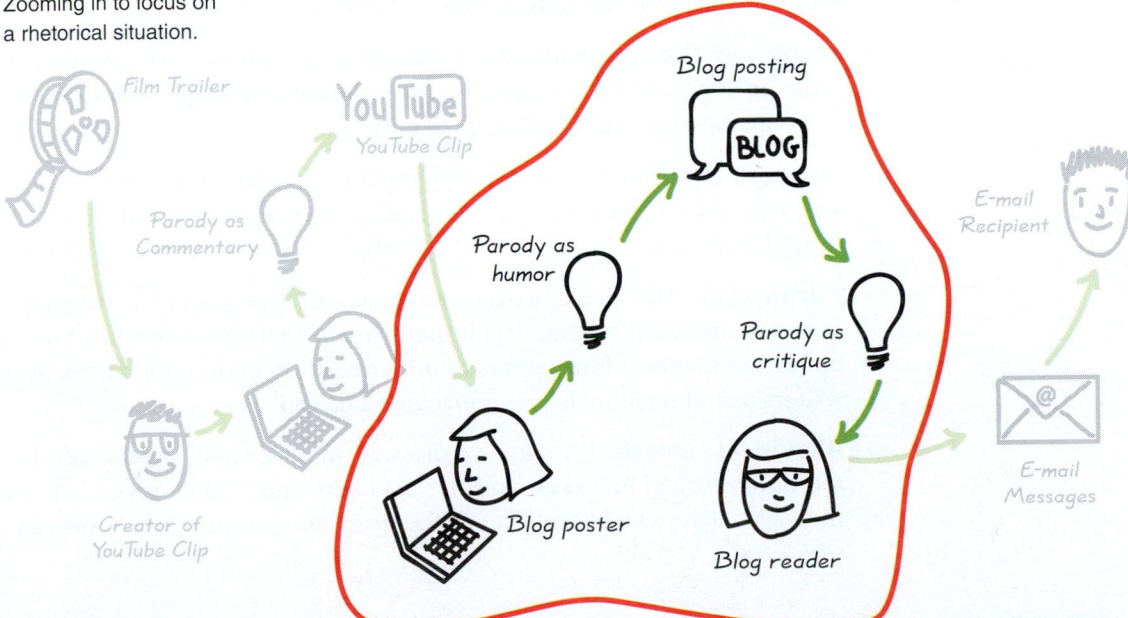

Zooming in and out helps you ask questions and make decisions about texts and culture

class discussion—takes place in a rhetorical situation, and you will need to become adept at analyzing and composing in a variety of these situations. (You probably are already skilled in many of them.) The chapter will also focus on some of the purposes and strategies people use when they write, whether they're persuading us to buy perfume or informing us about conflict in Afghanistan. Finally, we will look at choices concerning genres and mediums, thinking about how categories of writing, expectations, and materials influence readers and writers.

KEY TERMS

- **Cultural networks:** Collections of and relationships among people, ideas, and things. The elements in a cultural network influence one another. Examining the influences and connections among elements informs reading and writing.

- **Rhetorical situations:** Circumstances in which a speaker exchanges a message with an audience. Rhetorical situations are informed by different purposes and result in unique messages received by specific audiences.

- **Speaker:** The producer of a message in a rhetorical situation. Speakers can be individuals or larger groups or entities. Analyzing the speaker helps you read messages critically. The way you present yourself as a speaker influences the reception of messages you produce.

- **Audience:** The recipients of a message in a rhetorical situation. The makeup of an audience shapes the reception of a message, and speakers will craft messages with audiences in mind.

- **Message:** The text exchanged in a rhetorical situation. Messages consist of the material text that is composed and read as well as the ideas represented in the text.

- **Purpose(s):** The goals writers have when they create a message. Purposes include the practical impetus to write. (I need to warn hikers about the coyote.) Purposes also include the strategic objectives that writers use. (I need to deliver information clearly.)

- **Rhetorical analysis:** Examining a message in terms of its rhetorical situation. Rhetorical analyses consider speakers and audiences as well as messages. They can also look at concerns of genre or medium as they assess a text.

- **Genres:** Categories used to organize texts. Genres shed light on common features of texts and create expectations for readers and writers. Most texts are complex, often mixing elements of several genres which themselves are fluid, changing depending on rhetorical situations and cultural contexts.

- **Mediums:** The materials used to create a composition. Mediums enable and limit certain kinds of compositions. Mediums also account for the means through which a message is transmitted.

- **Zooming:** The process of narrowing or expanding your focus as you read and write. Zooming in helps you explore items and details. Zooming out helps you understand contexts and relationships. Zooming in and out helps you ask questions and make decisions about texts and culture.

Understanding Rhetorical Situations

LO

Learning
Objective 1.2

Let's look at a message to see how its meaning might shift based on changes in its rhetorical situation: who is speaking (or writing), who is listening (or reading), how the message is organized, and the contexts in which the message is shared.

Consider a simple message, such as "We need to sustain our resources." Imagine how the meaning shifts if the message is delivered by different speakers: if the CEO of a large retail corporation delivers the message, *resources* might refer to the financial assets of the company; if the head of Greenpeace makes the statement, *resources* might refer to natural habitat. A message is really a combination of a text and the ideas the message conveys. The exact same textual message takes on different meanings depending on who delivers it. (See Figure 1.3.)

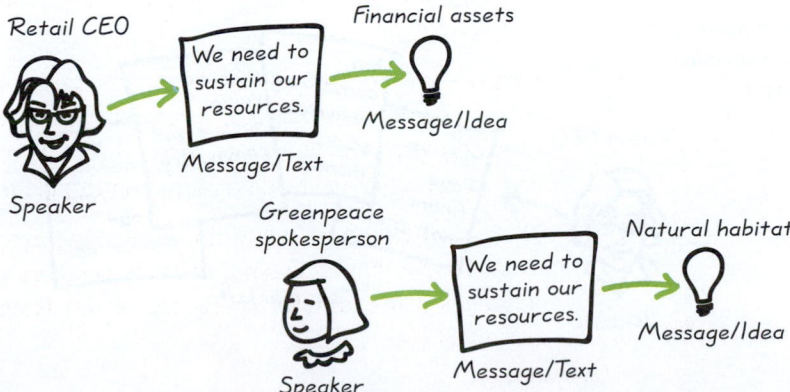

FIGURE 1.3
A change of speakers
influences messages.

Now, focus on how changes in audience affect rhetorical situations. Compare how the message delivered by the CEO will be received by corporation shareholders with the way the same message might be interpreted by a group of environmentalists. The shareholders might read the message as reassuring, while the environmentalists might greet the message with skepticism. A change in audience results in a new meaning for the message.

Because elements like audience have such an effect on communication, authors make decisions based on their rhetorical situations. For instance, the CEO would never simply present a message about sustaining resources to a group of environmentalists. Instead, she would assess her audience and craft a message designed to appeal to their values, perhaps linking financial motives with sustaining environmental resources. The message, then, would be shaped by the situation. (See Figure 1.4 and Lee Scott's speech below.)

Finally, rhetorical situations never exist in a vacuum containing only a speaker, a message, and an audience. Things are usually a bit messier, so you must zoom out to also consider the cultural network in which messages are exchanged (see Figure 1.5). Imagine that a government report on the environmental impact of global shipping had been splashed over the news during the week before the CEO delivers her speech. Or suppose a spokesperson for Greenpeace had addressed the same group about shipping waste the night before. Perhaps a new technology has just been invented to address shipping concerns. Historical events, people, texts, ideas, even physical things like inventions or technologies all make up the cultural network that must be considered to read and create messages.

Let's zoom in on our example to get a better feel for cultural networks and rhetorical situations. In this case, we will consider Wal-Mart's recent move toward environmental sustainability in its operations. In 2005, Lee Scott, the CEO of

WN

VIDEO
2. Rhetorical
Situations

FIGURE 1.4

Changes in audience
call for adjustments
of messages.

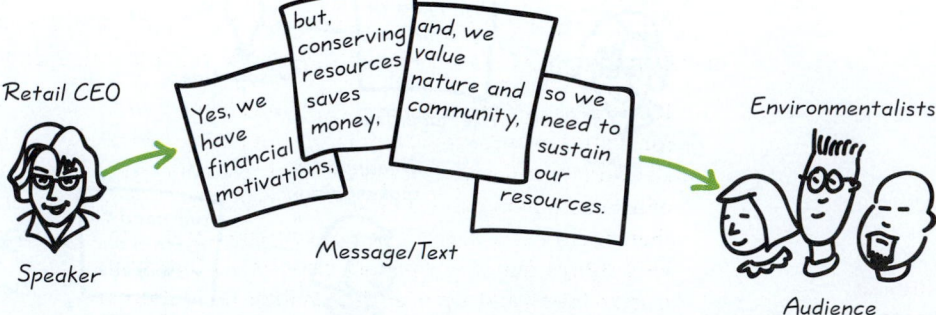

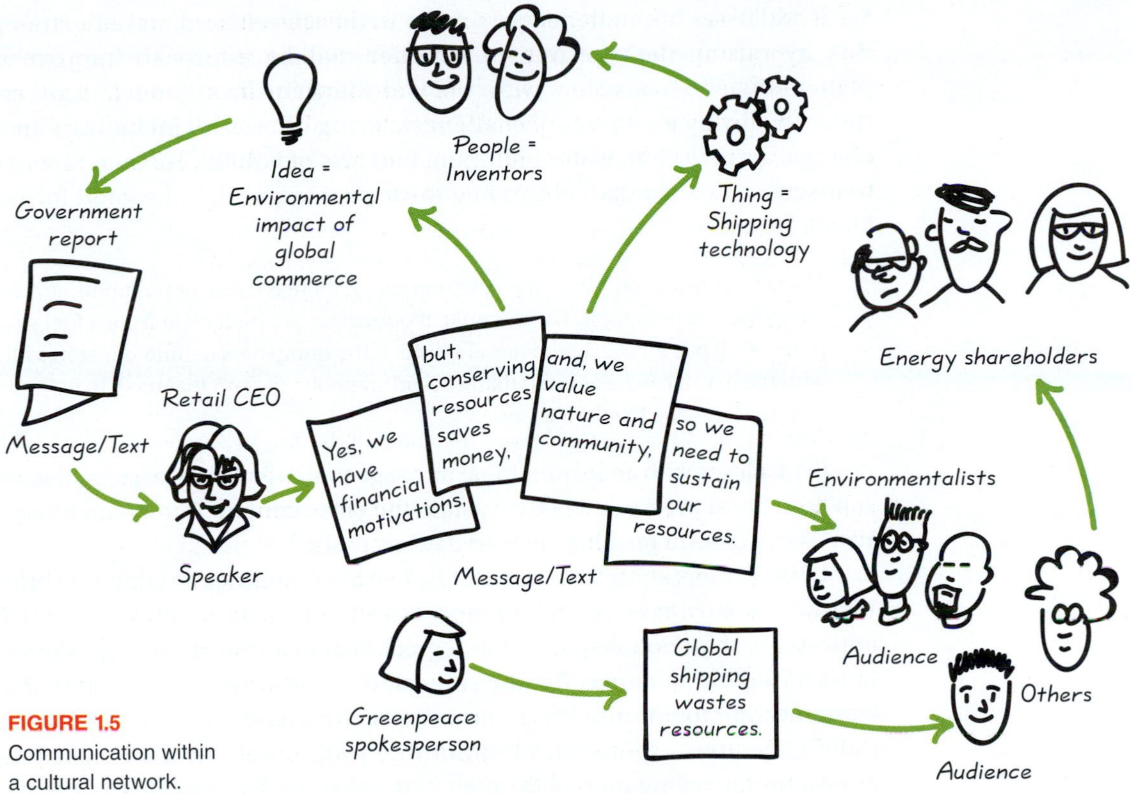

FIGURE 1.5
Communication within
a cultural network.

Idea =
Environmental
impact of
global
commerce

People =
Inventors

Thing =
Shipping
technology

Government
report

Energy shareholders

Message/Text

Retail CEO

Yes, we
have
financial
motivations,

but,
conserving
resources
saves
money,

and, we
value
nature and
community,

so we
need to
sustain
our
resources.

Environmentalists

Speaker

Message/Text

Audience

Global
shipping
wastes
resources.

Greenpeace
spokesperson

Others

Audience

LO

Learning
Objective 1.3

Wal-Mart Corporation, gave a presentation to shareholders titled "Twenty-First Century Leadership." In his speech, Scott discussed Wal-Mart's response to hurricane Katrina, suggesting that, in the response to the disaster, Scott "saw a company utilize its people resources and scale to make a big and positive difference in people's lives."

Scott used the speech to suggest that Wal-Mart should make similar efforts to respond to the twenty-first century problem of climate change:

> Katrina asked this critical question, and I want to ask it of you: What would it take for Wal-Mart to be that company, at our best, all the time? What if we used our size and resources to make this country and this earth an even better place for all of us: customers, associates, our children, and generations unborn? What would that mean? Could we do it? Is this consistent with our business model? What if the very things that many people criticize us for—our size and reach—became a trusted friend and ally to all, just as they did in Katrina?

Scott addresses his audience personally in the speech, and makes a strategic link by raising the question of whether making efforts to improve the planet might be "consistent with [the Wal-Mart] business model." Scott continues by listing a number of challenges facing the world, including climate change, air pollution, water pollution, and loss of habitat. He then moves on to discuss the ways that addressing these problems might be good for Wal-Mart's business:

> There is a simple rule about the environment. If there is waste or pollution, someone along the line pays for it. For example, if our trucks are inefficient from a fuel standpoint, we'll pay for that at the diesel pump. If the dumpsters behind our stores fill up with trash, you can be assured that we paid someone to send that trash to us, and we will pay someone to take it away.

Scott closes with an inspirational message to shareholders, arguing that they can both boost profits and better sustain the environment by implementing the Wal-Mart model of pushing for everyday low costs.

In his presentation to shareholders, Lee Scott outlines a vision for shifting Wal-Mart's business model to one based on sustainability. As a CEO addressing shareholders, Scott has a great deal of authority as a speaker and faces a friendly audience. But the subject of the address forces Scott to make some accommodations. Scott connects recommendations that might initially affect the corporation's bottom-line profitability with a longer-range argument for saving money through conservation. He provides evidence of potential savings in fuel and energy costs. He notes that reducing waste will save the company money. In a sense, he links environmental sustainability with economic sustainability: a smart rhetorical decision.

If we think of rhetorical situations as simple instances in which speakers pitch a message to an audience, we might declare Scott's presentation to shareholders a success. But even a speech delivered to such a specific audience is more complex. Wal-Mart is no doubt one of the most scrutinized corporations on the planet, and Scott knows that the audience for any corporate vision he might outline extends far beyond the walls of the shareholder's meeting.

You can see this broader cultural network in the way Scott opens his speech with a lengthy discussion of Wal-Mart's response to Hurricane Katrina. Scott suggests that the corporation should serve the public good and has benefited from doing so. He even discusses climate change, arguing that reducing greenhouse gasses is a corporate responsibility. Knowing he must advocate for Wal-Mart to the world at large, Scott crafts a message likely to appeal not only to shareholders interested in the return on their investments but also to environmentalists and advocates for social responsibility; Scott sounds as much like an Audubon spokesperson as he does a corporate CEO.

VIDEO
11. Understanding
Ethos

Lee Scott knows how to deliver a compelling presentation. But we can't completely assess the success of this message until we zoom out. Ultimately, this speech must be viewed as only one element in an extensive cultural network that includes many other texts and contexts. To get a sense of some of these contexts, let's look at an article by Sarah Irving.

 ## Don't Believe the Hypermarket
BY **SARAH IRVING**

Sarah Irving writes for Ethical Consumer *magazine. She also researches and publishes articles focusing on social concerns and issues of the environment. "Don't Believe the Hypermarket" appeared in 2006 in* New Internationalist *magazine.*

If you believe the hype, supermarkets the world over are going all green and cuddly. The British giant Tesco has announced that it is bolting renewable electricity generation on to its stores and rewarding customers for re-using plastic bags. French supermarket transnational Carrefour is advertising its reduction of toxic chemicals in cleaning products. The Real Canadian Superstore chain is giving a high profile to its range of "environmentally friendly" household goods. Most dramatically of all, Lee Scott, CEO of the much-criticized Wal-Mart, has announced a whole raft of environmental initiatives, including selling certified "sustainable" seafood and a massive commitment to organic food and clothing. What's more, he has pledged that such products will only cost 10 percent more than their less sustainable alternatives.

"It is clearly good for our business," says Scott. "We are taking costs out and finding we are doing things we just do not need to do, whether it be in packaging, or energy usage . . . there are a number of decisions we can make that are great for sustainability and great for bottom-line profit."

But is the "pile 'em high, sell 'em cheap" business model really compatible with sustainable development? Or are supermarkets projecting friendly images to divert attention from accusations that they are causing great harm to our society, health and environment? A small number of supermarkets control what much of the world eats. In Australia, two companies, Woolworths and Coles, sell a third of all food consumed. In Britain, the "big four" sell 75 percent of the country's groceries, with Tesco alone controlling 30 percent of the market. In the U.S., Wal-Mart, the largest retailer in the world, controls 20 percent of a $450 billion market.

These trends are rapidly embedding themselves in Majority World countries too, with a third of Mexico's food expenditure going to Wal-Mart alone, and Brazil's domination by supermarkets going from 30 percent to 75 percent in just 10 years. This power means that supermarkets are effectively deciding what we eat and how much suppliers will get paid for it.

And they're not planning to stop there. The ultimate dream is to dominate all so-called "non-food" sectors as well: clothes, insurance, pharmaceuticals, electrical goods, you name it. Tesco's deputy chair, announcing record profits in 2003, complained: "It's not good enough. We have got only 5 percent of the non-food market. We have 18 percent of the grocery market and there's 90 percent of the non-food market to go for."

CORPORATE ORGANICS

Providing supermarkets with organic produce is now big business, and the world's agro-industrial behemoths are muscling in on a sector which once belonged to a fringe movement of small-scale farmers seeking out ways of producing food more sustainably.

What you are buying when you choose an organic product from a supermarket is probably not the crop of a local farmer. Despite being infamous for pollution, land rights abuses and genetically engineered crops, the corporations which already control much of the globe's food supply, such as Cargill and Archer Daniels Midland, are increasingly buying up organic companies.

Many organic brands marketed as if they are small, independent, benevolent firms are actually owned by transnationals. They include Seeds of Change, bought by Mars in 1997, Green & Black's, snapped up by Cadbury Schweppes in 2005 and Back to Nature, held since 2003 by Kraft (a subsidiary of Altria, which owns tobacco giant Phillip Morris).

In Britain, supermarkets are quite unashamedly appropriating the methods used by small organic farmers to sell their produce. Tesco and Sainsbury's both recently announced that they were starting "veg box" delivery schemes, which have long been one of the most effective means of directly linking organic producers and consumers while cutting out the supermarket intermediaries.

WATERING DOWN STANDARDS

The concentration of leading organic brands in the hands of transnationals is steadily turning organics from a progressive movement into a label supermarkets can charge higher prices for. Sadly the hiked prices do not necessarily feed back into more ecological practices or better conditions for workers. Quite the opposite. According to Mike Green of the UK Soil Association, "Small and medium producers are being squeezed out because it becomes financially unviable for them to sell to supermarkets that are pushing down prices and cutting margins."

Meanwhile corporate interference has been compounding the problems. In 2002, the U.S. Department of Agriculture relaxed organic regulations, allowing supermarkets to increase the availability of produce labeled "organic" without the expense of genuinely improving standards. Conscious consumers have been fighting a rearguard action ever since. The U.S. Organic Consumers Association has launched a boycott of several supermarkets' own-brand "organic" milk because, it says, the companies are buying it from producers who keep cows under factory farming conditions.

In another attack on organic standards, in 2005 the EU announced plans, currently being fiercely opposed, to allow food labeled "organic" to contain up to 0.9 percent contamination with genetically modified materials. In Britain, Marshall's, one of the largest suppliers of vegetables to supermarkets, is rapidly moving into large-scale organic provision as demand grows. The company has been fined over £30,000 for pollution incidents between 2004 and 2005.

PERMANENT GLOBAL SUMMERTIME

For many people, the term "organic" evokes images of small producers, farming in tune with nature. But the standard range offered in supermarkets means chasing the seasons around the world, to give us a "permanent global summertime" where anyone can buy summer fruit and vegetables in the depths of winter.

In Northern supermarkets this means importing fresh produce from countries like Argentina, Chile and South Africa, where costs and labour standards are lower, and regardless of the massive contribution these "food miles" make to climate change.

The eternal availability of unseasonal food is also a concern raised by critics who see people increasingly disconnected from nature and lacking basic awareness of where their food comes from. A 2005 survey of 8–14 year olds by the British Heart Foundation found that 37 percent did not know that cheese was made from milk, and 36 percent weren't aware that chips come from potatoes.

UNREFORMED CHARACTERS

The negative impacts of supermarkets provide fodder for campaigns across the globe. Aggressive pricing which drives small local businesses into bankruptcy, encouragement of car culture, the environmental implications of building large superstores on out-of-town sites, squeezing small supplier firms, using wasteful packaging, and poor treatment of workers on the shop floor and in Majority World sweatshops are just some of the criticisms leveled against the big players.

Despite claims of reform, the evidence suggests that supermarket business continues very much as usual. A report by the National Labour Committee on Jordanian garment factories supplying Wal-Mart stores in 2005 and 2006 found horrific practices, including sexual and physical abuse of female workers. In April 2006, Hong Kong environmental groups

Don't Believe the
Hypermarket
(continued)
BY **SARAH IRVING**

staged protests at supermarket packaging waste and plastic bags clogging up the cramped environment of the island.

In August 2006, the BBC accused Tesco of "dragging out the planning process, challenging enforcement orders, manipulating the planning laws, and breaking them on occasion after the supermarket built massive out-of-town stores which exceeded planning permissions, and dumped 27,000 tonnes of rubble on an official Area of Outstanding Natural Beauty." The UK's independent Competition Commission is currently conducting a wide-ranging investigation into the big supermarkets, taking into account planning, pricing and supplier relationships.

Supermarket PR departments are working hard on improving their image—and let's hope we are seeing a genuine move to minimize some environmental impacts. But their interest in organics is far from altruistic. The "green dollar" has become very lucrative, and the need to win back consumers' approval is pressing.

The danger is that supermarkets, far from being reformed by their exposure to organics, are transforming an environmental movement striving to provide a sustainable alternative into a meaningless brand. Wal-Mart, which boasts in its 2006 annual report that its marketplace is clearly the world, has its sights not only on aggressive global expansion, but also the meaningless commodification of sustainable values.

Reflect on the Reading

Questions About "Don't Believe the Hypermarket"

1. How would you characterize Sarah Irving as a speaker? Do you find her credible? What about the article colors your sense of the speaker?
2. What is the main argument that Irving makes about corporations and the environment? Does Irving suggest the problem is with the corporations or with the hype?
3. Does "Don't Believe the Hypermarket" change your reading of Lee Scott's speech? If so, what about the article shifts your opinion? If not, what prevents the article from swaying you?
4. How would you relate the rhetorical situations in which Scott's speech and "Don't Believe the Hypermarket" appear? What approaches must you use to compare a public speech with a magazine article?

We've already thought about how the affiliation of Lee Scott with Wal-Mart might influence his message. We should make similar assessments about the author of "Don't Believe the Hypermarket." We can start by learning more about Sarah Irving. Discovering that Irving has also written about topics ranging from green building practices to women's issues to poverty reveals something about her interests (and possible biases) as the speaker behind the piece.

Further, since "Don't Believe the Hypermarket" appeared in the magazine *New Internationalist*, we can investigate the publication source as an element of the cultural network. The magazine's mission statement claims that "the *New Internationalist* is renowned for its radical, campaigning stance on a range of world issues, from the cynical marketing of babymilk in the Majority World to human rights in Burma." We might ask about the assumptions conveyed by the statement. These discoveries would help us better understand the article's intended audience, in this case readers interested in progressive social issues such as ending poverty and protecting the environment.

Like the CEO or Greenpeace spokesperson, then, the author and sponsoring entity behind "Don't Believe the Hypermarket" shape the way we perceive the message. This analysis can help us draw conclusions about the purposes that prompt the author to address the message to the audience, something we look at in more detail later in the chapter.

WN

RESOURCES
Wal-Mart and
Sustainability

Know It · Strategies for Understanding Rhetorical Situations

- Learn as much as you can about the author or speaker. Conduct research into the person's background. Look for other things the person has said or written. Develop a sense of the identity of the person behind the message.
- Understand the makeup of the audience. Consider the variety of positions you might find in the audience: are they mostly a homogenous group or do they have a range of perspectives? Think about what belief systems the audience is likely to have.
- Zoom in to analyze messages in rhetorical situations. Consider aspects of the message meant to appeal to the audience. Explore how the message represents the speaker. What can focusing on the details of the message tell you?
- Take a position on the message you are analyzing, and then examine that stance in terms of the rhetorical situation. How do your individual beliefs as an audience member influence your reading? How well do you identify with the speaker? What aspects of the message appeal to you?
- Connect rhetorical situations to the larger contexts in which they exist. Look at complementary or competing messages related to the topic. Consider other voices providing different messages. Examine how alternative audiences might react to the message. What can you discover when you zoom out?

Exercises for Understanding Rhetorical Situations

1. Identify a text, and create a graphic map representing the cultural network in which the text is situated. Think about people, ideas, things, and other texts related to the item. Use a piece of scratch paper to trace the key connections you discover.

2. Think about situations in which you have had to speak publicly. Did you use any strategies to help establish your authority as a speaker? What role did your audience play in the shaping of your message? Make a list of things you might change if you had a chance to go back and revise the presentation.

3. Choose a text (for example, a film, song, phone call, lab report, research essay, or Facebook message, to name a few options) and write a page or so analyzing the piece in terms of its rhetorical situation.

4. With a group of peers, take a stand on an issue (perhaps related to sustainability, social justice, personal freedoms, or another topic), and then develop a list of talking points that might be used in a debate. Think about how the points will represent your group as speakers, how an audience might respond, and how the talking points might be used to construct a larger message.

Understanding Rhetorical Purposes and Strategies

If you zoom out, you can identify a number of writing purposes (expressing, entertaining, informing, inquiring, persuading) that relate to most rhetorical situations. If you zoom in, you can discover strategies that can help you develop compositions. You will respond to specific rhetorical situations. (I'm going to try to get this library fine waived.) You will make choices about purposes and strategies. (I'm going to make rhetorical decisions meant to persuade.) These choices lead to further composing decisions. (I'm going to show my history of returning books on time to establish myself as a responsible borrower.)

Most messages reflect multiple purposes and strategies

But you need to remain flexible as you think about how various purposes inform rhetorical situations. Just think of the annual ritual of rating Super Bowl commercials. The television advertisement that is meant to persuade might also work hard to entertain. It turns out that most messages reflect multiple purposes and strategies. The best way to understand purpose is to think of the moment when a writer makes a decision about what to compose and how to proceed, and then ask questions about that moment as you analyze texts and produce your own messages.

Keeping in mind, then, that you need to constantly make composition decisions based on your situation (there are no hard and fast rules), let's look into some common strategies for writing. You can then learn to zoom in and out, mix and match, and make choices about these modes of communicating as you read and write.

LO

Learning
Objective 1.4

- **Writing to express ideas or experiences.** Sometimes we write to share our thoughts and experiences. The most obvious instance of such expressive writing is a journal. It's easy to dismiss this kind of writing as simply personal, and, indeed, in college classes the focus is usually on other forms of writing. Still, expressive writing often has public dimensions. Think of the number of memoirs (see Chapter 5) on bestseller lists or the number of blogs that feature personal writing. You might also bring an expressive purpose to other writing situations—for instance, you might begin or end a persuasive essay with a personal anecdote to engage readers or provide evidence.

- **Writing to entertain or engage the senses.** Sometimes writing to entertain is associated with literature. Works of fiction, for instance, use narration (see Chapter 20) and description (see Chapter 21) to tell stories. Among these techniques are the careful sequencing and pacing of events, the use of dialog, and the use of details to bring writing to life. And these strategies are helpful in many situations. Even a piece of persuasive writing like Lee Scott's speech uses details and tells a story. Fiction or music might specifically set out to entertain and delight readers, but you will use strategies like narration and description in many rhetorical situations.

- **Writing to inform or explain.** A staple in most writing classes, explanatory compositions help readers and writers make sense of concepts. Explanatory writing strives for clarity, focusing on facts, definitions, descriptions, and straightforward presentation. We discuss explanatory compositions in Chapter 10. Sometimes, writing to explain may be solely concerned with presenting information clearly (think of the quick start guide for a cell phone). But explanatory writing often is shaped by multiple purposes. Carla Farmar's essay on self-esteem and body image (pages 264–69) *explains* current research findings concerning body image and women's health. At the same time, the essay *persuades* readers that society should focus on issues of self-esteem as it addresses health problems such as eating disorders.

- **Writing to inquire or evaluate.** This strategy is likely the most flexible kind of writing you will encounter or produce. Some evaluative writing focuses on analysis and judgments; for example, a film review (see Chapter 11) looks at aspects of a movie (the acting, cinematography, editing, etc.) and offers an opinion on the film's value. Often, however, writing to evaluate is part of a process of inquiry that helps you develop and express ideas about a topic. To develop evaluative writing, you might use strategies of comparing and contrasting (see Chapter 23) and describing (see Chapter 21).

- **Writing to persuade.** Some persuasive communication may have only one purpose; for example, an advertisement might be designed to appeal strictly to your emotions to sell a product. In most cases, though, persuasive writing is one of the more complex forms you will encounter and is likely to incorporate a range of strategies from other types of writing. No doubt you will write to *evaluate* ideas as you persuade. You will need to *explain* evidence and *inform* readers. And you may need to *entertain*. You might compose persuasive pieces as letters to an editor, as proposals, or as position arguments (see Chapter 8). You will likely use strategies of argumentation (see Chapter 4) as you compose persuasive writing.

Ask Questions & Make Decisions

Exercises for Understanding Rhetorical Purposes and Strategies

1. Check your local newspaper or an online news source for letters to the editor. Identify a letter you find to be particularly persuasive. Make a list of the persuasive strategies used in the letter. (You can find examples of persuasive strategies on pages 109–14.)
2. Locate an item from popular culture meant to entertain. A YouTube clip, a pop song, or a TV show might be some possibilities. Think about other communication purposes and strategies used in the piece—informing, persuading, describing, analyzing, etc. Write a paragraph discussing the mixture of purposes and strategies you discover.
3. Find several reviews of a film, TV show, or CD. Make a list of the different strategies and purposes you find in the reviews. Select one review you find to be successful in weaving multiple purposes and strategies into its composition. Write a paragraph or two explaining what makes it more effective than the other reviews.

Understanding Genres

Genres are categories that organize forms of communication based on common features or qualities. Think of the typical television situation comedy. Most demonstrate some familiar characteristics like a recurring cast of (often quirky) characters, a real-world setting (coffee shop, police station, hospital), and an episodic structure in which problems play out and resolve themselves in thirty minutes—actually twenty-two minutes when you factor in commercials. Of course, even among the genre of situation comedies, you will find sub-genres and specific features for individual shows. Some comedies emphasize the everyday foibles of their characters while others steer toward more serious personal problems or social commentary.

Knowing about the conventions and variations among genres will enable you to make decisions about how best to read and communicate in different rhetorical situations. In college courses, you need to learn a good deal about the conventions of a number of written genres—the profile essay, the explanatory research report, the position argument, to name a few. These genre choices relate to your purposes as a writer: a profile essay calls for entertaining and informative writing that uses narrative strategies to tell the story of the subject of the profile; a research report asks for informative writing that provides details or explains ideas. The research report genre also creates expectations like the use of citations and careful documentation of sources.

Understanding the conventions associated with a genre helps you meet the expectations of your readers. But you still need to understand the decision making that takes place as you compose; even when you work with genres that seem to have reasonably fixed features and conventions, there is room for variation, and writers must mold the composition to meet their needs. Let's look at a brief article to think more about these complexities.

 # Genre Jumping Pays Off
BY **JON WEISMAN**

Jon Weisman is a features editor with Daily Variety. *He covers entertainment news, frequently reviewing new shows and reporting on the latest television and movies. "Genre Jumping Pays Off" first appeared in* Daily Variety *in 2006.*

You wouldn't expect many shows to be audacious enough to reinvent one of television's classic half-hours, "MASH," and only a few would expect to succeed.

However, critics and devoted viewers have found that from its very first stitch to tonight's 100th episode, "Scrubs" has combined slapstick and sophisticated comedy with earnest and devastating drama like no other medical show since the days of Hawkeye.

"I kind of thought of 'Scrubs,' as the new 'MASH,'" says *TV Guide* senior critic Matt Roush. "It never became a sensation like 'MASH,' but 'Scrubs,' I think, will go on and have a reputation that could live on."

Though "Scrubs" diverts from the "MASH" formula in a few areas—it's not set in a war zone—series creator Bill Lawrence deadpans that he "cribbed" straight from the 1970s classic. Like "MASH," "Scrubs" is fearless in aiming for laughter and tears alike.

Genre Jumping
Pays Off
(continued)
BY **JON WEISMAN**

"If you look at 'MASH,' they were able to get the best of both," Lawrence says. "Because they were in a hospital setting, they had this added ammo that you believed every character on 'MASH,' and, hopefully, every character on 'Scrubs,' really cares. . . . You are able to do some really silly comedy without indicting the characters."

Still, the idea for "Scrubs" didn't arise from a TV Land "MASH" marathon, but, rather, conversations that Lawrence had with old friends who became doctors.

"On American television, we like our doctors to be very serious," Lawrence says. "We like them to yell 'stat' a lot and bust through doors. One thing I noticed about these guys was that they were all the same goofballs I knew when I grew up with them."

As his friends told stories of their days fresh out of medical school, a CT scan went off around Lawrence's head.

"Imagine it's your first day of work at any new job and how nervous you are, (with) the added pressure that you're supposed to be responsible for people living or dying," Lawrence says.

The concept was golden, and remained so as the characters matured. Even as the characters age, they're still learning.

"The minute that 'Scrubs' completely grows up, it's over," Roush says.

With its raison d'etre in place, the surpassing achievement of "Scrubs" was one of tone. Laying the groundwork, Lawrence chose to employ a single-camera show at a time when network comedies rarely did that.

"Every time someone had tried to do a medical sitcom," Lawrence recalls, "it seemed like fake actors pretending to be doctors. . . . One of the things we thought early on was (if) we occasionally showed actual patients and actual people dying and things with emotional stakes, working in single camera, that it might be enough to combine with broad comedy."

The other key element in the evolution of "Scrubs" followed the decision to tell stories principally from the point of view of Dr. John "J.D." Dorian, played by then-unknown Hollywood hyphenate Zach Braff. Lawrence and his staff struggled to keep Braff's voiceover from becoming a mere crutch for story exposition.

The brainstorm: Put J.D.'s daydreams onscreen as well.

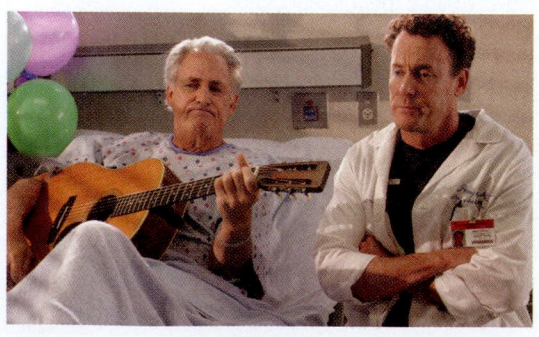

"What we decided was, rather than have it be a monotone narration, if it's going to be told through Zach's voice, we're going to do everything through J.D.'s eyes," Lawrence says. "It opened up a visual medium that those of us as comedy writers were not used to."

The attention to detail infused every character on "Scrubs," from series regulars Braff, Sarah Chalke, Donald Raison, Neil Flynn, Ken Jenkins, John C. McGinley and Judy Reyes, to even the one-line guests, all of whom are precisely drawn characters.

"Somebody brought up that 99% of sitcoms expect [minor characters] to deliver exposition," Lawrence says. "They're there only to make the main characters funny. We wanted them to all be oddly and weirdly funny in their own right."

While the future of "Scrubs" beyond 2007 is cloudy, its legacy is much less so. Roush says appreciation for "Scrubs" will grow in its afterlife.

"Because of its creativity, 'Scrubs' has earned its place among the really significant shows of our time, if not all time," Roush says. "I don't know if the show makes history the way 'MASH' does, but it sure makes for some good times."

Reflect on the Reading

Questions About "Genre Jumping Pays Off"

1. What does "Genre Jumping Pays Off" teach us about genres? Does the article suggest that *Scrubs* simply jumps between the genres of comedy and drama or that it creates a new kind of genre? What might be the difference?

2. Jon Weisman suggests that one of the greatest achievements of *Scrubs* is its tone. What do you suppose Weisman means by tone? (For more on tone, see Part 6.) If you've seen *Scrubs* how would you describe its tone? If not, what other shows can you think of that have a distinct tone? How do television shows establish a tone?

3. According to the article, what is significant about the use of cameras or voiceovers in *Scrubs*? How might these innovations help you discuss the show in terms of genres?

4. *Scrubs* has not achieved the level of popularity of other sitcoms. Do you think this has to do with its genre jumping? Why or why not?

"Genre Jumping Pays Off" demonstrates that you need a nuanced understanding of genres as a reader and writer. Often, compositions blend elements of several genres: a television show like *Scrubs* combines elements of comedy and drama; the humor becomes a vehicle for delivering serious messages. And our understanding of genres often depends on our knowledge of other genres. You might make sense of a hospital comedy in part by comparing it with a medical drama. Similarly, you can consider one kind of writing (a memoir, say) in terms of another kind (perhaps a research paper) to learn more about each.

Genres are often determined in large part by historical situations and culture

Further, genres are often determined in large part by historical situations and culture. In the first half of the twentieth century, a mystery novel would feature a hard-boiled male detective saving the day for a vulnerable woman. Today, you're just as likely to find a hard-as-nails female protagonist hauling the bad guy off to jail. Although jazz and hip hop may differ a good deal musically, they share similar historical traits as expressions of counterculture. So, genres can be understood in terms of their historical contexts and can serve as lenses for thinking about culture.

Finally, genres are connected to social and rhetorical situations. Think of the five-paragraph essay. In high school or when sitting down for a standardized test, a five-paragraph essay might be the genre of choice. However, in a college writing class, a five-paragraph essay will likely be viewed as too formulaic and simple. The same form might be highly valued in one situation, but disregarded in another. For this reason, thinking about genres must be accompanied by thinking about rhetorical situations and cultural networks.

Genres are built around conventions but also shift, blend, and change. You must ask questions about conventions and types of writing and pursue those questions in terms of specific rhetorical situations. You can then make choices about genre expectations as you read and compose. You may need to track more closely with the conventions of the genre (e.g., in a résumé). You may be working in a genre in which the conventions are clear, but also more flexible (e.g., a profile). Or you may have to make adjustments to the way you work with a genre as you encounter less familiar forms, all the time thinking about conventions, purposes, audiences, and contexts (e.g., in a playlist or photo essay).

Know It Strategies for Understanding Genres

- Think about how genres relate to other communication categories and constraints. The medium of film or the venue of the public speech, for instance, enable certain kinds of genres—the horror thriller or the wedding toast. How can genres enable and limit certain kinds of communication?
- Identify the features that characterize a given genre. Lists of characteristics will be hard to pin down completely, but thinking about common traits can help you discover key elements of a genre. What do these features tell you about texts or writing decisions?
- Explore the ways in which variations from genre conventions help you understand communication. An Outkast song might stand out for the way it modifies familiar expectations for hip hop. What do exceptions to the rules tell you?
- Think about the ways genres change over time or in response to elements of culture. Game shows have evolved into reality television. Science fiction films retain some genre elements, but they have also changed in response to computer-generated effects. What can you learn by zooming out to ask about history or related people, things, ideas, and texts?
- Understand the social dimensions of genres. The Western is no longer a mainstay of popular culture. In fact, many of the genre elements of earlier Westerns—savage Indians, helpless women, and macho men—will even appear offensive to contemporary viewers. What do genres tell us about culture and values?

Ask
Questions
& Make
Decisions

Exercises for Understanding Genres

1. Explore some genres that might be thought of as reasonably stable—the sonnet, the business letter, the romantic comedy, the pop song, etc. Select one genre, and then make a list of its key features. Next, list examples of variations of these features. Write a paragraph or two explaining whether you find the genre to be more stable and predictable or more fluid and variable.

2. Working with a group of peers, explore the genre of the five-paragraph essay. Begin by listing its key features and any significant variations on these features. Next, think about how the genre relates to other forms of writing. Identify two related forms, and then write a few sentences comparing the five-paragraph essay to them. Finally, think about the social dimensions of the five-paragraph essay, making a list of all of the ways in which the essay shapes and is shaped by cultural networks.

3. Think about a television show, film, or song that you find to be particularly innovative. Write a paragraph exploring the innovations in the item in terms of genre.

4. How can genres help us think about other phenomena? Can genres help us understand fashion, sports, college life? Choose an area that wouldn't normally be thought about in terms of genre, and then write a one-page analysis of the phenomenon as a genre.

Understanding Mediums

Learning Objective 1.5

A medium refers to the materials you use when you compose and to the way your compositions are transmitted. Often, you will use more than one medium as you work—bringing images into a research report, for instance. To make things more complicated, materials can be both abstract and physical: in a speech, words can be your materials; in a sculpture, clay. To get a sense of the questions raised by mediums, let's explore a reading.

 ## The Whole Damn Bus Is Cheering
MICHAEL BIERUT

Michael Bierut practices for the Pentagram design consultancy in New York. He is also the editor of several design journals and publishes regularly at the Web site DesignObserver.com. He teaches at the Yale school of art. "The Whole Damn Bus Is Cheering" first appeared on DesignObserver.com.

Stuck in horrible traffic on the New Jersey Turnpike last weekend, I didn't have much to look at other than the other slowly moving cars. Then I started noticing them, everywhere: those ribbon stickers.

While they come in different colors, the most popular is yellow. While they bear different messages, the most common is "Support Our Troops." And while the sentiments they espouse are noble, the design of these things is just plain awful.

The history of the yellow ribbon is sometimes traced back to a Civil War legend or a 1940s John Wayne movie, but for most of us it started with a 1973 pop song of excruciating banality: "Tie A Yellow Ribbon" by the ludicrous Tony Orlando and Dawn. Written by Irwin Levine and L. Russell Brown, the song combined a cloying, maddeningly unforgettable melody with lyrics no one would mistake for Cole Porter. [The lyrics to the song depict a man who is on his way home after a long absence. The singer is worried that his love will have abandoned him, but when he arrives home there are hundreds of yellow ribbons awaiting him, prompting all the passengers on the bus to let out a cheer.]

Particularly unnerving to me, along with the cheesiness of the fermata before the climactic line, was the implication that the narrator managed to tell "the whole damn bus" about the pre-arranged signal. I mean, shut up already. I also thought, as did most of my friends, that the singer was a newly released prisoner, rather than a returning hero.

The 1980 capture of fifty-two American hostages in Iran provided the yellow ribbon with its first entree into mainstream culture. The ribbon, literally tied around trees, became a way of signaling support for the hostages and faith that they would be safely returned. The advent of the AIDS crisis in the mid-eighties enabled the next transition, from literal ribbon to symbolic ribbon. Folded back upon itself and pinned to a lapel, the simple red ribbon was a grass roots creation, a wearable symbol of concern for the AIDS/HIV crisis and of solidarity with its victims. There was no "official" version, so anyone could make one. Then the folded-over-ribbon form got a further boost, and its final codification, when jewelry designer Margo Manhattan created the "official" red enamel ribbon lapel pin for AmfAR in 1991.

This basic form is the progenitor for the dozens of bewildering variations that have sprung up in recent years. There are now ribbons for and against virtually everything. Often, one colored ribbon can stand for (or against) several things. Green, for example, is connected to bone marrow donation, childhood depression. regular depression, the environment, eye injury prevention, glaucoma, kidney cancer, kidney disease, kidney transplantation, leukemia, lyme disease, mental retardation, missing children, organ donation, tissue donation, and worker safety. Whew! If it helps, the alternate color for leukemia is orange, and the alternate color for missing children is yellow.

FIGURE 1.6
Support our troops ribbon.

So comes, at last, the deluge: the transfiguration of the folded-over ribbon into ubiquitous bumper sticker, coming full circle to serve as a signal of support, a heartfelt one to be sure, for American servicemen and women in Iraq and Afghanistan. In my six-hour drive on Sunday (this was New York to Philly, with flooding on the Garden State and the NJ Turnpike closed south of Exit 4 due to "congestion," traffic fans) I saw dozens, if not hundreds, of them. There were a few pink ones (signifying concern about breast cancer, I hesitantly assume), more red, white, and blue ones (general patriotism). But of course the overwhelming majority were yellow, just like the song. And the most common design? A doggedly literal drawing of that crossed and folded-over ribbon, enhanced with some crappy Photoshop effects straight out of the Hallmark cardboard birthday-party decoration playbook, squashed as flat as a pancake on the fender of every other Honda Odyssey and Lincoln Navigator. A metaphor? A symbol? Exactly! But just to make sure, let's add "Support Our Troops" in case anyone misses the point. And in a world of nearly infinite choices, what typeface would be better to signal our steadfastness than . . . what is that, anyway? Nuptial Script?

Graphic designers used to know how to develop beautiful, simple, universal symbols capable of rallying millions of people to a cause. Regardless of how you feel about this war, or about war in general, the men and women who fight deserve our support. They also deserve a better symbol.

Reflect on the Reading

Questions About "The Whole Damn Bus Is Cheering"

1. What are your thoughts on the ribbon phenomenon in Western culture? Do you believe the proliferation of ribbons for multiple causes diminishes their effect? Why or why not?
2. Bierut claims that "men and women who fight . . . deserve a better symbol." Do you agree? What alternative symbol might you suggest?
3. Can you think of ways in which the cars that carry magnetic ribbons serve as mediums? What other non-traditional mediums deliver messages?
4. How does the medium of the written essay enable Bierut to express his ideas? What challenges might arise were Bierut to try to deliver the essay's message in a pop song or through a bumper sticker or magnetic ribbon?

Michael Bierut's brief reflection on the phenomenon of magnetic ribbons on cars tells us a great deal about mediums. Bierut traces the development of the ribbon symbol from ribbons tied around trees to references in pop songs to lapel pins to magnetic stickers for vehicles. We need to investigate how these mediums influence readers and writers. A ribbon tied around a tree might convey a message through the choice of fabric (colors, size, texture) or its placement (at the end of a driveway or in public view). Songs often offer a message through lyrics, but also deliver meaning through their vocal performances and musical accompaniments. And what if a song is recorded, transmitted over the Internet, then heard over headphones, versus, say, performed to a crowd in a public park?

We can't think of mediums without asking about rhetorical situations and cultural networks

It turns out that we can't think of mediums without asking about rhetorical situations and cultural networks. Think of graffiti artists who compose on the sides of buildings using spray paint. The materials might enable their work to become instantly public, but the situation might require painting in secrecy or painting very quickly. The materials might demand painting over existing art or constrain the composition to a small space. The situation even has physical implications. Windy conditions might hinder the ability to use the materials. A redesigned aerosol nozzle might enable new compositions. Regardless of your views on graffiti, you can easily see how the medium is linked to rhetorical situations and cultural elements that can quickly call forth some complicated composing choices.

Mediums raise complex questions about materials and tools. Think of something as seemingly straightforward as a written essay. You might use a pad and pencil to create the essay, but is it possible to determine whether your materials are the pad and paper or the words you combine to create your message? What if you decided to switch to a word processor? The word processor or pad and pencil might be thought of as *tools* used to work with the materials (words), but still these tools are in some ways like materials, and they influence how you compose. If you switch to crayon, it will likely reshape your message—making it seem more childish, creative, informal, etc. Switching to crayon won't pose too many skill problems as you compose written words, but what if you are working in the medium of sound or images? You may have to learn to use tools like image editors or microphones. Again, dozens of complications and decisions can arise from the medium in which you compose.

Additionally, it's impossible to think of mediums without considering them as *means of transmission* that enable others to receive and read what you write. Paint graffiti on the side of a train instead of a building, and the medium shifts from a fixed outdoor painting space to a rolling public canvas. The differences between pad and pencil and word processor become huge if you wish to share your essay with a large group of people. So, mediums require you to think about potential audiences and the ability to share what you create with others.

Finally, to fully understand mediums, we need to think through their cultural dimensions. The magnetic ribbon on the side of an SUV might not be the most nuanced method of conveying a message, but it has become the socially accepted means of showing support for a cause—the cultural associations of the ribbons are now more meaningful than their simple color and basic shape. Mediums create different kinds of meanings for different groups and over time. Fifty years ago a story told through ink drawings and cartoon bubbles would have been called a comic book. Today we might label the story a graphic novel—the term implies a shift in perspectives and values. This evolution reflects changing reading habits, and it shows how mediums and genres also influence and shape those habits.

Know It   Strategies for Understanding Mediums

- Think of the ways a medium facilitates some kinds of messages and limits others. A written essay does not lend itself to displaying moving images. An image may not provide the depth of analysis found in a written report. Ask what a medium enables, but also prevents.
- Be aware of the ways materials and tools influence composing processes. Audio essays might require recorded interviews while a literature review essay might call for written summaries and paraphrases. Essays composed with a word processor can be revised more easily than those written on pad and paper. What are the relationships between a medium, its materials and technologies, and the kinds of reading and composing the medium makes possible?
- Remember that mediums are also means of transmitting messages. The means of transmission influences how permanent a message might be as well as how publicly it might be shared. A painting changes when hung on the wall of a museum or when digitized and posted on the Web. What matters about the way a medium transmits its message?

- Investigate the ways mediums are also shaped by history and cultural networks. Graphic novels, now considered serious compositions, might have once been viewed as childish entertainment. How can you zoom out to better understand a medium and its messages?

Ask
Questions
& Make
Decisions

Exercises for Understanding Mediums

1. Make a list of the ways in which your word processor shapes how you write. Open your word processor and explore some of the Tools, Options, and other settings, refining your list as you go. Compose a paragraph or two summarizing the influence this tool has on your writing.
2. Working with a group of peers, think of some alternative methods of composing messages in written words—skywriting, wood burning, chisel and stone, etc. Select one alternative, and then make a two-columned list; in one column note the benefits of using this medium; in the other column list the challenges.
3. Search online for free comic-making software or try your hand at drawing, and then create a short comic strip. Use your comic strip to explain something about mediums or writing.
4. Find a new medium of expression—podcasts, Facebook postings, YouTube videos, and so on. Compose an analysis of the medium, concentrating on the kinds of communication facilitated by the medium, the materials, the tools needed to compose, and the social dimensions of the medium. (Consider composing in the medium you are analyzing.)

Learning from Other Mediums: Composing with Words and Images

 ## Writing with Pictures
BY **SCOTT MCCLOUD**

RESOURCES
Scott McCloud
and Comics

Scott McCloud created his best known comic, Zot, *in 1984. He has since been recognized as a leading voice calling for recognition of comics as a serious form of expression. His* Understanding Comics *appeared in 1993 and outlined his thinking about the genre. The excerpt here is from his third book,* Making Comics, *published in 2006.*

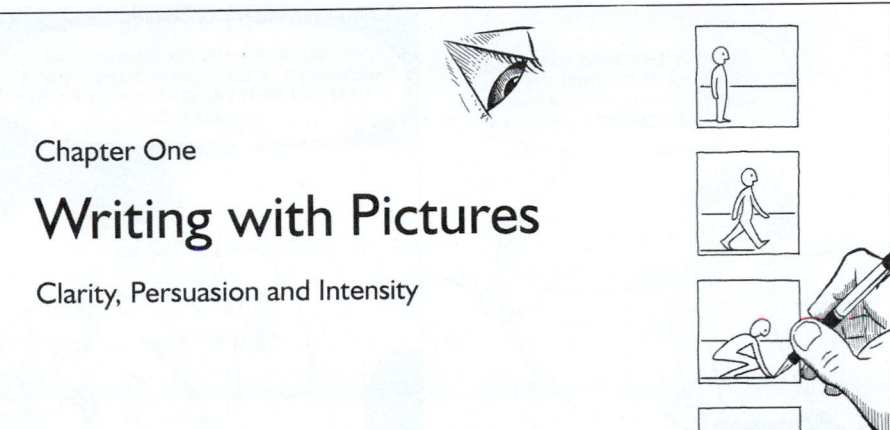

Chapter One

Writing with Pictures

Clarity, Persuasion and Intensity

It was a dark and stormy night...

tap
tap
tap

APOLOGIES TO C. SCHULZ.

Reflect on the Reading

Questions About "Writing with Pictures"

1. McCloud suggests that the goals of clarity and persuasion are necessary to connect with the audience of comics. Is it fair to say that these goals are necessary in any rhetorical situation? Why or why not?

2. The excerpt suggests that five types of decision making are required to compose comics—choices of moment, frame, image, words, and flow. Can you think of specific parallels when it comes to decision making required to compose stories made entirely of words? What about decision making to compose in other genres using words?

3. How does McCloud's comic relate to rhetorical purposes and strategies? Can you determine what might have prompted McCloud to compose this piece? How many broad strategies—like writing to express, entertain, inform, inquire, and persuade—can you recognize in the comic?

4. What comes to mind when you ask questions about McCloud's work in terms of genre. If you view comics as a genre, what questions arise in terms of expectations, readership, historical influences, and similar concerns?

5. What kind of medium is the comics form? Would it be fair to say that the words in the comic are one medium and the images another? What happens when you combine the words and images? Should we call comics multimedia? If so, how should we respond when asked to read or compose in such a form?

Respond

Write About Rhetorical Situations, Genres, and Mediums

To review some of the concerns covered in this chapter, consider the following writing opportunities:

1. **Compose a rhetorical analysis.** Find a text or message that inspires, angers, intrigues, or otherwise appeals to you. Write an analysis in which you discuss the text in terms of its rhetorical situation. What can you say about the speaker and the audience? What about the purposes or strategies you discover in the text? Zoom in to discuss the details of the message. Zoom out to explore contexts and choices about genre and medium. (For more on composing rhetorical analyses, see Chapter 7.)

2. **Experiment with rhetorical purposes and strategies.** Think of an interesting rhetorical situation: you have to break up with someone, you need to auction oddities from Uncle Walter's attic, you want your teachers to cancel class the day after Halloween, etc. Choose a writing strategy, and then compose a paragraph or two responding to the situation. Next, switch strategies (perhaps deciding to be entertaining instead of—or in addition to—being persuasive) and compose another response. Write a final paragraph reflecting on your two compositions.

3. **Explore alternative mediums.** Think of some examples that might qualify as unusual mediums—a boxcar covered with graffiti, a matchbook, a rock garden, clothes, food, etc. Think about some of the challenges and opportunities afforded by composing in this medium, and then write up your thoughts in a brief response. (Consider composing your response in the medium you are discussing.)

4. **Practice combining words and images.** Find an image online that engages you—a favorite photograph, humorous ad, a beautiful landscape, etc. Insert the image into a composition—a word processor will work fine, or you can try other tools—and then use words to respond to the message of the image. You might analyze the image, use it as a prompt for a story, or explain personal or cultural connections, to name some options. (For more on analyzing images, see Chapter 25.)

Zoom Out   Reflecting on Rhetorical Situations, Genres, and Mediums

- **Reading and writing are all about asking questions and making choices.** Adjusting your focus—zooming in and out—helps you discover problems and questions. Readers think about the decisions informing texts; writers make choices as they compose.

- **Rhetorical situations also involve the larger contexts of any act of communication, the cultural network.** Lee Scott's speech to Wal-Mart shareholders was launched into a world with preconceptions about the retail giant. This world includes additional messages, a host of people interested in the topic, and cultural concerns related to climate, economics, politics, consumerism, and so on.

- **The purpose and strategies informing any message relate to its rhetorical situation.** Authors have specific purposes in mind as they compose (to stop development in the local marsh, for instance). Authors also use rhetorical strategies for writing including writing to express, to entertain, to inform, to inquire, or to persuade.

- **Genres help us make sense of what we read and write.** While genres possess characteristic features, individual texts will present variations of those features. Variations might lead to sub-genres. Further, genres are not fixed categories. They take shape based on the influences of other genres and on elements of culture.

- **Mediums include the materials one uses to create a message.** These materials influence the kinds of communication that can take place and call for specific tools and skills to be used by writers. Mediums also account for the means of transmission through which messages can be exchanged.

For additional information and practice with the learning objectives in this chapter, go to www.mycomplab.com, Resources > Writing > The Writing Process > Planning.

2

Understanding Composing Processes

Zoom In Key Concepts and Learning Objectives

After studying this chapter, you should be able to:

2.1 Understand the stages of the composing process.

2.2 Explore questions and develop ideas by using prewriting strategies.

2.3 Record your thoughts quickly without getting bogged down in surface-level details by using effective drafting strategies.

2.4 Revise your compositions by thinking about your overall purpose, approach, and organization.

2.5 Edit and polish your compositions, using appropriate formats and conventions.

Have you ever had ideas for a project come to you while you were on your bicycle, in the shower, or maybe even making a sandwich? If so, you have experienced one of the ways in which the composing process can't be limited to the moment when you draft a piece of writing. Most big projects involve multiple intellectual tasks that can happen at various times. You might read for days, write for hours, put things aside, discover an insight on the bus, revise ideas, write some more, read again. Who knows exactly how things will play out?

Composing processes differ from writer to writer and from situation to situation. Some writers shun outlines while others couldn't work without one. A lengthy essay calls for serious planning while a Twitter message might be dashed off. Although everyone's approach will vary and there are no hard and fast rules, we need to draw some conclusions and use some common language to help make sense of how composing happens. To this end, this chapter talks about composing by dividing it into four familiar categories.

In some ways, these categories can help you work through a project by giving you starting places and possible paths to pursue. These categories include prewriting, the activities that take place prior to composing and during any part of the process in which ideas need to be discovered or invented; drafting, the composing that takes place as you figure out the connections between ideas and put thoughts on paper (or on screen); revising, the large-scale adjustments you make to improve what you have already drafted; and editing and polishing, the stylistic and surface-oriented adjustments that make the project easier to read.

> **Most big projects involve multiple intellectual tasks that can happen at various times**

KEY TERMS

- **Composing process:** The activities authors undertake as they develop a writing project. There are no absolute rules for how writers work, but there are some core activities that include prewriting, drafting, revising, and editing and polishing. These activities can occur at varying times, overlap, and inform one another.

- **Prewriting:** The activities you undertake before putting thoughts down on screen or paper. Prewriting generally happens early in the writing process, but can be employed to generate and refine ideas at any time. Prewriting activities include listing, outlining, drawing, freewriting, journaling, conversing, and asking questions.

- **Drafting:** Writing that is primarily concerned with recording ideas. When drafting, writers should have some notion of what they intend to say, but should remain flexible, letting thoughts flow and avoiding too much emphasis on surface-level issues.

- **Revising:** Activities through which you make large adjustments to a writing project. Generally, you zoom out when revising, thinking about how well the piece responds to the assignment, about your rhetorical situation, and about organization, missing pieces, and possible new directions.

- **Editing and polishing:** Writing activities that help prepare a project for viewing by others. Editing involves tightening language and addressing stylistic or mechanical problems. Polishing addresses surface-level concerns like formatting.

Identifying Composing Processes

LO

Learning
Objective 2.1

To make sense of composing processes, let's explore an example, an essay written by student Marcus Bynum.

➘ Where Are My Beats?
BY **MARCUS BYNUM**

Marcus's essay looks at the relationship between slam poetry and reggaeton music. He composed the essay in response to an assignment calling for an analysis of a genre. He adjusted his focus using a comparison strategy (see Chapter 23), discussing two genres in terms of each other. Marcus also conducted a good deal of research to learn more about his topic. He includes sources from his research to support his points, cites his sources in parenthesis in the essay, and then includes a list of works cited at the end of the paper. (You can learn more about research and about using sources in your writing in Chapters 14–17.)

Marcus Bynum

Professor Anderson

English 102

15 Mar. 2007

Where Are My Beats?

The genres of reggaeton and slam poetry at first might seem to have little in common. Reggaeton is a form of dance music first popularized in the Caribbean and Latin America and now part of mainstream popular music. Slam poetry is a kind of performance art once found only in college coffee shops and bookstores. But both genres share features and say a lot about their social groups. In fact, comparing the two reveals how genres develop from background influences but also rely on innovative artists to become popular. Further, reggaeton and slam poetry illustrate how genres evolve and influence other genres. Finally, reggaeton and slam poetry show that, despite having unique features, many genres have enough similarities to give them a common link.

What makes reggaeton interesting as a genre is how it blends together the influences of reggae and American hip hop to create a new style of music. The newness of this style is clear in the Latin focus of reggaeton. Most of the lyrics (at least in early reggaeton) were sung in Spanish and the beat combines reggae and hip hop beats with a Latin rhythm that sets the music apart. Many trace the reggaeton beat to a particular song that has become synonymous with the genre. "Dem Bow," released in 1991 by Shabba Ranks on his *Just Reality* CD, popularized the minimal driving beat repeated endlessly that forms the backbone for reggaeton music. This feature can't be overemphasized when discussing the genre. The steady looping of the single-minded drum beat has made reggaeton instantly recognizable and popular on the dance floor. Still, many have complained that the genre has become stagnant because there is so little variation on this feature. For instance, Luis Bode complains in an editorial to *Billboard* magazine that "it becomes so easy for the artists, musicians, producers and remixers to create under the banner of 'ley del menor esfuerzo' (the law of least effort). Which could lead many fans to tire of the sound—unless it can do a Madonna and reinvent itself" (Bode 4). It's true that the reggaeton rhythm is so steady it makes one worry that it will become a fad. You can hear samples of the reggaeton dem bow beat in the online article, "The Rise of Reggaeton" at http://www.thephoenix.com/article_ektid1595.aspx.

While the reggaeton beat emerged in the early '90s and can be recognized in particular songs, the history of the genre is harder to trace. Some people will trace reggaeton to earlier songs like "El Meneaito" by Gaby, which does not have the essential dem bow beat, but maintains a steady drum-backed rhythm and emphasizes Latin rap. Others cite Panamanian artists like El General as early precursors of reggaeton; these Panamanians began adapting dancehall reggae for Latin audiences in the 1980s (Marshal). Without major trendsetters like artists from Panama, Gaby, and Daddy Yankee, reggaeton may not have formed as genre. But we also need to look at how these artists were influenced by trends in music. The strongest influence is reggae, which spread during the '70s and '80s throughout Latin America and into Puerto Rico. These reggae sounds blended with other forms of Latin music like Plena (featuring a regular kick drum beat). On top of these influences, American hip hop seeped into reggaeton in the form of rapped lyrics layered over the beats. Overall, we can see reggaeton as a genre that grew out of these influences and was driven by several innovative artists (Marshal).

Like reggaeton, slam poetry has a complicated history. The genre originated in Chicago in the mid-1980s during performances in bars and jazz clubs. The performances were meant to be rowdy, open to anyone who wanted to participate, and based on a principle of competition. These slams grew in popularity and soon spread to college towns like Ann Arbor, Michigan, and to cities like New York and San Francisco. But the influences of the slam movement stretch back before the 1980s. It's possible to find resemblances of the slams in the beat poets of the 1960s who often gave readings featuring rowdy performances and improvisation. Contemporary performance poet Gary Glazner explains that the beats "brought a lot of energy to their readings, and that's what they have in common with slam poetry" (Reel). Others find earlier versions of the slam in late 1970s poetry readings modeled after boxing matches. These competitive readings formed the backdrop of the Chicago scene where slam poetry emerged in the mid-1980s. Elaine Equi was an early participant in these competitions and ties the development of slams to the cultural movements of the times: "We were with the punk scene. A lot of forces were converging in Chicago at the same time. . . . Suddenly there was an audience for poetry. There really isn't anything that close to the experience today except in rap music" (Heintz).

While beat poets and earlier performers no doubt shaped the genre of the poetry slam, the classic examples of slam poetry are often traced to a single person, Marc Smith, or Slampapi to use his stage name. Smith established the regular poetry performances at the Green Mill Jazz club in Chicago and put in place the key features of slams that are present today. Readings are generally limited in time (often to three minutes)—no poet is allowed to dominate the stage. Random members of the audience are chosen to judge the readings, usually on a scale of 1–10. Readings proceed in rounds until there is a winner. The genre of the slam has also developed some conventions for style and subject matter. Helena Echlin observes that

> although there are no restrictions on what you can recite, a slam style has evolved (run-on sentences, emphatic repetition and blunt vernacular) and so has a typical slam subject matter. Bittersweet confession is popular and so is bitter social commentary, partly because the slam poet has to keep one eye on his scorecard, and it's easier to whip up an audience with words like "revolution." (Echlin)

Slams have always been a part of underground culture, but their current associations also include ethnic and urban identities. Some of this evolution relates to the development of slams in large cities. The latest hot spot for slams is the Nuyorican café in New York, run by a nonprofit organization to give minorities an outlet for their expressions (Echlin). The urban *Def Poetry Jam*, created by HBO, features Mos Def hosting a number of readings by up-and-coming poets. In many ways, *Def Poetry Jam* might represent a new genre, one that builds on the slam, but incorporates more hip hop themes and approaches to performing. It's interesting that early slam poet Elaine Equi compared the atmosphere of early slams with the excitement of today's hip hop culture. While it's impossible to draw a direct line between slams and hip hop, rappers like Sage Francis, who brings a slam poetry background and social messages to hip hop, show how, like reggaeton, the genre of the slam continues to evolve.

Although there are differences between reggaeton and slam poetry (reggaeton is much more focused on dance beats and arguably has gone more mainstream), the similarities between the genres are more interesting. Both reggaeton and slam poetry illustrate the ways that genres grow out of their influences and reflect parts of culture. Reggaeton took reggae, Latin beats, and American hip hop to form a new genre. This new genre provided a vehicle for expressing Latin American culture. Slam poetry began in bars and clubs as an expression of underground artists. Further, both reggaeton and slam poetry relied on key individuals to develop. Marc Smith gave the slam poetry movement enough momentum to become a genre. Songs like "Dem Bow" by Shabba Ranks helped spark the birth of reggaeton. It's impossible to completely trace the genres to these individuals or songs, but these examples are helpful milestones for learning how genres get started.

Finally, both genres have evolved to take on new features or influence other genres and parts of culture. When R. Kelly released "Burn it Up" in 2005, it demonstrated how far reggaeton had shifted toward the mainstream ("Genre Watch"). Similarly, in 1998, when Nike asked slam poets to contribute poems to advertisements to be run during the Winter Olympics, the movement could be said to have also run into the mainstream (Echlin). Even more interesting are recent developments that show slam poetry blending into hip hop genres. The *Def Poetry Jam* and artists like Sage Francis represent the spoken word being translated into the culture of hip hop and the form of music. If hip hop influenced reggaeton, and now slam poetry is influencing hip hop, we can see that these genres have a common link. It turns out that, despite their differences and unique histories and features, reggaeton and slam poetry both fit into a larger category that gives them meaning and continues to influence our culture. They both share the qualities of expressing ideas about society with beats and spoken words.

Works Cited

Bode, Luis. "Reggaeton Needs Revamping." Letter. *Billboard* 14 Oct. 2006: 4. Print.

Echlin, Helena. "Open Nike." *New Statesman*. 17 Nov. 2003. Web. 15 Mar. 2007.

"Genre Watch: Reggaeton." *Remix*. (Jan 5, 2007). *InfoTrac*. Davis Lib., U of North Carolina. Web. 15 Mar. 2007.

Heintz, Kurt. "An Incomplete History of Slam." *The E-Poets Network*. 2007. Web. 15 Mar. 2007.

Marshal, Wayne. "The Rise of Reggaeton." *The Phoenix*. 19 Jan. 2006. Web. 15 Mar. 2007.

Reel, James. "The Beat Goes On: Ghosts of the Beat Generation Crash a Poetry Slam." *Tucson Weekly*. 25 Apr. 2002. Web. 15 Mar. 2007.

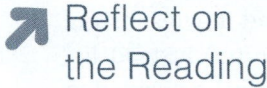

Reflect on the Reading

Questions About "Where Are My Beats?"

1. What are your thoughts on the two genres Marcus has selected to compare in "Where are My Beats?" Do these choices shed light on each other? What other possible choices might you recommend?

2. How well does the essay demonstrate the features of the genres? Are there any important features of reggaeton or slam poetry that have been overlooked?

3. What do you think of the examples chosen to illustrate the points made in the essay? Are the examples discussed in enough detail? Is the discussion connected to the explanations in the essay? What other examples might be discussed?

4. How well does the essay compare and contrast the two genres? Are there important distinctions or comparisons that have been overlooked? Does the comparison help you understand something about genres?

Think about Marcus's essay on reggaeton and slam poetry. The essay demonstrates a good deal of knowledge on the subject and explains its points clearly. It is well organized, uses evidence, documents its sources, and has few stylistic problems. But Marcus was by no means an expert when he started the project. And the first drafts of his essay didn't explain all of his points clearly and were in fact quite messy. From the essay, you might conclude that Marcus is an expert on literature and music and an accomplished writer, but he only got to this point after a good deal of composing. Let's take a closer look at Marcus's composing process.

Prewriting

There are almost as many ways of prewriting as there are of thinking

There are almost as many ways of prewriting as there are of thinking; you might get ideas for your project while you ride your bicycle or mow your lawn. But there are some concrete strategies as well that can help you get started on a project. These strategies include making lists, outlines, or graphic organizers; conducting research; freewriting; journaling; holding conversations; and asking questions.

Before writing his essay, Marcus began listing possible ideas for his genre comparison. His initial list appears in Figure 2.1.

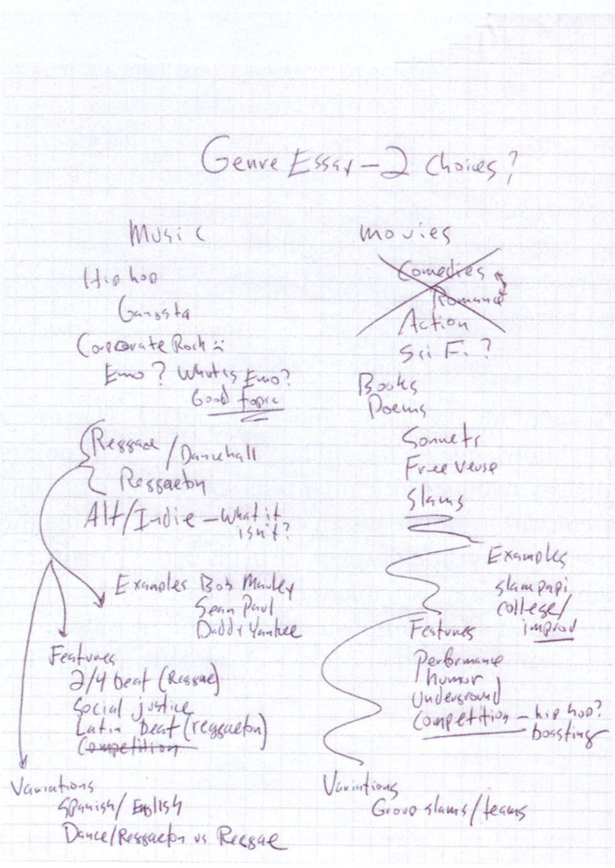

FIGURE 2.1

Marcus's list of possible ideas for his essay.

Marcus began by thinking about comparing music and movies, listing some movie genres. He decided to abandon the movies topic and, instead, list genres of literature. Eventually he decided to focus on slam poetry (a topic about which he had an interest), and he began to list details related to slam poetry. Note how Marcus has been exploring elements of culture and zooming in and out as he brainstorms about the essay (see Chapter 1). Listing has helped him focus on specific characteristics of genres. Arrows and the space on the page have helped him identify connections and organize ideas.

Some writers prefer to extend this method into graphic maps that use shapes, lines, colors, and arrangement to organize ideas visually. Some writers prefer to use a journal where they can explore ideas and keep a record of their thinking. Find a method that works best for you, and then understand that the process of exploration or invention is connected to your ability to zoom in and out to focus your thinking. Marcus zooms in to identify specific artists to discuss. He zooms out to explore cultural networks, finding connections with topics like social justice or humor. And he zooms in and out as he develops the comparison between reggaeton and slam poetry.

Eventually, Marcus decided to compare slam poetry with reggaeton. To think about how he came to that decision, you can look at some notes he took on one of the readings he collected when he began researching the project (see Figure 2.2). Notice how he concludes his notes by reacting to what he has read. He has doubts about the claim that Latino music is more likely to blend genres and he decides he needs to know more about the history of reggaeton. Earlier, he commented on the claim that reggaeton is a hybrid genre. At this point, we can see that Marcus is arriving at his more limited focus on reggaeton (instead of reggae or dancehall) by virtue of his interest and concerns about the topic.

FIGURE 2.2
Marcus's annotations and notes on a reading.

We can see that Marcus is already developing some questions that can help him further explore his topic. In addition to the questions that occur as you read and brainstorm, you can ask yourself some deliberate questions to help grease the wheels of your thinking. You might use the journalist's questions (who, what, when, where, why, and how) to generate ideas. You might ask questions about your rhetorical situation. (Who is my audience? What is my purpose? What do I know about my subject?) Or you might ask about elements of culture. (Who is connected to my topic and how does my subject relate to other texts, things, or ideas?)

Another prewriting strategy is to experiment with freewriting—timed writing exercises in which you record your stream of ideas as you explore a topic. And you can take up your topic with others in conversation to help you develop ideas. You might see whether the topic has been discussed in online forums, you can sit down with a family member or classmate to talk through your topic, or you can exchange some instant messages with a friend to ask and answer questions.

GENRE WATCH: REGGAETON. *Remix (Online Exclusive)* (Jan 5, 2007)

If you stop and think about it, there are few areas of the world that have spawned as many influential genres of music as the Caribbean. Salsa, merengue, cumbia and reggae were all born there. Expand a few miles out, and you'll find some of the regional Mexican styles like norteno and tejano as well. All of those genres are pretty much unassailable musical traditions, right? Well, not if you're a rebellious, urban Latino with access to a sampler and some software to shake things up.   *Genres can be revised!*

Case in point: the mix of dancehall reggae, hip-hop, salsa, cumbia and other Caribbean beats, known as reggaeton. While Latinos are the main audience, reggaeton's popularity is reaching even those who do not speak Spanish. Blame it on the beat.   *Beat is key feature of reggaeton*

A few years ago, reggaeton was barely a trend; now it's everywhere. There are whole radio formats built around it. The latest hits play in clubs and bars, on MTV and over the loudspeakers at baseball games. Pop artists such as R. Kelly, Alicia Keys and even Evanescence are trying to steal a little thunder from these upstarts by putting out reggaeton remixes. But some upand- coming Latin artists are sick of the phenomenon. Just as many countries have their own versions of reggaeton, they also have their own backlashes to it, resulting in vibrant musical subcultures.   *mainstream*

Reggaeton is a true hybrid. It's hard synth sounds and dancehall merengue-flavored rhythms get cues from all the previous genres it steals from without really sounding like any of them. But with a style of music that is so easy to make in a home studio with limited equipment, is it here to stay? Or is there a kid with a bootleg of Fruity Loops, a Boss drum machine and a distortion pedal just around the corner with the next big new style?   *Interesting. Guy you steal from other kinds of music am still be a genre?*

Latin America has a long tradition of the mash-up. Most Latin American music is a mix of European, indigenous and African music. So new genres such as reggaeton and Brazil's baile funk are not really breaking from the mold of their traditional music; they are simply branching out by incorporating new techniques, new technology and new perspectives. Reggaeton is as much traditional as it is modern, and in some parts of the world, it has supplanted rap in terms of popularity. With a sharp divide between lovers and haters of the genre, it was only natural that reggaeton become the music for rebellious young Latinos.

Are Latinos more likely to blend and mix genres? I doubt it. Plus reggaeton is such a hip hop genre — to me. Maybe not. Need more history of reggaeton

---

Know It **Strategies for Prewriting**

LO

Learning Objective 2.2

- Know that prewriting can take place at any time during a project. You might find that you need to go back to prewriting before you make revisions, for example. Remain flexible and use prewriting strategies anytime you need them.
- Zoom in and out as you explore ideas for a topic. Trace connections through cultural networks and train your focus on specific elements to examine the big picture as well as the details.

- Use freewriting, listing, journaling, outlining, and mapping to generate and focus ideas. Experiment with using pad and paper or other tools to force yourself to explore informally in the early stages of a project.
- Ask questions to drive your prewriting. If you discover questions related to your topic, they will lead you toward an area of focus. If you are stuck, you can query yourself using set questions (like the journalist's) to generate ideas.
- Join conversations to help generate and focus ideas. Explore online conversations to learn more about topics. Find a partner to help you discover and refine your topic.
- Use research and reading as forms of prewriting. As you look for sources, pay attention to how your thinking becomes more focused. Mark up your sources and take notes as you read to extend and concretize your thinking.

Ask Questions & Make Decisions

Exercises for Prewriting

1. As you begin thinking about a writing project, try this experiment: Open a new word processor document and place your cursor at the top of the page. Think about your topic, and then turn off your monitor or partially close your laptop screen. Compose freely about your topic for five minutes. When finished, look at what you have written and think about how this unseen typing affects your writing process.

2. Use a set of colored pens or pencils the next time you begin a project. Create a graphic organizer or map that details the main areas you will cover. Use colors to associate similar items and to demonstrate your thinking. (You can also use software like Inspiration, Freemind, or Cmap.)

3. As you begin thinking about a writing project, list on paper or on note cards the journalist's questions (who, what, where, when, why, and how). For each of the questions, develop a list of further questions (e.g., *Who cares about my topic? What matters about my subject? Why do people disagree?*, and so on). Working from your cards, develop a response to several of the questions.

4. For projects that require working with sources, annotate the texts you are reading. In addition to highlighting or underlining passages, add notes in the margins that distill key points, record questions that come up for you, and offer possible avenues you can explore as you write. When finished reading, look over these annotations and write several sentences exploring how you might discuss the source in a larger essay.

Drafting

Drafting should be primarily concerned with getting ideas onto screen or paper

Have you ever had the automated grammar or spell checker of your word processor influence your drafting? Maybe you stopped in the middle of a thought to go back and remove the green or red squiggle beneath a word or phrase, and then, when you returned to finish your thought, it had dissipated. If so, you might experiment with your drafting process. Drafting should be primarily concerned with getting ideas onto screen or paper. If there are small mechanical issues in your drafts, you can clean them up later.

Look at the first draft of Marcus's opening to his genre comparison essay (see Figure 2.3). Notice the words and phrases that have been flagged by the word processor. Were he to stop and worry about getting just the right phrasing of a sentence or fixing every problem on the first try, he might hamper his flow of ideas. Instead, Marcus has composed the draft with the intent of getting his ideas out. Obviously you need to make adjustments as you draft, but the point is that you should strive to use drafting as an opportunity to explore and express ideas with as little interference as possible.

Of course, drafting is not exactly the same as prewriting. If you have no sense at all of what you want to say or how you will say it, you might be better served by exploring more informal ways of getting at your ideas. Drafting generally calls for some focus in your thinking. Although you are only getting started with your composing, you should have already done some thinking about your topic and identified an angle you might use to discuss things.

You should also consider the timing of your assignment as you think about how best to draft your project. Don't begin drafting the night before your project is due; there simply won't be enough time for drafting, revising, and editing. Also, think about what sections you will draft and when. You might save the introduction for last, if you are having trouble forecasting what you want to say. If you have research sources to discuss, you might start with a summary (pages 375–76) and then translate that into the draft of a section of an essay. (It can help to make a work schedule with deadlines when you have a large project to complete.)

Eventually, you will need to get down to the nitty-gritty work of drafting paragraphs. Concentrate on organizing your paragraphs into coherent chunks so that you can draft the information quickly and convincingly. Have a focus for each paragraph, and then use examples and evidence to explain your focus and to illustrate your points. You can spell out the focus of your paragraphs using topic sentences (pages 417–19). Discuss any quotations you use to connect them with your points and to bring out your angle of approach to your topic.

VIDEO
12. Drafting

FIGURE 2.3

An early draft of Marcus's essay.

Comparing the genres of reggaeton and slam poetry at first might seem to have little in common. Reggaeton is a form of dance music first popularized in the Caribbean and Latin America and now part of mainstream popular music. Slam poetry is a kind of performance art found in college coffee shops and bookstores. But both genres share features and say a lot about their social groups. In fact, comparing the two teaches us how genres develop from background influences but also rely on leaders or trends to become popular.

It can be difficult to define the genre of reggaeton. Mostly because the genre mixes so many influences. It builds upon the Jamaican and reggae music and culture that has permeated the Caribbean. But it also picks up on American hip hop beats and themes. What makes reggaeton interesting as a genre is how it takes these influences and creates a new style of music by blending them together. The newness of this style is clear in the Latin focus of reggaeton. Most of the lyrics (at least in early regaeton) were sung in Spanish and the beat adds to the mix of regge and hip hop sounds a Latin rhythm that sets the music apart.

Many trace the reggaeton beat to a particualar song that has become synonymous with the the genre. "Dem Bow," by Shabba Ranks released in 1991. (Just Reality) popularized the minimal driving beat repeated endlessly that forms the backbone for reggaeton music. This feature can't be overemphasized when discussing the genre. The steady looping of the single-minded drum beat has made reggaeton instantly recognizable and popular on the dance floor. Still, many have complained that the genre has become stagnant because there is so little variation on this feature.

Know It   Strategies for Drafting

LO

Learning Objective 2.3

- Use drafting at any time during a project. You might find that you begin drafting materials as soon as you start taking notes on your readings. Remain flexible and draft materials whenever it becomes necessary.
- Know that drafting will benefit from your having done some exploration ahead of time. Have an angle or area of focus for your topic. Map out your project, listing ideas to be covered or sections you intend to compose.
- Focus on getting ideas out. Don't worry about small mechanical issues or get bogged down in finding the perfect phrasing as you compose. Draft to get the main points sorted out, and then go back and clean things up later.
- Be flexible. If you get writer's block, try beginning with a different section. Consider composing your introduction after you have a better sense of the shape of your project.
- As you draft paragraphs, concentrate on writing strategies (analyzing, describing, comparing, etc.) that will best meet your purpose. Be clear about the main points or focus to be covered in each paragraph. Discuss examples and quotations to make your points.

Ask Questions & Make Decisions

Exercises for Drafting

1. Working with a partner, select a topic for an essay and then engage in a conversation to brainstorm ideas and draft sections of the essay. Have one of you ask an initial question about the topic and then collaboratively compose a few sentences in response to the question. Look over what you have written together, and then revise it into a paragraph. Continue this process until you have drafted several paragraphs of an essay.

2. Put yourself in a non-writing situation where you can think freely about a topic (walking to school, bicycling through the park, taking a shower, etc.). Compose in your head either an outline for a paper discussing your topic or the opening section of such a paper. After you have finished your activity, write down as much of the composition as you can recall.

3. Take the results of one of the prewriting activities you have conducted for a project (a piece of freewriting, a list, a graphic map, etc.) and then identify some ideas in the prewriting that you wish to pursue. Draft paragraphs expanding on these ideas.

4. Use note cards or open a word processor as you work through a collection of sources for a research project. After you have completed a reading, develop a brief summary of the source (see pages 375–76). Incorporate your summaries later into a draft of your composition.

Revising

VIDEO
13. Revising

The composing process is rarely a series of steps that proceeds in a logical sequence. This becomes clear when you think about revision. To really revise your work, you need to return to prewriting, perhaps conducting new research, sketching out ideas, and generally rethinking your approach. You will also need to return to drafting, creating new materials based on the refined vision of your project. To get a sense of how revision calls for these prewriting and drafting activities, take a look at a page from Marcus's second draft of his essay (see Figure 2.4).

Marcus has used the Track Changes function of his word processor. (See the video in our e-book for more on this feature.) This feature allows you to make major changes to your composition, and then decide later if you wish to accept or reject those changes.

The comment by Carla has been embedded in the draft of Marcus's essay using the Insert Comments feature of her word processor. (You can also see our

FIGURE 2.4

A comment from a reader and revisions to Marcus's essay.

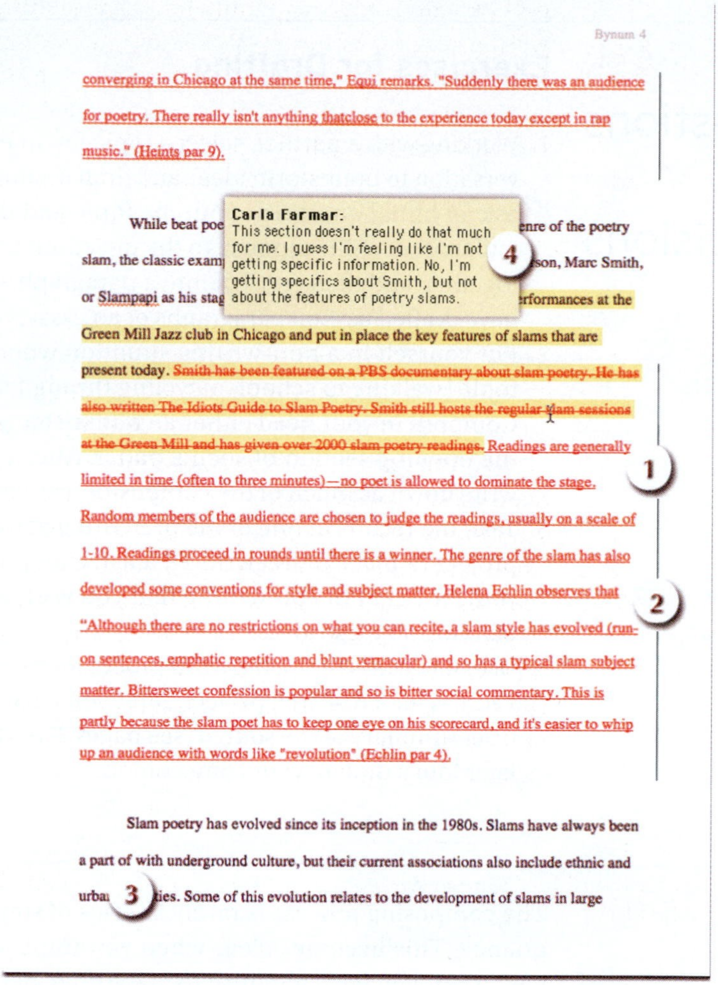

Bynum 4

converging in Chicago at the same time," Equi remarks. "Suddenly there was an audience for poetry. There really isn't anything thatclose to the experience today except in rap music." (Heints par 9).

While beat poe[...] enre of the poetry slam, the classic exam[...]son, Marc Smith, or Slampapi as his sta[...] erformances at the Green Mill Jazz club in Chicago and put in place the key features of slams that are present today. Smith has been featured on a PBS documentary about slam poetry. He has also written The Idiots Guide to Slam Poetry. Smith still hosts the regular slam sessions at the Green Mill and has given over 2000 slam poetry readings. Readings are generally limited in time (often to three minutes)—no poet is allowed to dominate the stage. Random members of the audience are chosen to judge the readings, usually on a scale of 1-10. Readings proceed in rounds until there is a winner. The genre of the slam has also developed some conventions for style and subject matter. Helena Echlin observes that "Although there are no restrictions on what you can recite, a slam style has evolved (run-on sentences, emphatic repetition and blunt vernacular) and so has a typical slam subject matter. Bittersweet confession is popular and so is bitter social commentary. This is partly because the slam poet has to keep one eye on his scorecard, and it's easier to whip up an audience with words like "revolution" (Echlin par 4).

Slam poetry has evolved since its inception in the 1980s. Slams have always been a part of with underground culture, but their current associations also include ethnic and urba[...] ies. Some of this evolution relates to the development of slams in large

Carla Farmar:
This section doesn't really do that much for me. I guess I'm feeling like I'm not getting specific information. No, I'm getting specifics about Smith, but not about the features of poetry slams.

1 Tracking the changes in this document shows text that has been deleted with a strikethrough font in red. You can see that Marcus has deleted much of the text in his paragraph on Marc Smith. Sometimes you may just need to move information that does not seem to fit in a given paragraph, but also be willing to let ideas go if they don't further the main points you wish to make.

2 The tracked changes in this document show new text in an underlined red font. Here, Marcus has essentially drafted most of this paragraph anew. You can also see that he has returned to his readings to identify examples and quotations to put into this revised section. You can see how prewriting and drafting play out even in the revision process.

3 Notice the small mechanical error in the second sentence of the third paragraph, "part *of with* underground culture." When drafting, you often move quickly to get the ideas out, generating small surface errors like the double prepositions "of" and "with" in this sentence. But notice also that Marcus has not stopped to fix this glitch in the sentence. Revision should zoom out, concentrating on clarifying, organizing, and generating ideas; there will be time to clean up the document later.

4 All the major changes in this paragraph have been prompted by a comment offered by Carla Farmar. Often it takes the perspective of another to notice ideas that don't make sense or to recognize that something might be missing. Marcus has taken this feedback to heart, strengthening the essay in the process.

e-book videos to learn more about this feature.) Whether embedded using a word processor or just sketched into the margins of a paper, these comments from readers are a key aspect of the revision process. You can evaluate your own work and improve it a great deal, but to get the most out of revision, you should get feedback from other readers.

To get the most out of revision, you should get feedback from other readers

When asking for or giving feedback, it helps to keep some strategies in mind. Notice how Carla has phrased parts of her comment: "This section doesn't really do much for me." This kind of personal response is fine because it shows the thinking of a reader as she encounters the paragraph. But Carla doesn't just discuss her feelings, she goes on to list details about the paper: "I'm feeling like I'm not getting specific information. No, I'm getting specifics about Smith, but not about the features of poetry slams." You can almost see Carla thinking through her evaluation of what is and isn't working for her as she composes her response.

Notice also that Carla has not told Marcus how to fix this problem. Sometimes a concrete suggestion can be shared with the author of a paper, but for the most part readers can point out problems and allow the author to return to the drafting process to sort through revisions. Similarly, Carla has not commented on surface errors like the double prepositions "of" and "with" at the bottom of the page. She is focusing on the big picture, knowing that Marcus can go back and fix the details on his own.

Know It   **Strategies for Providing Feedback**

- Read the paper through once quickly to get a sense of the ideas being discussed and any large problems. If you provide feedback too soon you might not be aware of information that comes later in the paper, or you might miss larger concerns that should be addressed.
- Focus on your reactions to the paper. Think of the review process as an opportunity for the author of a paper to gauge the impact of her work on real readers. Offer feedback that makes this reader's perspective available to the author: "I'm not understanding this section"; "This part really grabs me," etc.
- Take notes either on a printout or by adding comments to an electronic file. You can jot down the topics of paragraphs, creating an outline of the ideas covered. Sketch out any questions that arise as you read. As you work to understand what you are reading, mark up the document to illustrate your thinking.

- Concentrate on the big picture. Forego comments on surface errors to offer feedback about the organization and ideas in the essay. Note areas where the paper is unclear. Think not only about what is covered in the essay, but also about what might be added to make it stronger.

VIDEO
14. Peer Review

- Help the writer discover avenues for revision. As you point out problems with the essay, you can suggest some approaches to revision, but don't try to fix the problems for the author. For larger concerns about the ideas and direction of the paper, pose questions that get the author thinking about the topic in fresh ways.
- Be selective in offering feedback and advice. You can comment on every paragraph, but don't nitpick. Identify which issues in the paper are minor and which are serious, and then concentrate on helping the author fix the most pressing problems.
- Compose a final comment in which you summarize your reactions to the paper—listing things you find successful and your moments of confusion or concern. Summarize your recommendations for revising the paper. Offer questions that help the author discover a sharper focus or develop missing elements of the project. Identify a few of the most pressing changes needed to help with the organization or clarity of the essay.

Know It   Strategies for Revising

LO

Learning Objective 2.4

- Use a system for keeping track of the revisions you make. Try features of your word processor for tracking changes and creating versions. Rename documents as you revise. Save printouts from drafts while working on a project.
- Solicit and take to heart feedback about your work. Collect feedback early in the process and use it to emphasize the big issues. When giving feedback, provide the voice of an interested reader, emphasizing large concerns and helping the writer discover avenues for revision.
- Let go of ideas as you revise. Be willing to shift your focus or rethink your topic, even if it means some starting over. Don't hesitate to delete text that is not working.
- Return to prewriting and drafting as you revise. Conduct more research, take notes, make lists, freewrite, or otherwise brainstorm as needed to develop ideas and to move forward. As you compose new materials maintain a healthy drafting process, focusing on getting ideas out rather than getting them just right.

Ask Questions & Make Decisions

Exercises for Revising

1. Re-read Marcus Bynum's paper on pages 37–40. Use a blank sheet of paper to make a list or a graphic map representing the organization of the essay. Revise the list or map to reflect recommendations you might make for strengthening the paper.

2. Working with a group of peers, develop a list of guidelines for giving feedback on papers. Make five or more concrete recommendations readers can use when commenting on papers. Use these recommendations the next time you conduct a review of a peer's work.

3. Open a draft of a paper in your word processor, and then experiment with the Track Changes options under the Tools menu. (See our e-book for help with these features.) Once you have a sense of how these features work, use them as you revise a paper.

4. Think about writing projects you have done in the past and identify a few that stand out. Use these projects to develop a paragraph in which you explain and then reflect on your typical revision process.

Editing and Polishing

You can see how drafting and revising are connected to thinking: you are developing and refining your ideas as you compose and revise your essay. When it comes time to edit and polish the paper, you begin to focus on how clear your explanations can be and on the styles that will enable you to engage readers. You can think of the editing process as a slow progression through which you move away from the messier drafting and revising and toward a more limited polishing. You will always shift your focus as you read and write, but now the process will favor zooming in to concentrate on the style and the surface. Look at the two samples from Marcus's work on his essay that are shown in Figure 2.5 (page 52).

Notice that even after making the major revisions to his paper, Marcus produces some pretty messy edits on his third draft. In the paragraph on the top you can see that he is not really thinking anymore about the larger organization of his essay—he knows he wants to talk about innovative artists and musical influences in terms of reggaeton. He essentially knows what to say, but now must edit to figure out how to say it. Here, strategies like combining sentences and writing for concision will come in handy.

By the time Marcus reaches his fourth draft, he can more clearly focus on polishing the surface of his paper. He fixes typos, checks spelling, and makes stylistic adjustments to help the paper read more smoothly. He also begins to ensure that the documentation and formatting of the essay is thorough and correct, adding a parenthetical reference for the background information he has

FIGURE 2.5

Marcus's third and fourth drafts of his essay.

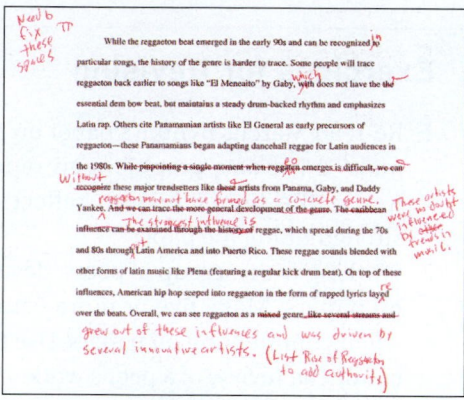

Marcus's Third Draft

Marcus's Fourth Draft

listed on reggaeton. Polishing is often the most straightforward component of the composing process. You can find information about how to fix sentences in the handbook in Part 6 and about how to format your documents and cite sources in Chapter 17.

Know It

LO

Learning Objective 2.5

Strategies for Editing and Polishing

- Wait until you edit and polish to address stylistic or surface level concerns. Of course, you can fix things as you go, but know that getting the big picture into focus first will make it easier to clean up the details later.
- Concentrate on issues of style as you edit. Learn to combine sentences to make your writing more efficient. Revise sentences to make them more clear and compelling.
- Use the polishing stage to make sure you meet all of the expectations of your genre and audience. Check that sources are documented and that figures and charts are labeled. Format your work to meet the style requirements of the assignment or genre.

Ask Questions & Make Decisions

Exercises for Editing and Polishing

1. Take a piece of writing on which you are working, then look over the first paragraph or two to identify two sentences that can be combined, and then revise them into a single sentence. Repeat the process for the rest of the paper, and then continue to combine or cut repetitive sentences.

2. For an essay you are composing with a word processor, use the Find function (usually under the File menu) to locate any sentences containing "is" or "are" constructions (e.g., *it is important. . . .* or *there are many reasons. . . .*). For each instance, check whether the sentence can be revised into active language (see Part 6).

3. Read the text of a completed composition aloud. As you read the text, take note of any awkward sounding passages. Go back and revise the passages, and then repeat the process.

4. Beginning at the end of a completed composition, read each sentence of the text in isolation. (Use a note card or folded paper to block out surrounding sentences.) Beginning with the last sentence and working backward, revise each sentence for clarity and concision.

Learning from Other Mediums: Composing Visually

 ## Excerpts from "Pollock Paints a Picture"
BY **ROBERT GOODNOUGH**

For many, the paintings of Jackson Pollock represent the pinnacle of abstract expression and innovation; for others, Pollock's canvases lead to head scratching and questions about the nature of art. In any case, it's hard to deny the unique nature of Pollock's composing process. This excerpt from the journal, Artnews, *discusses some of the ways Pollock went about composing his well-known works.*

To enter Pollock's studio is to enter another world, a place where the intensity of the artist's mind and feelings are given full play. It is the unusual quality of this mind, penetrating nature to the core yet never striving to show its surface, that has been projected into paintings which captivate many and agitate others by their strange, often violent, ways of expression. At one end of the barn, the floor is literally covered with large cans of enamel, aluminum and tube colors—the boards that do show are covered with paint drippings. Nearby a skull rests on a chest of drawers. Three or four cans contain stubby paint brushes of various sizes. About the rest of the studio, on the floor and walls, are paintings in various stages of completion, many of enormous proportions. Here Pollock often sits for

FIGURE 2.6
Jackson Pollock painting (Hans Namuth).

hours in deep contemplation of work in progress, his face forming rigid lines and often settling in a heavy frown. A Pollock painting is not born easily, but comes into being after weeks, often months of work and thought. At times he paints with feverish activity, or again with slow deliberation.

After some years of preparation and experimentation, during which time he painted his pictures on an easel, Pollock has developed a method that is unique and that, because of its newness, shocks many. He has found that what he has to say is best accomplished by laying the canvas on the floor, walking around it and applying the paint from all sides. The paint—usually enamel, which he finds more pliable—is applied by dipping a small house brush or stick or trowel into the can and then, by rapid movements of the wrist, arm and body, quickly allowing it to fall in weaving rhythms over the surface. The brush seldom touches the canvas, but is a means to let color drip or run in stringy forms that allow for the complexity of design necessary to the artist.

In his recent show, at the Parsons Gallery, Pollock exhibited a very large work, titled *Number 4, 1950.* (Pollock used to give his pictures conventionally symbolic titles, but—like many contemporary abstractionists—he considers them misleading, and now simply numbers and dates each work as it is completed.) It was begun on a sunny day last June. The canvas, 9 by 17 feet, was laid out flat, occupying most of the floor of the studio and Pollock stood gazing at it for some time, puffing at a cigarette. After a while he took a can of black enamel (he usually starts with the color which is at hand at the time) and a stubby brush which he dipped into the paint and then began to move his arm rhythmically about, letting the paint fall in a variety of movements on the surface. At times he would crouch, holding the brush close to the canvas, and again he would stand and move around it or step on it to reach to the middle. Within a half hour the entire surface had taken on an activity of weaving rhythms. Pools of black, tiny streams and elongated forms seemed to become

FIGURE 2.7
Still from the film *Jackson Pollock* (1951).

transformed and began to take on the appearance of an image. As he continued, still with black, going back over former areas, rhythms were intensified with counteracting movements. After some time he decided to stop to consider what had been done. This might be called the first step of the painting, though Pollock stresses that he does not work in stages. He did not know yet when he would feel strongly enough about the picture to work on it again, with the intensity needed, nor when he would finally be finished with it. The paint was allowed to dry, and the next day it was nailed to a wall of the studio for a period of study and concentration.

It was about two weeks before Pollock felt close enough to the work to go ahead again. This was a time of "getting acquainted" with the painting, of thinking about it and getting used to it so that he might tell what needed to be done to increase its strength. The feverish intensity of the actual painting process could not be kept up indefinitely, but long periods of contemplation and thought must aid in the preparation for renewed work. In the meantime other paintings were started. When he felt able to return to the large canvas with renewed energy, Pollock placed it back on the floor, selected a light reddish brown color and began again to work in rhythms and drops that fell on uncovered areas of canvas and over the black. Occasionally aluminum paint was added, tending to hold the other colors on the same plane as the canvas. (Pollock uses metallic paint much in the same sense that earlier painters applied gold leaf, to add a feeling of mystery and adornment to the work and to keep it from being thought of as occupying the accepted world of things. He finds that aluminum often accomplishes this more successfully than greys, which he first used.) Again the painting was allowed to dry and then hung on the wall for a few days' renewed consideration.

FIGURE 2.8
Number 4, 1950 by Jackson Pollock (© Pollock-Krasner Foundation/Artists Rights Society (ARS), New York/Carnegie Museum of Art, Pittsburgh; Gift of Frank R. S. Kaplan).

The final work on the painting was slow and deliberate. The design had become exceedingly complex and had to be brought to a state of complete organization. When finished and free from himself the painting would record a released experience. A few movements in white paint constituted the final act and the picture was hung on the wall; then the artist decided there was nothing more he could do with it.

Pollock felt that the work had become "concrete"—he says that he works "from the abstract to the concrete," rather than vice versa: the painting does not depend on reference to any object or tactile surface, but exists "on its own." Pollock feels that criticism of a work such as this should be directed at least in terms of what he is doing, rather than by standards of what painting ought to be. He is aware that a new way of expression in art is often difficult to see, but he resents presentation of his work merely on the level of technical interest.

Such a summation of Pollock's way of working is, of course, only part of the story. It has developed after years of concentrated effort, during long periods when nothing was satisfactory to him. He explains that he spent four years painting "black pictures," pictures which were unsuccessful. Then his work began to be more sure. There was a period of painting symbols, usually of figures or monsters, violently expressed. Of them, *She Wolf*, now owned by the Museum of Modern Art, was a crucial work.

Excerpts from
"Pollock Paints a
Picture" *(continued)*
BY **ROBERT GOODNOUGH**

Here areas of brush-work and paint-pouring were combined, the painting being done partly on the floor and partly on the easel. The change to his way of working today was gradual, accompanying his various needs for expression, and though there is a sense of the brutal in what he does this gradually seems to be giving way to greater calm.

↗ Reflect on the Reading

Questions About "Pollock Paints a Picture"

1. How well does the article capture the composing processes of Jackson Pollock? Is there anything that stands out about the way Pollock goes about composing?
2. What projects have you completed that might be considered creative or innovative? How would you describe the processes through which the projects came into being? How would you compare them to Pollock's composing processes?
3. What do you think of the painting *Number 4, 1950*? Can you recognize in the painting elements that represent Pollock's composing processes? Does the work seem finished?
4. How important are innovations in art or in other forms of communication? What is the relationship between new forms of expression and composing processes? Hold a discussion with classmates about innovations and composing, using the work of Pollock as a starting point.

Respond   Write About Composing Processes

To think more about composing processes, consider the following writing opportunities:

1. **Explore your writing processes.** Write a two- to three-page essay in which you detail elements of the processes you go through as you compose. You might use your experience with a print essay as the basis for the exploration. You might zoom in to analyze and explain your writing process, and then zoom out, exploring how an awareness of this process can benefit yourself and other writers. (For more on analyzing see pages 179–84 and for more on explaining a process see pages 440–41.)
2. **Compose an audio essay.** Use audio to discuss the creative processes of an artist or writer. You might interview a classmate or acquaintance about their creative processes. You could also find interviews and other materials online regarding the composing processes of musicians, writers, filmmakers, etc. Audio essays require you to blend audio samples, sound effects, and your own voice to create a composition. (For more on audio essays see our e-book.)
3. **Translate a composition to another medium.** Select an essay or some other composition that you have recently completed. Choose an alternate medium, and then compose the project again. You might turn a print essay

into a photo essay, translate a PSA flyer into an oral report, etc. Consider any additional prewriting that is needed. Experiment with new composing skills required by the shift in medium. Revise and edit, keeping the constraints and opportunities of the medium in mind. When finished write a brief reflection on the composing processes.

4. **Develop and maintain a blog.** Select an issue that concerns you, and then write about it using a blog. Blog writers often compose regularly, sometimes posting links to and brief discussions of things they have discovered online or reflections on daily occurrences. (As an alternative, you could focus on a daily posting to a social networking site like Facebook.) Try writing on the blog regularly for a month or so, and then think about how the experience relates to your usual composing processes.

Zoom Out   Reflecting on Composing Processes

- **Every project calls for authors to undertake a process of composition.** Composing processes will vary depending on the project. All of the components of the composing process feed into one another and may be used at any time during a project.

- **Each individual has unique composing processes.** However, there are often some common components including prewriting, drafting, revising, and editing and polishing.

- **Prewriting includes the activities that a writer engages to discover or invent ideas.** Freewriting, asking questions, holding conversations, journaling, researching, and making lists or maps are common forms of prewriting.

- **Drafting is concerned with getting ideas out rather than getting them just right.** Having an approach and a sense of the areas you will cover ahead of time will benefit drafting.

- **Revising is concerned with making adjustments to the big picture.** Make sure that all the necessary ideas are included and that the organization is coherent when revising. Often more prewriting or drafting is required when revising.

- **During editing and polishing the composing process becomes less messy.** Editing emphasizes style and how to best say things. Polishing emphasizes cleaning up the surface of the document and fixing details to meet genre and audience expectations.

 For additional information and practice with the learning objectives in this chapter, go to www.mycomplab.com, Resources > Writing > The Writing Process > Drafting.

Understanding Critical Reading and Thinking

Key Concepts and Learning Objectives

After studying this chapter, you should be able to:

3.1 Practice critical reading by using analysis, synthesis, and evaluation.

3.2 Analyze topics and texts by breaking up ideas and zooming in to focus on particulars.

3.3 Develop complexity in your approaches to topics by synthesizing sources, ideas, and texts.

3.4 Evaluate texts and ideas by making decisions about their value.

3.5 Use writing to develop your critical thinking abilities.

Look back over your life in school. Is it possible to discover your toughest school challenge? Was it middle school, junior year in high school, second grade? Was it math class, biology, maybe the fifth-grade writing test? You can probably identify at least one aspect of your early education that gave you fits. And, once you've identified a challenging moment, you can zoom in and out to explore what made it so tough. How did the situation relate to you personally? What made the moment different from other parts of your schooling? What do you know about education that helps you understand the moment?

Situating the moment and asking questions helps you to think critically. Soon you can come up with an explanation for the school challenge. It might have been your level of maturity or the constraints of formalized education. It could have had something to do with your aptitudes with language or math. It could have been a teacher or classmate. Or, more likely, it may have been some combination of factors. If you were intrigued enough by this brief reflection, you could push the exercise further, writing up your thoughts. You could look for new information, examine contexts, and come to some conclusions. You could refine all of this thinking and share your explanations by composing a paper on problems in K–12 education.

This simple exercise reveals the ways in which critical thinking not only can be a regular part of your daily reflections but also can be used more deliberately to help develop and share ideas. You explore ideas by asking questions, in this case surveying the past. You focus your thinking—here, identifying an educational challenge and examining its causes. You connect this thinking to other possibilities, looking at implications and explanations. And you can compose, bringing all of these complexities together into a form you can share with others.

KEY TERMS

- **Critical thinking:** A process through which we make sense of and offer judgments about people, things, and ideas. Core components of critical thinking include analyzing, synthesizing, and evaluating. Zooming in and out, asking questions, and making decisions drive critical thinking.

- **Analyzing:** Breaking things apart to examine their details. Analysis is linked with zooming in, identifying elements and looking at them closely.

- **Evaluating:** Examining and drawing conclusions about elements. Evaluation yields judgments about people, ideas, and things.

- **Synthesizing:** Connecting and combining elements to explore their relationships. Synthesis is linked with zooming out, identifying connections, influences, and relationships.

- **Critical reading:** The process of applying critical thinking to texts. You must zoom in and out, ask questions, and make decisions as you read texts. Critical readers become conscious of and deliberately engage in these activities.

- **Multiple perspectives:** The varying approaches people take to a topic. Most complex concerns evoke not either/or positions but an array of competing and complementary perspectives.

- **Scholarly sources:** Articles and other texts written for an academic audience. Scholarly sources tend to use specialized terminology and include extensive research.

- **Evidence:** Facts, statistics, and statements used to support a point. Critical thinking helps readers analyze and evaluate evidence.

Exploring Sources and Focusing Ideas

Learning
Objective 3.1

Memory exercises like the one opening this chapter can invoke the processes of critical thinking; they allow you to analyze events and synthesize ideas. But more commonly, the critical thinking you do in school will play out in specific projects. A big part of this formalized thinking will involve reading sources and exploring and focusing ideas. Let's take a look at a sample reading to think more about this process.

What Boy Crisis?

BY **JUDITH WARNER**

Judith Warner has written a number of books including You Have the Power: How to Take Back Our Country and Restore Democracy in America *and the biography,* Hillary Clinton: The Inside Story. *She has also written for* Newsweek, The New Republic, *and* The Washington Post. *Warner also hosts a weekly radio show. "What Boy Crisis" first appeared in the* New York Times *in 2006.*

It's been muttered for some time now in feminist academic circles that the "boy crisis"—the near-ubiquitous belief that our nation's boys are being academically neglected and emotionally persecuted by teachers whose training, style and temperament favor girls—is little more than a myth.

Now a major study has confirmed it. According to "The Truth About Boys and Girls," a report from the nonpartisan group Education Sector, most boys aren't just not failing; they're doing better than ever on most measures of academic performance. The only boys who aren't—the boys who skew the scores because they're doing really, really badly—are Hispanic and black boys and those from low-income homes.

"But the predominant issues for them," wrote Sara Mead, who based her conclusions in the study on decades of government statistics, "are race and class, not gender." Mead's conclusions echo those of Prof. Caryl Rivers of Boston University and Prof. Rosalind Chait Barnett of Brandeis.

"White suburban boys," they wrote in *The Washington Post* earlier this year, "are not dropping out of school, avoiding college or lacking in verbal skills. Among whites, the gender composition of colleges is pretty balanced. In Ivy League colleges, men still outnumber women."

Given these facts—which, when you think of it, were always pretty obvious—why is it that the notion that their sons are "in crisis" has persisted among affluent, educated (mostly) white parents and the similarly privileged journalists, experts and politicians who shape their opinions?

Blame anti-girl "backlash." Blame media navel gazing. I think, though, that there's more to it than that.

The notion that boys are in crisis rings true to many middle- and upper-middle-class parents because it feels true to them. And that's because these parents are sick of being told that their preschool sons need occupational therapy because they can't apply stickers with the right fine-motor finesse. These parents are sick of seeing their kindergarten boys referred to reading specialists. They're sick of suggestions that their 9-year-olds have A.D.H.D. if they can't sit still through school days from which recess has been cut, gym has been eliminated and even lunch, sometimes, has been all but eradicated to cram in more hours of test prep.

Many dads recall that when they were in school, they were restless, sometimes turbulent, sometimes aggressive, sometimes disruptive in class. When they channeled their energy into the workplace, they thrived—and they don't want their sons pathologized, or girlified, for the sake of big-size classroom control.

I sympathize with much of this. But what I don't see happening among parents who complain that their boys are being disserved by educators is a calling into question of their own complicity with high-pressure schools that demand way too much of their sons.

Talk of the boy crisis is a diversion. It draws attention from the real reasons so many white suburban parents sense that their sons are in trouble. Those reasons aren't academic; they're behavioral and emotional. Researchers have found in recent years that anxiety, depression and self-medicating through drugs and alcohol are disproportionately on the rise in rich communities, as kids seek escape from excessive pressures to succeed.

This isn't unique to boys. Girls in these communities are showing an increased incidence of eating disorders (female athletes are in particular trouble on that score), and also a disturbing rise in escapist behaviors like binge drinking and cutting. Experts say

What Boy Crisis?
(continued)
BY **JUDITH WARNER**

girls are showing crisis signs for the same reasons as boys: because they're stressed out, overextended and pushed beyond the limits of normal human endurance. But since girls' forms of acting out tend to be self-destructive rather than disruptive and often coexist with excellent academic performance, they often pass under the radar.

The notion that there's a universal boy crisis is expedient for well-off parents in other ways as well. Talk—about anti-boy discrimination, about boy-only learning styles—is cheap. Doing the things necessary to address the real crisis among black, Latino and rural and poor city boys isn't: it requires money for smaller classes, better-trained teachers and more support. I'm not sure that white suburban taxpayers are eager to pay the price. But I do know that if we can get past gender turf battles, we might be able to address what's really going wrong with our nation's kids.

Reflect on the Reading

Questions About "What Boy Crisis?"

1. How would you describe the tone of "What Boy Crisis?" What does the tone suggest about the author? How does the tone influence your impression of the essay?

2. What are your thoughts on the research cited in the essay? Does the evidence provided in the essay give you enough knowledge of the topic? What else might you like to know?

3. How many groups with an interest in the topic can you discover in the essay? Does the essay prioritize any of these stakeholders above others? Does it ignore or make light of the concerns of any group?

4. Is it fair to say that this essay suggests that there are no real differences between boys and girls when it comes to school experiences? Why or why not?

5. "What Boy Crisis?" suggests that instead of the progress of boys, we should be focusing on "what's really wrong with our nation's kids." What are some of these real problems according to the essay? Do you agree with this assessment? What other problems would you identify?

This process of analysis is a key component of critical thinking

Let's take a closer look at "What Boy Crisis?" to see how we can explore ideas and focus thinking. We can start with some questions: *What is the subject of the article? What can we learn from its rhetorical situation? What claims does it make?* This article discusses a study, "The Truth About the Boy Crisis." It appeared in the *New York Times*, written by an author concerned with public policy and politics. It claims that the real educational achievement gaps relate to race and class, not gender. "What Boy Crisis?" uses this claim as a springboard to pose a different problem for education, the stressful demands of "high-pressure schools." Already we have broken the article down into some of its pieces. This process of analysis is a key component of critical thinking.

Learning
Objective 3.2

As we investigate the piece, we can always stop and expand on these initial moments of analysis. We might look into the suggestion that there is a "boy crisis" in schools. The article quickly dismisses this suggestion, but it does admit that "parents . . . [feel the concerns] to be true," and it goes on to list a number of potential problems for boys: trouble with fine motor skills, difficulties with early reading, diagnoses of ADHD (attention deficit/hyperactivity disorder). The article even suggests that, unlike girls, whose acting out might "pass under the radar," boys are more likely to be disruptive given the stresses of high-pressure education. We're zooming in, analyzing and summarizing this particular dimension of the article. But we can't stop there.

Focus requires selection and decision making

Another key aspect of exploration is conducting research. So far, we have based all of our thinking on this one article. To understand the "boy crisis" fully, we need to expand our investigation. A quick online search will reveal dozens of articles taking up the issue. Most of these seem to respond either to the same study ("The Truth About Boys and Girls") referenced in "What Boy Crisis?" or to a *Newsweek* cover story titled "The Trouble with Boys." You could follow up, reading the *Newsweek* piece online, or browsing through your library database to find the "The Truth About Boys and Girls" study. (See Chapters 14–17 for more on research.) All of this investigation will refine your understanding of "What Boy Crisis?" and of the topic in general.

Eventually, though, you will need to focus your thinking. Focus requires selection and decision making. Think of the way focus works on a camera; you might adjust the lens to bring an object into focus, say the sign in the center of the photograph shown here (see Figure 3.1), but other objects—the car or the boy—would move out of focus, though they would still be present in the image. You could swing the camera to the left to photograph the boy instead of the sign. With each decision about where to focus your attention, you will practice evaluation. You will make value judgments as you select and discard areas of focus.

FIGURE 3.1
An example of the concept of focus as it relates to the composition of a photo.

On one level, evaluations should be a very personal matter. If you have experience with high-pressure schools and make that your focus, you will have insights into the topic. In fact, you are going to have more success if you identify with, or "own your topic," in this way. Further, you will eventually have to take ownership of the ideas you develop and share. The summary of "What Boy Crisis?" above merely requires discovering and listing the main points in the article. But readers also need to see your perspective on these points. Do you think schools are no harder than in the past, but that our educational culture is too quick to medicate behavior problems? Decide what interests you about the topic and let this perspective come through in your work.

As you develop your perspective, you will engage in a process of prioritizing. Think of the way the camera maintains some awareness of all of the elements in its field. The sign is in focus, but the boy remains part of the picture. So, too, you will need to learn to entertain competing claims and possibilities. Yes, high-stress schools are causing behavior problems, but let's put that to the side for a moment to focus, for example, on the role of pharmaceutical solutions to problems in education. Prioritizing in this way means that, as you focus your thinking, you entertain (even address) competing possibilities.

Know It Strategies for Exploring Sources and Focusing Ideas

- Give yourself permission to simply react to readings or topics. You might start with whether you like or dislike an idea or text. Or just consider what pops into your head when you contemplate the topic or reading. Instead of looking for the final or correct answer, look instead to see where your reactions take you.

- Pursue questions to get a feel for the topic or make inroads into a reading. Explore questions that arise on their own as you think. Consider how additional stock questions might help generate exploration. Ask who, what, where, when, why, and how to help you explore: who cares about an issue, who wrote a text, why does the issue matter, what was a writer trying to accomplish, when was a text written, how does it deliver its message, and so on.

- Use some of the prewriting strategies discussed on pages 41–44 to help with your explorations. Freewrite, make lists, talk with peers, make outlines or maps, doodle, or use whatever other writing tasks you find helpful for brainstorming.

- Use analysis to make exploring a topic or reading manageable. Slice ideas into chunks so you can explore smaller components of a larger issue. Zoom in, taking up one piece of an argument or one aspect of a reading. Delve deeper into these smaller pieces to begin focusing your thinking.

- Be conscious of the decision making involved as you explore and refine ideas. Consider the criteria you use as you prioritize ideas or come to an understanding of a reading. Think about what elements in a larger cultural network get left out as you focus.

Ask Questions & Make Decisions

Exercises for Exploring Sources and Focusing Ideas

1. Think about all of the challenges related to K–12 education. Explore this topic broadly by creating a list of topics (peer pressure, testing, violence, and so on). Attempt to come up with at least eight areas of concern related to education.
2. Zoom in on one of the areas of concern you have listed related to K–12 education. Focusing on this area, make a list representing issues or questions related to this specific concern. (For a concern like violence, you might list bullying, video games, contact sports, and so on.)
3. Write a three- or four-sentence summary demonstrating the key dimensions of the concern you have selected. Outline the issues that must be addressed to gain an understanding of the topic.
4. Write three or four sentences offering your evaluation of the issue. Identify what matters most when thinking about the concern. If there is a debate related to the topic, take a side and explain your stance.

Connecting and Composing

The process of exploring and focusing represents a kind of zooming in on a subject; you survey an issue and then identify and focus on particular dimensions of the topic. Traditionally, this process of surveying and then identifying particulars has been called analysis. Alternatively, the process of connecting represents a zooming out; you look for relationships, examine alternative possibilities, and think about contexts. Traditionally, this kind of thinking has been called synthesis, the process of bringing concepts together to create new knowledge. We've separated out these dimensions of critical thinking in order to discuss them, but in practice this zooming in and out overlap and inform each other. To get a better sense of how this process can work, let's look at another article related to the boy crisis in education.

 ### Re-Examining the "Boy Crisis"
BY **KATHLEEN PARKER**

Kathleen Parker has been a journalist for over twenty years. She frequently writes about family, race, and gender and appears on television to discuss contemporary issues. She also teaches at the Buckley School of Public Speaking and Persuasion in South Carolina. "Re-examining the 'Boy Crisis'" first appeared in the Lowell Sun *in 2006.*

Re-Examining the "Boy Crisis" *(continued)* BY **KATHLEEN PARKER**

America's "boy crisis" has been canceled.

It was all hype, we're now told by Education Sector, a nonpartisan education research group.

In a new study titled "The Truth About Boys and Girls," researcher Sara Mead concludes that the failing-boys mantra was politically motivated hooey advanced by anti-feminist pundits and others who cherry-picked data to advance their own ideological agendas.

Boys aren't so much in crisis, says Mead, who analyzed data from the National Assessment of Educational Progress. They're just not doing very well. That is, middle- and upper-class white boys generally are doing fine, while blacks, Hispanics and the poor (some of whom surely are white) are doing badly to terribly.

We have a class and race problem, in other words, not a boy problem. Maybe.

Mead seems most concerned that education funds might be misdirected in response to recent noises that school programs are unfriendly to males and that teaching styles should be adjusted to accommodate brain differences—and, hence, learning styles—in males and females.

The study, though filled with intriguing information—not much of which undermines the case of males-doing-badly—seems mostly aimed at halting trends away from policies that were put in place to advance girls. Mead makes clear that any disagreement with her conclusions constitutes Neanderthal "hysteria."

"While most of society has finally embraced the idea of equality for women," she writes, "the idea that women might actually surpass men in some areas (even as they remain behind in others) seems hard for many people to swallow."

Fine. Let's call a truce for the moment on who is or isn't politically motivated, and take a look at the data. It is apparently true that boys do pretty well in elementary and middle school but tend to go wobbly in high school and college.

We may need to give social scientists a few more decades to pin down possible reasons for that, but I'm willing to bet my two cents on a combination of testosterone and a lack of disciplined guidance from fathers. A subject worthy of research not addressed in this study might be the correlation between poor academic performance among these same black, Hispanic and impoverished boys and the absence of fathers in the home.

Meanwhile, here are some of the statistics that say "not a crisis," just "not that great."

Only 65 percent of boys who start high school graduate four years later, compared with 72 percent of girls; 42 percent of boys are suspended from school at least once before age 17, compared with 24 percent of girls. (This is the most alarming statistic in the Mead study and deserves a closer look.)

Elementary-school boys are more likely than girls to be held back a year, while high-school boys' achievement is declining in most subjects (although it may be improving in math).

A "substantial" percentage of boys are diagnosed with disabilities, while boys comprise two-thirds of special education students, as well as 80 percent of those diagnosed with emotional disturbances or autism. Boys also are 2 1/2 times as likely as girls to be diagnosed with attention deficit hyperactivity disorder.

Mead notes that while these are troubling statistics, they don't tell the whole story. With what seems like relief, she adds that the number of girls with disabilities is growing, so it's not just a "boy issue."

She finds further consolation in the fact that though boys are not doing as well as girls in many categories, overall academic achievement and attainment for boys is higher than it's ever been. And, "while academic performance for minority boys is often shockingly low, it's not getting worse." Phew.

In fairness, Mead may be right that the "crisis" rhetoric has served its useful purpose. Nevertheless, defining "crisis" down doesn't alter the fact that girls are doing better, while boys (except for the luckiest white boys) are lagging. However you cut it, degrees of bad are still bad.

Moreover, the declining status of boys—or the ascent of girls, if you prefer—is at least in part the product of political pressures that led to policy changes and cultural adjustments that have benefited girls. No one wishes to take away those accomplishments or to turn back the clock on girls.

That we might wish to exercise the same political clout in the interest of our sons and our nation's future fathers isn't a symptom of political one-upmanship, but a necessary search for balance.

No matter how much we tweak the data, one reliable truth is that successful women will always want to meet and mate with successful men. At this rate, they will be hard-pressed to find them.

↗ Reflect on the Reading

Questions About "Re-Examining the 'Boy Crisis'"

1. How would you describe the tone of "Re-Examining the 'Boy Crisis?'" What examples can you cite to demonstrate the tone? Do you find the tone effective? Why or why not?

2. What do you think of the way the essay cites the study, "The Truth About Boys and Girls"? Are there places where you feel as if you need more information about the original study? Do you feel as if the study is represented fairly?

3. What do you make of the claim that, "one reliable truth is that successful women will always want to meet and mate with successful men?" What does this claim say about the author or article? How does it relate to the boy crisis?

4. Both "What Boy Crisis?" and "Re-Examining the 'Boy Crisis'" refer to the same study, but come to different conclusion about the significance of the study. How do you explain their different approaches? Which do you find more compelling? Why?

Already you can see an opportunity to draw connections between the two articles. We might begin to look for patterns that emerge when examining readings. "What Boy Crisis?" opens by citing feminist concerns that the boy crisis might be a "myth." "Re-Examining the 'Boy Crisis'" also addresses these feminist concerns, suggesting that the study itself argues that, "the failing-boys mantra was politically motivated hooey." You can see that thinking through this topic will require you to address concerns of feminism or gender.

You can also begin to compare and contrast the two pieces. On the one hand, they both refer the same study. They both acknowledge that there are race and class dimensions to the boy crisis and that politics informs the debates over the issue. On the other hand, "What Boy Crisis?" seems to accept the results of the study, while "Re-Examining the 'Boy Crisis'" challenges them, or at least seeks to draw different conclusions from them. You can sense a kind of opposition developing between the two articles.

You can also zoom out to think about contexts to better understand readings. Both articles introduce the study in terms of political debates and gender issues, and both acknowledge the historical disparities between women and men when it comes to educational success. Both acknowledge the relationships between race, class, and school performance. Both articles discuss behavioral differences between boys and girls. And both discuss medications and the growing tendency to treat attention problems pharmaceutically. So, thinking about history, politics, race, class, medicine, and so forth is needed to fully understand the issue or the articles.

Finally, the ability to make connections allows you to entertain competing perspectives. On the simplest level, you can weigh opposing points of view—one piece says the boy crisis is real and the other says it is a myth. On a more complex level, you will consider and address multiple perspectives—the boy crisis is (or is not) real, and it is related to race and class, and it is connected to high-pressure schooling. It is the ability to make sense of multiple connections and relationships that leads to thinking and projects with complexity. Complexity matters because it not only holds a reader's interest but also more accurately reflects the nature of knowledge and relationships among people, ideas, and things.

The process of composing represents the culmination of all of the aspects of critical reading and thinking

The process of composing represents the culmination of all of the aspects of critical reading and thinking. It can be hard to know when thinking ends and composing begins. For instance, as you explore and gradually focus on a specific dimension of a topic, you are already composing your thoughts. If you take notes or begin some kind of writing, then this composing becomes concrete. When you sit down at the keyboard to draft, you call

WN

VIDEO
15. Summarizing

forth the thought processes that will help you create your project, and you probably re-read the sources you have collected.

When it comes to composing major projects, you will move back and forth among the components of the writing process discussed in Chapter 2—prewriting, drafting, revising, and editing and polishing. This movement is obviously integral to critical thinking as you ask questions, explore, focus, make decisions, and come to conclusions throughout the composing process. In addition, there are other kinds of writing you can undertake to assist critical thinking.

Creating a summary, for instance, provides an opportunity to practice critical reading. Often, you can use a summary to identify the main point or points made in an article. A summary tries primarily to accurately represent the article, rather than challenge its position. Consider this summary composed by student Tara Joss.

"Re-Examining The 'Boy Crisis'" Summary
BY TARA JOSS

In "Re-Examining the 'Boy Crisis,'" Kathleen Parker responds to the study, "The Truth About Boys and Girls" conducted by Sara Mead. Mead reports that the "failing boys crisis" is politically motivated by anti-feminists. Mead's study, sponsored by the Education Sector, a nonpartisan research group, instead suggests that the 'failing boys crisis' is all hype. The study cites statistics from the National Assessment of Educational Progress to show that the boys who are not doing well are mostly blacks, Hispanics, and poor whites.

Parker does not disagree with the assessment of the study that claims poor and minority boys are struggling. But she does question the claims that all boys no longer face challenges in school. Instead, "Re-Examining the 'Boy Crisis'" suggests that boys do pretty well in elementary and middle school, but hormones, lack of strong male role models, and lack of guidance, make high school boys "go wobbly."

According to Parker, statistics show 65 percent of boys who start high school graduate four years later compared with 72 percent girls. Boys are suspended more often than girls. Boys are more likely to be held back, and boys are 2 1/2 times more likely to be diagnosed with ADHD than girls.

Parker suggests that even if the "crisis" may have been exaggerated, the fact is that boys are not doing well. Girls continue to do better. Political pressure and policy adjustments help girls but a balanced policy would also help boys.

Reflect on the Reading

Questions About Tara's Summary

1. How well do you think Tara's summary handles the original "The Truth About Boys and Girls" that Parker cites in her article? What suggestions would you make regarding addressing the original study?
2. How clear and concise is the language in Tara's summary? What recommendations would you make for simplifying the writing?
3. Are there aspects of "Re-Examining the 'Boy Crisis'" that the summary overlooks? What might be added to bring out any additional complexities in the article?

VIDEO
16. Paraphrasing

Composing does not always require that you hatch fully formed ideas or that you even have responses to questions that arise as you think. Tara's summary merely tries to make sense of the reading she has encountered. (See pages 375–76 for more on summaries.) As you continue to write, you will further refine your thinking. Eventually, you will need to take ownership of your topic. You can complement summaries by paraphrasing sources as you integrate them into your compositions. You will need to draw conclusions in order to have something concrete to say. You will need an angle or area of focus for your project (a thesis), and you will need to evaluate and make statements about ideas along the way. Writing will help you with all of these aspects of thinking.

Know It   Strategies for Connecting and Composing

Learning Objective 3.3

- Look for patterns as you think about topics or engage with readings. Does an article return regularly to certain points or perspectives? Are there similarities between the ways different articles or individuals approach a topic? What relationships come into view as you learn more about the topic or engage multiple readings?
- Identify contrasts between ideas or readings. Where opposing points of view emerge, stop and consider the motivations and ideas behind the different perspectives. When smaller variations emerge in perspectives or readings, think about how these points relate to larger patterns and to the topic as a whole.
- Examine the central conflicts related to your topic. What do people usually argue about when they discuss your topic? Do points of disagreement seem clearly marked out (e.g., in debates about abortion), or are the perspectives more gray and nuanced (e.g., in debates about homeland security and personal freedom)?

- Explore the links between what you are reading and other pieces that have been written on the topic. Are there common assumptions that all writers share about a topic? What points in the piece you are reading diverge from other perspectives?
- Use summaries, notes, and other prewriting opportunities. Compose informally to make sense of readings. Use writing to help explore the complexities of the topic and the connections between ideas and readings.

Ask Questions & Make Decisions

Exercises for Connecting and Composing

1. Participate with a mixed group of peers to compare and contrast the educational experiences of boys and girls. Take turns discussing challenges and opportunities, and then develop a list containing observations about girls and education and a second list with observations about boys. Discuss your findings as a class.
2. Identify an invention from the last hundred years that changed educational practices. Examine the historical contexts of education before the invention, and then write a paragraph summarizing the effect of the invention.
3. Watch a news/talk show in which two guests discuss opposing sides of an issue. Pay attention to the way the guests interact and the substance of their remarks. Write a paragraph summarizing the topic based on the statements of the guests. Write a second paragraph, analyzing the format of the news/talk show.

Exploring Multiple Sources and Ideas

So far we've been talking about reading one or two articles. But we've already been developing some relatively complex ideas. Our readings introduced the possibility that there is a boy crisis in education. Both readings referred to a research study challenging the existence of a boy crisis. One of our initial readings agreed with the claims of the study, while another rejected those claims, reaffirming the challenges faced by boys in education. Finally, our first reading offered an alternative area of focus, high-pressure schooling (see Figure 3.2 on the next page).

You can see that critical thinking really kicks in when you have to work with multiple sources and weave several ideas together. To think about this process, let's extend our exploration of the boy crisis by taking up the suggestion that high-pressure schools are the root of many educational problems. We'll start with another reading.

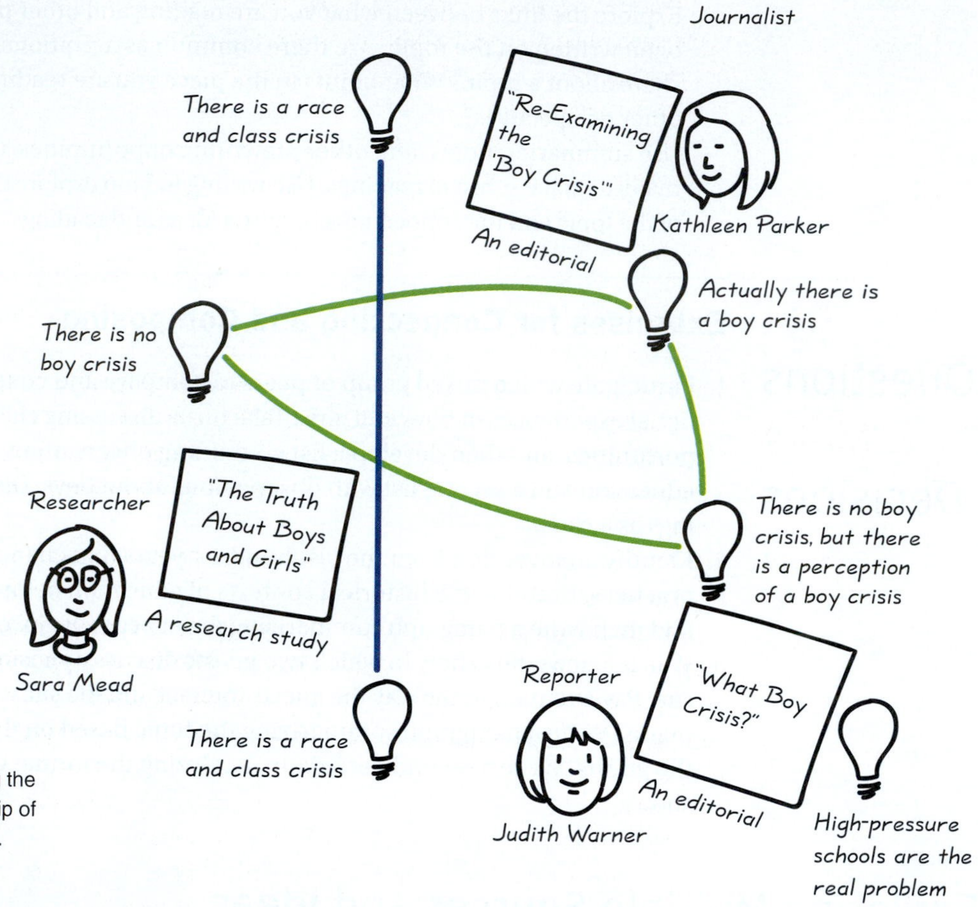

FIGURE 3.2
A diagram showing the flow and relationship of ideas in three texts.

Students Set the Rules at New York City School

BY **NAHAL TOOSI**

Nahal Toosi began her career in journalism at her college newspaper, the Daily Tar Heel. *She has worked as an embedded reporter covering the Iraq war and now writes for the* Milwaukee Journal Sentinel. *"Students set the rules at New York City School" was released by the Associated Press in 2006.*

One recent day at the Brooklyn Free School, the "schedule" included the following: filming horror movies, chess, debate and making caves for Teenage Mutant Ninja Turtles.

Not that the students had to go to any of these sessions. At this school, students don't get grades, don't have homework, don't take tests, and don't even have to go to class—unless they want to.

"You can do basically anything at any time, and it's just a lot more fun because sometimes when you need a break at regular schools you can't get it," said Sophia Bennett Holmes, 12, an aspiring singer-actress-fashion designer. "But here, if you just need to sit down and read and have time to play, then you can do that."

"Free schools," which had their heyday decades ago, operate on the belief that children are naturally curious and learn best when they want to, not when forced to. Today, the approach is getting another look from some parents and students tired of standardized testing, excessive homework, and overly rigid curriculums.

"Every kid here is definitely motivated to learn something, there's no doubt in my mind," said Alan Berger, a former public school assistant principal who founded the Brooklyn school in 2004. "Our belief is that if we let them pursue their passions and desires, they'll be able to get into it deeper. They'll be able to learn more how to learn."

Hundreds of free schools opened in the U.S. and elsewhere in the 1960s and 1970s. Most shut down, but some, such as the Albany Free School and Sudbury Valley School in Massachusetts, have persisted. Overall, it's unknown how many free schools operate today.

The ones still in operation often use a "democratic" model, giving students a say in running the institution.

At the Brooklyn Free School, much of that decision-making occurs in a mandatory (yes, as in required) weekly gathering called the Democratic Meeting. Here, students air grievances, pose challenges, propose rules and set policy. Even the youngest kids have a vote equal to staffers. One agreed-upon rule? No sword-fighting allowed inside.

The school—granted a provisional charter by the state to run as a private educational institution—occupies two floors of a Free Methodist church.

Students are required to show up for at least 5 1/2 hours a day, partly so that the school can meet legal definitions, but what they do with their time is up to them. The student population—42 students, ages 5 to 17—is diverse racially, economically and in terms of ability, and the students are not separated by age.

On any given day, a student might be playing chess, reading a book, practicing yoga or helping mummify a chicken.

Even among some champions of alternative education, free schools are considered a bit too radical.

"You don't throw the baby out with the bath water," said Jeanne Allen, president of the Center for Education Reform, a leading advocate of charter schools. "You don't get rid of all structure and standards if you want your child to be able to deal with all different settings."

Others say free schools could gain popularity if the emphasis on testing and regimented curriculums keeps up.

"Not only is there more interest, this is the wave of the future," said Jerry Mintz, director of the Alternative Education Resource Organization. "The other approach doesn't work, and everybody knows it."

Students Set the
Rules at New York
City School
(continued)
BY **NAHAL TOOSI**

The Brooklyn Free School isn't free in the financial sense. Tuition is $10,000 a year, but many parents just give what they can. There's a waiting list of about 35 students.

Watching the change in her son, David Johnston, has been worth the risk for Randy Karr.

While David did well "statistically" at previous schools, he hated going, sometimes crying when she dropped him off. Getting him to do homework was a struggle, and in Karr's opinion, the homework was useless anyway.

"There's very little about learning that goes on in school," Karr said. "A lot of it is being still, being quiet, not talking to your neighbor, not moving around too much. Especially if you're a boy, it's lethal."

At the Brooklyn Free School, David, now 12, is blossoming. He helps run a class on pharmacology and carries a notebook where he writes down things he's learning.

But what about the basics? Long division, spelling, algebra? Is it enough to let a child decide when to learn those things? That troubles a few parents who use outside tutors for their children, Berger said.

Some students said the flexibility made sense for the youngest and oldest, but not as much for those in the middle.

"I feel like they're definitely going to have a hard time with college, where you have to sort of do that sitting down and shutting up thing," said Victoria Rothman, 17, a public school refugee who now spends much of her school day studying music. "There are kids who sit here and play video games all day. I'd put a limit to that or ban it."

Others disagree, noting most adults can barely remember, or rarely use, most of what schools pounded into them.

In some ways, as the Brooklyn school evolves, it is becoming more structured. Students will soon have to meet a set of graduation "requirements," where they must present a portfolio showing proficiency in areas such as communication, investigation and reflection.

But the definition of proficiency, like much of the school, is flexible.

↗

Reflect on the Reading

Questions About "Students Set the Rules at New York City School"

1. Do you agree with the premise behind the Brooklyn Free School, that "children are naturally curious and learn best when they want to, not when forced to?" How would you relate this belief to your own educational experiences?

2. What connections can you discover between "Students Set the Rules at New York City School" and the boy crisis? Does it seem counterintuitive that more freedom in school might lead to fewer behavior problems? Why or why not?

3. Is it fair to say that because we don't use something we learned in school it is unnecessary? What is your response to the claim that "most adults can barely remember, or rarely use, most of what schools pounded into them?"

4. What should be the purpose of K–12 education? If you had the chance to create your own school, what would you require? What learning methods would you choose? How would you design your perfect school?

"Students Set the Rules at New York City School" raises some interesting questions about alternatives to high-pressure schooling. The article suggests that "children are naturally curious" and contrasts this possibility with concerns about standardized testing and excessive homework. A key question raised by the article, then, is whether learning should be driven by an internal, personal sense of motivation that comes from students, or by external forms of motivation like test performance or grades. The article also asks about the role of requirements and rigor, suggesting that some standards may be a good thing when it comes to reforming education.

We can show the increasing complexity of our understanding of the boy crisis topic, then, with another image representing our thinking so far (see Figure 3.3).

FIGURE 3.3
The flow and relationship of ideas in four texts.

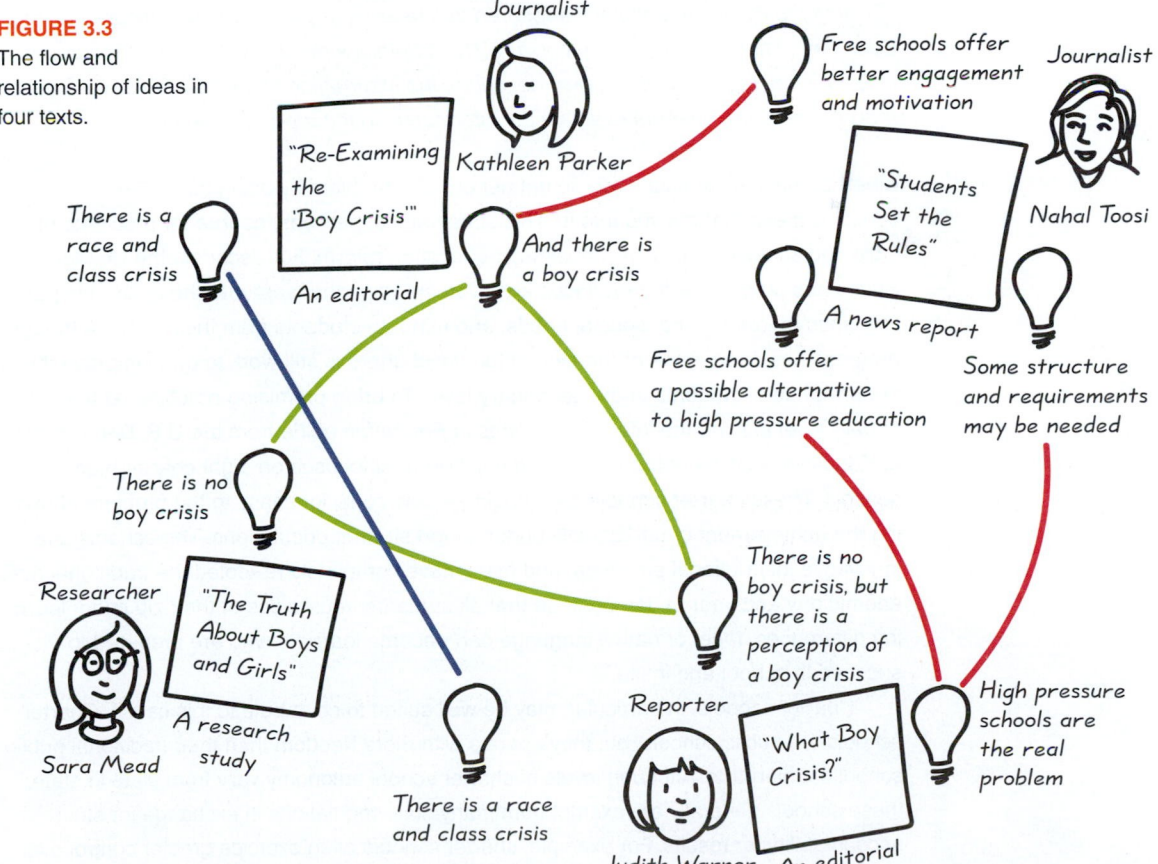

Scholarly Sources

LO

Learning
Objective 3.4

As you read critically, you must learn to identify and then evaluate the claims and evidence you come across. "Students Set the Rules at New York City School" suggests that internal motivation and a democratic model can help improve education. If we look at the article, though, we will see that much of the evidence is anecdotal—students and parents report on their experiences with the school. To understand this kind of evidence in more detail, let's look at one additional source of information, a short piece that takes a more scholarly approach to reporting on education reform.

Closing the Achievement Gap by The U.S. Department of Education

"Closing the Achievement Gap" appeared in a newsletter put out by the Department of Education, The Education Innovator, *in 2006. It details a report by the U.S. Department of Education, but warns that it only describes the information shared by the government report. It asks that readers evaluate the information in the report for themselves.*

Albert Einstein once said, "You do not get out of a problem by using the same consciousness that got you into it." This statement is, perhaps, as true for problems of logic and science as it is for problems of education reform. For decades, the United States has grappled with pernicious achievement gaps that separate the academic performance of low-income, special needs, and minority students from their peers. Although progress has been made at the elementary level, there is still work to do to improve the performance of students at the secondary level. To bring promising practices at the secondary level to light, the latest *Innovations in Education* guide from the U.S. Department of Education's Office of Innovation and Improvement focuses on eight charter high schools. These charter schools are bringing a new consciousness to the problem of raising the achievement of traditionally underserved student populations. The schools use innovative instructional practices, and many have completely re-tooled the traditional academic day and year to demonstrate that all students, regardless of their zip code, learning differences, race, or native language can become learners who are prepared to succeed in school and in life.

Charter schools, in particular, may be well suited to contribute to this cause. Charter schools are public schools, but they operate with more freedom than their traditional public school counterparts. Although levels of charter school autonomy vary from state to state, these schools generally are exempt from many state regulations in exchange for strict accountability for results. For example, charter schools often exercise greater control over their budgets, they may have more input regarding staffing decisions, and they have the ability to initiate cutting-edge programs.

As a result of charter schools' potential to improve the educational establishment as well as the prospects of students who need innovative, effective instructional programs the most, the latest *Innovations in Education* guide focuses on *Charter High Schools Closing the Achievement Gap*. The schools included in the guide were chosen in 2005 from over 400 charter high schools that are meeting academic targets under the No Child Left Behind Act (NCLB) and are closing achievement gaps by holding students to high academic standards. To be considered, the schools had to have graduated at least one cohort of students and have data to show that, for the most part, students were moving on to postsecondary education or employment. Eight schools were ultimately selected for the guide: Gateway High School (CA), Media and Technology Charter High School (MA), Minnesota New Country School (MN), The Preuss School (CA), The SEED Public Charter School (DC), Toledo School for the Arts (OH), YES College Preparatory School (TX), and North Star Academy Charter School of Newark (NJ). Each of these schools is college preparatory in intent, and each is developing creative solutions to problems faced by high schools across the country.

PROFILED SCHOOLS SHARE SIMILAR ELEMENTS

Although all the schools are unique, six similar characteristics unite them. Across the board, the schools are mission-driven; focus on college preparation; teach for mastery; provide support; value professional learning; and hold themselves accountable.

The first unifying factor among the schools is that they are mission-driven because they were created in response to what their founders believed was a lack of high-quality secondary school options in their local communities. Because the schools were created with the intent of meeting students' needs as their primary objective, teachers, school leaders, parents, board members, and community partners maintain a laser-like focus on ensuring that their missions ensure students' success. All adults have a clear understanding of and commitment to the mission of their schools, and all decisions from staffing to budget allocations are made based on whether the mission is furthered. Along with a relentless focus on goals, these schools also work to build a positive school culture where students and staff feel valued.

One way of ensuring that students feel valued is to offer them a rigorous, college-preparatory curriculum that keeps them engaged and excited about learning. Most of the profiled schools offer Advanced Placement courses along with additional support services. In these schools, there is no such thing as a "college track;" there is only a "success track." In addition to academic rigor, the schools promote internships and enrichment opportunities that allow students to apply the lessons they learn in the classroom to experiences that enhance their understanding of the world that extends beyond their local communities.

Closing the
Achievement
Gap by
The U.S.
Department of
Education
(continued)

To ensure that all their students are prepared for higher education and the "real world," teachers in the profiled schools teach for mastery, expect their students to work hard, and do not accept social promotion. If learning requires more time than a teacher initially anticipated, more time is provided. Lesson plans are flexible, evolving instructional guides—not documents set in the stone of an immovable curricular timeline. All schools have developed longer academic days or years, and some have added summer and weekend sessions.

It is important to note that these schools not only offer students more rigor and more time on task—they also offer more support. This support is exemplified in advisory programs, academic tutoring, mentoring, and college counseling. Each of the schools provides a relatively low student-to-teacher ratio (22:1) and employs part-time specialists, social workers, special education teachers, and parent volunteers who work daily with students. Indeed, parents are considered an invaluable resource at these schools, whether they are serving on the governing boards, fundraising, or participating in parent-teacher conferences.

The idea of support also extends to teachers. A number of the schools have built in regular opportunities either during the academic day or year for teachers to plan, reflect, and collaborate with one another. The principals at these schools value professional learning by working closely with teachers to improve instruction. Principals act as instructional leaders by conducting classroom observations, providing feedback on lesson plans, and collaboratively organizing intervention strategies for struggling students.

The final unifying factor among these schools is that they hold themselves accountable. Strong, active governing boards are at the helm of these schools, generating creative solutions to problems and empowering school leaders to make and implement decisions in a manner that is both expeditious and beneficial to students. The schools are fiscally responsible, and they regularly use student achievement data and information gathered from their constituents to improve their operations.

A STUDY IN CLOSING GAPS: NORTH STAR ACADEMY CHARTER SCHOOL OF NEWARK

The high graduation and college-going rates at these profiled schools belie the notion that traditionally underserved students cannot perform to high standards. One of the profiled schools, North Star Academy Charter School of Newark (NJ), named for Frederick Douglass's abolitionist paper *The North Star*, promotes higher education as the guiding "north star" of success for its inner city students, the majority of whom are African-American. The story of North Star Academy begins with James Verrilli, a teacher in the Newark public schools, and Norman Atkins, a journalist with a private foundation, both of whom set out to improve the gloomy outlook for students living in the second poorest city in the United States. In 1997, the year that North Star was founded, only 50 percent of freshmen that enrolled in Newark high schools reached their senior year and, of those, only 26 percent planned to attend college, six percent actually enrolled, and only two percent earned degrees. Now in its ninth year of operation, North Star is improving the life chances of Newark students with its 100 percent graduation rate and 95 percent college-going rate for the class of 2005.

NO ACADEMIC TRACKING LEADS TO A "SUCCESS TRACK" FOR ALL

North Star began as a middle school, but was expanded to serve high school students at the request of local parents who wanted better school options for their students after the eighth grade. The school currently serves 384 students in fifth through twelfth grade, with 125 students in the high school section. Ninety-nine percent of the students are African-American or Hispanic. All students who are accepted through the school's lottery system understand that they will be required to work hard throughout North Star's 11-month academic year. To graduate, students must take four years of English, mathematics, science, and history, and three years of foreign language, physical education, and the arts. North Star also encourages its students to enroll in Advanced Placement calculus, U.S. history, U.S. government, and English. None of the classes at North Star are tracked in terms of academic rigor because all classes offer honors-level, college-preparatory work. Additional graduation requirements include passing the New Jersey High School Proficiency Assessment, completing a senior thesis and composition, taking the SAT at least twice, engaging in 40 hours of community service, and applying to at least two colleges.

As if North Star students were not busy enough, the school also offers internships and special programs. For example, there is a journalism project in partnership with Princeton University, a Junior Statesman program through Georgetown University , and an FBI Summer Training Institute. Students who keep up their grades may spend a month off campus on work sites or traveling to foreign countries. Through a partnership with AFS Intercultural Programs, Inc., North Star students can spend time in China, Paraguay, Costa Rica, and Argentina. A relationship with VISIONS Service Adventures enables students to volunteer in Ecuador and the Dominican Republic.

HIGHLY DISTINCTIVE FEATURES

Two of North Star's most innovative features are its use of data to inform instruction and its commitment to ensuring that all students understand the subject matter they are taught. Every six to eight weeks, teachers administer a set of interim assessments that are aligned with state standards and the school's curriculum. Teachers, department chairs, and the school principal examine the results and determine which students need additional help. Teachers then re-teach key concepts to the whole class or offer tutoring to individual students before, during, or after the school day. North Star also offers a Saturday tutoring session, so that no student slips behind. Another distinctive element at the school is the

Closing the
Achievement
Gap by
The U.S.
Department of
Education
(continued)

principal's presence as an instructional leader. Every day, high school principal Julie Jackson and the principal at North Star's sister middle school visit at least 85 percent of classrooms. The principals observe classes, provide informal feedback to teachers, and use data from the interim assessments to draw connections between instruction and student learning.

NORTH STAR'S RESULTS

The hard work of principals, teachers, and students at North Star Academy Charter School of Newark appears to be paying off with 100 percent of twelfth grade students in the class of 2005 passing the New Jersey High School Statewide Assessment, compared to 85.1 percent of students statewide, 44.2 percent of students in the district, and 19.5 percent of students in neighborhood schools. With the highest rate of four-year college acceptance and attendance of any school in New Jersey, North Star has truly become a guiding light for Newark's most needy students and a model for other schools across the country trying to eliminate the achievement gap.

Reflect on
the Reading

Questions About "Closing the Achievement Gap"

1. Does "Closing the Achievement Gap" undercut the claims in "What Boy Crisis?" that high-pressure schools are a problem in education today? Why or why not?
2. How does "Closing the Achievement Gap" make you rethink your reading of "Students Set the Rules at New York City School?" Is it fair to say the claims made in "Students Set the Rules at New York City School" are uninformed? Why or why not?
3. How would you compare the writing style in "Closing the Achievement Gap" with the earlier articles in this chapter? Which do you prefer to read and why? Which do you find more convincing?
4. How would you summarize "Closing the Achievement Gap" in one or two sentences? How would you relate the summary to the flow charts in this chapter mapping the topic of education reform?

Really thinking through the topic of alternative schools will require us to evaluate—to make decisions about—the various claims concerning education. At some level, turning to sources written for scholarly audiences can provide additional information needed to make evaluations. Scholarly sources tend to employ specialized terminology and aim their claims at a limited group of readers who tend to be immersed in the questions and problems related to a subject.

"Closing the Achievement Gap" assumes that its readers know something about concepts like college preparation, professional learning, or teaching for mastery. As a reader less familiar with these terms, you can still get the gist of the points the piece is trying to make. The more specialized the audience the more challenging it can be to engage with scholarly sources, but the payoff will come as you focus attention on a topic and explore the reasoning put forward in this rhetorical situation. (For more on using scholarly sources, see pages Chapter 16.)

Evidence

The sources in this chapter range from short informative pieces written for a general audience (like "Students Set the Rules at New York City School") to articles written for academic fields containing specialized language (like "Closing the Achievement Gap"). It can be tempting to give the claims in "Closing the Achievement Gap" more validity. First, the source tends to refer to research studies conducted by education professionals. Second, the article incorporates the statistics and conclusions from those studies in its text. In most scholarly rhetorical situations, this use of evidence is necessary. But that doesn't mean you can take such evidence at face value or that other kinds of evidence are not worthwhile.

For instance, consider the article's use of evidence on page 77:

> To be considered, the schools had to have graduated at least one cohort of students and have data to show that, for the most part, students were moving on to postsecondary education or employment.

Looking closely, we might ask what the report means by "for the most part." How many is most? Is 90% necessary to meet the criteria? 75%? Would 51% qualify as most? It's not likely that the report would claim that 51% qualifies as most, but based on this evidence, we can't really tell.

You must work with multiple sources to fully understand the perspectives and evidence in a single source

Further, a single study can't by itself demonstrate the validity of a particular view of education reform. "Closing the Achievement Gap" presents the perspective that is reflected in the original government report. But other studies exist that challenge the benefits of charter schools. For this reason, you must work with multiple sources to fully understand the perspectives and evidence in a single source.

Finally, evidence should not be dismissed simply because it does not come from a research study. Recall one of the suggestions made in the earlier "Students Set the Rules at New York City School" article: "David, now 12, is blossoming. He helps run a class on pharmacology and carries a notebook where he writes down things he's learning." First, we must consider what is being claimed here. The statement doesn't actually say that David is performing better in school. Instead, this piece offers a personal insight into David's attitude about school. If a big piece of the educational reform puzzle has to do with motivation, then this evidence can still be compelling, and David's mother is probably the best source for this kind of information. The key is connecting the claims made with the evidence provided to support those claims.

Let's stop and look at how our thinking has evolved while reading these sources with one final flow chart (see Figure 3.4).

This final flow chart can help us revisit all of the readings we have covered. Look at the main features of charter schools represented by the figure— a clear mission, high levels of support, low student-teacher ratios, a focus on college preparation. These qualities relate to high-pressure schools; they shed light on issues of motivation linked with free schools; and they offer potential solutions to achievement gaps based on race, class, or gender. All of these sources help us zoom out to understand the many concerns at play in conversations about educational reform.

Know It   Strategies for Exploring Multiple Sources and Ideas

- Find sources that take up opposing positions as you work. If you are still exploring, look for sources with competing perspectives to better understand a topic. If you have already taken up a position, be deliberate about finding and reading sources with an alternative stance.
- Look for positions that synthesize or take more complex views on your topic. Move beyond black and white representations of issues and instead try to explore the gray areas.
- Locate a range of sources to inform your thinking about a topic. Use popular sources to get a handle on the issues and on major positions. Find scholarly sources to continue evaluating the topic. Explore potential strengths and weaknesses of each kind of source.
- Examine the evidence and logic of your sources. Locate any cited sources that seem important. Critique the arguments put forth in your sources. (See Chapter 4 for more on argument.) Weigh the value of different types of evidence.
- Compose notes as you work with sources. Print out and mark up key sources. Compose summaries of important sources. Sketch out ideas for making sense of and writing about your topic. Create lists, maps, charts, or outlines to organize ideas.
- Keep track of sources as you work. Keep printouts of important sources. Bookmark Web sites. Save links to database sources. Copy citation information. Take notes and try to stay organized.

FIGURE 3.4
The flow and
relationship of ideas in
five texts.

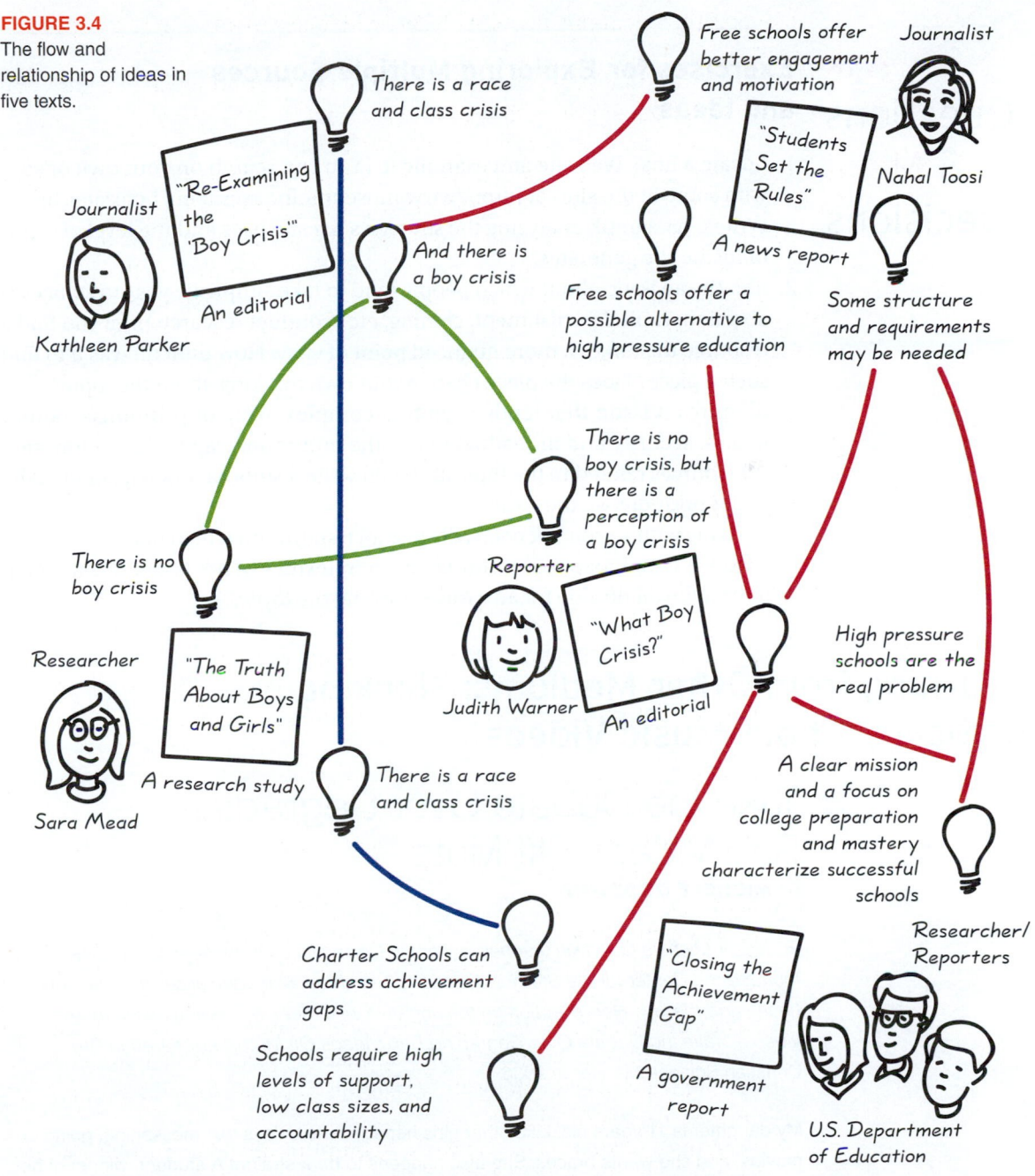

There is a race
and class crisis

Free schools offer
better engagement
and motivation

Journalist

"Students
Set the
Rules"

Nahal Toosi

Journalist

"Re-Examining
the
'Boy Crisis'"

An editorial

Kathleen Parker

And there is
a boy crisis

A news report

Free schools offer a
possible alternative to
high pressure education

Some structure
and requirements
may be needed

There is no
boy crisis, but
there is a
perception of
a boy crisis

Reporter

There is no
boy crisis

Researcher

"The Truth
About Boys
and Girls"

"What Boy
Crisis?"

High pressure
schools are the
real problem

Judith Warner

An editorial

A research study

Sara Mead

There is a race
and class crisis

A clear mission
and a focus on
college preparation
and mastery
characterize successful
schools

Charter Schools can
address achievement
gaps

"Closing the
Achievement
Gap"

Researcher/
Reporters

Schools require high
levels of support,
low class sizes, and
accountability

A government
report

U.S. Department
of Education

Ask
Questions
& Make
Decisions

Exercises for Exploring Multiple Sources and Ideas

1. Locate a hoax Web site and examine it. (You can search on your own or start with some of the sites at http://www.museumofhoaxes.com/hoaxsites.html.) Write a paragraph analyzing the strategies the site uses and the level of credibility the site generates.

2. Identify an issue about which people tend to take simplistic yes/no stances—abortion, capital punishment, cloning, etc. Conduct research until you find a resource that takes a more nuanced point of view. How difficult was it to find such a piece? Does the piece change your own thinking about the topic?

3. Identify an issue that lends itself to a complex array of positions—border fences, security and individual rights, the minimum wage, etc. Explore several sources related to the topic and then write a summary encapsulating the major positions on the issue.

4. Working with a group of peers, discuss an issue about which people disagree. Create a visual map representing the complexities of the issue. Use the map to develop an outline for an essay exploring the topic.

Learning from Other Mediums: Thinking Critically About Music Videos

 ## Take the Debate Over Degrading Rap Videos Off Mute

BY **MICHELE GOODWIN**

Professor Michele Goodwin teaches law at the University of Minnesota, where she founded the Center for the Study of Race and Bioethics. She specializes in issues of health and the law. Her reflection on the negative influences of stereotypes in music videos, "Take the Debate Over Degrading Rap Videos Off Mute," appeared in The Christian Science Monitor *in 2006.*

My daughter is 11 years old. Like other girls her age, she enjoys text messaging, going to movies, and she wants braces. She also happens to be a straight A student, winner of her school's science fair, and an accomplished classical dancer at a premier ballet school in Chicago. She is also African-American. Despite her accomplishments and what some might say is a "good start," I am a helicopter parent (I hover constantly).

FIGURE 3.5
Girl dressed as entertainment personality.

Because the horrible images portrayed of black girls and women as gyrating, hypersexual, insolent, irresponsible, and utterly available prey may stigmatize her and could lead to violence against her, I worry. Naively, I assumed this could be managed by monitoring the MTV, VH1, and, worst of all, BET television channels in our home. Yet, I shouldn't have been surprised when my daughter's new classmate from the Philippines, unprovoked, called my daughter a "stupid ho" and "b-ch," terms of endearment used by some black men in videos and rap music. When confronted by the principal, the boy admitted addressing my daughter that way, but argued in his defense that he learned it from black men on TV.

A controversy earlier this summer involving Troi Torian (aka DJ Star), a popular New York disc jockey, and his spate of on-air sexual and violent threats against a little girl illustrates the perverse state of affairs. To taunt a rival disc jockey, DJ Star asked callers to reveal the whereabouts of Rashawn Casey's 4-year-old daughter. He made highly descriptive, on-air references to possible sexual interactions with her. He offered a $500 reward for any information about where the little girl attends school.

This kind of lewd public commentary demonstrates a certain kind of 21st-century minstrelsy and reveals a complex state of intraracial affairs. Within the African-American community, issues of sexual violence, including rape, incest, and abuse are typically closeted. Black people seem to fear that if whites were to get wind of such problems it might exacerbate racism and perpetuate stereotypes.

For example, Michael Eric Dyson, winner of the 2006 NAACP Image Award, has publicly criticized Bill Cosby for exposing dirty little secrets such as drug use, parental neglect, and other issues in the black community. Professor Dyson describes Mr. Cosby as being insensitive and pushing a "destructive" agenda. Dyson claims Cosby won't admit that racism exists. Nothing could be further from the truth than the notion that accountability, integrity, and self- growth are "destructive" to black Americans. Neither are these right-wing, Republican, or "white" values.

FIGURE 3.6
The Pussycat Dolls at the 2008 Q102 Jingle Ball.

Moreover, we are only deluding ourselves to think no one notices this terrible self-destruction. After all, BET is quite public, as are videos on MTV and the criminal records of those caught in the matrix of celebrity and "gangsta" life. Ironically, it remains black men who primarily portray black women as hypersexual. From once exporting images of respected if not noble civil rights leaders and activists, the black image now includes desperate sexual depravity. Most important, I wonder why these conversations must happen in the race closet when the videos and behavior are very public, unapologetic, and ubiquitous.

➹ Reflect on the Reading

Questions About "Take the Debate Over Degrading Rap Videos Off Mute"

1. What claims does Goodwin seem to be making in the piece? What counter-arguments or additional claims can you think of to complicate Goodwin's position?
2. How does Goodwin's status as an African-American relate to the critique offered in the essay? How would you discuss the image in Figure 3.5 in terms of the essay? How would you relate Goodwin's points to larger concerns about ethnicity?
3. Goodwin specifically targets BET and videos on MTV or VH1 that have a negative impact on young black women. What similar concerns arise related to stereotyping that takes place in other mediums?
4. How would you relate music videos to the discussion in this chapter on the boy crisis in education? Can either of these concerns help us understand the other? How much more complex would your approach to either topic be if it included the other?

Respond   Write to Explore Critical Reading and Thinking

You should attempt to use and strengthen your critical thinking and reading every time you take on a writing project. The following assignments provide some targeted opportunities:

1. **Compose a report of four or more pages in which you use multiple sources to educate readers about an issue.** Your report will provide analysis and synthesis of your sources in order to give readers an overview of the topic. Although you will want to select an area of focus that you can call your own, the report should entertain multiple perspectives on the topic. The report should also use evidence to demonstrate its points. Use citations and document your sources as needed to provide evidence for your points. (For more on research essays, see Chapter 10.)
2. **Write a comparison/contrast essay in which you explore two or more sources that have significant differences in their rhetorical situations.** You

RESOURCE
Music Videos

might use a scholarly source and a source directed to the general public. You could use a source primarily meant to entertain and a source mostly meant to persuade. You could use sources representing different perspectives on an issue. Read each piece critically. Develop a list of points of similarity or difference between the two articles. Discuss your findings in an essay of three or more pages. (See Chapter 23 for more on comparisons.)

3. **Compose an essay in which you analyze music videos in terms of a cultural concern.** Zoom in to sharpen your focus. You might narrow your approach by looking at hip hop, country, or indie videos. You could look for genre differences among videos—live performance, choreography and dance, storytelling, etc. You could narrow things based on your cultural concern—looking at videos promoting gender stereotypes, consumerism, or substance abuse, for instance. Use the videos to explore several dimensions of your topic and write up your findings. You can compose the essay on a word processor or online. Insert or link to samples to demonstrate your points. To push the assignment, consider composing a video essay (see Chapter E8).

Learning
Objective 3.5

4. **Create an online portal page to combine and collect multiple sources.** An online portal or profile page allows you to customize the way you interact with Internet resources. Begin by creating an account with Google, Yahoo!, or some other Internet portal. Log into your account and then look for the link that will let you customize or add options and features to your account. (On Google, this might be listed as iGoogle; on Yahoo! this might be listed as MyYahoo!) Once logged in, find the options for personalizing your page. Add and arrange modules or widgets to customize the page; you might put world news or weather near the top to suit your interest, find show times for your local theater, or add updates to news related to outdoor sports. Experiment with the selection and layout until you have a sense that the information matches your interests. When finished, reflect on the portal in terms of critical thinking and composing.

Zoom **Out**   Reflecting on Critical Reading and Thinking

- **Reading, thinking, and writing are related.** You practice critical thinking all the time, but reading strategies such as looking for evidence or considering competing perspectives can further the process. Writing culminates the process of critical thinking, helping you to sort through ideas and explain your perspectives to others.

- **You can start with simple exploration.** You can survey your own ideas about topics, getting your bearings. You might begin with your responses to readings, getting the gist of what is said. Soon, you will identify specific elements to analyze in more detail.

- **Research is a big part of critical reading and thinking.** Reading several sources on a topic ensures that you have the background necessary to judge the articles you encounter. You also refine your thinking as you engage in the research process.

- **You need to prioritize ideas and information.** Like taking a picture, you must decide what elements to include in the frame and which might be brought into sharpest focus. These decisions require you to take ownership of ideas, making judgments through evaluation.

- **You can connect ideas through a process of synthesis.** Look for patterns in and among your sources. Compare and contrast ideas and readings. Examine the contexts that inform your thinking and your sources.

- **Critical thinking asks you to entertain multiple perspectives.** Often these perspectives are more nuanced than simple either/or positions. (Education might have problems related to class, but also related to high-pressure, and sometimes to gender.) Learning to work with multiple sources helps you entertain these complexities.

- **Zooming in and out helps you practice critical thinking and reading.** As you explore elements of culture, you must ask questions and make decisions about the connections you discover. You must also zoom in to focus your thoughts. As you analyze, summarize, synthesize, evaluate, and draw conclusions about a topic, you zoom in and out.

For additional information and practice with the learning objectives in this chapter, go to www.mycomplab.com, Resources > Writing > Writing Purposes > Writing to Analyze.

Reading and Understanding Arguments

 Zoom **In**   **Key Concepts and Learning Objectives**

After studying this chapter, you should be able to:

4.1 Break arguments into their component parts to show the logic behind claims, reasons, and evidence.

4.2 Identify ethical, logical, and emotional appeals.

4.3 Identify logical fallacies in arguments.

4.4 Analyze arguments to discover hidden assumptions.

4.5 Respond to opposing points of view.

Spend some time reading the letters section of a newspaper or magazine, and you will quickly develop a sense of the way arguments get formed. A source such as the *Los Angeles Times* or *Newsweek* publishes a story, maybe a piece about government health policies for the elderly. The article might lay out some concerns related to the issue. The writers who respond in the letters section might voice their agreement, take issue with the article, or offer some additional perspectives. You can tell something about the complexity and importance of the issue by the number of responses the story generates. A simple report with the latest figures on life expectancy might not generate much interest at all. A story about age discrimination, however, might provoke more responses, and a piece advocating caps on medical access for the elderly would produce a storm of letters.

The more responses the stories generate, the easier it is to see them as arguments. A report on aging statistics is pretty straightforward: there might be disputes about how the statistics were gathered, but the factual nature of the story leaves little to argue about. The topic of ageism is more complicated. Most people would never argue that ageism is a good thing, but there might be disagreements about the extent of the problem or root causes. When it comes to the elderly and limited health care resources, however, the topic gets trickier. We're talking about the implications of an aging population, an array of medical policies and technologies, and ideas about the responsibilities of society—an interrelated collection of cultural elements.

So, arguments are really about the complexities that come up when we address issues. The facts are all one color. The two sides of ageism might be mostly black or white. But the ways in which society should respond to some of the more difficult implications of aging are gray (no pun intended) and murky. People will disagree about the extent of the problem, the feasibility of any solutions, and the ethical dimensions of the issue.

Of course, a letter to the editor is a real-world writing opportunity. You can examine messages that take the shape of arguments, but in practice, you will use elements of arguments to write persuasively in a number of rhetorical situations. You may be asked to argue about a controversy as a way of exploring a topic and sharpening your writing skills. But just as likely you will need to compose persuasively as you write proposals, evaluate texts you have read, or discuss academic topics. We will look at some of these possibilities in this chapter.

> ## Arguments are really about the complexities that come up when we address issues

WN

VIDEO
6. Complexity in Arguments

KEY TERMS

- **Arguments:** Compositions that seek to persuade an audience to act, feel, or believe a certain way. Arguments are created using claims, reasons, and evidence. Although meant to sway readers, arguments also explore the complexities of topics.

- **Claim:** A statement or assertion about a topic. A central claim can form the thesis of an argument. Additional claims can further the central claim or make related points.

- **Reasons:** Statements offered in support of a claim. Reasons provide explanations for why a claim is worth considering. The organization and relevance of the reasons offered creates the logical appeal of the argument.

- **Evidence:** Information offered in support of a claim or reason. Evidence provides the authoritative weight that makes claims and reasons believable. Evidence takes the form of facts and statistics, the statements of others, and anecdotes and observations.

- **Appeals:** Strategies for persuading an audience. Appeals can be made to the ethical status of the speaker (ethos), to the logic of the argument (logos), and to the emotions of the audience (pathos).

- **Toulmin system:** Terminology borrowed from legal studies to help understand and develop arguments. Toulmin terms include *grounds* (evidence), *warrants* (assumptions), and *backing* (rebuttals).

- **Fallacies:** Faulty reasoning used in arguments. Fallacies include ad hominem (personal) attacks, faulty assertions about causes and effects, distracting red herrings, misleading analogies, slippery slope claims, circular reasoning, disingenuous either/or arguments, and non sequitur claims that don't follow from their reasons.

Finding Complexity in Arguments

Arguments generally touch on topics about which people will disagree. When you take up a topic like genetic research or gay marriage, you will quickly discover vocal advocates on either side of the issue. But you will also soon recognize the many layers of complexity that make up such topics, as you can see in the argument below in which Bill McKibben urges us to take action against global warming.

⬊ Meltdown: Running Out of Time on Global Warming
BY **BILL MCKIBBEN**

Bill McKibben has written about global warming for decades. He also writes about religion and issues of social justice. In 2007, he released the book Deep Economy: The Wealth of Communities and the Durable Future. *"Meltdown: Running Out of Time on Global Warming" first appeared in* The Christian Century *in 2007.*

WE NEED A MOVEMENT to combat climate change, we need it fast, and we need it to involve as many churches as possible. And you can help make it happen the Saturday after Easter.

How's that for a blunt and artless beginning? But that's the point. The time is so short, and the task so large, that eloquence seems almost frivolous. I wrote the first book about global warming for a general audience way back in 1989, and I've been writing about it ever since. But now—though I'm not very good at it—I'm trying to organize. And I need help. Here's why.

The climate crisis is bearing down on us much faster than most people realize. A decade ago most experts thought of global warming as the largest challenge civilization faced—but they also thought that it would happen relatively gradually. So far, by burning coal and gas and oil, we've released enough carbon dioxide to raise the temperature of the planet about a degree Fahrenheit. Which doesn't sound like much, and indeed the early computer models predicted that such an increase would just bring us to the threshold of noticeable change—really big impacts seemed still a few decades down the road. But that cautious optimism has faded in the past few years as one study after another has proved that the earth was more finely balanced than we'd understood.

For instance, the temperature rise has been enough to start melting every frozen thing on earth, which in turn creates its own problems. In the Arctic Ocean, nice white ice that reflected lots of the sun's rays back to space is quickly turning into nice blue water that absorbs much more of the sun's heat, amplifying the warming. The thawing tundra is releasing huge quantities of methane, which is another potent global warming gas. Scariest of all, the great ice sheets above Greenland and the West Antarctic appear to be melting faster than predicted. There's the very real chance of a catastrophic rise in sea level, one that would endanger the world's coastal cities, inundate much prime farmland, and drive hundreds of millions from their homes.

The bottom line: we have much less time to act than we thought, and that action has to be dramatic. James Hansen is the country's foremost climatologist, a man who will doubtless win the Nobel Prize for his decades as a NASA researcher running the most powerful computer model of the climate, and he said last year that we have a decade to reverse the flow of carbon into the atmosphere or else we will live—his words—on a "totally different planet." There's enough theology in that phrase for a month of sermons, but let me concentrate on the politics. It means that the changes we make in our homes and churches as individuals and congregations, vital as they are, can't deliver the speed or magnitude of change that will slow climate change. It means that we need to change light bulbs—but we also need to change laws. It means that Washington, after two decades of a very successful bipartisan effort to do nothing, needs to spin on a dime.

It would be easier, nicer and in many ways more reasonable to put in effect the kind of tepid and gradual program envisioned a few years ago by politicians like John McCain. But "politically realistic" turns out, with what we now know, to be scientifically unrealistic. By Hansen's calculation, and that of many other scientists, we need to be reducing carbon emissions more than 2 percent a year in this country to have any chance of staying on the right side of catastrophe. We need—at the very least—a federal commitment to cut carbon emissions 80 percent by 2050.

That's a hard target, but by no means an impossible one. New technologies are steadily appearing—second- and third-generation solar and wind systems, ever-better hybrid cars. We understand how to make appliances far more efficient than the ones we use today, and how to change building codes so that new construction stops wasting energy and indeed begins to produce it. And, of course, we know how to build trains and buses, how to grow some of our food closer to home. We don't lack for science or engineering, nor indeed for economic mechanisms to make a transition more efficient, or policy proposals to guide our work. What we lack is simply political will.

Imagine your average representative or senator. He or she hears constantly from the lobbyists representing the most profitable interests on earth (Exxon Mobil, for instance, last year made more money than any corporation in the history of corporations, and it used some of that revenue both to lobby and to spread disinformation about global warming). The congressperson may also hear occasionally from the lobbyists for the Washington environmental groups, but he suspects that most of the people in his home district don't consider climate change a top priority. I sat in John McCain's office three years ago, when he was trying, without success, to pass his extremely modest bill—a bill that would not begin to meet the scientific test for taking climate seriously. Still, he said, "all of the manufacturing sector is opposed to significant measures being taken. People like the National Association of Manufacturers, the automobile industry. There's a broad array of powerful opposition to doing anything." There was no great mystery about what needed to happen: "Until enough citizens who are voters care, then these special interests will be able to block any meaningful policy change. It's as simple as that."

So we need—and quickly—a movement. We need a movement as urgent, as morally committed, as willing to sacrifice, as creative, as passionate as the civil rights movement was a generation ago. And we have to build it almost from scratch. The environmentalism of the moment is vibrant and wonderful—but it's built for other tasks. It's built for acting on the local level (saving watersheds and scenic views) and for lobbying on the national level (changing toxics regulations or winning new wildernesses). It's not built for mobilizing

Meltdown: Running
Out of Time on
Global Warming
(continued)
BY **BILL MCKIBBEN**

masses of Americans around a moral challenge. The possibility of a movement exists—Hurricane Katrina blew open the door, and Al Gore walked through that door with his powerful movie, *An Inconvenient Truth*. The national mood has changed, but so far national policy hasn't shifted. And it won't shift enough without a powerful shove.

SO HERE'S THE PLAN. On Saturday, April 14, a coalition of environmental activists and organizations will be staging rallies around the country. Local rallies will all hoist the same banner: "Congress: Stop Global Warming. Cut Carbon 80% by 2050." Those rallies will be linked electronically, through both the new technologies of the Web and the traditional media. (Only ten days after the Stepitup07 Web site was launched, 196 actions were scheduled in 43 states.) Some of the rallies will be in places everyone will recognize—the melting icefields at Glacier National Park, the levees above New Orleans' Ninth Ward, the endangered coral reefs off Maui and Key West. Some rallies will be in places less famous but equally iconic and special for those involved. Town parks, League of Women Voters meetings, City Hall plazas. Church steps.

Why church steps? Because, to put it crudely, politicians pay attention to people on church steps.

But why should churchpeople be at the forefront of this movement? Here's my best shot at explaining:

1. If you care about social justice, this is the biggest battle we've ever faced. Computer models suggest that climate change will soon be creating hundreds of millions of refugees, fleeing rising waters or fields turned to desert (more refugees than we managed to create with all the bloody wars of the century we've just come through). I've wandered the lowlands of Bangladesh, fertile homeland for 150 million people. Imagining it underwater is ghastly enough. And then remembering that these people have done nothing to create the problem, that the 4 percent of the world living in America creates 25 percent of the carbon dioxide—well, suffice it to say, it makes me feel sad and angry and guilty all at once. And determined, which is the most useful emotion on that list.

2. If you care about the rest of God's creation, then get to work. God made (in whatever way) the creatures of the earth and of the sea; we're now engaged in a massive, rapid act of decreation. Coral reefs may be gone soon, and with them an entire corner of God's brain. Huge amounts of DNA are simply disappearing—the best predictions say that the extinctions from a rapid warming will rival those that happened the last time an asteroid slammed into the planet. Except that this time the asteroid is us, and—blessed with free will—we can prevent its impact if we so choose.

3. If you care about the future—about 10,000 generations yet unborn—then this is your cause. The residence time of carbon in the atmosphere is long, and the

changes we're now causing are, on human time scales, probably permanent. It's hard to see what's going to freeze Greenland once we've melted it. We are permanently degrading and impoverishing the earth for all who follow us—and we're doing all that to prolong for another quarter century the lifestyle that a fifth of humanity has enjoyed for maybe 50 years.

4. If you care about the selfish individualism that has come to define too much of our culture, then this is the chance to act. This movement is the first in which people will be demanding something more than simply extending participation in "the good life" to more people. It's a movement that will force us to answer deep questions about what that good life is. Eighty percent less fossil fuel use means a different America by mid-century—perhaps one where people depend more on their neighbors than they do now. That's scary, but also hopeful. The church which can still posit some goal for human life other than accumulation—must be involved in the search for what comes next.

CHRISTIANS WON'T BE alone in this movement. The nascent religious environmental movement—which already includes noble efforts like Interfaith Power and Light and the Evangelical Environmental Network—has found allies in Judaism, in Islam, in Buddhism and in many other traditions (which makes sense, since this issue inevitably involves questions of origin, of end, of right behavior; it's theological at its core). There's also a swiftly emerging student movement on hundreds of campuses—not angry this time so much as dogged and hardworking. Some enlightened corporate chieftains have begun to join in as well—they know that the insurance sector, the part of our economy that we ask to deal with risk, is (to use the technical term) freaking out over global warming. The November elections removed from power congressional committee chairs who called climate change a hoax—but in so doing they probably opened the door to the kinds of too-weak compromise that might keep us from doing what we need to do.

Which is: set a target and get to work. Reams can and will be written about precisely what technologies and what taxes and what subsidies and what regulations will and won't be needed in the years ahead. But without a vision the effort will perish, and with it the blooming, buzzing, mysterious, gorgeous, cruel world we were given.

Even with a vision there's no guarantee of success. Some scientists are already saying we've waited too long, that a runaway greenhouse effect is now a real possibility. And the fact that China and India are now starting to burn fossil fuel in appreciable (if not American) quantities makes the task harder (and the need for our leadership all the greater). But faith in a living God allows us hope. Not hope that everything will come out OK, that God will simply override our reckless greed and keep the temperature down. That's not hope, that's wishing. But hope that if we make a real effort, the best effort we're capable of, it will matter. Somehow.

↗
Reflect on
the Reading

Questions About "Meltdown: Running Out of Time on Global Warming"

1. How would you summarize in one sentence the argument offered by the article? Is it possible to capture the complexities of the argument?

2. "Meltdown: Running Out of Time on Global Warming" first appeared in *The Christian Century*. The article also makes a number of appeals based on religious beliefs. How would you relate these elements to the argument in the article?

3. Often, arguments will include a section acknowledging (and sometimes refuting) opposing positions. "Meltdown: Running Out of Time on Global Warming" doesn't explicitly contain such a section. What might this element do for the strength of the argument? Can you recognize any acknowledgements of opposing sides in the article?

4. How effective do you find the four reasons for acting against global warming that McKibben offers toward the end of the article? Are you convinced? Are you likely to make changes or take action? Why or why not?

Arguments consist of a series of claims, reasons, and evidence that support a conclusion that the author hopes will be convincing to readers. You can see this basic structure in Figure 4.1.

FIGURE 4.1
The basic structure of an argument.

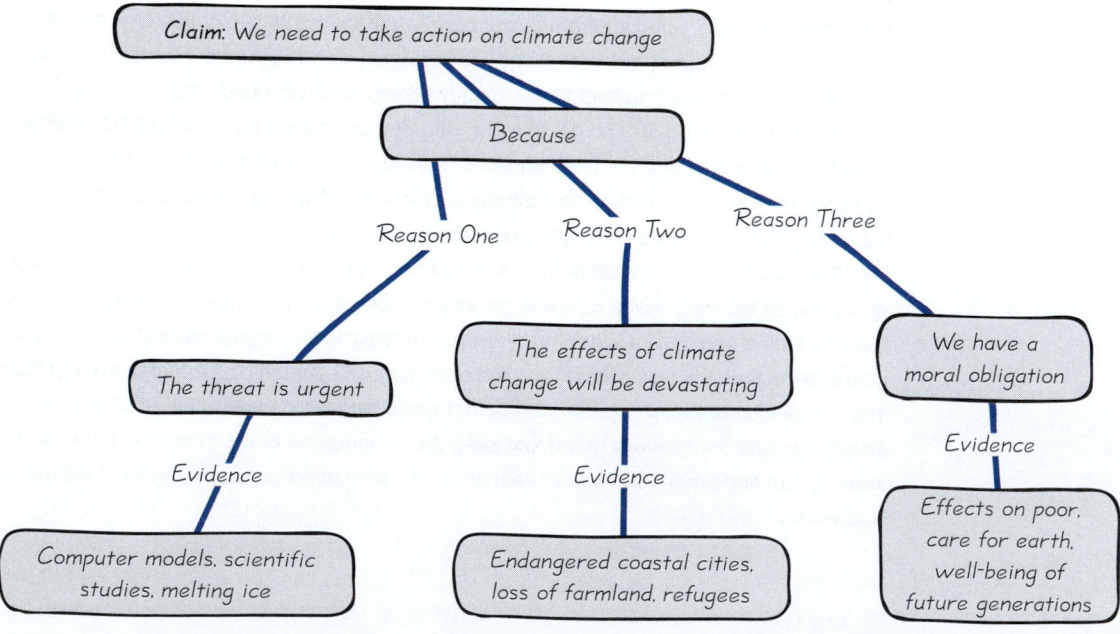

A claim is merely a statement. In arguments, the major claims try to sway readers to believe or to act a certain way. On one level, McKibben's claim is straightforward: We need to take action against climate change. He supports this claim by offering some compelling reasons: the threat is urgent, the effects of climate change will be devastating, and there is a moral obligation to take action. McKibben also supports these reasons by providing evidence: he cites examples of rapid climate change and references "the country's foremost climatologist," and he calls upon theological tenets to bolster his reasons.

Beginning with a topic about which people might disagree, McKibben establishes a claim, identifies reasons to support the claim, and then offers evidence to back up those reasons. You can see how following this formula would help you write persuasively. But an argument should do more than press readers toward a pre-defined conclusion. Notice how McKibben provides background information about the topic. He discusses previous predictions, histories, and statistics regarding carbon release. We can see how arguments serve to educate readers and clarify the complexities of a topic.

Arguments serve to educate readers and clarify the complexities of a topic

Further, complex topics can rarely be reduced to arguments that might be represented with a single claim. Let's look again McKibben's argument to see how multiple claims must sometimes be layered into an argument to bring out the complexities of a topic, as seen in Figure 4.2 (page 98).

In many ways, our initial analysis of the argument simply rehearses the debate on climate change that has been taking place for the last twenty years. Those advocating for responses to climate change argue that the problem is real, it's urgent, and specific action is needed. But the second claim calling for social organization represents an evolution of this familiar argument and becomes as central to the article as the earlier debate about whether climate change is real.

LO

Learning
Objective 4.1

Notice how McKibben's article also develops the two claims simultaneously. He introduces both claims right up front and then weaves together the reasons and evidence needed to make the claims convincing as he discusses the topic. As you move through the piece, additional complexities are layered over the discussion: we need to take action, that action is social organization, the problem is urgent, the challenges are political, and the movement must be global. Already you can see that most topics require a nuanced and organic development of arguments, one that educates readers and clarifies the topic for them rather than one that simply twists them toward a conclusion.

There's one more layer of McKibben's argument that bears closer examination—his personal engagement with the topic. Some of McKibben's personal investment is reasonably predictable; for example, when he lists his experience with the topic of climate change, it helps establish his authority, giving the argu-

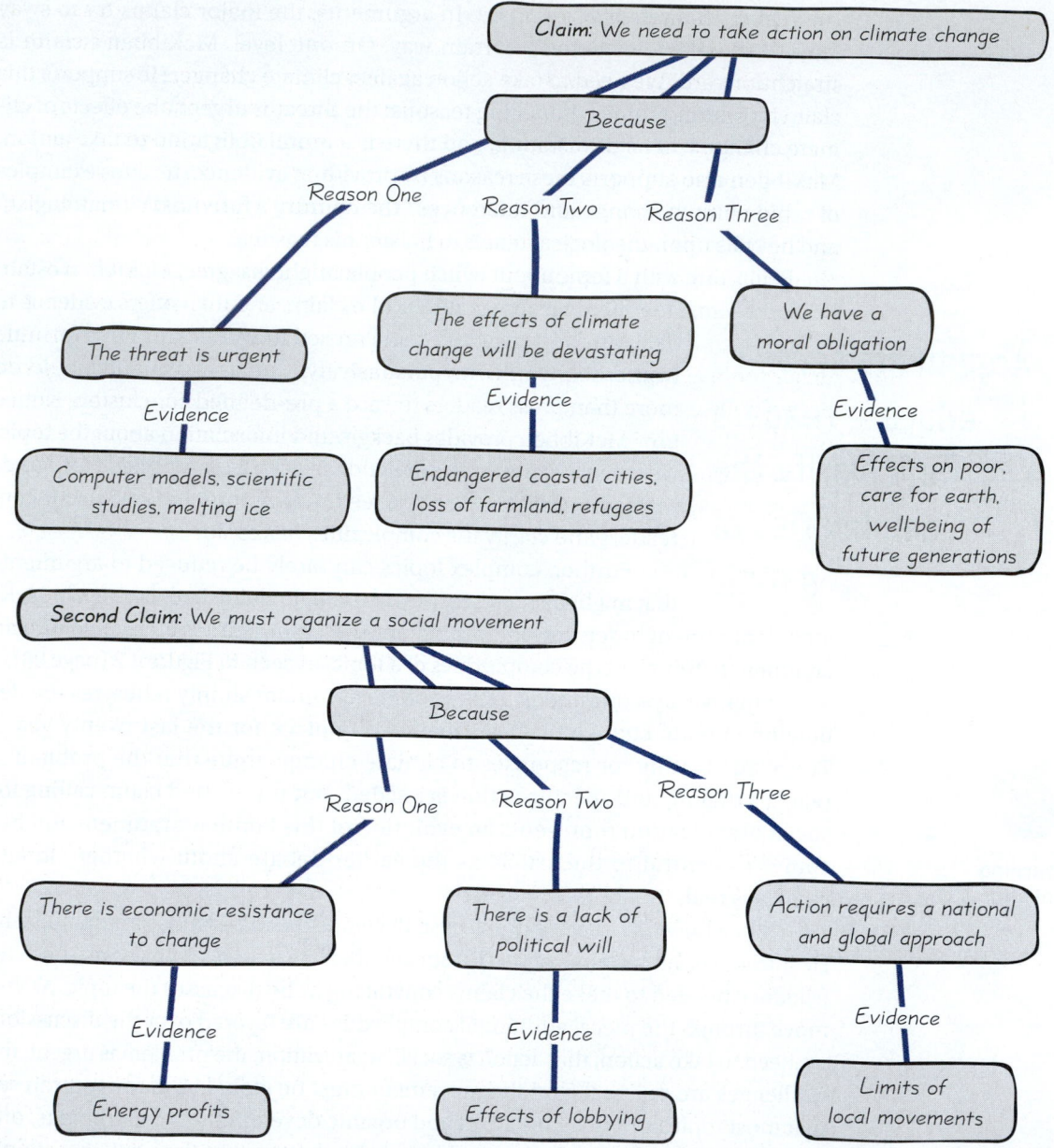

FIGURE 4.2
Another claim layer in
McKibben's argument.

ment a stronger sense of credibility. Similarly, McKibben's revelation about his religious background tells us something about his ethos; we learn about the identity and values of the person delivering the argument (see page 109 below). You may not want to include such personal revelations in all of the arguments you compose, but you should try to establish a sense that you are a credible speaker with a genuine and open-minded interest in your topic.

But what should we make of the way McKibben's argument is addressed directly to a religious audience? Here the move tells us a good deal about the rhetorical situation in which the argument exists. Having such a specific audience reveals the importance of appealing to the values of potential readers. These assumptions or beliefs in part determine the claims and evidence that readers will accept. McKibben touches on some of the scientific and economic dimensions of the topic in his argument, but focuses most of his energy on the moral and spiritual concerns that are more likely to sway his intended readers. In many ways, this personal, religious dimension represents yet another layer in the argument; we could zoom in to evaluate McKibben's beliefs in more detail or zoom out to situate climate change among elements of culture like religion (as McKibben does).

Know It   Strategies for Finding Complexity in Arguments

- Think about assumptions and belief systems that support positions on issues. After identifying major assumptions, think about variations that add complexity to the issue. What happens when positions on climate change, for instance, are supported by religious beliefs?
- Stop to scrutinize the reasons offered in support of the major claim made in an argument. Think of these reasons as additional claims. What assumptions underlie them? What additional reasons might be needed to support them, and what objections to the reasons might be raised?
- Use sketches or maps to unpack the parts of an argument. Create bubbles representing multiple positions. Draw connections between claims and reasons. Use a visual representation to bring out the facets of the issue.
- Think about how positions on an issue shift with changes in context. Do positions differ depending on where groups are located? Have views of the issue shifted over time? Increase the complexity of your understanding by zooming out to think about contexts.
- Explore additional sources of information to bring out the complexities of an argument. Find enough sources to move your thinking beyond either/or positions on your topic.

Ask Questions & Make Decisions

Exercises for Finding Complexity in Arguments

1. Choose a topic about which people clearly disagree—gun control, drug legalization, pornography, immigration, etc. Conduct research into historical views on the topic. Write a paragraph comparing points of view today with those from an earlier era.
2. Identify an issue that lends itself to either/or positions—capital punishment, abortion, prayer in schools, etc. Develop a list of at least three perspectives that look past either/or positions on the issue.
3. Consider the assumptions that lie beneath a position on an issue. Next, think about the assumptions that lie beneath an alternative perspective on the issue. Finally, keeping the beliefs and assumptions in mind, develop a list of things that both sides would agree upon regarding the issue.
4. Participating with a group of peers, create a visual representation of a position on a topic. Next, think about additional topics that share similarities with your first topic. Develop visual representations for at least two more topics, and then discuss the relationships you can discover between all of the topics.

Responding to Alternative Points of View

McKibben's call for social organization as a means to take action against climate change demonstrates how arguments often evolve organically as they explore a number of claims. But the piece does not reveal one other key component of arguments, their need to consider multiple perspectives and address opposing points of view. To think about these dimensions of arguments, let's look at an additional reading, an essay by Steven Johnson.

Yes, People Still Read, but Now It's Social
BY **STEVEN JOHNSON**

Steven Johnson writes regularly for the New York Times. *He is interested in the impacts of media on culture and ideas and has recently published the book,* Where Good Ideas Come From: The Natural History of Innovation. *"Yes, People Still Read, but Now It's Social" appeared in the* New York Times *in 2010.*

"THE POINT of books is to combat loneliness," David Foster Wallace observes near the beginning of "Although of Course You End Up Becoming Yourself," David Lipsky's recently published, book-length interview with him.

If you happen to be reading the book on the Kindle from Amazon, Mr. Wallace's observation has an extra emphasis: a dotted underline running below the phrase. Not because Mr. Wallace or Mr. Lipsky felt that the point was worth stressing, but because a dozen or so other readers have highlighted the passage on their Kindles, making it one of the more "popular" passages in the book.

Amazon calls this new feature "popular highlights." It may sound innocuous enough, but it augurs even bigger changes to come.

Though the feature can be disabled by the user, "popular highlights" will no doubt alarm Nicholas Carr, whose new book, *The Shallows*, argues that the compulsive skimming, linking and multitasking of our screen reading is undermining the deep, immersive focus that has defined book culture for centuries.

With "popular highlights," even when we manage to turn off Twitter and the television and sit down to read a good book, there will a chorus of readers turning the pages along with us, pointing out the good bits. Before long, we'll probably be able to meet those fellow readers, share stories with them. Combating loneliness? David Foster Wallace saw only the half of it.

Mr. Carr's argument is that these distractions come with a heavy cost, and his book's publication coincides with articles in various publications—including *The New York Times*—that report on scientific studies showing how multitasking harms our concentration.

Thus far, the neuroscience of multitasking has tended to follow a predictable pattern. Scientists take a handful of test subjects out of their offices and make them watch colored squares dance on a screen in a lab somewhere. Then they determine that multitasking makes you slightly less able to focus. A study reported on early this month found that heavy multitaskers performed about 10 to 20 percent worse on most tests than light multitaskers.

These studies are undoubtedly onto something—no one honestly believes he is better at focusing when he switches back and forth between multiple activities—but they are meaningless as a cultural indicator without measuring what we gain from multitasking.

Thanks to e-mail, Twitter and the blogosphere, I regularly exchange information with hundreds of people in a single day: scheduling meetings, sharing political gossip, trading edits on a book chapter, planning a family vacation, reading tech punditry. How many of those exchanges could happen were I limited exclusively to the technologies of the phone, the post office and the face-to-face meeting? I suspect that the number would be a small fraction of my current rate.

I have no doubt that I am slightly less focused in these interactions, but, frankly, most of what we do during the day doesn't require our full powers of concentration. Even rocket scientists don't do rocket science all day long.

To his credit, Mr. Carr readily concedes this efficiency argument. His concern is what happens to high-level thinking when the culture migrates from the page to the screen. To

Yes, People Still
Read, but Now It's
Social *(continued)*
BY **STEVEN JOHNSON**

the extent that his argument is a reminder to all of us to step away from the screen some-times, and think in a more sedate environment, it's a valuable contribution.

But Mr. Carr's argument is more ambitious than that: the "linear, literary mind" that has been at "the center of art, science and society" threatens to become "yesterday's mind," with dire consequences for our culture. Here, too, I think the concerns are overstated, though for slightly different reasons.

Presumably, the first casualties of "shallow" thinking should have appeared on the front lines of the technology world, where the participants have spent the most time in the hyperconnected space of the screen. And yet the sophistication and nuance of media com-mentary has grown dramatically over the last 15 years. Mr. Carr's original essay, published in *The Atlantic*—along with Clay Shirky's more optimistic account, which led to the book *Cognitive Surplus*—were intensely discussed throughout the Web when they first appeared as articles, and both books appear to be generating the same level of analysis and engagement in long form.

The intellectual tools for assessing the media, once the province of academics and professional critics, are now far more accessible to the masses. The number of people who have written a thoughtful response to Mr. Carr's essay—and, even better, published it online—surely dwarfs the number of people who wrote in public about "Understanding Me-dia," by Marshall McLuhan, in 1964.

Mr. Carr spends a great deal of his book's opening section convincing us that new forms of media alter the way the brain works, which I suspect most of his readers have long ago accepted as an obvious truth. The question is not whether our brains are being changed. (Of course new experiences change your brain—that's what experience is, on some basic level.) The question is whether the rewards of the change are worth the liabilities.

The problem with Mr. Carr's model is its unquestioned reverence for the slow contemplation of deep reading. For society to advance as it has since Gutenberg, he argues, we need the quiet, solitary space of the book. Yet many great ideas that have advanced culture over the past centuries have emerged from a more connective space, in the collision of different worldviews and sensibilities, different metaphors and fields of expertise. (Gutenberg himself borrowed his printing press from the screw presses of Rhineland vintners, as Mr. Carr notes.)

It's no accident that most of the great scientific and technological innovation over the last millennium has taken place in crowded, distracting urban centers. The printed page it-self encouraged those manifold connections, by allowing ideas to be stored and shared and circulated more efficiently. One can make the case that the Enlightenment depended more on the exchange of ideas than it did on solitary, deep-focus reading.

Quiet contemplation has led to its fair share of important thoughts. But it cannot be denied that good ideas also emerge in networks.

Yes, we are a little less focused, thanks to the electric stimulus of the screen. Yes, we are reading slightly fewer long-form narratives and arguments than we did 50 years ago, though the Kindle and the iPad may well change that. Those are costs, to be sure. But what of the other side of the ledger? We are reading more text, writing far more often, than we were in the heyday of television.

And the speed with which we can follow the trail of an idea, or discover new perspectives on a problem, has increased by several orders of magnitude. We are marginally less focused, and exponentially more connected. That's a bargain all of us should be happy to make.

↗
Reflect on the Reading

WN

VIDEO
7. Alternative Points of View

Questions About "Yes, People Still Read, but Now It's Social"

1. How would you describe the tone of the article? What would you say to someone who felt the piece was too combative? What if someone said it was too conciliatory?
2. How well does Johnson present the position of Nicholas Carr, the person behind the claim that the Internet is damaging the ability of individuals to think deeply? Do you feel like you need more information about Carr's perspective? Why or why not?
3. How convinced are you by Johnson's response to Carr? If you are swayed, what parts of the piece moved your opinion? If you are skeptical, what questions do you have?
4. What are your thoughts on the ways in which the Internet influences our ability to think? Do you agree that we are more distracted as a result of the Internet? Why or why not?

"Yes, People Still Read, but Now It's Social" represents some typical strategies for responding to alternative perspectives in the way it lists a claim, and then develops an argument in response to the claim. You can get a better understanding of how this movement develops from Figure 4.3.

Johnson begins by paraphrasing the claim offered by Carr, that "the compulsive skimming, linking and multitasking of our screen reading is undermining the deep, immersive focus that has defined book culture for centuries." Johnson presents Carr's position that the Internet is limiting the ability of individuals to think deeply. Further, Johnson discusses the scientific studies on multitasking that support the opposing point of view. The key here is that Johnson is offering readers a clear picture of Carr's perspective. Arguments that respond to alternative positions are stronger when they give the opposing point of view a fair hearing.

Johnson does not, however, simply accept the opposing stance. Instead, he explores the various elements that make up the Carr's argument. Here, understanding the structure of arguments is helpful. You can respond to an overall claim. Or you can challenge the reasons and evidence offered to support that claim. Johnson does this by zooming in to focus on the scientific studies. Note, however, that Johnson does not dismiss the studies outright. He does question their artificial nature (test subjects "watch[ing] colored squares dance on a screen"), and he points out that the studies only claim a 10–20% loss of focus. In

FIGURE 4.3

The structure of the argument "Yes, People Still Read, but Now It's Social."

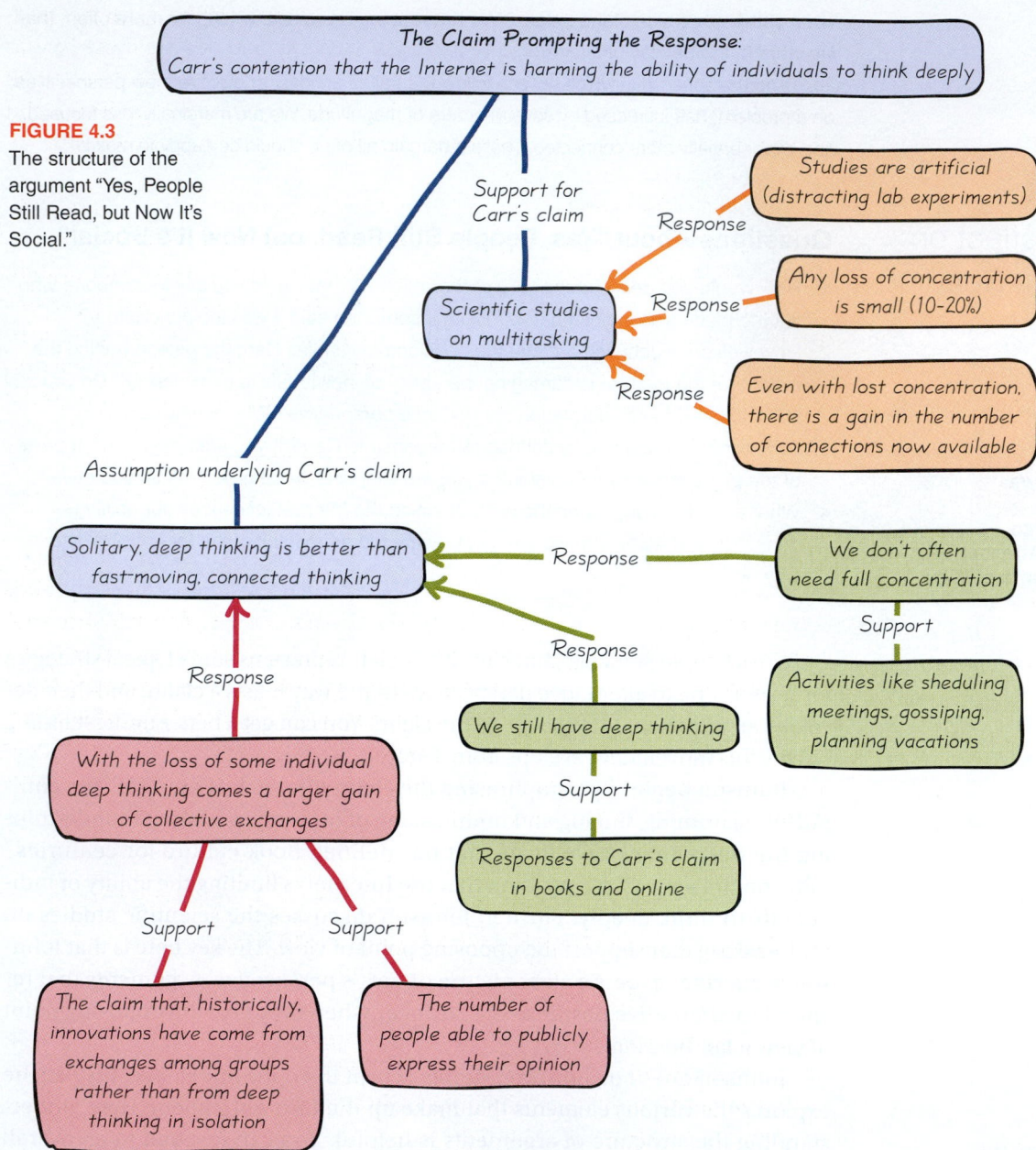

the end, though, Johnson admits that there is some validity to the claim that multitasking limits attention. But Johnson goes on to say that despite these limitations, the benefits that might come from multitasking outweigh these small losses. Johnson uses the strategy of accepting and countering an opposing point of view, demonstrating that an argument can sometimes be made stronger by acknowledging alternative positions.

Johnson takes a similar approach as he moves on to the core of Carr's argument, the assumption that solitary, deep thinking is the better than group exchanges. To further develop his argument, Johnson challenges Carr's suggestion that deep thinking is no longer happening in the age of the Internet, citing books that have been written and lengthy online exchanges that have developed even in response to Carr's claim. As he closes out his response to Carr, Johnson goes on to suggest that, while solitary deep thinking can be a good thing, it may not be the only (or even the best way) to promote innovation and sustain culture. He provides counter arguments showing how inventions like the printing press were driven by collaboration, challenging the assumption that isolated, extended deliberation is necessarily better than the alternatives.

Again, Johnson does not argue with the contention that an extended engagement with ideas can be a good thing. Instead, he acknowledges the basic claims being made by Carr, but goes on to show how the assumptions and evidence supporting those claims can be questioned, softening Carr's claims as a result. As a whole, his essay enacts the strategy of considering alternatives, accepting those that make sense, questioning those that seem problematic, and extending alternatives to offer a new perspective. All of these moves culminate in an essay that agrees that there is some loss of focus with the Internet, but argues that the corresponding benefits outweigh the costs.

WN

VIDEO
3. Outlining
Alternative
Points of View

Know It   Strategies for Responding to Alternative Points of View

LO

Learning
Objective 4.5

- To discover potential objections to arguments, explore the points of contention related to a topic. Ask, *When people discuss the topic, what do they normally disagree about?* Before developing your own position, survey the range of perspectives on the topic.
- Think about assumptions that people who disagree with your approach might hold. What beliefs characterize opponents of your stance? Which of these beliefs and attitudes deserves to be addressed in your argument? Where can you find common ground between opponent's assumptions and your own position?

- Try to prioritize potential objections to your topic. Identify a range of positions that might need to be addressed. Once you have a list of possibilities, consider which represent valid challenges to your approach. Prioritize these alternatives so that you can respond to the most pressing ones.
- Think about ways in which people might object to both the claims and reasons you provide and the evidence that supports them. In some instances, you may need to revise your position. In others, though, you may simply need to provide better evidence.
- Decide when to rebut and when to acknowledge and embrace opposing points of view. If alternative positions don't undermine your major claim, you may be able to accept them. For serious challenges to your stance, see whether you can develop a compelling refutation. If not, reevaluate your own position.

Ask Questions & Make Decisions

Exercises for Responding to Alternative Points of View

1. Identify a position that you hold strongly; for example, perhaps you have always been opposed to high-stakes school testing, space programs, minimum drinking ages, or violent sports. Develop a list of reasons and evidence that might support someone arguing against your standard position.
2. Think of a group that is readily associated with a policy position—feminists and birth control, fundamental Christians and abortion opposition, sportsmen and gun ownership, etc. Write a paragraph exploring the assumptions and beliefs that underlie the position of the group.
3. Watch a debate on a cable news program regarding a current event. Write a paragraph exploring the behavior of the participants in terms of their responses to alternative points of view.
4. Participating with a group of peers, identify a topic for an argument and then agree on a position regarding the topic. Think of possible objections to the group's position, and then develop an outline for a paper that responds to those objections.

Understanding Key Components and Assumptions in Arguments

We have been dissecting arguments to analyze them. In practice, things are always less clear cut. But for now, we can continue thinking about some of the usual elements that are found in arguments. These elements are sometimes talked about with language developed by legal scholar Stephen Toulmin, using terms like *grounds, warrants,* and *rebuttals*. You can almost hear the courtroom clacking of a stenographer's machine.

Let's zoom in and start with the most basic structure, what we have been calling a claim. Recall that in his piece on climate change, Bill McKibben offered the claim that we need to take action on global warming. And he put forth some key reasons why we should believe the claim. We need to take action because the threat is urgent, the effects of climate change will be devastating, and we have a moral obligation. Let's zoom in some more. Figure 4.4 shows an illustration of the claim and just one of the reasons.

Visualizing McKibben's essay in this way helps us recognize how arguments develop strength through their structure. The reason helps explain the rationale behind the claim and the evidence provides support for both. The evidence answers the question, *On what grounds do you offer this claim and its supporting reason?* Here we can see how these structural elements can be described using terminology derived from legal contexts. The computer models and studies offer support for the reason and the claim. We need all three components—the claim, the reasons, and the grounds—for the argument to hold up.

Arguments develop strength through their structure

And there's another component that we must consider, one that is a bit trickier to pin down but equally important to the argument's structure. Hidden beneath the surface of the claim and the reason is an assumption that taking action will stop the threat (see Figure 4.5). This assumption is like a link in the chain of the argument that allows McKibben to make his claim. If our efforts would be futile, then no matter how urgent the threat, the claim would not follow from the reason; that is, it would not be warranted.

McKibben offers evidence that new technologies can alleviate the dangers of climate change. He provides examples to show that efforts will not be futile, that taking action has the potential to create change. This additional evidence supports or provides backing for the assumption.

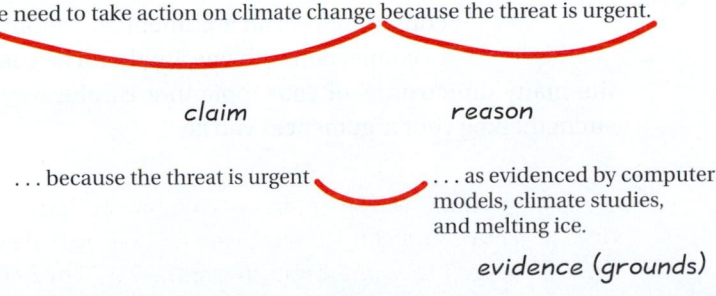

FIGURE 4.4
A diagram linking a claim, reason, and evidence.

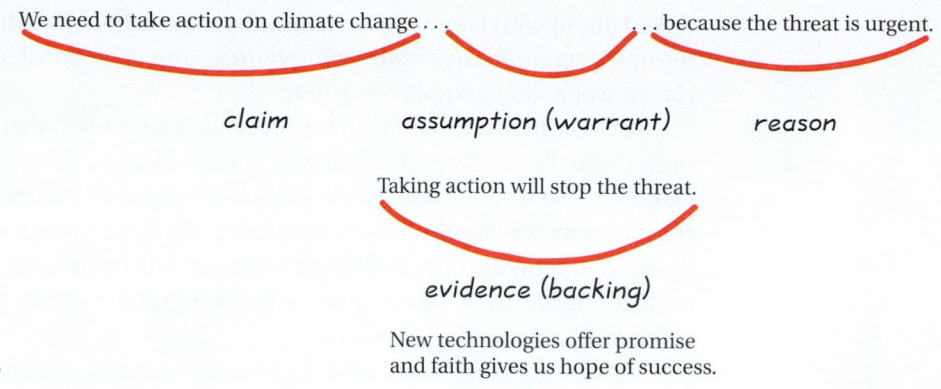

We need to take action on climate change . . .   . . . because the threat is urgent.

claim   assumption (warrant)   reason

Taking action will stop the threat.

evidence (backing)

New technologies offer promise
and faith gives us hope of success.

FIGURE 4.5
A diagram linking a
claim, assumption,
reason, and evidence.

And the structure of arguments gets even more complex. You can see how
identifying not only reasons behind a claim but also any assumptions that lie
beneath a claim offers great opportunities to challenge and strengthen an argument. You can see that objections might be raised to both the reason and the
assumption. These objections are sometimes called rebuttals, challenges to
the major elements of the argument. Figure 4.6 illustrates how
rebuttals and responses are expressed in McKibbon's article.

We can use these basic terms and structures to anticipate objections and develop possible responses to the rebuttals someone
might make to an argument. These responses can come in the
form of providing additional evidence to support the argument or
as refutations that take issue with possible objections.

You can't be too formulaic when composing, but as an exercise in organizing your thoughts and developing possible structures for your arguments, you can see how these kinds of models
can help. Identifying reasons and assumptions helps you make
your case. You can extend this process by considering possible objections, and then develop responses that anticipate and address
these concerns. Remember, you can zoom in to focus on specific
components of an argument and zoom out to consider elements
in connection with one another. The goal is really to think through
the many dimensions of your topic in a careful way, adding complexity and
strengthening your argument as you go.

**Remember, you can
zoom in to focus on
specific components
of an argument
and zoom out to
consider elements
in connection with
one another**

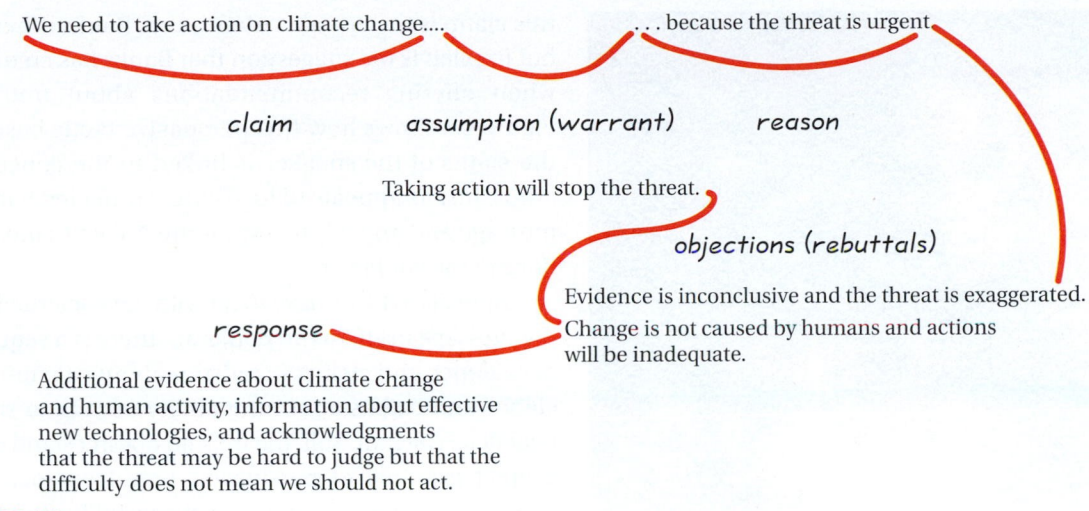

We need to take action on climate change....   . . . because the threat is urgent.

claim   assumption (warrant)   reason

Taking action will stop the threat.

objections (rebuttals)

Evidence is inconclusive and the threat is exaggerated.
Change is not caused by humans and actions
will be inadequate.

response

Additional evidence about climate change
and human activity, information about effective
new technologies, and acknowledgments
that the threat may be hard to judge but that the
difficulty does not mean we should not act.

FIGURE 4.6
A diagram linking
claim, assumption,
reason, objections, and
response.

Understanding Appeals, Evidence, and Fallacies

LO

Learning
Objective 4.2

Based on the figures we have been providing and the discussion of claims, reasons, and evidence, you might assume that arguments are simply formal structures that lead readers through a logical sequence of points until they reach a pre-defined conclusion. Actually, things are usually more fluid when you encounter or compose an argument. A big part of this fluidity comes from the varying kinds of appeals and evidence that can be used in arguments.

In Chapter 1, we discuss how rhetorical situations encompass and influence relationships between the creator of a message (the speaker), the audience for a message, and the message itself. A message like "We need to sustain our resources" can mean different things depending on the speaker and audience. Some specific types of appeals that correspond with the elements of rhetorical situations are frequently made in arguments.

Arguments generally make appeals based on ethos, logos, and pathos. The word *ethos* is related to ethics and describes the credibility and appeal of the speaker of a message. Typically, spokespeople promoting products rely on ethos for their appeals. Consider the claims made in the milk ad in Figure 4.7. The argument goes that we should drink milk because Tyra Banks says so. Explicit in

Girls, here's today's beauty tip. Think about you and your 10 best friends. Chances are 9 of you aren't getting enough calcium. So what? So milk. 3 glasses of milk a day give you the calcium your growing bones need. Tomorrow— what to do when you're taller than your date.

MILK

Where's your mustache?

FIGURE 4.7
Tyra Banks as a spokesperson in a milk ad.

this claim is the visual evidence that Banks is healthy, but implicit is the suggestion that Banks has credibility when offering recommendations about nutrition. Figure 4.8 shows how this persuasive tactic based on the status of the speaker is linked to the concept of ethos, just as appeals to logos are connected with the message and appeals to pathos are linked to the emotions of the audience.

Appeals to logos have to do with the construction of the message itself. In the Banks ad, there is a sequence of evidence and claims—statistics about calcium deficiency and claims about the ability of milk to supply beneficial calcium. Still, the milk ad doesn't stand out as a great example of persuasion based on logic. For contrast, consider arguments composed for academic rhetorical situations. An academic argument will spend the bulk of its time dealing with logical appeals. And the care that an academic author puts into the logical structure of a message affects the reader's view of the ethos behind the argument.

The term *pathos* is related to the word pathetic, but does not describe something necessarily sad. Instead, appeals to pathos are geared toward inciting the emotions of the audience. The reaction might be sadness, but it could also be frustration, anger, or any other emotion that could influence someone's actions. Public service announcements frequently make use of these kinds of appeals, often using images that grab the emotions. The Banks ad plays on pathos by choosing to use an alluring photo of Banks to get attention and sway thinking.

Appeals based on ethos, logos, and pathos are not mutually exclusive. You will establish ethos even as you work on the logical dimensions of arguments, and you will always be thinking about your audience and their emotional responses to what you create. The key to working with the various kinds of appeals is using the rhetorical situation as a guide. If you are creating a public service announcement, you might emphasize appeals to the emotions. If you are asked to write an argument for an academic situation, you are going to focus on its logic, which will in turn enhance your credibility (ethos).

You can use a similar flexibility as you think about the kinds of evidence that can be used to write persuasively. Arguments provide examples that illustrate their points. These examples serve as evidence. In academic situations, evidence

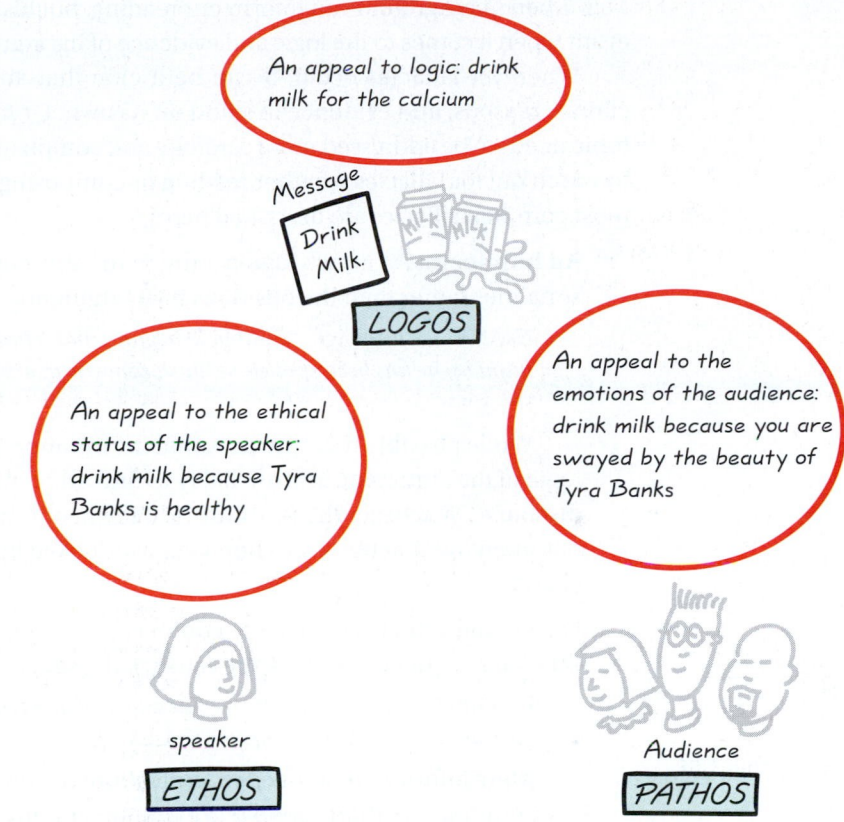

An appeal to logic: drink milk for the calcium

Message

Drink Milk.

LOGOS

An appeal to the ethical status of the speaker: drink milk because Tyra Banks is healthy

An appeal to the emotions of the audience: drink milk because you are swayed by the beauty of Tyra Banks

speaker

ETHOS

Audience

PATHOS

FIGURE 4.8
The rhetorical situation and types of appeals.

often takes the form of quotations that show the views of authorities. Evidence can also include facts or statistics taken from reliable sources. In general, academic arguments privilege evidence that is verifiable. The requirement that authors document their sources stems from this tendency; careful documentation allows readers to examine the evidence for themselves. Again, this care reflects on the ethos present in the argument, depicting the speaker as being conscientious about evidence. (For more on evidence, see pages 114–15.)

Fallacies appear convincing on the surface but, on closer inspection, are revealed to be illogical appeals that can't hold together

A related area concerning arguments has to do with what are considered fallacies. Fallacies appear convincing on the surface but, on closer inspection, are revealed to be illogical appeals that can't hold together. Were people to argue against Bill McKibben's claim that we need to take action on climate change by suggesting that McKibben is a granola-eating, sandal-wearing hippie, they would be making an *ad hominem,* or personal, attack.

McKibben's background can inform our reading, but his personal tastes are irrelevant when it comes to the logic and evidence of his argument.

Wherever fallacies occur, it can be a clue that an argument lacks sound claims, reasons, and evidence to stand on its own. Or it could be a sign that the topic needs to be addressed more carefully and completely. In any case, you need to watch out for fallacies whether reading or composing arguments. Eight of the most common fallacies are described here.

Ad hominem. An attack "against the man," this fallacy focuses on the personalities rather than the positions in an argument.

> EXAMPLE: *Although McKibben argues that climate change is caused by humans, he has been spotted at Phish concerts in a tie-died T-shirt so his word is suspect.*

While possibly true, the personal information has little bearing on the logic of the argument. You are likely to find ad hominem attacks in political discourse. Whenever the focus turns to the people involved in an argument, pay attention that the issues don't get overlooked in the heat of personal exchange.

Cause and effect. This fallacy confuses one thing that precedes the next thing in a sequence as being the cause of the second element.

> EXAMPLE: *The number of hikers has fallen off in recent years because mining has been allowed in the local wilderness area.*

WN

VIDEO
17. Logical Fallacies

More information is needed to attribute the drop in the number of hikers to mining. Perhaps people are hiking less often in general. Perhaps a new trailhead or rafting area elsewhere has reduced the number of hikers. Sometimes called *post hoc, ergo propter hoc* (after this, therefore because of this) this fallacy may appear in messages discussing problems and solutions. Whenever you encounter claims about effects, check that a relevant causal link exists.

Red herring. This fallacy is a distraction that appears in an argument.

> EXAMPLE: *Stricter copyright laws will restrict our personal freedoms. Look at what happened during the 1950s: people were persecuted out of fears of communism.*

It's possible that a connection might be developed between copyright legislation and personal freedom, but it would take much more work. As this statement stands, it is a distraction. Whenever you find parts of an argument that seem out of place or tangential, check that the claims are relevant to the topic at hand.

False analogy. Comparing two or more dissimilar things or offering insights based on unfair comparisons results in this type of fallacy.

EXAMPLE: *Adding an unpaved access road in the local wilderness will be the equivalent of setting up the Berlin Wall.*

The comparison is unfair. A major interstate complete with fences and non-stop traffic might divide a wilderness area in such a severe way, but a small gravel road would not. As with red herrings, keep an eye out for comparisons that are not relevant to the claims made in an argument.

Hasty generalization. This fallacy draws conclusions based on insufficient evidence or on evidence not relevant to the topic.

EXAMPLE: *We are already seeing the devastating effects of climate change. The 2010 hurricane season has already seen two major storms.*

There may be a link between strong storms and climate change, but two storms provide little real insight into any climate trends. Always examine evidence to make sure that it is sufficiently detailed.

Slippery slope. This fallacy assumes that a small action or event will lead to the most severe consequences.

EXAMPLE: *Failure to enact new emissions legislation will raise sea levels, quickly flooding our coastal cities and killing millions.*

Though climate change models can predict dire consequences, linking those directly to a single piece of legislation places too much at stake, using a worst case scenario as a kind of scare tactic. You may find slippery slope fallacies in discussions of policy or of cultural trends. Whenever you encounter dire predictions or claims that seem too absolute, watch out for slippery slope fallacies.

Circular reasoning. This type of fallacy restates claims as support for initial positions.

EXAMPLE: *The new mine will prevent any use of the wilderness for leisure because mining limits recreation possibilities.*

The whole question here is whether mining limits recreation, so the statement returns back on itself by offering its own claim as a reason for believing the statement. Sometimes called begging the question, this fallacy can show up in all kinds of writing situations. Arguments should offer detailed chains of claims, reasons, and evidence, rather than restatements of a single claim.

Either/Or. These fallacies offer false, simplistic responses to complicated concerns.

EXAMPLE: *If you are for recreation in the wilderness, you must be opposed to the mining operations.*

As we have been discussing, making decisions about complicated concerns requires weighing multiple, often competing perspectives. A person could easily be in favor of both recreation and mining. You are likely to encounter either/or thinking in all kinds of contexts. Watch out for a claim that oversimplifies a complex issue or tries to force readers toward an either/or perspective.

Non sequitur. This fallacy "does not follow" logic but links two unrelated items as a claim and a reason.

> EXAMPLE: *Emissions legislation should be enacted because automobile accidents are on the rise among teen drivers.*

While the rise of accident rates among teen drivers is a compelling reason to make changes in legislation, it is unconnected to climate change . You can encounter non sequiturs in all kinds of situations. Check that any reasons offered are relevant to the claims they are meant to support.

Know It   Strategies for Understanding Appeals, Evidence, and Fallacies

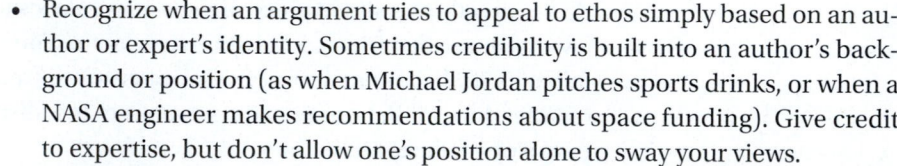

Learning Objective 4.3

- Recognize when an argument tries to appeal to ethos simply based on an author or expert's identity. Sometimes credibility is built into an author's background or position (as when Michael Jordan pitches sports drinks, or when a NASA engineer makes recommendations about space funding). Give credit to expertise, but don't allow one's position alone to sway your views.
- Look for ways authors establish ethos through their arguments. Are authors fair minded about their topics, giving legitimate weight to opposing points of view? Is the logic of an argument acceptable? Is the use of evidence honest and careful?
- Use visual representations, outlines, or whatever other methods will help you unpack the structure of arguments. List the major claims offered in an argument. Sketch out the reasons supporting those claims. Take note of evidence provided. Develop your own sense of the major components of an argument.
- Learn to recognize appeals to emotions. In ads or propaganda, appeals to pathos are easy to pick out, but lots of other messages try to move the feelings of readers. Distinguish between uses of emotion that bring out the human dimensions of a topic and disingenuous attempts to sway readers and play on feelings.
- Take care as you evaluate the evidence offered in arguments. Verify facts and statistics put forward in support of an argument. When the statements of others are offered as evidence, evaluate the credibility of the people making the statements.

- For evidence that uses anecdotes and observations, keep the nature of the claims and evidence in mind. Providing personal insights or experience to support a point is legitimate in some instances, but it can't substitute for facts and expert opinion in most cases.
- Watch out for fallacies in arguments you read or compose. Don't assume that a fallacy completely discounts an argument, but use the recognition of a fallacy as an opportunity to scrutinize or develop an argument more fully.

Ask Questions & Make Decisions

Exercises for Understanding Appeals, Evidence, and Fallacies

1. Think about a number of ad campaigns that rely on spokespeople. Identify a campaign that you think makes an appropriate use of the ethos of the spokesperson and then write a paragraph explaining why.
2. Find a political ad that you think is effective but that provides few reasons to support its position. Look at the points offered in the ad and then rewrite the ad to deliver the same message using claims and evidence. Make an outline demonstrating the logic of your revised ad.
3. Look through online discussions and identify a statement that uses one or more fallacies. Consider whether these fallacies completely undermine the claims offered or where they call for more development of the argument. Post a response either challenging the position or asking for clarification.
4. Do you believe arguments should ever use feelings to persuade readers? Hold a discussion with classmates regarding the appropriate uses of pathos in arguments.

LO

Learning
Objective 4.4

Learning from Other Mediums: Video Persuasion

 Where Did That Video Spoofing Gore's Film Come From?

BY **ANTONIO REGALADO AND DIONNE SEARCEY**

When Al Gore released An Inconvenient Truth *in 2006, many praised the film for adding a sense of urgency to climate change discussions. Alternative perspectives also rose up. And some of these alternatives took the form of amateur videos. Or so it seemed. The medium of the video documentary provided a vehicle that reinvigorated debate on the topic. And subsequent amateur spoof videos raised even more questions about the*

Where Did That
Video Spoofing
Gore's Film Come
From? *(continued)*
BY **ANTONIO REGALADO
AND DIONNE SEARCEY**

ways we produce and encounter persuasive messages. This piece from the Wall Street
Journal *offers some insights.*

EVERYONE KNOWS Al Gore stars in the global warming documentary "An Inconvenient
Truth." But who created "Al Gore's Penguin Army," a two- minute video now playing on
YouTube.com?

In the video, Mr. Gore appears as a sinister figure who brainwashes penguins and
bores movie audiences by blaming the Mideast crisis and starlet Lindsay Lohan's shrinking waist size on global warming. Like other videos on the popular YouTube site, it has a
home-made, humorous quality. The video's maker is listed as "Toutsmith," a 29-year-old
who identifies himself as being from Beverly Hills in an Internet profile.

In an email exchange with *The Wall Street Journal*, Toutsmith didn't answer when asked
who he was or why he made the video, which has just over 59,000 views on YouTube. However, computer routing information contained in an email sent from Toutsmith's Yahoo!
account indicate it didn't come from an amateur working out of his basement.

Instead, the email originated from a computer registered to DCI Group, a Washington,
D.C. public relations and lobbying firm whose clients include oil company Exxon Mobil Corp.

A DCI Group spokesman declines to say whether or not DCI made the anti-Gore penguin video, or to explain why Toutsmith appeared to be sending email from DCI's comput-
ers. "DCI Group does not disclose the names of its clients, nor do we discuss the work
that we do on our clients' behalf," says Matt Triaca, who heads DCI's media relations shop.

Dave Gardner, an Exxon spokesman, confirms that Exxon is a client of DCI. But he
says Exxon had no role in creating the "Inconvenient Truth" spoof. "We, like everyone else
on the planet, have seen it, but did not fund it, did not approve it, and did not know what its
source was," Mr. Gardner says.

The anti-Gore video represents a less well-known side of YouTube. As its popularity
has exploded, the public video-sharing site has drawn marketers looking to build buzz for
new music releases and summer blockbusters. Now, it's being tapped by political
operatives, public relations experts and ad agencies to sway opinions. Ogilvy & Mather, for
example, says it plans to post amateur-looking videos on Web sites to spark word-of-
mouth buzz about Foster's beer.

For marketers and pranksters of all sorts, online video is the latest venue for tactics
"they've been doing for years," says Fred Wertheimer, president of the watchdog group
Democracy 21. "What we don't know is will this have any impact. In the political arena it's
the great experiment right now."

Politicians and marketers already make wide use of email lists and blogs, and it has
long been possible to distribute information over the Internet while disguising its origins.
But Web video operates on a different level, stimulating viewers' emotions powerfully and
directly. And because amusing animations with a homespun feel can be created just as
easily by highly paid professionals to promote agendas as by talented amateurs, caveat
emptor is more relevant than ever.

Hurricane Katrina
August 29, 2005

Photo: NOAA

FIGURE 4.9

A shot of Al Gore in his film *An Inconvenient Truth*.

One politically charged issue has drawn dueling YouTube videos recently: whether phone giants should be able to charge Internet companies for speedier delivery of their content. One of the videos features a slide show and tinny voiceover, and takes the side of phone companies. At the end, it directs viewers to go to www.netcompetition.org, a Web site backed by AT&T Inc. and other phone and cable companies with a stake in the issue. On the other side are consumer groups, one of whose YouTube videos features musician Moby warning of the dangers of a two-tier Internet.

Mr. Wertheimer thinks videos like the Gore spoof, whose sponsorship is vague, can be disingenuous. "They're coming in under false pretenses—under the guise of being a clever video you might be interested in," he says. For its part, AT&T says its affiliation with the group is clearly listed on netcompetition.org, just a few clicks away.

DCI is no stranger to the debate over global warming. Partly through Tech Central Station, an opinion Web site it operates, DCI has sought to raise doubts about the science of global warming and about Mr. Gore's film, placing skeptical scientists on talk-radio shows and paying them to write editorials.

Of course, Mr. Gore and his allies have also used the Internet to great advantage. To stoke interest in his film, the distributor of *An Inconvenient Truth*, Paramount Classics, created its own YouTube video by cartoonist Matt Groening, creator of *The Simpsons*. Called "Al Gore's Terrifying Message," the video, which features a cartoon version of Mr. Gore arguing with a robot, has had more than a million views. Paramount is identified as the source next to the video.

Meanwhile, critics of Mr. Gore have frequently sought to get their message out through conservative bloggers, talk radio and Internet news services. Marc Morano, communications chief for Republican Sen. James Inhofe of Oklahoma, who has led opposition to climate legislation on Capitol Hill, says an Internet strategy is both effective and necessary because mainstream news organizations are "promoting the message of Gore uncritically."

Internet videos could prove particularly potent, because they may influence watchers in ways they don't realize. Nancy Snow, a communications professor at California State University, Fullerton, viewed the penguin video and calls it a lesson in "Propaganda 101." It contains no factual information, but presents a highly negative image of the former vice president, she says. The purpose of such images is to harden the views of those who already view Mr. Gore negatively, Dr. Snow says.

YouTube has an estimated 20 million viewers daily, but with thousands of videos on the site, it can be difficult for marketers to reach their audience, says Brian Reich, a consultant for Mindshare Interactive Campaigns, who helps nonprofits and political candidates learn to use YouTube and other video sites effectively. "You still have to micro-target

WN

RESOURCES
Parody as Argument

Where Did That
Video Spoofing
Gore's Film Come
From? *(continued)*
BY **ANTONIO REGALADO
AND DIONNE SEARCEY**

your information and make it compelling and relevant and timely to get people to pay attention," he says.

Traffic to the penguin video, first posted on YouTube.com in May, got a boost from prominently placed sponsored links that appeared on the Google search engine when users typed in "Al Gore" or "Global Warming." The ads, which didn't indicate who had paid for them, were removed shortly after *The Wall Street Journal* contacted DCI Group on Tuesday.

Diana Adair, a spokeswoman for Google, says the search giant doesn't allow advertising text that "advocates against any individual, group or organization." However, the policy doesn't apply to the Web sites or videos that such ads point to. Although most advertisers want their identities known, Ms. Adair says Google will protect the identity of advertisers who want to remain anonymous, only releasing that information under a subpoena or court order.

↗ Reflect on the Reading

Questions About "Where Did That Video Spoofing Gore's Film Come From?"

1. How would you discuss the phenomenon of the release of the Gore spoof video in terms of rhetorical situations? What can you say about the authorship, purpose, and message of the video?
2. Watch *Al Gore's Penguin Army*. (Search online to locate the video.) What can you say about the video in terms of fallacies? How many of the fallacies listed on pages 112–114 come to mind? Can you think of additional fallacies or problems raised by the piece?
3. The article suggests that Web videos are a particularly powerful means of persuasion. What, according to the article, makes them so? Do you agree? Why or why not?
4. Watch *Al Gore's Penguin Army*, *Al Gore's Terrifying Message*, or the South Park episode "Man Bear Pig." (They should be available online.) Hold a discussion with classmates about these videos in terms of argument.
5. Watch *An Inconvenient Truth*. How many persuasive strategies can you identify in the piece? How would you discuss the film in terms of it structure, appeals, and uses of evidence? Write up your analysis in a short essay.

Respond   Write to Explore Arguments

You will no doubt need to be persuasive in all kinds of situations. These writing prompts offer some specific opportunities and can help you practice writing arguments in many contexts.

1. **Write an essay in which you take a position while exploring a topic about which people can disagree.** Your argument should consider and respond to alternative perspectives on your topic and objections to your position. You may

FIGURE 4.10

A comic offering an argument about climate change.

begin with a strong claim and then develop the argument around that claim, or you may explore your topic from multiple positions to arrive at a major claim. As you work, provide reasons to demonstrate the logic of your thinking and incorporate evidence to support your points. Document any sources that you use (Chapter 17).

2. **Compose a collage that offers a visual argument about an issue.** The collage will include multiple images that have been cropped and layered over one another to create a new composition. The collage might also include text, but the focus will be on combining images to create an argument. You can collect images for the collage online. Be sure to keep track of the location of the images you collect; you will include this information in a supplemental list of sources for your collage. Refer to the information on pages 345–47 to ensure that you use images fairly.

3. **Create a mock-up of a public service announcement (PSA) poster.** Using a word processor or image editor, combine one or more images and text to create an argument about a topic of importance to you. Survey potential topics. Are there pressing problems for which you wish to advocate? Do existing PSAs miss the point about a topic? What topics strike your interest? Examine other PSA posters (like the example on page 211) to learn more about the genre and the medium you will be working with.

4. **Create a short comic strip meant to persuade readers about a topic of importance to you.** Before beginning, review the advice offered by Scott Mc-Cloud on pages 28–32. Find a topic and then identify a major claim that you would like to make regarding the topic. Using either paper and drawing tools or comic creation software, compose at least a three-panel comic that delivers a persuasive message about your topic. Select one or more characters for the comic. Create frames for the comic strip. Fill the frames with settings, characters, and objects. Add words to help express your message. Figure 4.10 shows a comic created on the topic of climate change.

Zoom **Out**   Reflecting on Arguments

- **Arguments are built around topics about which people can disagree.** Issues that evoke either/or responses are too simplistic for arguments. Facts and opinions similarly don't lend themselves to arguments. Instead, the gray areas where multiple perspectives on topics can be found make the best spaces for arguments.

- **Arguments are structured around claims, reasons, and evidence.** A claim makes a statement about an issue—like the thesis statement for the argument. Reasons explain why the claim is worth considering, and evidence provides further support for the reasons offered in an argument.

- **Looking at the structure of arguments helps us scrutinize and strengthen persuasive writing.** Borrowing legal terms, we can explore evidence (grounds), assumptions (warrants), and objections (rebuttals) as we encounter and compose arguments.

- **Most arguments in some way respond to alternative points of view.** Even arguments that don't explicitly acknowledge opposition are generally constructed around disagreements. Arguments often discuss and then try to refute opposing points of view, but they can also acknowledge alternative perspectives as part of their persuasive strategy.

- **Arguments can contain additional layers of complexity.** An argument might pursue two or more claims. It might accept an alternative perspective, but argue for looking past that perspective. Arguments serve not only to win debates but also to explore and clarify topics.

- **Arguments frequently make appeals to ethos, logos, and pathos.** The ethical dimensions or credibility of the speaker behind an argument shape the way in which the argument is received. The logical structure of an argument reflects on the speaker and forms the basis of organization for the claims, reasons, and evidence of the argument. Appeals to pathos strike the emotions of readers. All of these appeals can be woven into arguments in different ways, depending on rhetorical situations.

- **Academic situations emphasize the logical dimensions of arguments.** They call for discussion of alternative possibilities and compelling reasons presented in an organized fashion. Academic arguments emphasize verifiable evidence and formal elements that represent a fair-minded and careful speaker.

- **Learning to identify fallacies can help you become more critical about arguments.** Check your own arguments for fallacies to ensure that you are fair in your own persuasive compositions.

For additional information and practice with the learning objectives in this chapter, go to www.mycomplab.com, Resources > Writing > Writing and Visuals > Reading Visual Arguments.

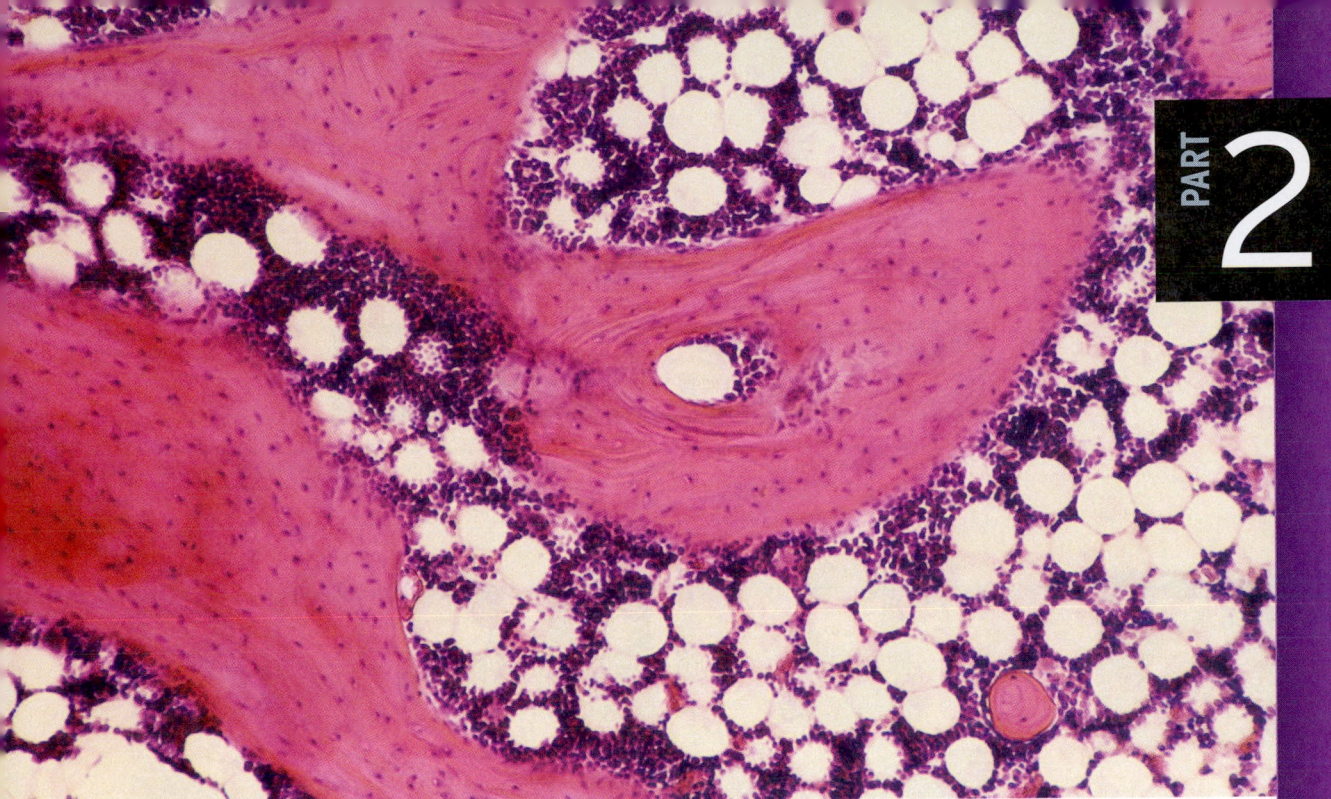

Composing Projects

CHAPTER 5

Memoirs

Zoom In   Key Concepts and Learning Objectives

After studying this chapter, you should be able to:

5.1   Analyze and understand memoirs as a genre of personal writing focused on events in the author's life.

5.2   Compose a memoir that takes some creative license but maintains a focus on real events in your past.

5.3   Offer insights on themes such as change, challenges, conflict, relationships, family, and community and share them with your readers.

Y ou may have heard about the controversy that erupted when Oprah Winfrey promoted James Frey's *A Million Little Pieces* for her Book of the Month Club. Frey's book described struggles with alcohol and drug addiction and a criminal past that destroyed many lives. It was later discovered that many of the events had been greatly exaggerated or were simply untrue. Because Frey and his publisher had promoted the book as a memoir, a nonfiction account of Frey's life, the fallout was intense. Frey initially suggested that some artistic license was necessary to make the memoir more dramatic. As the extent of the fabrication in the book came out, however, Frey confessed to lying. His publisher also admitted that they never did any fact-checking for the book and agreed to include in all future editions an apology for the distortions.

What can the James Frey controversy teach us? If we zoom out, we can see that the controversy reveals much about how contemporary culture views these personal stories. We see a culture fascinated with the lives of others and quick to elevate people to the status of celebrities. But we also see a culture angered by deception, a culture that wants compelling stories but wants them to be real. We see that questions about the value of truth are central to these autobiographical accounts. And, if we zoom in, we can see that genres heavily influence the ways we read and write; if *A Million Little Pieces* had been classified as a work of fiction, none of its claims would have been challenged. As we look more closely, we will discover that memoirs select real episodes (details about a life) to discuss, and then explain how those episodes reveal more general truths. Memoirs, then, blend facts, interpretations, and artistry to create a sense of drama.

KEY TERMS

- **Memoir:** A genre of personal writing that focuses on an episode or a time frame within an individual's life. Memoirs strike a balance between documenting events and entertaining or instructing readers with larger lessons.

- **Episodes:** In the memoir genre, events in the life of the author. A short memoir might revolve around a single event. These episodes range from momentous events to everyday occurrences.

- **Narration:** A writing strategy used to relate events or tell a story. Narratives make use of details and descriptions and they often include dialog.

- **Truth value:** The level of credibility that can be assigned to a piece of writing; this criteria is important in memoirs because they are a nonfiction genre that also seeks to entertain.

Understanding Memoirs

To think more about memoirs, let's take a look at an excerpt from *An American Childhood* by Annie Dillard.

 ## An Excerpt from *An American Childhood*
BY **ANNIE DILLARD**

Annie Dillard was born in Pittsburgh, Pennsylvania, and grew up in an affluent household where she was encouraged to read and write. Dillard won the Pulitzer Prize in 1975 for her nonfiction book A Pilgrim at Tinker Creek, *in which she recounts her experience of living at Tinker Creek and reflects on nature, religion, and life. This excerpt is taken from* An American Childhood *(1987), in which Dillard documents her life as a child in Pittsburgh.*

One Sunday afternoon Mother wandered through our kitchen, where Father was making a sandwich and listening to the ball game. The Pirates were playing the New York Giants at Forbes Field. In those days, the Giants had a utility infielder named Wayne Terwilliger. Just as Mother passed through, the radio announcer cried—with undue drama—"Terwilliger bunts one!"

"Terwilliger bunts one?" Mother cried back, stopped short. She turned. "Is that English?"

"The player's name is Terwilliger," Father said. "He bunted."

"That's marvelous," Mother said. "'Terwilliger bunts one.' No wonder you listen to baseball. 'Terwilliger bunts one.'"

For the next seven or eight years. Mother made this surprising string of syllables her own. Testing a microphone, she repeated, "Terwilliger bunts one"; testing a pen or a typewriter, she wrote it. If, as happened surprisingly often in the course of various improvised gags, she pretended to whisper something else in my ear, she actually whispered, "Terwilliger bunts one." Whenever someone used a French phrase, or a Latin one, she answered solemnly, "Terwilliger bunts one." If Mother had had, like Andrew Carnegie, the opportunity to cook up a motto for a coat of arms, hers would have read simply and tellingly, "Terwilliger bunts one." (Carnegie's was "Death to Privilege.")

She served us with other words and phrases. On a Florida trip, she repeated tremulously, "That . . . is a royal poinciana." I don't remember the tree; I remember the thrill in her voice. She pronounced it carefully, and spelled it. She also liked to say "portulaca."

The drama of the words "Tamiami Trail" stirred her, we learned on the same Florida trip. People built Tampa on one coast, and they built Miami on another. Then—the height of visionary ambition and folly—they piled a slow, tremendous road through the terrible Everglades to connect them. To build the road, men stood sunk in muck to their armpits.

They fought off cottonmouth moccasins and six-foot alligators. They slept in boats, wet. They blasted muck with dynamite, cut jungle with machetes; they laid logs, dragged drilling machines, hauled dredges, heaped limestone. The road took fourteen years to build up by the shovelful, a Panama Canal in reverse, and cost hundreds of lives from tropical, mosquito-carried diseases. Then, capping it all, some genius thought of the word Tamiami: they called the road from Tampa to Miami, this very road under our spinning wheels, the Tamiami Trail. Some called it Alligator Alley. Anyone could drive over this road without a thought. Hearing this, moved, I thought all the suffering of road building was worth it (it wasn't my suffering), now that we had this new thing to hang these new words on—Alligator Alley for those who liked things cute, and, for connoisseurs like Mother, for lovers of the human drama in all its boldness and terror, the Tamiami Trail.

Back home, Mother cut clips from reels of talk, as it were, and played them back at leisure. She noticed that many Pittsburghers confuse "leave" and "let." One kind relative brightened our morning by mentioning why she'd brought her son to visit: "He wanted to come with me, so I left him." Mother filled in Amy and me on locutions we missed. "I can't do it on Friday," her pretty sister told a crowded dinner party, "because Friday's the day I lay in the stores."

(All unconsciously, though, we ourselves used some pure Pittsburghisms. We said "tele pole," pronounced "telly pole," that splintery sidewalk post I loved to climb. We said "slippy"—the sidewalks are "slippy." We said, "That's all the farther I could go." And we said, as Pittsburghers do, "this glass needs washed," or "the dog needs walked"—a usage our father eschewed; he knew it was not standard English, nor even comprehensible English, but he never let on.)

"Spell 'poinsettia,'" Mother would throw out at me, smiling with pleasure. "Spell 'sherbet.'" The idea was not to make us whizzes, but, quite the contrary, to remind us—and I, especially, needed reminding—that we didn't know it all just yet.

"There's a deer standing in the front hall," she told me one quiet evening in the country.

"Really?"

"No. I just wanted to tell you something once without your saying, 'I know.'"

Reflect on the Reading

Questions About An Excerpt from *An American Childhood*

1. How does the inclusion of specific events help carry forward Dillard's memoir? Is it fair to say the events tell the story?
2. What does Dillard's description of their trip to Florida say about the connection between Dillard and her mother? What other parts of the memoir speak to their relationship?

3. How would you characterize the voice in the memoir? Does the narrator come across as sarcastic, friendly, formal, distant, close, etc.? How does this voice relate to any messages you recognize in the memoir?

4. How does the last line relate to the rest of the memoir? Does the final line represent a different kind of truth than the details and events presented earlier? Why or why not?

This short excerpt from Dillard's *An American Childhood* reveals some key characteristics of a memoir. Above all, the role of memory is central to the piece. A memoir documents the past, not so much with historical details, but rather with the personal experiences of the writer. Because memories drive these personal records, memoirs also tend to focus on themes like families, relationships, personal struggles, or life lessons. Dillard's piece emphasizes what she learned from her mother while growing up.

> A memoir documents the past, not so much with historical details, but rather with the personal experiences of the writer

Memoirs also focus on key events or anecdotes. Notice how Dillard's piece, however, does not treat an intense episode or personal tragedy—no earthquake, car crash, or childhood trauma here. Instead, the memoir begins with something as mundane as a baseball game on the radio. What is key is that the piece has deliberately selected episodes that hold the memoir together; the baseball phrase, the naming of the Tamiami Trail, and the Pittsburghisms tighten the focus of the memoir to shared memories about language.

But Dillard does not stop there. She also establishes connections between the episodes and insights about her life and family. The memoir recounts an episode in which Dillard's mother asks Dillard to spell words such as *sherbet*. Then the memoir reveals the episode's significance (a lesson about humility). These links between episodes and insights make the memoir meaningful beyond the personal level. They also help establish a connection with readers, a reason for readers to be interested in the memoir. Most memoirs deliver insights or lessons about life. Memoirs reveal the connections between people and ideas.

Finally, Dillard's excerpt demonstrates a number of narrative strategies (see Chapter 20) writers can use to tell their stories. The memoir develops a sense of character for the figures it discusses—for example, the way in which Dillard's mother "improvise[s] gags" and pokes fun at French or Latin phrases. Settings (Florida and Pittsburgh), plot devices (the Tamiami Trail flashback in the middle), and dialog make the memoir not just a list of events but rather an engaging story. The memoir relies on description (see Chapter 21) to bring the story to life. Notice the details about those who built the Tamiami Trail, such as "They fought off cottonmouth moccasins and six-foot alligators."

Know It   Strategies for Understanding Memoirs

Learning
Objective 5.1

- Connect the experiences in the memoir with the insights they represent. Identify any larger themes the memoir takes up. How do the details in the memoir speak to thematic concerns?
- Notice the expressive nature of memoir writing. Expect fewer formal elements (such as footnotes or citations) and more personal observations. Listen for the author's voice. Identify some of the strengths and weaknesses as well as advantages and disadvantages inherent in the expressive nature of personal writing.
- Analyze the narrative and descriptive strategies used in the memoir. Does the memoir use setting, plot, character development, or dialog to tell its story? How does description of these elements influence your understanding of the piece?
- Weigh the truth value of the memoirs you encounter. Does the memoir make explicit claims about its factuality? Does it trend more toward fiction? What kinds of truth can you find in the piece?

Ask Questions & Make Decisions   Exercises for Understanding Memoirs

1. Childhood memories make great starting places for memoirs because they can lead to insights about relationships or life lessons. Practice linking specific episodes with life lessons by making a list of three or more children's books and the insights they offer.
2. Think of television shows or films that tell stories about people (VH1's *Behind the Music*, A&E's *Biography*, *JFK*, *Seabiscuit*, *Miracle*, etc.). How do these works accomplish the task of providing insights into life and living? Write a paragraph exploring how elements of their storytelling might be adapted to writing memoirs.
3. The episodes in memoirs can range from the mundane to the tragic. Working with a small group of peers, develop a list of challenges related to including

traumatic episodes in memoirs. Develop a second list of challenges related to including everyday events in memoirs.

4. What do you make of the tension between classifying memoirs as nonfiction and the advice to engage readers by using narrative strategies? How far can memoirs stray from the facts and remain "true"? What ethical guidelines can you identify for memoir writers? Hold a discussion with classmates about memoirs, narration, and truth.

Readings and Resources for Exploring Memoirs

Memoirs often take familiar forms like autobiographies or printed essays. But memoirs need not always rely only on printed words. You may also be able to find alternative forms of memoirs in graphic novels or in blogs or video postings online. Below you can find a couple of examples. Marjane Satrapi delivers a memoir using the medium of comics in an excerpt from *Persepolis*, and Jimmy Santiago Baca uses a memoir essay to recount literacy experiences in "Coming into Language."

 ## The Veil

BY **MARJANE SATRAPI**

Marjane Satrapi's Persepolis *is recognized as a prime example of memoir writing presented in the form of a graphic novel. Satrapi combines images and words to relate her experiences growing up in Iran at the time of the fall of the Shah and during the Iran–Iraq war. The novel has been turned into a feature film. The excerpt below is from the opening chapter of the book.*

THE VEIL

EVERYWHERE IN THE STREETS THERE WERE DEMONSTRATIONS FOR AND AGAINST THE VEIL.

AT ONE OF THE DEMONSTRATIONS, A GERMAN JOURNALIST TOOK A PHOTO OF MY MOTHER.

I WAS REALLY PROUD OF HER. HER PHOTO WAS PUBLISHED IN ALL THE EUROPEAN NEWSPAPERS.

AND EVEN IN ONE MAGAZINE IN IRAN. MY MOTHER WAS REALLY SCARED.

HAVE YOU SEEN THIS?

DON'T WORRY, DARLING.

SHE DYED HER HAIR,

AND WORE DARK GLASSES FOR A LONG TIME.

From "The Veil," from PERSEPOLIS: THE STORY OF A CHILDHOOD by Marjane Satrapi, translated by Mattias Ripa and Blake Ferris, translation copyright © 2003 by L'Association, Paris, France. Used by permission of Pantheon Books, a division of Random House, Inc. For online information about other Random House, Inc. books and authors, see the Internet web site at http://www.randomhouse.com.

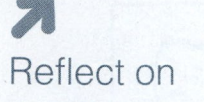

Reflect on the Reading

Questions About "The Veil"

1. What are your thoughts on using the medium of the graphic novel to present a memoir? Do you find that the visual representations help make the memoir more engaging? How might you translate the images into words?
2. What themes can you recognize in "The Veil?" Is it fair to say that this memoir is not based on everyday events? Why or why not?
3. What do you make of the fact that "The Veil" is told from a child's perspective? Do you feel as if memoirs have more meaning when they present the perspectives of children?
4. What other forms might be used to present memoirs? Can you imagine a memoir presented as a musical? As a radio broadcast? As a billboard? What is the relationship between memoirs and the mediums used to convey them?

WN

RESOURCE
Multimedia
Memoirs

Coming Into Language
BY JIMMY SANTIAGO BACA

Jimmy Santiago Baca was born in New Mexico and spent time with his grandmother and in an orphanage before running away at age thirteen. While serving a five-year prison sentence, he discovered a love for language and writing. By the time of his release, he had written and published several poems. He went on to author three novels and dozens of poetry collections. In addition to working on his own books, he currently devotes his time to helping others overcome hardships through writing.

On weekend graveyard shifts at St. Joseph's Hospital I worked the emergency room, mopping up pools of blood and carting plastic bags stuffed with arms, legs, and hands to the outdoor incinerator. I enjoyed the quiet, away from the screams of shotgunned, knifed, and mangled kids writhing on gurneys outside the operating rooms. Ambulance sirens shrieked and squad car lights reddened the cool nights, flashing against the hospital walls: gray—red, gray—red. On slow nights I would lock the door of the administration office, search the reference library for a book on female anatomy and, with my feet propped on the desk, leaf through the illustrations, smoking my cigarette. I was seventeen.

    One night my eye was caught by a familiar-looking word on the spine of a book. The title was *450 Years of Chicano History in Pictures*. On the cover were black-and-white photos: Padre Hidalgo exhorting Mexican peasants to revolt against the Spanish dictators; Anglo vigilantes hanging two Mexicans from a tree; a young Mexican woman with rifle and ammunition belts crisscrossing her breast; Cesar Chavez and field workers marching for fair wages; Chicano railroad workers laying creosote ties; Chicanas laboring at machines in textile factories; Chicanas picketing and hoisting boycott signs.

From the time I was seven, teachers had been punishing me for not knowing my lessons by making me stick my nose in a circle chalked on the blackboard. Ashamed of not understanding and fearful of asking questions, I dropped out of school in the ninth grade. At seventeen I still didn't know how to read, but those pictures confirmed my identity. I stole the book that night, stashing it for safety under the slop sink until I got off work. Back at my boardinghouse, I showed the book to friends. All of us were amazed; this book told us we were alive. We, too, had defended ourselves with our fists against hostile Anglos, gasping for breath in fights with the policemen who outnumbered us. The book reflected back to us our struggle in a way that made us proud.

Most of my life I felt like a target in the crosshairs of a hunter's rifle. When strangers and outsiders questioned me I felt the hang-rope tighten around my neck and the trapdoor creak beneath my feet. There was nothing so humiliating as being unable to express myself, and my inarticulateness increased my sense of jeopardy. Behind a mask of humility, I seethed with mute rebellion.

Before I was eighteen, I was arrested on suspicion of murder after refusing to explain a deep cut on my forearm. With shocking speed I found myself handcuffed to a chain gang of inmates and bused to a holding facility to await trial. There I met men, prisoners, who read aloud to each other the works of Neruda, Paz, Sabines, Nemerov, and Hemingway. Never had I felt such freedom as in that dormitory. Listening to the words of these writers, I felt that invisible threat from without lessen—my sense of teetering on a rotting plank over swamp water where famished alligators clapped their horny snouts for my blood. While I listened to the words of the poets, the alligators slumbered powerless in their lairs. The language of poetry was the magic that could liberate me from myself, transform me into another person, transport me to places far away.

And when they closed the books, these Chicanos, and went into their own Chicano language, they made barrio life come alive for me in the fullness of its vitality. I began to learn my own language, the bilingual words and phrases explaining to me my place in the universe.

Months later I was released, as I had suspected I would be. I had been guilty of nothing but shattering the windshield of my girlfriend's car in a fit of rage.

Two years passed. I was twenty now, and behind bars again. The federal marshals had failed to provide convincing evidence to extradite me to Arizona on a drug charge, but still I was being held. They had ninety days to prove I was guilty. The only evidence against me was that my girlfriend had been at the scene of the crime with my driver's license in her purse. They had to come up with something else. But there was nothing else. Eventually they negotiated a deal with the actual drug dealer, who took the stand against me. When the judge hit me with a million-dollar bail, I emptied my pockets on his booking desk: twenty-six cents.

One night in my third month in the county jail, I was mopping the floor in front of the booking desk. Some detectives had kneed an old drunk and handcuffed him to the booking bars. His shrill screams raked my nerves like a hacksaw on bone, the desperate

Coming Into
Language
(continued)
BY **JIMMY SANTIAGO
BACA**

protest of his dignity against their inhumanity. But the detectives just laughed as he tried to rise and kicked him to his knees. When they went to the bathroom to pee and the desk attendant walked to the file cabinet to pull the arrest record, I shot my arm through the bars, grabbed one of the attendant's university textbooks, and tucked it in my overalls. It was the only way I had of protesting.

It was late when I returned to my cell. Under my blanket I switched on a pen flashlight and opened the thick book at random, scanning the pages. I could hear the jailer making his rounds on the other tiers. The jangle of his keys and the sharp click of his boot heels intensified my solitude. Slowly I enunciated the words . . . p-o-n-d, ri-pple. It scared me that I had been reduced to this to find comfort. I always had thought reading a waste of time, that nothing could be gained by it. Only by action, by moving out into the world and confronting and challenging the obstacles, could one learn anything worth knowing.

Even as I tried to convince myself that I was merely curious, I became so absorbed in how the sounds created music in me and happiness, I forgot where I was. Memories began to quiver in me, glowing with a strange but familiar intimacy in which I found refuge. For a while, a deep sadness overcame me, as if I had chanced on a long lost friend and mourned the years of separation. But soon the heartache of having missed so much of life, that had numbed me since I was a child, gave way, as if a grave illness lifted itself from me and I was cured, innocently believing in the beauty of life again. I stumblingly repeated the author's name as I fell asleep, saying it over and over in the dark: Words-worth, Words-worth.

Before long my sister came to visit me, and I joked about taking her to a place called Xanadu and getting her a blind date with a vato named Coleridge who lived on the seacoast and was malias* morphine. When I asked her to make a trip into enemy territory to buy me a grammar book, she said she couldn't. Bookstores intimidated her, because she, too, could neither read nor write.

Days later, with a stub pencil I whittled sharp with my teeth, I propped a Red Chief notebook on my knees and wrote my first words. From that moment, a hunger for poetry possessed me.

Until then, I had felt as if I had been born into a raging ocean where I swam relentlessly, flailing my arms in hope of rescue, of reaching a shoreline I never sighted. Never solid ground beneath me, never a resting place. I had lived with only the desperate hope to stay afloat; that and nothing more.

But when at last I wrote my first words on the page, I felt an island rising beneath my feet like the back of a whale. As more and more words emerged, I could finally rest: I had a place to stand for the first time in my life. The island grew, with each page, into a continent inhabited by people I knew and mapped with the life I lived.

---

*In Chicano dialect, *vato* means a dude or man; *malias* means strung out on. (JSB)

I wrote about it all—about people I had loved or hated, about the brutalities and ecstasies of my life. And, for the first time, the child in me who had witnessed and endured unspeakable terrors cried out not just in impotent despair, but with the power of language. Suddenly, through language, through writing, my grief and my joy could be shared with anyone who would listen. And I could do this all alone; I could do it anywhere. I was no longer a captive of demons eating away at me, no longer a victim of other people's mockery and loathing, that had made me clench my fist white with rage and grit my teeth to silence. Words now pleaded back with the bleak lucidity of hurt. They were wrong, those others, and now I could say it.

Through language I was free. I could respond, escape, indulge; embrace or reject earth or the cosmos. I was launched on an endless journey without boundaries or rules, in which I could salvage the floating fragments of my past, or be born anew in the spontaneous ignition of understanding some heretofore concealed aspect of myself. Each word steamed with the hot lava juices of my primordial making and I crawled out of stanzas dripping with birth-blood, reborn and freed from the chaos of my life. The child in the dark room of my heart who had never been able to find or reach the light switch, flicked it on now; and I found in the room a stranger, myself, who had waited so many years to speak again. My words struck in me lightning crackles of elation and thunderhead storms of grief.

When I had been in the county jail longer than anyone else, I was made a trustee. One morning, after a fistfight, I went to the unlocked and unoccupied office used for lawyer-client meetings, to think. The bare white room with its fluorescent tube lighting seemed to expose and illuminate my dark and worthless life. When I had fought before, I never gave it a thought. Now, for the first time, I had something to lose—my chance to read, to write; a way to live with dignity and meaning, that had opened for me when I stole that scuffed, second hand book about the Romantic poets.

"I will never do any work in this prison system as long as I am not allowed to get my G.E.D." That's what I told the reclassification panel. The captain flicked off the tape recorder. He looked at me hard and said, "You'll never walk outta here alive. Oh, you'll work, put a copper penny on that, you'll work."

After that interview I was confined to deadlock maximum security in a subterranean dungeon, with ground-level chicken-wired windows painted gray. Twenty-three hours a day I was in that cell. I kept sane by borrowing books from the other cons on the tier. Then, just before Christmas, I received a letter from Harry, a charity house Samaritan who doled out hot soup to the homeless in Phoenix. He had picked my name from a list of cons who had no one to write to them. I wrote back asking for a grammar book, and a week later received one of Mary Baker Eddy's treatises on salvation and redemption, with Spanish and English on opposing pages. Pacing my cell all day and most of each night, I grappled with grammar until I was able to write a long true-romance confession for a con to send to his pen pal.

Coming Into
Language
(continued)
BY **JIMMY SANTIAGO
BACA**

He paid me with a pack of smokes. Soon I had a thriving barter business, exchanging my poems and letters for novels, commissary pencils, and writing tablets.

One day I tore two flaps from the cardboard box that held all my belongings and punctured holes along the edge of each flap and along the border of a ream of state-issue paper. After I had aligned them to form a spine, I threaded the holes with a shoestring, and sketched on the cover a hummingbird fluttering above a rose. This was my first journal.

Whole afternoons I wrote, unconscious of passing time or whether it was day or night. Sunbursts exploded from the lead tip of my pencil, words that grafted me into awareness of who I was; peeled back to a burning core of bleak terror, an embryo floating in the image of water, I cracked out of the shell wide-eyed and insane. Trees grew out of the palms of my hands, the threatening otherness of life dissolved, and I became one with the air and sky, the dirt and the iron and concrete. There was no longer any distinction between the other and I. Language made bridges of fire between me and everything I saw. I entered into the blade of grass, the basketball, the con's eye and child's soul.

At night I flew. I conversed with floating heads in my cell, and visited strange houses where lonely women brewed tea and rocked in wicker rocking chairs listening to sad Joni Mitchell songs.

Before long I was frayed like rope carrying too much weight, that suddenly snaps. I quit talking. Bars, walls, steel bunk and floor bristled with millions of poem-making sparks. My face was no longer familiar to me. The only reality was the swirling cornucopia of images in my mind, the voices in the air. Midair a cactus blossom would appear, a snake-flame in blinding dance around it, stunning me like a guard's fist striking my neck from behind.

The prison administrators tried several tactics to get me to work. For six months, after the next monthly prison board review, they sent cons to my cell to hassle me. When the guard would open my cell door to let one of them in, I'd leap out and fight him—and get sent to thirty-day isolation. I did a lot of isolation time. But I honed my image-making talents in that sensory-deprived solitude. Finally they moved me to death row, and after that to "nut-run," the tier that housed the mentally disturbed.

As the months passed, I became more and more sluggish. My eyelids were heavy, I could no longer write or read. I slept all the time.

One day a guard took me out to the exercise field. For the first time in years I felt grass and earth under my feet. It was spring. The sun warmed my face as I sat on the bleachers watching the cons box and run, hit the handball, lift weights. Some of them stopped to ask how I was, but I found it impossible to utter a syllable. My tongue would not move, saliva drooled from the corners of my mouth. I had been so heavily medicated I could not summon the slightest gestures. Yet inside me a small voice cried out, I am fine! I am hurt now but I will come back! I'm fine!

Back in my cell, for weeks I refused to eat. Styrofoam cups of urine and hot water were hurled at me. Other things happened. There were beatings, shock therapy, intimidation.

Later, I regained some clarity of mind. But there was a place in my heart where I had died. My life had compressed itself into an unbearable dread of being. The strain had been too much. I had stepped over that line where a human being has lost more than he can bear, where the pain is too intense, and he knows he is changed forever. I was now capable of killing, coldly and without feeling. I was empty, as I have never, before or since, known emptiness. I had no connection to this life.

But then, the encroaching darkness that began to envelop me forced me to re-form and give birth to myself again in the chaos. I withdrew even deeper into the world of language, cleaving the diamonds of verbs and nouns, plunging into the brilliant light of poetry's regenerative mystery. Words gave off rings of white energy, radar signals from powers beyond me that infused me with truth. I believed what I wrote, because I wrote what was true. My words did not come from books or textual formulas, but from a deep faith in the voice of my heart.

I had been steeped in self-loathing and rejected by everyone and everything—society, family, cons. God and demons. But now I had become as the burning ember floating in darkness that descends on a dry leaf and sets flame to forests. The word was the ember and the forest was my life. . . .

Writing bridged my divided life of prisoner and free man. I wrote of the emotional butchery of prisons, and my acute gratitude for poetry. Where my blind doubt and spontaneous trust in life met, I discovered empathy and compassion. The power to express myself was a welcome storm rasping at tendril roots, flooding my soul's cracked dirt. Writing was water that cleansed the wound and fed the parched root of my heart.

I wrote to sublimate my rage, from a place where all hope is gone, from a madness of having been damaged too much, from a silence of killing rage. I wrote to avenge the betrayals of a lifetime, to purge the bitterness of injustice. I wrote with a deep groan of doom in my blood, bewildered and dumbstruck; from an indestructible love of life, to affirm breath and laughter and the abiding innocence of things. I wrote the way I wept, and danced, and made love.

Reflect on the Reading

Questions About "Coming into Language"

1. What messages can you find in "Coming into Language?" What would you say to someone who argued that the insights in the memoir were only relevant to someone who had experienced prison?

2. Do any episodes from the memoir stand out? If you had to pick a key moment in the memoir, which would you select, and why?

3. What do you make of the fact that Santiago Baca had to steal the secondhand book he used to learn to read? How would you discuss the memoir in terms of access to literacy?

4. What narrative strategies can you recognize in "Coming into Language"? Which strategies do you find most effective and why?

Writing Assignment: A Memoir

Learning
Objective 5.2

Compose a memoir essay in which you recount one or more episodes from your past. Use the episodes to present larger lessons about life to your readers. Use narrative strategies to describe settings and characters and use details or dialog to bring the episode to life. When you have a draft of the memoir ready, share it with others, asking for comments about the truths revealed by the memoir and the way the story is told.

Ask Questions & Make Decisions

Exercises for Composing Memoirs

1. Search your memory for episodes that might make good examples to include in a memoir. Think of events that speak to themes of change, to conflicts you may have had, to challenges you have overcome, or to lessons about life. Develop a list of at least four episodes that might be used in a memoir.

2. Think about the people you know with the most interesting stories. Identify one person, and then write a couple of paragraphs detailing one of the stories related to this person. Use strategies of narration (see Chapter 20) and description (see Chapter 21) to bring the story to life.

3. Develop a dialog between two characters that brings a concept or lesson—courage, humility, the value of friendship, love, chance, etc.—into focus for your readers.

4. Take an everyday event from your life and develop a paragraph or two describing the event. Add creative details that make the description of the event engaging. Push the boundaries of creative license and embellishment, while still maintaining the truth value of the episode.

Plan It   Invention Strategies for Memoirs

As you plan your project, think about your rhetorical situation and the nature of memoirs. A good memoir is less a diary entry and more a statement about human experience meant to enlighten and engage an audience. The identity of the memoir writer (your ethos as a speaker) will be central. Think also about how the episodes you discuss will connect with your audience. An epiphany about a snowboarding technique might be translated into an insight that can be shared with mountain bikers, surfers, even parents and grandparents. Consider the following steps to begin your work:

- Look over the memoirs in this chapter. What models might you wish to emulate? What aspects of the memoir form appeal to you? What promises to be the most challenging aspect of composing a memoir?
- Think about the audience for your memoir. Are you writing for a limited group (like classmates)? Will your memoir be made public? How will readers react to what you have to say and how will you adjust your memoir to relate to their expectations?
- Consider your own memories as possible starting places for a memoir. Looking back, what do you appreciate or wonder about? Remember that memoirs can treat both milestone and everyday events. What episodes from your past might be good to write about?
- Think about some themes that might organize a memoir. How might topics like relationships, challenges, or moments of personal growth help you explain something about your life to readers? How might concerns of family, tradition, community, love, work, or similar topics organize a memoir?
- Make good use of prewriting (pages 41–44). Use doodles, IMs to friends, lists, or any other strategies that might let you explore freely.
- Make a list of possible themes and insights you might discuss. Make a second list of possible episodes you might cover.
- Think about relationships between people, ideas, and things. How have past events, items, and people shaped you? What ideas are connected to these elements?

CONNECT IT   More Resources for Memoirs

For more detailed information about some of the strategies you might use in memoirs, consider the following resources:

For more on rhetorical situations, see Chapter 1

For more insights into writing about people, see Chapter 6.

For more on narrating, see Chapter 20.

For more on describing, see Chapter 21.

For more on analyzing, see pages 62–65.

For more on comparing and contrasting, see Chapter 23.

✳ Compose It Draft a Memoir Essay

As you begin drafting your memoir, keep in mind the connections you need to establish between episodes and insights. For most memoir assignments, you will focus on one or more episodes that form the heart of the story. You will then share insights about those episodes with a broader set of readers. You will also need to employ strategies of narration and description to entertain readers. Use the following steps as guidelines for your memoir writing:

- Select the episodes you wish to focus on for the memoir. You can always make adjustments later, but you will need to hone in on one or two specific memories or moments to get started.
- Identify the insights you wish to explore in the memoir. Insights might begin with focused statements like "my sister taught me to fight" and extend to truisms like "struggle makes one stronger."
- Compose an opening section. You might jump right into a key episode. Or you could begin by discussing insights and then take up events. Just remember, a key goal is to engage and entertain your readers.
- Use descriptive writing strategies as you work (see Chapter 21). Elaborate the details of the examples you discuss. Think about the senses of your readers and make decisions that help them see, hear, smell, taste, and feel the details you describe.
- Use narrative writing strategies to bring the memoir to life (see Chapter 20). Describe settings and people using detailed language. Incorporate dialog to demonstrate interactions between people. Follow the creative writer's credo of "Show, don't tell."
- Check that you are drawing connections between the episodes you discuss and themes and life lessons. You might want to save the big insights for later in the memoir. Or you can offer ideas along the way.
- Check the language to make sure it is compelling. Think about your voice. Polish the piece and share a draft of it with peers.

Focus on Student Writing

The Laughter of Our Children
BY ANN GILLINGHAM

Memoirs touch on personal subjects, so sharing them can sometimes be difficult. The name of the author of this memoir has been changed, as have some of the other names in the book. Because memoirs are concerned with the value of truth, the author notes that she has artistically expanded on the core events in the memoir. She has dramatized the opening episode to emphasize points that come up in the later episodes.

Ann Gillingham

Professor Anderson

English 102

May 21, 2009

The Laughter of Our Children

At first it wasn't even an argument. Just the usual give and take between my Dad and my Mom's brother, my Uncle Sean, at one of the many get-togethers that spilled out of our shoe-boxed sized living room and onto the patio behind our house. We lived in the suburbs outside of Boston in a three-bedroom house with a small yard. Nothing special. I don't even remember the occasion— a birthday, I guess. We sat outside on the patio, Dad over the grill, Sean at his side, the sounds of burgers sizzling and barbecue smells promising another warm afternoon that would soon blend into the long and forgettable stretches of early summer in the life of a thirteen-year-old girl.

And then it was an argument. Sean stepped back from the barbecue and folded his arms across his chest. "You've got to be kidding me," he burst out. "Bobby Sands was a saint. A true martyr. He did more for his people in jail in those two months than all of your politicians have in the last twenty years."

Dad stepped back as well. "I'm just saying, he missed his opportunities. He was stubborn. He died, and for what?"

Sean stepped forward, uncrossing his arms and clenching and unclenching his hands into fists. Dad set down the barbecue tongs and pushed his face next to Sean's.

Sean raised his arms to shove Dad backwards into the grill, the lid slamming shut and bottles of sauce falling and breaking on the hard patio cement.

Mom rushed from the kitchen side door, screaming, "No, Sean. Robert. Stop it." She pulled Dad into the yard. Sean stepped away and pushed through the side gate. Ten seconds later his car started, then sped away. As Mom walked back toward the kitchen I saw something in her face I'll never forget. Her eyes were moist, but it seemed as if some belief had set itself up inside her that afternoon, a belief no less firm than the tight set of her jaw as she walked past. She also seemed strangely distant from me and Dad, as if the conviction she had discovered were hers alone.

What was happening? What could make Mom, if even just for a moment, feel so separate from us? What could bring these two friends, brothers really, so close to blows? It would take me eight years to fully understand.

* * *

We had almost made the circle. We had started our vacation in Dublin City, Ireland, a thriving, bursting-at-the-seams kind of place, with young professionals and expensive European cars. We hopped from Dublin to London where we discovered more opulence. Wealth oozed from every street, storefront, and passerby. Our hotel overlooked the Marble Arch, and through it many a Lamborghini, Ferrari, Bentley and Aston Martin purred its way toward, I'm sure, a swanky address. After London, we toured Scotland, which in its own right is on the upward swing, then headed over the waters back to Ireland, this time to Belfast.

When we first docked in Belfast we told our taxi driver we had only a short time in the city. His advice: "If you only do one thing while you are here—take the Black Taxi Tour." He gave my Dad a card. "When you're ready," he said, "give this number a call." We checked into our hotel, and then Dad made the call. Within ten minutes we had our tour guide with his black taxi, and off we went to understand a little bit more about the history of Belfast.

Ian, our driver, with his thick Irish accent, was, I am guessing, a former member of the IRA. He explained that this tour was not one-sided. He would give us both accounts of the conflict so

Gillingham 3

we could formulate our own opinions; much like the Palestinian/Jewish struggle, you have to be there, know the people, see the devastation to understand the pain of both groups.

Ian showed us many points of interest, including the Crown—a beautiful pub covered with colorful tile, glass, and wood. Mom told me that during the Troubles, this landmark survived forty-two bombings. We drove around the city taking in the sites, but instead of the brisk pace of Dublin or the affluence of London, the streets of Belfast were more somber. We saw the Hotel Europa—the most bombed hotel in Belfast, the Titanic Memorial near the House of Parliament, then the actual site where the Titanic was built. We were interested in everything, but Mom seemed distracted. While the cab sat idling in front of it Irish Press building, Mom asked, "Where is the mural of Bobby Sands?"

Ian laughed. "Alright," he said. "We'll see it, but first a little history."

The lesson begins with the uprising of 1916. Ireland has been fighting with the British for 800 years. The strife became even more pronounced with William of Orange, but the 1916 uprising was the catalyst for Irish Independence. The year 1916 saw intellectuals, businessmen, and ordinary people trying to win back their freedom. Freedom was gained in all but the north of Ireland. We drive past boarded-up buildings. Ian tells us that almost 60% of the people are "on the dole." What I am seeing in Belfast is a struggle to breathe the air of independence and to reap its rewards. Belfast is gasping.

We drive along with Ian into the Protestant/Unionist/Loyalist neighborhood of Hopewell Crescent in Lower Shankill where murals decorate walls and buildings. It begins to drizzle but we step out of the car. In front of us is an alarming mural of a man, wearing green, orange, and black fatigues as well as black stocking mask and gloves, holding an Uzi, with his sites trained on us. Written above his head in black letters is UFF Member. As we walk from one side of the mural to the other, the point of the gun follows us. It is rather eerie—like being hunted. On a building to the right of the Uzi is a larger-than-life picture of Jackie Coulter, who was killed in 2000. The mural reads: *In proud memory of Lt. Jackie Coulter.* Coulter was shot down by the UVF (Ulster Volunteer Force). Ian tells us of the UVF, the UDA, the PUP, the IRA, and those are only a few of the players in this bitter game. It is confusing, and like I said, it will take a long time to understand it all.

Now we are driving up Shankill Road, still on the Protestant side of the Peace Wall. This corrugated steel and cement structure reminds me of the Berlin Wall. It is incomprehensible that a civilized Western country could still have such a monument to division. But here it is covered with graffiti and drawings posted by people from all over the world.

We turn the corner. Now we are on the Catholic side of the wall. We are in the Clonard community and visit a red brick alcove where a Celtic Cross stands a few feet in front of a black chunk of marble. Colorful wreaths and flowers decorate the base. This memorial to the Clonard Martyrs is in memory of innocent people gunned down by British soldiers. Names and ages are etched into the stone. There is a child as young as four and so many others. It is a sobering sight. I find my chest tightening and I have to step away.

There are murals everywhere. On Bombay Street a mural of Gerard McAuley reads, *Never Again*. On we drive to see a mural of a revolver with a statement about her majesty's government in bold letters, *Collusion is not an Illusion*. We see more and more depictions of martyrs. Now we drive past a wall with drawings of the men who are the central characters in the so-called Troubles. It reads: *This is dedicated to the ten brave hunger strikers who sacrificed their lives in 1981. Their cause is our cause, freedom . . . The struggle goes on still.*

Finally we drive along Falls Road and there it is. In bright colors covering the entire side of a two story building, large as life, a mural of Bobby Sands. And there again is the look I remember in my Mom's face. Eyes moist, jaw set, she turns to me and says, "There it is. The Bobby Sands mural."

I smile at Mom. "What does it mean?"

She smiles back. "I was twenty-two when he went on hunger strike. I watched along with the rest of the world as a young man died. People didn't understand why someone would starve himself to death. What cause would be worth your life? I knew. Bobby Sands believed freedom was worth every breath and he gave up the most precious gift in the world to prove that point."

I remember the barbecue, Uncle Sean and Dad arguing over something I still didn't fully comprehend. I turned to my Dad and asked, "So, that's what you and Sean were fighting about? Why?"

Gillingham 5

Dad shakes his head. "I don't know either. I guess I just didn't understand. I watched on television. I remember Bobby Sands was elected to Parliament just before he died. The news was filled with it. One-hundred thousand people attended his funeral. I can't remember a world leader anywhere having that kind of power. Why not use it? I didn't understand."

"It's hard to imagine the emotions of that time," Mom explains. "Dad thought it was a waste, but Sean and I felt that it was an act of freedom. Starving to death was like saying that freedom matters more than anything in human existence. Without it we are mere cogs in someone else's wheel."

I notice that Mom again has that look in her eyes, but now her jaw is loose and her mouth turned up at the corners. Dad scoots a bit closer toward her on the bench seat in the back of the black taxi and they both smile, then we all turn one more time to study the face, painted brightly over the bricks. While Belfast still moans in birthing pangs, I truly feel this man made a difference. He must have. On his mural one line stands out: *our revenge will be the laughter of our children*. As we drive out of the Falls Road neighborhood, I look back at the green rolling hills that sit above the city. There is beauty in this place. More murals line the road, people chat with one another, and the shops seem to buzz with life.

But inside our black taxi no one says a word.

Reflect on the Reading

Questions About "The Laughter of Our Children"

1. What narrative strategies does the memoir use to tell its story? What would you say to Ann about the descriptions, dialog, characters, settings, and plot of her memoir?

2. In her memoir, Ann reflects on the history of Northern Ireland. What do you think of this strategy of weaving historical information into the personal memoir?

3. Would you say Ann's memoir is more concerned with family or with insights into politics and freedom? How are these insights related to one another?

4. "The Laughter of Our Children" ends with the phrase "no one says a word." Does this ending lessen the force of the insights the memoir is trying to get across? What are some strategies for demonstrating insights?

Revise It   Strategies for Revising Memoirs

In addition to general strategies for revision, concentrate on these areas as you revise your memoir:

- Can the audience relate to the episodes, and do the episodes lead to larger insights?
- Are the insights relevant and compelling? Do the lessons in the memoir address concerns that others might share? Do they touch on human relationship, challenges, conflicts, or change? Do they address some other concern that will have large appeal?
- Does the memoir hold readers' interests? Does it use narrative strategies to provide a sense of setting and context? Does the detail provided about the characters in the memoir help the reader to know them?
- Is there too little or too much description or dialog? Does the description appeal to multiple senses of the reader? Is the dialog realistic and compelling? Does the dialog reveal aspects of the larger message the memoir is trying to convey?
- Is the organization of the events and the narration logical and engaging? Does the chronology of the episodes make sense? Could episodes be broken into smaller pieces in the narration?

RESOURCE
Sample Memoirs

Push It   More Possibilities for Memoirs

1. Create a memoir using the medium of comics. Pinpoint an episode you would like to discuss. Identify larger insights that can be associated with the episode. Create a storyboard for the comic, putting in frames and sketching out ideas for images and text. Use comic creation software or drawing tools to compose the memoir. (See the excerpt from *Persepolis* on pages 129–35 and the advice of Scott McCloud on pages 28–32 for more insights into comics.)

2. Compose a playlist memoir. Playlists can represent all kinds of subjects. Pick an event or specific time in your life about which you would like to reflect. Develop a list of songs that deliver a message about the time. Add explanations to your list to help readers understand the relationships between the songs and your life. (See Chapter E5 for more on playlists.)

3. Develop and maintain a personal blog where you inform readers about your life. Decide what kind of audience you imagine as readers of your blog. Use a Web service like livejournal.com, blogger.com, or wordpress.com to create the blog. Invite members of your intended audience to read and respond to the blog.

Learning
Objective 5.3

Zoom Out   Reflecting on Memoirs

- **Memoirs are personal.** Writing a memoir requires that you tell a story that has some connection to you. This process may not be completely comfortable if you've been in the habit of composing documented research reports, but remember that memoirs should also focus on larger lessons and concerns.

- **Memoir writers balance the need to be artistic with the demands of accuracy and truth.** Being honest in your selection of episodes and genuine in your voice enables you to maintain credibility while using creative license to compose compelling stories.

- **Memoir writers don't include every scuffed knee or high-school dance.** Instead, writers focus on events that might teach readers something about life. These episodes don't have to be earth shattering. Often, everyday experiences provide insights that readers can recognize.

- **Memoir writers use narrative strategies (developing characters, establishing settings, pacing plots, and composing dialog) to bring their stories to life.** Memoirs also call for descriptive writing that "shows, not tells," using details that engage the senses of readers.

- **Memoirs are about memories.** They often treat topics that engage readers on emotional levels, topics like families or relationships, lessons learned, struggles, and changes in perspective. Memoirs give writers a chance to look back and think about what matters in a life.

For additional information and practice with the learning objectives in this chapter, go to www.mycomplab.com, Resources > Writing > Writing Purposes > Writing to Reflect.

6

Profiles

 Zoom **In** **Key Concepts and Learning Objectives**

After studying this chapter, you should be able to:

6.1 Compose a profile that focuses on key moments or episodes to capture a portrait of a person.

6.2 Make larger points by discussing episodes to illuminate the focus of a profile.

6.3 Use storytelling and description to creatively treat profile subjects and situations.

6.4 Understand how profiles can be developed in multiple genres and mediums.

If you are like most people who have uploaded a picture or filled out a list of favorite songs on a Web site, you have given some thought to the ways in which profiles can define people. Do you like cats or dogs? Folk or hip hop? Should you upload the image with you wearing the serious smirk or the one with the cowboy hat? We make choices all the time about the ways we present ourselves. A written profile is similarly composed through a series of decisions meant to deliver a message about a person.

You can keep in mind this connection between decision making and identity as you read or write profiles. A profile engages readers with details that bring a person's story to life. Rather than try to cover everything there is to know, however, a profile will focus on one or two telling aspects of the person. Profiles offer a kind of story that helps readers grasp an important idea about someone. As you think about reading and writing profiles, you might want to look over the materials on memoirs in Chapter 5.

KEY TERMS

- **Profile:** A composition that illuminates aspects of a person. Profile subjects don't have to be public figures (though they often are). Profiles provide a focused point or angle that helps readers understand the person or discover insights into an important concern.

- **Biography:** A story that captures the life of a person. Most biographies are more extensive than a profile, and cover a longer period of a person's life.

- **Episode:** A key event in a person's life. Episodes need not be life changing, but they usually do offer a lesson that can be translated into a point related to the subject of a profile.

- **Narration:** A means of telling a story by sequencing and discussing events. Most profiles use a third person perspective, providing the voice of a narrator (the profile author) who relates and comments on key events in the profile subject's life.

- **Description:** A means of composing that engages readers by providing details. Descriptions can shed light on people and things through the word choices that authors use. Descriptions appeal to the senses of readers.

Understanding Profiles

To get a better sense of the ways in which profiles reveal insights into a person, consider the following profile of Jenny Fulle.

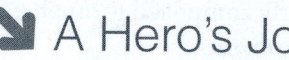

A Hero's Journey
BY **NEIL BROVERMAN**

Neil Broverman is an associate editor of The Advocate, *a print and online magazine devoted to issues of interest to the gay and lesbian community. "A Hero's Journey" was published in* The Advocate *in February 2007.*

When Jenny Fulle was 18 she scrubbed George Lucas's toilet. It was 1980 and Fulle was already a minor celebrity, half-remembered as the baseball prodigy whose determination forced Little League Baseball to allow girls to play.

But Fulle's rubber gloves were merely creating the backstory for an amazing second act of a modern Horatio Alger story in which a gay protagonist goes from janitor to executive vice president of a movie studio with not so much as a black eye in the process.

As executive VP of production at Sony Pictures Imageworks—the company responsible for all three Spider-Man pictures, both Charlie's Angels films, *The Chronicles of Narnia*, and other marvels of special effects and animation—Fulle is one of the most powerful lesbians in Hollywood. And she's pulled herself to the top without the help of nepotism or a formal education.

"I had just dropped out of college and wasn't quite sure of what I wanted to do. I was floundering a bit," she remembers. "So someone said to me, 'Would you like to clean toilets for George Lucas?' and I said, 'Hey, that sounds cool.'"

She started working at Industrial Light and Magic, George Lucas's special effects compound in the San Francisco Bay area, and became captivated by the energy of the studio. At 23 she became a production assistant, a coveted stepping-stone that can lead to bigger things if you're smart and tenacious enough.

"After a couple of years in production, it was, 'Oh, little Jenny—she used to be a janitor and now she's a coordinator. Isn't that cute?'" Fulle says. "People were putting me in a box, and it wasn't because of my sexuality or my gender but the fact that a few years earlier I was emptying their trash."

Tired of being known as the cleaning lady, Fulle packed her bags and moved to Los Angeles. It was as much a personal choice as a professional necessity: "Up in Marin County, I was the only gay."

Fulle landed production gigs on many hypermasculine films, including Arnold Schwarzenegger movies *Total Recall*, *Eraser*, and *True Lies*, and surprisingly didn't experience much sexism. "Certainly, I've felt like I've come up against the boys' club, but it hasn't been impenetrable," she says. In fact, occasionally she's gleaned confidence from the most unlikely experiences.

Once, in her early days in Los Angeles, she found herself on a movie set feeling out of place and trying desperately to look like she belonged.

"Whoopi Goldberg was there," Fulle recalls, "and she came up to me in front of all these people and said, 'Didn't I #$##% you at Woodstock?' I felt all the blood drain from my face. It was definitely an icebreaker."

To Fulle, Hollywood's homophobia is directed largely at actors; players behind the camera aren't subjected to the same degree of hostility. "I've been out publicly since I came out of the womb, and I've never been closeted at work," she says. "In the film industry you want something that people will remember you by, and I think my outness has only helped me."

It certainly hasn't hurt. The promotions continued with Fulle advancing at Hollywood's premier digital studios, such as DreamWorks SKG, before being tapped by Imageworks president Tim Sarnoff for her current position.

"Jenny is everything this industry should stand for," Sarnoff says via e-mail. "She's gotten to where she is today with hard work, determination, and a sense of humor. Her strength is important as well—she can lift more than I can."

The executives' working relationship produced hits like *Superman Returns*, *The Aviator*, and the Spider-Man movies. What's next? The brand-new *Ghost Rider*, starring Nicolas Cage.

Fulle likes to have a lot on her plate, and she freely admits that she's "always been a type A personality from the time I was a child."

After all, it's not just anyone who could accomplish what Fulle did, beginning as a 9-year-old tomboy from Mill Valley, Calif. A natural leader, Fulle was known as one of the best young baseball players in Northern California. And she wanted in on Little League, open only to boys.

"[The Little League] told me I couldn't play because I was a girl," Fulle remembers. "It just didn't make sense to me." So she went straight to the top.

"I can still remember writing a letter to President Nixon at my kitchen table. I sent it off and forgot about it. But a few months later, I got a letter back from the Department of Health, Education, and Welfare and they gave me the guidelines to handle that sort of discrimination."

Fulle's mom, Donna Lyons, whom her daughter calls a NorCal hippie type, took matters to the Mill Valley Parks and Recreation Commission. But when Little League Baseball threatened to take away Mill Valley's affiliation if the city allowed a girl to play, the commission caved. The family turned to the National Organization for Women, whose Marin County chapter president was an idealistic young woman named M. Lee Hunt. Their complaint advanced to the Mill Valley city council, and things turned ugly as the town began to air its prejudices.

A Hero's Journey
(continued)
BY **NEIL BROVERMAN**

"There were Boy Scouts who turned out [at the city council meetings], definitely not in favor of Jenny playing baseball," Hunt recalls. "There were guys who spoke whose faces were red and had veins standing out on their neck. I was speaking to the media, and tomatoes and eggs were being thrown."

Today, Marin County is a liberal enclave that starts at the end of the Golden Gate Bridge. But back in the early '70s the area—like the rest of country—was going through severe growing pains, particularly when it came to female equality. When the Mill Valley city council ruled against Jenny, she and her allies dug their heels in deeper. With the help of the American Civil Liberties Union, they sued Little League Baseball and were vindicated by the Marin County superior court. Thus, in 1974, Little League Baseball integrated itself. Girls could now prove their worth alongside the boys. And Fulle did just that—she led her league in home runs her first season.

"*The Bad News Bears* came out a few years later, and I always thought, OK, that's not fair, I played for the [Mill Valley] Bears," Fulle says. "I thought the Tatum O'Neal character should have been me. A few years later, I worked with Michael Ritchie—the director of the movie—and I told him the story and he said, 'Oh, my God, I remember that. We were reading about it in the newspaper and we were changing the script as the story was coming out.'"

Fulle's fight also inspired Hunt, now a family lawyer in nearby San Rafael, California. "The impetus for me to go to law school was this case because I saw how much a person could do as a lawyer."

In 2000, Fulle was honored in Mill Valley for her forward-looking achievements. She led the Little League opening-day parade and threw out the first ball as part of the city's centennial celebration.

Fulle's 6-year-old son, Wyatt (she and her ex-partner share custody), may not comprehend the magnitude of his mother's many accomplishments, but he reaps the benefits. The little tee ball player will soon graduate to the Little Leagues, where he'll play alongside both girls and boys.

Reflect on the Reading

Questions About "A Hero's Journey"

1. What have you learned about Fulle from the profile? If you had to sum up Jenny Fulle with two or three adjectives, which ones would you select? Why?

2. What kinds of storytelling strategies does the piece use to deliver the profile of Fulle? Are there particular strategies that you find to be more or less effective?

3. What are your thoughts on the ways the profile discusses two major aspects of Fulle— her filmmaking and her childhood experiences with baseball? What would you say to someone who argued that discussing both of these elements causes the profile to lose focus?

4. Is it fair to say that Fulle is exceptional? What elements of the profile speak to her position as a common person? What elements suggest she is unique? What strategies does the profile writer use to help readers identify with Fulle?

"A Hero's Journey" demonstrates some of the key elements of profiles. The profile does not simply list random biographical details about Jenny Fulle. Instead, it explores events in Fulle's life—a start as a janitor, a stint as a production assistant, and the move to heading up major films—with the intent of highlighting some of the characteristics that have made her successful. The piece also takes an angle on the profile subject by focusing on her struggles and achievements. This angle represents a key component of the profile.

The profile also shows how writers can engage their audiences using narrative strategies. The piece includes quotations from people who have insights into Fulle or from Fulle herself. There are also detailed descriptions of heated city council meetings. These storytelling strategies help bring out the profile subject, much as one might find in a novel emphasizing aspects of a character. Details of this kind bring the person to life in the profile.

Often, the hardest part about writing a profile, or anything for that matter, is coming up with an angle, or a meaningful perspective on the topic. In "A Hero's Journey," readers are given lots of details that all help develop the sense that Fulle is an inspirational figure who has overcome barriers to achieve success. This focus takes the project from a mere collection of information to a compelling composition.

WN

VIDEO
49. Chronology
and Narrative

Know It   Strategies for Understanding Profiles

- Consider the subject of the profile. Often profiles will describe a public figure, but they can also treat more personal subjects—a sister or a parent, for instance. Occasionally, profiles will treat larger, people-related topics such as hobbies or professions through the lens of a particular person.

- Look for an angle or focus. Profiles might not make an explicit announcement of their angle (a kind of thesis statement), but a focus should emerge through the details and discussion in the project.

- Examine research in the piece. Profiles often include excerpts from interviews. (See pages 362–63 for more on interview research.) Profiles will also include biographical information, but effective profile authors will be careful not to overwhelm readers by just dumping facts into the essay.

- Look for narrative strategies as profiles discuss their subjects. They may include anecdotes or other storytelling techniques like descriptions of settings or characters.

- Examine connections with larger issues. Profiles may speak to contemporary trends or human traits and concerns (culture, technology, politics, courage, families, and so on). A good profile can make a larger statement about the world.

Exercises for Understanding Profiles

1. Explore some user profiles posted to online social sites (Facebook, MySpace, etc.). What do these profiles have in common with the profile essay? How do they differ? What can you learn about writing profiles based on these sites?

2. What makes someone a good subject for a profile? Are the qualities of a person more important than their status as a public figure? Why or why not? Work with a group of peers to develop a list of criteria for a good profile subject.

3. Working with a small group of peers, think of a stereotype often applied to a person (jock, nerd, hippie, preppie, etc.). Work together to write an opening paragraph for a profile of a stereotyped person. Use details to make the paragraph engaging for readers. When finished, revise the paragraph to include a trait that does not fit the stereotype.

4. Watch a television show that serves as a profile (*Behind the Music, Biography, Cribs*). How do these profiles present their stories? What strategies might be adapted from television profiles to other formats?

Readings and Resources for Exploring Profiles

A great way to find examples of profiles is by looking through news magazines or Web sites. Publications like *Time* or *Newsweek* frequently include pieces on figures ranging from scientists to politicians. You can also try sources with more specialized audiences depending on your topic—*Runner's World* for athletes, *Rolling Stone* for musicians. And a number of sources now include profiles in audio forms—NPR's StoryCorps, series, for instance. You can also explore the examples below, a profile from *USA Today Magazine* featuring cartoonist Steve Brodner and a piece by Tara Cady Sartorius discussing quilter Yvonne Wells.

❯ Raw Nerve: The Political Art of Steve Brodner

Steve Brodner is well known as a political cartoonist. His illustrations have appeared in publications ranging from Sports Illustrated *to* The New York Times Book Review *and have been a regular feature of* Harper's *magazine. His political cartoons were published in the book* Freedom Fries. *He teaches at the School of Visual Arts in New York. "Raw Nerve" appeared in* USA Today Magazine *in September 2008.*

FIGURE 6.1
"The Full Rudy"
(Copyright © Steve
Brodner. Used by
permission.).

Explosive is an apt term to describe the art of Steve Brodner, whose deftly executed drawings cast a spotlight on the American political scene as it unfolds. Working on a national political stage, Brodner perhaps is the most successful, influential, and widely read of today's political illustrators. His wry humor and unique ability to conceive visual form inspired by icons of popular culture resonate through our shared societal memory. Powerful images speak to us with precision and directness, offering fresh perspectives and revealing sometimes painful truths about our world and the influential leaders of our times.

"Raw Nerve! The Political Art of Steve Brodner" draws upon a celebrated tradition of political caricature that harks back to the 18th century. Beginning with the work of English illustrator James Gilray, whose satirical art cast a critical eye on the British government and the governing classes, political illustration has served to inform, motivate, and sometimes incite the public. During the past two centuries, great cartoonists like Francisco Goya, Honoré Daumier, and Thomas Nast have offered distinctive political and social perspectives, keeping their messages before the public through constant innovation and compelling imagery that posed significant questions about the events of their day. Like his predecessors, Brodner's political illustrations define and comment on society, challenge our ideas, and profoundly influence public opinion on a mass scale.

Brodner has been a satirical illustrator for more than 30 years. Born in 1954 in Brooklyn, N.Y., he studied art at Cooper Union, graduating in 1976. As a young artist, he entered and won first place in a major illustration competition sponsored by the Population Institute—an award presented by *New York Times* caricaturist Al Hirschfeld, an individual he admired greatly. Brodner cut his teeth at *The Hudson Dispatch*, a small newspaper in Union City, N.J., where his talent for political satire first was recognized. In 1977, *The New York Times Book Review* began publishing his art, and from 1979 through 1982, he produced his own journal, *The New York Illustrated News*. Brodner developed a distinctive style in the early 1980s, and began creating illustrations for nearly every major American periodical of the day. By the end of the decade, he emerged as one of the

Raw Nerve: The
Political Art of Steve
Brodner
(continued)

nation's foremost political artists, a distinction he maintains to this day. In fact, he is the *New Yorker's* official political illustrator for the 2008 presidential campaign.

"For me, caricature is part of what goes on in illustration: finding essences that are useful in storytelling," Brodner explains. "The exaggeration is not the destination, but rather the train you take to get there. What will you find to help you make your point?"

Dictionaries define satire as "biting wit, irony, or sarcasm used to expose vice or folly." In his art, Brodner combines satire with caricature, "a deliberate distortion of features or parts to create a ridiculous effect," he says. Through these devices and, with a unique ability to envision a particular moment in American popular culture, Brodner challenges us to see the world through his eyes. Because he responds to events in a near-instantaneous fashion, much of his art is ephemeral. After an event has faded from the now ubiquitous 24-hour news cycle, Brodner's art serves as a kind of political and cultural landmark. The best of the artist's work stands the test of time and continues to resonate long after the spotlight of publicity has dimmed.

FIGURE 6.2
"Gas Bag" (Copyright
© Steve Brodner. Used
by permission.).

"The last 30 years in American political life have been characterized by war, scandal, deception, hypocrisy, and corruption, followed by . . . more war and scandal. It's been fun—at least it has to me because I am a caricaturist," he notes. "Professional satirists are endowed with a perverse pleasure mechanism; we're like bloodhounds who become elated at closing in on a body—and we provide, I think, a similar public service."

Brodner describes himself as an art journalist. He seeks reporting assignments from national publications, researches topics, and produces compelling images that provoke an emotional response. These always are done in series form to create an expansive visual narrative that speaks to a greater truth. His topics of choice are evidence of society's most pressing concerns, whether they address the plight of the American farmer, gun violence in U.S. cities, or the machinations of government at the state level. Unlike his overtly political images, satire is not universally present in his art journalism, providing a complete and authentic picture of issues and events.

Brodner's singular ability to capture the essence of a politician's public persona, and his unique insight into the visual language and metaphors of popular culture, result in profound commentary that immediately is comprehensible and often hilarious. During his career, Brodner has garnered intimate knowledge of the political class, shining a bright light

FIGURE 6.3
"Hot in Here" (Copyright © Steve Brodner. Used by permission.).

on presidents and their people, whether Democrats or Republicans. His pointed visual evaluations of Ronald Reagan, George H.W. Bush, Bill Clinton, George W. Bush, and their administrations, have influenced public opinion and raised imperative questions for discourse.

From scandals and wars to natural and manmade disasters, the events of each presidency make a lasting impression. Though Brodner's illustrations of political figures appear daily, these exhibition selections of more than 100 drawings represent the most memorable events of the past 15 years. From the early days of Bill Clinton's presidency to his subsequent impeachment, Brodner's images form a continuous narrative through the years of George W. Bush's administration, including the monumental events of Sept. 11, 2001, and the ongoing Iraqi war.

How does a political illustrator create? Brodner begins with a sketch book, crafting portraits of potential subjects in pencil and developing ideas. Like most caricaturists, he exaggerates specifically recognizable features, providing his audience with a particular frame of reference. Then, he overlays a pop culture reference, creating an instantly understandable image from disparate elements. Though usually humorous, sobering or ironic truths about a particular individual, situation,

FIGURE 6.4
"The World" (Copyright © Steve Brodner. Used by permission.).

or political event often are evident. Brodner's powerful character studies provide profound insights into his subjects' personas and sometimes are empathetic. For example, 1996 Republican presidential candidate Bob Dole was wounded severely during World War II and has limited use of his right hand, yet this issue never was exploited by the candidate. The artist's images convey a sense of deep respect for his subject, despite his disagreement with Dole's political philosophy.

Over the years, Brodner's representations of key political figures evolve naturally. A case in point is his approach to drawing George W. Bush, who first was put to paper by the artist in 1998, while he was governor of Texas. A representational image developed into multiple caricatures, including variations on *Mad* magazine's Alfred E. Neuman and Disney's Mickey Mouse, culminating in what Brodner describes as "Simple" Bush. This elemental form is created with just a few lines on paper, but still is recognizable as the President.

Some of Brodner's works share a goal of expounding on who Americans are as a people. He revels in extolling the absurd and loves to remind us of how our past informs our present. In a homage to Norman Rockwell, Brodner offers an updated version of "Freedom from Want." Rather than expressing convivial chatter around a holiday table, he depicts a group of self-absorbed caricatures. Fast food stands in for the home-cooked turkey in a work intended to lampoon the changes in American society since Rockwell's time.

Brodner's drawings, as seen in "Raw!," reflect his unique blend of wit and acerbic, laser-like vision of American society, politics, and contemporary leaders. This is the first major museum exhibition for Brodner, who wryly describes himself as an "equal opportunity offender" of all politicians, political parties, and creeds.

"Steve Brodner is one of the most important political illustrators working today," notes Charles Sable, exhibition curator. "His singular ability to capture the essence of a politician's public persona and his unique insights about popular culture result in profound commentary. His illustrations are immediately comprehensible and often are absolutely hilarious."

Reflect on the Reading

Questions About "Raw Nerve: The Political Art of Steve Brodner"

1. What is the effect of connecting the profile of Brodner with the succession of presidents he has lampooned over the years? Is it fair to call these presidential eras episodes in Brodner's life? Why or why not?

2. The piece in *USA Today Magazine* reports on an exhibition of Brodner's works, "Raw Nerve." What can you say about the ways in which the profile is shaped by this connection?

3. The original version of "Raw Nerve" appeared in *USA Today Magazine* with a total of fourteen images. Four of the images are reproduced here as Figures 6.1 through 6.4. How would you discuss the piece in terms of its visual portrayal of Brodner's work? How would you construct a visual profile of a person?

⬎ Soulful Survivor Sewing
BY **TARA CADY SARTORIUS**

Tara Cady Sartorius is an artist based in Montgomery, Alabama. She is the curator of education at the Montgomery Museum of the Arts. Sartorius writes numerous articles exploring artists and offering suggestions to teachers for arts education as part of a series called Arts and Activities, *in which "Soulful Survivor Sewing" was published in February 2009.*

My, how far we have come! The 20th of January 2009, will always be known as the date of the inauguration of the first African-American President of the United States. The journey—historically, socially and emotionally—has been a long one. The story of race relations in America, from exploitation to excellence, has been told by many in various forms, from song and dance to narrative fiction and expository history. The style of storytelling of the artist who made the quilt [on page 165] is one approach that deserves closer consideration.

Blur your eyes and glance at the overall composition. It looks a little like a playground with a game of ring-around-the-rosie in the lower right and a long Slip 'N Slide on the left. Looking just a little closer, though, brings to the foreground the image of a lynching and other historic events that happened during the Civil Rights Movement in the American South.

The artist, Yvonne Wells (birth date undisclosed, but c. 1942), used appliquéd and quilted fabric to create a portrait of an era and an acknowledgment of individuals who contributed, either through their negative or positive deeds, to important social change in the United States.

The quilt is full-sized, and could be placed on a bed to keep someone warm on a cool winter night, yet it is hardly intended for such use. "I do make quilts that are not made for warming," says Wells. "The quilts that I make and create are . . . considered wall hangings. They represent pictures, as a painter puts his pictures on the wall."

The soft fabric matches Wells' soft-spoken personality. While she does not shy away from harsh subjects, Wells does not approach such realities in a harsh manner. On the contrary, she has always chosen a gentler tactic when expressing her political views.

Where Yvonne Wells grew up had a perfect vantage point. "During that time it was the most tense time that I have ever experienced between the races. You could just almost cut it."

Her hometown, Tuscaloosa, Ala., is where, on June 11, 1963, Alabama's Governor George Wallace stood in the doorway of Foster Auditorium at the University of Alabama attempting to stop two young African-Americans from registering for school. That event is depicted at the top of Wells' quilt. Back then she was attending the "HBCU" (Historically Black College/University), Stillman College, in Tuscaloosa.

Soulful Survivor
Sewing
(continued)
BY **TARA CADY
SARTORIUS**

The importance of education was a long-standing tradition in Wells' family. Yvonne's mother was an elementary school teacher and she and all of her eight siblings attended Stillman College. In 1964 Wells graduated with a major in Physical Education and a minor in English.

Her first job, in 1965, was at her alma mater, Druid High School, in Tuscaloosa. She taught there for five years and then, in 1970, Wells was selected by the district office to be transferred across town to a "white school" (Tuscaloosa High School) as part of the integration efforts in the early 1970s. "Coach Wells" taught PE at Tuscaloosa High School for more than 20 years. In her "spare" time, she attended evening classes at various colleges in the area until, in 1973, she earned her master's degree.

Wells' first quilt was made in 1979 for an entirely functional purpose: to keep her legs warm in a drafty room. Quilting became nearly a compulsion for her, and two years later she placed an ad in the newspaper, "Quilts for Sale, $20 and up. Call after 4 P.M."

Art dealer Robert Cargo saw the ad, called and bought. His support over the years helped Wells' confidence grow, and as her quilting "voice" grew, so did her base of admirers.

In 1985 Wells exhibited her work for the first time at the Kentuck Art Festival (best known for its folk or self-taught artist exhibitors) in Northport, Ala. Wells was surprised and delighted to win Best of Show. She won the same honor in 1990, 1991, 1995 and 1997.

Wells has the wonderful ability to express herself clearly both visually and verbally—important qualities that make her the terrific artist she is today. She's self-taught, self-motivated and very articulate. Her style is completely her own, and she takes pride in her individuality.

> My work is not traditional. I like it that way. If people tell me to turn my ends under, I'll leave them raggedy. If they tell me to make my stitches small and tight, I'll leave them loose. Sometimes you can trip over my stitches they're so big. You can always recognize the traditional quilters who come by and see my quilts. They sort of cringe. They fold their hands in front of them as if to protect themselves from the cold. When they come up to my work they think to themselves, "God, what has happened here—all these big crooked stitches." I appreciate these quilters. I admire their craft. But that's not my kind of work. I would like them to appreciate what I'm doing. They are quilters. But I am an artist. And I tell stories.

Wells sews, and also tells out loud the stories connected to her quilts. Reminiscing about her life during the turbulent Civil Rights era in Alabama, she recalls a day she was teaching softball to her PE class.

> I remember ... I was with my class outside and people were going to whatever event it was ... and they would yell out of the car at me with my class out there ... "You need to get away from out there, you ain't got no soul."

FIGURE 6.5
Yesterday: Civil Rights in the South, III by Yvonne Wells, 1989. (Montgomery Museum of Fine Arts, Montgomery, Alabama, Gift of Kempf Hogan).

I will never forget that phrase . . . that statement will always remain with me. Why [was] he saying that? As time went on I came to the realization people were thinking everybody should be doing the same thing at the same time . . . [but] . . . there are different types of protest, [there's] the physical, there's the quiet,

"Soulful Survivor Sewing" by Tara Cady Sartorius from Arts & Activities, February 2009. Reproduced with permission of Arts & Activities magazine, www.artsandactivities.com.

Soulful Survivor
Sewing
(continued)
BY **TARA CADY
SARTORIUS**

there's all kinds, but everybody does not have to do the same things, as long as
the end is what you are looking for.

In some ways, in January 2009, both an end and a new beginning are here. Even
before the vote in November of 2008, Wells remarked, "It came because of a lot of hard
work that has been done by so many people, so many foot-soldiers, so many people who
gave up lives . . . I think it's great. It's a time for a change . . . It's good for the nation and it's
good for the world."

The story is not over, and it never will be. Soulful storytellers such as Yvonne Wells
keep the narrative alive, and all the while, the good or not-so-good that comes from our
deeds is sewn into the textured fabric of history.

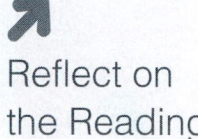

Reflect on
the Reading

Questions About "Soulful Survivor Sewing"

1. The profile of Wells discusses the quilter in terms of the Civil Rights movement and issues of race. Is it fair to say this is a political profile? Why or why not?
2. What do you think it means when the profile refers to Wells's quilting "voice"? What can
   you say about the way the profile addresses the art of quilting? How does the focus on
   the art influence the profile of Wells?
3. The profile contains a number of quotes from Wells. What is the effect of incorporating
   the words of the profile subject into the piece?
4. Conduct research online concerning Wells or the art of quilting. After some
   investigation, think about additions you might make to "Soulful Survivor Sewing" or
   about a profile you might compose related to some form of art.

Writing Assignment: A Profile

> Compose a profile of a person. The subject can be a public figure or an important person in your life. Conduct some research to learn more about your profile subject. Identify an angle you can use to focus the profile. Pinpoint episodes you can discuss to shed light on your profile subject. Include quotations as needed and use narrative strategies to bring the profile subject to life.

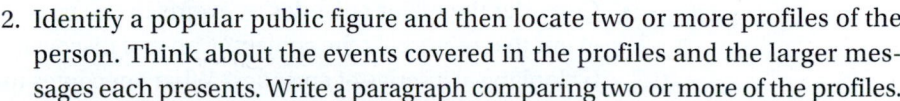

Ask
Questions
& Make
Decisions

LO

Learning
Objective 6.1

Exercises for Composing Profiles

1. Find a profile essay you like, and then write a one-page analysis exploring the strategies used in the essay. What connections does the essay draw with larger issues? How does the essay demonstrate its focus? How is it organized? What styles and techniques work well in the essay and what details does it include? What makes it an interesting essay?

2. Identify a popular public figure and then locate two or more profiles of the person. Think about the events covered in the profiles and the larger messages each presents. Write a paragraph comparing two or more of the profiles.

3. Select a person who is often covered in profiles—Lance Armstrong, Hillary Clinton, Kanye West, etc. Identify an aspect of the person's life that is not typically discussed in these profiles. Think about why the aspect you have discovered is often overlooked. Do most profiles have a standard focus? Are there human qualities that don't make good subjects for profiles? Write up your reflections in a paragraph.

4. Identify a person who might not automatically be a first choice for a profile— your neighbor, sister, guitar teacher, etc. Brainstorm about ways to develop a profile of the person you have selected. What strategies might you use to demonstrate aspects of the profile subject? How might you make the profile of interest to a wide range of readers? What larger issues could you address through the profile? Write up a brief outline for a profile of the person.

5. Explore a number of audio essays profiling people. (Visit online sites like npr.org or search for resources related to oral history.) Make a two-column list, populating the first column with strategies these audio essays use to bring their subjects

to life. In the second column, list alternative strategies for print-based essays or ways in which the audio strategies might be translated into print essays.

Plan It   Invention Strategies for Profiles

It's not necessary to choose a celebrity, politician, or historical icon as the subject of your profile, although these are certainly good possibilities. The main objective is to create a profile of a person that also speaks to a human concern. Here are some steps to get started:

LO

Learning
Objective 6.2

- Think about profiles you have read in the past or browse through some profiles. What do you like and dislike about the profiles you read? What aspects of other profiles might you emulate?
- Consider broad topics that interest you. Are there hobbies, trends, careers, or other concerns that might lead you to a subject?
- Identify a subject for your profile, and then brainstorm freely, perhaps creating a list of adjectives or key terms that represent the person. You can then prioritize or expand on items in the list to continue the invention process.
- Try visualizing aspects of the subject. Are there iconic images related to the person that might launch your thinking about the profile? If you were to make a montage or collage of images that represent the subject, what images would you choose and why?
- Consider the major episodes or events in the person's life. Is there a signal event that represents the subject? Can you discover a progression or growth by looking at a series of episodes? What anecdotes might be included in the profile?
- Conduct research about the person to discover ideas. Capture as much key biographical information as possible. Look for existing profiles. What is covered more deeply and what is overlooked?
- Think about what you might ask the person if you had a chance to sit down for an interview. What is the most interesting aspect of the person's life? What unanswered questions do you have about the subject of your profile?

CONNECT IT   More Resources for Profiles

- For more detailed information about some of the strategies you might use in profiles, consider the following resources:
- For more on rhetorical situations, see Chapter 1.

- For insights into writing about life events, see Chapter 5.
- For insights into using photographs to write about people see Chapters 13 and 25.
- For more on narrating, see Chapter 20.
- For more on describing, see Chapter 21.
- For more on analyzing, see pages 62–65.
- For more on comparing and contrasting, see Chapter 23.
- For options concerning video profiles, see Chapter E-8.

WN

RESOURCES
Video Profiles

Compose It **Write a Profile**

To begin, think about the angle you will take. Has your profile subject not been discussed enough, in your opinion? Alternatively, has the person been discussed, but from a perspective you find puzzling, annoying, or otherwise dissatisfying? Make sure you have identified not only a subject who matters to you but also an area of focus, and then keep these strategies in mind as you compose:

- Draft a quick plan for organizing the profile. You may want to organize the essay around the aspects of your subject that make him or her worth writing about. You might also think about events, themes, or subtopics that could organize the essay—for instance a section on struggles and then a section on triumphs. Compose an outline, map, or sketch of ideas for the project.
- Write an opening paragraph that connects with readers. Demonstrate early the approach to the person you wish to emphasize. You can always create a placeholder introduction and return to that section later, but get down some ideas that suggest your angle—the main impression you hope to put across.
- Compose the body segments of the essay. Use your outline and episodes or aspects of the profile subject to organize the sections. Add enough detail to explain key points about the subject. Use narrative strategies as you compose. Be sure that you have conducted enough research to write authoritatively about the topic.
- Include quotations as needed to further your points as you draft the sections of the essay.
- Compose a closing section that wraps up the profile. You might reiterate the focus of the essay. You might use a representative anecdote that

LO

Learning
Objective 6.3

reinforces the points you have made. Think about how quotations or a larger lesson might create a good takeaway message for readers.

- Consider how formatting or design strategies might be applied to the profile. Can you use pull-quotes or columns to help readers take in the profile? Are there images that might be incorporated into the essay? (See Chapter 26 for more on design.)

Focus on Student Writing

The Challenge Question

BY **SUSAN RAMOS**

Susan composed this essay in response to an assignment calling for a profile of a local figure, a close friend, or relative. She conducted an interview with her profile subject, allowing her to use many quotations. Because she has a personal relationship with the subject of her profile, she includes some of her own experiences, bringing some aspects of memoir (see Chapter 5) into the piece.

Susan Ramos

Professor Anderson

English 101

28 January 2008

The Challenge Question

One of the first lessons you'll learn if you spend any time with Trace Waters is that it's never a good idea to judge people based on stereotypes. I thought most guitar players were laid back, their practice rooms stacked with back copies of *Rolling Stone* magazine, their nights spent jamming with local musicians in smoky dives. As my mom drove me to my first lesson (with a guy named Trace, of all things), I could almost picture the shaggy-haired figure in black band-shirt and sandals that would great me at the door. I couldn't have been more wrong. Trace wears generic khaki slacks. He generally sports a button up shirt and a pair of leather loafers. He shook my hand and invited me into a well-lit practice room. Instead of music magazines and old sofas, the room held two straight-back chairs. Along the far wall was a wooden workbench beneath a large peg board filled with hooks holding wrenches, pliers, screwdrivers, meters, clamps, and implements that seemed like they'd be more at home on some surgical tray in an operating room. That was my first lesson: don't take anything for granted. It sounds corny, but it turns out that Trace Waters was not meant to teach me about guitar (though I have learned to play), but about life.

I knew Trace was not your typical teacher when our lesson began with him pointing to the workbench and asking me to lay down my guitar. "Your guitar needs some work," he said.

The guitar was brand new (a "starter pack" Epiphone model just unwrapped on my twelfth birthday the week before), but not wanting to argue I laid down the instrument and managed a vague response. "Okay."

"Let's get started."

"I've never played an instrument," I admitted, trying to lower any expectations.

"That's why we're here." He smiled and pointed to the peg board with its perfectly arranged tools. "This is a Phillips head screwdriver, sometimes called a cross-drive or cross-head screwdriver. These are needle-nose pliers. This is a peg winder. These wipes remove oil from your skin. . . . "

Trace knows everything about every tool because he once apprenticed with a Mercedes mechanic. After high school, he decided to forego the straight-to-college route and move to California. With no contacts and few prospects he cold-called every business in Manhattan Beach until the owner of a small import auto repair shop took pity on him, giving him his first job washing parts and mopping the garage floor. "I spent my first six months up to my elbows in the solvent tank," he recalls. "But I learned a lot. I'd show some kind of gear or chain to my boss, Albert, and he'd bark out something like 'not clean enough; do it again.'" Trace briefly scrapes his top teeth over his lower lip, thinking. "Albert might yell, but then he'd explain how the gear and chain worked together to open the valves, how the valves brought the fuel into the engine, how it all had to be timed just right and we needed to see all the marks on the gear. Even cleaning some random car part became a lesson in the workings of the internal combustion engine."

Trace credits the three years spent working on cars with his philosophy toward life. He sounds like some kind of figure from a 1950s family sitcom as he explains. "You have to take pride in everything. If you skimp anywhere, it will seep into other areas of your life and come back to bite you." He recalls once forgetting to check the fit of a valve cover and the near-disastrous consequences. "There was oil everywhere, but it could have been a lot worse. I could have ruined a five thousand dollar engine. You have to be focused and precise. You check and recheck. And you pay attention to details. It matters."

After California, he moved back east to study music in New York. He got his degree in classical music, putting himself through school by playing in bands and working the kitchen at a restaurant called the Cedar Tavern. "I met all kinds of great people—musicians, artists, just great people." Trace tells me this as we're making guacamole in his kitchen. I'm interviewing him for this profile and realizing that what makes Trace an amazing teacher is he brings his philosophy of pride and precision to everything he does. And he never misses an opportunity to turn the littlest things into a lesson. "When you add the lime juice to the avocado, the citric acid will keep the dip from browning as much. It's oxidization that makes it brown. We'll use these plastic knives and forks to chop and stir—less metal in the process can help." Anyone can make guacamole, I think to myself. And we'll probably eat it all before it even has a chance to go brown. But Trace has to make it just so, every detail just right, every move thought through.

But there's more to Trace Waters than a sharp mind and an attention to detail. I ask Trace why he left New York, why he dropped the bands and started giving lessons full time. "That's easy," he responds. "I was challenged. When I worked on cars, Albert told me one day I'd have a chance to make something of myself and he said, 'I challenge you. Push yourself to do something more than what seems easy or obvious.'" In New York, Trace's career was about to take off. Things were lining up perfectly. "I was wrapping up my school and making connections. I had a nice job lined up making soundtracks for a media company. But something was off." Trace explains that he kept thinking about the way that Albert pushed him and about the challenge he had been given years earlier to look beyond the easy solution. Just as he was about to embark on the path to become a working musician, Trace realized exactly what his challenge would be: to carry forward the advice that he himself had been given by his mentor.

As I listen to Trace, I can't help but recall my own experience. It was sometime during my second year of lessons when I told Trace I was thinking about putting the guitar aside. "There aren't many band opportunities for girls," I said. "My chorus teacher wants to move me up to concert choir."

"Whoa, no way," he shot back. "Keep singing, but don't quit guitar. It might be tough, but that's exactly why you have to do it."

It was hard trying to become a girl who plays electric guitar and I was ready to walk away, but Trace would have none of it. The very next week he introduced me to a drummer, Bridgette. Three weeks later Megan and Paige joined us. The next month, Trace signed us all up for the local battle of the bands concert. For the next seven years we played together, eventually landing the headlining act at our homecoming dance. It turns out people wanted to hear from girls who could play music. It turns out we had a lot to say. I now see why Trace took the path he did, why we went from wanderer to mechanic to New York artist to the best teacher I have known in my life. He had responded to his own personal challenge, which was helping me discover and respond to mine.

Reflect on the Reading

Questions About "The Challenge Question"

1. In some ways, Susan's profile also contains elements of a memoir, since she discusses the profile subject in terms of her own experiences. What can you say about this blending of genres? Does it make the profile more or less successful, in your opinion?

2. How well does Susan's profile take an angle on its subject? Are there spots where it goes out of focus? What suggestions would you make for adjusting the focus of essay?

3. What strategies of narration or other techniques stand out in the essay? What suggestions might you offer for bringing the profile subject to life?

4. How important are the details included in Susan's profile. Do you feel like the focus on everyday episodes like the making of guacamole diminishes the impact of the profile's message? Why or why not?

WN

RESOURCE
Sample Profiles

Revise It   Strategies for Revising Profiles

As you revise your profile, consider a few areas that can help improve your composition. First, be sure to gather feedback. You might seek feedback from someone who is unfamiliar with your profile subject so he or she can give you a sense of how well you communicate key points. Also keep these strategies in mind:

- Make sure you have an angle that distills the aspects of your subject's life into a focused topic for the profile.
- Think about the narrative structure of the essay. Developing the essay around a sequence of events can help provide a logical structure. Still, you might break up this kind of sequencing to grab the interest of your readers or emphasize a key episode.
- Check that you are providing enough details and descriptions of the subject. Profiles should bring the person to life for your readers. Consider key traits of the subject, and then use language that offers enough detail to make those traits palpable for readers.
- Check that you have used quotations or dialog to give the essay interest and bring out aspects of the subject of the profile.
- Use images or formatting elements to further engage your readers. Be sure that the underlying structure and content of the essay convey a clear message about your subject. Extend this message by adjusting the look and arrangement of the profile.

- Revise many times, refining your focus and bringing the profile subject to life as you go. As you move into the later stages of revision, tighten language, and polish the surface-level and mechanical details of the essay.

Push It   More Possibilities for Profiles

VIDEO
33. Composing a Playlist

1. Compose a playlist that represents the identity or tells the story of a person. Begin by identifying a subject for your profile. Next, create an annotated list of songs that provides a profile of your subject. If your subject, for instance, had trouble in school, struggled with addiction, and then overcame those obstacles, you could collect a list of songs that represents that journey. Compose your list of songs and brief annotations demonstrating the ways the songs convey a message about your profile subject. Excerpt passages from the lyrics of the songs to help get across your message. You can compose this list and explanations in a word processor or on a class Web site. You can also make links to any song samples available online and to copies of the songs' lyrics. (See Chapter E5 for more on playlists.)

Learning Objective 6.4

2. Compose an audio essay profiling a person. Identify a subject, keeping in mind the need to find audio samples for the essay. Look first to see whether there are interviews or audio essays discussing a public figure. For a personal acquaintance, you can conduct your own interviews. Develop a plan for the essay and then create an opening segment that engages your listener and introduces your profile subject. Add your own narration and interview segments to develop the profile. Incorporate additional relevant audio materials—song samples for musicians, speech excerpts for politicians, ambient sounds, etc. Edit the essay to ensure that it flows and tells the profile subject's story while pointing to a larger issue. Polish the piece, and then post it online for listeners. (See Chapter E3 for more on audio essays.)

Zoom Out   Reflecting on Profiles

- **Profiles are about one of the key elements of cultural networks: people.** Profiles can zoom in on this element, but they can also draw connections with things or ideas, demonstrating how culture has shaped an individual and how that person illuminates concerns like perseverance, success, compassion, etc.

- **Profiles tell stories.** A good profile uses narration strategies to demonstrate events. Profiles also use description and details to bring the subject to life.
- **Profiles zoom in, highlighting key episodes rather than providing a birth-to-deathbed account of a person's life.** Identifying these episodes and discussing them to make deliberate points brings out the focus of the profile.
- **Profiles are suited to a range of media.** Audio profiles work well at integrating interview materials and giving voice to a profile subject. Images, similarly, can make the subject of a profile visually present for an audience.

For additional information and practice with the learning objectives in this chapter, go to www.mycomplab.com, Resources > Writing > Writing Purposes > Writing to Describe

Rhetorical Analyses

 Zoom **In**   **Key Concepts and Learning Objectives**

After studying this chapter, you should be able to:

7.1 Compose a rhetorical analysis that looks carefully at the ways in which a text delivers its message.

7.2 Analyze rhetorical situations and appeals in order to offer insights into texts.

7.3 Find and select print and non-print texts for analysis.

7.4 Discuss contexts and larger concerns when composing a rhetorical analysis.

Do you remember taking reading comprehension exams during your early school years? You were likely given a couple of paragraphs and then asked a series of questions to see how well you understood the passage. In some ways, a rhetorical analysis is a more extended version of the assignment. You train your attention on some kind of text and discuss what you see.

What sets a rhetorical analysis apart is that you also focus on the way a text works. You might, for instance, examine how the text makes appeals to its audience. You would look at other elements of the rhetorical situation—the authority of the speaker or the purposes informing the text. You would also look at specific strategies used in a text and at other details. Does a text appeal to your emotions, to your intellect, or perhaps to both? In what ways? Does it use description, narration, statistics, or quotations, and if so, to what end?

And you will want to think of texts in flexible ways. Often a text tries to accomplish more than one thing. Sometimes the contexts surrounding what you study require detailed analysis. And sometimes you will have to make decisions about what kinds of texts to analyze. An advertisement certainly makes a good subject for a rhetorical analysis. You could also consider a nonprofit's promotional pamphlet, a street sign, or even a recyclable shopping bag. The more skilled you become at conducting rhetorical analyses, the more you will discover the interesting texts that surround you.

KEY TERMS

- **Rhetorical situation:** The setting in which any act of communication takes place. Rhetorical situations typically consist of a speaker, an audience, and a message. They are also connected with elements of culture (other texts, ideas, speakers, and readers, etc.).

- **Appeals:** The ways in which a text seeks to engage its readers. Common approaches are appeals to ethos (the credibility of the speaker), appeals to logos (the logic of the message), and appeals to pathos (the emotions).

- **Rhetorical strategies:** Methods of communicating the details of a message. Common strategies include narration, analysis, description, comparison, and persuasion.

- **Genres:** Categories used to classify, engage, and compose texts. Genres establish conventions that create expectations. Texts meet and adapt these conventions as they deliver their messages.

- **Medium:** The materials and mode of transmission used to create and deliver a message.

- **Text:** Any item crafted by humans that communicates a message. Familiar texts include essays, stories, and advertisements. A number of less familiar texts (films, songs, video games, etc.) can also be analyzed rhetorically.

- **Visual analysis:** Examining the rhetorical dimensions of images. Visual analysis considers arrangement, balance, contrast, emphasis, cropping, size, shape, line, color, and other elements of images.

Understanding Rhetorical Analyses

As you become more adept at conducting rhetorical analyses, you will find that you can apply the skill to a range of items. From music to films to product packaging to T-shirt slogans, all kinds of texts and messages reveal insights and rhetorical dimensions as you subject them to analysis. Here we will look specifically at strategies for analyzing words and images.

Analyzing Texts Made of Words

Let's take a closer look at how a rhetorical analysis can work when applied to written or spoken words. We will start with a reading, an analysis of two political speeches from the 2008 U.S. presidential campaign.

Reading the Speeches of McCain and Obama Has Made Me Ashamed of Our Political Class
BY **MATTHEW PARIS**

Learning
Objective 7.1

Matthew Paris writes for the British newspaper, The Times. *He has worked for almost two decades on the paper's political beat. He is also the author of numerous books on travel and politics. "Reading the Speeches of McCain and Obama Has Made Me Ashamed of Our Political Class" appeared in* The Times *on March 29, 2008.*

Rather less than two years ago, bored and with time to kill at a Conservative party conference, I decided to do what is for a British journalist a rather unusual thing. I decided

Reading the
Speeches of
McCain and Obama
has Made Me
Ashamed of Our
Political Class
(continued)
BY **MATTHEW PARIS**

to read a whole speech, a long speech by a politician, a speech with no particular news value. I decided to read every word.

The full text happened to be lying on my bed. I had taken it from a huge pile left largely untouched on the counter of the Press Office. It was Senator John McCain's speech to the Tory conference. I knew that it had not caused much of a stir, had said nothing new, and that fellow journalists had reported it as ponderous, overlong and dull.

So I read it. And it was ponderous, overlong and often dull. Nor did the speech say anything surprising or new. There was nothing there worth remembering for future reference, or quoting to you now, two years later, nor any passage that seemed worth noting down. This was a speech cluttered with heavy furniture.

But it was his. You knew that at once. It had a certain old-fashioned style and respect for language that I admire. And it turned me into a convinced admirer of the Senator that I shall always now be. I finished reading, certain that an honourable and honest man was behind the writing, certain of his strength of mind and will, and certain of his almost abrasive sense of right and wrong.

I suppose the qualities that came through most were an uncompromising nature, and a certain thrilling carelessness whether or not he was keeping his reader with him. There were quaint, somewhat antique turns of speech that any Alastair Campbell would have removed at once; long, convoluted sentences with precarious dependent clauses; and an almost solemnly scholarly tone that reminded me of my dear, self-educated, bookish grandfather. Without being able to say how, I gained from it the strongest sense of a stiff-necked integrity that seemed both refreshing and different, and wholly admirable.

One of the ways that integrity came through, I remember noting, was in a stubborn if subliminal reluctance to overstate his case for the sake of effect; he never picked the easy, vulgar word. And (though I know McCain's reputation for impatience and sudden anger) an essential intellectual modesty came through: this speaker did not believe and so would not pretend that politics was easy or obvious; that every question had a clear answer; or that his opponents were wicked or stupid. I feel I learnt more about McCain in that quiet 20 minutes with his text in my hotel bedroom than I have since from months of reading news reports and commentaries.

Today I have repeated the experiment. I've just read an entire speech by Barack Obama: the Illinois Senator's recent speech in Philadelphia about race.

In many ways this speech could hardly be more different from Senator McCain's. Obama's text is crisp, modern, elegant, moving and stylish. It is also lucid—at times almost painfully so—and very much conceived as an exercise in communication. The speech has been drafted with its audience in mind at every turn, speaking clearly and carefully to the listener, anxious to keep us on board, and to keep our sympathy too.

But, however different, this speech, like McCain's, comes from the heart and the mind of the man who wrote it. It is his speech, and every word suggests he cares how he expresses himself and respects language. And, like McCain's, the speech has the confidence never to swagger or stoop; and the courage and intelligence to see and confess that the world, and America, is a complicated and ambivalent thing, and the easy answers often wrong.

Senator Obama's speech in Philadelphia is nearly 5,000 words long and should really be read in full and at a sitting, for its argument is sequential, gathering force as the text proceeds. You will find it easily on the internet. I shall restrict myself here to quoting his remarks about his church. Obama's campaign has been embarrassed, and his enemies handed ammunition, by this African-American church, and its retired black pastor's strident comments about race. The easy thing would have been to dissociate himself in simple terms from all three. Instead, he says this:

> The church contains in full the kindness and cruelty, the fierce intelligence and the shocking ignorance, the struggles and successes, the love and, yes, the bitterness and bias that make up the black experience in America.

> And this helps explain, perhaps, my relationship with Reverend Wright. As imperfect as he may be, he has been like family to me. He strengthened my faith, officiated my wedding, and baptised my children . . . He contains within him the contradictions— the good and the bad—of the community that he has served diligently for so many years. . . . I can no more disown him than I can disown the black community.

> I can no more disown him than I can my white grandmother—a woman who helped raise me, a woman who sacrificed again and again for me, a woman who loves me as much as she loves anything in this world, but a woman who once confessed her fear of black men who passed by her on the street, and who on more than one occasion has uttered racial or ethnic stereotypes that made me cringe.

> These people are a part of me.

You may agree on reading this that here is more than mere eloquence and more than mere emotion, however heartfelt. Behind the language lies such an intelligent recognition of the ambiguity of public and private life, and so honest an instinct to risk expressing it, that I shall never be able to think this would-be president a less than admirable person.

And before we British sneer, as is our habit, at the crudities of U.S. politics, maybe we should ask ourselves when we last saw a leading British politician invest such care and honesty—and such risk—in a speech. Turning aside from Senators Obama and McCain I return to Westminster, Blackpool, Bournemouth and Brighton, and the shallow reasoning and moral monochrome of our own political class, with their underlying assumption that a speech is for tonight's TV clips and tomorrow morning's newspapers, and nothing more; that thought clad in any permanent record is dangerous; and that the public recognition of ambivalence or complexity is an admission of weakness.

I know next to nothing about U.S. politics, and neither envy nor would try to emulate those journalistic colleagues who can speculate on the likely effect on this or that sector of

RESOURCES
Political Speeches

the American electorate of a would-be presidential candidate's remarks. I only know the effect of Obama's and McCain's speeches on me. They convince me that alongside the cynicism and shallow populism that democratic politics always brings, there can still subsist depth and integrity, and—yes, it matters—discernment and style.

"Reading the Speeches of McCain and Obama Has Made Me Ashamed of Our Political Class" by Matthew Paris from The Times, March 29, 2008. Copyright © 2008 The Times, nisyndication.com. Used by permission.

Reflect on the Reading

Questions About "Reading the Speeches of McCain and Obama Has Made Me Ashamed of Our Political Class"

1. What do you find most effective about the way the piece is written? What seems least effective?
2. Do you feel as if you have gotten enough information from Paris's article to make your own judgment about the two speeches? What additional analysis would you like to see?
3. What are your thoughts on the excerpts from Obama's speech that are included in Paris's piece? What points would you make in a rhetorical analysis of the excerpts?
4. Paris's piece suggests that both speeches reveal "honorable" or "admirable" men and that both speeches have refreshing elements of honesty. How would you relate this assessment to the kinds of judgments generally made about political speeches?

You can see in Paris's short assessment of the two speeches the key approach of a rhetorical analysis. The piece is primarily concerned with how the speeches work to deliver their messages. This focus on the methods used in a text takes a reader through much of the territory covered in the opening chapters of this book. Recall that in Chapter 1 we discuss the elements of rhetorical situations, situations in which a speaker presents a message to an audience. Paris focuses on the status of the speaker, on the audiences for the speeches, and on the contexts in which the speeches are delivered. This first level of analysis allows Paris to look at the texts in terms of big picture questions—who is speaking, in what context, to whom, and for what purpose.

You can use this initial assessment to think about the kinds of appeals made in a text. (See pages 109–11.) Texts often make appeals to readers based on ethos (the status of the speaker), pathos (emotions), or logos (logic). Paris suggests that the texts gave him a sense of the person "behind the writing," of the ethos or credibility and "honor" of the speakers. He also hints at appeals to logos, or logic, as he analyzes the way Obama's speech makes points about the complexities of his topic to help sway readers.

Recall also the advice about critical reading offered in Chapter 3. The author of a rhetorical analysis will ask questions and carefully read a text, zooming in to look at features in detail. Paris celebrates the way both speakers respect and care for language. He notes the sequential organization of Obama's speech. He discusses the "turns of speech" and language used by McCain, contrasting McCain's "scholarly tone" with the "crisp, modern" mood represented by Obama's words. In short, he zooms in to detail the way the speeches deliver their messages.

Finally, Paris zooms out to connect the speeches to a larger context and offer some conclusions. He makes comparisons between the speeches and what he sees in British political culture. He touches on the tendency of most British political speeches to avoid risks and honesty and to strive for sound bites fit for TV news. He makes a broader claim about the links between rhetorical style and complexity and integrity. In short, he extends the detailed discussion of how the speech works to offer insights into how it relates to elements of culture.

WN

VIDEO
4. Rhetorical
Appeals

Analyzing Images

When you analyze images, you will follow many of the same steps you take when you read anything critically. You will start with an open mind and broad focus, and then you will zoom in on specifics while you refine your thinking. You will eventually discover questions and identify rhetorical strategies suited to the visual medium. And you will zoom back out to think about connections and contexts as well as about the significance of the ideas you uncover.

Still, there are some strategies for reading visual materials that can come in handy as you explore. (See Chapter 25 for more on understanding visual compositions.) Begin by thinking about genre and medium (see pages 18–28). When reading a photograph, for instance, you might pay particular attention to how the image is framed or to the ways light is used to emphasize elements of the image. Examining a poster or magazine spread might involve thinking about layout or the mixing of words and images in the text.

Look at the arrangement of the elements in the image. It can be helpful to imagine a grid layered over an image so you can think about the placement of elements. Note any visual elements that stand out. A bright or dark color, or an object that jumps out might help you begin a reading of an image. Recurrent shapes, or odd shapes that strike the eye as well as bold or interesting lines might provide an entry into an image. Look also for points of contrast. Uses of light or color can create contrasts, as can shapes or objects.

Explore the focal points in the image. Often lighting is used to create focal points or points of emphasis. Sometimes the arrangement or use of shapes, colors, or lines can create focal points, and these focal points often pull your attention in a particular direction. Look also at the way the image is cropped or the way objects in the image are framed. Discover any messages that begin to

Learning
Objective 7.2

emerge as you examine the image. These messages may differ from what you would find in an essay, but nonetheless, you should be able to analyze them rhetorically using visual terms.

Figure 7.1 demonstrates some of the possibilities for performing this kind of analysis on an image. The figure is annotated to help illustrate how you can use critical reading strategies to think and write about images.

Know It   Strategies for Understanding Rhetorical Analyses

- Explore the ways in which a text delivers its message. Examine any larger contexts or concerns through the lens of careful reading of the rhetorical moves in the text.
- Consider the rhetorical situation associated with a text. Ask questions about speaker and audience to open avenues for exploring a text. Think about the purposes that inform a text to help you understand the message.
- Extend analysis of the rhetorical situation by thinking about appeals made by a text. Think about the ways texts play to your emotions or rely on the ethos of their speakers. Examine the logic of the claims made in a text.
- Ask questions about genre and medium to guide your rhetorical analysis. Ask how conventions shape a text. Consider how the text resists or modifies expectations.
- Zoom in to critically read the details of a text. How does a text use description, narration, dialog, comparison or some other writing strategies? What can be said about the use of language or the tone of the text?
- Learn to analyze a range of texts. Understand how to read and write about images, sounds, and videos. Consider how media elements mix in a text.
- Zoom out to make connections and offer conclusions based on your rhetorical analysis. Don't stray too far from the primary work of analyzing rhetorical moves, but do extend your analysis to consider associations with people, ideas, and things.

Ask Questions & Make Decisions   Exercises for Understanding Rhetorical Analyses

1. Search online for political speeches and select one to analyze. Write a paragraph analyzing the speech in terms of Paris's claim that most political speeches lack depth and integrity.
2. Watch at least ten advertisements on television or on the Web, analyzing them to identify appeals made to ethos, pathos, or logos. Make a chart listing the number of each type of appeal that you discover.

FIGURE 7.1
Poster for Buffalo Bill's
Wild West Show
(Library of Congress).

❶ Because this image takes the form of a poster, it includes a number of pieces of text. The banner at the top is meant to quickly grab the attention of viewers. The smaller print at the bottom provides specifics about the touring Buffalo Bill show advertised by the poster. What other things can you say about the image based on its status as a promotional poster?

❷ Notice the use of color in the image. The leg in the foreground emphasizes the Native American with a none-too-subtle saturation of dark red color. Look elsewhere at the use of red in the image. What messages does this color send? What other colors are interesting in the image and why?

❸ The repetition of the Native American figures forms a visual and thematic pattern. How would you relate the repeated figures with the series of wagons stretching into the distance? What other patterns stand out and what messages do they convey?

❹ Notice how the horse in the lower-left quadrant of the image is painted using sharp contrasts

between white and reddish brown. The use of contrast helps the horse stand out and creates a focal point for the eye. Is it fair to say that the reddish brown also resonates with the use of red in the image?

❺ You can read images like other texts, looking for stories and messages. What story can you come up with based on the figure in the center of the image on the black horse? What other stories or messages can you discover in the image?

❻ The poster creates several direct links to its context. Buffalo Bill is mythologized in the poster as a courageous frontiersman, but if we look deeper into the historical figure of William Frederic Cody, we will soon uncover questions about nineteenth-century frontier encounters as well as interesting topics about early forms of media promotion and showmanship. How might what you know or learn about frontier history or entertainment influence your reading of the image?

Exercises for Understanding Rhetorical Analyses
(continued)

3. Identify a text with which people are familiar (for instance, "The Gettysburg Address," *Star Wars*, *Moby Dick*, "Letter from Birmingham Jail," an ad campaign advertisement). Write a page or more connecting the text with elements of culture.

4. Find a contemporary image promoting a public figure or media event—a movie poster, video game ad, concert promotion, or similar item. Compare the visual composition in the contemporary item with that of the Buffalo Bill poster on page 185. What visual elements or persuasive strategies do they share? Are the pieces more similar or different?

5. On a sheet of paper, make two columns. Working with a small group of peers, list in the first column all of the things that make reading printed texts difficult. In the second column, list all of the challenges related to reading images. Decide which you find more difficult, texts or images, and for what reasons. Report your findings to your other classmates.

Readings and Resources for Exploring Rhetorical Analyses

Texts flow through our cultural networks in every direction. When people stop to consider the ways these works deliver their messages, they create careful readings that examine these texts and their contexts. You can discover these analyses as you encounter reviews, reports, and analyses everywhere. A few examples are provided below: Jennie Yabroff and Susan Elgin analyze the television series *Mad Men* and Francine Prose examines Car Girls, a series of photographs depicting female auto show models.

⬎ A Word From our Sponsor
BY **JENNIE YABROFF (WITH SUSAN ELGIN)**

Jennie Yabroff is freelance author who contributes regularly to a number of magazines including Newsweek *and* Salon. *She focuses on society with a special emphasis on culture and the media. "A Word from Our Sponsor" appeared in* Newsweek *in August 2008.*

"Mad Men" may be set in the 1960s, but the show's period-piece ads tell us plenty about ourselves.

This week on "Mad Men": an American Airlines flight has crashed into Jamaica Bay just after takeoff. All 95 passengers are dead, but that doesn't stop the Sterling Cooper ad agency from engaging in a bit of gallows humor. One junior staffer says that because of the number of golfers onboard, the bay turned plaid. Another riffs on a new slogan for American: "Idlewild to Rockaway in less than eight minutes." And then (slight spoiler alert here) one young ad man learns that his own father was on the plane. He—we won't spoil it entirely by telling you which one—stumbles out of the office in a daze, only to find out when he returns the next day that the higher-ups now want to go after American for real—and they want him to lead the campaign to rehabilitate the airline's image after the crash. He says that would be inappropriate: "I haven't even cried yet." But viewers familiar with AMC's hit drama know that the normal constraints of decency rarely apply at Sterling Cooper. In the end, the young staffer not only shows up for the pitch to American, he uses his personal tragedy as a calling card.

The first season of "Mad Men" sought to simultaneously celebrate the creativity of advertising and reveal the underside of the American Dream. But this new season—with its stories of plane crashes and prostitution in the first two episodes alone—looks darker. "Mad Men" pointedly blurs the line between the way the characters sell their products and the way they sell themselves. The show is a period piece—at times self-consciously so—that traffics in our modern, dystopian view of America as a nation of sellouts. Balancing the vintage and the contemporary is all the more challenging given how different the world of advertising was in the "Mad Men" era from today. "Advertising back then was still largely visible as a blight on the landscape, a billboard or an annoying interruption of your favorite TV or radio programs," says Mark Crispin Miller, an NYU professor who is writing a history of the Marlboro Man campaign. "It's not that way anymore."

The notion of selling yourself hasn't always been linked to advertising. In the industry's early days, the focus was on logic. Earnestly worded, essay-length "reason why" ads carefully spelled out a product's benefits. By the era of "Mad Men," consumers had become sophisticated about marketers' methods—or so they thought. "Advertising doesn't work on me," a date boasts to Peggy in one episode. She snaps back that when advertising is good, people never think it works. In fact, advertisers have long exploited consumers' sense of themselves as insiders, says Miller. "People who work in advertising are smart enough to recognize that people like to think they are too clever to be taken in by commercials. So a lot of commercials goof on advertising," he says. "Mad Men" gives a nod to one of the most effective examples when the staff at Sterling Cooper passes around Volkswagen's celebrated "lemon" ads. The ads cheekily copped to producing the occasional bad product. "That campaign is famous for having an attitude that acknowledged consumers' skepticism," says Rob Walker, author of "Buying In: The Secret Dialogue Between Who We Are and What We Buy." "It communicates that the audience is sophisticated enough to understand the language of advertising."

The 1960s, when the series is set, are known as a "golden age" of advertising because of the creativity in art and copy. But the period might just as well be called the

A Word From our
Sponsor *(continued)*
BY **JENNIE YABROFF**
(WITH SUSAN ELGIN)

age of polished brass, since the idea of truth in ads was just then giving way to the primacy of emotional persuasion. Instead of touting a product's merits, advertisers in the '60s strove to evoke a feeling or philosophy—there's a good reason those Marlboro Man ads are considered to be the most successful campaign ever (and notice how everyone on "Mad Men" smokes, even though they're privy to some of the early studies on smoking and health). The stealth approach rules today, when ads sometimes don't even show the product, let alone spend paragraphs explaining why we should buy it. It's how we've arrived at the era of the viral ad video, which marketers post on the Web in hopes that it will take on a life of its own. Remember the Levi's clips featuring young men doing back flips into their jeans? The mystery around their origin—the brand is never mentioned—only fueled their popularity. "Images don't make claims," says Peggy Kreshel, a professor of advertising at the University of Georgia. "You can't argue with an image the same way you argue with a printed word."

Critics of "Mad Men" say that the show makes the job appear effortless, as though brilliant ad copy is the result of happy inspiration while playing with your kids or chatting with your waiter. "'Mad Men' makes creativity look like it is serendipitous. It's true that ad ideas come from anywhere, but it's not as easy as it looks," says Kreshel. But it's just this sense that any spontaneous sentiment or offhand remark can be put to use to sell a product that makes the show so insidious. In one of the signature scenes from the first "Mad Men" season, Kodak is looking for a campaign for its new slide projector "wheel." It wants to focus on the technology, but the head of creative understands that advertising has become about making an emotional connection with consumers. In the pitch meeting, he loads the wheel—which he's romantically renamed the "carousel"—with pictures of his wife and kids, essentially selling his family to win the account. In this week's episode, Peggy states the equation more bluntly. When a guy she meets at a party asks her to go home with him, she says: "I'm in the persuasion business, and frankly I'm disappointed by your presentation." The power of advertising doesn't get more personal, or painful, than that.

Reflect on the Reading

Questions About "A Word from Our Sponsor"

1. Do you agree that contemporary advertising is no longer primarily concerned with logic? Why or why not?

2. What do you find most effective about the way "A Word from Our Sponsor" is written? What seems least effective?

3. Yabroff's piece analyzes the television show *Mad Men,* but also discusses advertising in general. How does this strategy impact your understanding of the show itself?

4. Yabroff quotes a number of advertising scholars in her piece. How does the use of these citations relate to the impact the article has on you as a reader?

⤷ Auto Erotic: Jacqueline Hassink's Car Girls
BY **FRANCINE PROSE**

Francine Prose teaches literature at Bard College. She is the author of several novels, including Blue Angel, Household Saints, *and* The Glorious Ones. *Her work frequently takes up themes of gender and sexuality. "Auto Erotic: Jacqueline Hassink's Car Girls" was published in the journal* Aperture *in 1997.*

By now, to point out that car manufacturers use sex, or the promise of sex, to sell automobiles seems as self-evident—as banal—as saying that the purpose of advertising is to create desire. Who has not seen a TV commercial in which a hot, beautiful woman slides into the passenger seat of an equally hot, beautiful sports car, her short skirt rucking up as her dashing male companion reaches for the gearshift?

Yet the photographs in Jacqueline Hassink's Car Girls series have the power to make us rethink the association between auto and eros as if it had never occurred to us, and to see it newly in all its sheer outrageous strangeness. Shot in the high-tech, futuristic, glossy, and elaborately stage-managed glare of car shows in the United States, Europe, and Asia, these photographs seem like stills from an otherworldly porn movie in which the participants are not just fully clothed but elaborately costumed, a film in which a changing cast of voyeurs are invited to observe a sex act involving a woman and a V8 engine.

These images make you long to have been a fly on the wall at the board meeting at which it was decided what the women would wear, outfits (like those worn by "Jeep girl" in Shanghai and the "Ferrari girl" in Geneva) that are not only color-coordinated to match the car, but designed to mimic the experience of driving it. Sporty or elegant, racy or refined, these women put a new spin on the concept of commodification. Dressed to complement the vehicles they represent, they seem like auto-accessories, like the air fresheners and floor-mats you can buy while you're killing

FIGURE 7.2
Ferrari Girl, Paris
(Jacqueline Hassink).

time at the car wash or the garage—air fresheners and floor-mats that might have sex with you if you can afford it.

What's so daring about these photographs is how they approach, almost recklessly, the territory of the car advertisement, and then veer away, as if at the last moment, to suggest everything that has gone into producing that ad: focus groups, market research, all the glories, excesses, and anxieties of end-stage capitalism. It's fascinating to track the differences between countries and cultures: in Tokyo the women are pure male fantasy, while in New York the car girls' all-business power-suits mean that someone has noticed that a growing number of potential buyers are women, with their own ideas about what it might mean to buy and drive a certain make or model.

In her work, the Dutch-born Hassink has long been engaged by the stark contrasts and shifting borderlines between the public and the private, the corporate and the domestic, the individual and the collective. Finally, what gives her Car Girls series its resonance is her continuing exploration of that divide. While some of the car girls exist in airy isolation, breathing the ether of the gauzy consumer dream, others—in Detroit and Geneva—must put up with the intrusions and incursions of the customer looking back, or—in Shanghai—taking pictures. Meanwhile, the static perfection of these women's public selves makes the glimpses of them chatting or thinking or just standing around—off-duty, and a little slumped—seem startlingly intimate.

With subtlety and humor, Hassink succeeds in showing us that these women are, in fact, neither air fresheners nor sex dolls, but actual human beings. You look at these beautiful, strangely dressed women posed alongside gorgeous vehicles, and you can almost see them wondering how much longer they have to stand there until the show ends and they can change back into their own clothes, and get into a bus or a taxi, or their own unstylish, second-hand cars, and go home.

Reflect on the Reading

Questions About "Auto Erotic: Jacqueline Hassink's Car Girls"

1. The article claims that Hassink's photographs have the power to make us "rethink the association between auto and eros." After looking at the image in Figure 5.2, would you agree or disagree? Why?

2. How much time does Francine Prose spend discussing the details of Hassink's images? Do you feel as if the discussion is adequate for demonstrating the points Prose wishes to make?

3. The piece touches on several elements of culture—cars, sexuality in advertising, boundaries between public and private life, etc. What are your thoughts on the ways the article balances analysis of photographs with discussions of culture? What recommendations might you give to Prose along these lines?

4. Search online for Jacqueline Hassink's Car Girls series of photographs. Explore a number of the images and then think about how you would compose your own analysis. What points from Prose might you reiterate or extend? What points of your own would you offer?

Writing Assignment: A Rhetorical Analysis

Write an essay in which you analyze the way a text delivers its message. Consider the rhetorical situation that relates to your text. What can you say about the speaker, the audiences for the text, and purposes informing the piece? Think about genre and medium conventions and about appeals offered in the text. Examine the strategies used and the details that are present in the text. Use the detailed discussion you provide of the rhetorical moves made in the text to offer insights into larger concerns. Make good use of critical thinking strategies as you begin, allowing careful reading of the text to drive your project.

Ask Questions & Make Decisions

LO

Learning Objective 7.3

Exercises for Composing Rhetorical Analyses

1. Write a summary of two or more paragraphs for any of the readings in this book. Include discussion of the rhetorical situation, details about the way the text delivers its message, and some thoughts about larger concerns related to the text.

2. Search online for an image that lends itself to analysis. Review the advice for reading images in Chapter 25 and then make a list of all the visual communication strategies you can discover in the image.

3. Select a well-known text—something like the Declaration of Independence, an important political speech, or a famous work of literature. Look over the item and then identify two rhetorical elements that you believe give the text its staying power.

Plan It   Invention Strategies for Rhetorical Analyses

Remember that rhetorical analyses should rely heavily on careful reading. Focus on zooming in and out as you engage a text. Think about the cultural contexts and the rhetorical situation of the text. How can you tell who is writing and for whom? Think also about the purposes informing the piece and appeals made in the text. Ask questions about genres and mediums. Here are some helpful strategies:

- Consider what you know about rhetoric and communication. What makes a text interesting in how it delivers its message? What kinds of rhetorical strategies do you like to encounter and why? What ways of communicating make you most suspicious or concerned?
- Think about possible texts to be analyzed. Ask about texts that have not been frequently discussed by others. Or think of texts that have been discussed, but about which you think people have missed the point. Think about texts that have always troubled or confused you. Consider a favorite text that others should know about.
- Choose a text to write about. Check with your instructor if you are unsure about your selection. Get a copy of the text and any information about its authorship and publication.
- Read the text carefully. Identify the key rhetorical features that strike you. Ask questions about the rhetorical situation, about genre and medium, about appeals that are directed at readers, and about the details of the text.
- Think about how the text compares to related items. Conduct research to find out more about the text or the topic. (See Chapters 14–17.)
- Ask questions about the cultural elements associated with the text. Does the text respond to anything specific? What larger concerns inform the text?

CONNECT IT   More Resources for Rhetorical Analyses

For more detailed information about some of the strategies you might use in rhetorical analyses, consider the following resources:

For more on rhetorical situations, see Chapter 1.

For more on critical reading and thinking, see Chapter 3.

For more on analyzing books, music, and films, see Chapter 11.

For more on analyzing works of literature, see Chapter 12.

For more on reading and composing with visuals, see Chapters 25 and 26.

For more on describing, see Chapter 21.

For more on analyzing, see pages 62–65.

For more on comparing and contrasting, see Chapter 23.

✳ Compose It Write a Rhetorical Analysis

As you compose your rhetorical analysis, you will zoom in and out. From the word choices to the structure of the text, you will need to describe the details of the piece you are looking at. Act as the eyes and ears of your reader. Help them see the facets of the text you wish to highlight, rather than assume they have already read the piece or will interpret it just as you do. Also spell out connections with the big picture. Does the piece respond to a specific event? Is there a history of similar texts that might be traced to better understand the item you are studying? Compose a response that allows you to explore the larger significance of the text you are analyzing. Consider the following steps:

- Situate the text for readers. You might open the analysis with background information—provide details about the authorship and publication of the text.
- Demonstrate associations that illuminate the text. Trace the lineage of a text—for instance, showing precursors like *Pocahontas* as you begin to analyze *Avatar*. Compare and contrast the text with related items.
- Spend some time discussing the rhetorical situation of the text. Identify and explore connections with the speaker. Explore the audience and examine purposes informing the text.
- Identify specific strategies used in the text. Zoom in on one or two strategies in particular and discuss their details.
- Look for points where you can evaluate what you see. Analyses strive to be objective, but you should still take ownership and offer conclusions about what you discuss.
- Zoom out to consider how the text relates to elements of culture. Should you address the text in terms of people associated with it? What cultural concerns deserve discussion? Balance the emphasis on reading the text with some consideration of the bigger picture.

LO

Learning
Objective 7.4

✳ Focus on Student Writing Organic Labeling and Rhetorical Situations

BY **KRISTEN WILLIAMS**

Like all genres, rhetorical analyses are flexible, sharing some solid conventions, but also allowing authors to adjust their approach and produce a message in tune with their rhetorical situations. In this essay, Kristen Williams is particularly interested in the marketing of organic products. She expresses that interest through an analysis that focuses heavily on rhetorical situations related to product labeling.

Kristen Williams

Professor Anderson

English 102

15 Dec. 2007

Organic Labeling and Rhetorical Situations

Most companies have gotten pretty sophisticated about pitching products. Take the packaging for Stonyfield Farm's yobaby yogurt. From the earth tones in the carton to the fruit and flowers in the artwork to the angelic faces of the babies, the packaging is well designed to deliver the message that yobaby is natural and healthy. But the package contains one other detail that asks us to think more deeply about the rhetorical situations in which products like this one get produced and marketed. This extra detail is the organic label displayed prominently at the top of the carton. Unlike the images or package design, the organic label must be approved by the United States Department of Agriculture (USDA) before it can be applied. But how do we know when something is organic? Environmental groups have a different idea about what qualifies as organic from that of many corporations, even natural food corporations. If we look at the way these groups debate the organic label, we can make better judgments about specific products and learn more about this larger context in which companies, consumers, and environmental groups exchange messages about organic foods.

In late 2007, a number of consumers filed a lawsuit against several grocery chains. The suit claimed that the stores knowingly sold milk that had been labeled organic, despite the fact that the company producing the milk, Aurora Farms, had been cited by the USDA for deliberately ignoring organic standards. A recent article in the *Seattle Post-Intelligencer* points out that there is a discrepancy between the conditions under which the milk is produced and the way it is marketed to the public:

> Stores sell Aurora's milk under their own in-house brand names, such as Costco's Kirkland and Target's Archer Farms, in cartons marked "USDA organic," typically with pictures of pastures or other bucolic scenes.

"That's not even close to the reality of where this milk was coming from,"
said Steve Berman, a Seattle lawyer whose firm is among those suing.
"These cows are all penned in factory-confinement conditions." (Johnson)

The lawsuit reinforces the lessons we can gather from simply looking at packaging and marketing practices related to organic foods. It makes sense for corporations to create messages that emphasize a natural, even innocent environment where products come from the land and animals are well cared for, even happy. This friendly farm myth is a big part of the appeal of organic packaging because it matches with the values of the consumers of most of these products. This audience is interested in the back-to-nature story because it offers a counter example to contemporary urban or suburban culture based on consumerism: the message is that the products represent a simpler, almost utopian time. Further, the messages target the ethical concerns of their audience. The idea that animals are not mistreated appeals to the sense of moral right and wrong held by most consumers of organic products.

But thinking about the producers of these messages helps us see that the back-to-nature story may well be more myth than reality. The Web site of Aurora Organic Dairy, for instance, includes many details that further the organic story. The menu is set over a background of rolling hills sparsely populated with a handful of grazing cows, complete with a rustic barn in the background. The opening page even includes a video with more open fields and happy cows. The site makes a clear emotional appeal. In one screen from the video, an adult cow (the mom) gently cleans the face of a calf with her tongue. Even in this image, however, we can see the disparity between the myth of the natural farm and the reality of the production of many organic products. The mother cow sports an ear tag bearing the number 1514. It's impossible to know how many cows make up the herd at Aurora, but the tag raises questions about the scale of the operation even as it tries to convey the family farm message. Other pages on the Aurora Web site raise further questions. The products page contains a category for "bulk/industrial" products and the milk page features packaging containing the label "Your Brand," inviting potential distributors to make large purchases and sell the product under their labels, the practice targeted in the 2007 lawsuit.

Looking at the discrepancies between the myth and the realities in the messages shows us that it's difficult to understand the debates about labeling organic products without also understanding the economics of the situation. Much of the debate about standards has to do with the scale of organic farming. Aurora foods, the producer of the milk, is one of the largest suppliers of organic dairy products. As the *Post-Intelligencer* tells us,

> The legal disputes are the latest front in the battle over the organic food movement, with large corporate players insisting that they can do organic farming on a large scale, and sustainable family farms complaining that such operations aren't really organic and contribute to surpluses that drive down prices, making it harder for them to compete. (Johnson)

We see that discussions about the organic label must also take up questions about economics. The conversation turns into a debate about the motives of organic corporations and the nature of USDA certification. Are farms like Aurora simply using larger scale operations to meet a growing demand for organic products? Aurora Dairy has maintained USDA organic certification for its facilities since 2003, and the lawsuits reported in the article have been dismissed based on Aurora's USDA certification. We see that the debate moves to what it means to be certified by the USDA. And we see many groups eager to join the debate. The nonprofit group the Cornucopia Institute, for instance, produces and distributes a report titled "Maintaining the Integrity of Organic Milk." The report exposes "factory farms that are employing suspect practices that skirt organic regulations and negatively impact human nutrition and the health and well-being of livestock" (4). The Institute distributes the report and shares other resources about family-scale farming on their Web site.

Of course, the Cornucopia Institute is just one among many groups pouring out information about organic farming. Entities like the Organic Trade Association (OTA) serve to promote organic products but represent not organic consumers but the organic industry. The OTA

Williams 4

has encouraged the USDA to allow a number of nonorganic products to be included in foods that are still given the organic label. These developments are reported on by consumer organizations and on blogs or Web sites like *The Daily Green*, which cites among the organizations lobbying for the inclusion of nonorganic ingredients Stonyfield Farms, which has requested that nonorganic Inulin (a substance that comes from chicory plants) be allowed in organic products "to increase the nutritional value of calcium in yogurt by making it easier for the body to absorb" ("38 Non-Organic Ingredients"). So the debate about organic labeling brings us back to Stonyfield yogurt and their packaging. The point is not that Stonyfield should be included among the groups criticized by organizations like the Cornucopia Institute, but that the organic labeling debate reveals a much larger rhetorical situation in which many groups communicate. The USDA sets guidelines about labeling products. Organic providers lobby government entities like the USDA. Consumer groups expose what they see as bad practices. News groups report on lawsuits. Looking over the offerings in the grocery store is just the first step in understanding a whole range of communication that extends far beyond decisions about how to design a yogurt package.

Works Cited

Aurora Organic Dairy. Home page. 2007. Web. 14 Dec. 2007.

Cornucopia Institute. "Maintaining the Integrity of Organic Milk." *Cornucopia Institute*. Cornucopia Institute, 2007. Web. 14 Dec. 2007.

Johnson, Gene. "Lawsuits: Costco, Others Sold 'Organic' Milk That Wasn't Organic." *Seattle Post-Intelligencer*. Hearst Seattle Media, 13 Dec. 2007. Web. 14 Dec. 2007.

"38 Non-Organic Ingredients Found in 'USDA Organic' Foods." *The Daily Green*. Hearst Communications, 19 July 2007. Web. Dec. 14 2007.

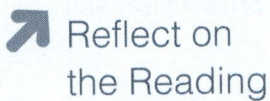

Reflect on
the Reading

Questions About "Organic Labeling and Rhetorical Situations"

1. Kristen's essay looks at the rhetorical situation in which organic dairy packaging is produced. Do you feel as if the essay captures the essential elements of this rhetorical situation? Does the essay adequately look at the speaker, audience, message, and context? Which of these elements might be covered in more depth?

2. As an analysis essay, "Organic Labeling and Rhetorical Situations" should provide opportunities for Kristen and the reader to zoom in on the details of the text under study. Did the essay help you understand the rhetorical moves made in the yogurt packaging? If so, how? If not, what changes might you suggest?

3. What strategies can you discover in Kristen's essay for conveying information? Do you find the strategies effective? Why or why not?

4. Are you able to pick out Kristen's position on organic farming among the analysis in the essay? What would you say to someone who argued that the essay is really a persuasive piece of writing meant to argue against factory farms?

Revise It Revision Strategies for Rhetorical Analyses

When you have a draft finished, share it with peers and revise the analysis based on feedback. Like any kind of composition, rhetorical analyses benefit most from multiple revisions. Here are some additional strategies that can help:

- Check that you discuss rhetorical elements of the text you are studying. You should be able to use rhetorical terminology to identify several elements such as the speaker, audience, genre, medium, language use, and style of the text.

- Provide specific examples from the text under study. Are the examples discussed in detail? Are you overlooking evidence from the text that might bolster your points?

- Connect your analysis to larger questions. Do you consider the context in which the text is situated? How are you handling any controversies or points of discussion related to the topic as a whole?

- Be aware of your own rhetorical strategies and the techniques you are using in your analysis. Have you thought enough about your rhetorical situation? Is your composition appropriate for your audience? How are you working with the conventions of your genre and medium? How are you handling the details of your message?

- Check that you are meeting the expectations of your assignment. Are you documenting any sources you use? Are you formatting your work properly? Are the mechanical and surface level elements of your project clear and correct?

Push It   More Possibilities for Rhetorical Analyses

1. Think of an item that you might not normally consider to be a text—a plastic shopping bag, a burger, a car, or a haircut, for instance. Compose an analysis in which you explore the ways this item delivers a message to an audience.

2. Develop a research project in which you explore the ways in which personal histories and contexts shape an individual's engagement with a text. Select an interesting text for analysis. Interview at least three people, taking note of their readings of the text in question. (For this task, you may want to choose a shorter text or something well known, so that your subjects can offer informed insights.) Write an essay in which you compare reader reactions to the text's rhetorical strategies.

3. Find an online conversation concerning a topic about which you have an interest. You might look through discussion group postings or search for an active blog or social network where multiple participants are debating an issue. Find a conversation thread that consists of at least ten postings by at least three people. Analyze the conversation as a text, considering the rhetorical strategies used, the nature of online conversations, and the topic under consideration.

RESOURCES
Sample Rhetorical
Analyses

Zoom Out   Reflecting on Rhetorical Analyses

- **Rhetorical analyses are concerned with how a text delivers a message.** The focus is on the strategies and techniques used by an author to appeal to an audience.

- **All of the rhetorical terms and advice in this book can be applied to composing a rhetorical analysis.** You can think about rhetorical situations, about appeals, about writing strategies, and about the details of the text as you create your analysis.

- **Critical thinking drives the process of composing a rhetorical analysis.** You can zoom in and out as you ask questions about a text and its message and as you make decisions about how to compose your response.

- **Any number of texts can be put through a rhetorical analysis.** You will want to think about the genre of any text you assess. Nonprint texts will call for you to identify communications strategies related to the mediums in which they are composed.
- **Rhetorical analyses can also take up larger contexts and concerns.** You can make connections between the details and the strategies used in a text and other elements of culture.

For additional information and practice with the learning objectives in this chapter, go to www.mycomplab.com, Resources > Writing > Writing Purposes > Writing to Analyze.

Position Arguments

Zoom In · Key Concepts and Learning Objectives

After studying this chapter, you should be able to:

8.1 Use arguments to clarify your perspective and learn more about an issue.

8.2 Compose position arguments that sway readers toward your perspective.

8.3 Understand how appeals to ethos, pathos, and logos are made in arguments.

8.4 Offer statements, stake out positions, and provide compelling reasons supporting your statements and positions.

8.5 Use evidence to help bolster arguments.

8.6 Compose arguments that address complexity.

What do you suppose makes spectacles like the *Jerry Springer Show* compelling? It could be the topics taken up each day: pornography, gender identity, or infidelity, to name a few. It could be the presence of the bouncer-bodied security guards, suggesting that, at any moment, debate over the topic of the day might turn into a knock-down brawl. In either case, such shows provide a good negative example of what you should understand about arguments.

An effective argument doesn't use trash-talk confrontations but, instead, uses critical thinking to help writers and readers explore and come to some agreement about a topic. If you had to state your own position about the show's ineffective argument approach, for instance, you might posit that Jerry Springer trivializes personal problems by exploiting them for entertainment. Such an argument would zoom in to make claims about the show's topics, format, guests, and viewers and zoom out to make points about cultural concerns. Your purpose would be to help readers see the show from your perspective, and you would use persuasive rhetorical strategies to meet your goal.

Most of the strategies needed to compose a compelling argument are discussed in detail in Chapter 4. You must discover an arguable topic and stake out a position. You will make claims about the topic and offer reasons for supporting the claims. You will provide evidence to bolster your points. You will also look at assumptions that underlie your take on the topic. You will address potential objections to your position. And you will pay heed to rhetorical situations and strategies. Following these guidelines will let you take up topics and discover their complexities. You may even sway others to agree with your perspective without ever having to raise your voice or chest bump a talk-show bouncer.

WN

VIDEO
Finding an
Arguable Topic

KEY TERMS

- **Arguable topic:** A topic about which people are likely to disagree. Position arguments require areas of disagreement for debate and discussion to take place.

- **Claim:** A statement that stakes out a position or makes an assertion. Arguments are woven together using a series of claims.

- **Reason:** An explanation offered in support of a claim. Reasons can be thought of as the "because clauses" of a claim; for example, we should lower the drinking age because it will curb binge consumption of alcohol.

- **Evidence:** Facts, statements, and observations offered in support of claims and reasons. In academic situations, facts and statements from authorities usually carry the most weight.

- **Opposing points of view:** Competing perspectives on a topic. Good topics for argument support not one but multiple positions.

- **Rebuttal:** A response to an opposing point of view. Successful arguments try to either accept and accommodate or refute opposing points of view.

Understanding Position Arguments

Learning Objective 8.1

To get a better sense of how you might compose a position argument, let's look at an example.

Let's Talk About Sex

BY **ANNA QUINDLEN**

Anna Quindlen writes regularly for Newsweek, *frequently concluding each issue with short essays on culture and politics. She is also a bestselling novelist with books such as* Object Lessons, One True Thing, *and* Blessings *to her credit. "Let's Talk About Sex" appeared as a* Newsweek *"Last Word" column in March 2009.*

Congress loves abstinence-only programs so much it has thrown big bucks at them. The public? It's got better ideas.

It is a truth universally acknowledged that there is a deep schism in this country, a schism between those many Americans who support comprehensive sex education in the schools and an equal number who believe that only abstinence should be taught, between those who want teenagers to be told about masturbation and HIV prevention and the like, and those who believe they mostly need to hear that true love waits.

It is one of those universally acknowledged truths that happen to be utterly false.

The poll results are astonishing. While respondents in some surveys are divided over whether more emphasis should be on contraception or on abstinence, nearly 90 percent of those sampled in several recent polls support the notion of sex ed in schools. I'm not sure that many people would agree about teaching long division.

But none of this is what you would hear if you put your ear to the ground in Washington, D.C. In yet another example of how things can go horribly awry within that zone of magical thinking, Congress has poured $1.5 billion into what is essentially anti-sex ed, abstinence-only programs, despite the following facts:

1: They don't work. A study conducted for the Department of Health and Human Services during the last Bush administration showed that teenagers who took abstinence-only classes were just as likely to have sex as those who didn't.

Let's Talk About Sex
(continued)
BY **ANNA QUINDLEN**

2: They're actually counterproductive. Other studies have shown that adolescents in abstinence-only programs were less likely to use contraception, perhaps because those programs emphasize only the failure rates of even the best methods.

3: Everyone understands this. A growing number of states are turning down federal funds for abstinence-only education. Yes, that's right: states are being offered money and saying no. (I wanted to write that in capital letters but restrained myself.) Texas leads the nation in spending for abstinence-only programs. It also has one of the highest teen birthrates in the country. Those two sentences together sound like the basis for a logic question on the SAT, but a really easy one.

President Obama's budget seems to reflect the sentiment of most Americans, promising to "stress the importance of abstinence while providing medically accurate and age-appropriate information to youth who have already become sexually active." In other words, we can indeed walk and chew gum. But not in abstinence-only education, in which students must be taught little more than that married sex is good and unmarried bad. Homosex? Not even an issue. In the human-sexuality curriculum in Utah, for instance, guidelines say teachers cannot "advocate homosexuality," which if I were a teacher would translate as "leave well enough alone." Or well enough for all but the gay kid in the classroom, who is probably wondering how he's going to handle the waiting-for-marriage part, since Utah won't let him get married. The guidelines also forbid discussing "the intricacies of intercourse, sexual stimulation or erotic behavior." I'm not sure what that means, but I do love that word "intricacies." It sounds as though teachers shouldn't teach the Kama Sutra, or Cirque du Soleil.

In our current straitened economic atmosphere, there must be no more of what our grandmothers called "throwing good money after bad" for junk virginity pedagogy that emphasizes the eww factor with photographs of lesions. It's the eww factor that causes a lot of the problem here; it's remarkable how many parents think sex education should be handled in the home, then are so queasy they leave the teaching of it up to episodes of "The Real World." Even some of the comprehensive sex-ed curricula are incomplete. With their emphasis on HPV, STDs and problem pregnancies, they seem to ignore one critical point: pleasure. It's the equivalent of talking about salmonella and forgetting to mention that food tastes good.

Because we hear so often that there are two sides to an issue, we've become accustomed to thinking there are two equal sides to most of them, especially the ones on which people scream the loudest. You can see this reflected in coverage of demonstrations, in which tens of thousands can march against the war, or for gay rights, and a chunk of the story will be taken up by quotes from 11 people with American flags or verses from Leviticus on their signs.

In Washington this fallacy is taken as gospel because there really are two sides to every issue, and both of them belong to lobbyists. Even if they are arguing nonsense, as they once did when they said that tobacco didn't cause cancer, as they still do when they say cigarettes are not marketed to the underage, they do it in nice shoes, sometimes at a cocktail party. Good grooming and mini-quiches make their arguments seem plausible.

Perhaps this issue offers an opportunity for elected-official ed, too. It's worth looking past the dueling paid faces to actual public opinion about what appear to be contentious issues—but sometimes aren't. Common sense dictates that schools should offer a comprehensive view of sexual behavior, including a guide to those measures that can help sexually active students avoid visiting an abortion clinic or experiencing burning during urination. And elected officials might try a comprehensive view, too, before they use scarce resources on programs they've embraced mainly because they do not offer the inconvenience of complexity.

↗ Reflect on the Reading

Questions About "Let's Talk About Sex"

1. How would you articulate the main position taken by Quindlen in the piece? Do you generally agree or disagree with her stance? Why?
2. What argumentative strategies stand out in the piece? Does the essay provide a compelling argument about sex education?
3. How does the article zoom out to make larger points? How successful do you find the argument regarding these larger points?
4. Is it fair to say the article is dismissive of opposing points of view? Why or why not?

"Let's Talk About Sex" represents a fairly typical position argument. A reader should be able to come away from the piece with a clear statement about what exactly is being advocated, in this case, the idea that comprehensive sex education should be offered in schools. Quindlen's piece fits the model of an argument because she extends the main claim with a series of additional claims, reasons, and evidence explaining why she is offering her perspective to readers. She suggests that the public mostly disagrees with the approach offered by congress. She offers evidence in the form of poll numbers to support this point. She provides additional claims and reasons: abstinence-only programs are counterproductive and economic concerns call for an end to ineffective programs. In short, she appeals mostly to our sense of logic, weaving together a series of claims and providing evidence to support them.

"Let's Talk About Sex" also touches on some larger concerns. One of the reasons Quindlen offers for her position, for instance, relates to the influence of lobbying on legislation. She also suggests that Washington, D.C. is out of synch with the general public when it comes to sex education. Both of these points further her larger project of getting readers to support comprehensive sex education programs in schools. And these claims expand the scope of the argument, extending it into areas of government reform.

Quindlen's piece does not go into great detail about opposing points of view. In fact, her position implies that there is little real disagreement about the issue,

WN

VIDEO
8. Rebuttal/
Opposing Points
of View

and her citation of evidence from polls supports this point. Given the genre and rhetorical situation of the essay (a one-page piece in a popular magazine) this approach to the complexity of the topic makes sense, but, in most academic position arguments, writers make deliberate moves to address multiple positions on the topic.

Know It   Strategies for Understanding Position Arguments

- Begin by identifying the main claim offered in the piece. Sometimes arguments will stake out more than one position, but you should be able to pick out the key points that are advocated by an author.
- Ask questions about the rhetorical situation and the kinds of appeals offered in an argument. What can be said about the speaker? What groups are likely target audiences? How does the piece appeal to logic, to emotions, or to the credibility of the speaker?
- Examine the components of arguments that appear in a piece. Think about the relationships between claims, reasons, and evidence. Consider how the piece works with assumptions that underlie positions on a topic. (See Chapter 4.)
- Pay attention to the ways in which evidence is used. What types of evidence are provided? How well is the use of evidence documented? Can you think of counterexamples that are not presented by the piece?
- Explore the way the argument handles opposing points of view. Does it give opponents a fair hearing? Is there a legitimate presence of multiple perspectives in the piece? Does the piece accept or reject compelling alternatives?
- Consider the rhetorical strategies used in the piece. Conduct a rhetorical analysis (see Chapter 7). Think about structure and organization. Look for comparisons, analogies, analysis, description, or other details used to make points in an argument.

Learning
Objective 8.2

Ask Questions & Make Decisions   Exercises for Understanding Position Arguments

1. Read through the editorials in a local news source. Identify an editorial or letter to the editor that seems particularly weak in its argumentation. Write a rebuttal letter, submitting it if you wish.
2. Think about some of the other forms of communication that stake out a position—bumper stickers, billboards, T-shirts, etc. Make a list of steps designers might take to make these items more compelling as arguments.
3. Choose one of the topics typically taken up in position arguments—same-sex marriage, immigration, social services, or education policies, for instance.

Make a list of all the possible positions that might be advocated related to the topic. Write a paragraph or two exploring the relationships between the positions you have discovered

4. Using the resources of your library, conduct a search for articles related to a topic about which people argue—gun control, government reform, environmental concerns, etc. (See Chapters 14–17 for more on research.) Identify at least two sources related to the topic that can be classified as position arguments. Write a paragraph exploring the rhetorical situations, genres, and mediums of those sources.

Readings and Resources for Exploring Position Arguments

LO

Learning
Objective 8.3

Position arguments range from the sloganeering found on bumper stickers to the nuanced logic contained in public policy documents. You will find a few samples below. Elizabeth Muhlenfeld articulates the position of college administrators regarding an initiative to open the debate on the drinking age. And a photograph of a protest and a public service announcement offer examples of advocating for a position in other mediums.

Seeking a Drinking Age Debate: Perspectives from an Amethyst Initiative Signatory About Moving the Dialog Forward
BY **ELISABETH MUHLENFELD**

Elisabeth Muhlenfeld is the President of Sweet Briar College, one of 135 colleges currently endorsing the Amethyst Initiative, an effort by college leaders to spark debate about alcohol issues on campuses. "Seeking a Drinking Age Debate: Perspectives from an Amethyst Initiative Signatory About Moving the Dialog Forward" appeared in the journal University Business *in October 2008.*

As an enthusiastic signatory to the Amethyst Initiative, a joint statement issued by college and university presidents and chancellors urging public debate on the National Minimum Drinking Age Act, I am pleased to say the discussion is certainly underway.

Seeking a Drinking
Age Debate:
Perspectives from
an Amethyst
Initiative Signatory
About Moving the
Dialog Forward
(continued)
BY **ELISABETH
MUHLENFELD**

Reaction to our call for a dispassionate exploration of the relationship between the legal drinking age and the problems associated with underage drinking has been swift, vehement, sometimes reasoned, often emotional, and occasionally misleading or false. When the Associated Press broke the story, voices pro and con erupted in news briefs and editorials, in the blogosphere, and on the airwaves. Despite the fact that our statement takes no position one way or the other on changing the current drinking age, most early reports asserted, "College presidents want to lower the drinking age to 18." Some suggested that our motive was to get out of work: We just don't want to go to the trouble of upholding the law; we're trying to avoid the unpleasant task of policing frat parties.

Mothers Against Drunk Driving—an organization that I have always admired and that has had a powerful and positive impact on our societal understanding of the evils of drunk driving—expressed outrage, even suggesting that parents should think twice before sending a child to a college whose president had signed the statement. It was hardly a reasoned response to our call for debate.

TROUBLING NUMBERS

So why did we choose this fight in the first place? College and university presidents are not given to diving into such controversial waters. We know this issue is fraught with pain and frustration. But we also know that 21 simply isn't working. We live in a society where underage drinking is pervasive (fully 72 percent of those aged 18 to 20 report using alcohol in the last year, according U.S. Department of Health and Human Services statistics).

Worse, over the last three decades, our teens have developed an increasingly dangerous culture of clandestine binge drinking. Every day, we see the tragic costs of that culture. It is the lucky college president who has not had to telephone parents to report that their child has been the victim of date rape exacerbated by alcohol abuse, or killed in an automobile accident coming back from an alcohol-fueled all-night party.

Binge drinking is drinking to get drunk. Defined by statisticians as consuming five or more drinks in a row (and by students as "getting completely wasted"), binge drinking within the last month is reported by 36 percent of our young adults between 18 and 20, according to government studies. The Harvard School of Public Health puts the number at nearly 50 percent. Those who engage in binge drinking are at risk for a sad litany of problems, the least of which is poor academic performance.

According to the National Institute on Alcohol Abuse and Alcoholism, underage drinking annually contributes to some 1,700 deaths, 599,000 injuries, and 97,000 cases of sexual assault. SAMHSA, a division of the U.S. Department of Health and Human Services, states that nearly one in five teenagers (16 percent) "has experienced 'black out' spells where they could not remember what happened the previous evening." This is not good clean fun. It is a national shame that demands our attention.

Research tells us that binge drinking has been on the rise since the National Minimum Drinking Age Act went into effect, which was largely championed as an antidote to alcohol-related traffic fatalities. Indeed, there is abundant research indicating that the higher drinking age laws have coincided with a decrease in traffic deaths since the mid-1980s—though declines in alcohol-related deaths actually began in the 1970s, well before 21 became the norm. Some of that decrease is surely due to fewer adolescent drinkers behind the wheel, but the evidence is unclear whether our higher drinking age has, on balance, saved many lives.

The past two decades have seen other major changes, from improved highways and safer cars to mandatory seatbelt usage and, in some jurisdictions, stiffer legal penalties for driving under the influence. These factors and greater awareness of the consequences of drunk driving likely combine to account for declines in overall alcohol-related vehicular deaths across age groups. Furthermore, other industrialized nations with lower drinking ages than the United States saw even greater declines during this period.

The one positive trend I can report among underage drinkers is, I think, a result of the efforts of MADD and similar groups in the 1970s and 1980s: a wider acceptance among young people that it is no longer "cool" to drink and drive. Students often take along a friend who does not drink as a designated driver. I once overheard two college students talking about how they knew they would get drunk at an upcoming party and thus had made plans to spend the night rather than drive home. I didn't know whether to applaud their maturity or sputter in horror that they found planning to get drunk acceptable—or for that matter, desirable.

EARLY EXPOSURE, CULTURE OF ACCEPTANCE

College officials work hard to combat the culture of underage drinking, and particularly binge drinking. But we often feel like the little Dutch boy with his finger in the dyke. For one thing, students don't wait until they get to college to take their first drink. Most of them have had some experience with alcohol in high school—nearly always unsupervised, with no one modeling responsible behavior or teaching moderation. A recent government study indicates that among 17-year-olds, 25 percent had binged within the last month.

Students have no trouble obtaining alcohol. Many ask older friends to buy it for them, but untold numbers think nothing of using a fake ID. Students reason that if they are legally adults, old enough to serve on juries (and render judgment on the death penalty), purchase property, vote, or serve in Iraq, they ought to be able to buy a beer.

At Sweet Briar College (Va.), nearly 30 percent of students study abroad at some point during college. In many places, alcohol consumption is not policed, wine or beer is a normal accompaniment to a meal, and binging, American style, is rare. Here at home, respect for the "21 law" among the young is almost nonexistent, an unsettling fact in a nation that regards itself as law-abiding. Students simply become adept at not getting caught, which means they steer clear of authority figures while drinking.

In other words, given this law that college students ignore, we find ourselves unable to educate them effectively about drinking. At Sweet Briar, more than 70 percent of our

Seeking a Drinking
Age Debate:
Perspectives from
an Amethyst
Initiative Signatory
About Moving the
Dialog Forward
(continued)
BY **ELISABETH
MUHLENFELD**

students are underage. For those students, the college can only preach abstinence, which we know is unrealistic, or urge responsible behavior when imbibing—which acknowledges they will be breaking the law. Both postures seem hypocritical.

FRESH APPROACHES

There must be a better way. The organization whose members developed the Amethyst Initiative, Choose Responsibility (www.chooseresponsibility.org), has a number of interesting suggestions about stepped education and licensing approaches that are worth considering. And once we turn our attention to this issue, other ideas will present themselves that might help us dissolve the culture of clandestine binge drinking. The Amethyst Initiative, named for the stone the Greeks believed prevented intoxication, seeks only to provoke a national debate about the efficacy of the Minimum Legal Drinking Age Act, which comes up for renewal in 2009.

If after a rigorous examination of the existing public policy lawmakers and constituents believe 21 still makes sense, so be it. But we need to put this issue under a microscope. If we discover that the 21 law is contributing to clandestine binge drinking, then we will need to weigh benefits against risks. That's the kind of thing we do well. Small liberal arts colleges are of many stripes, but all of us take seriously our responsibility to educate the whole student—and that includes inculcating in students the ability to think deeply about ethical issues and to take personal responsibility for every aspect of their lives.

My e-mail inbox has been jammed for three weeks with more than 3,000 outraged form letters, thanks to MADD, and in truth I expected some significant pushback from my own college community. But the message that our current policy is not working has resonated with our students, staff, faculty, and alumnae. I've been impressed with the thoughtful support, including one letter from a 91-year-old alumna saying simply, "I am with you."

Reflect on the Reading

Questions About "Seeking a Drinking Age Debate"

1. What is being proposed by Muhlenfeld and other Amethyst Initiative signers? What would you say to someone who suggested that their proposal is not a position?
2. How would you analyze the rhetorical situation of "Seeking a Drinking Age Debate"? What would you say about the piece in terms of purposes and audiences? How does Muhlenfeld respond to this situation as a speaker?
3. What are your thoughts on the elements of argument in the piece? What kind of claims does Muhlenfeld make and what reasons and evidence does she provide to support the claims?
4. Where do you find yourself in the debate over college drinking? What points do you find significant from the perspective of students? What happens if you shift to the perspectives of parents or college administrators?

FIGURE 8.1
Demonstrators in Argentina protest the Iraq War (AP).

⤵ Images Arguing Positions

While logic represents a primary form of appeal in arguments written for academic settings, it is not the only means of persuading an audience. Nor are essays and print the sole genre and medium for staking out a claim. The photograph and the public service announcement below demonstrate alternative possibilities for advocating a position.

FIGURE 8.2
PSA opposing violence to animals (PETA).

Reflect on the Reading

Questions About "Images Arguing Positions"

1. What kinds of decisions might have gone into taking the photograph in Figure 8.1? Is it fair to say the photographer is the author of an argument? Why or why not?

2. Figure 8.1 captures a nonviolent protest. Can a protest or performance be analyzed in ways similar to reading other texts? How would you explain the human actions in the image in terms of position arguments?

3. The photograph in Figure 8.2 splices together human and animal faces. What can you say about this modification of the image?

4. Recall that arguments can make appeals (see pages 109–11) based on their speaker (ethos), their logic (logos), and emotions (pathos). How would you analyze the PSA in terms of these various appeals?

Writing Assignment: A Position Argument

Write an essay in which you take a position while exploring a topic about which people can disagree. Your argument should consider and respond to alternative perspectives on your topic. You may begin with a major claim and then develop the argument around that claim, or you may explore your topic from multiple positions to arrive at a major claim. As you work, provide reasons to demonstrate the logic of your thinking and incorporate evidence to support your points.

Ask Questions & Make Decisions

Exercises for Understanding Position Arguments

1. Search through the databases of your library until you find a position argument on a topic about which you have an interest. Analyze the argument to identify the kinds of appeals it presents. Write a paragraph detailing appeals to ethos, logos, or pathos in the piece.

2. Working with a group of peers, select a broad topic that might be used to develop an argument—immigration reform, violence in schools, health care crises, stereotypes in the media, global commerce, and so on. From this broad topic, develop a claim that might serve as the basis for an argument, for example, schools have a right to monitor private student communications,

Hispanics should boycott the World Bank network, The United States should increase trade tariffs on China, and so on. Once you have an arguable topic, develop a list of supporting reasons that might be used to compose an argument.

3. Conduct research about a topic of interest. (You might use the topic from the previous prompt.) As you explore, locate at least one example of three kinds of evidence: (1) facts and statistics, (2) statements of others, and (3) anecdotes or observations. Write a paragraph comparing the uses and effectiveness of the various kinds of evidence.

4. Find a piece of communication designed to appeal to the emotions—an advertisement, a piece of propaganda, a public service announcement. Identify the main claim being made in the piece. Develop a list of reasons and possible evidence that might be used to create an argument supporting (or arguing against) the claim.

Plan It   Invention Strategies for Position Arguments

Selecting the right topic for a position argument is crucial. Some topics may prove difficult because there is little grey area where productive debate might happen. Aim for a topic that lends itself to multiple perspectives on a complex issue. Here are some concrete steps:

Learning Objective 8.4

- Think about possible topics for your argument. Start with controversial local, national, or global issues, and then identify several possibilities. Look for topics that can be discussed with complexity rather than topics that divide too starkly into black or white approaches.
- Survey one or more of these topics to see if it will lend itself to an argument. Is it complex enough? Can you find enough sources of information? Does it appeal to your interests?
- Identify the topic you wish to take up and, more specifically, the claim or position for which you wish to argue. To help yourself identify an angle you can pursue, ask the question, *When people discuss my topic, what do they normally disagree about?*
- Develop a list of reasons that might be offered in support of your position. Look over the list to identify any reasons that seem particularly convincing, thinking about how they might be organized in support of your claim.
- Conduct research to learn more about your topic and to gather evidence. Take notes and keep track of sources you discover. Identify specific evidence to support the reasons you might use in your argument.

- Consider which parties have an interest in your topic. Make a list of interested parties. Are there groups who are more likely than others to accept your position? Are there groups you must address if your argument is to make a difference? Are there groups you can ignore? What can the assumptions and beliefs of the interested parties tell you about your argument?
- Think about the position you are taking, and then consider counterarguments. Are there stances that directly oppose your position? Are there additional layers of complexity that complicate the points you wish to make? How can you integrate these perspectives into your argument?
- Zoom out to the contexts that are relevant to your topic. Does your argument address race, class, gender, or other concerns? How will you account for connections with key people, texts, and elements of culture as you develop your argument?
- Create an outline, a set of note cards, a graphic map, or any other device that can help you concretize a plan for developing your argument. Think about the structure of arguments (pages 96–99) as you map out possible directions for your work.

CONNECT IT   **More Resources for Position Arguments**

For more detailed information about some of the strategies you might use in position arguments, consider the following resources:

For more on rhetorical situations, see Chapter 1.

For more on arguments, see Chapter 4.

For insights into using research in position arguments, see Chapters 14– 17.

For more on thesis statements for position arguments, see Chapter 18.

For insights into organizing structures for position arguments, see Chapter 19.

For insights into using definitions in position arguments, see Chapter 22.

For more on analyzing, see pages 62–65.

For more on comparing and contrasting, see Chapter 23.

For more on exploring causes and effects in position arguments, see Chapter 24.

For insights into using visuals in position arguments, see Chapter 25.

For information on design strategies, see Chapter 26.

For insights into developing annotated bibliographies for position arguments, see Chapter E4.

Compose It   **Write a Position Argument**

As you begin to compose, remember the flexible nature of genres and rhetorical situations. You will be persuading readers, but you will also often write to explore. And you will likely use explanatory strategies (Chapter 10) to provide information for readers, even as you write to persuade. Know also that position arguments (at least those composed in college writing courses) come with some clear expectations. You should make judicious use of evidence to support your claims, and you should cite and document your sources. Focus on the structure and logic of your composition. Below are some strategies to keep in mind:

- Revisit your sources. Identify key statistics, passages, or other evidence you will use to support your claims. Think about what kinds of evidence will be most convincing for the major points you want to make.
- Continue zooming in on the logic of your argument. Use lists, maps, or other strategies to explore and track ideas. Begin with the claim or claims you wish to make. List reasons that can be used to support the claim. Note evidence that can be used to bolster the reasons.
- Write summaries (pages 375–76) of alternative points of view you wish to address. Be fair in articulating the strengths of opposing perspectives. Include examples from research to further explain alternatives.
- Working from a sketch of the structure of your argument, begin drafting sections that explain the elements of the argument in detail. You might begin with one of the reasons supporting the main claim. Discuss the reason, supplying evidence to strengthen your explanation. Detail any assumptions underlying the reason.
- Compose text addressing possible objections to the points you are making, to the assumptions supporting your points, or to your evidence. Make decisions about how best to integrate this discussion into your text, perhaps using any summaries of opposing positions that you have composed. Decide whether to try to refute opposing points, or to acknowledge and accept them.
- Look for opportunities to incorporate research into the argument. Examine your sources for crucial information that readers should have. Look over what you have written so far to identify sections that require more evidence.
- Continue drafting the argument. Develop or revise your introduction and conclusion. Keep track of the evolving structure of your work, perhaps revising your outlines or maps.
- Document any sources and adjust the format of the essay using an approved style guide, e.g., MLA style (pages 384–99) or APA style (pages 400–10).

WN

VIDEO
15. Summarizing

LO

Learning Objective 8.5

Focus on Student Writing

Interest Only: The Problem with Student Loans
BY **TARA JOSS**

Tara composed this essay in response to a research assignment. Her initial plan was to develop a research report on problems with the student loan system. Her own experiences with loans, however, prompted her to take a more forceful stance on the topic, so she revised her work to more clearly stake out a position as she offered information about the topic. Tara wrote the piece prior to the latest legislation, which has moved subsidies for student loans toward government-backed lending, as Tara advocates.

Tara Joss

Professor Anderson

English 102

11 February 2010

Interest Only: The Problem with Student Loans

The federal direct loan program, a government subsidized program to help students and their parents pay for college, has been nearly squashed by powerful national lenders. These lenders—Citibank, Sallie Mae, and Bank of America, just to name a few—have muscled the government-run program to the sidelines in the game of loaning students college funds. The problem is the government program costs less, around $3.85 per every $100 lent. The big private lenders are costing the government $13.81 per $100 (Glater and Arenson). So, why are taxpayers subsidizing the private lenders as the banks and corporate interests take over the student loan industry? And why hasn't the free market worked to make student loans more affordable? There are many possible answers to these questions but they all lead to a clear conclusion: money and influence have corrupted the student loan system and the government needs to move now to take back student loans.

There is a long history of government involvement with student loans, a history that combines regulations and subsidies with the goal of helping to open educational opportunities for students. The subsidies consist primarily of guarantees against defaults. When lenders provide federally guaranteed loans to students, they know that if the borrower fails to pay back the loan, the government will cover the costs. "The lender is willing to make the loan, despite the student's lack of employment, credit history or collateral, because a guarantor stands behind the loan" ("The Federal Family Education Loan Program"). Proponents of these guaranteed FFELP loans claim that the limited risk encourages lenders to participate in a market that might otherwise be too risky while it enables them to keep costs down because they don't have to pass on the expenses of bad loans to students or their parents. But others argue that the system is a sweetheart deal for lenders. As the Progressive Policy Institute points out, "In the guaranteed loan program, the government gives the student-paid interest income to the lenders, but puts all of the risks on the shoulders of taxpayers. The risks include the costs of defaults and the costs associated with rising interest rates" (Shireman 3). The subsidies are an important piece in the puzzle when it comes to helping make loans available to students. But, since private lenders have clearly profited over the last four decades (the industry did $85 billion in business last year and Sallie Mae had a return on investments of 43%), it seems that the subsidies have tilted too far toward smoothing the way for private lenders to make profits.

But to fully understand the issue, we need to distinguish between the two main types of government-supported loans. The government subsidizes two kinds of loans. Through the direct student loan program, the federal government lends money directly to students—usually through the William D. Ford Federal Direct Loan Program (at a cost of just under $4 per $100 lent). The government assumes the risks of defaults, and then after graduation, loan recipients make payments directly to the government. Under the Federal Family Education Loan Program (FFELP), the "guaranteed" loan program, the government still covers the risks of the loans, but the loans themselves originate from private lenders (at a cost of just under $14 per $100 lent). Of course, the higher costs to the government associated with the FFELP loans might not be a problem if it meant a better deal for students and their parents. In fact, arguments for the private lenders hinge on the possibilities of competition between lenders leading to more options for consumers. It's possible to argue that the huge growth of the FFELP segment demonstrates the ability of private lenders to do a better job. In the early 1990s there was a big push to transition the bulk of the subsidized lending into direct federal loans. A program to make the transition was put into effect in 1994. According to the *New York Times*, "private lenders began

Joss 3

offering schools and students a variety of benefits like scholarship money and lower interest rates and fees" (Glater and Arenson). A spokesperson for Sallie Mae told the *Times*, "the private sector program has better prices, better product selection, better service and better technology" (Glater and Arenson). So, on the surface, it seems as if the private lenders can compete with and even provide stronger service than the government.

However, the assumption that competition in the free market will provide more economical choices doesn't hold true. In fact, when it comes to student loans, the free market doesn't really exist. The government subsidies do more than make it easier for banks to offer loans to students without credit histories. Because the loans are guaranteed by the government, banks have little incentive to invest in collecting loans that go into default or to help struggling borrowers with their payments. In fact, the government itself has set up and subsidized a number of collection agencies to address just this problem (Shireman). Further, the head start that lender Sallie Mae was given with initial subsidies makes it the 800-pound gorilla in the student loan market, making it hard for smaller, independent banks that might compete to even enter the arena. Sallie Mae's 10 million student loan customers owe a total of $142 billion. With the recent sale of Sallie Mae to J.P. Morgan and Bank of America and the continued consolidation of big lenders, the question is, will they compete against themselves? With Sallie Mae being bought out by a group of lenders who are in business together, student's choices along with competitive rates are reduced.

The lengths that banks go to in order to succeed in the student loan market eventually lead to The United States Congress. In 2006, the Congress enacted a change that set up a favorable fixed-rate scheme for private lenders. *The New Republic* points out that the decision to scale back the less costly direct loan program was political. The program was expanding until the congressional takeover of Congress by Republicans in 1994 tilted policy back toward private lenders under the guise of choice for students. The government-run program was cheaper for students and saved the nation money, but lobbying and political pressure have pushed the program closer toward extinction (Clark). Today, less than 25% of subsidized loans are direct federal loans. Private educational lenders have given more than 3.5 million to members of Congress in the form of campaign donations. Alternative plans put before Congress have been ignored because they conflict with pro-business members who receive generous donations from private lenders. One of those members is John Boehner. His alterations to the federal student loan program will cut subsidies

Joss 4

for student loans by $13 billion over a five-year period. The increase will be passed on to students and their parents.

The government once gave guaranteed loans to everyone. Now the government-direct program is on life support and big lenders jockey for position as the preferred lender. Banks pay off university officials and government officials. The argument coming from the big lenders that the private sector provides more choice and better options just isn't true. And now with the buyout of Sallie Mae, consumers will have fewer choices when it comes to lenders. Foreshadowing things to come Senator Edward Kennedy argues, "clearly, banks and investors see student loans as a very profitable business. It's more urgent than ever to enact reforms to our student loan system to ensure that students, not profits, are our top priority" (Hilzenrath and Paley). Abuse of the system by bankers is a breach of trust to a sector of Americans who can scarcely afford it. What appears to be a good competitive deal will, over time, cost lower class and middle-class families more to send their children to school. To advocate for yourself or your student, make sure you tell your congressman how you feel about private lenders cornering the market on student loans. Also, let him or her know that there should be strict guidelines and oversight to ensure that the so-called free market is not rigged in favor of special interests. The best first step would be to reinvigorate the direct loan program. This movement may now be underway as the government is now considering an overhaul that would shift the focus back toward the direct loan program. If we keep moving in this direction, perhaps the private lenders might have some real competition.

Works Cited

Clark, Kim. "Loan Shark." *New Republic*. New Republic, 12 Feb. 2006. Web. 12 May 2008.

"The Federal Family Education Loan Program." USA Funds, 14 May 2007. Web. 5 May 2008.

Glater, Jonathan D., and Karen W. Arenson. "Lenders Sought Edge Against US in Student Loans." *New York Times*. New York Times, 15 April 2007. Web. 8 May 2008.

Hilzenrath, David S., and Amit R. Paley. "Private Investors to Buy Sallie May for $25 Billion." *Washington Post*. Washington Post, 17 Apr. 2007. Web. 5 May 2008.

Shireman, Robert. "Straight Talk on Student Loans." *Progressive Policy Institute*. Progressive Policy Institute, 14 Sept. 2004. Web. 9 May 2008.

Reflect on the Reading

Questions About "Interest Only"

1. How would you relate your experiences with college finances to the argument in "Interest Only?" Do the problems appear as pressing as the essay makes them out to be? What insights into the topic do you have?

2. How would you describe the structure of Tara's argument? Are there ways in which additional complexities might be layered over the existing claims?

3. "Interest Only" provides a lot of information about loan programs. Is this evidence compelling? What other kinds of evidence might make the argument stronger?

4. Tara advocates for government reform of the student loan system. Would you say that she fairly considers alternative perspectives? Why or why not?

Revise It   Revision Strategies for Position Arguments

In addition to general strategies for revision, including asking peers to read your draft, concentrate on these areas as you return to your position argument for rewrites:

LO

Learning
Objective 8.6

- Think about the ethos or ethical appeal of the essay. Do you come across as fair and careful? Are the authors of sources used in the essay credible? What can be done to strengthen the authority of the essay?

- Honestly assess how thoroughly multiple perspectives are addressed in the essay. You need not take up every possibility, but serious alternatives to your position should be covered carefully. Check that opposing points of view are treated fairly and are addressed in the subsequent claims of your own argument.

- Stop to consider the makeup of the audience for the essay. Especially when it comes to people who might be skeptical about your claims, think about their belief systems and assumptions they might make about the topic. How can you adjust your essay to better resonate with these readers?

- Examine the logic of the essay. Map out the structure of the argument using a reverse outline. Are there gaps in the reasoning? Do any of the reasons offered in support of your major claim seem questionable? How can you strengthen the logical structure of the argument?

WN

RESOURCES
Sample Position
Aruguments

- Test that the essay uses evidence effectively. Are there spots where the evidence seems thin? Does the essay use both facts and statistics and statements from experts? Where will additional evidence make the argument more persuasive?

- Check the formal elements of the essay. Ensure that formatting and visuals are used effectively (see Chapter 26). Is all of the evidence integrated smoothly into the essay? Are the sources properly documented?

- Revise several times, concentrating on strengthening the credibility of the essay and the logic of the argument. Tighten the language to ensure you are making points clearly and providing information economically. Polish the surface-level features of the essay.

Push It   More Possibilities for Position Arguments

WN

VIDEO
23. Images and Intellectual Property

1. Create a public service announcement that stakes out a position on an arguable topic. Use a word processor, publishing software, or an image editor to compose the PSA. Identify an image that offers a visual argument. You may want to use multiple images to develop a collage or collection of images that makes your points. (Refer to the information on pages 345–47 to ensure that you use images fairly.) Complement the image with text that delivers key claims, reasons, and evidence for your position. Within the genre of the PSA, adjust your approach to meet the expectations of your audience.

2. Design a bumper sticker that advocates a position by making one or more valid points. Use publishing or image editing software to create the sticker. (Common bumper sticker dimensions are three by eleven inches.) Identify images for the sticker and develop a short phrase that captures your position on the issue. When finished, consider composing a sticker for an alternative perspective on the topic. (You can order prints of your designs from an online bumper sticker site.)

Zoom Out   Reflecting on Position Arguments

- **A good position essay begins with an arguable topic.** An issue must come with enough room for disagreement to make a successful starting point. You may have to further adjust your topic to avoid simple black and white disagreements.

- **Position arguments are meant both to clarify and persuade.** You should adjust your own thinking as you explore perspectives on a topic, and then prompt readers to consider the position you stake out.

- **When you read the position arguments of others, practice critical thinking.** Learning to read carefully (Chapter 3), examining rhetorical situations (Chapter 1), and analyzing writing strategies allows you to critically evaluate the arguments of others.

- **Arguments require logical organization.** Position arguments make a major claim and then offer additional claims, reasons, and evidence to support the stance. (See Chapter 4 for more on the elements of arguments.)

For additional information and practice with the learning objectives in this chapter, go to www.mycomplab.com, Resources > Writing > Writing Purposes > Writing to Argue or Persuade

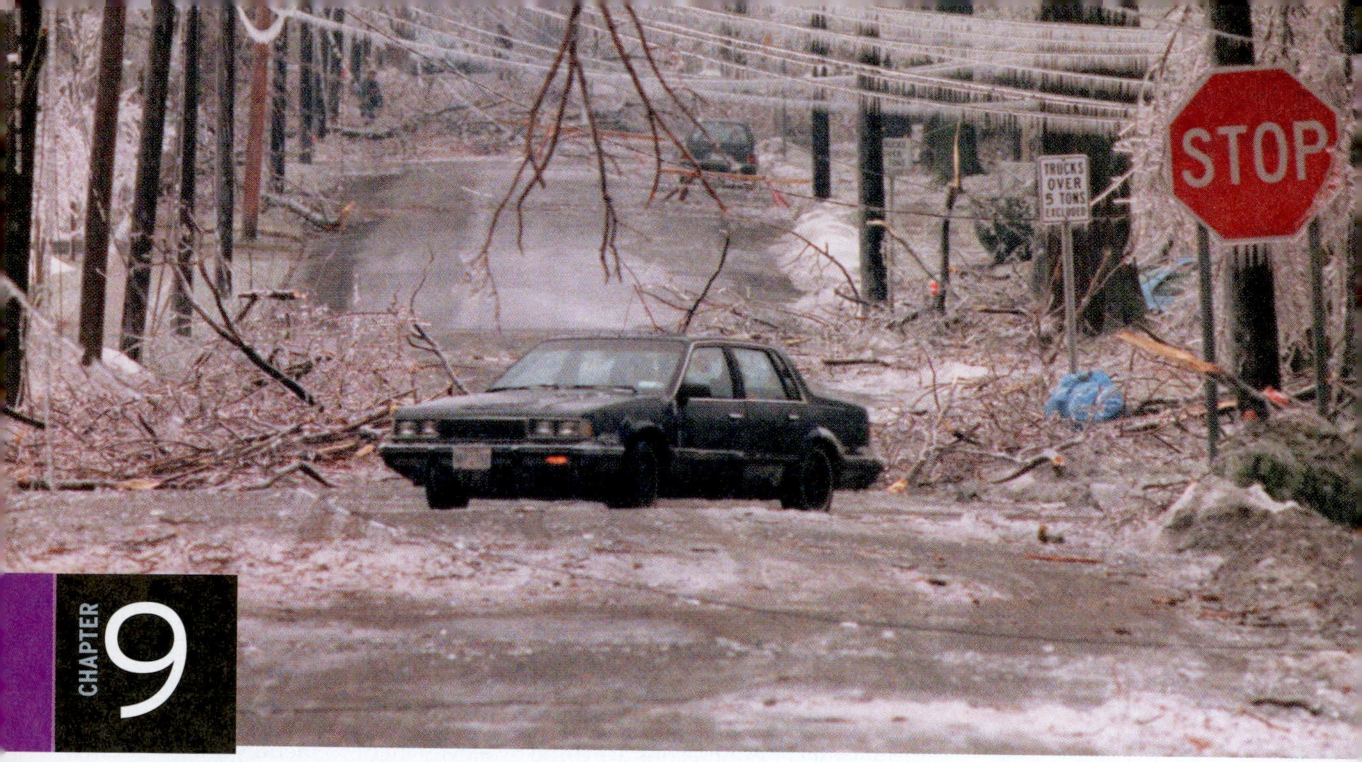

CHAPTER 9

Proposals

Zoom In — Key Concepts and Learning Objectives

After studying this chapter, you should be able to:

9.1 Identify problems that can drive the development of proposals.

9.2 Employ critical thinking to identify possible solutions to complex problems.

9.3 Develop claims that justify a proposed solution for readers.

Suppose you have just moved to a new apartment complex on the edge of town, and you're looking forward to the chance to hike or bike into work. You hit the trail heading out of the complex. The trail cuts through a subdivision, crosses a small city park, and then dead-ends at the edge of a second subdivision. There is short fence and a sign saying, *Posted—No Entry*. You know the trail picks up again at the opposite side of the neighborhood. You know the streets in the subdivision are public roads, but you're stuck here at the edge, unable to connect with the trail just a few dozen yards away.

How might you respond to the situation? Some responses would require little effort. You could turn around and try to find an alternate route to work. Or you could ignore the sign, hop the fence, and continue on your way. But other responses will require a bit more effort. You could try to convince the neighborhood to add a gate in the fence and allow you (and other hikers and bikers) to cut through and reach the trail on the opposite side. If you choose this option, though, you're going to have to develop and sell others on a proposal.

As in any rhetorical situation, you will need to make some concrete decisions. You will need to figure out the audience you will address and then decide how to explain the extent of the problem. You will have to spell out the solution you propose. And you will need to spend a good deal of time justifying your solution, convincing your audience that following your proposal would be a good idea. It might be tough to convince the residents to allow outsiders to cut through their neighborhood; you might think about potential partners who could help—perhaps the city council or your new neighbors in the apartment complex. You will need to come up with some compelling reasons for opening the trail beyond simply stating that it will be more convenient for you.

You can see that proposals are similar to the arguments discussed in Chapter 4. The main differences have to do with the goals and outcomes you hope to achieve when writing a proposal and the specific forms that proposals can take. If the city council decided to hold an open meeting on the issue, you might have to develop flyers or brochures to outline your solution and build support in the community. If the neighborhood agreed to open the trail but declined to pay for it, you might have to develop a grant or funding proposal to get things done. In all of these situations, you would be dealing with a problem (unconnected trails) and trying to convince people to enact a solution.

KEY TERMS

- **Proposal:** A composition that outlines a problem and proposes a solution. Proposals urge readers toward action by demonstrating the significance of the problem and the feasibility of the solution.

- **Justification:** The aspects of a proposal that convince readers that the solution is likely to address the problem effectively. Justification sections might also construct an argument for acting on a proposal by including information about costs and consequences.

- **Alternative solutions:** Sections of a proposal that consider alternative approaches to solving the problem. Sections that weigh alternatives can show why those options might not work or why they might be less desirable.

- **Causes and effects:** Particular actions one might take and the subsequent consequences. Proposal authors can persuade others to accept their solutions by projecting the consequences of acting or not acting on the solution. (See Chapter 21 for more on causes and effects.)

Understanding Proposals

There are many kinds of proposals, but most will offer variations on the problem–solution format. The bulk of some proposals are focused on detailing the problem, with an emphasis on educating readers. Other proposals will concentrate on justifying the solutions that are being put forth; for example, a grant proposal might have detailed budgets and impact studies meant to demonstrate the feasibility of the solution. You can get a sense of this problem–solution movement from the following proposal by The Center for Science in the Public Interest.

Taxing Sugared Beverages Would Help Trim State Budgets, Consumers' Bulging Waistlines, and Health Care Costs

BY **THE CENTER FOR SCIENCE IN THE PUBLIC INTEREST**

The Center for Science in the Public Interest is an advocacy group focused on issues of health, nutrition, and the environment. The organization concentrates on educating the public and advocating for government legislation. "Taxing Sugared Beverages" was published as part of the Liquid Candy campaign in 2010.

STATE BUDGETS ARE IN TROUBLE

Tax receipts are falling around the country and state budgets are in real trouble—possibly for years to come. The Center on Budget and Policy Priorities, a think tank that studies budget issues that affect moderate and low-income people, reports that 48 states have or are facing budget shortfalls this fiscal year (2010) and predicts that a majority will experience shortfalls in 2011 as well. States' aggregate budget gaps through 2011 may exceed $350 billion.

Those budget gaps put enormous pressure on governors and state legislators to make the hard choices necessary to balance their budgets. Politicians, interest groups, and the public have been consumed by battles over how much to cut vital state programs, many of which are already seriously underfunded, and how much to raise in new revenue. Dozens of states have already implemented budget cuts that hurt the most vulnerable of their residents, and more than 30 states have raised taxes. Given the current economic crisis, more such actions are anticipated over the next few years to keep budgets in balance and maintain governmental solvency.

TAXING SOFT DRINKS WOULD REDUCE BUDGET WOES

Despite the dire economic condition of almost every state in the union, lawmakers have largely ignored one important potential source of revenue that would also improve the public and reduce health care costs. Imposing taxes on sugar-sweetened beverages would yield billions of dollars in new revenue and counter the alarming risks of obesity, poor nutrition, and displacement of more healthful foods and beverages. The burgeoning consumption of relatively cheap sugared beverages increases risk for obesity and diabetes, which are among the most significant causes of ill health and escalating health care costs.

Many states already impose modest taxes on sugared beverages and snack foods, but those small taxes bring in little revenue and have little, if any, effect on the consumption of those products and the health of consumers. The current budget crisis calls for bold action to balance state budgets without hurting the state's most vulnerable residents. Imposing reasonable taxes on soft drinks—which are the only food category that has been shown to promote overweight and obesity—would provide needed new revenue and actually improve the health of the most needy citizens—by saving vital state programs and by reducing excessive consumption of unnecessary products that result in serious and costly diet-related diseases. Levying special taxes on soda pop and other sugar-sweetened beverages would trim budget deficits and state health care costs, while also shrinking the waistlines of teens and others who gorge on unhealthy drinks.

Although taxing soft drinks will not—by itself—balance state budgets or wipe out diet-related diseases and health care costs, the revenue potential from a modest new (or extra) tax of five cents per 12-ounce serving is considerable. Nationally, states would see increased revenues of more than $7 billion annually, ranging from about $13 million in Wyoming to about $878 million in California. Currently, 25 states (and the City of Chicago) levy special taxes on soft drinks, typically in the form of a sales tax. New York State's sales tax on soda brings in several hundred million dollars each year, while Arkansas' soda excise tax yields more than $40 million per year.

Taxing Sugared
Beverages Would
Help Trim State
Budgets,
Consumers' Bulging
Waistlines, and
Health Care Costs
(continued)
BY **THE CENTER FOR
SCIENCE IN THE PUBLIC
INTEREST**

OBESITY, SOFT-DRINK TAXES, AND HEALTH

Aside from the revenue implications, there are numerous good reasons to tax soft drinks (including those sweetened with sugar, corn syrup, or other caloric sweeteners) and other carbonated and non-carbonated drinks, such as fruit drinks, sports drinks, and energy drinks):

- Sugared soft drinks are the only food or beverage that has been shown to increase the risk of overweight and obesity, which increase the risk of heart disease, stroke, cancer, diabetes, and other costly and debilitating chronic diseases.[1]
- More than two-thirds of Americans are overweight or obese.[2]
- Sugared beverages are marketed aggressively, especially to children and adolescents, whose intake of those drinks surpassed their intake of milk in the 1980s. Those beverages now account for around 10% of the calories consumed by children and adolescents.[3]
- For each additional sugared drink consumed per day, the likelihood of a child's becoming obese increases by 60%.[4]
- Americans spend roughly $150 billion a year on medical expenses related to obesity, of which about half is paid with Medicare and Medicaid dollars.[5]
- Like the steep taxes now levied on tobacco products, which have significantly reduced tobacco use, modest taxes on sugared beverages would tend to reduce soda consumption. Taxes on sugar-sweetened drinks would encourage consumers to switch to more healthful beverages, leading to reduced calorie intake and less weight gain. And though the somewhat higher prices would have only a modest effect on consumption, some of the revenues could be used to promote healthier diets and more physical activity.
- Although soft-drink taxes would affect lower-income consumers more than higher-income consumers, low-income folks would be the prime beneficiaries of expanded health care and any prevention programs funded by the new revenue, and would reap the benefits of better health and reduced risk of serious chronic diseases.

---

[1]Vartanian LR, Schwartz MB, Brownell KD, Effects of soft drink consumption on nutrition and health: a systematic review and meta-analysis, Am J Public Health 2007;97:667–75.
[2]http://www.cdc.gov/nchs/products/pubs/pubd/hestats/overweight/overwght_adult_03.htm (accessed 9/20/09).
[3]Brownell KD, Frieden TR, Ounces of Prevention—The policy case for taxes on sugared beverages, N Engl J Med 2009; 10.1056/NEJMpo902392.
[4]Nielsen SJ, Popkin BM, Changes in beverage intake between 1977 and 2001, Am J Prev Med 2004; 27:205–10. [Erratum, Am J Prev Med 2005; 28:413.]
[5]Finkelstein EA, Trogdon JG, Cohen JW, Dietz W, Annual medical spending attributable to obesity: payer- and service-specific estimates, Health Affairs 28, no. 5 (2009): w822–w831(published online 27 July 2009; 10.1377/hlthaff.28.5w822).

↗ Reflect on
the Reading

Questions About "Taxing Sugared Beverages"

1. What groups have the ability to act on the proposal offered in "Taxing Sugared Beverages?" How would you describe the rhetorical situation in which the Center for Science in the Public Interest is writing?
2. How effective is "Taxing Sugared Beverages" in bringing the problem of sugary drinks to light? What additional strategies would you suggest for demonstrating the problem?
3. What elements of arguments can you recognize in the article? How does the piece address opposing points of view? How effective is the use of evidence in the article?
4. What solution does "Taxing Sugared Beverages" propose to the problem it outlines? Do you find that the solution proposed is presented effectively? What elements of the proposal do you find most convincing and why?

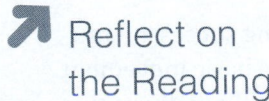

WN

VIDEO
19. Identifying a
Problem

"Taxing Sugared Beverages" represents a clear example of a proposal meant to offer a solution to a problem. Initially, proposals will concentrate on demonstrating the nature of the problem. The report demonstrates the pressing nature of the problem by focusing on two main elements, economics and health. The report references a think tank and offers statistics to point out the extent of state budget difficulties. It also asks readers to consider the impact of budget problems by detailing trends toward cutting programs and raising taxes.

The report uses headings to guide readers and moves quickly to discuss the ways in which a soft drink tax might alleviate state budget problems. Of course, as with most topics, the sugary drink problem is complex. The report addresses this complexity by beginning to discuss the link between these drinks and health issues. And the report points out that some solutions, such as small taxes on sugared beverages, have been tried. This move acknowledges the complexity of the problem; not only should we consider a possible tax on sugary beverages, we need to think about the most effective kinds of taxes.

The rest of the proposal lays out potential benefits from enacting the right kind of tax on sugary beverages. Here the piece creates a back and forth movement between discussing the problem and the solution. Statements that show the negative health impacts of sugary drinks continue to demonstrate the extent of the problem. Statements that point out the potential costs of these negative health consequences help justify the solution being offered.

LO

Learning
Objective 9.1

In proposals, authors describe ways of addressing problems while they also justify the solutions they propose. The organization of such proposals can vary. Often proposals will clearly separate sections outlining the problem, the solution, and the justification of the solution. Or they may weave discussion of these concerns together, as does "Taxing Sugary Beverages." Creating successful proposals, then, requires a flexible approach that understands the basic movement of proposals from problems to solutions to justifications, but that adjusts this movement based on the rhetorical situation.

Know It   Strategies for Understanding Proposals

- Evaluate the nature of the problem addressed by the proposal. Is the problem a local issue—the need for a new toll road? Or is the problem a matter of public policy—the need to change medical research priorities? The nature of the problem will determine the audience and purpose of the proposal as well as the kinds of solutions offered.
- Think about the approach to the problem outlined in the proposal. Is the proposal identifying a new problem or offering a new way of looking at an existing problem? How have others viewed the problem in the past? If it is a longstanding problem, what might account for its pervasiveness?
- Consider the layers of complexity inherent in the problem. Does the proposal concentrate on the big picture or does it also consider smaller contributing factors? What aspects of the problem might the proposal overlook?
- Weigh the nature of the solution offered in the proposal. Has the solution been tried already? If it's a new solution, what makes it particularly viable at this time? Are there analogous situations that might help you understand the solution?
- Identify layers of complexity in the solution. What parties are interested in the solution and how are they likely to respond? Will implementing specific aspects of the solution require additional actions (organizing, political action, fundraising, etc.)?
- Consider how the proposal justifies the solution. Does it make ethical or emotional claims that call us to action? Does it spell out potential benefits of implementing the solution or consequences of not acting?
- Examine the feasibility of the solution. Does it seem logistically practical? Does the proposal discuss economic aspects of the solution? Are you convinced that the proposal could be implemented?
- Ask about assumptions that underlie the proposal. Will all people agree that there is a problem? Does the proposal honestly consider alternative solutions to the problem?

Ask
Questions
& Make
Decisions

Exercises for Understanding Proposals

1. Select a problem that has been discussed for many years (high-school dropout rates, environmental degradation, teenage pregnancy, school violence, etc.). Search online for proposals meant to address the problem, looking for proposals written several years ago. Write a two-paragraph analysis of a proposal meant to address the problem; describe any of its solutions that have been implemented effectively or explore why those solutions have not been effective.

2. Revisit Bill McKibben's argument about climate change in Chapter 4. What elements of the problem–solution format can you identify in the essay? Is it fair to call the piece a proposal? Why or why not?

3. Find a selection of compositions in varying genres—flyers, brochures, podcasts, infomercials—that address problems or propose solutions. Evaluate several examples, and consider their similarities and differences. Write a paragraph or so on your findings.

4. Choose a topic that most people don't recognize as being a problem (fish farms and nutrition, bee depletion, low personal savings rates, etc.). Think about the reasons people don't have an interest in the problem, and then find several proposals related to the problem. Make a list of strategies these proposals use to convince readers of the significance of the problem.

Readings and Resources for Exploring Proposals

Anywhere you find arguments, you are likely to also encounter proposals. But proposals also include an element of problem solving, an added dimension that persuades readers that they should take a specific course of action. You can find these kinds of proposals as you explore topics relating to politics, society, economics, engineering, and education, to name just a few possibilities. You can also think further about proposals by considering the examples below. George Will and the Institute for Public Policy both offer proposals related to the drinking age.

Drinking Age Paradox
BY **GEORGE WILL**

George Will is a regular columnist for Newsweek. *He has also written regularly for* The Washington Post *and was the editor of* National Review, *a conservative magazine devoted to politics. He won the Pulitzer Prize in 1976 for his journalistic column work. "Drinking Age Paradox" appeared in* The Washington Post *in 2007.*

Drinking Age
Paradox
(continued)
BY **GEORGE WILL**

Public policy often illustrates the law of unintended consequences. Society's complexity—multiple variables with myriad connections—often causes the consequences of a policy to be contrary to, and larger than, the intended ones. So, when assessing government actions, one should be receptive to counterintuitive ideas. One such is John McCardell's theory that a way to lower the incidence of illness, mayhem and death from alcohol abuse by young people is to lower the drinking age.

McCardell, 57, president emeritus of Middlebury College in Vermont and a professor of history there, says alcohol is and always will be "a reality in the lives of 18-, 19- and 20-year-olds." Studies indicate that the number of college students who drink is slightly smaller than it was 10 years ago, largely because of increased interest in healthful living. But in the majority who choose to drink, there have been increases of "binge drinking" and other excesses. Hospitalizations of 18- to 20-year-olds for alcohol poisoning have risen in those 10 years.

This, McCardell believes, is partly because the drinking age of 21 has moved drinking to settings away from parental instruction and supervision. Among college students, drinking has gone "off campus and underground," increasing risks while decreasing institutions' abilities to manage the risks.

Although all 50 states ban drinking by persons under 21, technically there is no national drinking age. Each state has the right to set a lower age—more than half had lower age limits in the 1970s—but doing so will cost it 10 percent of its federal highway funds and cause significant uproar from contractors and construction unions.

This pressure on the states by the federal government was put in place in 1984, under Ronald Reagan. He was famously susceptible to moving anecdotes, and Mothers Against Drunk Driving, founded in 1980, had a tragically large arsenal of them. MADD has been heroically successful in changing social norms, nudging society toward wholesome intolerance of the idea that intoxication is amusing (today, the 1981 movie *Arthur*, featuring Dudley Moore as a lovable lush, is embarrassing) and that drunken driving is a peccadillo.

The hope was that a drinking age of 21 would solve two problems. One was that of "blood borders" between states with different drinking ages: People from age-21 states drove into neighboring states with lower drinking ages, then drove home impaired. The other problem was immature and reckless drinking. The hope was that proscribing drinking by people under 21 would substantially delay drinking until that age.

That theory, McCardell believes, has been slain by facts. What is needed now is some "mechanism other than moral suasion" to regulate alcohol use by the under-21 cohort.

The drinking age of 21 was one of 39 measures proposed during the 1980s by a presidential commission on drunken driving; various measures adopted did dramatically reduce the problem. But according to the National Institute on Alcohol Abuse and Alcoholism, about 5,000 people under 21 die every year from vehicular accidents, other injuries, homicides and suicides involving underage drinking. Supporters of the drinking age of 21 say there is nothing wrong with the law that better enforcement could not cure.

McCardell thinks that, on campuses, a drinking age of 21 infantilizes students, encouraging immature behavior with alcohol and disrespect for law generally. Furthermore, an "enforcement only" policy makes school administrations adversaries of students and interferes with their attempts to acquaint students with pertinent information, such as the neurological effects of alcohol on young brains. He notes that 18-year-olds have a right to marry, adopt children, serve as legal guardians for minors and purchase firearms from authorized dealers, and are trusted with the vote and military responsibilities. So, he says, it is not unreasonable to think that they can, with proper preparation, be trusted to drink.

McCardell—gray hair, gray suit, soft voice; he says he is a "social drinker"—and his group, Choose Responsibility, suggest merely that drinking by 18-year-olds be treated like driving by young people: as an activity requiring a license earned after instruction, with provisions for suspending the license when the right it confers is abused.

Students may not care about McCardell's cause because they have little trouble finding fake IDs or getting older friends to purchase their alcohol. His strongest argument, however, may be that delaying legal drinking until 21 merely delays tragedies that might be prevented with earlier instruction in temperance. The age that has the most drunken driving fatalities? Twenty-one.

Reflect on the Reading

Questions About "Drinking Age Paradox"

1. What do you identify as the problem being addressed in "Drinking Age Paradox?" Is Will saying that underage drinking is not a problem?
2. What solution does Will propose? Do you believe the solution will address the problem? Why or why not?
3. Are there enough details provided to determine the chance of the solution succeeding? What kind of information would you need to be convinced?
4. How does "Drinking Age Paradox?" address any opposition to its proposed solution? Do you feel the opposing points have been treated fairly? Have the opposing points been defused?

Adult Accountability for Underage Drinking: The Case for Social Host Laws
BY **THE INSTITUTE FOR PUBLIC STRATEGIES**

"Adult Accountability for Underage Drinking: The Case for Social Host Laws" was released as an Issue Briefing by the Institute for Public Strategies, an organization devoted to supporting education and change in areas of public and private policy. The Issue Briefing was released in 2003.

ISSUE BRIEFING | Institute for Public Strategies

Adult Accountability for Underage Drinking: The Case for Social Host Laws

East County Community Change Project • May, 2003

Research indicates that most underage drinking takes place in private settings such as home parties. To reduce youth access to alcohol effectively, social access must be addressed in addition to retail and bar sales.

This issue briefing details the problem of social hosting — adults providing alcohol or allowing underage drinking to occur in private settings — and proposes a social host ordinance as a solution.

The Top Threat to Youth

Alcohol is the drug of choice for youth[1] and the leading cause of death among teenagers.[2] It's involved in the

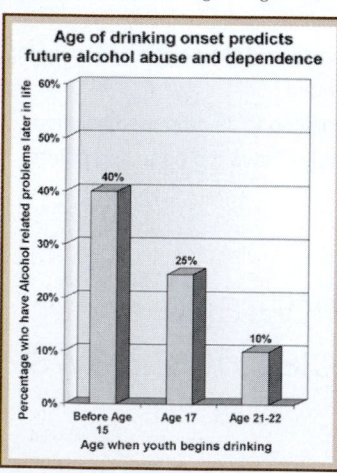

Age of drinking onset predicts future alcohol abuse and dependence

Percentage who have Alcohol related problems later in life

Before Age 15: 40%
Age 17: 25%
Age 21-22: 10%

Age when youth begins drinking

deaths of more teens than all other illicit drugs combined — by a four-to-one ratio.[3] Underage drinking is a factor in nearly half of all teen automobile crashes and 50 to 65 percent of youth suicides.[4] Alcohol abuse is linked to as many as two-thirds of all sexual assaults

and date rapes of teens and college students, and it contributes substantially to homicides, suicides and fatal injuries.[2] It is also a major factor in unprotected sex among youth.[2]

While many believe that underage drinking is an inevitable "rite of passage" that adolescents can easily recover from because their bodies are more resilient, exactly the opposite is true. The brain changes dramatically during adolescence, and this growth can be seriously inhibited by alcohol consumption. The damage alcohol can cause to the adolescent brain is often long-term and irreversible. Even short-term or moderate drinking impairs learning and memory far more among youth than adults.[5] Adolescents need to drink only half as much as adults to suffer the same negative effects.[6]

Youth who begin drinking alcohol before age 15 are four times more likely to become dependent on alcohol than those who wait to begin drinking until age 21. Those who begin drinking before age 13 are twice as likely to have unplanned sex during college, and more than twice as likely to have unprotected sex

> **Youth access to alcohol must be addressed through all sources, including social sources.**

during college, as those who do not start drinking until after age 19.[8]

Because of the negative consequences of underage drinking — coupled with the fact that, on average, young people first use alcohol at 13.1 years of age[9] — youth access must be addressed proactively through all sources, including social sources. Even if young people do not drive after drinking at a home party, the long-term consequences pose unacceptable risks to youth.

At local and national levels, home parties have repeatedly been identified as the primary source by which youth obtain alcohol.[10,11,12] Studies indicate that most underage drinking does not occur in commercial establishments.[12] National research shows that 57 percent of minors reported drinking at friends' homes,[11] and local surveys suggest that 60 to 80 percent of junior and senior high school students obtain alcohol from home or home parties, with 30 percent

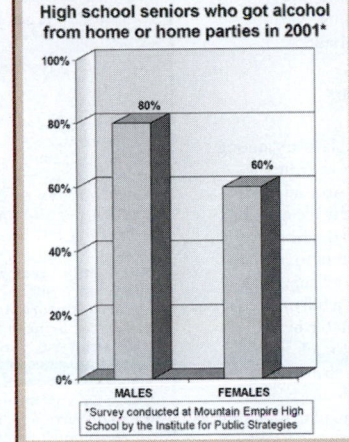

High school seniors who got alcohol from home or home parties in 2001*

*Survey conducted at Mountain Empire High School by the Institute for Public Strategies

reporting that they consume alcohol at home with their parent's permission[13].

A Costly Problem for Communities

The economic cost of alcohol use by youth in California — including traffic crashes, violent crime, burns, drowning, suicide attempts, fetal alcohol syndrome, alcohol poisonings and treatment — is more than $6.5 billion per year.[14] In the City of San Diego, 7,519 law enforcement calls to home parties were documented in 2001, many of them involving alcohol and underage drinking. The expense to taxpayers for the thousands of hours of police service involved is conservatively estimated to be several hundred thousand dollars.[15]

Support for policy change to prevent alcohol problems in San Diego is broad-based. A local poll released in March of 2002 found that more than six out of seven residents of San Diego (86 percent) say underage drinking in the region is a serious concern.[10]

Communities large and small have begun to address the problem of social hosting through dialogue and local policymaking. In 2002 the City of Poway adopted an ordinance holding adults accountable for serving alcohol to minors in private settings — the first of its kind in San Diego County. In April of 2003, Oceanside adopted a similar law, followed by the cities of San Diego and La Mesa.

Social host liability laws are being implemented across the nation to impose civil penalties, usually in the form of monetary damages, on social hosts for injuries caused by their intoxicated guests. New Jersey was the first state to adopt a social host liability law.[16] Since

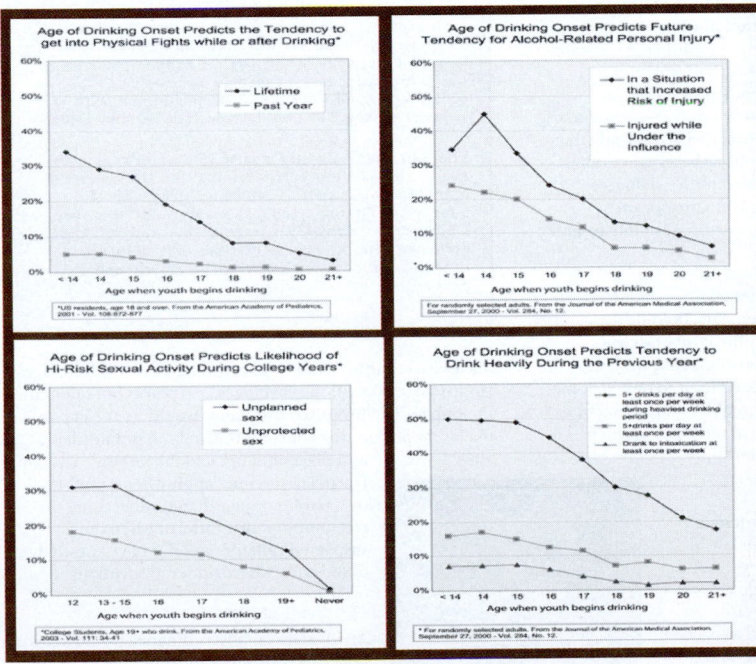

then Delaware, Georgia, Idaho, Indiana, Massachusetts, North Carolina, North Dakota, New Hampshire, New Mexico, Oregon and Vermont have followed suit.

Putting a Stop to Social Hosting

According to current research, social host laws are among the most effective forms of public policy in reducing binge drinking and drinking and driving.[16] Around the country, lawmakers and courts are increasingly recognizing that underage drinking is a serious threat to the health and safety of their communities and are taking steps to reduce it.

Lawmakers are recognizing that underage drinking is a serious threat to health and safety.

The Kansas State Senate recently passed a bill making it a crime (punishable by six months in jail) for adults to allow underage drinking in their homes.[17] Pennsylvania sentenced a woman to four and a half years in prison after she allowed a party that led to the drunk driving deaths of three teenagers.[17]

In California, the assignment of civil penalties to social hosts is precluded by the state Civil Code, which requires an injured third party to prove that his or her injury was caused by the host's illegal service of alcohol rather than the drinker's own consumption of alcohol.[18] In addition, the California Civil Code states that "no social host who furnishes alcoholic beverages to any person shall be held legally accountable for damages suffered by that person, or for injury to the person or property of, or death of, any third person, resulting from the consumption of those beverages." [19]

Therefore, local municipalities are taking a slightly different approach to social hosting. Current laws holding social hosts accountable in San Diego County focus on hosts who provide alcohol to minors. Instead of sanctioning civil penalties after a third party has been injured or killed, the social host laws hold adults accountable by imposing fines and allowing police departments to recover costs incurred in breaking up private parties where underage drinking occurs.

The problems associated with underage drinking in homes are difficult for law enforcement agencies to resolve without greater authority. As the San Diego City Attorney's Office reported to the city council before the council passed a social host law: "Currently there is no law which

Public Policy and Community Change

In the spring of 2000, discussions in many community sectors around San Diego County began to focus on reducing the social availability of alcohol to youth. The San Diego Policy Panel on Youth Access to Alcohol formed a Social Availability Committee to apply that momentum in the policy arena.

Meanwhile, data on youth alcohol access were collected from local high schools in Poway, where community forums helped organize a response to underage drinking at house parties. High-profile Operation Safeguard law enforcement efforts later that year and in 2001 brought more attention to adult providers of alcohol. Links between community prevention advocates, law enforcement and elected officials were further strengthened when the Policy Panel hosted a legislative forum that focused on social availability issues.

With guidance from the North Inland Community Prevention Project, Poway City Councilmember Jay Goldby introduced the county's first social host ordinance in the fall of 2002. After the ordinance was passed, members of the Social Availability Committee followed up with San Diego City Councilmember Brian Maienschein, who in the spring of 2003 led a successful effort to adopt a more stringent social host law in the county's largest municipality. An even stronger ordinance was simultaneously passed in Oceanside, prompted by Police Chief Mike Poehlman with the support of the Tri-City Prevention Collaborative.

The San Diego County Board of Supervisors soon began considering a similar law for the county's unincorporated areas. Chairman Greg Cox and Supervisor Dianne Jacob sponsored the measure, which would not only assess a fine and full cost recovery after the first offense, but also direct those funds back into law enforcement and prevention efforts.

---

makes it a crime for a minor to consume alcoholic beverages [or to] possess alcoholic beverages ... in places not open to the public. The proposed ordinance would fix the gap in the law by prohibiting consumption in both public places and places not open to the public." The San Diego law does not apply when a minor's own parent or guardian is supervising the consumption of alcohol or when the suspected violator does not have knowledge of the party where underage drinking occurs.

An ideal social host ordinance would allow police to issue misdemeanor citations with

COMMUNITY RESOURCES

East County Community Change Project
(619) 660-6233, www.publicstrategies.org/east

North Inland Community Prevention Project
(858) 391-9303, nicpp@mhsinc.org

Oceanside Police Chief Mike Poehlman
(760) 435-4493

S.D. County Policy Panel on Youth Access to Alcohol
(619) 692-8475, www.alcoholpolicypanel.org

San Diego County Sheriff's Captain Glenn Revell
(619) 956-4001

San Diego Police Detective Larry Darwent
(619) 531-2429

Tri-City Prevention Collaborative
(760) 757-8211, jbyrom@vistacommunityclinic.org

fines attached to any adult who permits underage drinking in his or her home. Further, it would permit law enforcement to recover service costs from the adult offender the very first time police are called to the residence. Repeat offenders would face escalating fines. Social host ordinances give law enforcement a tool to control private parties where underage drinking occurs, and they serve as a significant deterrent to hosting the parties in the first place.

The Institute for Public Strategies is a nonprofit organization that advances public health through changes in policy and community norms. The East County Community Change Project, which is conducted by IPS, serves El Cajon, Santee, Lemon Grove, La Mesa and the unincorporated areas of the East County. The project is funded by the San Diego County Health and Human Services Agency, Alcohol and Drug Services. For more information, please contact Brenda Simmons at (619) 660-6233, ext. 16, e-mail info@publicstrategies.org or visit www.publicstrategies.org/east.

References

1. *Teen Tipplers: America's Underage Drinking Epidemic* (2002). National Center on Addiction and Substance Abuse.
2. American Medical Association, Office of Alcohol/Drug Abuse (2001).
3. Drug Strategies, 1999.
4. National Institute on Alcoholism and Alcohol Abuse.
5. Brown, S.A., Tapert, S.F., Granholm, E, & Delis, D.C. (2000). "Neurocognitive functioning of adolescents: Effects of protracted alcohol use." *Alcoholism: Clinical and Experimental Research.* 24(2): 164-171.
6. Pyapali, G.K., Turner, D.A., Wilson, W.A., & Swartzwelder, S.H. (1999). "Age and dose-dependent effects of ethanol on the induction of hippocampal long-term potentiation." *Alcohol.* 19(2): 107-11.
7. Grant, B.F., and Dawson, D.A. (1997). "Age of onset of alcohol use and its association with DSM-IV alcohol abuse and dependence: Results from the National Longitudinal Alcohol Epidemiologic survey." *Journal of Substance Abuse,* 9: 103-110.
8. Hingson, R.W., Heeren, T., Winter, M.R., & Wechsler, H. (2003). "Early age of first drunkenness as a factor in college students' unplanned and unprotected sex attributable to drinking." *Pediatrics,* 111(11): 34.
9. National Household Survey on Drug Abuse: Main Findings 1998, U.S. Department of Health and Human Services (2000).
10. The San Diego Alcohol Survey, Poll on Alcohol Promotions and Youth (2001). Institute for Public Strategies.
11. Combating Underage Drinking Survey (1999).
12. Mayer, Forster, Murray, and Wagenaar (1998).
13. The East County Rural Project: Underage Drinking in the Mountain Empire (2002). Institute for Public Strategies.
14. Pacific Institute for Research and Evaluation (1999).
15. San Diego Police Department.
16. Stout, E.M., Sloan, F.A., Liang, L., & Davies, H. H. (2000). "Reducing harmful alcohol-related behaviors: Effective regulatory methods." *Journal of Studies on Alcohol.*
17. Prichard, O. (Mach 31, 2003). "A growing number of states seek to send a strong message that prison time will result." *Philadelphia Inquirer.*
18. California Civil Code, Section 1714(b).
19. California Civil Code, Section 1714(c).

Institute for Public Strategies

409 Camino del Rio South, Ste. 305, San Diego, CA 92108
Phone: (619) 296-3311 / Fax: (619) 296-3322

3835 Avocado Blvd., Suite 265, La Mesa, CA 91941
Phone: (619) 660-6233 / Fax: (619) 660-6234
E-mail: info@publicstrategies.org

www.publicstrategies.org

Reflect on the Reading

Questions About "Adult Accountability"

1. How would you relate the "Adult Accountability" article to George Will's article "Drinking Age Paradox?" Is there any overlap between the solutions proposed by the two articles?

2. How does the problem of social hosting of home parties relate to the larger problem of teen drinking? How well does the "Adult Accountability" article address this larger problem?

3. Do you believe that social host ordinances will solve the problem outlined in "Adult Accountability?" How does the article justify this proposed solution?

4. Do you feel that the article treats opposing points of view fairly? What tone does it take regarding alternative positions? Can you think of alternative solutions that would address the problem of teen drinking?

Writing Assignment: A Proposal

> Write an essay in which you identify a problem and propose and justify a solution. The proposal might address a specific local situation or it could take up a larger public policy issue. Compose for an audience that might take action on the proposal—perhaps policy makers with the ability to enact the proposal or a public that might be spurred to action. Consider alternative solutions and possible opposition to your proposal.

Ask Questions & Make Decisions

Exercises for Composing Proposals

1. Working with a group or peers, develop a list of possible topics that could be addressed in a proposal essay. Think of problems at the local, national, and global levels, adding several possibilities from each category to your list. Select one topic from the list, and then develop an outline detailing how you would demonstrate the problem and justify a solution. Report your findings to your classmates, asking them to respond to your proposed solution with questions and ideas of their own.

2. Revisit "Adult Accountability for Underage Drinking: The Case for Social Host Laws" (pages 232–35). Think about the way informational graphics and the design of the document contribute to the message of the proposal. Make a list of alternative ways a writer might propose a solution to a problem—a video, a billboard, etc.

3. Identify what you feel to be a long-term problem that has been discussed in detail but has not been solved—homelessness, teen alcohol abuse, school violence, etc. Brainstorm about possible reasons behind the difficulty in addressing this problem—a lack of will, insufficient knowledge, resources, priorities, etc. Does it seem as if these hurdles can be overcome? Write up your findings in a paragraph or so.

4. Taking the problem you identified in the previous exercise, make a list of all of the interested parties who might be involved in addressing the issue. For each of the key stakeholders, jot down ideas about what might motivate that group. Write a paragraph reflecting on how these motivational factors might fit into a proposed solution to the problem.

Plan It   Invention Strategies for Proposals

As you prepare to write a proposal, focus on the problem and possible solutions. Most problems require detailed solutions because they are complicated and entrenched. You need to get an honest assessment of the problem before going forward. And you need to apply similar thinking to the solution. Consider these steps to get started:

- Look over the proposals in this chapter or review additional proposals online. Get a sense for the ways in which proposals cover the problem, the solution, and the justification for the solution. Think about the ways in which proposals are organized.

- Think about potential topics for your proposal. Are there local issues in which you are invested? Are you frustrated with any systems or institutions? Are there public policies you believe need to be changed? Explore several possibilities until you identify a problem you would like to address.

- Brainstorm about the problem you have selected. What personal perspectives can you bring to the problem? What are the most challenging aspects of the problem? Why hasn't the problem been addressed in the past or, if it has, why didn't the problem get resolved?

- Conduct research to learn more about the topic. Are there other, related problems you need to consider? Can you find enough information to compose the proposal?

Learning
Objective 9.2

- Identify information that might be effective when presented in a graph, table, or other visual mode.
- Consider the rhetorical situation in which you are working. To whom will you address your proposal? What do you know about your audience and their values? How will you project yourself as a speaker? What will you try to achieve?
- Identify any additional layers of complexity related to your topic. Are there factors that contribute to the larger problem? How will you address the complexity of the problem in the proposal?
- Think about the specific solution you will offer to address the problem. How complex must the solution be? Will it be possible to convince people that the solution is desirable and feasible?
- Identify any analogies or scenarios that might be used in the proposal. What analogies might help people understand the problem? Can you predict possible consequences to enacting or not enacting the solution that will help make the proposal stronger?
- Zoom out to think about cultural concerns related to the problem and your proposal. Are there ethical issues you need to address? Can social issues help you justify your proposal?
- Consider similar issues or problems. Have related concerns been addressed in the past? Will related issues complicate the solution you propose? How might public perceptions concerning similar issues influence readers of your proposal?
- Think about alternative solutions to the problem. Are there possible approaches that can be folded into your proposal? Will you need to explain why your approach should be favored over others? Are there opposing viewpoints to your overall topic that you need to consider?

CONNECT IT **More Resources for Proposals**

For more detailed information about some of the strategies you might use in proposals, consider the following resources:

For more on rhetorical situations, see Chapter 1.

For more insights into writing arguments, see Chapter 4.

For more on position arguments, see Chapter 8.

For more on conducting research, see Chapters 14–17.

For more on describing, see Chapter 21.

For more on analyzing, see pages 62–65.

For more on examining causes and effects, see Chapter 24.

Compose It **Write A Proposal**

As you begin drafting your proposal, let the work you've done with prewriting and your rhetorical situation guide you. What will you need to produce given the make-up of your readers, your goals, and the nature of your problem? A well-known issue might require less focus on the problem and more emphasis on the solution. An overlooked issue might require calling attention to the problem as the main focus. Here are some possible steps to follow:

- Think about how you will organize and shape your essay. You will likely take up the problem and then offer and justify a solution, but the amount of time you spend on each element of the proposal can vary.
- Create an outline or map of the areas you will address in your proposal. List any contributing factors and layers of complexity in the problem. Spell out all the dimensions of your solution.
- Collect as much research and evidence as needed to compose the proposal. Statistics can help show the extent of the problem. Reports or the perspectives of experts can help justify your solution. Anecdotes and analogies can help illustrate the problem and the solution.
- Draft the sections of the proposal. Be aware of the movement from problem to solution that makes up proposals, but be flexible in your approach to organizing the essay. Give readers a strong sense of the problem. Be clear about the solution. Discuss benefits and consequences as you justify your solution.
- Make sure that you address opposing perspectives and alternative solutions in the proposal. You might list these after you have offered your own solution. Or you could survey the possibilities before spelling out your approach. Acknowledge and build upon valid alternatives. Show why your approach should be considered over, or in addition to, others.
- Close with a section reiterating the solutions you are suggesting. If there is a need for public awareness and action, detail what you expect from readers. Indicate any concrete steps you would like readers to take after finishing the proposal.

Focus on Student Writing

Laura began this essay as a memoir reflecting on a tragic episode related to an ice storm in her community. After giving the project some thought, she began looking into possible responses that might mitigate the effects of such storms. Her essay evolved into a research project and the resulting proposal below.

Laura Davis

Professor Anderson

English 102

7 Mar. 2008

Burying the Problem

As I drive down Homestead Road in Chapel Hill, North Carolina, I'm struck by the beauty of the open fields, the carefully landscaped entrances to neighborhoods, and the abundance of trees, but then I have to stop and ask myself, *Why does this perfect picture have to be tarnished by a jumble of power lines?* Before I know it, however, I'm no longer thinking of the way these lines clutter the sky and interrupt the natural beauty of our neighborhoods. Instead, I begin to think about the tragic history associated with overhead power lines over the years. I'll never forget the fire that started in a local home in 2002 as a family tried to keep warm during a power outage after an ice storm damaged overhead power lines. A kindergartener was killed in that fire, and I wonder whether these unsightly overhead power lines weren't partially to blame. The more we learn about overhead transmission lines, the more we realize that they pose significant problems for our community. Overhead power lines have been shown to lower property values. Some scientists wonder whether there may be links between the power lines and cancer. Yearly, hundreds of people are killed nationwide in accidents with overhead power lines. And these lines are primarily responsible for regular power outages that are inconvenient and sometimes deadly. Clearly, these lines are not only an eyesore but also a threat to the well-being of our community. The solution? Invest in burying power lines.

Some of the problems associated with power lines might seem trivial at first. Sure, it might be more aesthetically pleasing to have power lines buried, but that doesn't justify the high cost of placing lines underground. According to a study by Edison Electrical Institute, which did a cost analysis in Virginia, the cost of putting lines underground and maintaining them would not be worth the aesthetic value (Johnson). In most of the newer neighborhoods, the power lines have been buried and the aesthetics can't be lauded enough, but burying existing overhead lines would be much too expensive. Or so opponents of burying power lines suggest. What these studies fail to take into consideration, though, is the link between aesthetics and property value. A recent study in the Journal *Land Economics* found that "High voltage electric transmission lines do have an effect on property value" (Hamilton and Schwann 443). The study found two factors that impacted property values: concerns over dangers related to proximity to power lines and aesthetics. For homes closest to power lines, property values were lowered an average of 6.3%. Concerns about the costs of burying lines fail to take into account the economic benefits that would come from increased property values.

Costs are the number one reason power lines remain above ground. Estimates put the cost of burying existing lines at around $1 million per mile (Johnson 1). The argument goes that those expenses would be passed on to consumers who are struggling already with the rising costs of energy bills. But these arguments don't also consider the costs associated with the current system of overhead power lines. I have noticed every year as I drive through my neighborhood the line of Duke Power trucks with workmen pruning the vast array of pines, oaks, and walnut trees. Burying power lines would create a significant savings from not having to trim trees. The annual savings for the state of Virginia would be $50 million per year (Johnson 17). Similar savings could be had by protecting power lines from storm damage. The same Edison Electric study estimated a savings of $40 million if the state were to experience two severe storms in a year. In fact, many of the economic benefits of burying power lines extend beyond simply maintaining the electric grid. Chapel Hill suffered tremendous damage from Hurricane Fran. People were without power for up to two weeks. Food spoiled. Workers stayed home.

Businesses closed down. Estimates place the costs of Fran at $5 billion ("Major US Weather Disasters"). No doubt those costs would have been significantly lower had more utilities been protected underground. Further, utilities would profit from the resulting sales created by increased reliability. In Virginia, these profits were projected at $12 million per year (Johnson). In North Carolina, we could see the same savings. Homes and businesses that lose power represent not only an inconvenience but also an economic challenge, especially in a state that regularly sees severe weather events caused by hurricanes and ice storms.

In many ways, the problems concerning the costs of burying power lines have less to do with long-term economic impacts and more to do with short-term disputes about who would pay for the work. In Dare County, North Carolina, some utilities have been placed underground mostly due to hurricanes and bad weather. In Duck and South Shores, the residents have paid the cost, but the rest of Dare County has not. Clearly, for those in economically advantaged areas, the cost is less of a problem. In other areas, the concerns of placing too high a burden on those who are less advantaged must be addressed. But many cities have come up with workable plans for burying power lines. Funding models range from passing expenses on to customers to using government subsidies to asking utility companies to foot the bill to, in most cases, some combination of these options. Cities that have developed plans and made the choice to place their utilities underground include San Antonio, Texas; Colorado Springs, Colorado; New Castle, Delaware; Saratoga Springs, New York; Williamsburg, Virginia; Tacoma, Washington; Frederick, Maryland; and Boulder, Colorado. Each city has a different way of paying for installing underground lines. Boulder assists property owners by sharing costs of burying existing overhead lines through the Xcel Energy Undergrounding Credit. Property owners pay 50% of the cost while Xcel sets aside funds from the preceding year's revenue to be used to defer the rest of the cost up to $100,000 (Johnson). Xcel doesn't provide unlimited funds for the program, but the cooperation between Xcel and property owners reveals that, really, what is needed—more than bundles of money to pay for trenching and laying cable—is leadership. The problem is not so much economic as it is strategic: developing and implementing plans requires collaboration between utilities, government, and the community.

While it's good to know that solutions to the aesthetic and economic problems caused by overhead power lines need not be derailed simply because of economics, it is disturbing to think that we talk about money at all when we consider the more significant dangers of power lines. You may recall the recent news story covering four Boy Scout leaders who were electrocuted during the annual scout jamboree in Virginia. The scout leaders were putting up a tent when one of the poles came in contact with a high power line. That the incident happened at all is tragic, but more troubling is the fact that accidents involving overhead power lines take place all the time. The Consumer Product Safety Commission estimates that "between 1990 and 1998, more than 300 people in the U.S. were electrocuted when an antenna or pole they were holding touched a high-voltage power line" ("National Electric"). These figures don't include the high number of electrocutions that take place among construction, landscaping, or agricultural workers. Any industry that works outdoors invests heavily in overhead wire safety programs, but still accidents happen, frequently resulting in death. Further, the threat from downed power lines hits those who are least prepared to handle dangerous situations involving electricity. Three residents were recently killed in Ipswich, New Zealand. A woman and her three-year-old daughter were clearing brush on a footpath when they ran into live power lines. A neighbor rushing to their aid was also electrocuted. After the incident, the local coroner expressed his frustration with arguments citing the expense of burying power lines: "Because it's so expensive should not cause it to be shelved. It is a challenge, but at the end of the day . . . what price can be put on a human life?" (Keim).

We can't put a value on a human life. And we know that overhead power lines are costly in human and economic terms. Think of the residents killed when ladders and tent poles accidentally contact live power lines. Consider the electrocution injuries and fatalities among construction workers and tree trimmers. Think about those power poles and pylons that contribute to deaths by traffic accident each day. Think of the money invested in power line avoidance education programs, in tree pruning around power lines, in helping communities recover after major storms. There really is no reason not to begin the process of eliminating this dangerous and costly problem. Duke Power was accused of under reporting about $123 million in pretax income from 1998 to 2000. We might want to ask, *How much profit should these companies make and why are we paying exorbitant amounts to look at unsightly, dangerous, and antiquated technology?* In our world, burying power lines should be techno-efficient, safe, and affordable in the long term. We need leadership at the government, community, and utility corporation levels to make this change happen. I for one would rather pay a bit more for my utilities to be able to drive down Homestead or any road in Chapel Hill knowing I have done something to make it safer for the people I see working and playing among the lush green landscape, a landscape with no wires attached.

Works Cited

Hamilton, Stanley W., and Gregory M. Schwann. "Do High Voltage Electric Transmission Lines Affect Property Value?" *Land Economics* 71.4 (1995): 436–45. Print.

Johnson, Bradley W. "Out of Sight, Out of Mind?: A Study on the Costs and Benefits of Undergrounding Overhead Power Lines." *Edison Electric Institute,* July 2006. Web. 5 Mar. 2008.

Keim, Tony. *Coroner Calls for Overhead Powerline Ban. The Rivermouth Action Group,* n.d Web. 5 Mar. 2008.

"Major US Weather Disasters by Estimated Costs and Deaths." *All Countries* Web site, 2006. Web. 3 Mar. 2008.

"National Electric Safety Month: CPSC Alerts Consumers to Electrocution Hazards from Overhead Power." *News from Consumer Product Safety Commission,* 1 May 2002. Web. 3 Mar. 2008.

Reflect on the Reading

Questions About "Burying the Problem"

1. Laura's proposal essay opens with a personal focus. Do you find the strategy effective? Why or why not?

2. In what ways does including a quotation from a source in New Zealand affect the message of the essay? Are there other aspects of the piece that raise questions for you?

3. Much of the solution sections of the paper concentrate on responding to economic arguments about the cost of burying power lines. Do you feel as if the essay provides enough information about the economic dimensions of the problem? What kinds of information might make the essay stronger?

4. How well does the proposal address opposing points of view? Can you think of additional objections to burying power lines?

5. The essay closes by emphasizing the human costs of overhead power lines. Is it possible to argue that the paper is needlessly playing on the emotions of readers? How would you respond to such an argument?

Revise It   Strategies for Revising Proposals

When you revise your proposal, make sure that your project is on track in terms of the big picture questions. Have you identified a pressing problem? Do you propose a viable solution? Are readers likely to be persuaded? Think also about these strategies:

- Review your proposal, trying on the perspective of a skeptical reader. Where might you flag sections of the proposal with questions or disagreements? Take note of these potential problem areas and revisit them later to address the concerns.

- Focus your attention on the discussion of the problem. How clear are the key concerns laid out in the proposal? Does your discussion of the problem reveal it to be significant enough to warrant people's attention? If not, does the topic need adjusting or can you revise the composition to better illustrate the problem?

- Zoom in as well on the solution. Have you outlined enough specifics to give readers a clear sense of what you propose? How can you make the solution more concrete?

- Pay particular attention to the justification section. Have you considered the costs of the solution? Do you detail the consequences? Are readers likely to walk away from your piece feeling convinced that the solution could work?

Learning Objective 9.3

- Review your proposal to ensure that it will resonate with those who are likely to be most involved with your solution. Have you gotten their attention? Have you detailed the problem and offered a solution viable enough to make your readers want to help?
- Look over the design of your proposal. Could headings, informational graphics, and other elements of document design (Chapter 26) make the proposal more compelling?
- Examine the research you have integrated into the proposal. Are there areas where more information will benefit the proposal? Are quotations smoothly woven into the text? Are they properly documented?

Push It   More Possibilities for Proposals

1. Compose a grant proposal. Grant proposals are similar to problem–solution proposals in that they are written to address a problem or pressing need. They may also detail aspects of a solution, explaining what will be accomplished with any funding provided. They require a good deal of explanation to demonstrate their feasibility, including budgets and other lists of deliverables that show what will come from enacting the proposal. The key to composing a grant proposal is to match the problem with a funding agency that will likely have an interest in the issue. A proposal that is well matched with the mission and expertise of the funding agency has a much better chance of success. You will also need to be deliberate about following all of the criteria listed in the Request for Proposals (RFP) put out by the funding agency. Agencies receiving hundreds of competitive proposals will eliminate those that don't follow the protocols for submission.

2. Compose a public service announcement like the one on page 211. Public service announcements (PSAs) represent a kind of distillation of the key components of a problem–solution proposal, with an emphasis on the call to action. A PSA might take the form of a flyer, a poster, or a brochure, to name some possibilities. As you develop a PSA in one of these visual forms, think about elements of document design. You may want to include some of the details that help justify a solution—perhaps a few statistics or quotations—but in general, your message will focus on demonstrating the problem visually and urging viewers to act. Strive to provide a compelling image that grabs a viewer's attention and that reveals the nature and extent of the problem. You might then use a textual statement to suggest the kind of action that you propose viewers should take. For more on creating visuals, see Chapters 25 and 26. For more on creating flyers and brochures, see Chapter E7.

RESOURCES
Sample Proposals

Zoom Out   Reflecting on Proposals

- **Proposals address problems.** You may have personal experience with a problem. There may be local issues that frustrate you. You may have convictions about a policy issue. All of these situations can be met with a proposal that demonstrates the problem and offers a solution.

- **Proposals offer justifications for the solutions they put forward.** They may make ethical claims related to the problem or they may detail the feasibility of solutions as a way of arguing for their approach.

- **Proposals allow you to learn a good deal about issues.** Problems often have many layers of complexity—for example, large social concerns layered with specific challenges that must be addressed layered with contributing factors that must also be considered to solve the problem.

- **Proposals follow a problem-solution movement but can take a variety of forms.** Some issues require you either to emphasize a problem more and the solution less or vice versa. Problem-solution compositions also consider opposing points of view. They weigh and respond to alternative solutions and consider assumptions that underlie their positions.

- **Some situations require alternative forms of proposals.** Publicity documents like flyers or brochures can be used to demonstrate problems and prompt viewers toward action.

For additional information and practice with the learning objectives in this chapter, go to www.mycomplab.com, Resources > Writing > Writing Purposes > Writing to Argue or Persuade

CHAPTER 10

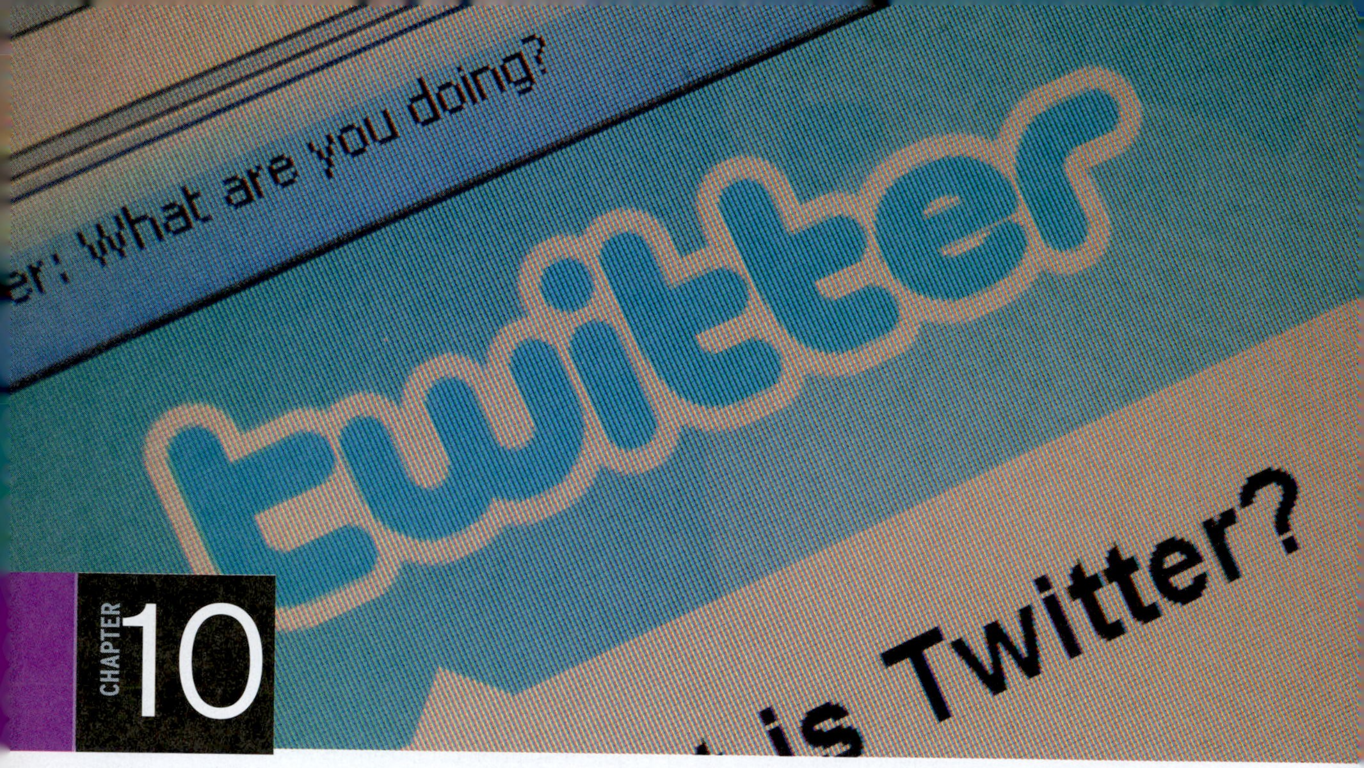

Explanatory Research Essays

Zoom In

Key Concepts and Learning Objectives

After studying this chapter, you should be able to:

10.1 Present information clearly, and then make decisions about when and where to do so.

10.2 Use an inquiry-based approach to learn as much as possible about a topic.

10.3 Conduct research to make sense of and present complex information to readers.

10.4 Use graphics and formatting elements to organize and present information.

Y ou will find explanatory writing in all kinds of situations. Sometimes a piece of writing simply needs to deliver information. When you encounter the "Quick Start Guide" for your cell phone or a flyer for this weekend's 5k road race, you really just want to quickly grasp a concept or gather crucial facts. But explanatory writing will also frequently address other purposes and take more complex forms. Explanatory research essays can help you explore questions, identify concerns, and pursue leads as you examine a complex issue. You should keep an open mind, be ready to learn, and think critically as you read explanatory research pieces, and you must be flexible as you compose them.

You will need to understand the key role of research in explanatory writing. It is possible to investigate and explain a topic based on your own firsthand knowledge, but in most reading and composing situations, explanatory writing requires that you conduct research. If you are reading explanatory essays, you may have to track down sources to follow up on questions and check a writer's facts. If you are composing, research should pave the way for you to explore the concerns circulating around a topic. This chapter covers explanatory essays in several forms. Most include formal uses of sources and all of them reflect extensive research. (You can learn more about research in Chapters 14–17.)

KEY TERMS

- **Explanatory writing:** Writing that focuses primarily on providing information. In essays, explanatory writing often strives to help readers make sense of a concept or concern.

- **Informational graphics:** Charts, graphs, images, and illustrations that help readers make sense of information. Charts and graphs provide a visual representation of data. Images and illustrations provide visual evidence and offer detailed examples of processes or items.

- **Formatting elements:** Features in texts that help readers make sense of information or move through a document. Tables help organize data. Headings, bullets, numbered lists, and text boxes help organize and display textual information.

- **Informational strategies:** Writing strategies that can be used in explanatory situations. Helpful strategies include comparison, discussion of processes or causes and effects, description, analysis, and evaluation.

Understanding Explanatory Research Essays

To get a better sense of the key features of explanatory essays, let's look at an example. In this piece, Ingrid Caldwell reports on the use of the Internet by terrorist organizations.

 ## Terror on YouTube: The Internet's Most Popular Sites Are Becoming Tools for Terrorist Recruitment
BY **INGRID CALDWELL**

The Forensic Examiner publishes research articles related to the field of forensic science. It frequently also includes pieces related to law enforcement. Ingrid Caldwell is a freelance writer. "Terror on YouTube: The Internet's Most Popular Sites Are Becoming Tools for Terrorist Recruitment" was published in 2008.

Since its creation, the Internet has been viewed as a symbol of democracy and free speech, a tool for communicating, networking, and learning. But there is a dark side to the unregulated sprawl of the World Wide Web, and it doesn't take a computer forensics expert to find it. The very same features that make it convenient for the average user to socialize with friends or research for a school paper are now being used by terrorist organizations to recruit, raise funds, and attract a whole new generation of supporters.

The terrorist presence on the Web concerned Homeland Security and Governmental Affairs Committee chairman Joe Lieberman (ID-Conn.) so much that he wrote a letter to Google chairman Eric Schmidt, urging him to remove from YouTube all videos with ties to terrorist organizations. In his letter, Lieberman wrote that terrorists use YouTube and similar sites to "disseminate their propaganda, enlist followers, and provide weapons training" and that they unintentionally "permit Islamist terrorist groups to maintain an active, pervasive, and amplified voice, despite military setbacks or successful operations by the law enforcement and intelligence communities" (Senate Committee on Homeland Security and Governmental Affairs, 2008).

"Protecting our citizens from terrorist attacks is a top priority for our government," Lieberman continued. "The private sector can help us do that. By taking action to curtail the use of YouTube to disseminate the goals and methods of those who wish to kill innocent civilians, Google will make a singularly important contribution to this important national effort."

MANY TERRORIST VIDEOS

YouTube responded to Lieberman's request by taking down some videos that the company said violated its policies on content. But *The Forensic Examiner* found that on June 18, weeks after the Lieberman initiative, many videos remained on YouTube that appeared to promote or affiliate with terrorist groups such as Hamas, Hezbollah, Al-Qaeda, and the Iraqi insurgency.

One disturbing YouTube video featured Star Wars action figures recreating the beheading of American journalist Daniel Pearl. Though the actual Pearl execution is not on YouTube, it can easily be found elsewhere on the Internet.

YouTube videos posted by supporters of the Iraqi insurgency show American soldiers being shot and flag-covered coffins en route to the United States.

Other YouTube videos found by *The Examiner* included tributes to suicide bombers, propaganda promoting Hamas and Hezbollah leaders, and statements alleging that the U.S. is covering up its actual casualties in Iraq. One cartoon image showed a bloody U.S. soldier caught in a mousetrap that featured the Iraqi flag. Osama bin Laden's message praising the attacks of 9/11/2001 also can be found on YouTube.

FREE SPEECH DEBATE

Lieberman's plea re-ignited the nationwide debate about when—if ever—security should override freedom. Civil libertarians ask: Terrorists on the Web pose a very real threat, but would harshly regulating Internet content in an attempt to stop them do more harm than good?

In his report "How Modern Terrorism Uses the Internet," Gabriel Weimann (2004a, p. 2) states that security agencies have focused too much on potential acts of cyberterrorism (such as virus attacks and hacking) and have failed to widely address the more common ways in which terrorists use the Internet every day. Although cyberterrorism is a real threat that needs to be handled seriously, terrorists more commonly use the Internet to recruit new supporters, mobilize current supporters, raise funds, find information on potential targets, and wage campaigns of intimidation and disinformation.

Weimann (2004a, p. 2) states that in 1998 "around half of the 30 organizations designated as 'Foreign Terrorist Organizations' under the U.S. Antiterrorism and Effective Death Penalty Act of 1996 maintained Web sites; by 2000, virtually all terrorist groups had established their presence on the Internet."

Modern terrorist organizations have changed with the times, operating more like a PR-savvy corporation than a stereotypical bunch of nomads hiding in a back room. One of Hezbollah's sites targets international journalists directly and encourages them to contact the organization's press office (Weimann, 2004a, p. 4). According to Weimann, Web sites

Terror on Youtube:
The Internet's Most
Popular Sites Are
Becoming Tools for
Terrorist Recruitment
(continued)
BY **INGRID CALDWELL**

maintained by terrorist groups use similar methods of propaganda, aiming their messages at current and potential members, the global public, and citizens of enemy states in order to gain sympathy and financial support.

"Typically, a [terrorist organization] site will provide a history of the organization and its activities, a detailed review of its social and political background, accounts of its notable exploits, biographies of its leaders, founders, and heroes, information on its political and ideological aims, fierce criticism of its enemies, and up-to-date news," said Weimann in his report. "Despite the ever-present vocabulary of 'the armed struggle' and 'resistance,' what most sides do not feature is a detailed description of their violent activities" (p. 4).

Using sophisticated rhetorical methods, online terrorists attempt to convince their audiences that their violent acts are necessary to achieve "greater peace," that they have no other choice. Their tactics are undeniably successful: Since Sept. 11, numerous threats of big attacks on U.S. soil have appeared on al Qaeda's Web site, and while none of these threats came into fruition, they attracted significant media attention and managed to perpetuate the nationwide feelings of fear and insecurity that arose post-9/11.

In a 2003 speech, former Secretary of Defense Donald Rumsfeld read the following passage from an al Qaeda training manual recovered in Afghanistan: "Using public sources openly and without resorting to illegal means, it is possible to gather at least 80 percent of all information required about the enemy" (as cited in Weimann, 2004b). "Public sources," of course, refers primarily to the Internet, where the average user can find anything from maps of the New York subway system to commercial flight schedules to the current whereabouts of a particular U.S. politician—all without sacrificing anonymity.

Because there is no question that terrorists use the Internet every day to further their plans, the solution seems fairly straightforward: shut down their sites, take their videos off YouTube, closely monitor their chat rooms, and censor their blogs and news articles. But, as Dan Gillmore, a panelist at the 2005 International Summit on Democracy, Terrorism, and Security in Madrid, pointed out, it's often more complicated than that. In some countries, the line between terrorist rebellion and legitimate political dissent is hard to distinguish, and heavy regulation of the Internet could actually backfire and endanger innocent people.

"We believe that an attempt to end anonymity would be highly unlikely to stop a determined terrorist or criminal of any kind, but it would certainly have a deeply chilling effect on political activity in places where speaking one's mind is dangerous and where certain kinds of unpopular speech could jeopardize someone's livelihood or perhaps life," Gillmore said (as cited in Ito, 2005).

Another case for a free and open Internet rests on the idea that it is best to keep enemies in plain sight. As long as terrorist organizations uphold their presence on the Web, it is possible to keep track of their whereabouts, plans, and new campaigns. Rebecca MacKinnon, also a panelist at the 2005 summit, argued that the general public can play a useful role in the fight against terrorism—keeping a watchful eye on those corners of the Web that security agencies are not able to monitor constantly.

"Terrorism is a problem of armies, it is a problem faced by police forces, but it is also a problem faced by ordinary citizens everywhere," she said. "The best way to combat terrorism is to involve the general public in that fight and the best way to do that is through the open Internet" (as cited in Ito, 2005).

On May 8, 2008, the Senate Committee on Homeland Security and Governmental Affairs released a report, "Violent Islamist Extremism, the Internet, and the Homegrown Terrorist Threat," detailing the threat of terrorists on the Internet. Authored by Lieberman and Ranking Minority Member Susan Collins (R-Maine), the report calls on federal agencies to unify their scattered attempts into a single, comprehensive plan for responding to the terrorist Web presence.

"Despite recognition in the National Implementation Plan (NIP) that a comprehensive response is needed, the U.S. government has not developed nor implemented a coordinated outreach and communications strategy to address the homegrown terrorist threat, especially as that threat is amplified by the use of the Internet," Lieberman and Collins (2008, p. 16) wrote.

The committee's report proposes no specific solution but stresses the immediacy of the problem, concluding that the "use of the Internet by al-Qaeda and other violent Islamist extremist groups has expanded the terrorist threat to our homeland. No longer is the threat just from abroad, as was the case with the attacks of September 11, 2001; the threat is now increasingly from within, from homegrown terrorists who are inspired by violent Islamist ideology to plan and execute attacks where they live. One of the primary drivers of this new threat is the use of the Internet to enlist individuals or groups of individuals to join the cause without ever affiliating with a terrorist organization" (Lieberman & Collins, 2008, p. 15).

Because complete censorship is difficult and dangerous, perhaps what we need to do is not regulate but reign in the Internet as a tool—not impose heavy restrictions, which could hurt everyone, but utilize the freedom and global connection provided by the Internet to further the goals of democracy and peace.

"The fundamental democratic values that are embedded in the architecture of the Internet are the same fundamental democratic values that will enable us to defeat terrorism," said Andrew McLaughlin, head of Global Public Policy and Government Affairs for Google, Inc., at the 2005 summit. "They are openness, they are participation, they are distribution of authority, accountability; these are the essential features of the Internet, and if we view this medium properly, we can see that it is in fact the best ally that we have in fighting the scourge of terrorism."

References

Ito, J., moderator. (2005, March 10). Democracy. Terrorism and the Internet. International Summit on Democracy, Terrorism and Security. Retrieved June 9, 2008, from http://english.safe-democracy.org/keynotes/democracy-terrorism-and-the-internet.html#transcrip

Terror on Youtube: The Internet's Most Popular Sites Are Becoming Tools for Terrorist Recruitment *(continued)*
BY **INGRID CALDWELL**

Lieberman, J., and Collins, S. (2008, March 8). Violent Islamist extremism, the Internet, and the homegrown terrorist threat. Senate Committee on Homeland Security and Governmental Affairs. Retrieved June 9, 2008, from http://hsgac.senate.gov.libproxy.lib.unc.edu/public/_files/IslamistReport.pdf

Senate Committee on Homeland Security and Governmental Affairs. (2008, May 19). Lieberman calls on Google to take down terrorist content. Senate Committee on Homeland Security and Governmental Affairs. Retrieved June 8, 2008, from http://hsgac.senate.gov/public/index.cfm?Fuseaction=PressReleasesDetail&PressRelease_id=8093d5b2-c882-4d12-883d-5c670d43d269&Month=5&Year=2008&Affiliation=C

Weimann, G. (2004a, March). How modern terrorism uses the Internet. U.S. Institute of Peace. Retrieved June 10, 2008, from http://www.usip.org/pubs/specialreports/sr116.html

Weimann, G. (2004b, April 30). Terrorism and the Internet. Computer Crime Research Center. Retrieved June 8, 2008, from http://www.crime-research.org/news/30.04.2004/254/

Reflect on the Reading

Questions About "Terror on YouTube: The Internet's Most Popular Sites Are Becoming Tools for Terrorist Recruitment"

1. How would you describe the responsibilities of private organizations like Google or YouTube when it comes to personal freedom? When, if ever, should these organizations respond to requests to remove materials?

2. The article reports that among the items posted on the Internet are photographs of American casualties in flag-covered coffins. How would you respond to someone who argued that this is necessary in an age when governments tightly control information?

3. The article provides a good deal of information about its topic. What other purposes can you recognize informing the piece? Do you find these instances complementary or distracting?

4. How do you respond to the claim that "regulating Internet content in an attempt to stop [terrorists] would do more harm than good"? Hold a discussion with classmates about the claim.

Let's look more closely at "Terror on YouTube: The Internet's Most Popular Sites Are Becoming Tools for Terrorist Recruitment." In many ways, the piece serves as a kind of clearinghouse for information. It summarizes and highlights key points from a report by Gabriel Wiemann. Like most research reports, the piece cites instances where it refers directly to outside sources, and then it documents those sources in a reference list at the end of the essay. "Terror on YouTube" uses APA format for citing sources. Depending on the format of the essay, these source citations can follow different styles. (You can learn more about citing sources in Chapter 17.)

But the article does not simply dump information on readers. Instead, it passes along key points in a sequence that helps illuminate the topic. From the Wiemann source, it pulls out statistics about the extent of terrorist activity online and picks out distinct examples that help illustrate the concerns it discusses. The article also identifies telling quotations from the Wiemann source and includes those to help bring the issue into focus. The article also weaves information from this source together with highlights from additional resources. It uses a quotation from a congressional report, cites panelists from a conference on Internet terrorism, and offers facts and statistics as necessary.

Note also how "Terror on YouTube: The Internet's Most Popular Sites Are Becoming Tools for Terrorist Recruitment" generally takes an objective stance as it explores the topic. It details the position of those who are opposed to Internet regulation to combat terrorism. It surveys the main concerns that arise related to the topic, and then illustrates these concerns with information and examples. The piece does move in some additional directions toward the end, when it begins to highlight the possible use of the democratic structure of the Internet to combat terrorist efforts. Here, the beginnings of a proposal or an argument emerge, but they serve to create closure for the exploration of the topic. The main aim of the piece is to lay out the key concerns as clearly as possible for readers.

Know It Strategies for Understanding Explanatory Research Essays

- Think of explanatory essays as one among many kinds of writing. A poem or song might try to move your emotions. An argument might try to sway your decisions. Explanatory essays will try to clearly present information. All of these types of writing can borrow from and blend with one another.

- Learn more about the author of an explanatory essay—what motives might he or she have in composing the article? What knowledge and authority does the author possess?
- Evaluate critically the evidence used in explanatory essays. Information may be presented as examples, statistics, or quotations. Look beyond the face value of the evidence and make decisions about its reliability. (For more on evaluating sources, see Chapter 16.)
- Learn more about the topic of the essay. Ask others what they think about the topic. Conduct research to verify the information that is presented.
- Examine the strategies used to deliver information. How are comparisons, definitions, analogies, or claims about causes and effects used to provide information? Are visual or formatting strategies used to share information? How effective are these elements?

VIDEO
20. Informational
Graphics

Ask Questions & Make Decisions

Exercises for Understanding Explanatory Research Essays

1. Find an item that seems to be primarily concerned with delivering information—a manual for an electronic device, a pamphlet with information on a medical condition, a flyer, etc. Examine the item to discover purposes beyond the simple presentation of information. Write a paragraph about your findings.

2. Identify something about which you are an expert—pottery, Web building, skateboarding, making an omelet, etc. Focus on a task related to your expertise and then make a list of all the steps you would need to write about to explain that task to readers.

3. Choose a complex concept—propaganda, capitalism, journalism, unionization, instant messaging, etc. Explore the definition of the concept using several reference sources (manuals, dictionaries, and encyclopedias). Make a list of the controversies you discover as you examine definitions of the concept.

4. Using the concept you chose above, explore articles that you find through your library. Identify an article that focuses heavily on providing information related to the concept. Write a paragraph comparing the piece to what you discovered using reference sources.

Readings and Resources for Exploring Explanatory Research Essays

RESOURCES
Sample Explanatory
Research Essays

Research essays that present information are some of the most common forms you will encounter. You can find research essays in most academic journals and many newspapers, books, and magazines. You can also explore the example below, in which Hadley Ferguson explains how educators can make use of Twitter.

Join the Flock!

BY **HADLEY FERGUSON**

Hadley Ferguson teaches history at Springside Middle School in Philadelphia. She also blogs regularly about technology and education. She explains how Twitter can help educators keep informed and create connections in "Join the Flock," which was published in 2010 in the journal Learning and Leading with Technology.

A year ago, I had no idea what a PLN was. Before I built my professional learning network, I did all my learning by myself. If I needed to understand something for a new unit, I researched it on my own. That was before I discovered Twitter, the virtual meeting place where your PLN comes together.

A PLN is a community of individuals around the world who are learning together. They can start out as strangers, people you couldn't pick out in a crowded room. But Twitter helps these strangers come together to create a community built on communication and collaboration dedicated to making learning and education the best it can be.

TAKE TIME TO BUILD YOUR COMMUNITY

The first thing to know is that developing a PLN on Twitter takes a commitment—not necessarily a huge one, but it does take some time. It is a bit like starting a new friendship: You cultivate a relationship by chatting over coffee in the faculty room or sharing an anecdote in the hall. It is the kind of commitment that causes you to pause rather than walk on, and that's what it will take to develop and maintain a PLN using Twitter.

The amount of time you set aside to build your PLN depends on you. It can be 10 minutes a day or an hour on a Saturday, but it is necessary, or you will never begin to learn from the people you are following.

Join the Flock!
(continued)
BY **HADLEY FERGUSON**

As with any process, it can be broken down into several steps:

Set up your account. Once you sign up for a free account on Twitter, you'll be asked to write a 140-character bio and post a photo. It is important that you have a photo or avatar rather than simply the Twitter-bird default. That image makes you more real to your PLN. Also, make sure that you include in your bio what you are interested in, as people who are deciding whether to follow you will look at that to get a sense of what you care about. Mine reads: "History teacher, tech enthusiast, lifelong learner, Mom and Grandmom."

Learn to follow. Following someone requires nothing more than clicking the Follow button. Twitter then notifies that person that you are following him or her. It's a bit like offering a compliment. It means that you are interested in what he or she thinks. Generally, they will check out your profile and decide whether they want to follow you too.

When the people you follow post something, it shows up in your Twitter stream. Choose people you want to learn from. I look for educators, history teachers, and middle school teachers. You can search for a person you know in the Twitter search box, or you can search for keywords and find people who are interested in the same topics. Check out the person by reading the bio under the picture. Some people include their hometowns, their favorite sports, or their hobbies. Look for people you share a common interest with, whether it's an enthusiasm for baseball, lifelong learning, or ed tech.

I have one Twitter account set up for my professional development and one for my personal interests. That way, when I want to learn about teaching and new ideas about education, I go to my twitter.com/hadleyjf account. When I want to hear from the president or learn what is happening in Philadelphia, I go to twitter.com/hadleynana. For me, there is too much information to have only one account.

Tap into great lists. A good way to find people to follow is to check out the lists that other people create. A few of my favorites from fellow educators are: Shelly Terrell (http://twitter.com/ShellTerrell), Paula White, (http://twitter.com/ PaulaWhite), Tom Whitby (http://twitter.com/tomwhitby), and Milton Ramirez (http://twitter.com/tonnet). They have identified people who are committed to learning and growing in a Web 2.0 world. Choose as many people as you want from their lists and begin to follow them.

Watch and listen. The wonderful thing about Twitter is that you can simply follow people and not say a word. Just read the tweets, click on links to blogs, and learn. There is no need to put yourself into the conversation until you are ready to be visible. You can spend hours and days lurking without tweeting anything. You never need to be the awkward person at a party, standing on the outside of a group, listening in, and wishing you could participate. On Twitter, all of the conversation comes to you. You are invited in from the start. The level of participation is up to you.

Very quickly, you will begin to find links to interesting blog posts or new tools for the classroom. It is a forum where educators post what they are thinking and what they stumble upon.

Give generously. The next step is to move beyond simply taking from the Twitter stream and start retweeting. When you retweet someone's post, it shows up in the stream of the person who posted it. That person "sees" you and will often thank you for sending his idea along. He may have no idea how many followers you have. He only knows that you liked what he posted. Often that person, or someone who follows him, will start to follow you, and you will begin to build your own following. The more you retweet, the more people will begin to follow you, because you will have made yourself visible to the PLN world.

Once you feel comfortable becoming part of the conversation, you might want to add a comment before retweeting the link or comment. Do this by typing something such as "Yes!" or "Gr8 idea" before you retweet. As you do this, you show yourself a bit more. If you want to remain invisible and simply learn without commenting, you can do that, but if you want to enter the conversation, then these are small steps to build your confidence. You can simply add "Good idea" with little concern that you might make a mistake, though from my experience, the educators who take time to have conversations on Twitter rarely point out mistakes. Even when there is disagreement, it is generally in the context of trying to provide the best for kids.

Expose yourself. This is where it can get a little scary, because the next steps require you to begin to expose yourself and your thinking. You can do a tremendous amount of learning without going any further, but there is so much more available if you share your ideas with the people who are now following you. Begin by tweeting the links to tools and sites that you find in your daily work as an educator. If you read a good article, copy the link and send it out. If you use a tool effectively, tweet about it. "Used Wallwisher with 8th grade today. Loved it." You will develop the habit of including your PLN in your thinking. The wonderful part about having only 140 characters is that there isn't much room to make a fool of yourself. And if you do, as I have, it passes quickly and no one remembers.

Tag your tweet. Using a hashtag—another word for the pound sign (#)—in your tweet will give it even more exposure. A hashtag will add it to the streams of the educators who follow that hashtag. Some of the education hashtags I find useful are #teachers, #educators, #web20, and #pln. When you add a hashtag to your post, more people will see what you are sharing.

At this point, you may find yourself becoming addicted to Twitter and to conversations with your PLN. Using Twitter to tap into my PLN has made my teaching suddenly come alive. I have discovered people who wanted to help me succeed or help me figure out what went wrong. When I have a question, I turn to my PLN and wait to hear back. It may seem like 140 characters does not allow enough room to communicate, but those few characters connect me to blogs and websites. Over time, I have built relationships with people I know only by their photos or avatars, but they are real people to me nonetheless. I look for them in my stream of tweets and recognize them as they scroll by. They are my PLN, and I am part of theirs. So join the flow of ideas and learning and watch it change how you see yourself as a teacher and your students as learners.

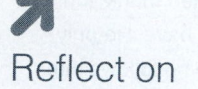

Reflect on the Reading

Questions About "Join the Flock!"

1. What strategies does Ferguson use to make it easy to take in information? Can you think of other possibilities for making the materials more clear?

2. How clearly does "Join the Flock!" explain the process of interacting on Twitter? What would you say to someone who argued the piece is not technical enough?

3. Ferguson's focus is on using Twitter to communicate with educators. Does this emphasis limit the appeal of the article? Why or why not?

4. The piece suggests that participating in a personal learning network can change our habits of thinking. Do you agree? How would you explain this kind of change?

Writing Assignment: An Explanatory Research Essay

Compose an explanatory essay in which you provide information to readers about a concept or concern. Since you will be offering knowledge to readers, you may wish to write about something with which you are already familiar—dance, woodworking, the Civil War, soccer, music, DNA, etc. Regardless of your level of expertise, you should conduct research to explore and help explain key dimensions of the topic. (See Chapters 14–17 for more on research.)

Your emphasis should be primarily on providing information, but you may also focus some of the essay on complementary goals—perhaps persuading readers about an aspect of your topic or entertaining them to engage their interests. Familiarize yourself with strategies for conveying information, and then compose your essay, making decisions about how best to explain your concepts.

Ask Questions & Make Decisions

Exercises for Composing Explanatory Research Essays

1. Consider possible topics for an explanatory research essay. Some possibilities will work better depending on your expertise and interests (service learning over particle physics) or on their complexity and relevance (corporal punishment over corduroy styles). Make a list of at least eight possible topics for an explanatory research essay.

2. Pick a concern for a possible explanatory research essay, and then think of aspects related to the concern that might be illustrated using comparisons. Write a paragraph sketching out possible comparisons that could be used in an essay.

3. Think about a task with which you are familiar. Write a page or so explaining the task to readers. When finished, think about how describing a process might be used in an explanatory research essay.

4. An explanatory research essay often tries to not only inform but also engage its readers. Other forms of explanation often forego this advice in order to concentrate only on information—DVR manuals or cake recipes. Identify an example of this kind of instructional writing, and then revise the instructions so that they engage readers.

Plan It

Invention Strategies for Explanatory Essays

You will have to adjust what you compose based on decisions about your rhetorical situation, but be aware of the core process of delivering information. As you plan, think of opportunities to use graphs, charts, or illustrations to help make information evident. You will also want to organize your work clearly. Your overarching goal is to help others make sense of your topic. Here are some steps to get started:

Learning Objective 10.1

- Begin by thinking of your rhetorical situation. Strive to present yourself as a credible source of knowledge on your topic. Assess the knowledge levels of your audience, adjusting your essay plan based on their needs and ability to handle the complexity of your information.

- Learn as much as you can about your topic. See Chapters 14–17 for more on conducting research. Synthesize the sources of information you encounter, identifying key strands of knowledge to share with readers.

- Select the most important points to share with your readers. As you pinpoint pieces of knowledge to share, remember that explanatory research essays should not simply dump data on their readers. Consider how to organize your key points so readers will find them easy to understand.
- Collect the best evidence you can find to convey your information. Take notes from sources you have read and strategize about how you will weave facts, quotations, or examples into the essay.
- Think about how the details and information you provide can be used to make larger points about your topic. You're not trying to win an argument, but your information can connect with cultural concerns and help you draw conclusions.
- Look at the way your topic is treated in other contexts. Can you refer to some of these other messages to help readers understand the topic? Will you need to address competing claims about your topic?
- Develop an outline, graphic organizer, or some other planning document. Try to map out a clear and logical sequence.

CONNECT IT   Helpful Connections for Explanatory Research Essays

For more detailed information about some of the strategies you might use in explanatory essays, consider the following resources:

For more on thesis statements, see pages 413–17.
For more on organizing structures, see pages 422–30.
For more on research, see Chapters 14–17.
For more on evaluation, see pages 80–82.
For more on analyzing, see pages 62–65.
For more on describing, see Chapter 21.
For more on defining, see Chapter 22.
For more on comparing and contrasting, see Chapter 23.
For more on examining causes and effects, see Chapter 24.
For more on presenting information visually, see Chapters 25 and 26.

Compose It **Write an Explanatory Research Essay**

When drafting, work from your plan or outline to ensure a helpful organization for your essay. Remember that you need to distill information and pick out the key details. Finally, rely on whatever writing strategies will be most helpful in presenting your information and making points. Use comparisons, discuss causes and effects, consider processes, analyze, and evaluate as needed to develop the body of your essay. Consider these steps:

LO

Learning
Objective 10.2

- Create introductory text that engages readers as it conveys information. Show the relevance of the topic as you open your essay. Zoom out to draw connections with concerns readers may have.
- Develop the body of your essay using explanatory strategies. Offer definitions when helpful. Provide relevant examples. Make comparisons and discuss causes and effects as appropriate to make your information concrete. Write clear and compelling sentences.
- Use formatting strategies to help readers navigate your information. Use headings to organize materials. Use lists and text boxes to highlight key points.
- Include visuals to reinforce and present information. Use charts, tables, and graphs (pages 474–77) to make complex information easier to take in. Use images to engage readers and make information relevant.
- Document any sources using an appropriate style (see Chapter 17).

Focus on Student Writing   Self-Esteem and Body Image
BY **CARLA FARMAR**

Carla wrote this essay in response to a personal interest in women's health issues. She conducted some brief research to bolster her understanding about possible links between self-esteem and body image. She then composed the essay with the idea of sharing her knowledge, and also possibly helping readers with issues of self-esteem.

Carla Farmar

Professor Anderson

English 102

21 Mar. 2007

Self-Esteem and Body Image

You've no doubt seen the spoofs of some of the magazine ads featuring whisper-thin supermodels selling perfumes and cosmetics. One image depicts a ghastly scene with an emaciated model forcing herself to throw up with the caption *Obsession* (Figure 1). These images point to a disturbing truth about women and eating disorders. Dieting and thinness in our culture truly have become obsessions, and these satirical images ask us to think about it.

But too often our attention focuses on eating disorders such as anorexia nervosa or bulimia. Even satires, meant to raise our awareness, miss the mark. They reveal pencil-thin arms and protruding ribs, drawing our attention again and again to the bodies of women without concentrating on the root of the problem: women's self-esteem.

WHAT IS SELF-ESTEEM?

Self-esteem reflects the way people feel about themselves. When thinking about the health of women, starting with self-esteem makes sense because most of the beliefs women have about body image are related to their sense of self. Self-esteem also accounts for a number of other behaviors for women that can contribute to an overall healthy demeanor. According to a recent report discussing a Girls' Circle program designed to support adolescent girls, "lower levels of self-esteem have been correlated with a wide range of negative outcomes, including higher rates of teen pregnancy, alcohol and drug abuse, juvenile delinquency, suicide, depression, social anxiety, and alienation, dissatisfaction, and dieting" (Steese et al. 58). Since self-esteem establishes a foundation for personal well-being, focusing our attention on the self-esteem of women—especially young girls—makes more sense than starting with a secondary behavior like dieting.

A healthy sense of self-esteem, however, can be difficult to achieve for women. According to a study by Laura Esch and Keith J. Zullig, "Societal, peer, and parental pressures to achieve

Farmar 2

the thin cultural norm can lead to impaired feelings of well-being, unhealthful weight control and food consumption behaviors, and poor body weight perceptions" (345). The study exam-

Fig. 1. A spoof ad on eating disorders (Adbusters.org).

ined a group of fourth and fifth graders. They were the most vulnerable groups who were sensitive to parental influences on appearance and weight. And not surprisingly, girls were much more aware of body weight than their male counterparts. Self esteem has been linked to parenting and to quality of life. When one has meaningful attachments and a solid foundation from parents, then the influences of school, peer pressure, and the media seem to have less sway over young women. And quality of life tends to track from infancy into adulthood (Esch and Zullig).

The transition from child to adult is a challenge for anyone, but research shows that it can be especially difficult for girls. The Girls' Circle report states that depression is "disproportionately high among

adolescent girls, with about 2 to 1 ratio of girls to boys" (Steese et al. 56). Sexual abuse and the damaging after-effects of such abuse are three times as likely to take place among girls than boys. According to Lisa A. Sjostrom and Catherine Steiner-Adair, there are a number of gender differences among boys and girls related to self-esteem: "When boys are asked to identify their strengths and things they like best about themselves, without pause, most boys launch into a list of talents and things they can do in the world. . . . Ask girls the same question and often you are met with a pause. Or giggles. Or silence" (141). Clearly, self-esteem lies beneath many of the problems faced by young girls and women, including eating disorders.

WHY DOES BODY IMAGE MATTER?

Body image stands for the way a person feels about his or her appearance. Knowing how important self-esteem is to all aspects of a woman's feelings, it might be tempting to concentrate our attention on the feelings and beliefs of young girls in an attempt to strengthen their self-esteem. Research has shown that "children with poor self-esteem were more dissatisfied with their bodies" (Steese et al. 59). Body image is also closely linked to issues of perception. According to a recent study, "women overestimate the size of their hips by 16% and their waists by 25%, yet the same women were able to correctly estimate the width of a box" (Wardenburg Health Center). Because perceptions are so crucial when it comes to body image, addressing the feelings and beliefs related to self-esteem can go a long way toward changing body image and subsequently reducing eating disorders.

However, things are not quite so simple. For one thing, many of the psychological transformations girls undergo during puberty are directly tied to changes taking place in their physical bodies. Further, research shows that body image and self-esteem usually influence each other. Yes, strong self-esteem can improve body image, but at the same time problems with body image can damage self-esteem: "Perception of one's physical appearance has been consistently recognized to be the number one factor in predicting self-esteem (Steese et al. 59). Finally, although best practice is to avoid fixating on the media's fascination with thin bodies, cultural influences still make body image a major factor when it comes to concerns of women's health: "What remains sadly consistent is how many girls refer to their bodies as the ultimate measure of their worth—how many literally weigh their self-esteem" (Sjostrom and Steiner-Adair 142).

WHAT APPROACHES WORK BEST?

While untangling the relationship between body image and self-esteem is difficult, as is over-coming cultural influences that shape perceptions, there are some approaches that seem to be helping address these issues of women's health. Key to most of these successes is adopting a holistic approach that avoids focusing primarily on behaviors like eating disorders, which might be seen more as symptoms of a larger problem with self-esteem. For instance, one eating disorder prevention program is tellingly titled *Full of Ourselves: A Wellness Program to Advance Girl Power, Health, & Leadership*. The program seeks to prevent eating disorders by focusing on the "mental, physical, and relational health" of young girls. As the program emphasizes the themes of power and leadership, it encourages participants "to confidently state their own opinions, to practice positive self-talk, to create and sustain healthy connections with others, and to mentor and lead activities with younger girls" (Sjostrom and Steiner-Adair 143).

Similarly, the Girls' Circle program focuses on issues such as self-efficacy. Research indicates that a sense of self-efficacy—a sense of competence and belief in one's abilities to take action and handle situations—plays a central role in determining one's behavior and self-esteem. The program, therefore, "attempts to promote safe spaces in which girls can take risks and gain mastery through a variety of social-emotional and skill-building activities" (Steese et al. 63). Assessments of the program have found "significant changes in self-efficacy" among girls who have participated. The program also emphasizes social connections and the ability to develop and maintain relationships as a key factor in overall personal health and well being for young women. The Full of Ourselves program similarly emphasizes components meant to foster relationships and promote a sense of efficacy among participants.

Another study suggests teaching hunger-based eating and not deprivation dieting. This focus places control with the individual and raises self-esteem by providing a choice in food consumption. The study was conducted in connection with a college course where students were taught "strategies for resisting media influences, developing greater body acceptance,

Farmar 5

overcoming negative dieting practices, and learning how to eat in response to hunger" (Hawks et al. 365). Students in the course were better able to resist media pressure, modify restrictive dieting in favor of hunger-based eating, and develop a positive body image, all translating into a healthier self-esteem (Hawks et al.). Similar benefits have been found for women who engage in organized exercise regimens. According to recent research into a women's running program, "running provided experiences which led to enhanced self-esteem, notably through perceived improvements to the physical self, but also through increases in mastery/achievement and physical competence" (Bond and Batey 69).

Clearly, these programs represent a step forward in the way we think about women's health issues such as eating disorders. It's not that serious problems such as anorexia don't deserve our attention. In fact, these problems serve as warning flags, asking us to focus even more diligently on what can be done to promote healthy attitudes and behaviors for girls and women. But by asking bigger questions and looking for root causes, these approaches may hold more promise for creating lasting change.

Farmar 6

Works Cited

Bond, Katherine A., and Joanne Batey. "Running for Their Lives: A Qualitative Analysis of the Exercise Experience of Female Recreational Runners." *Women in Sport & Physical Activity Journal* 14.2 (2005): 69–83. Print.

Esch, Laura, and Keith J. Zullig. "Middle School Students' Weight Perceptions, Dieting Behaviors, and Life Satisfaction." *American Journal of Health Education* 39.6 (2008): 345–54. Print.

Hawks, Steven R., Hala Madanat, TeriSue Smith, and Natalie De La Cruz. "Classroom Approach for Managing Dietary Restraint, Negative Eating Styles, and Body Image Concerns among College Women." *Journal of American College Health* 56.4 (2008): 359–67. Print.

Sjostrom, Lisa A., and Catherine Steiner-Adair. "Full of Ourselves: A Wellness Program to Advance Girl Power, Health, and Leadership: An Eating Disorders Prevention Program That Works." *Journal of Nutrition Education and Behavior* 37.2 (2005): 141–44. Print.

Steese, Stephanie, et al. "Understanding Girls' Circle as an Intervention on Perceived Social Support, Body Image, Self Efficacy, Locus of Control, and Self Esteem." *Adolescence* 41.161 (2006): 55–74. Print.

Wardenburg Health Center. "Shocking Statistics." *Student Wellness*. University of Colorado, Boulder, 15 Dec. 2006. Web. 4 April 2009.

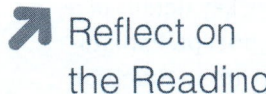 Reflect on the Reading

Questions About "Self Esteem and Body Image"

1. How easily were you able to pick out the main focus of "Self Esteem and Body Image"? How would you summarize Carla's essay in one sentence? What suggestions would you offer Carla about her area of focus?

2. How well does the essay convey specific information about its topic? What strategies does the piece use to provide specifics? Is any unnecessary information included?

3. How successful do you find the essay in terms of engaging readers? What works and what doesn't when it comes to holding your interest? What suggestions would you give for making the piece more engaging?

Revise It   Strategies for Revising Explanatory Essays

As you revise, remember that you need to leave readers with an improved understanding of your concept or concern. Your essay will succeed in large part based on the amount of information it provides and on the ease with which readers are able to take in the details. Keep these considerations in mind:

LO

Learning
Objective 10.3

- Think about the organization of the essay. Use reverse outlines or other strategies to chart and consider the way the essay is put together. How are explanations sequenced? Are there points where the reader will lose track? What changes can you make to the structure to make it easier to take in the information?

- Examine the writing strategies that you have used. Are you consciously trying to analyze, describe, or evaluate information? Are you trying to draw conclusions or persuade readers? How effective are these strategies?

- Think about what might be missing from the essay. It can be easy to cover the obvious points, but there may be information that readers require to fully understand the topic. Does the essay forego any explanations because they are tricky or difficult to integrate into the text? If so, how might you account for the missing information in the piece?

- Look at how effectively the essay uses charts, graphs, or illustrations to convey information. Are figures labeled and discussed? Are they clear and relevant?

- Check that formatting and organizational elements are present and well implemented. Does the piece use headings to section out the essay? Do text boxes or other features help present information? How can adjustments to the look and features make things more clear?

- Consider the way the essay zooms out to connect with associated elements of culture. In general, explanatory essays focus on clarifying key details of a concept. But you will also explore what matters about the concept. Explaining a concern like autism, for instance, might require a writer to touch on connections with parenting, education, even the media.

- Check that the essay meets the goals of its rhetorical situation. Does it clearly provide information? Does it explore the complexities of a topic? How well does the piece respond to the assignment?

- Clean up all the surface details of the work. Check that quotations are accurate. Ensure that all research is cited and documented, including visuals. Edit to tighten the language. Polish the look and feel of the piece.

Push It   More Possibilities for Explanatory Research Essays

A number of genres are geared heavily toward delivering information. Posters, flyers, and brochures are frequently used to articulate key facts and insights to readers. You can also use video, audio, and other mediums to create explanatory compositions.

LO

Learning Objective 10.4

1. Create a brochure related to a concept or concern. Use research to identify an important concern. Plan a three-panel brochure. Think about the genre of the three-panel brochure. The folding pattern calls for an engaging first outer panel and a back panel that provides contact or other background information. The inner panels can be used to provide more details, including charts and illustrations. Sketch out ideas for the organization of the panels, and then use publishing software to compose the brochure. See Chapter E7 for more information.

2. Compose a video slide show in which you provide information about a concept, event, or process. The slide show will sequence images and text to deliver your information. You can also add an audio track with narration or other sound elements. You can use images that you collect online. Refer to the information on pages 345–47 to ensure that you use materials fairly. You will use a video editor (for example, Microsoft's Movie Maker or Apple's iMovie) to create the slide show. Integrate images, record voices or import audio, and use text in the form of titles. You will need to think about timing, sequencing, and how to deliver information with images, audio, and text. Refer to Chapter E8 for more on composing with video.

WN

RESOURCES
Sample Explanatory Essays

Zoom Out   Reflecting on Explanatory Research Essays

- **Explanatory essays represent a complex genre.** They center on providing information, but also promote exploration for readers and writers. They can also be persuasive or fulfill other goals. As you encounter the range of texts that deliver information, you will begin to appreciate the variety of forms explanatory writing can take. As you compose in various rhetorical situations, you can call on explanatory writing strategies to help you meet your goals.

- **When articulating information, a number of strategies can be helpful.** Making comparisons and providing examples can help illustrate concepts. Describing processes or discussing causes and effects can help clarify information about a concern.

- **A number of related genres can be used to provide information to readers.** Flyers, brochures, and PSAs all deliver facts and can serve as explanatory compositions.

- **Formatting elements (lists, headings, tables, etc.) and other visual strategies are important when providing explanations.** Documents must be prepared with care if readers are to make sense of your information.

For additional information and practice with the learning objectives in this chapter, go to www.mycomplab.com, Resources > Research > The Research Assignment > Writing the Research Paper.

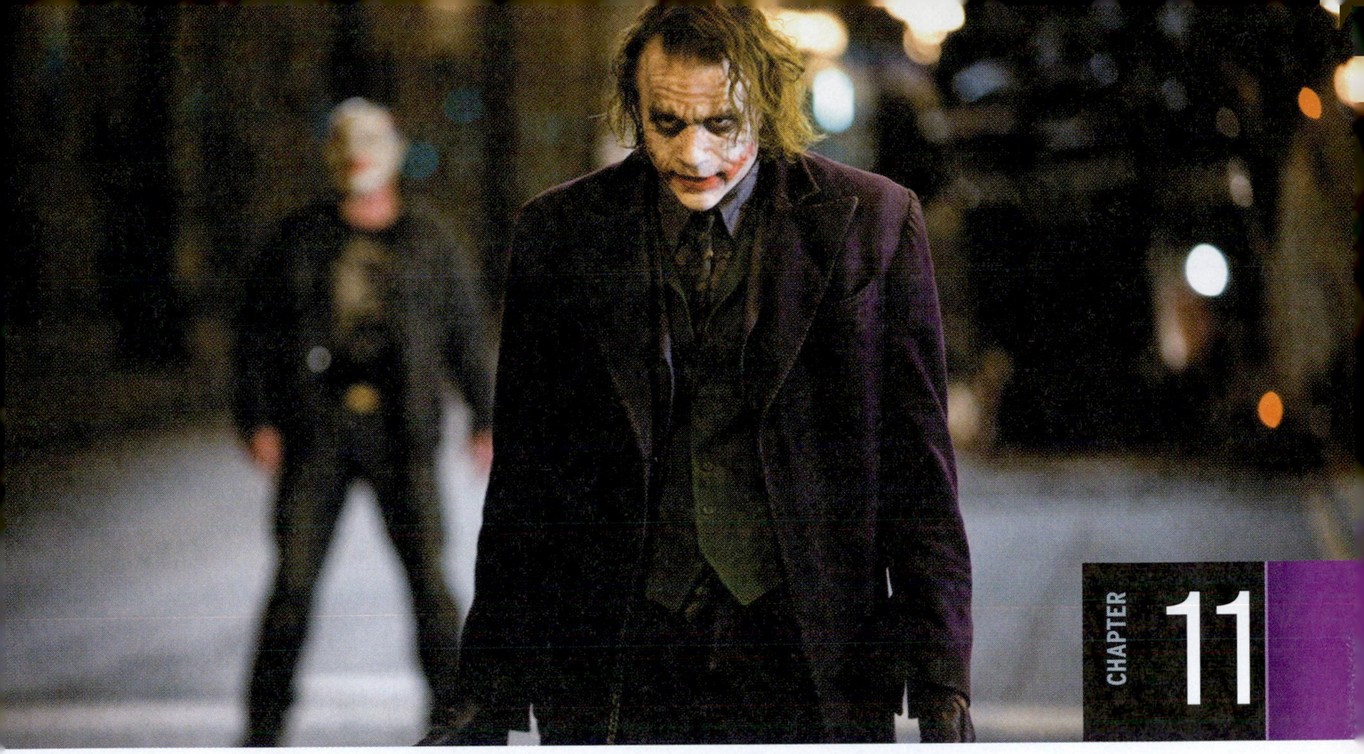

CHAPTER 11

Book, Music, and Film Reviews

Zoom In Key Concepts and Learning Objectives

After studying this chapter, you should be able to:

11.1 Practice critical reading by analyzing and evaluating books, music, and films.

11.2 Make comparisons and trace the history and influences informing a book, piece of music, or film.

11.3 Use details to support the assessments you make in a review.

11.4 Make judgments about the value of books, music, and films.

Listen to any conversation on the way out of a movie theater and you're likely to discover a review. On one level these responses reflect casual opinions: "That movie sucked." "Really? I kind of liked it." On another level, these moments represent more serious judgments: "I'm tired of villains based on political figures." And on a third level, these exchanges offer detailed evaluations: "I thought the use of natural light added a sense of realism." The more detailed filmgoers are in their descriptions, the more their reactions become reviews.

The same holds true for books and music. You can listen to a new CD with an ear attuned to offering a quick reaction. Or you can assess the details (evaluating lyrics, vocals, and instruments) and make statements about what you hear. You can read a novel for pleasure or you can examine a text with an eye trained on what makes a story successful, on settings, characters, and language. In fact, you can conduct a review of most any element of culture—an airport security guard, a pizza, a museum exhibit, etc., although the focus here is on books, music, and films.

When you compose a review, you put this more careful approach into action. You will begin by thinking about rhetorical situations, genres, and mediums. When looking more closely at the latest blockbuster, for instance, you will think about the characteristics of the medium of film and about different film genres. You will zoom in, then, as you discover and discuss the details of the item under review. And you can zoom out, making connections and offering insights about the work as a whole and about larger questions and concerns.

KEY TERMS

- **Review:** An evaluation of an item. Reviews are commonly written about books, films, music, and performances.

- **Background:** Contextual information that helps readers understand the significance of a review. Background can include details (like author or publisher information) or comparisons and insights about related items.

- **Criteria:** Characteristics used to evaluate an item under review. Often criteria are developed by thinking about similar items or about genres and mediums.

- **Themes and concerns:** Topical and cultural issues that are addressed by a book, film, piece of music, etc. Discussing the way an item handles themes and cultural concerns gives a review a larger focus.

Understanding Reviews

To get a better sense of how you might compose a review, let's look at an example.

LO

Learning
Objective 11.1

Too Many Rules
BY **ROSS DOUTHAT**

Ross Douthat writes for a number of venues. He is a conservative blogger and opinion writer for the New York Times. *He is also the co-author of the book* Grand New Party. *He has been a senior editor for* The Atlantic *and writes film reviews regularly for* National Review. *"Too Many Rules" appeared in* National Review *in 2008.*

If we can all agree to pretend that *Batman Forever* and *Batman and Robin* never happened—and with apologies to George Clooney's nippled, codpieced Batsuit and Arnold Schwarzenegger's indelible performance as Mr. Freeze, I'm pretty sure we can— then just two directors, Tim Burton and Christopher Nolan, have had a crack at the Batman mythos in the last two decades, and they've taken radically different approaches to the iconic vigilante. In *Batman* and especially *Batman Returns*, Burton took the essential unrealism of a comic-book landscape and deliberately heightened it, creating a stylized alternative universe populated by caricatures and freaks—its Gotham an out-of-time blend of gothic and Art Deco, the thirties and the eighties; its villains campy and sinister all at once; and its overall sensibility seemingly drawn, like much of Burton's oeuvre, from the fever dreams of a black-humored, bloody-minded adolescent.

Fifteen years later, Christopher Nolan has taken Batman in precisely the opposite direction—toward a harrowing realism that owes as much to Sidney Lumet or Quentin Tarantino as it does to the world of Batmobiles and supervillains. *Batman Begins* tiptoed uneasily along the realism-fantasy divide: One moment it was a gritty urban crime drama, pitting a not-yet-super Bruce Wayne against the Gotham Mob; the next it was, well, a comic book, in which an ancient Tibetan order of warrior monks was plotting to dump a hallucinogenic toxin into Gotham's water supply and then vaporize the water so that . . . oh, you get the idea. But with *The Dark Knight*, Nolan delivers a Batman movie that's largely purged of silliness—a raw, dark, gripping narrative about politics and crime, terrorism and corruption, in which the fact that the hero happens to be wearing a Batsuit often feels almost incidental to the story.

The critics have already anointed *The Dark Knight* the finest Batman movie ever, and perhaps the finest superhero film, period. But in the long run, I think Burton's approach may hold up slightly better. His Batman movies were considerably less ambitious than what Nolan is attempting here—as much as I love *Batman Returns*, I wouldn't use the word "Shakespearean" to describe its ambitions—but they had the advantage of cutting with the grain of the genre he was working in. Burton aimed to fulfill the superhero movie; Nolan wants to transcend it. But no matter how dark *The Dark Knight* gets, or how high it ratchets up the stakes, he keeps bumping his head on the ceiling.

Here's a capsule summary of the great film that *The Dark Knight* wants to be. By dressing up in a Batsuit and fighting crime by night, the billionaire Bruce Wayne (Christian Bale) has brought some semblance of order to a lawless modern city. But the order he's achieved is transient, and when a new hero emerges—the white-knight district attorney Harvey Dent (Aaron Eckhart)—who seems capable of fighting crime within the system, Batman contemplates retirement. In an ideal world, Gotham wouldn't need a costumed freak to handle lawbreaking; moreover, taking off the Batsuit would give him the chance to woo back his lost love, Rachel Dawes (Maggie Gyllenhaal)—who doesn't care to date a vigilante and is cuddling up to Dent.

The difficulty with this plan is that by wounding the Mob, the Batman-Dent one-two punch has made Gotham's gangsters desperate—desperate enough to make a deal with the devil, and let him drag the whole city down to hell. That devil would be Heath Ledger's Joker, a shambling, hissing, lipsmacking Iago in facial scars and clown makeup, and one of the scariest nihilists ever to slither into a summer popcorn film. (Ledger deserves all the posthumous accolades he's received; indeed, I suspect that his untimely death actually means that this performance will end up being underrated, its greatness slightly undercut by the sense of obligation that attends the praise that's heaped upon it.) The Joker is a man from nowhere: He doesn't want money, he doesn't want power, and he doesn't care if he lives or dies. He just "wants to see the world burn," as Wayne's butler, Alfred (Michael Caine), puts it. And stopping him will come at a cost—in laws broken, liberties trampled (not for nothing have the movie's post-9/11 themes been read as essentially pro-Bush), lies embraced, and lives destroyed—that may be more than anyone can bear.

"Welcome to a world without rules," *The Dark Knight*'s most arresting poster promises. That's precisely what the set-up I've just sketched out promises the audience—a rare $185 million blockbuster in which it seems as though anything can happen, and nothing, not even the hero's triumph, feels rote or foreordained.

But it's also precisely what Nolan can't quite deliver, because he's making a Batman movie, after all, and no matter how dark things get there are rules you have to follow. You have to introduce some totally ridiculous technologies (like a sonar-based surveillance system that lets Batman spy on all of Gotham) and some snazzy new gadgets (the "Batpod" motorcycle) so that all the fanboys in the audience can scream, "Yeah! Wicked!" (Given the gravity *The Dark Knight* otherwise aspires to, these comic-book touches feel like the equivalent of Michael Corleone's whipping out a laser gun midway through *The Godfather*.) You have to include at least one extended action sequence where Batman performs jujitsu on the laws of physics—in this case, an assault on a mobster's Hong Kong skyscraper—even if it's superfluous to the plot. And you have to end the film with a climactic face-off between the hero and the villains, even if it drags the movie out for an unnecessary 40 minutes and saps away the tragic momentum the first two acts have built.

What's more, there are things you just can't do. When the Joker promises to blow up a hospital, you know the building will be evacuated before the bombs go off. When Batman promises to give up his surveillance powers once the present emergency is over, you know he'll follow through. And when the Joker tells Batman, in one of the film's most chilling scenes, "I'll show you. . . . When the chips are down, these civilized people will eat each other," you know he'll be proven wrong.

These predictabilities are not a problem for the top-of-the-line superhero movie that *The Dark Knight* succeeds in being. They're only problems for the still-better movie that it clearly wants to be. I like what Christopher Nolan has done here; I'd just like to see what he can do in a film with slightly fewer rules.

Reflect on the Reading

Questions About "Too Many Rules"

1. What is your reaction to Douthat's use of terms like *oeuvre* or to his references to other directors? Do these moves strengthen or hinder your engagement with Douthat as a speaker?

2. "Too Many Rules" reviews *The Dark Knight* by placing it in the context of other Batman films. Do you find the strategy effective? Why or why not?

3. What does Douthat mean by the title, "Too Many Rules"? Does the rest of the review support the ideas offered in the title?

4. Do you agree with the assessment of the film offered by Douthat? What points would you make in your own review of *The Dark Knight* that would challenge or extend those made in "Too Many Rules"?

In "Too Many Rules," you can see some elements that turn up in most reviews. The piece begins by providing some background that helps readers understand the context of the film, in this case, discussing the various Batman movies and asking us to consider those directed by Tim Burton and by Christopher Nolan in more detail. The piece also offers a brief encapsulation of the film, making sure to highlight the key thematic concerns rather than trying to summarize every detail of the plot.

"Too Many Rules" also provides insights into the genre of the item under discussion. In fact, the premise of the review is that the genre of the superhero film constrains the efforts of Nolan. And the review zooms in to explore aspects of the film in more detail, focusing, for instance, on the performance of Heath

Ledger. Film reviews generally discuss acting, the uses of sound, the ways in which the camera is used (cinematography), special effects, editing, and other elements of filmmaking.

And the piece zooms out. It touches on thematic elements of the film, citing political dimensions of the movie's treatment of surveillance and personal liberties. The piece also offers larger conclusions about the film as a whole, suggesting that as a superhero movie, *The Dark Knight* succeeds, but questioning whether the film works as a more realistic crime drama. In short, "Too Many Rules" places the film being studied in a context, offers evaluations of details of the film, and then provides larger insights and an overall assessment of the movie. This general pattern will prove helpful for the reviews you might write.

Know It Strategies for Understanding Reviews

- Begin with your own knowledge of the item under review. If you are unfamiliar with the subject of a review you are reading, consider examining it on your own before trying to make sense of the review.
- Look at the way the author of a review provides background information about the item for readers. Does the author compare the item with similar works? Does she trace the history of the item?
- Think about the way the review summarizes the item for readers. Reviews must give enough information about the item for readers to make sense of the discussion, but should not bore readers with plot summary or unnecessary description.
- Look for the review to provide insights about genres or mediums. Does the piece help readers understand what matters about the genre under discussion? Are characteristics of the medium considered?
- Ask questions about the details. A film review should examine acting, sound, lighting, and so on. A music review should discuss lyrics, instrumentation, production, etc.
- Examine the review in terms of thematic and cultural concerns. Does the review identify key themes? Does it offer insights into the way the reviewed item or event addresses these concerns?
- Identify the overall assessment offered by a review. Does it reduce things to a simple thumbs up or down? Does it posit a more complex assessment? What is the takeaway message?

Ask Questions & Make Decisions

Exercises for Understanding Reviews

1. Think of a film you have always thought to be overrated. Go to an online Web site devoted to film reviews (e.g., rottentomatos.com or imdb.com) and look through reviews of the film. Keep an open mind, but also think about your own judgment, and then post your own review.

2. Choose a movie that you enjoy but don't think about too deeply. Watch the director's commentary on a DVD version of the film and then write a couple of paragraphs exploring your fondness for the film in terms of the director's vision.

3. Go to an online music source (Amazon, iTunes, Rhapsody, etc.) and look at the reviews for several artists. Make a list of all of the musical terms that are discussed in the reviews.

4. Use your library database or the Web to find published reviews of a favorite book. Read two or more reviews, and then write a paragraph exploring the ways in which the reviews situate the book for readers and discuss the details of the text.

Readings and Resources for Exploring Reviews

A review zooms in to examine in detail the characteristics of an item and then zooms out to situate that item among related elements or in a larger context, offering evaluations along the way. Below, Michiko Kakutani reviews the book *Extremely Loud and Incredibly Close*.

RESOURCES
Sample Reviews

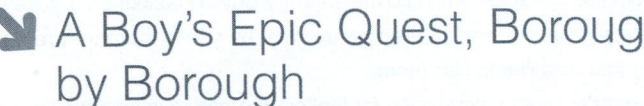

A Boy's Epic Quest, Borough by Borough
BY **MICHIKO KAKUTANI**

Michiko Kakutani has written for The Washington Post *and* Time *magazine and contributes regularly to the* New York Times. *She is known for her often biting criticism and has garnered the hostility of some of the authors she has reviewed. "A Boy's Epic Quest, Borough By Borough" appeared in the* New York Times *in 2005.*

Extremely Loud and Incredibly Close
By Jonathan Safran Foer
Illustrated. 326 pages. Houghton Mifflin. $24.95.

A Boy's Epic Quest,
Borough by Borough
(continued)
BY **MICHIKO KAKUTANI**

With his new book, *Extremely Loud and Incredibly Close,* 28-year-old Jonathan Safran Foer demonstrates the same high-flown ambition that brought his 2002 debut novel, *Everything Is Illuminated*, bouquets of critical kudos but with decidedly more cloying results.

That earlier book tackled the subject of the Holocaust and the uses of memory; this novel explores the nature of grief and the difficulty of human connection through the prism of 9/11 and the World War II firebombing of Dresden. While it contains moments of shattering emotion and stunning virtuosity that attest to Mr. Foer's myriad gifts as a writer, the novel as a whole feels simultaneously contrived and improvisatory, schematic and haphazard.

The core problem has to do with the novel's 9-year-old hero. Oskar Schell, whose father died in the World Trade Center on Sept. 11, should be a highly sympathetic character: a clever, sensitive boy, grief-stricken over his father's death, neglected by his self-absorbed mother, and beset by insomnia, depression and panic attacks. Unfortunately, he comes across as an entirely synthetic creation, assembled out of bits and pieces of famous literary heroes past. Like J.D. Salinger's Holden Caulfield, Oskar wanders around New York City, lonely, alienated and on the verge, possibly, of an emotional breakdown. Like Gunter Grass's Oskar Matzerath in "The Tin Drum," he plays a musical instrument (in his case, a tambourine) while commenting on the fearful state of the world around him. And like Saul Bellow's Herzog, he writes letters to people he doesn't know.

To make matters worse, Mr. Foer has endowed Oskar with an exasperating precocity that's reminiscent less of Salinger's Glass-family kids than those annoying child guests on late-night talk shows. A devotee of the Internet, Oskar is a chatty font of trivia on everything from the number of birds that die smashing into windows to the number of locks installed every day in New York City. He hands out calling cards that identify him as an "inventor, jewelry designer, jewelry fabricator, amateur entomologist, Francophile, vegan, origamist, pacifist, percussionist, amateur astronomer, computer consultant, amateur archeologist, collector." And like the smarmy Eddie Haskell on "Leave It to Beaver," he's constantly flattering women his mother's age by telling them they're beautiful, sometimes adding that he'd like to kiss them.

Oskar's favorite expression for feeling depressed is wearing "heavy boots," a phrase he repeats endlessly throughout the novel. His favorite pastime is inventing things that don't exist, like "a kite-string bracelet," little microphones that would play "the sounds of our hearts through little speakers" and "incredibly long ambulances that connected every building to a hospital." "What if you had to water skyscrapers," he wonders, "and play classical music to them, and know if they like sun or shade?"

After his father's death, Oskar discovers in his dad's closet a blue vase containing an envelope marked Black; inside is a key to what appears to be a safe-deposit box. Oskar becomes obsessed with finding out whom the key belongs to, and his quest takes him on a journey through the five boroughs of New York. He begins calling on all the people named Black he can find, asking if they knew his father or if they know anything about his father's key.

Oskar's mother never really inquires about his wanderings. In fact, no one seems to think it's terribly odd or dangerous for a 9-year-old boy to be trundling about New York at all hours of the day and night, or visiting complete strangers.

But then, Mr. Foer appears to want his tale to inhabit a limbo land located somewhere just beyond the world as we know it. Indeed his main subplot, involving Oskar's grandparents, reads very much like a fable. We're asked to believe that his grandparents marked off in their apartment multiple "Nothing Places" "in which one could temporarily cease to exist" and that this caused all sorts of philosophical complications: "It became difficult to navigate from Something to Something without accidentally walking through Nothing, and when Something—a key, a pen, a pocketwatch—was accidentally left in a Nothing Place, it never could be retrieved."

We're also asked to believe that Oskar's grandfather, who lost his fiancee, Anna, during the firebombing of Dresden, was so traumatized by his experiences that he stopped speaking and took to writing down everything instead: "If something made me want to laugh, I'd write 'Ha ha ha!' and instead of singing in the shower I would write out the lyrics of my favorite songs, the ink would turn the water blue or red or green, and the music would run down my legs."

There is something precious and forced about such scenarios, as though Mr. Foer were trying to sprinkle handfuls of Gabriel Garcia Marquez's magical realism into his story without really understanding this sleight of hand. Similar difficulties attend Mr. Foer's other attempts to employ razzle-dazzle narrative techniques: playful typography, blank pages (meant to signify pages from a memoir Oskar's grandmother supposedly wrote on a typewriter with no ribbon) and photographs Oskar has pasted into his scrapbook: images of everything from doorknobs to mating turtles to a man falling to his death from one of the World Trade Center towers.

Clearly Mr. Foer has used these techniques as writers in Latin America and Eastern Europe have used them to try to get traction on horrific events that defy both reason and conventional narrative approaches, but all too often his execution verges on the whimsical rather than the galvanic or persuasive. In fact, *Extremely Loud and Incredibly Close* tends to be at its most powerful when Mr. Foer abandons his willful use of experimental techniques and simply writes in an earnest, straightforward manner, using his copious gifts of language to limn his characters' state of mind.

His depiction of Oskar's reaction to phone messages left by his father as he awaited rescue in the burning World Trade Center, his description of Oskar's grandfather's love affair with Anna and his experiences during the bombing of Dresden—these passages

A Boy's Epic Quest, Borough by Borough *(continued)*
BY **MICHIKO KAKUTANI**

underscore Mr. Foer's ability to evoke, with enormous compassion and psychological acuity, his characters' emotional experiences, and to show how these private moments intersect with the great public events of history. Sadly, these passages are all too few and far between in what is an admirably purposeful but ultimately mannered and irritating novel.

Reflect on the Reading

Questions About "A Boy's Epic Quest, Borough by Borough"

1. From reading the piece, are you able to gather why Kakutani is sometimes faulted for her harsh criticism? What messages do you receive about the ethos of the author of the piece?
2. What aspects of the review do you find most helpful? Does the piece provide enough information about the novel for you to make a decision about possibly reading it?
3. How would you compare this book review with the review of the film offered on pages 275–77? Is it fair to say the reviews are more similar than different? Why or why not?

Writing Assignment: A Book, Music, or Film Review

Write an essay in which you review a book, film, musical artist, song, CD, or performance. Situate the item for readers, offering background information (release dates, authors, titles, publishers, and page length for books; directors, actors, running times for films; labels and producers for music, etc.) and drawing connections with related items. Consider connections with thematic concerns or other elements of culture. Develop a discussion that makes judgments about the item's value and significance. Provide details that bring the item to life for readers and that support your evaluation. Document your sources and gather feedback as you work.

Ask Questions & Make Decisions

Exercises for Composing Reviews

1. Recall an exceptional concert that you have attended. Write a page or so exploring what made the concert special.
2. Identify a film that does not fit easily into a single genre. Develop a list of criteria that might be used to evaluate the item.
3. Choose a favorite book and then conduct research to locate a review that is critical of the work. Write a paragraph or two responding to the review.
4. Think about a film, book, or CD that stands out as groundbreaking or unique. Conduct research to identify similar examples or items that might have influenced the work. Write up your findings in a paragraph or two.

Plan It

Invention Strategies for Reviews

The planning activities for your review will require you to zoom out and in. You will want to get familiar with some of the larger concerns related to the genre and medium of the item you are considering. You will also want to understand the item in terms of related examples. A review of a new gangster film, for instance, is likely to reference classics like *The Godfather* or *Scarface*. Additionally, you will need to become an expert in the item under review. Revisit the item several times and develop a list of specifics that you might discuss. Here are some possible steps:

- Think about the pros and cons of reviewing different types of items. What challenges and opportunities arise depending on whether you examine a book, a film, a CD, etc.? (Check with your instructor, too, as you explore possibilities.)
- Conduct research to locate several examples of reviews that have been written about the type of item you choose, and then explore those reviews as models.
- Identify a specific item for your review. Look beyond obvious examples; *The Godfather* or Pink Floyd's *The Wall* have been well covered already. Consider controversial items, pieces you would like to learn more about, or items you believe to be misunderstood. You might choose something you rate highly or something you dislike; just pick something you feel strongly about.
- Explore other reviews that have been written on your particular item. Look for points of agreement or consensus. Relate your own assessment to what you discover.
- Think about the item in terms of genres and mediums. Develop a list of criteria you might discuss in reviewing the item.

- Consider examples of similar works that will help readers better understand your review. Investigate works that might have influenced your item. Think about historical trends related to the item.
- Develop an outline, a graphic map, or some other organizing option that will help you to plan your composition.

CONNECT IT   More Resources for Book, Music, and Film Reviews

For more detailed information about some of the strategies you might use in reviews, consider the following resources:

For more on rhetorical situations, see Chapter 1.

For more on arguments, see Chapter 4.

For insights into using research in reviews, see Chapters 14–17.

For more on thesis statements, see Chapter 18.

For insights into organizing structures, see Chapter 19.

For insights into using definitions, see Chapter 22.

For more on analyzing, see pages 62–65.

For more on comparing and contrasting, see Chapter 23.

For insights into using visuals, see Chapter 25.

For information on design strategies, see Chapter 26.

Compose It   Write a Review

As you compose your review, be careful not to merely summarize what takes place in a film or book or to try to capture every aspect of a musical piece. Think about how you can offer conclusions about the relative merits of the piece, consider the item in a larger context, and address thematic elements or cultural concerns. Here are some more ideas for getting started:

- Begin by introducing the item under review for readers. Offer key background information (release dates, authors, titles, publishers, and page length for books; directors, actors, running times for films; labels and producers for music, etc.). Provide informational details, but also compose an opening that engages readers.
- Help readers see the item as it fits within a larger cultural network. Trace lineages of films, songs, paintings or other works of art. Explore connections with elements of culture. Situate the item within a larger picture.

- Develop a rationale for evaluating the item. Spend some time bringing criteria to light, perhaps discussing related examples and the genre or medium. Be thoughtful about the characteristics you choose to consider. Most romantic comedies, for instance, have a conflict between lovers that gets resolved at the end of the film. But that criterion might be too basic to offer much help. Instead, you might think about the supporting cast, the comedic elements, or the soundtrack.

Learning Objective 11.3

- Discuss the details of the item. Don't assume that readers have heard the CD or read the book. Pick out illustrative examples that allow you to demonstrate the characteristics of the item and its strengths and weaknesses. Watch out for too much summary. Instead, identify key elements and offer assessments.
- Examine thematic elements related to the item. How does the item address these concerns? What questions does its treatment of issues raise or answer?
- Draw conclusions about the item. You can draw conclusions about the details along the way; for instance, the horns add a sense of melancholy to the song. And you will want to offer broad assessments about the item as a whole; for instance, the computer-generated special effects are cheesy, but the characters are well developed and the way in which the film addresses questions of personal privacy makes it worth seeing.

Focus on Student Writing

Marcus Bynum

Professor Anderson

English 102

29 May 2007

Reading Spots of Ink

When David Gibbons and Alan Moore released the first installment of their twelve-issue comic series, *Watchmen*, insiders at DC Comics were overwhelmed. They did not know exactly what to make of the story, but were sure they had something special on their hands. As the comics began to be snapped up from newsstands, the reactions of readers only amplified the sense that the series was a hit. But what is it about the collaboration between artist Gibbons and writer Moore that is so compelling? *Watchmen* was not the first serialized comic story to be taken seriously. Art Speigelman's *Maus* broke onto the scene some six years earlier. While *Watchmen* lacks the memoir-like qualities of *Maus*, it does present a sense of realism in the way it takes on the human dimensions of superheros. In fact, *Watchmen* works because it tears away the fantasy façade, revealing a mix of lust, depravity, insecurity, and struggle that complements the typical mix of superhero qualities with dimensions that can only be called human.

The story can't be said to center around a single character or plot element, but roughly traces the interconnecting stories of several superheros, including the Comedian (a violently flawed man of action), Ozymandus (a super-intelligent do-gooder) Doctor Manhattan (a physicist given god-like powers through a nuclear accident), the Nightowl (a gadget-building geek figure), and Laurie Juspeczyk (a second-generation female force). The events open with the death of the Comedian, so much of the rest of the reading involves flashbacks and backstory, adding a nice sense of complexity to the narrative. The relationships between the characters also drive much of the action. Doctor Manhattan can't maintain his relationship with Laurie, who heads to the arms of the Nightowl for consolation. These personal foibles become key points of tension as they interact with the thematic twists that have been established by Moore. The book creates a world with a revisionist's sense of history. The United States has won the Vietnam War but hostilities with the Soviet Union push the two countries to the brink of nuclear war and global annihilation. Only Doctor Manhattan can intervene with his god-like powers, but he becomes lost in fits of jealousy and isolation as the story races toward its conclusion.

The unanswered questions in the main story translate into a traditional page-turner. Additionally, the dismantling of the superhero myth keeps us engaged with the characters as they come to grips with their all-too-human dilemmas. Shortly after the release of the

Bynum 3

twelfth installment, DC comics compiled the episodes into a bundle and marketed it as a graphic novel. But the intellectual weight of *Watchmen* does not derive from the sum of its pages or even from the addition of front and back covers and binding. It is the way that Gibbons and Moore deliver their story that has prompted countless reviewers to place it among their lists of best books ever. The storytelling can be attributed to some of the most creative uses of the medium of the graphic novel and to careful weaving together of themes and story elements.

Moore and Gibbons were no strangers to the medium of comics when they began their collaboration on *Watchmen*. Their expertise can be seen in the way they skillfully use the panel structure to establish the pacing of the story. While each of the twelve installments can be considered to be an episode, the panel structure is cleverly used to create mini-installments. Often a single page spread will relate a key part of the action—for instance, when the death of the Comedian is depicted in the opening scenes. But just as often these spreads will be combined with others through clever arrangements and juxtapositions. We end up with a woven structure that layers multiple actions over one another in ways as complex as any that might be found in the prose structures of Joyce or Faulkner.

The book makes similar connections as it works with the visual medium of comics. Gibbons, for instance, has placed numerous iconic nuggets among the pages that provide clues to readers about both the action and the themes in the story. The careful placement of a photograph, for instance, prompts a series of flashbacks where Doctor Manhattan relates the history of his accident and of his romantic relationships. Photographs similarly launch backstory episodes featuring first-generation crime fighters. Iconic elements like flyers, blimps, protest signs, and graffiti create similar threads of narration that weave throughout the book.

As if that weren't enough, Moore and Gibbons take deliberate measures to draw our attention toward a new way of reading. The book features a comic within a comic, a series of episodes prompted by a character reading a pirate comic, *The Black Freighter*, at a local newsstand. *The Black Freighter* episode appears strategically throughout the novel, pushing

Bynum 4

forward the action. But it also operates as a kind of interpretive lens, offering lessons about hubris and isolation. As such, it illuminates the actions of the main characters as they wrestle with their human emotions. The lesson Moore and Gibbons offer is one in postmodern meaning, a suggestion that readers need not be pulled along as with a string from point A to B, but that interpretations can accumulate over time, building upon and informing one another.

It is this lesson in contemporary approaches to meaning making that sets *Watchmen* apart as more than a simple novel, graphic or otherwise. But there is still more. The character of Rorschach holds a special place in the novel. Another human-heeled hero, Rorschach carries with him a past tainted by a prostitute mother and his own gutter sensibilities. But clever guides Gibbons and Moore have hidden a clue to reading this sorry character. Rorschach has been inspired by the story of Kitty Genovese, the Brooklyn woman who was killed in 1964 while her neighbors looked on. Subsequent psychological studies have termed the phenomenon of not intervening Genovese syndrome, or the bystander effect. Rorschach stands as the anti-bystander, a person of principle ready to intervene no matter how fraught with human cynicism and frailty. The novel, then, not only dismantles the superhero façade but also offers Rorschach as a substitute. But a Rorschach test really just reflects the psyche of its subject. So, *Watchmen* is good because it offers a new way of reading and new knowledge about the need for (not super) human action in the face of difficulty. It is great because, like Rorschach and a Rorschach test, the novel puts the onus on the reader as it prompts us to consider how we will respond to this new knowledge.

Reflect on the Reading

Questions About "Reading Spots of Ink"

1. What is your initial response to Marcus's review? Can you identify his overall assessment of the book? What elements of the review seem successful? Where might it miss the mark?

2. How well does Marcus provide background information about the book? What suggestions might you offer for the opening of the essay?

3. What are your thoughts on the level of detail offered in the review? Do you feel like you need more information at any time?

4. Based on Marcus's review, do you feel as if you would like to read *Watchmen*? If you have read the novel, would you agree or disagree with Marcus's review?

Revise It **Strategies for Revising Reviews**

LO

Learning
Objective 11.4

In addition to general strategies for revision, including asking your peers to read your draft, concentrate on these areas as you return to your review for rewrites:

- Check that the introduction engages readers and places the item within a larger context? Are comparisons illustrative? Is the item situated within a historical framework?
- Consider how the review addresses concerns related to genres or mediums. Does the review account for genre expectations or for instances where an item does not fit easily within a single genre?
- Stop to consider how the review relates to those of others. Do you cite other critics? Are there adjustments that you can make based on alternate readings?
- Examine the discussion of the details of the item. Ensure that you are not summarizing too much. Instead, tie the focused discussion of details to points you wish to make in the review.
- Ask about the way the review treats thematic concerns. Are any controversies addressed? Does a judgment of the item rest on the way it treats cultural issues?
- Check that you offer a concrete assessment of the piece. More than likely, you will not boil things down to a simple good or bad assessment but will consider what was effective and what was not. Be sure you are offering conclusions as you wrap up the review.
- Revise several times, concentrating on zooming in to elaborate details and zooming out to offer evaluations.

RESOURCES
Sample Reviews

Push It   More Possibilities for Reviews

1. Compose a film review using multimedia that you find online. Rely on the wealth of materials on the Web (film trailers, interviews with actors or directors, still images, etc.) to include examples that can be discussed in the review. Use an online space (a class Web site or blog, for instance) to compose the review. Embed clips of samples from the film or other video materials. Add images or audio files as relevant. Develop your discussion around these items, extending them by offering evaluations of the film or using the items to support your points.

2. Create an audio essay in which you offer a review of a song, musical artist, or CD. In the essay, blend samples from the CD with your own narration. Make decisions about the fair use of audio in the essay. Use an audio editor to import and cut samples that represent key elements of the music. Add narration to develop the review. Fade items in and out and adjust the volume to create an effective audio composition. (For more on audio essays, see Chapter E3.)

WN

VIDEO
21. Multimedia
Film and Music
Reviews

Zoom Out   Reflecting on Reviews

- **Reviews offer judgments about the value of an item.** Most reviews take up films, books, or music, but you can also review performances and other items.

- **Situating an item within a historical context or in terms of similar examples helps readers make sense of an item.** Reviews don't assess in a vacuum; instead, they create connections and comparisons.

- **Reviews bring out the details of the items under discussion.** They don't get bogged down in summary, but they do serve as the eyes and ears for readers who may not be familiar with the piece.

- **Reviews address larger issues.** They consider how books, films, music, and other forms of art express thematic concerns. They also look at the ways in which items relate to culture and contexts.

For additional information and practice with the learning objectives in this chapter, go to www.mycomplab.com, Resources > Writing > Writing Purposes > Writing to Evaluate.

Literary Analyses

 Zoom **In**   **Key Concepts and Learning Objectives**

After studying this chapter, you should be able to:

12.1 Examine literary elements to develop interpretations of poems, plays, stories, and novels.

12.2 Identify thematic concerns as you to read and write about literature.

12.3 Zoom out to connect works of literature with with larger social issues.

12.4 Develop arguments to explain interpretations of works of literature.

12.5 Integrate, discuss, and document quotations as you analyze works of literature.

Have you ever walked away from a work of literature with the feeling that you are missing some profound message about a poem, story, or play? It is not an uncommon experience. In fact, interpreting literature is sometimes viewed as a mystical activity requiring you to discover some elusive meaning that is hidden beneath the surface of the text. But there is no real mystery. You simply need to learn to examine the details of texts and then to connect those details with elements of culture. A passage from a poem might link with ideas about gender, tradition, innocence, or family. A text might be connected to historical contexts, with people, ideas, and things associated with its authorship or publication.

The key is in knowing what to look for and how to go about drawing connections between the details in texts and elements of culture. When reading poetry, for instance, you can look at structure, rhyme, rhythm, word choice, and figurative language. For fiction, you can focus on settings, characters, and narration. For drama, sets, stage directions, and dialog. For all literary texts, you can think about themes and symbols. Already you can see how zooming in on any of these aspects helps you to begin developing an interpretation.

You can also zoom out. The practice of literary studies is concerned with the ways in which texts reflect and shape culture. You can think about the authors of texts, about readers, and about conventions related to genres and mediums. You can connect themes and symbols with other works and with culture. You can look at the historical dimensions of works of literature and explore other aspects of the contexts in which literature is written and read.

There is no need to keep a literary analysis simple. In fact, a successful literary analysis will depend on finding linkages between the details of a text and the significance of its themes and contexts. Zoom in and out.

KEY TERMS

- **Literary analysis:** A composition that explores a literary work. Most analyses offer an interpretation of the work, examining details and offering conclusions about messages and contexts.

- **Poetry:** Literature that uses compressed language and imagery to deliver a message. Most poems are shorter than other works and use rhyme, rhythm, and figurative language.

- **Fiction:** Literature written in prose that tells a story. Most fiction traces events that happen to characters, focusing on themes and messages in the process.

- **Drama:** Literature written to be performed on a stage. Most drama is divided into acts and scenes and is developed through dialog between the characters.

- **Themes:** Sometimes called motifs, the shared human and cultural concerns that appear in literature. Common themes include love, work, community, nature, family, friendship, tradition, change, and so on.

- **Literary elements:** Aspects of literary works that can be examined in detail. Particular genres feature specific elements; for instance, fiction features settings, plot, and characters.

- **Contexts:** The cultural elements that are associated with a work of literature. Contexts include the historical situation in which a text is produced, the historical reception texts have had, information related to the authorship or development of a text, and contemporary elements of culture that influence a text.

WN

VIDEO
9. Interpreting
Literature

Understanding Literary Analyses

To get a better sense of how you might compose a literary analysis, let's look at an example. Here, we include a poem by Richard Wilber and an analysis of the poem written by Isabella Wai.

 The Writer
BY **RICHARD WILBUR**

Richard Wilbur has written numerous books of poetry, including 1956's Things of This World, *which received the Pulitzer Prize. In 1987, he was appointed U.S. Poet Laureate. "The Writer" is taken from his* New and Collected Poems, *published in 1988.*

In her room at the prow of the house
Where light breaks, and the windows are tossed with linden,
My daughter is writing a story.

I pause in the stairwell, hearing
From her shut door a commotion of typewriter-keys
Like a chain hauled over a gunwale.

The Writer
(continued)
BY **RICHARD WILBUR**

Young as she is, the stuff
Of her life is a great cargo, and some of it heavy:
I wish her a lucky passage.

But now it is she who pauses,
As if to reject my thought and its easy figure.
A stillness greatens, in which

The whole house seems to be thinking,
And then she is at it again with a bunched clamor
Of strokes, and again is silent.

I remember the dazed starling
Which was trapped in that very room, two years ago;
How we stole in, lifted a sash

And retreated, not to affright it;
And how for a helpless hour, through the crack of the door,
We watched the sleek, wild, dark

And iridescent creature
Batter against the brilliance, drop like a glove
To the hard floor, or the desk-top,

And wait then, humped and bloody,
For the wits to try it again; and how our spirits
Rose when, suddenly sure,

It lifted off from a chair-back,
Beating a smooth course for the right window
And clearing the sill of the world.

It is always a matter, my darling,
Of life or death, as I had forgotten. I wish
What I wished you before, but harder.

Reflect on the Reading

Questions About "The Writer"

1. What examples of similes, metaphors, and other imagery can you identify in the poem? What can you say about these elements?

2. What themes are most prevalent in the poem? How can these themes be used to develop possible interpretations?

3. How do you interpret the phrase "It is always a matter, my darling / Of life or death"? How does your reading of that passage shape your view of the poem as a whole?

Richard Wilbur's "The Writer"
BY **ISABELLA WAI**

Isabella Wai teaches English at Auburn University. She has written many pieces on Richard Wilbur and also conducts research on Asian literature. "Richard Wilbur's 'The Writer'" was published in The Explicator *in 1995.*

> *Poetry's prime weapon is words, used for the naming, comparison, and contrast of things. Its auxiliary weapons are rhythms, formal patterns, and rhymes. It is by means of all these that poets create difficulties for themselves, which they then try to surmount.*
>
> —Richard Wilbur, "The Bottles Become New, Too"[1]

An artist struggling to translate the elusive reality into verbal patterns is a recurring theme in Wilbur's poetry. He needs metaphors to formulate his impression of, and establish a relationship with, the fugitive events that excite him. Such an interest in the interplay between imagination and reality belongs, of course, to the general poetic movement initiated by the nineteenth-century British romantic poets, especially William Wordsworth and Samuel Taylor Coleridge.

The title of the poem "The Writer" refers to Wilbur's daughter, who is composing a story on the typewriter, and to the poet himself, who attempts to organize his observations into verse.[2] The poem is based upon a contrast of two metaphors, one rejected and the other accepted. Flurries of noise from the "typewriter-keys" provoke the poet to look for an image to embody his experience of hearing. The typing sounds "like a chain hauled over a gunwale." This image of the ship is continued in his comparison of "the stuff / Of her life" to "a great cargo." The poet wishes his daughter "a lucky passage."

But she seems to reject the analogy of writing to delivery of goods and to an ocean voyage:

> But now it is she who pauses,
> As if to reject my thought and its easy figure.
> A stillness greatens, in which
> The whole house seems to be thinking,
> And then she is at it again with a bunched clamor
> Of strokes, and again is silent.

The first "figure" is "easy" because the poet seems to have formulated his impressions as a matter of habit or because the voyage-life analogy is quite facile and stale. The simile "a chain hauled over a gunwale," which imitates only the sound of typing, oversimplifies the complexities of writing and fails to demonstrate the intensity of a vigorous struggle associated with the creative process or with the imposition of an artistic order upon reality.

The contrast of noise and silence reminds the poet of a bird "which was trapped in that very room, two years ago." The physical manifestations of "the dazed starling"

Richard Wilbur's
"The Writer"
(continued)
BY **ISABELLA WAI**

battering "against the brilliance" and dropping "like a glove / To the hard floor, or the desk-top" are similar to the flurries of "typewriter-keys" followed by short periods of thinking. More important, both the bird and the girl are in agony, literally or metaphorically "humped and bloody," searching for "the right window," which means a passage to freedom for the "iridescent creature" and a successful projection of her "heavy" thoughts for the writer.

Moreover, both metaphors of ship and bird—which suggest the idea of "breaking through" or "getting through"—do not bear only on her writing, but on her life in general. The word "iridescent" implies that the movements of the bird, like the girl's composition, are elusive of "easy" figures. The colors of its plumage changed with the different positions it took. Literally the bird fought against the confining wall; and, figuratively like the birds in Wilbur's "An Event" (274), it has been resisting the poet's attempt to translate its physical presence into words. The caged bird becomes an image for both the poet and his daughter, struggling for expression.

In helping the bird escape, both father and daughter were united in spirit with the bird. They shared the same happiness that the bird must have experienced when it finally found its way to the opened window. The father-and-daughter union is suggested by the use of the first-person plural pronouns "our" and "we": "we stole in, lifted a sash / And retreated, not to affright it"; "We watched the sleek, wild, dark / And iridescent creature"; and

> . . . how our spirits
> Rose when, suddenly sure,
> It lifted off from a chair-back,
> Beating a smooth course for the right window
> And clearing the sill of the world.

The poet's concern for the bird is a reflection of his love for his daughter. The bird "clearing the sill of the world" becomes an image for his daughter finding the needed expressions and surmounting the looming barriers in her life. The love between father and daughter is strengthened by their concern for a fellow creature and by their common passion for writing. The "reins of love" ("All These Birds": 269) inspire the poet to creativity. He synthesizes these provocative events, past and present, into a new poetic experience.

"The Writer," which ends with a prayer for his daughter, implies a broad parallel with W. B. Yeats's poem so titled. Wilbur's prayer, like Yeats's, serves also as a philosophical reminder to himself:

> It is always a matter, my darling,
> Of life or death, as I had forgotten. I wish
> What I wished you before, but harder.

Notes

1. Richard Wilbur, "The Bottles Become New, Too," *Responses, Prose Pieces: 1953–1976* (New York: Harcourt Brace Jovanovich, 1976) 220.
2. Richard Wilbur, *New and Collected Poems* (San Diego: Harcourt Brace Jovanovich, 1988) 53–54. Additional references to this work are by page number in the text.

Works Cited

Wilbur, Richard. "The Writer." *The Mind-Reader: New Poems*. New York:
    Harcourt, 1976.

Reflect on the Reading

Questions About "Richard Wilbur's 'The Writer'"

1. How would you summarize Wai's reading of the poem? Do you find her interpretation compelling? Why or why not?
2. Wai begins her analysis with a quotation from Wilbur as an epigraph. What are your thoughts on this strategy?
3. How successfully does the piece use quotations from the poem as evidence? What suggestions might you give Wai about the use of quotations?
4. What are your thoughts on the reference to Yeats's poem toward the end of the analysis? Is it fair to say the reference is a distraction? Why or why not?
5. The analysis ends with a quotation from the closing lines of the poem. What would you say to someone who argued that this ending is a missed opportunity to draw further conclusions about the poem?

LO

Learning
Objective 12.1

Looking at Isabella Wai's response to Richard Wilbur's poem demonstrates several key elements of a literary analysis. First, Wai offers a reading or interpretation of the work, suggesting that the poem ultimately represents a father's love for his daughter. She also discusses broadly the movements in the poem that account for this message, the synthesizing of images from the past (the bird trapped in the room) and the present (the daughter at the typewriter). You can see how Wai offers a viable interpretation of the work that drives the analysis.

Wai also zooms in to demonstrate how the details of the poem relate to the larger message she has discovered. She looks closely at the imagery used to describe the daughter at the typewriter, noting literary elements such as similes ("Like a chain hauled over a gunwale") and symbols (the trapped bird). She also explores the language, highlighting and discussing words like *iridescent* and the use of plural pronouns. Wai identifies elements of poetry and then zooms in to examine them in detail. She is also diligent about properly incorporating these details into her writing, quoting from the poem and citing and documenting her sources.

Wai complements this careful focus on literary elements with movements that zoom back out to make connections and draw conclusions. She links her analysis of the imagery and language with the thematic concerns of fathers, daughters, and writing. And she zooms out further to place the poem in the context of other works by Wilbur and by W.B. Yeats. She also places Wilbur's work within a tradition of poetry that is concerned with the relationships between the imagination and reality. Her response examines the big picture, but also zooms in to analyze the way the poem delivers its message and fits within a larger context.

Know It   Strategies for Understanding Literary Analyses

- Begin by thinking about the work being analyzed. If you are familiar with the work, identify points where your own reading relates to that of the analysis. If you have not read the work in question, then consider the insights into the text that the analysis provides.
- Understand the literary elements unique to the genre being analyzed. For fiction, consider plot, narrative points of view, setting, and characters. For poetry, consider speakers, structure, rhyme, rhythm, word choice, and figurative language. For drama, consider stage elements (sets, costumes, lighting, music, etc.) stage directions, and dialog.
- Examine how the analysis addresses common literary elements like themes. Does the piece identify key motifs and consider symbolism?
- Look to see whether the analysis draws connections with larger literary concerns and with elements of culture. Does the piece discuss allusions or links with similar works? Does it trace the relationships between the work and cultural and historical contexts?

Ask Questions & Make Decisions   Exercises for Understanding Literary Analyses

1. Think about essays you have written about literature in school assignments. Make a list of aspects of these essays that have been successful.
2. Choose a story with which you are familiar, and then explore Web sites that offer essays written about the story. Think about all of the qualities that make a successful literary analysis, and then look closely at several of the essays on the Web. Write a paragraph discussing your findings.

3. Choose a well-known literary text about which you have questions. Locate the resources for literature offered through your library's Web site; good databases include Literature Online (LION) and Magill's Literary Resources (MagillOnLiterature). Examine these resources and then write a paragraph exploring the ways in which they illuminate the literary text.

Readings and Resources for Exploring Literary Analyses

WN

RESOURCES
Sample Literary
Analyses

You can discover published analyses of literature in journals available from your school's library and on the Web. You can also explore the example below, in which Kieko Dilbeck offers a reading of Zora Neale Hurston's *Their Eyes Were Watching God*.

Symbolic Representation of Identity in Hurston's *Their Eyes Were Watching God*
BY **KEIKO DILBECK**

Keiko Dilbeck received her graduate degree from Northern Arizona University. She currently teaches English at Red Mountain High School in Mesa Arizona. "Symbolic Representation of Identity in Hurston's Their Eyes Were Watching God" *was published in* The Explicator *in 2008.*

In *Their Eyes Were Watching God*, the celebrated novel by Harlem Renaissance writer Zora Neale Hurston, the audience is provided a window into the development of the black female psyche through specific symbols. Hurston's reliance on symbolism in her literature has been emulated by writers such as *The Color Purple* author Alice Walker and studied by numerous researchers such as Rachel DuPlessis and Lillie Howard. These individuals and others have examined the symbols used in Hurston's literature and the personal relevance of symbols in the author's life, but they have not explored the relationship of these symbols to the main character, Janie—or what Hurston might call the New Negro Woman.[1] Through the symbolic use of the pear tree, mule, and hair, Hurston shows the development of her main character's identity as a woman and an African American.

Symbolic
Representation of
Identity in Hurston's
*Their Eyes Were
Watching God*
(continued)
BY **KEIKO DILBECK**

By the end of the novel, Janie realizes that a woman is to be loved, respected, and self-sufficient, which is manifested through Hurston's use of the pear tree symbol. An anthropologist by training and practice, Hurston may well have known that "in primitive cultures pear trees […] symbolize the sexuality/fertility of women" (Howard 47). The young Janie's sexuality takes shape as she relaxes underneath a pear tree: "She saw a dust-bearing bee sink into the sanctum of a bloom; the thousand sister-calyxes arch to meet the love embrace and the ecstatic shiver" (Hurston 11). Attuned to the connection between man and woman, Janie desperately wants the love and affection from a man that the tree receives from the pollen-bearing bee: "Oh to be a pear tree—any tree in bloom!" (11). As the novel progresses, this connection becomes fleshed out as she experiences marriage with Logan, Jody, and Tea Cake. Her first marriage with Logan is devastating: "Logan Killicks was desecrating the pear tree" (13). Janie recognizes that, along with being sexually desired, a woman should be treated with respect and dignity. In Janie's next marriage, with Jody, Hurston builds on the symbolism of the pear tree. Although Jody provides for her financially, he is jealous of the attention Janie receives from other men. In this marriage, Janie realizes that a man should have faith in his wife and give her freedom to experience life: "Janie pulled back a long time because [Jody] did not represent sun-up and pollen and blooming trees" (28). It is not until her final marriage that the dream of the tree is realized. This realization is important because it comes when Janie is nearly forty years old, ripe with life and experience. With Tea Cake, Janie achieves womanhood: "[Tea Cake] looked like the love thoughts of women. He could be a bee to a blossom—a pear tree blossom in the spring" (101). Not only does he appreciate Janie's beauty, intelligence, and independence, but he also shows her tenderness, trust, and respect.

One of the most curious symbols in *Their Eyes* is that of the mule, which Hurston uses to develop female identity. Early in the novel, Janie's grandmother explains, "De nigger woman is de mule of de world so far as Ah can see" (Hurston 14). Nanny provides Janie with old-fashioned insight while trying to explain Janie's place in the world as a woman. This correlation between woman and mule appears repeatedly, but never with more meaning than when Janie tires of her first husband, Logan, and runs off with Jody Starks to Eatonville for a life where she is only expected to "sit on de front porch and rock and fan" (28). In Eatonville, she is again disappointed—it is a town full of men who believe that "[s]omebody got to think for women and chillun and chickens and cows. I god, they sho don't think none themselves" (67). Matt Bonner, one of the residents, is ridiculed for his failure to control his stubborn mule, which is also taunted and abused by the townspeople. Hurston inserts this subplot as a metaphor of Janie and Jody's marriage. Janie expresses empathy for the animal and this is often seen as Janie's "own sense of gender entrapment" (DuPlessis 112). It is interesting to note that once Jody dies and Janie is free to do as she pleases, there are no further references to mules; Janie is free of her "load," no longer required to bear the expectations of men or others. Janie can escape her grandmother's words and realize her true power as a woman and human being—she belongs to no one but herself.

Hair is the most prominent symbol used throughout the text to expound femininity and identity. Janie's hair is what makes her stand out as independent and powerful, as demonstrated when she returns to Eatonville: Hurston notes "the great rope of hair swinging to her waist" (2). The townspeople wonder, "[w]hat dat ole forty year ole 'oman doin' wid her hair swingin' down her back lak some young gal?" (2). While married to Jody Starks, the most domineering of Janie's husbands, she was made to bind her hair up: "Joe never told Janie how jealous he was. He never told her how often he had seen the other men figuratively wallowing in it […]" (51). When Jody dies, "[s]he tore off the kerchief from her head and let down her plentiful hair" (83). During their twenty-year marriage, Jody asserted himself over Janie: "The tying up of Janie's hair is clearly an exertion of power on Joe's part […] he sends a message to Janie that her hair is not hers to wear the way she wants" (Ashe 3). The last man in Janie's life is unlike her first two husbands. He says to her shortly after their first meeting: "Ah ain't been sleepin' so good for more'n uh week cause Ah been wishin' so bad tuh git mah hands in yo' hair. It's so pretty. It feels jus' lak underneath uh dove's wing next to mah face" (Hurston 99). Tea Cake treats Janie's hair (womanhood) with considerate devotion, and it is under these circumstances that Janie's identity is her own. One scholar notes, "Tea Cake is expressing his love by glorifying in Janie's beauty. He is loving her as she is—not trying to make her into a creation of his own" (Ashe 4). Janie's hair is also a marker of her ethnic identity. She is different from the rest of the Eatonville citizens and those in the muck because she is three-quarters Caucasian and one-quarter African American. Mrs. Tucker, a black woman who "can't stand black niggers," admires Janie's "coffee-and-cream complexion and her luxurious hair" (Hurston 135, 134). Despite Mrs. Turner's request to "class off," Janie refuses. "Janie's reaction to Mrs. Turner's racial bias, however, indicates that, although Janie's hair is vital to her self-esteem, her racial identity is intact" (Ashe 5).

Examining these significant symbols in *Their Eyes* is necessary to fully understand Hurston's development of the black female. Historically, these women had been treated like animals, more specifically mules, to carry the burdens of men. Hurston encourages women to rise above this situation; she shows women that it is possible to realize their potential and achieve their aspirations.

Notes

1. Male authors of the Harlem Renaissance often contemplated the struggles and examined the development of the "New Negro." Philosopher and critic Alain Locke stated the New Negro "had to 'smash' all of the racial, social and psychological impediments that had long obstructed black achievement" (Institute for International Visual Arts).

Symbolic
Representation of
Identity in Hurston's
*Their Eyes Were
Watching God*
(continued)
BY **KEIKO DILBECK**

Works Cited

Ashe, Bertram D. "'Why Don't He Like My Hair?': Constructing African-American
    Standards of Beauty in Toni Morrison's Song of Solomon and Zora Neale Hurston's
    Their Eyes Were Watching God." *African American Review* 29.4 (1995): 579–92.

DuPlessis, Rachel Blau. "Power, Judgment, and Narrative in a Work of Zora Neale
    Hurston: Feminist Cultural Studies." *New Essays on Their Eyes Were Watching God*.
    Ed. Michael Awkward. New York: Cambridge UP, 1990. 95–123.

Howard, Lillie P., ed. *Alice Walker and Zora Neale Hurston: The Common Bond*. Westport:
    Greenwood, 1993.

Hurston, Zora Neale. *Their Eyes Were Watching God*. New York City: Perennial, 1990.

Institute of International Visual Arts. "The New Negro." Harlem. 8 May 2007
    <http://www.iniva.org/harlem/negro.html>.

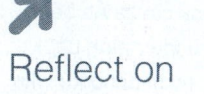

Reflect on
the Reading

Questions About "Symbolic Representation of Identity in Hurston's *Their Eyes Were Watching God*"

1. Dilbeck concentrates on just one literary element (symbolism) in her analysis of *Their Eyes Were Watching God*. Do you find this strategy effective? Why or why not?

2. What are your thoughts on the use of quotations in the piece? Are they smoothly integrated and well discussed?

3. Dilbeck incorporates information from a number of outside sources, scholars who have also written on the novel. How does this move influence your reading of the analysis?

4. The piece concludes with some points about the treatment of black women. Do you think that enough connections and context have been provided? What are your thoughts on the conclusion?

Writing Assignment: A Literary Analysis

Compose an essay in which you analyze a work of literature. Your analysis should offer an interpretation of the work—an angle, or over-arching message, that you provide, which expresses your reading of the text. Consider related texts as well as historical and cultural contexts as you develop your reading. You should also discuss the literary elements in the work to support your interpretation. (Explore literary elements unique to the genre as well as elements like themes and symbols.) Use quotations from the work to support your points, and consider using quotations from outside sources. Connect detailed analysis with points related to your interpretation. Document your sources and gather feedback as you work.

Ask Questions & Make Decisions

Exercises for Composing Literary Analyses

1. Identify a piece of literature you like, but about which you have not thought too extensively. Consider the themes and literary elements of the work, and freewrite for five minutes about possible interpretations of the text.

2. Choose a poem or short story. Think about possible annotation strategies, and then read the text with a pen or pencil in hand, marking up the document to help you develop an interpretation.

3. Working with a group of peers, choose a genre of literature, and then develop a list of literary elements that are key to understanding the genre. For each, write three or more statements offering recommendations that will help readers examine these literary elements.

4. Choose a literary text with which you are familiar. Imagine that you have been tasked with delivering a lecture on the text to your peers. Develop an outline for the lecture. If possible, present the lecture to a group of classmates.

Plan It

Invention Strategies for Literary Analyses

Learning
Objective 12.2

Preparing to write a literary analysis will go more easily if you have an angle that you can use to get started. You will also need to become an expert on the work in question. Expertise will come from reading (and re-reading!) the text, examining its details. You can also conduct research to learn more about the work, which will lead you to additional sources that can be used to provide evidence when you compose. Finally, you will need to become comfortable with the literary elements that you will analyze. To start the planning process, try the following approach:

**Learning
Objective 12.3**

- Start with your response to the text. What is your gut reaction to the work being analyzed? How can you translate that response into a more comprehensive reading? Work to develop an interpretation, and then check that you can articulate your take on the text in a few concrete statements.
- Conduct research to refine your thinking. Look into the historical and cultural contexts connected to the text. Find out more about the author or literary movements related to the text. Read what others have said about the work.
- Make a list of the literary elements you will be looking at in your analysis. Include general aspects like themes and symbols and then identify those elements unique to the genre with which you are working.
- Re-read the text. Keep an open mind about your initial angle of interpretation, using your approach to guide your reading, but adjusting your thinking as you make new discoveries. Annotate the text as you revisit the work.
- Identify several passages that you wish to discuss in the analysis. Think about how you might sequence your discussion of the passages to guide readers through your interpretation.
- Zoom out to consider points you might make to situate the text in terms of larger concerns. Note any background information readers might need. Sketch out points to be made about the author, cultural contexts, or literary history.
- Develop an outline, graphic map, or some other planning document to help you think about the organization of the essay.

CONNECT IT **More Resources for Literary Analyses**

For more detailed information about some of the strategies you might use in literary analyses, consider the following resources:

- For more on rhetorical situations, see Chapter 1.
- For more on arguments, see Chapter 4.
- For insights into using research in literary arguments, see Chapters 14–17.
- For more on thesis statements, see Chapter 18.
- For insights into organizing structures, see Chapter 19.
- For insights into using definitions, see Chapter 22.
- For more on analyzing, see pages 62–65.

- For insights into integrating quotations into literary analyses, see pages 377–83.
- For more on comparing and contrasting, see Chapter 23.
- For insights into using visuals in literary analyses, see Chapter 25.
- For information on design strategies, see Chapter 26.
- For insights into developing annotated bibliographies for literary analyses, see Chapter E4.

Compose It **Write a Literary Analysis**

**Learning
Objective 12.4**

As you begin drafting, remember the importance of analysis to this assignment. In many ways, you will be enacting a process of reading or analyzing as you write. It might be helpful to begin with a detailed discussion of some of your key passages; you can always draft the introduction and conclusion later. Or you can sketch out your main points and then discuss the text as you explore these points in the body of the essay. Keep a few things in mind:

- Remember that readers may not be familiar with the text. You will want to include background information (text, author, date of publication, etc.) and you will need to give basic information about the text, without bogging down in summary.
- Think about the organization of the essay. Most literary analyses open with background, sketch out a reading, and then proceed to discuss the text in the body of the essay. If you bring in outside sources, you can weave them in as needed.
- Integrate and discuss quotations from the literary piece. Become adept at smoothly weaving quotations into your prose (see pages 377–81). Remember that every quotation should serve as a springboard for discussing your own insights. For every quotation, follow up with extensive discussion.
- Be sure to weave together your analysis of the details of the text with relevant points of your interpretation. As you use quotations, zoom in to analyze them, then zoom back out to relate them to your overall reading of the text.
- Compose with an eye toward illuminating the contexts and larger concerns related to the text. You may wish to bring out much of this discussion toward the end of the analysis. Or you can establish the relationship between the text and larger concerns initially, and then draw connections throughout.

Focus on
Student
Writing

The Love Factory: "Womanhood," Sex, and Marriage
BY **TARA JOSS**

Tara wrote this piece in response to the poem "Womanhood" by Catherine Anderson. Tara offers a reading of the poem in terms of feminist scholar Diana Leonard's claim that marriage is a relationship based on labor. We include with Tara's essay a reprint of Anderson's poem.

Womanhood
BY **CATHERINE ANDERSON**

She slides over
the hot upholstery
of her mother's car,
this schoolgirl of fifteen
who loves humming & swaying
with the radio.
Her entry into womanhood
will be like all the other girls'—
a cigarette and a joke,
as she strides up with the rest
to a brick factory
where she'll sew rag rugs
from textile strips of kelly green,
bright red, aqua.

When she enters,
and the millgate closes,
final as a slap,
there'll be silence.
She'll see fifteen high windows
cemented over to cut out light.
Inside, a constant, deafening noise
and warm air smelling of oil,
the shifts continuing on. . . .
All day she'll guide cloth along a line
of whirring needles, her arms & shoulders

rocking back & forth
with the machines—
200 porch size rugs behind her
before she can stop
to reach up, like her mother,
and pick the lint
out of her hair.

Tara Joss

Professor Anderson

Contemporary Literature

30 Apr. 2009

The Love Factory: "Womanhood," Sex, and Marriage

The feminist scholar Diana Leonard has called marriage a "labour relationship" but has argued that "marriage, however, differs from other labour relations in being shrouded in talk of love, companionship, and sharing. . . ." (261). This sometimes-mysterious relationship between women, labor, and the language of love offers a helpful lens for viewing the poem "Womanhood" by Catherine Anderson. The poem appears in Anderson's collection *Work of Hands*. It centers on the maturation of a fifteen-year-old girl as she begins work at a rug factory. The young girl seems to first be excited about her venture into the labor force, but is then thoroughly disappointed by the drudgery of the mill. The poem could serve as a contemporary critique of exploitive labor practices in its depiction of a teenage girl pressed into the textile industry. But looking more closely at the imagery of sexuality in the poem helps us understand the work on another level. Yes, there is drudgery and exploitation in the poem, but it is also linked to the sexual dimensions of womanhood. The poem ultimately suggests that something that we normally think of in positive terms, like marriage or sexuality, can be easily lined up with something as obviously negative as a sweatshop.

The poem is organized into two stanzas, with the difference between the stanzas accounting for a loss of innocence. In the first stanza, the entry into womanhood has traditional associations:

> Her entry into womanhood
> will be like all the other girls'—
> a cigarette and a joke,
> as she strides up with the rest
> to a brick factory
> where she'll sew rag rugs
> from textile strips of kelly green,
> bright red, aqua. (7–14)

The reference to "a cigarette and a joke" lulls the reader into a comfortable view of the potential future of the young girl, the cigarette suggesting youthful transgressions that are pictured as mostly harmless or at least humorous. There is some foreboding that seeps into the first stanza, as evidenced by the setting and activity (sewing in a factory). Still, the main picture is one of possibility and youthful potential, brought home by the touches of color that close out the stanza, "kelly green / bright red, aqua" (13–14).

Unfortunately, this mostly upbeat initial view is reversed in the second stanza. This reversal takes place instantly in the opening lines of stanza two:

> When she enters,
> and the millgate closes,
> final as a slap,
> there'll be silence. (15–18)

The personification of the millgate hammers home the point that this entry into womanhood will be nothing like the youthful picture alluded to in stanza one. A loss of

Joss 3

possibility not only comes but also hints at violence and pain, "final as a slap" (17). Of course, the movement from innocence to experience has long been a motif in literature (think snake and apple). Further, the critique of factory life put forth in the poem might resonate as strongly with a reader from the nineteenth rather than the twenty-first century. The poem joins a long list of works charting a loss of innocence and charging an uncaring mechanized society with the crime.

However, under an alternatively modern interpretation of Anderson's poem, one that is highly sexualized, the thematic significance of "Womanhood" becomes much more provocative. The opening lines depicting the girl's motion as she "slides over / the hot upholstery" (1–2) set the stage for this sexualized reading. Words like *hot*, *humming*, and *swaying* all contribute to the tone of the first stanza. Later in the poem, the speaker characterizes the factory as dimly lit and filled with "warm air." Yet what goes on in the factory seems stimulating, "whirring needles" (25) and "rocking back & forth" (26). The abundance of sexual connotations throughout the poem, might lead some to believe that "Womanhood" is simply a poem about a girl's entry into sexuality conveyed, in a metaphorical sense, through a description of her first day at a textile factory.

A closer look at this sexual interpretation, however, also reveals the movement to be one of loss and pain. Any sexual connotations are undercut by the fact that they are made mechanical by the factory setting. Although there is a kind of sexualized awakening given to the young girl, the endless repetition associated with it and the inhuman connections responsible for her movements translate the sexual promise into still another critique of the factory system:

> All day she'll guide cloth along a line
> of whirring needles, her arms & shoulders
> rocking back & forth
> with the machines— (24–28)

This negative twist on sexuality is strengthened by a number of literary elements in the poem. There is a parallel structure established between the fifteen-year-old girl and the "fifteen high windows" (19) in the factory. Yet the windows are "cemented over to cut out light" (20). While the factory is dim and warm, it is also "deafening." Instead of the scent of flowers or perfumed candles, we have "warm air smelling of oil" (22). Everything that might offer the promise of sexuality is perverted by the factory into something dull, cease-less, and mechanical.

The poem completes the link between the drudgery of the factory and sexuality through the representation of another kind of labor, the labor that produces children. Here the negative connotations of the sweatshop allow us to consider Leonard's perspective on marriage as a labor relationship. Just as the mother must introduce her young daughter to the mechanized state of sexuality represented by the mill in Anderson's poem, the young girl must look forward and recognize her future as she

> stop[s]
> to reach up, like her mother,
> and pick the lint
> out of her hair. (29–32)

The gesture adds a sense that the link between sexuality and labor creates a vicious cycle for women. Just as the rows of rugs line up endlessly and the needles whir ceaselessly, mothers and daughters are destined to labor through their sexuality. The imagery of sexual-ity quickly moves toward drudgery and mechanical repetition as the poem transitions from innocence in stanza one to experience in stanza two. More important, the movement from innocence to experience is linked to institutions. On one level, these institutions are easy to see and criticize, as in the demeaning labor of the factory. On another level, these forces must be seen beneath surfaces like the language of love, as when sexuality becomes mecha-nized toil through institutions like marriage.

Joss 5

Works Cited

Anderson, Catherine. *The Work of Hands*. Shutesbury, MA: Perugia, 2000. Print.

Leonard, Diana. *Sex and Generation: A Study of Courtship and Weddings*. London: Tavistock, 1980. Print.

Reflect on the Reading

Questions about "The Love Factory: 'Womanhood,' Sex, and Marriage"

1. Tara uses a claim from an outside source to establish the main angle of her interpretation. What are your thoughts on this strategy?
2. What can you say about the way the essay discusses elements of poetry like rhyme, rhythm, and figurative language? What suggestions might you give Tara about the details of the poem?
3. How well does "The Love Factory: 'Womanhood,' Sex, and Marriage" address broad literary concerns like themes and symbols? Does the piece tie a reading of these elements into a larger interpretation of the poem?
4. Look over the poem "Womanhood" on page 306. After developing your own reading, what advice would you give to Tara about revising her analysis?

Revise It   Strategies for Revising Literary Analyses

As you revise your literary analysis, try to approach your work from the perspective of potential readers. Imagine readers who have not read the work, and check that you provide enough information for them to make sense of what you are saying. Think also about these strategies:

- Re-read your piece starting with the last paragraph and working backward. Are there any sections that seem confusing? Create a reverse outline, and then look it over to check your organization.

Learning
Objective 12.5

RESOURCES
Sample Literary
Analyses

- Examine your use of quotations in the analysis. Check that you are including the most relevant passages. Ensure that you are discussing each quotation in detail.
- Consider alternative readings that might undercut your interpretation. Are there places where you might need to adjust your approach?
- Ensure that you are zooming out, not just discussing the details of literary elements. As you use quotations or examine an element of the text, check that you are tying that discussion to larger points of your interpretation. Make sure you are looking at contexts and cultural concerns.
- Examine the formal elements of the analysis. Check that quotations are integrated smoothly. Ensure that you are citing and documenting sources. Examine the format of the essay. Polish all of the surface-level aspects of the text.

Push It   More Possibilities for Literary Analyses

1. Compose a playlist representing the identity of a literary character. Music is well suited to represent insights into humans. Select a literary character, and then identify songs that shed light on him or her. Return to the story, and develop a reading that explores themes in terms of the character. Sequence the songs into a playlist that charts the development of the character and reveals the thematic concerns of the text. Add explanations that demonstrate your thinking for each of the song entries. (For more on playlists, see Chapter E5, especially the playlist on Jane Eyre.)

2. Choose an expressive work that does not fall into the categories traditionally associated with literature. You might look at dance, painting, photography, or music, for instance. Consider the genre and medium of the text, developing an understanding of the features that set the form apart—for instance, lyrics, rhythm, melody, and instruments for music. Examine the work you have chosen, developing a reading that offers an interpretation. Compose a literary analysis discussing the text in terms of its features and presenting readers with your interpretation.

Zoom **Out**   Reflecting on Literary Analyses

- **Literary analyses offer a reading of a text.** You will present an interpretation and discuss the details of a work to develop a literary analysis.

- **Literary analyses examine key elements of literature.** These elements differ from one genre to another. Think of literary analyses as a chance not only to explore a text, but also to learn about genres and the study of literature.

- **Outside reading can benefit literary analyses.** Familiarize yourself with sources appropriate for literature and then conduct research (Chapters 14–17) to help you explore literature with more complexity.

- **Literary analyses also zoom out as they examine a text.** Think about the ways in which texts relate to their contexts, to their authors, and to literary history. Make connections between the details you discuss and elements of culture.

For additional information and practice with the learning objectives in this chapter, go to www.mycomplab.com, Resources > Writing > Writing Purposes > Writing to Analyze

CHAPTER 13

Photo Essays

 Zoom **In**   **Key Concepts and Learning Objectives**

After studying this chapter, you should be able to:

13.1 Identify relevant images that can be used for documenting events, discussing cultural concerns, or explaining concepts.

13.2 Analyze visuals when composing photo essays.

13.3 Compose captions that discuss the details of images and make connections with the larger topic of an essay.

13.4 Conduct research to add depth and provide insights in a photo essay.

13.5 Use video and Web editors, online spaces, or word processors to create a photo essay.

Taking photographs (or writing about them) challenges you to make all kinds of composing decisions. First, you must select a subject. Your choice may be relatively simple and specific (for example, I know I want to focus on that fire hydrant). Or your decision might take more work (for example, there is something that needs to be said about this neighborhood; let's see if I can capture it). The difference between snapping an image of a fire hydrant and trying to develop a record of a neighborhood is one of scale and context. On a small scale, you might take a picture to make a statement about a single object. On the larger scale, you might combine a photograph of the hydrant with a picture of a child or an abandoned car to document the overall feel of an area.

Photo essays allow you to think about a topic using these differing scales. By selecting a number of images, authors create a message based on combinations, a message that represents a larger context or subject. But photo essays must strike a balance between compiling this bigger picture and helping readers see its details. Each photograph offers an opportunity to explore a specific statement—for example, *Why this child?* And to draw connections—for instance, *How does this fire hydrant relate to urban decline?* The images comprise pointed details even as they convey ideas about the subject of the essay as a whole. Zoom in and out.

Some of the work of interpreting and composing photo essays involves analyzing images. You should refer to the instruction in Chapter 25 to get up to speed on reading visuals. But photo essays also generally include text in the form of titles and captions. Photo essays, then, require selecting, sequencing, and reading images as well as analyzing and explaining them using words. Selecting titles lets you point out relationships between individual images and the larger essay. Captions can both describe the image under discussion and situate that image in the context of the rest of the essay.

KEY TERMS

- **Photo essay:** Sometimes referred to as a slideshow, a collection of images and captions that provides information or delivers a message.

- **Caption:** The explanatory text that accompanies an image in a photo essay. Captions serve as a key means for analyzing images and making points in a photo essay.

- **Navigation:** The process of moving through a series of pages in a photo essay. Most photo essays include forward (next) and back (previous) options; sometimes essays use thumbnail images for navigation.

- **Sequence:** The order in which images appear in photo essays. The sequence of images should represent an organization consistent with the message of the essay as a whole.

- **Fair use:** The practice of ethically integrating the work of others into your compositions. To use images fairly requires a number of decisions related to copyright concerns. (See our e-book or pages 345–47 for more information.)

VIDEO
24. Web Photo Essays

- **Analyzing images:** The process of reading and writing about photographs and other visual items. Visual analysis asks questions about medium, genre, and rhetorical concerns like arrangement, contrast, color, scale, and emphasis (See Chapter 25).

Understanding Photo Essays

To get a better sense of the key features of photo essays, let's look at an example. Here, a series of images is used to organize a chronological exploration of the gay rights movement in America.

 Gay Rights, From Stonewall to Prop 8
PHOTOS BY **FRED W. MCDARRAH, TERRY SCHMITT, JOHN STOREY, AND SARA KRULWICH**

"Gay Rights, from Stonewall to Prop 8" was created by Time *magazine for inclusion on its Web site as an accompaniment to stories covering the passage of Proposition 8 in California. The proposition (passed in November 2008) re-instated a ban on same-sex marriages that had earlier been overturned by the California Supreme Court. The photo essay was published in 2009. We include here a selection of six photos from the essay.*

An unidentified group of young people outside the Stonewall Inn, 27 June 1969. The Stonewall was a bar in New York City's Greenwich Village known as a gathering place for gay men and lesbians. Anger at police harassment coalesced into a series of demonstrations and riots in June 1969. The modern gay rights movement often locates its origins in these protests.

One month after the demonstrations at the Stonewall Inn, activist Marty Robinson speaks to a crowd of approximately 200 people before marching in the first mass rally in support of gay rights, New York, 27 July 1969. The first gay pride march was born.

By 1977, the counter-reaction to the gay rights movement was in full swing. Anita Bryant, runner up in the 1959 Miss America pageant and a well-known pop singer, organized a group called Save Our Children. Bryant and her group succeeded in pushing for repeal of a Dade County, Florida ordinance that prohibited discrimination based on sexual orientation. Bryant described the opposition to gay rights as a "crusade."

Harvey Milk at the 1978 San Francisco Gay Freedom Day Parade. Milk was elected to the San Francisco board of supervisors in 1977, demonstrating the political clout of an organized gay constituency. Harvey Milk became the gay-rights movement's first visible martyr when he was shot and killed by Dan White on 27 November 1978.

On May 21, 1979, word spread that ex-cop Dan White, who had shot and killed Harvey Milk, had been given a seven-year sentence. White had been acquitted of first-degree murder by a jury. Community anger poured into the streets of San Francisco in the form of the White Night riots.

Larry Kramer, founder of ACT-UP and the Gay Men's Health Crisis group at his home in New York, December 1989. AIDS was first reported in the U.S. in 1981. Widespread fears and the perception of AIDS as a "gay plague" undermined many of the gains made by the gay rights movement in preceding decades. ACT-UP worked to promote awareness and to support medical research on AIDS and related conditions.

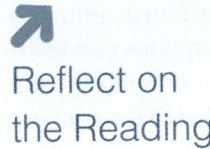

Reflect on the Reading

Questions About "Gay Rights, from Stonewall to Prop 8"

1. How would you describe the rhetorical situation represented by this photo essay? What can you say about the audience and the creator of the essay? What purposes can you identify for the piece?

2. What are your thoughts on the selection of images in the photo essay? What would you say to someone who argued that the images have been selected for their subject matter rather than for their visual qualities?

3. How effective do you find the captions to be? What types of decisions can you imagine the author of the captions making?

4. For the most part, the photo essay sequences images chronologically. What are your thoughts on this arrangement? What alternative organizational strategies might work for this subject?

"Gay Rights, from Stonewall to Prop 8" generates a number of questions. First, we might think about subjects for photo essays. Often, photo essays look at events or concepts because these subjects lend themselves well to visual representations. Images help illustrate what took place or how something works. But even subjects like cultural or political concerns can work well for photo essays. The key is to have an angle the can help organize the essay. The piece above traces the evolution of the gay rights movement, allowing its author to select photos that represent moments in that history and to organize the selections logically.

The online version of the piece (http://www.time.com/time/photogallery/0,29307,1900959,00.html) also includes other key features of photo essays. There are forward and back buttons allowing readers to move through the images. There are sources listed for all of the photographs. There are title provided for each image. There are also links to external Web pages. The titles provide information about the origin of the images. (If an artist has given an image a title, that name is preferred; if not, photo essay authors can provide titles.) The links send readers to Web sites with more information. (Most photo essays are delivered over the Web; for more on creating these compositions, see below.)

The captions do much of the work in photo essays. Captions can provide background information—for example, the fourth page in the essay offers details about its subject, Harvey Milk. And captions can make points that situate the image within the larger message of the essay. The challenge is to distill this information and explanation into a concise statement. Note how the caption identifies Harvey Milk and explains his significance to the gay rights movement, but does not go into great detail, which might overwhelm the flow of the essay as a whole.

Finally, through the combination of all of its pages, the photo essay creates a holistic message about the topic. The need to distill information in the captions is balanced by the ability to display multiple images and captions. For instance, the brief information about Harvey Milk in the caption for the fourth photo is extended in the discussion of the fifth image. Together, the two captions give readers enough information to understand the role of Milk in the gay rights movement. Selecting and sequencing the images while creating captions that make connections with one another gives the essay coherence and delivers a larger message.

Know It   Strategies for Understanding Photo Essays

- Consider the rhetorical situation of photo essays. Think about the author and audience of the essay. What elements of the cultural context should be considered when examining the piece?
- Spend time exploring the photographs. Who took the pictures? In what context? What more can you learn about the human and cultural connections related to the images?
- Evaluate the visual elements of the essay. Learn to read images (see Chapter 25). Think about decisions made by the photographer or artist. Consider the messages expressed in the images.
- Consider the formal elements of the photo essay. How are images titled? Are all sources cited? How do the navigation and other mechanical dimensions of the piece affect your reading?
- Think critically about the captions. How well do they discuss the image? How do they create connections with one another and with the larger message of the piece? How does the author handle the distilled nature of captions? Are there places where more (or less) information might be called for?
- Examine the overall message of the photo essay. Can you articulate a thesis for the piece? Often these compositions focus on providing information and on documenting events, concepts, or aspects of culture, but other purposes are possible. What is the essay trying to do or say?

Learning
Objective 13.2

Ask Questions & Make Decisions   Exercises for Understanding Photo Essays

1. Identify a topic that might work well for a photo essay. Search online for images related to the topic, examining at least ten photos. Make a list of things that might be said about the topic based on the images you have discovered.
2. Working with a small group of peers, explore an online photo site like flickr.com, photobucket.com, or photo.net. Identify a tag related to a topic (immigration, food safety, gay marriage, L.A. riots, Dresden bombings, etc.) Examine photographs that have been tagged with the topic, and then discuss the collection with your partners.
3. Search online for photo essays (also try the terms *slideshow*, *slide show* or *photoessay*). Examine five or more examples, and then identify what you

consider to be an excellent photo essay. Write a paragraph exploring your findings.

4. Search online and view photo essays related to several different disciplines (medicine, history, popular culture, art, technology, etc.). Identify two interesting examples, and then write a page or so comparing them.

Readings and Resources For Exploring Photo Essays

Learning Objective 13.1

The Web is full of photo essays. Some of the best collections are provided by the online sites for magazines like *Time*, *Newsweek*, or *Life*. This is no accident. *Life* magazine pioneered photo essays, publishing collections of photographs and accompanying text that covered topics ranging from war to travel to celebrity profiles. Below find excerpts from a classic photo essay, Eugene Smith's "Country Doctor."

 ## Country Doctor

BY **EUGENE SMITH**

On September 20, 1948, Life magazine released the photo essay "Country Doctor." The essay featured the work of photographer Eugene Smith. Smith spent twenty-three days documenting the life of Dr. Ernest Ceriani as he went about his work in the small town of Kremmling, Colorado. The collection became one of the best-known examples of a photo essay, the images capturing the drama of Ceriani's day-to-day experiences as a small-town doctor. We provide excerpts from the piece below.

Country Doctor Ernest Ceriani making house calls on foot in a small town.

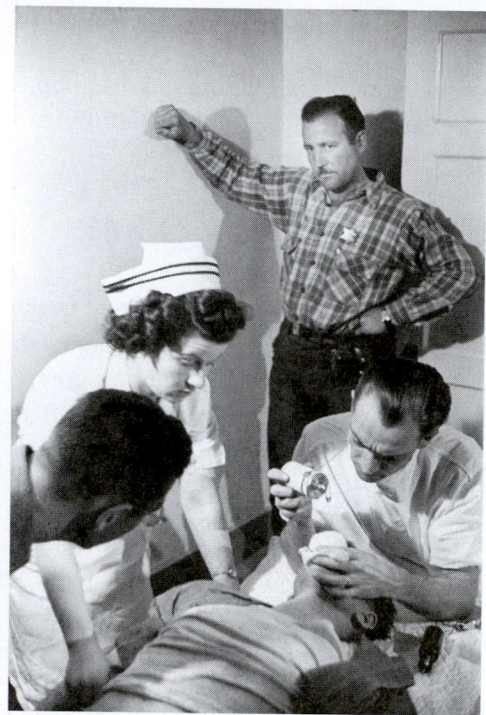

Doctor Ceriani administering anesthesia to a patient as a nurse and others look on.

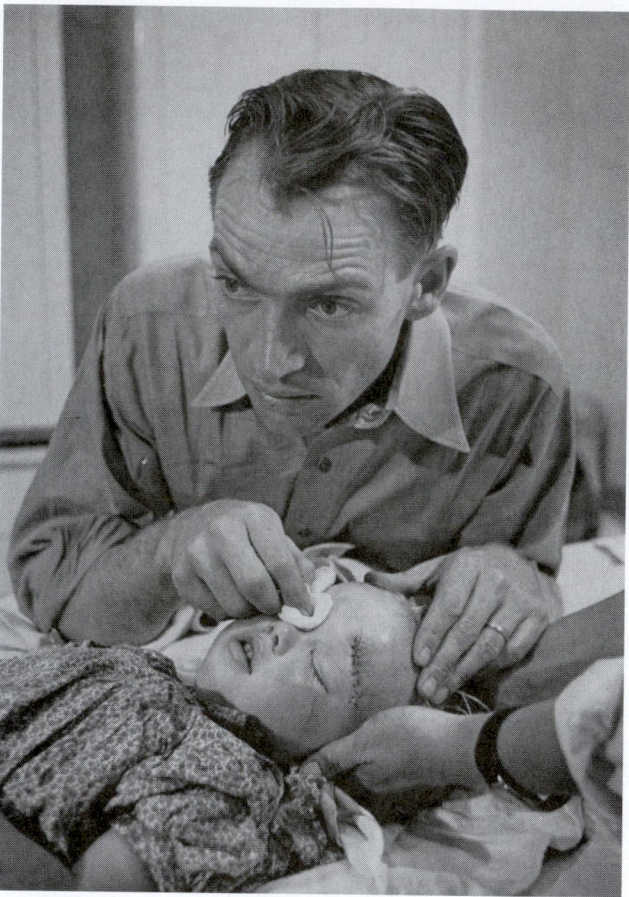

In a hospital emergency room, the doctor wipes the eye of a girl whose head he has just stitched up after she was kicked by a horse.

Doctor Ceriani, surrounded by nurses, bending down to examine a young girl who was kicked in the head by a horse. Her worried parents clutch each other in fear.

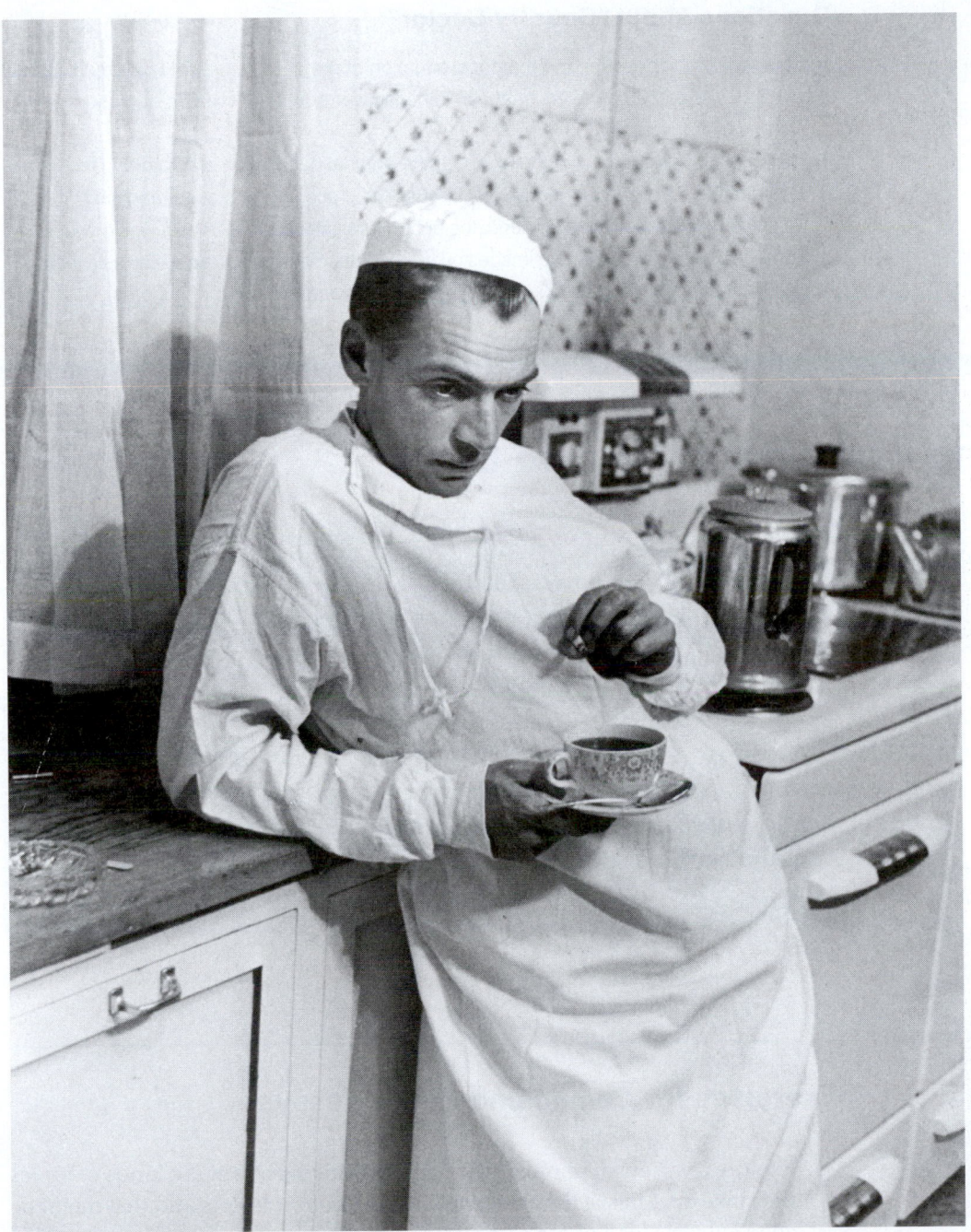

Doctor Ernest Ceriani in a dazed state of exhaustion, having a cup of coffee in the hospital kitchen at 2 a.m. after performing a cesarean section where the baby and the mother died due to complications.

Reflect on the Reading

Questions About "Country Doctor"

1. How would you describe the rhetorical situation of the photo essay? How would you evaluate the piece based on what you can discover about the creator, audience, and purposes of the essay?

2. What questions arise as you think about the original publication of "Country Doctor" as a magazine spread? How would you discuss the piece in terms of its medium?

3. What comments can you offer about the photographs themselves? What would you say to someone who argues that the images overwhelm the message of the essay as a whole?

4. Conduct some brief research into Eugene Smith. Examine some of his other photographs and photo essays. How would you discuss "Country Doctor" in relation to his other work?

Writing Assignment: A Photo Essay

WN

VIDEO
23. Images and Intellectual Property

> Compose a photo essay in which you select and sequence images and provide captions to deliver a message about a topic. Begin with your rhetorical situation, deciding what purposes you hope to achieve and for whom you will be composing. Create a sequence of six or more images. Follow guidelines for appropriate use of images (see pages 345–47). Compose captions for each of the images. Add navigation elements to the essay. Document your sources and gather feedback as you work. (See the Zoom Box on page 329 for more on composing options.)

Ask Questions & Make Decisions

Exercises for Composing Photo Essays

1. Explore a variety of photo essays online, thinking about the kinds of topics they take up. Make a list of topics that meet your interests and that might be good subjects for a photo essay.

2. Think about the issues related to fair use of images in your compositions (see pages 345–47). Keeping in mind the guidelines for using images, search

online and download a collection of at least ten images that might be used in a photo essay.

3. Search online to identify a well-known photograph (such as "Flag Raising at Iwo Jima," "Vietnam Napalm," or "Migrant Mother"). Conduct research about the image and its contexts, and then write a caption of no more than four sentences that situates the photo for readers.

4. Examine a number of photo essays online, looking at their formal elements. Where are the photos placed on the page? How are captions, navigation, and source information delivered? Bookmark two examples of essay designs that you find to be effective.

Plan It   Invention Strategies for Photo Essays

LO

Learning
Objective 13.4

Your planning will need to address the added complexity that comes from composing with images. You will also need a strong research focus to handle the task of finding and citing images and to learn more about your topic. That activity will require you to understand the ethical and logistical dimensions of image use (pages 345–47). You will also need to keep images in mind as you make decisions about potential topics. You might be eager to compose an essay on suburban bicycle traffic, but if you can't find relevant and usable images, you will have to make adjustments. Consider these specific strategies as you get started:

- Study the dimensions of locating, downloading, and documenting images. Learn the search strategies involved in finding images and understand the concerns of intellectual property related to using images. Ensure that you know how to save and document images.

- Think about the purposes that will inform your work. Check your assignment or talk with your instructor to get started. Understand that photo essays can deliver information, but also consider how you can compose photo essays to achieve other goals.

- Consider the nature of captions. Think about the benefits and challenges of composing using a limited amount of text. How can you distill information into small chunks but still make your points?

- Identify a model you can use for the formal elements of the photo essay. You will need a layout that supports navigation and provides spaces for captions and documentation. (See the Zoom Box on page 329 for specific suggestions.)

- Choose a topic for the photo essay. Think about the topic until you can articulate an angle that might organize your approach. Make sure that usable images are available for your topic.

WN

VIDEO
24. Web Photo
Essays

WN

VIDEO
25. Word
Processors and
Photo Essays

- Sketch out ideas for key points that you wish to make related to your topic. Think about the cumulative message that the photo essay might deliver and how individual images and captions can contribute to that message.
- Ask questions about the organization of your photo essay. Given your potential topic, what kind of sequencing of images makes sense? Sketch out a storyboard or other planning document to help you organize your essay.

VIDEO
26. Online Photo Sites

CONNECT IT Helpful Connections for Photo Essays

For more detailed information about some of the strategies you might use in photo essays, consider the following resources:

For more on analyzing images, see Chapter 25.

For more on presenting information visually, see Chapter 26.

For more on research, see Chapters 14–17.

For more on organizing structures, see Chapter 19.

For more on analyzing, see pages 62–65.

For more on narrating, see Chapter 20.

For more on describing, see Chapter 21.

Compose It Create a Photo Essay

There are some logistical steps you will need to complete as you create the photo essay. These steps will vary depending on the medium you select and the composing options available to you. The Zoom Box below gives more details related to these technical steps. (Be sure to check with your instructor if you have questions about the form of the essay.) In addition, work through the following steps:

- Collect the images for the project. Download materials to your computer, keeping track of source information. Follow guidelines for appropriate use of images.
- Create a template that can be used for the pages of the photo essay. (See the Zoom Box or our e-book for more information.)
- Create an opening page for the essay. Place the opening image on the page, adjusting the scale as needed and providing source information. Your opening page may serve to introduce your topic, or it might analyze your first image.

- Compose a caption for the image. If you have conducted research for the essay, look for opportunities to incorporate it into your caption, perhaps adding quotations or providing relevant facts. Be concise, but discuss the key points.
- Compose the remaining pages of the essay, making choices about sequencing and keeping in mind the way individual photos and captions can contribute to the message of the essay as a whole.
- Check that the navigation of the essay is user friendly and that it functions properly. Document your images and any other sources you cite (see Chapter 17).
- Check the layout of your pages. Does the placement of the images allow space for captions and other features? What effect would adjustments to the scale or arrangement of the items have on the layout?
- Examine your captions. If you are incorporating research, is it well integrated into the captions? Is the language sharp? Do the captions make connections with one another or with larger points? Make sure that quotations are accurate and that all research is cited and documented.
- Check that you are using images fairly. Do you include source information for each image? Have you studied fair use guidelines (pages 345–47) and made careful decisions about how and when to use images?
- Ensure that the mechanical and surface details of the piece are in order. Check that any links function.

Zoom Box   Technical Options for Composing Photo Essays

Learning Objective 13.5

You will need to adjust what you do depending on your own situation, but here are some ideas for possible approaches to putting together your photo essay:

1. **You can compose your photo essay as a series of Web pages.** The simplest way is to use an online composing option like Google's Sites tool. You can also use a Web editor. (You may have an editor already, or you can download a free editor like SeaMonkey.) Use tables to set up a page with spaces for an image, a caption, title and source information, and navigation options. Refine this page, and then use it as a template for creating additional pages. Create necessary pages, and then add links between them to allow readers to navigate through the essay. Insert your

images and compose your text. When you have finished, upload the files to the Web (if necessary) and test and troubleshoot everything.

2. **Use software like Photo Story, Movie Maker, or iMovie.** These media editors operate using a timeline with which you compose. You will arrange images along the timeline to create the sequence of photos for the essay. These programs might be limited in the way they allow you to arrange and provide captions. You can experiment with the title options, and consider using the audio capabilities to narrate your captions. When you have finished composing with a media editor, you can export the file using a video format. Likely options include mp4, QuickTime (MOV), Windows Media (WMV), or Flash (FLV) formats. You can also learn more about using video editors from our e-book.

3. **You can use an online site to create slideshows.** Picture sites like Flickr and Photobucket have slideshow options. You will likely have to edit the descriptions of the photos to create the captions and you may have to adjust other settings. When you are finished, you can easily publish and gather feedback, usually by sharing the URL for the slideshow.

4. **You can also create a photo essay using a word processor.** Use a separate page for each photo, and then use tables or text boxes to create a layout. You may not be able to include navigation features in a word processor document, but you can still develop an essay that organizes a selection of images and provides captions that discuss and draw conclusions from the images—the core work of the photo essay.

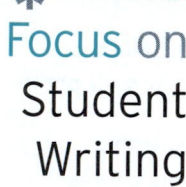

Focus on Student Writing

Nationalism and Persuasion: Group Identity, Motivation, and Images
BY **TREVOR JACKSON**

Trevor composed this photo essay as part of a research exercise. His goal was to explore images that convey persuasive messages. He discovered a wide variety of propaganda posters online, and conducted research about the posters before composing a set of Web pages that allowed him to discuss the images.

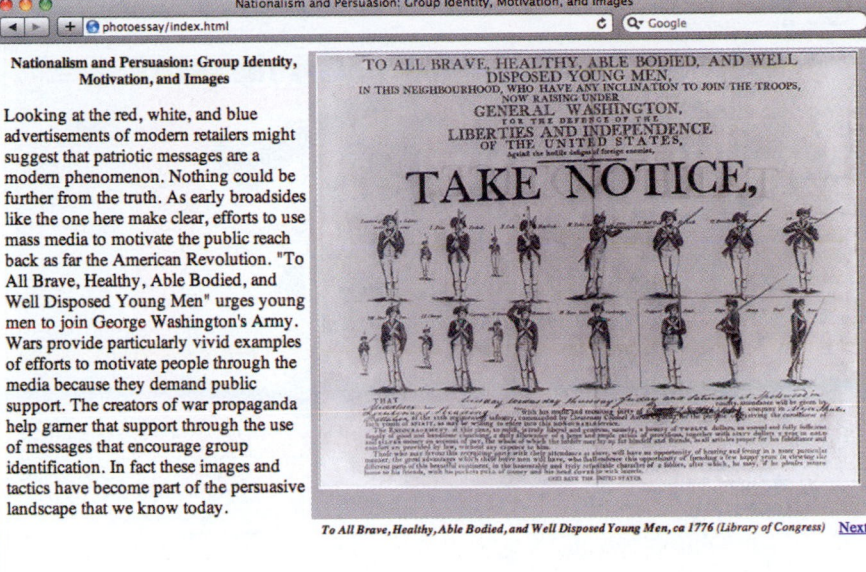

Nationalism and Persuasion: Group Identity, Motivation, and Images

Looking at the red, white, and blue advertisements of modern retailers might suggest that patriotic messages are a modern phenomenon. Nothing could be further from the truth. As early broadsides like the one here make clear, efforts to use mass media to motivate the public reach back as far the American Revolution. "To All Brave, Healthy, Able Bodied, and Well Disposed Young Men" urges young men to join George Washington's Army. Wars provide particularly vivid examples of efforts to motivate people through the media because they demand public support. The creators of war propaganda help garner that support through the use of messages that encourage group identification. In fact these images and tactics have become part of the persuasive landscape that we know today.

To All Brave, Healthy, Able Bodied, and Well Disposed Young Men, ca 1776 (Library of Congress)   Next

Nationalism and Persuasion: Group Identity, Motivation, and Images

Some of the most effective messages meant to persuade the public to support military causes took the form of propaganda posters. Early posters borrowed techniques from the art world. Grace-Ellen McCrann demonstrates how Jules Cheret and his contemporaries developed posters with "bolder strokes and less detail than work that had previously been judged to be art" (54). As Richard Moss explains "it was all about grabbing the attention in the quickest way with the simplest messages and imagery" (Moss). Posters like "Treat 'Em Rough" exemplify this approach. The focus is on the fierce image of the cat. Bold colors amplify the message, relying on imagery of fire. The statements are direct—attack like a fighting cat by joining the tank core.

Previous

Treat 'Em Rough, 1918 (Library of Congress)   Next

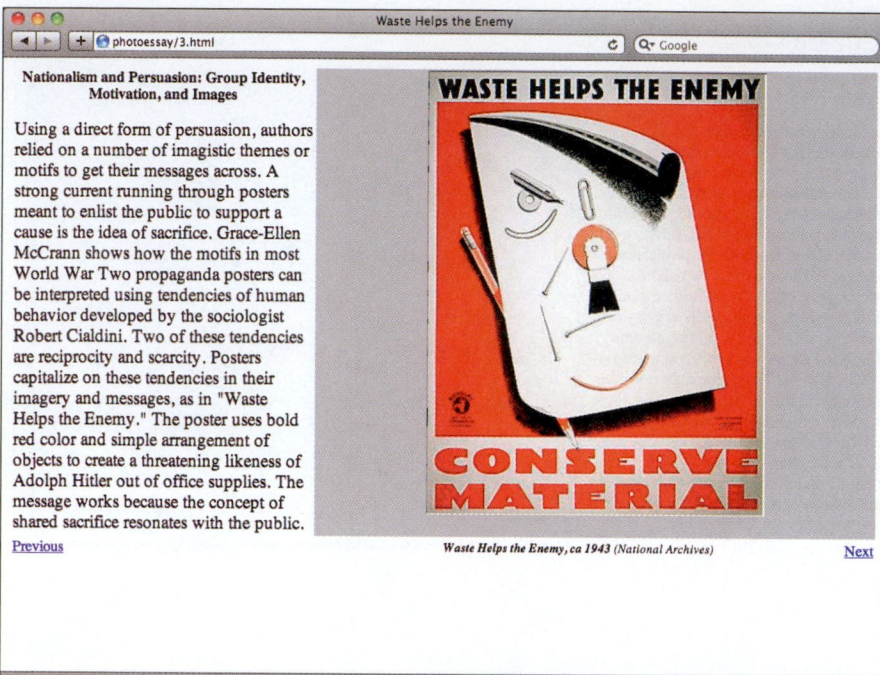

Waste Helps the Enemy

photoessay/3.html

Q- Google

Nationalism and Persuasion: Group Identity, Motivation, and Images

Using a direct form of persuasion, authors relied on a number of imagistic themes or motifs to get their messages across. A strong current running through posters meant to enlist the public to support a cause is the idea of sacrifice. Grace-Ellen McCrann shows how the motifs in most World War Two propaganda posters can be interpreted using tendencies of human behavior developed by the sociologist Robert Cialdini. Two of these tendencies are reciprocity and scarcity. Posters capitalize on these tendencies in their imagery and messages, as in "Waste Helps the Enemy." The poster uses bold red color and simple arrangement of objects to create a threatening likeness of Adolph Hitler out of office supplies. The message works because the concept of shared sacrifice resonates with the public.

Previous

Waste Helps the Enemy, ca 1943 (National Archives)

Next

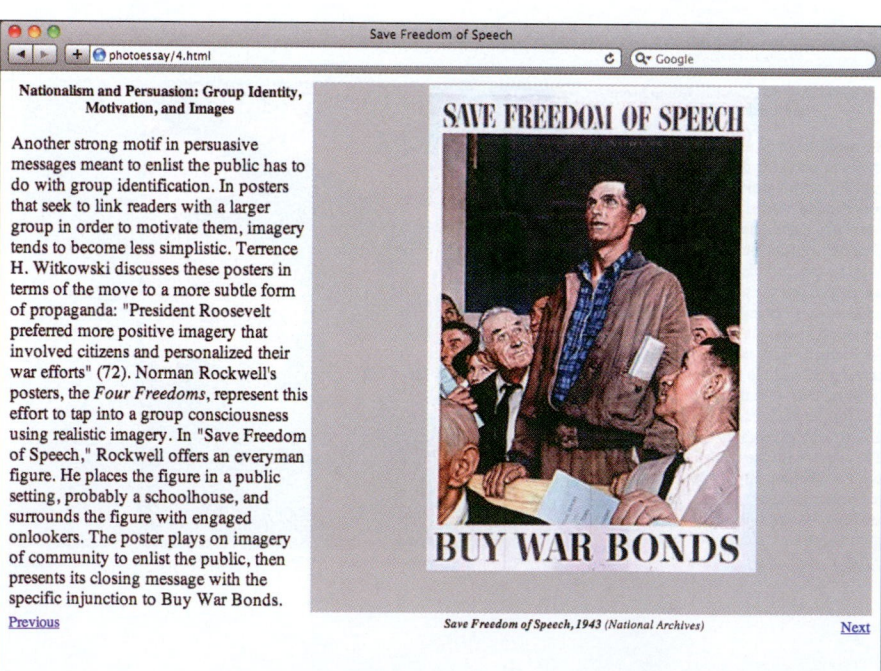

Save Freedom of Speech

photoessay/4.html

Q- Google

Nationalism and Persuasion: Group Identity, Motivation, and Images

Another strong motif in persuasive messages meant to enlist the public has to do with group identification. In posters that seek to link readers with a larger group in order to motivate them, imagery tends to become less simplistic. Terrence H. Witkowski discusses these posters in terms of the move to a more subtle form of propaganda: "President Roosevelt preferred more positive imagery that involved citizens and personalized their war efforts" (72). Norman Rockwell's posters, the *Four Freedoms*, represent this effort to tap into a group consciousness using realistic imagery. In "Save Freedom of Speech," Rockwell offers an everyman figure. He places the figure in a public setting, probably a schoolhouse, and surrounds the figure with engaged onlookers. The poster plays on imagery of community to enlist the public, then presents its closing message with the specific injunction to Buy War Bonds.

Previous

Save Freedom of Speech, 1943 (National Archives)

Next

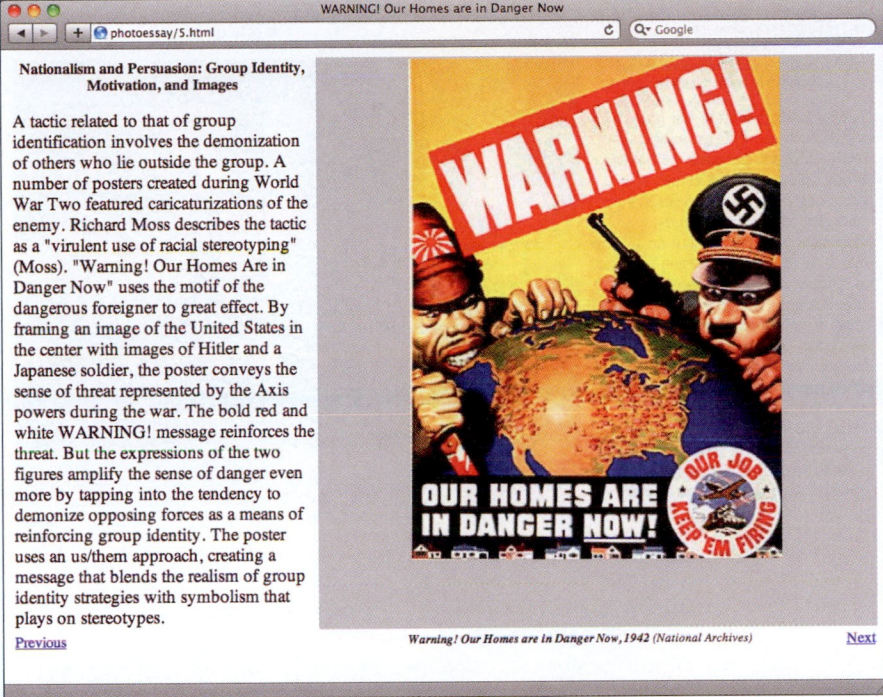

WARNING! Our Homes are in Danger Now

photoessay/5.html

Google

Nationalism and Persuasion: Group Identity, Motivation, and Images

A tactic related to that of group identification involves the demonization of others who lie outside the group. A number of posters created during World War Two featured caricaturizations of the enemy. Richard Moss describes the tactic as a "virulent use of racial stereotyping" (Moss). "Warning! Our Homes Are in Danger Now" uses the motif of the dangerous foreigner to great effect. By framing an image of the United States in the center with images of Hitler and a Japanese soldier, the poster conveys the sense of threat represented by the Axis powers during the war. The bold red and white WARNING! message reinforces the threat. But the expressions of the two figures amplify the sense of danger even more by tapping into the tendency to demonize opposing forces as a means of reinforcing group identity. The poster uses an us/them approach, creating a message that blends the realism of group identity strategies with symbolism that plays on stereotypes.

Previous

Warning! Our Homes are in Danger Now, 1942 (National Archives)

Next

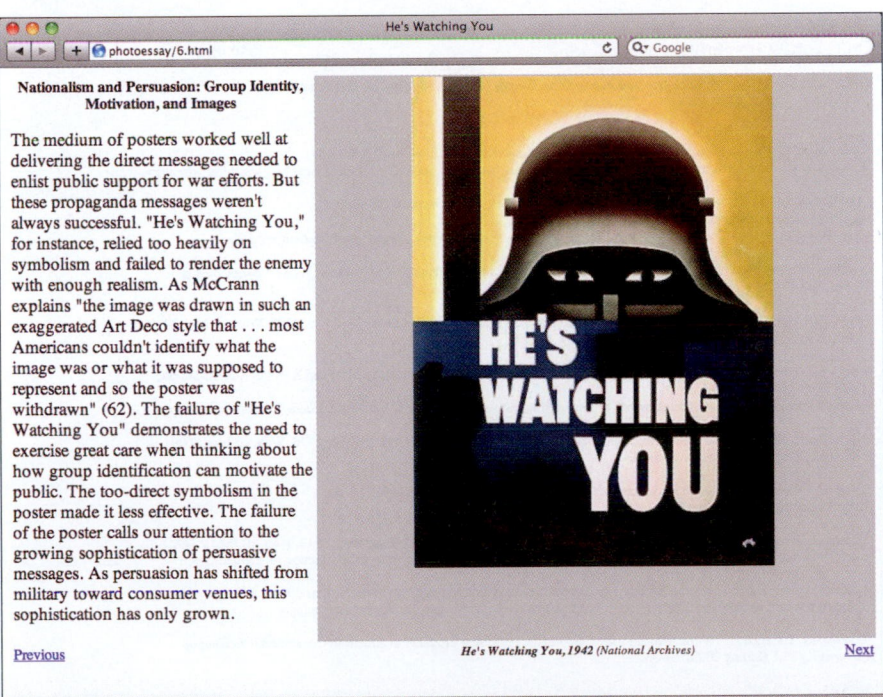

He's Watching You

photoessay/6.html

Google

Nationalism and Persuasion: Group Identity, Motivation, and Images

The medium of posters worked well at delivering the direct messages needed to enlist public support for war efforts. But these propaganda messages weren't always successful. "He's Watching You," for instance, relied too heavily on symbolism and failed to render the enemy with enough realism. As McCrann explains "the image was drawn in such an exaggerated Art Deco style that . . . most Americans couldn't identify what the image was or what it was supposed to represent and so the poster was withdrawn" (62). The failure of "He's Watching You" demonstrates the need to exercise great care when thinking about how group identification can motivate the public. The too-direct symbolism in the poster made it less effective. The failure of the poster calls our attention to the growing sophistication of persuasive messages. As persuasion has shifted from military toward consumer venues, this sophistication has only grown.

Previous

He's Watching You, 1942 (National Archives)

Next

Nationalism and Persuasion: Group Identity, Motivation, and Images

The methods present in war posters represent some of the growing pains felt by efforts to persuade the public. While bold colors and simple statements dominate the posters, their strategies became increasingly sophisticated over time. It is no surprise that these methods have been translated to modern contexts. Witkowski suggests that "the history of the poster medium is intimately entwined with the history of consumer culture" (70). Images like the Wal-Mart display shelf demonstrate two points: persuasion has grown more complex, with lunch box tie-ins and viral marketing, and many early techniques are still with us as persuasion continues to play on motifs of sacrifice and group identification.

Previous

Wal-Mart Display Shelf (Bonnie Kamin)

Sources

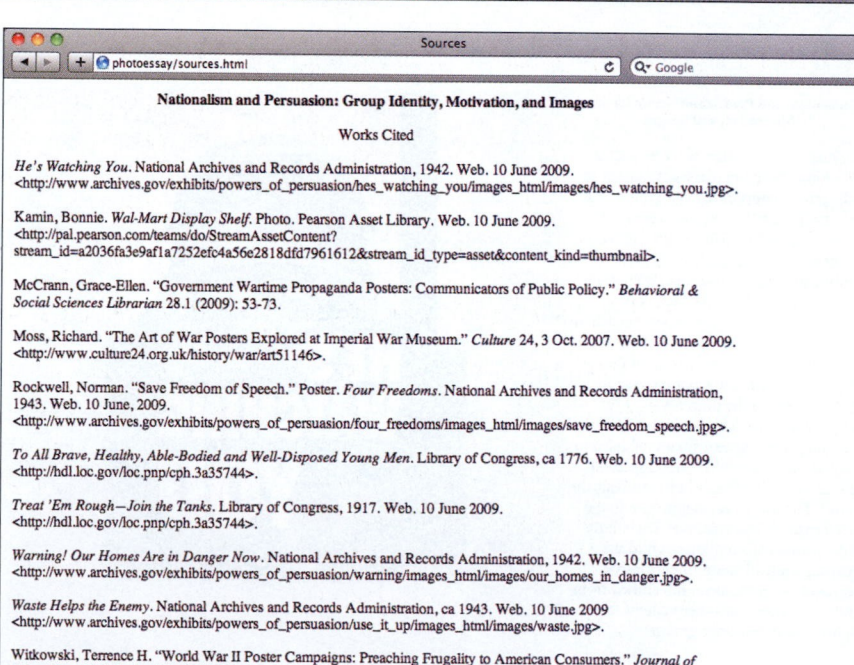

Nationalism and Persuasion: Group Identity, Motivation, and Images

Works Cited

He's Watching You. National Archives and Records Administration, 1942. Web. 10 June 2009.
<http://www.archives.gov/exhibits/powers_of_persuasion/hes_watching_you/images_html/images/hes_watching_you.jpg>.

Kamin, Bonnie. *Wal-Mart Display Shelf*. Photo. Pearson Asset Library. Web. 10 June 2009.
<http://pal.pearson.com/teams/do/StreamAssetContent?
stream_id=a2036fa3e9af1a7252efc4a56e2818dfd7961612&stream_id_type=asset&content_kind=thumbnail>.

McCrann, Grace-Ellen. "Government Wartime Propaganda Posters: Communicators of Public Policy." *Behavioral & Social Sciences Librarian* 28.1 (2009): 53-73.

Moss, Richard. "The Art of War Posters Explored at Imperial War Museum." *Culture* 24, 3 Oct. 2007. Web. 10 June 2009.
<http://www.culture24.org.uk/history/war/art51146>.

Rockwell, Norman. "Save Freedom of Speech." Poster. *Four Freedoms*. National Archives and Records Administration, 1943. Web. 10 June, 2009.
<http://www.archives.gov/exhibits/powers_of_persuasion/four_freedoms/images_html/images/save_freedom_speech.jpg>.

To All Brave, Healthy, Able-Bodied and Well-Disposed Young Men. Library of Congress, ca 1776. Web. 10 June 2009.
<http://hdl.loc.gov/loc.pnp/cph.3a35744>.

Treat 'Em Rough—Join the Tanks. Library of Congress, 1917. Web. 10 June 2009.
<http://hdl.loc.gov/loc.pnp/cph.3a35744>.

Warning! Our Homes Are in Danger Now. National Archives and Records Administration, 1942. Web. 10 June 2009.
<http://www.archives.gov/exhibits/powers_of_persuasion/warning/images_html/images/our_homes_in_danger.jpg>.

Waste Helps the Enemy. National Archives and Records Administration, ca 1943. Web. 10 June 2009
<http://www.archives.gov/exhibits/powers_of_persuasion/use_it_up/images_html/images/waste.jpg>.

Witkowski, Terrence H. "World War II Poster Campaigns: Preaching Frugality to American Consumers." *Journal of Advertising* 32.1 (Spring 2003): 69-83.

Beginning

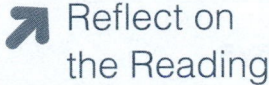 Reflect on the Reading

Questions about "Nationalism and Persuasion: Group Identity, Motivation, and Images"

1. How would you summarize the message of the photo essay as a whole? What suggestions might you offer Trevor in terms of the topic and his angle?
2. What are your thoughts on the use of research in the photo essay? Do you feel as if the piece provides enough information about the topic of propaganda posters?
3. What do you think of Trevor's selection of images? What about the analysis of the posters? What suggestions would you offer about the images?
4. Do the captions strike a balance between distilling information and discussing the topic? Where does the balance succeed or fail?

 Revise It   **Strategies for Revising Photo Essays**

The medium you use for your photo essay will determine some of your options for posting and collecting feedback. Gather feedback from classmates and peers. If you have composed the essay using Web pages or an online site, then solicit responses from potential online readers. As you revise, keep these considerations in mind:

- Revisit your topic. Does the photo essay form work well with your subject? Can you make adjustments to your approach to tighten the focus or add coherency to the piece?
- Examine the organization of the photo essay. Would the essay benefit from additional opening or closing screens? Does the sequencing of the images make sense and provide a coherent message? What effect would adding or deleting any images have on the structure?
- Check the layout of your pages. Does the placement of the image allow space for captions and other features? What effect would adjustments to the scale or arrangement of the items have on the layout?
- Examine your captions. If you are incorporating research, is it well integrated into the captions? Is the language sharp? Do the captions make connections with one another or with larger points? Make sure that quotations are accurate and that all research is cited and documented.
- Check that you are using images fairly. Do you include source information for each image? Have you studied fair use guidelines (pages 345–47) and made careful decisions about how and when to use images?
- Ensure that the mechanical and surface details of the piece are in order. Check that any links function.

Learning
Objective 13.3

Push It   More Paths and Possibilities for Photo Essays

1. Create a narrated slide show about your topic. Using a program like Microsoft's Photo Story or Movie Maker, or Apple's iMovie, sequence images to create a photo essay. Compose a script that offers readers information about your topic and about the images. Add a narration track to the slide show using your script. Make changes to the timing of the images and to your script, adjusting each to create a good flow. When you have finished, export the slide show and post it online. (See the samples in Chapter E8.)

2. Choose a contemporary local concern or event and then use a digital camera to capture images that can be used for a photo essay addressing the topic. Give yourself time to gather a large collection of images and then identify a selection of photos for the essay. Conduct research as needed; you might conduct field research (pages 361–65) as you take your photographs. When you have a good collection of images and a strong knowledge of the topic, compose a photo essay. Post the essay and invite members of the community to read it and respond.

RESOURCES
Sample Photo
Essays

Zoom Out   Reflecting on Photo Essays

• **Photo essays provide a way of discussing a number of topics.** Events, cultural issues, and concepts (like technical or medical innovations) all can benefit from presentation using images and text.

• **Research can inform and strengthen photo essays.** You need research skills to select images and to explain your topic.

• **Photo essays require new composing skills.** You can compose a photo essay using a word processor, a Web editor, an online site, or a video editor. You must consider layout, navigation, and other design concerns.

• **The selection process for images used in a photo essay requires critical thinking.** You must be deliberate in identifying images that illuminate the topic and that can be used fairly.

• **Captions deliver much of the message in a photo essay.** Captions call for tough choices because they must be concise, but at the same time make points and draw connections for readers.

For additional information and practice with the learning objectives in this chapter, go to www.mycomplab.com, Resources > Writing > Writing and Visuals.

Research
Strategies

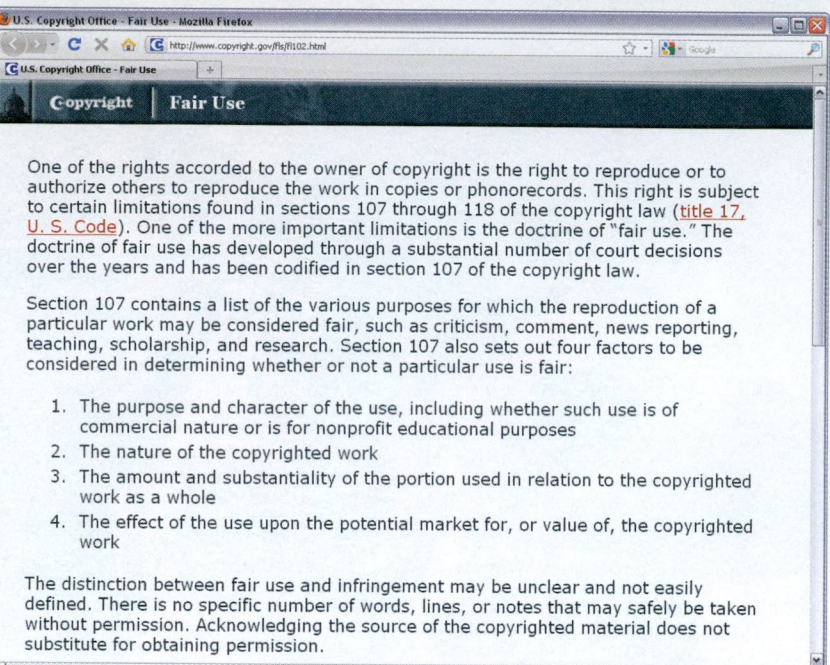

One of the rights accorded to the owner of copyright is the right to reproduce or to authorize others to reproduce the work in copies or phonorecords. This right is subject to certain limitations found in sections 107 through 118 of the copyright law (title 17, U. S. Code). One of the more important limitations is the doctrine of "fair use." The doctrine of fair use has developed through a substantial number of court decisions over the years and has been codified in section 107 of the copyright law.

Section 107 contains a list of the various purposes for which the reproduction of a particular work may be considered fair, such as criticism, comment, news reporting, teaching, scholarship, and research. Section 107 also sets out four factors to be considered in determining whether or not a particular use is fair:

1. The purpose and character of the use, including whether such use is of commercial nature or is for nonprofit educational purposes
2. The nature of the copyrighted work
3. The amount and substantiality of the portion used in relation to the copyrighted work as a whole
4. The effect of the use upon the potential market for, or value of, the copyrighted work

The distinction between fair use and infringement may be unclear and not easily defined. There is no specific number of words, lines, or notes that may safely be taken without permission. Acknowledging the source of the copyrighted material does not substitute for obtaining permission.

CHAPTER
14

Understanding Research

 Zoom In **Key Concepts and Learning Objectives**

After studying this chapter, you should be able to:

14.1 Identify questions that drive successful research.

14.2 Consider varying perspectives to better understand a topic.

14.3 Identify writing assignments that can benefit from research.

14.4 Recognize the strengths and weaknesses of different kinds of sources.

14.5 Make ethical decisions about research concerns.

Y ou may have heard of *twenty questions*. It's a simple game in which some-one holds a secret and participants take turns asking yes or no questions to narrow down the possibilities and guess the answer. In some ways, conducting research follows a similar pattern. The difference between the game and the process of research lies in the complexity of the answers that you receive as you explore. Rarely does research return yes or no responses. Instead, you're more likely to encounter a series of maybes that lead you closer to an understanding of the complexities of your topic but nowhere near a final answer.

In this chapter, we look broadly at this research process. While exploring a topic, you will likely further narrow your focus. And you will pursue a number of supporting questions. While investigating these and other questions, you must learn to work with a variety of sources in order to discover and explore the many perspectives and potential biases that circulate through any research project. This process must reflect an understanding of information ethics, practices through which writers learn to avoid plagiarism and to use sources fairly.

KEY TERMS

- **Research question:** A question that drives the inquiry for a research project and defines the scope of the investigation. A research question allows you to take a topic that would be too broad for a research essay and narrow the focus into something manageable.

- **Supporting questions:** Subsequent questions that must be explored as part of the investigation of a broader research question.

- **Sources:** Materials containing information to be used in a research project. Primary sources contain first-hand information, while secondary sources present the interpretations of primary sources.

- **Biases:** Limited perspectives or personal agendas related to a topic. All writers have biases, but a researcher must learn to recognize strong biases and to consider alternative perspectives.

- **Information ethics:** The practice and study of using information responsibly. Information ethics range from careful evaluation and documentation of sources to responsible decision making about when and how to use materials.

- **Plagiarism:** The improper use of information in sources or the failure to properly acknowledge the use of research materials.

- **Fair use:** the practice of responsibly using copyrighted materials in your own work.

WN

VIDEO
40. Fair Use and
Intellectual
Property

Asking Questions

LO

Learning
Objective 14.1

Research supports the way you ask questions and make decisions in all kinds of rhetorical situations. You might track down statistics to help figure out the best way to market a campus group in a brochure for new students. You might locate, collect, and evaluate a series of images for a photo essay covering a historical event. You might interview acquaintances for a memoir. In many academic research situations, this type of inquisitiveness is often built into the assignment itself. For instance, essay genres that call for research often ask you to explore the complexities of an issue. A research question can get you started. About a topic like alternative medicine, a writer might formulate a question such as, *Should the federal government support the integration of alternative medicine practices into the U.S. health care system?* Such a question helps determine the scope of the project—in this case, focusing on government support for alternative medicine and on the nature of the U.S. health care system. The process of developing the question allows the writer to take a topic that would be too broad for a research essay (alternative medicine) and narrow the focus into something more manageable (government support for alternative medicine in the United States).

Further, you can develop and explore subsequent questions as a means of discovering research sources. *What role should the government play in health care decisions? How viable is alternative medicine for mainstream care? Who might benefit or lose from more alternative medicine in the U.S. health care system?* All of these questions open additional avenues that can be pursued as you discover and evaluate sources.

Know It Strategies for Finding Research Questions

- Conduct some initial research related to your topic. What questions occur as you begin exploring sources? What positions do the sources have in common? Where do they differ? What questions does a comparison of sources raise?
- Revisit your research assignment. Does the assignment ask you to explore particular aspects of your topic? What questions can you formulate about your topic that will allow you to fulfill the assignment?
- Think about ways of narrowing down broad topics using questions. What questions will enable you to take a general subject—the environment, say— and turn it into a narrow topic for an essay such as, *Does climate change make nuclear power an environmentally friendly energy source?*

- Explore the conversations and debates circulating around a topic. What do people usually argue about related to the topic? What ideas are in favor and which are on the fringe? How can these perspectives translate into research questions?
- What are your interests regarding the topic? What do you feel has been overlooked? What are you unsure about? What matters most to you, and how can a research question help you explore and explain those issues?

Ask Questions & Make Decisions

Exercises for Finding Research Questions

1. Choose a topic about which people clearly disagree—gun control, drug legalization, censorship of pornography, immigration, etc. Conduct historical research into views on the topic held in the past. Write a research question that would help you compare points of view today with those from an earlier era.
2. Identify an issue that lends itself to either/or positions—capital punishment, abortion, prayer in schools, etc. Develop a question that might help you explore both sides of the topic (for instance, *How are medical advances shaping debates about abortion?*).
3. Consider the assumptions that lie beneath a position on an issue; for example, proponents of embryonic stem cell research might believe that life begins at birth. Next, develop a list of questions that would help you explore the assumption.

Joining Conversations

Learning Objective 14.2

People often talk about research as an opportunity to join a conversation and discover multiple perspectives on an issue or topic. This metaphor reveals the complexities of most issues. Think, for instance, of the people who might take a position on a topic like police brutality. We'd find on one side law enforcement spokespeople, of course, and on another side people speaking for victims of police brutality. But we'd also find people looking at the issue from perspectives ranging from civil rights to community organization to media studies to law to race relations.

As you explore a topic like police brutality, then, you have a chance to bring all of these voices together through your process of research. When you discover these different perspectives, you not only realize the levels of complexity inherent in a topic, you check against being unduly swayed by any single perspective. As you can

FIGURE 14.1

Online conversations regarding police brutality.

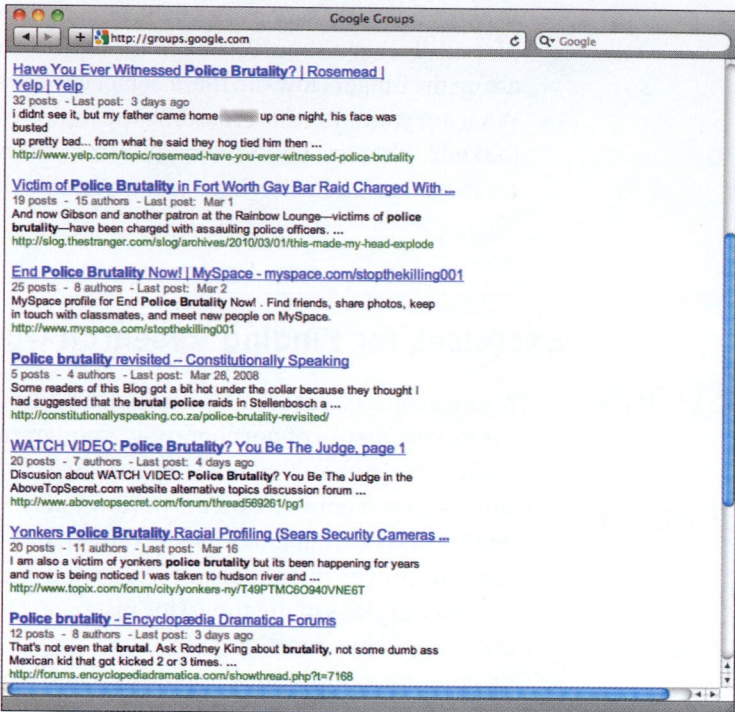

imagine, putting all of these competing voices together can get a bit chaotic. But it can also reveal how each of these voices has their own agendas and generally advocates for their own position; that is, they have their biases.

What's exciting is that the more you learn about the topic, the more you, too, can participate in these conversations. Having listened to and spotted possible shortcomings or biases among competing perspectives, you can offer your own, more broadly considered, take on the issues. When you write about the topic and share your work with others, you concretize this gesture, literally adding your voice to the mix.

Know It   Strategies for Joining Research Conversations

- Use questions to explore differing perspectives on issues. Ask who, what, where, when, why, and how to develop a list of people interested in your topic.
- As you look through sources on a topic, explore the reference lists showing sources or works cited, which you will find toward the end of the articles. Look at the range of perspectives represented in the sources. Identify any

sources that turn up regularly. What might give these items a stronger voice in the conversation?

- Look through the archives of online discussions as you explore topics. Start at http://groups.google.com/, http://technorati.com, or http://blogsearch.google.com/. What perspectives are represented by the participants in these online conversations? What can these exchanges tell you about your topic?

Ask Questions & Make Decisions

Exercises for Joining Research Conversations

1. Locate and read at least three articles related to a research topic. Write a paragraph detailing as many perspectives as you can find represented in the articles.

2. Identify two competing perspectives related to a topic. For each, develop a paragraph with a brief character sketch that describes a person connected to each perspective. What demographics would you assign to the person? What tastes or interests? How can you bring to life a representative person behind the perspective?

3. After having done some research into a topic, select a perspective that seems particularly prone to bias. Make a list of statements that might be offered from that biased perspective. Repeat the process for one or more alternative voices related to the topic.

4. Identify an online discussion group or blog currently debating a potential research topic. Read the postings fully to get a sense of the conversation, and then post your own thoughts, either responding to what has already been said or taking the discussion in a new direction.

Zooming in and out on a Topic

With all this talk of pursuing questions and joining conversations, you might think that research is all about open-ended exploration—which it is. But it's also about focusing and analyzing information. In fact, while you will need to zoom in and out as you conduct research, you will find that a key to success in research is narrowing your approach so that you can investigate some aspect of the topic in depth. For instance, the minute you begin raising questions about a broad topic, you start to narrow its scope. If you ask, *What do environmentalists and developers argue about?*, your topic on the environment narrows to habitat depletion. If you ask, *What is a key concern related to habitat depletion?,* your emphasis may become the loss of wetlands or threats to birds on waterways. Like zooming in with a magnifying glass, broad topics and conversations move out of your lens as you narrow your focus.

Learning Objective 14.3

Pay special attention to your research assignment as you narrow its scope. Often, assignments specifically ask that you treat certain dimensions of a topic. Also, watch that your scaling down doesn't prevent you from finding adequate sources or discussing your project in terms of the bigger picture. Is the runoff problem in a local neighborhood typical or atypical of what many communities face? Is the loss of wetlands only one of many competing threats to the environment, all of which need urgent attention? Usually, if you are savvy at locating materials (Chapter 15), you can find resources for narrow topics, but be ready to make adjustments if your focus becomes too limited. Finally, don't scope a project so extremely that it no longer fits your interests; writing about paved surfaces and water degradation might be manageable, but may limit you too much in discussing your original concern for wild birds on waterways.

Know It Strategies for Zooming in and out on Topics

- Recall the metaphor of zooming in and out. You can start with a narrow focus and broaden to find connections and larger directions for your research. Or, you can begin with a broad topic and zoom in until you arrive at a manageable project.
- Use questions to narrow your focus. Stating a research interest in the form of a question gets the ball rolling. Develop supporting questions, and then consider whether any of them might form the basis of a project.
- Refer to your assignment to get ideas about narrowing the project. Make sure your proposed research meshes with the scope called for in the assignment. Ask your instructor for ideas or input into the focus you have developed.
- Think about specific groups to help focus your project. Who is affected the most? Who is most responsible? Who do you identify with? How can you scope the project to respond to any of these questions?
- Remember to zoom out as you consider your research topics. Look for connections with related examples or topics. Think about how shifts in location can reshape your project. Are there issues that become more complex at the national, state, or local level?

Learning Objective 14.4

Ask Questions & Make Decisions

Exercises for Zooming in and out on Topics

1. Identify someone who is an expert about your topic. Conduct some initial research to help narrow your focus, and then develop a list of three or more questions for the expert. If possible, set up an interview and pose the questions to the expert. (See the information on conducting field research on pages 361–65.)

2. Scan the headlines in your local news, either in the paper or on the Web. Identify a story that strikes your interest. Conduct some initial research, and then develop a research question related to the topic.

3. Start with a broad topic, and then conduct some keyword searches (page 352) either using the Internet or a library database. Take note of the number and range of search returns. Refine the topic, and then conduct new searches. Repeat the process until you have difficulty finding adequate sources. Write up your experiences in a paragraph.

4. Identify a narrowly focused topic. (A local building project or ban against leaf blowers, for instance.) Make a list of at least five similar examples or related concerns. Use the list to reformulate the topic into something that is still manageable but a bit larger in scope.

Using Information Ethically

LO

Learning Objective 14.5

Conducting research raises several concerns related to the ethics of how you use information. First, you'll be borrowing materials produced by someone else. You need to put this information in your work to provide insights and evidence, so you have to carefully cite and document those efforts every time. Second, you'll need to ensure that readers of your work can access your sources, which allows them to check that you are using materials properly and to join the research conversation. Finally, you'll need to make decisions about how much of these materials you can honestly use in your work and where to best use them. Reuse too much of a source, and you not only misappropriate the materials but also water down the force of your own insights.

You also need to make decisions about using materials in light of the varying genres and mediums with which you are working. In many situations, you will be composing printed essays, and in most, you will need to work closely with the language and ideas in your sources. There are some distinct rules you need to follow.

VIDEO
40. Fair Use and
Intellectual
Property

The best way to work ethically with materials is to learn something about fair use. The fair use provision of U.S. copyright law allows the use of copyrighted material for commentary, criticism, reporting, teaching, scholarship, and research. This means that for your academic projects you can use materials like magazine ads, provided your use of those materials meets certain criteria. These criteria, however, must be weighed together as use decisions are made on a case-by-case basis. In discussing such decisions, The U.S. Copyright Office lists the following criteria:

1. the purpose and character of the use, including whether such use is of commercial nature or is for nonprofit educational purposes;
2. the nature of the copyrighted work;
3. the amount and substantiality of the portion used in relation to the copyrighted work as a whole; and
4. the effect of the use upon the potential market for or value of the copyrighted work. (Fair Use Guidelines)

All of these criteria place the responsibility on you to be deliberate and honest. You can't just say, *My project is for educational purposes, so I can use whatever I want.* If you use more than the minimal amount required to make your point—even in the most straightforward academic essay—you will be violating fair use. Instead, you will need to weigh the various factors that can determine fair use. Is the material you want to use necessary for your project? Does your project present commentary, reporting, or some other appropriate form? Are you using the appropriate amount, given the nature of the materials? What impact might your use have on the original? Decisions about fair use are made by considering the U.S. Copyright Office's four criteria and giving weight to each based on the specifics of the case. Using a whole ad to compose a critical analyses might have a negative effect on the entity behind the ad, but if the purpose of the use stems from a valid critique, the use might be fair, as when an essay reproduces a Camel cigarette advertisement to offer commentary or criticism of tobacco marketing aimed at children. The purpose and character of the use would outweigh the potential problems with the effect on the value of the ad.

Because these decisions require critical weighing of these factors, there are no hard and fast rules. Still, you can see how these criteria can help you not only to decide when and how to use materials but also to develop good habits as a writer. Using only the minimum source amount required, for instance, prompts you to expand on materials in your own words, allowing you to contextualize them and explain how they fit in with the points you are making. In short, using materials responsibly is not just ethical, it makes rhetorical sense. (You can find more information and resources for fair use in our e-book.)

CONNECT IT   More Resources for Research

As you conduct research and use sources in your writing, consider the following resources:

- For information on locating sources, see Chapter 15.
- For more on evaluating sources, see Chapter 15.
- To encapsulate ideas from a source in a summary, see Chapter 3.
- For more on paraphrases that restate ideas from a source in your own words, see Chapter 16.
- For more on quotations, see Chapter 16.
- For more on citation and documentation, see Chapter 17.

Know It   Strategies for Using Information Ethically

- Think of the rhetorical dimensions of the ethical use of information. How does using information fairly help your credibility? How can appropriate uses of information enhance your compositions?
- Dedicate yourself to honorable uses of information. Commit to applying the necessary time and energy to develop and share your own ideas. Educate yourself about plagiarism and strategies for integrating research into your compositions (see Chapter 15).
- Familiarize yourself with the guidelines and expectations of your school or instructor. Ask your instructor to explain her approaches to using information. Find out what resources are available to provide you with more insights into policies and expectations.
- Learn the ins and outs of summaries, paraphrases, and quotations (see Chapter 15). The words of others are one of your best resources; you just need to know how to integrate them into your own work.
- View citations and documentation as crucial elements of your compositions. Know that careful citation and documentation bolsters your credibility, but also helps turn your work into a resource for readers to use as they explore a research conversation.
- Understand the complexities of fair use. Think about how fair use doctrines apply to your print essays. When using any materials, weigh the fair use criteria as you make decisions.

Ask Questions & Make Decisions

Exercises for Using Information Ethically

1. Conduct research online into well-known cases of plagiarism or misuse of information (fictional news pieces, borrowed political speeches, falsified memoirs, etc.). Write a paragraph or two exploring these failings and reflecting on information ethics in society.

2. Working with a group of peers, develop a policy statement for ethical use of information in your class. Compare the statement with that of your instructor or your school. As a class, discuss and modify the statement into a course policy.

3. Conduct research on fair use, and then explore some remixed movie trailers online. Based on your understanding of the fair use doctrine, develop a paragraph arguing whether these compositions do or do not meet fair use criteria.

Zoom Out

Reflecting on Research

- **Research goes hand in hand with critical thinking and writing.** Zooming in and out develops and sharpens ideas while helping with the discovery of materials. Research benefits most writing projects, allowing authors to compose with expertise and understand the complexities of their topics.

- **Research is about exploring questions.** A large research question can give shape to a project. Supporting questions can help spur additional research. Pursuing questions can drive the composition of a project.

- **The best research is viewed as a conversation.** Most issues support multiple perspectives and voices. Engaged researchers participate in research by understanding the positions put forward, and then extending them with their own thoughts.

- **Research for many genres eventually requires a narrowed scope.** Although entire books are written about broad topics like a presidential election, shorter genres require a focused project that zooms in on a subtopic (Green Party bumper stickers from 2008, say).

- **Ethical issues arise regularly when conducting research.** Using the words of others in essays requires special care. Non-textual materials demand fair use decisions.

For additional information and practice with the learning objectives in this chapter, go to www.mycomplab.com, Resources > Research.

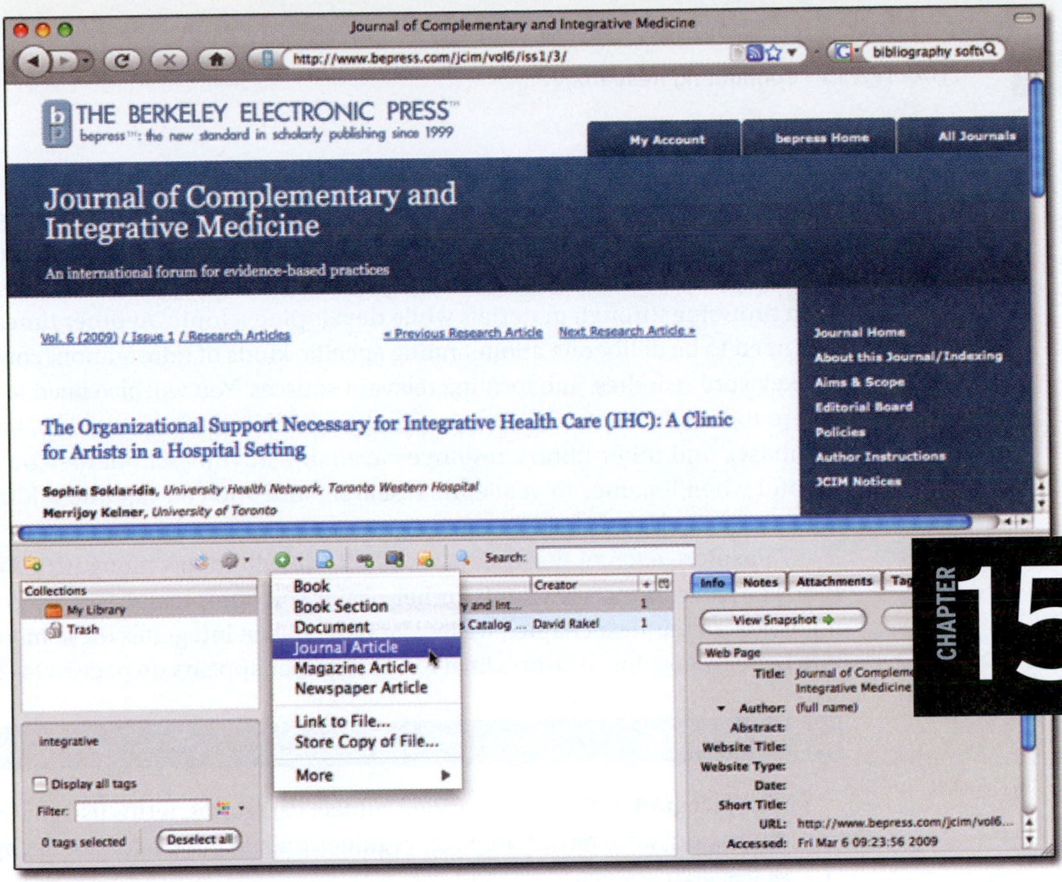

Conducting Research

CHAPTER 15

Zoom In   Key Concepts and Learning Objectives

After studying this chapter, you should be able to:

15.1 Understand how librarians organize information using subject headings.

15.2 Use keywords when searching databases and the Internet.

15.3 Use library databases to find relevant, authoritative sources of information.

15.4 Locate and evaluate information online.

15.5 Gather information resources for your projects through observations, interviews, and surveys.

This chapter takes an in-depth look at the research process and offers concrete advice to help you find and make sense of information. We begin by looking at search strategies. Sometimes you may want to take an open-ended approach to research, perhaps beginning with subject categories, and then browsing through materials while developing a topic. At other times, you will need to be deliberate about finding specific kinds of information, conducting keyword searches, and locating relevant sources. You will also need to learn where to look for materials. The Internet is chock full of information, but the databases and other library resources available at your school may be more helpful when it comes to academic research, and you can tap into additional sources by conducting field research.

To explore each of these skills in detail, we will follow along with Allison Johns as she conducts research for her project on complementary alternative medicine. In our next chapter, we look at how Allison integrates these materials into her composition. Allison's final research paper appears on pages 394–399.

KEY TERMS

- **Subject guides:** Sometimes called subject categories, terms used by librarians to organize resources. Subject guides make a good place for beginning a research project.

- **Keyword searches:** Queries made using terms chosen by a researcher. Keywords are used to locate specific materials within databases.

- **Library research:** Investigations conducted using the resources available through a library. In addition to materials in the physical library, databases containing electronic resources are available through library Web sites.

- **Internet research:** Searches for resources among the various materials of the Internet. Internet resources range from archives of electronic discussions, such as e-mail exchanges or blog messages, to Web pages to documents to audio and video.

- **Field research:** Primary research conducted to learn more about people, a place, or a topic. Field research includes observations, interviews, and surveys.

Subject Headings

Learning Objective 15.1

Allison Johns began her investigations with a research question (pages 340–41), asking, *Should the federal government support the integration of alternative medicine practices into the U.S. health care system?* From this question, she could cull a number of potential subjects or topics: *government regulations, alternative medicine,* and the *U.S. health care system.*

Figure 15.1 demonstrates how Allison began refining her topic by exploring these subjects. The figure has been annotated to explain something about the research process.

FIGURE 15.1
Browsing through subject categories.

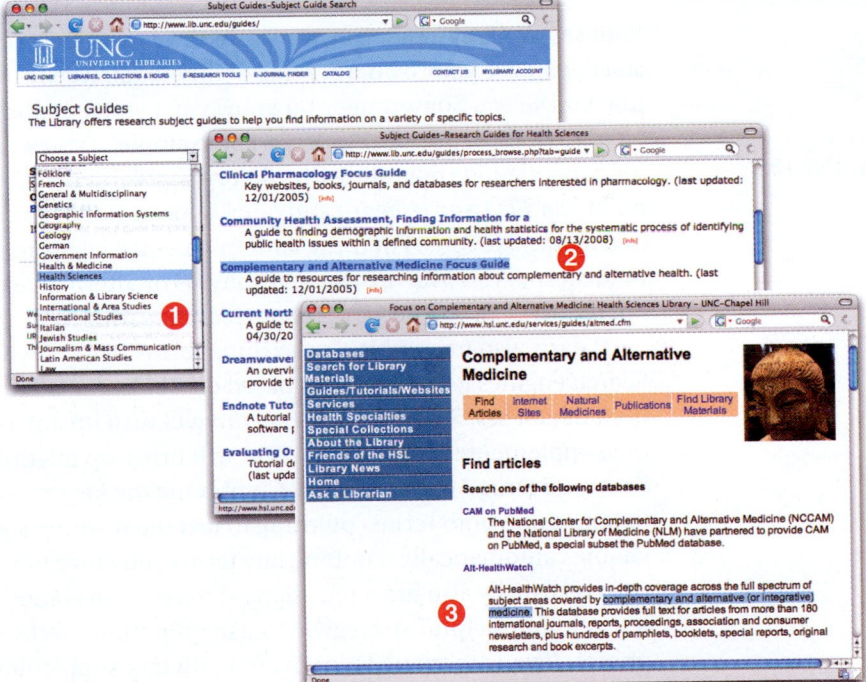

❶ Allison begins by locating the *Subject Guides* link on her library Web site, and then selecting a subject related to her topic. Subject guides are set up by librarians to organize resources into categories. Subject guides often begin with broad categories and then narrow their focus by collecting materials under sub-categories. As a result, you must sometimes drill down to hone in on more specific topics. Here, Allison selects the category of Health Sciences.

❷ Grouped beneath the Health Sciences category, Allison finds resources gathered under the subject heading Complementary and Alternative Medicine (CAM). This discovery proves crucial to her research

project because she had not yet heard of the term "complementary" medicine. Now, she not only has a new subject heading to use in further research but also adds a new dimension to her thinking about alternative medicine.

❸ As Allison pursues her discovery of this new subject, she moves to a collection of databases related to CAM. She learns that complementary medicine is a significant topic in discussions of health care, complete with its own acronym and national study center. She also discovers additional subject terms like "integrative" medicine that can further develop her thinking.

As you identify relevant sub-categories, you will begin to discover more specific topics. In Allison's case, for example, the discovery of the subject heading "Complementary and Alternative Medicine" refines her thinking about her topic; rather than considering traditional and alternative medicine as competing practices, she realizes that the two approaches might work together. (Her eventual research paper evolved from the topic of government regulations to focus on the definition of CAM.)

Keyword Searches

LO

Learning
Objective 15.2

With keyword searches, you don't explore categories set up by someone else. Instead, you use your own querying ability to retrieve resources related to terms that you select. Sometimes you know what you are after, and you can use keywords to locate specific resources. For example, if you wanted to refer to government regulations regarding the dietary supplement ephedra, you could search online for *FDA* and *ephedra* and quickly locate policy documents, press releases, and medical reports. For these kinds of targeted keyword searches, pay attention to the terms you use. Are there synonyms or alternative terms? If *ephedra* does not return what you need, perhaps *ephedrine* will.

Learn also to combine or exclude terms using keyword search strategies. Search engines use techniques based on Boolean math to locate information in their databases. Searching for *ephedra* will turn up any resource that mentions the supplement; searching for *FDA* will bring up anything at all related to the Food and Drug Administration. Combining the keywords will locate only items that mention both terms, pointing to just the resources you need. Most search engines automatically combine any terms you enter into their query fields, but you can usually also use a plus sign (+) to ensure a combined search.

Another helpful strategy is to use quotation marks to search for an exact phrase. If you are trying to learn about dietary supplements that might replace ephedra, you could search for *ephedra* and *alternative*, but you would uncover too many resources related to alternative medicine and ephedra in general. If you search for the exact phrase, "alternatives to ephedra," you will target resources discussing ephedra replacements. Most search engines require quotation marks around an exact phrase search, but you can usually also use the advanced options of search engines to query for specific phrases.

You can also exclude terms from searches. If you wanted to learn about ephedra warnings, but did not want to locate resources related to warning letters sent by the FDA to dietary supplement companies, you could exclude a term by adding a minus sign (−) before a keyword—*ephedra* and *warning -letter*.

WN

VIDEO
41. Library
Databases

Libraries and Databases

If you need information from the Web at large, Google and other search engines are a good choice. But if you want to find books, articles, reviews, research reports, or published news reports, you will have better luck looking in your library. The good news is that libraries are fully wired; you don't have to leave your computer to get to these published sources. You just need to know how to find the right database and conduct a subject or keyword search. The place to start is the Web site of your school library. Figure 15.2 shows some of the database possibilities available at most libraries. Your choices for databases will generally follow two possibilities: (1) meta collections of multiple databases for broad searches and (2) specialized databases with materials related to a single discipline, topic, or publication.

FIGURE 15.2

Searching meta collections of online databases.

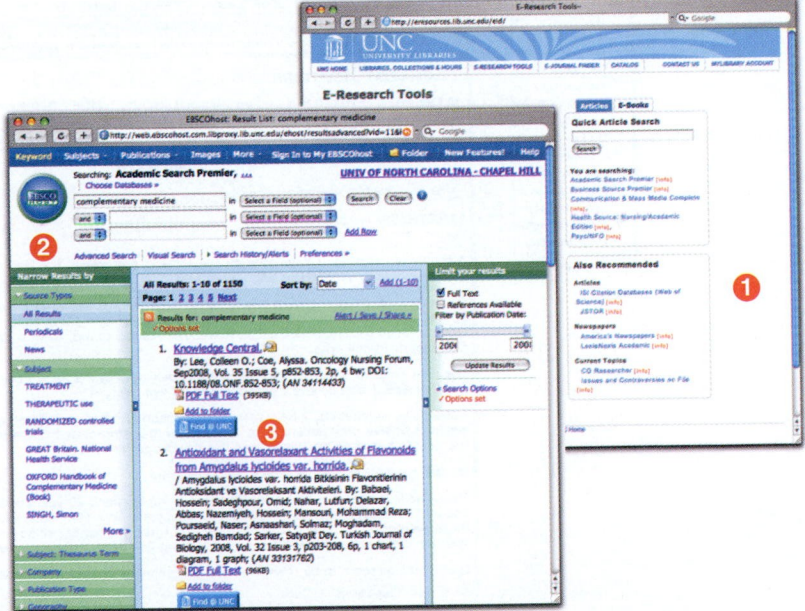

❶ Allison identifies the broad database options available. These include meta collections of databases covering academic articles, meta collections covering general interest and news articles, and broad collections related to research issues and controversies.

❷ Using a broad collection of academic articles, Allison searches for the terms *complementary* and

medicine. The form also provides fields for more terms that can refine the search and a link to an Advanced Search screen with even more options.

❸ The search yields 1,150 results, many of which provide brief descriptions and links to full text articles. Notice how some of the articles listed are published in academic journals and seem to be aimed at a specialized audience.

Searching broad collections initially can help you get a sense of the issues at play related to your topic and the kinds of resources that are out there. Remember to think about the genre and audience of the materials you are discovering. Compare the items returned in Allison's search of academic databases with those shown in Figure 15.3.

FIGURE 15.3
Searching meta collections for popular sources.

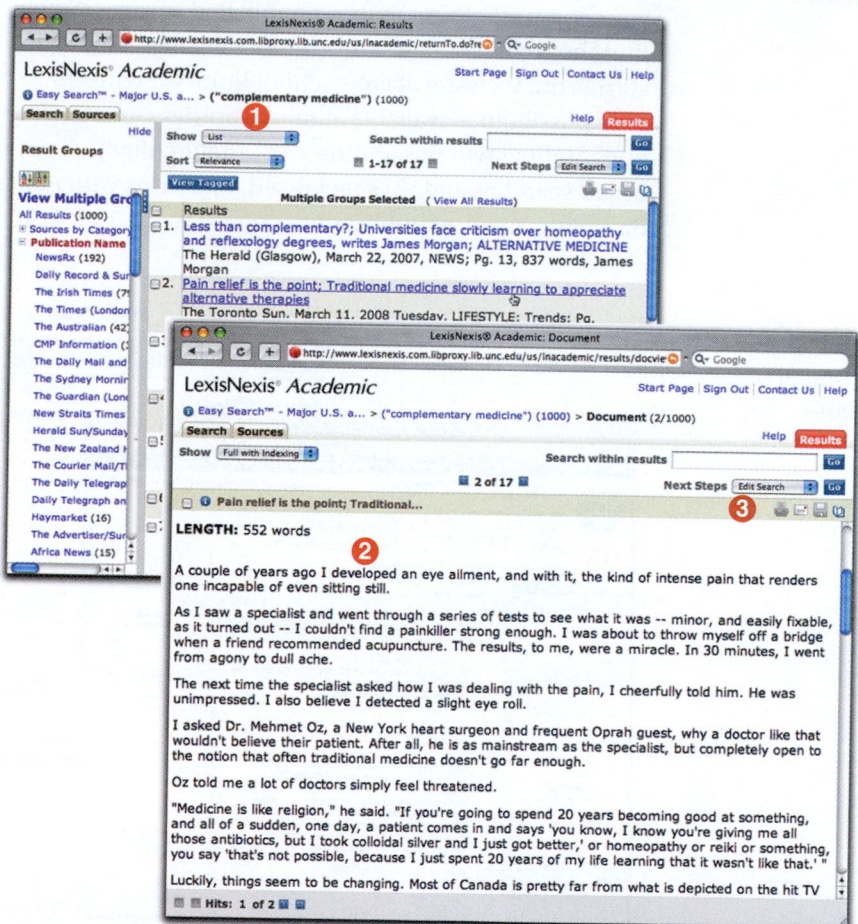

❶ Allison conducts the same search, but this time uses a broad collection of popular sources, in this case the Lexis Nexis database of news articles. Notice that Allison discovers through this broad query a sub-question related to her topic, the treatment of pain with complementary and alternative methods.

❷ The sources returned are written for a general audience. Notice the tradeoff between ease of

comprehension and depth of coverage. The article is 552 words—enough information to get some insights into pain treatments, but not enough detail to speak authoritatively on the topic.

❸ All databases provide options for managing the resources that you find. For all entries you should be able to save citation information and for full text pieces, you can usually print, e-mail, or save the article.

Some popular sources will go into more detail and offer enough helpful information to make it into your projects. You will need to look over enough sources to make judgments.

As a final step in narrowing your focus and strengthening your expertise on a topic, you can search through specialized databases, as in Figure 15.4.

FIGURE 15.4
Searching special collections of academic sources.

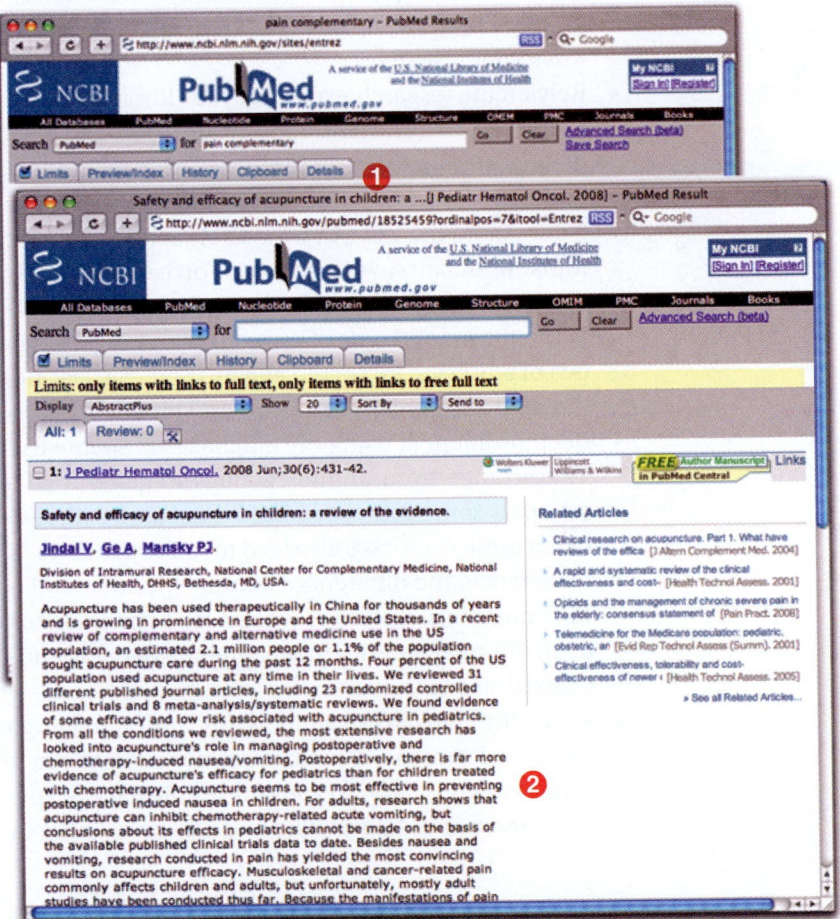

❶ Allison here queries the specialized database PubMed, which catalogs academic articles related to medicine. Because the database is already limited to the areas of medicine, she does not need to include that term in her query. Her search will return academic pieces in the field of medicine related to complementary approaches and pain.

❷ The search returns full text articles containing mostly facts and published research. Again, the genre and audience of these materials must be considered. Some academic sources may be highly specialized and difficult to use. Some will be very helpful. This source compiles the results of twenty-three studies and presents the research in language that can be understood by non-experts, so the piece might make a nice complement to the general sources Allison has uncovered.

Know It — Strategies for Using Subject Categories, Keywords, and Libraries and Databases

Learning
Objective 15.3

- Spend some time thinking through your topic before getting started. Develop research questions (page 340). Think about what people argue over concerning your topic. Try to come up with an angle or some questions to drive your research.
- Rely on the research experts at your library. Find out about library orientations. Talk to librarians about your topic. Get personalized help if you are having trouble locating resources or even getting started with a research project.
- Understand the ways in which subject categories can help you refine your thinking and discover resources. You can begin by browsing through subject categories, getting a feel for the issues and materials.
- Learn the ins and outs of keyword searching. Understand the specific methods of any keyword search engines you use. Develop a knack for identifying the right terminology to narrow and broaden your search results.
- Become adept at using the databases available from your library Web site. These range from online catalogs to general collections of popular and scholarly sources to specialized databases with resources on narrow topics. Often these databases also lead to full text articles.
- Understand the differences between popular and academic sources. Know the limitations of sources written for a general audience or sources that are of an informal nature. Understand the benefits and challenges of using specialized sources.
- Learn the steps involved in saving and managing resources you discover. Learn to download, e-mail, or print resources you find on library Web sites. (These options vary, so you will simply have to spend some time getting to know the tools.) Also explore and use any citation tools available.

Ask Questions & Make Decisions — Exercises For Using Subject Headings, Keywords, and Libraries and Databases

1. Locate a list of Library of Congress subject headings. (Do a Web search or start at http://lcsh.info/.) Spend ten minutes or so exploring the categories. Which categories make the most sense? Are there any that seem odd or unworkable? Report your findings in a brief presentation or a paragraph.

2. Go to the Web site of your school or local library. Locate the tutorials or how-to information related to research, and then read the instructions for locating electronic resources. Spend at least thirty minutes learning the workings of the site.

3. Use your library databases to locate three articles related to a topic about which you have an interest: (1) an article from a popular source, (2) a piece collected through a broad database of scholarly articles, and (3) a piece discovered through a specialized database. Use the tools of the Web site to download or e-mail the articles to yourself, saving them for future use and collecting citation information as you go.

Internet Sources

VIDEO
42. Internet Sources

Because you use a Web browser to reach almost any source, you can easily get confused about just what kinds of materials you are discovering. What's the difference between sources if they are all just items on the Internet? We've already talked about the unique nature of library sources you might access online. When it comes to materials on the Internet at large, there are similar distinctions you need to understand.

Remember to be inquisitive and deliberate as you scour the Internet. Spend some time examining the addresses of sites you visit. Watch what happens when you move from one kind of Web domain to another (e.g., moving from a .com to a .org to a .gov Web site). Does the quality of the resources change? Do you get a distinct sense of authorship or of the entities behind the information you discover? Think also about medium and genre questions that are revealed by materials you find: Are the resources you find Web pages, pdf files, image files, word processor documents? Are you locating reports, advertisements, articles, or message postings? As always, watch out, ask questions, and think critically.

You will also need to start making some decisions. For instance, knowing something about the types of materials online can help you find the right strategy for locating information. Instead of the basic strategy for locating anything on the Internet (i.e., type in a few words at Google, and—bam!—research at your fingertips), try targeting specific types of materials. For example, if you are looking for conversational research, you will have good luck querying archives of Internet discussion groups, as Figure 15.5 (page 358) demonstrates.

You will want to be strategic about the kinds of resources you choose as you develop a research project. Conversational resources, for instance, will be helpful in the early stages of a project as you brainstorm. Internet groups can also give good insights into the perspectives of the key positions that circulate around

FIGURE 15.5
Searching through Internet discussion groups.

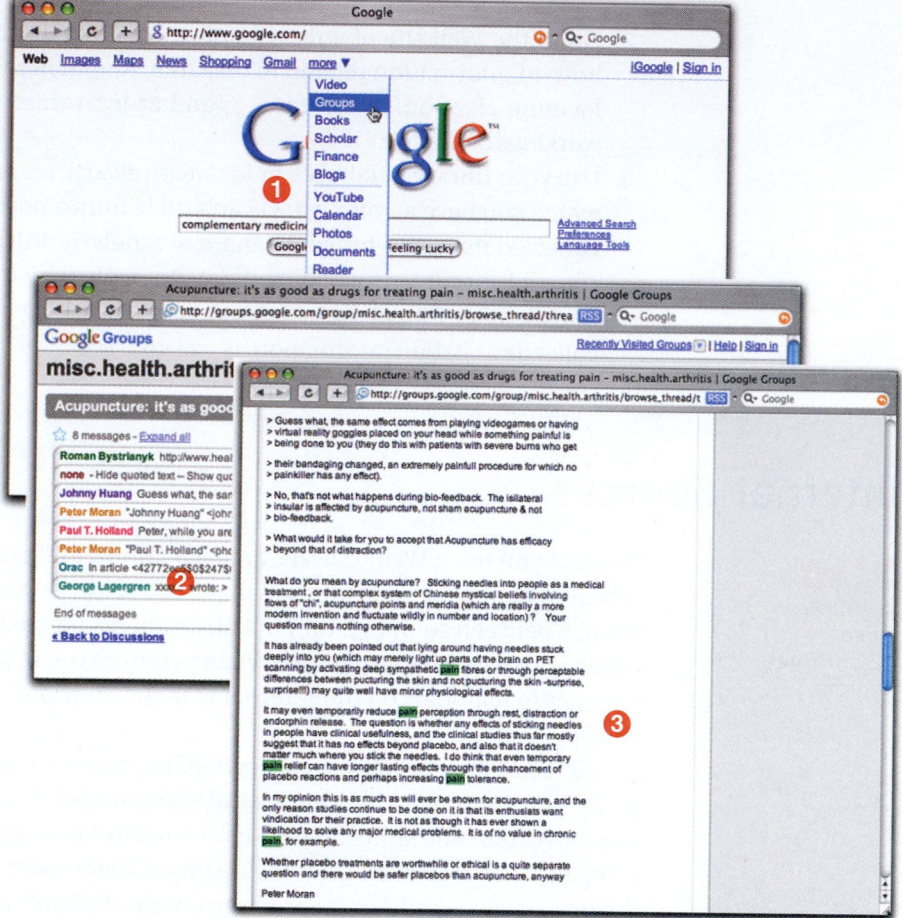

❶ Notice the number of options for searching different types of materials on the Internet. In addition to discussion groups, you can look through scholarly Web materials, blogs, books, videos, and more. Selecting the right type of resource to query is the first step.

❷ Discussion group conversations collect the insights of members of Internet communities. The postings to the group are organized in threads

related to specific topics. Here, members of the group *misc.health.arthritis* debate acupuncture.

❸ The postings that you find in conversations will be a mix of articles and expert and nonexpert opinion. You will need to sift through these postings critically, using extra doses of skepticism and thinking of conversations as potentially leading you toward resources, but also as windows into perspectives on topical issues.

a topic. If a group is active, you can sometimes use online discussion spaces to post queries and solicit feedback about a topic and potential resources.

Remember also to pay attention to the differences among the organizations and entities behind sources on the Web. The Web serves as a giant clearinghouse for all kinds of research reports, government information, organizational materials, and company-sponsored information (see Figure 15.6).

Figure 15.6 shows materials sponsored by government and organizational entities. It can be tempting to assign more credibility to these kinds of government or organizational sites. After all, they do have a nonprofit ethos, employ experts, and often focus on disseminating the results of research. Think twice, though, before granting too much authority to any site. The Mayo Clinic site, for instance, uses a .com domain but likely has information similar to what you would find at the Cleveland Clinic with its .org Web site. You need to scrutinize the materials you find, using the source of the information as a guide without too quickly jumping to conclusions.

You will also need to learn something about keeping track of and organizing sources you discover. Most Web browsers have a Bookmarks or Favorites function that will allow you to store the Web addresses (URLs) of sites that you find or use. There are also tools that can help you record more detailed information and organize sources while you work (see Figure 15.7).

FIGURE 15.6
Government and organizational Web sites.

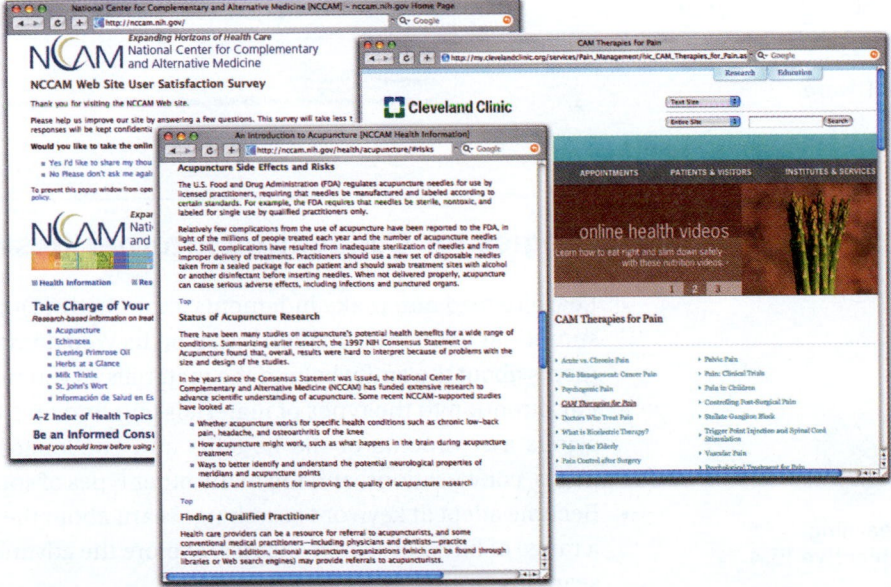

FIGURE 15.7

A social bookmarking site and Web browser research tool.

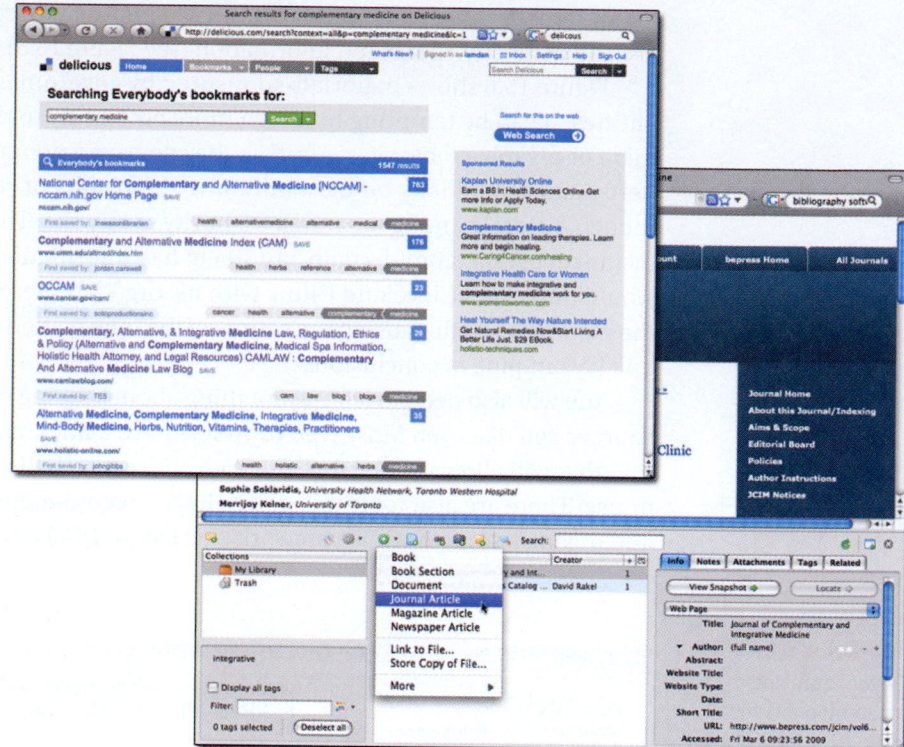

VIDEO

31. Bibliography Software

LO

Learning Objective 15.4

Know It   Strategies for Conducting Internet Research

- Learn to read and make judgments about URLs. Don't make knee-jerk assumptions about information based on its Web domain, but do weigh judgments about the entity behind the materials as you make evaluations.

- Pay attention to the types of materials you find on the Internet. Make conscious assessments of the benefits and challenges of using audio, Web pages, conversations, and the many other types of sources you will discover.

- Become adept at keyword searching. Learn about the variety and abilities of a range of Internet search engines. Explore the advanced options of Internet searches.

- Learn how to track and save the materials you discover. Use the Bookmarks or Favorites options of your Web browser. Experiment with online bookmarking sites and research tools. Save key resources and be deliberate about organizing your materials.

Exercises for Conducting Internet Research

1. Go to an Internet search engine and conduct a series of keyword searches. Begin with a broad term such as *health*, *politics*, or *entertainment*. Take note of the number and kind of materials returned with such a broad query. Identify more specific keywords and combinations of terms (e.g., querying for "libertarian foreign policy" instead of "politics"). Continue refining your queries until you reduce the number of search returns to triple digits.

2. Use a blog or discussion group search engine to find conversational resources. (You can start with the options at Google.) Explore the perspectives that play out in several conversations about a topic of interest. Write a summary of the conversation, focusing on the give and take between positions.

3. Explore the Internet for resources related to a topic of interest. Keep at it until you find materials from at least three different kinds of domains (.com, .org, .gov, .net, etc.). Analyze any differences you find and write up your thinking in a paragraph or so.

4. Go to an Internet bookmarking Web site. (You can start with http://delicious.com or http://citeulike.com.) Look at the collections of resources that have been gathered around a keyword related to a topic of interest. Learn how to use the tools at the Web site to create your own bookmarking records.

Field Research

LO

Learning Objective 15.5

Sometimes you will conduct research in which your own hand plays a larger part in the collection of materials. When you interview people, for instance, you become the recorder and archiver of sources before you even begin to sort through and make decisions about how to use the information. Often people label this kind of work primary research—research that you conduct yourself. (Looking through articles written by someone else would be secondary research.) When you conduct primary research, a key question is how much of yourself to allow into the process. Of course, researchers strive for objectivity, but you will shape the process as you conduct observations, interview people, or develop surveys to collect information.

Observations

You are most likely to use observations when you want to write about a location or a cultural phenomenon—perhaps for a research report on attitudes toward sustainability or a profile of life in your dorm. Observations can be fun because you get to see situations in ways you have likely overlooked before. You may shop at the local farmer's market regularly, but when studying the scene for a project on green consumers you might realize there are various categories of marketgoers—fitness and health nuts, ecology and "green" movement devotees, cruelty-free advocates, cooking aficionados. What do they have in common? What sets them apart? These are the kinds of questions you will explore as you conduct observational research.

Before you conduct an observation, make some decisions about the place. Be sure to select a location where your presence will be appropriate. For example, observing the farmer's market makes sense, but observing the mayor's office might be hard to pull off, and observing the local playground might be a bad idea. Also plan on visiting a place multiple times. Sure, Saturday is big at the market, but patterns might develop from one weekend to another and you might discover important finds on weekday afternoons.

When you conduct an observation, be sure to capture contextual information. Record the date, time, and place. But also take note of the circumstances. Describe the weather conditions. Detail the setting. Are there physical aspects of the place that shape behavior—comfy couches in the dorm TV room? Also let your senses guide you as you discover details to record. What do you see, hear, and smell? How are people dressed? How do they interact? What objects do they use?

Finally, you will need to take careful field notes. Bring a notebook and develop a system for entering information. Some researchers strive to record just the observations—woman, tie-dyed clothes, bought arugula. Others include interpretations or questions—woman, tie-dyed clothes, bought arugula; is there some connection with the cooking aficionados (usual purchasers)? You might divide your notebook into columns where you can jot down both observations and interpretations. You can also return to your field notes shortly after the observation and compose a more formal reflection with interpretations.

Interviews

Interviews can inform a wide range of research projects. You might collect reactions for a proposal essay or gather quotations for a podcast detailing a local artist. Really, any time the insights of another might prove useful, you can conduct an interview. Interviews also force you to think about your role in the research process. In fact, you will need to manage the exchange that takes place with your interview subject. Sometimes, you need to pull back and let your subject share insights, but at other times, you need to guide the session toward areas of your research. A good interview is like a modified conversation: focused on the interview subject, sometimes moving in unexpected directions, but circling around your research topic.

Preparation matters when it comes to interviews. Conduct initial research both about your topic and your interview subject (or subjects). You need to know what issues are at stake and what attitudes your subject might have before you begin a conversation. You will also need to prepare your questions in advance. The key is to make decisions about the kinds of things to ask. For one thing, avoid basic factual questions; you can look those up yourself. Instead, think about whether you seek responses that illuminate specific aspects of your project or whether you want to gather broad insights about your topic.

As with observations, you will need to spend some time planning an interview. Handle the logistics with your interview subject. Be sure to allow plenty of time and accommodate the schedule of your interviewee. Also tell your subject something about your project as you set things up. He or she may be able to offer some initial guidance and help you determine how best to use your time together. Think also about how you will record the interview. If you have a voice recorder, ask for permission ahead of time to capture the interview. Double check about permission to use the interview in your research and ask if you may present follow-up questions. Come prepared with notebook, recorder, and questions.

After the interview, reflect on the session. Use your notes or recording to review what was said. Make sure you have all the contextual information in place—date, place, name of interviewee spelled correctly. Write up a brief summary of the interview. Annotate your notes to indicate key responses or jot down the timestamps of interesting sections of your recordings. Develop any follow up questions and figure out how to submit them at a later date and gather additional responses.

Surveys

Surveys are somewhat like interviews, but they tend to target a wider group and require less back and forth between you and your subject. You can use survey data to support any point you might make in a project—backing up an argument about religious freedom or adding evidence to an oral report on bicycling on campus. With surveys, you will want to have a reasonably clear idea of your focus ahead of time. If you wanted to find out whether the dorm lounge was a place for watching TV or for sleeping and hanging out, you could survey people about their habits.

You will have two basic options for developing survey questions. First, you can use data-gathering questions to illicit specific responses. Yes or no questions, multiple choice questions, checklists, and ranking questions can all be used to collect specific information targeted to your concerns. Here are some possibilities:

1. [Yes/no question] Would you pay more for cruelty-free products?

   (circle one)   Yes   No

2. [Multiple choice question] In your opinion, which of the following animal testing activities should be allowed?
   ❑ Prescription drugs
   ❑ Cosmetics
   ❑ Behavior studies
   ❑ None

3. [Ranking question] On a scale of 1 to 5, please rank how cruelty-free products influence your buying decisions

   (Little influence) 1   2   3   4   5 (Great influence)

In addition to these data-gathering questions, you can provide questions requiring written responses on a survey. As with an interview, these questions or prompts should be focused (e.g., "How does the television set contribute to the atmosphere of the lounge?"). Perhaps the most important advice is to develop questions that do not lead respondents in a particular direction. An open-ended question might produce more reliable and useful responses (e.g., "Please share your thoughts on the purpose of the TV lounge"). There are lots of tutorials online for creating good data-gathering questions. Your task is to bring a clear sense of your project to bear on creating the survey. As always, ask questions and make decisions about what you need to know to develop your project. Then, formulate questions that will prompt survey takers to share the kinds of information you need.

Logistically, you will need to think about how to target a survey group. Who should you survey? If you ask only people who frequent the lounge, you might miss the insights of those who avoid the space because of the TV. Think also about how to deliver the survey and collect responses. You can compose and print out a survey with a word processor. You can wait for responses or have people return the survey to you. Another good option might be online survey tools like surveymonkey.com. You can use these tools to create, deliver, and collect responses in one fell swoop.

As with other field research, you will need to write up your results. For data questions, you may be able to calculate responses and deliver the information in a graph or table (see Chapter 26). You can also use what you find as evidence in your written work. For written responses, you can quote materials—which you will probably want to do anonymously since respondents may give more unvarnished answers if they are not sharing their names.

Know It   Strategies for Conducting Field Research

- Make decisions about how much of yourself to involve in the research process. No research is completely objective, but field research allows you to interact with your subjects. You will need to be aware of your own role and possible biases in the process.
- Think about what kinds of field research will best capture the information you seek. Observations can tell you something about people and places, but interviews and surveys will provide more insights into their perspectives.
- For observations, be thorough and persistent. Details might not seem important in the moment, but later could prove helpful. Capture as much information as you can. Also, conduct observations more than once.
- For interviews and surveys, learn the ins and outs of composing successful questions. Consult online guides to interviewing and question writing. Check that your questions do not lead respondents toward conclusions.

Ask Questions & Make Decisions   Exercises for Conducting Field Research

1. Spend a few minutes observing a place that you might normally overlook—the bus stop in front of your apartment, the checkout line at the store, the kitchen at work. Freewrite for five minutes about possible papers you could develop based on your quick survey of the place.
2. Search online for video of interviews. Watch at least three different interviews, taking note of the way questions are posed and of the interviewer's style. Write a paragraph outlining your philosophy toward conducting interviews.
3. Go to an online survey site like surveymonkey.com. Create an account, and then create a survey that you can give to friends or relatives. You might ask about food, music, or movies, or you could collect responses for a research topic. Send the survey out, examine the responses, and then share a brief summary of the results with your survey takers.

Zoom **Out**   Reflecting on Conducting Research

- **Research is best viewed in rhetorical terms.** Purposes shape research. Activities range from brainstorming and discovering topics to narrowing a focus to locating specific resources.

- **Critical thinking goes hand in hand with research.** A fluid sense of adjusting ideas characterizes a healthy research process. Multiple perspectives also reveal themselves through research. Evaluations and judgments emerge as the research process plays out (see Chapter 3).

- **Researchers make decisions constantly:** where to conduct research—the library, the Internet, or the field; what kinds of questions to pursue—research questions, supporting questions; how best to locate resources—browsing through categories, searching with keywords. As always, ask questions and make decisions.

- **Researchers pay close attention to the process of locating materials and the details of what they discover.** Taking note of topics, search terms, and findings helps you make sense of research sources. Closely examining the items discovered provides specifics for understanding and using materials.

- **Archiving and keeping track of research is as important as identifying materials.** Researchers record as much information as possible about sources, collect items, and organize materials as they go.

For additional information and practice with the learning objectives in this chapter, go to www.mycomplab.com, Resources > Research > The Research Assignment > Finding Sources.

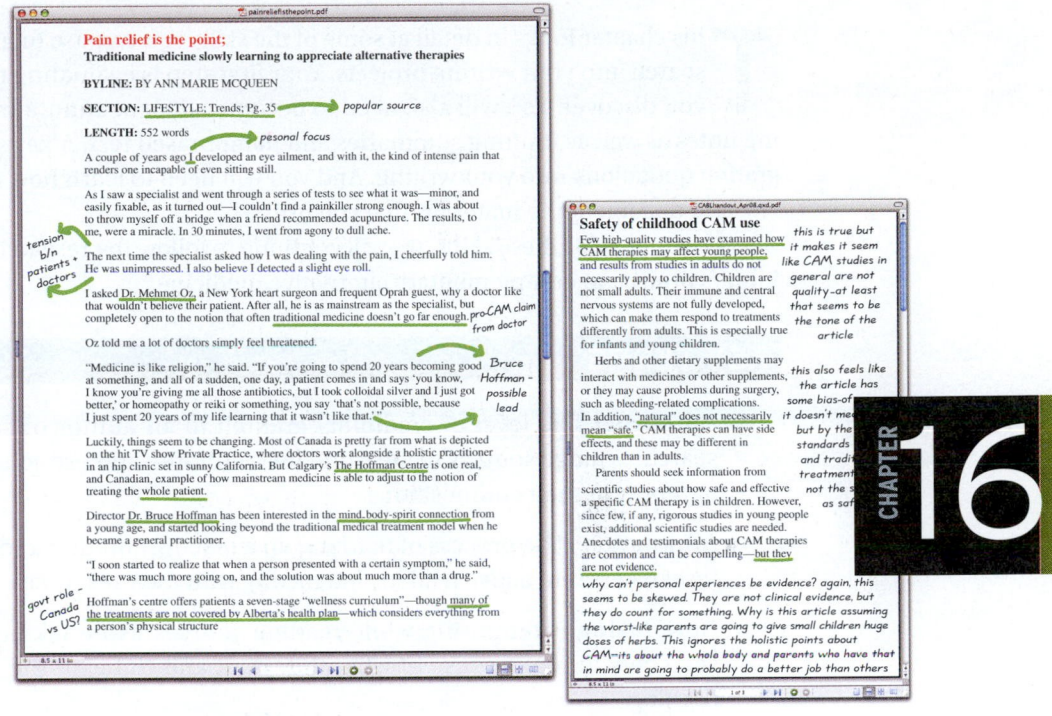

Evaluating and Composing with Sources

Zoom In   Key Concepts and Learning Objectives

After studying this chapter, you should be able to:

16.1 Consider authors, audiences, genres, mediums, and purposes to assess the authority of sources.

16.2 Deploy reading strategies to help you make evaluations.

16.3 Summarize and paraphrase sources by focusing on their key points.

16.4 Integrate quotations from sources into compositions.

16.5 Cite and document materials used in research writing.

This chapter looks in detail at some of the skills you can use to integrate research into your writing projects. Your first step is evaluating the sources you discover. You will also need to become adept at annotating and taking notes as well as drafting summaries and paraphrased text. A key skill is integrating quotations into your writing. And you will need to learn how to properly cite and document the materials that you use.

As we consider these skills, we will continue to follow the research of Allison Johns's project on complementary alternative medicine.

KEY TERMS

- **Authority:** The level of credibility granted to an author or source. Researchers judge sources to measure their authority and use sources to add authority to their compositions.

- **Annotation:** The process of marking up a text. Annotating a source turns researchers into active readers, interacting with their resources.

- **Note taking:** Composing while reading sources. Note taking helps researchers to make sense of what they read and to begin the process of drafting.

- **Summarizing:** Capturing the essence of a source. Summaries strive to objectively get the gist of materials and can range from short sketches to more detailed distillations.

- **Paraphrasing:** Translating the main ideas of a source into your own words. Paraphrases help authors emphasize aspects of resources as they incorporate them into their own compositions.

- **Quoting:** Using the words of others in your own writing. Quotations add authority to your work and enable you to place your ideas in conversation with those of others.

- **Attributive tags:** Sometimes called signal phrases, words used to introduce quotations and associate them with their author.

- **Citation:** References in the text that indicate the source of materials you incorporate into your writing. Citation combines with documentation to help readers identify and locate your research.

- **Documentation:** A listing or note that provides publication and other identifying information for sources. Usually, a list documenting sources appears at the end of a composition.

- **Plagiarism:** The inappropriate use of the work of others. Plagiarism can result from deliberate unacknowledged borrowings or from carelessness as you use research sources.

Evaluating Sources

VIDEO
43. Evaluating Bias and Credibility

Much of this book is based on the assumption that reading and writing should be driven by a process of asking questions and making decisions. Nowhere will this approach be more evident or necessary than when you evaluate research sources. It's relatively easy to find all kinds of materials once you have identified a topic for a project. It's harder to pass judgments about which of those materials are best to use. To do so, you will need to revisit core concerns of rhetorical situations (Chapter 1) and critical reading (Chapter 3). To get started, let's weigh the different meanings of the term *authority*.

Within the term *authority,* you can recognize the word *author*, prompting you to "consider the source" of materials. Begin by asking questions about the author (or authors) of sources; this author might be an individual or an entity or organization. Does the author have any apparent biases? Reports on potential problems related to acupuncture sponsored by the makers of Motrin must be read with considerable skepticism. Similarly, an online posting by the local acupuncturist about the dangers of ibuprofen might be biased. Conversely, authors can increase the value of sources; a health organization can affirm the credibility of clinical research, and an acupuncturist can bring expertise to claims about alternative methods of treating pain. Think critically about authors. Ask questions about *who* is behind a source, and then make judgments accordingly.

LO

Learning Objective 16.1

You also need to think about authority in terms of the currency of sources and of rhetorical situations. Sometimes well-established sources provide good insights, but generally more current sources will have more authority. Purposes, mediums, genres, and audiences, too, shape the ways in which sources can be used. And you need to move from evaluating sources in terms of their purposes and audience to using sources with an eye toward your own goals and readers. Get comfortable with the idea that some sources are better suited for some rhetorical situations than others.

Consider the online discussion forum postings encountered by Allison Johns (see Figure 16.1). There is a back and forth flow in the messages, with one author making a claim about the efficacy of acupuncture and another challenging the assertion. Additional respondents extend this conversation, sometimes posting links to and excerpts from articles or references to additional sources.

FIGURE 16.1

Online forum postings.

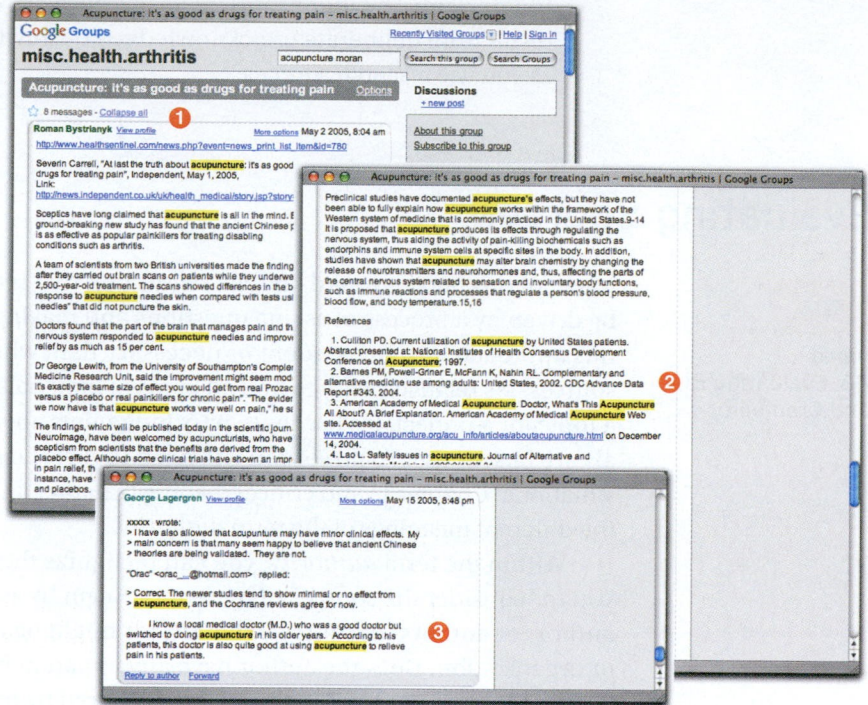

❶ This posting contains an article that has been copied from an online news site. You need to think about the genre of the messages you encounter as well as their authors and audiences.

❷ This posting contains a number of references and links to additional sources. When evaluating

sources, your research process will not stop; instead, you will uncover more avenues for investigation.

❸ Some sources lack the authority that comes from publication or citation. You will need to make decisions about when and how best to use these kinds of primary sources of information.

The medium of the online forum shapes these messages; the ability to post is unfiltered, the composition space lends itself to shorter, unedited messages, the threaded comment-and-response format promotes posts that challenge, extend, or clarify one another. Allison encounters a range of message genres even within the medium of the online discussion forum.

Someone who makes an initial post copies and pastes an entire article into a message. A respondent dashes off a quick counterpoint, a subsequent poster composes a bibliography-like message with a series of links—three postings, three different kinds of messages. And audience issues must also be considered. Perhaps some of these authors are frequent participants in the group. Others may be newcomers. The group may share certain assumptions about the value of alternative medicine that shape their responses. You need to weigh all of these concerns even as you evaluate a few messages posted online.

In other words, you need to focus on who is behind the message and how the message is received. And you need to think about the content of the message. Again, think of the term *authority*; the way the message is put together accounts for much of its authority. An article that cites and documents its information is more credible than one that simply makes assertions. A piece that acknowledges alternative approaches can carry more authority by virtue of its balance. You will also need to think about the logic and evidence behind messages. Does the piece contain any logical fallacies? Are claims backed up with evidence? Of what type and how credible is the evidence? (Review the discussion of arguments in Chapter 4 to get a feel for how to apply this kind of evaluation to your research sources.)

VIDEO
44. Evaluating
Primary Sources

Finally, you will need to consider your own rhetorical situations and purposes as you evaluate sources. Are you still in the brainstorming stages of a project? Perhaps you can use forum postings to better understand the issues at play in conversations about your topic. Perhaps you can post your own query to extend and refine your thinking. Are you focused on a specific topic? You need to find sources that treat the issue in detail to sharpen your expertise. Are you drafting an essay? You will want to discuss sources as you compose, analyzing, synthesizing, and drawing conclusions to help express your ideas.

Annotating, Note Taking, and Creating Bibliographies

LO

Learning
Objective 16.2

The key difference between annotating and taking notes is where the writing takes place. Annotating generally happens on the pages of materials you read. In this process, the reader (you) is in the role of responder, which makes you more active and ultimately allows you to weave your own insights into the texts you are considering. In a sense, you engage in a conversation with the text—sometimes noting small observations to clarify points and other times more forcefully pushing your own ideas into the mix.

Look at the two samples in Figure 16.2 (page 372). The annotator on the left seems to be concentrating on reading to learn, marking up the text with observations that analyze the source and that highlight information. The annotations on the right demonstrate a reader who is veering more toward writing as she marks up the text, objecting to points in the piece and spelling out her own perspectives on the topic. No doubt your own reading style and your situation will dictate the way you engage materials; however, be open to the idea that your reading is not a passive activity but a process through which you develop and compose your ideas.

Note taking extends this active response by moving your writing away from the surface of the resources you are investigating. You might take notes about a specific resource, using the opportunity to make sense of the reading and to cull

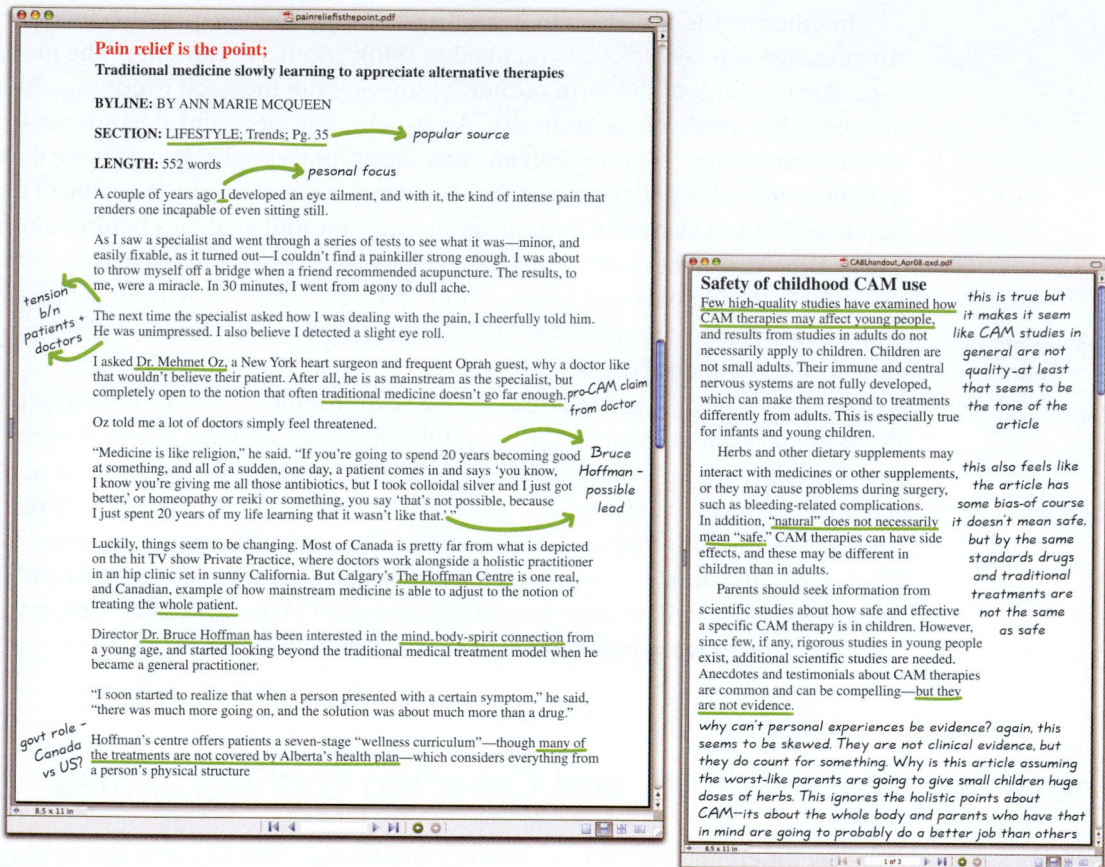

FIGURE 16.2
Different styles of annotation.

insights from the source. You can also use notes to zoom out and begin making sense of your topic as a whole. The page of notes in Figure 16.3 does both, listing specific readings and generating larger questions about the project.

In these notes, the author creates a mix of observations about the topic and responses to texts to help her understand her resources. At times, the notes pick up on specifics from a single source, even creating a list of information from a reading. At other times, the notes record ideas about the topic as a whole and sketch out additional research questions that can further refine the project.

You can also begin collecting and writing about sources in an annotated bibliography, a list of possible resources for a project that contains annotations encapsulating the ideas and commenting on the materials. (See Figure 16.4 and Chapter E4.)

FIGURE 16.3
A page of notes.

> There are really two-perspectives on CAM.
>
> 1   CAM is natural whole body approach to medicine that is not that different than what doctors recommend–eat well, exercise, take care of body and mind, etc.
> 2   CAM is just a way to ignore science and a financial opportunity for quacks.
> Two might be a bit harsh, but most of the research does break things into what can be proven–science, and what is just anecdotal. See Goode–"commonsense" or "mumbo jumbo"
>
> Really the question of how much weight to put into
> different kinds of studies is a biggie.
>
> Also on the two perspectives, CAM advocates sometimes see the pills and test heavy traditional medical practices as equally out of the mainstream. Have we gone too far in believing science and chemicals solve everything? Or really are they always the only or best solution? That seems like the better question.
> ✓ More thoughts on Goode (Whole Bodies, Divided Minds)
> ✓ Nothing new–see Hippocrates
> ✓ Connections to chronic, life concerns–arthritus, pain, etc.
> ✓ Connections to mind/spirit practices–Chinese, faith healing, etc.
>   ✓ Not anti science–welcome studies and willing to use medicines when appropriate
> Peter Clark–Ethics of Alternative Medical Therapies-points out how medical fear of CAM has legal and treatment problems. 46% of patients using alternative med do so without doctor advice or supervision. Doctors don't give CAM info as treatment options. Is there a legal problem? Doctors should be obligated to inform patients of all the options. Should CAM be one of them?

FIGURE 16.4
A section of an annotated bibliography.

> Annotated Bibliography
>
> Bhanoo, Sindya N. "Alternatives Enter the Mainstream: Unconventional Care Wins Some Converts." *Washington Post* 16 Sep. 2008, HE01+. Print.
>
>   This piece is written for a general audience but provides some statistics about efforts to integrate alternative therapies into hospitals and other mainstream treatment centers. Discusses the Johns Hopkins Integrative Medicine Center—a good example to show complementary approaches.
>
> Cassidy, Claire M. "Some Terminology Needs for Writers, Researchers, Practitioners, and Editors as We Move, Toward Integrating Medicines." Editorial. *The Journal of Alternative and Complementary Medicine* 14.6 (2008): 613–615. Print.
>
>   This editorial is aimed at health professionals but is clear and provides a helpful discussion of the issues related to labeling different forms of medicine—a useful source for showing the problems with the "us versus them" mentality often found in discussions of CAM.

Know It   Strategies for Evaluating Sources, Annotating, Note Taking, and Creating Bibliographies

- Become skilled enough that evaluating sources becomes second nature. Consider rhetorical situations as you examine sources, and ask questions: Who made the statement? When? For whom? For what purpose? In what genre or medium?

- Take apart the messages you encounter. What kinds of appeals do they make? How do they use evidence? Does the source acknowledge alternatives and place itself within a larger conversation?

- Read actively, making sense of and distilling information as you go. Use annotations to highlight key points in sources and mark ideas. Take notes to sketch out and synthesize your thoughts. Create bibliographies with annotations to make sense of your sources.

- Think of reading and writing as interconnected. Write while you explore materials, brainstorming ideas or capturing the essence of resources. Continue to research as needed after beginning to draft your thoughts.

Ask Questions & Make Decisions   Exercises for Evaluating Sources, Annotating, Note Taking, and Creating Bibliographies

1. Conduct research related to a topic of interest at an online collection of conversations, such as a blog or discussion group. (Try groups.google.com, or technorati.com.) Spend at least fifteen minutes exploring the kinds of materials exchanged in the postings. Write a paragraph explaining your findings.

2. Using your library Web site, locate several resources in an academic database. Look them over, assessing their authority. Browse the Internet for sources on the same topic, again evaluating them. On a sheet of paper, make a list with two columns. In the columns, list the pros and cons of each type of source.

3. Go to two or more Web sites that offer false or misleading information. (Search using the keyword "spoof Web sites" or try dhmo.org or martinlutherking.org for starters.) What strategies do the sites use? Do these sites change your assumptions about online information? Write up your reactions to the sites in a paragraph or an online posting.

4. Search the Web for the poem "Marginalia" by Billy Collins. Analyze the poem, and then think more about how the way we read tells us something about ourselves. Share your thoughts with your classmates.

Summarizing and Paraphrasing

VIDEO
45. Summarizing and Paraphrasing

When you create summaries and paraphrases of sources, you are moving more clearly into the realm of composition. A summary simply distills the information in a source into a manageable chunk. As you create a summary, you may want to include key quotations that you can later incorporate into your drafts. Here are some details to keep in mind regarding summaries:

- Summaries strive for accuracy. The goal is to capture what a piece says; you can challenge or interpret sources elsewhere, but the summary should objectively get the gist of a piece.
- Summaries focus on the main ideas. Sometimes a key detail is necessary, but generally the author of the summary does the work of identifying the points that matter and articulating those points economically in her own words. The process is one of tightening, helping you provide accurate snapshots of more extensive ideas in sources.
- Summaries are a genre of writing. They can include quotations and attributive tags (see pages 377–81). Summaries can be plugged into larger writing pieces to explain a topic, provide information, offer evidence, and so on. Depending on your rhetorical situation, summaries can range from loosely sketched explorations to carefully crafted distillations of sources.

LO

Learning Objective 16.3

You may find yourself composing summaries of individual paragraphs or of entire sources. The excerpts below demonstrate how Allison distilled a paragraph from a source.

Original paragraph: Practiced in China and other Asian countries for thousands of years, acupuncture is one of the key components of traditional Chinese medicine. In traditional Chinese medicine (TCM), the body is seen as a delicate balance of two opposing and inseparable forces: yin and yang. Yin represents the cold, slow, or passive principle, while yang represents the hot, excited, or active principle. According to TCM, health is achieved by maintaining the body in a "balanced state"; disease is due to an internal imbalance of yin and yang. This imbalance leads to blockage in the flow of qi (vital energy) along pathways known as meridians. Qi can be unblocked, according to TCM, by using acupuncture at certain points on the body that connect with these meridians. Sources vary on the number of meridians, with numbers ranging from 14 to 20. One commonly cited source describes meridians as 14 main channels "connecting the body in a weblike interconnecting matrix" of at least 2,000 acupuncture points (NCCAM).

Summary: Acupuncture has been part of traditional Chinese medicine (TCM) for thousands of years. TCM believes in "opposing and inseparable forces: yin and yang" (NCCAM). This belief underlies the practice of acupuncture. When an imbalance between yin and yang occurs, acupuncture can be applied to specific meridian points, unblocking the channels through which the life force (qi) flows (NCCAM).

Notice that the summary does not capture every detail of the original paragraph; it leaves out the number of meridian points, for instance. The focus is on the key information—the belief that acupuncture can help restore the balance between yin and yang.

Paraphrases are similar to summaries, except they articulate the gist of a source in your own words. With paraphrases, you might include more details and rephrase the source to integrate it with your own ideas. Consider this paraphrase of the same excerpt:

> The traditional Chinese medicine concept of balance between yin and yang informs the practice of acupuncture. Yin (cold or passive energy) and yang (hot or active energy) must be in balance, and blockages of crucial meridian points can inhibit the flow of energy, called qi, jeopardizing the health of the patient. Using more than 2000 points on the body, acupuncture targets between fourteen and twenty meridian channels to help restore the balance between yin and yang (NCCAM).

In the paraphrase, the author shifts the focus to match her own interests— the yin and yang and the concept of balance. She also provides more specifics, listing the number of acupuncture points and delineating the characteristics of yin and yang. The paraphrase includes some common terms from the original passage, but the emphasis has been adjusted and the passage no longer uses quotations from the original source.

For both summaries and paraphrases, you need to watch out for plagiarism. You will need to quote any materials that you take directly from a source. And you will have to check that your distillations restate the main ideas without borrowing too much from the originals. Consider the following example, which has some phrases highlighted to illuminate an unacceptable paraphrase:

> Acupuncture *has been practiced in China and other Asian countries for thousands of years. According to traditional Chinese medicine (TCM),* one must maintain a "balanced state" between yin and yang. *Blockage in the flow of qi* will create an imbalance. Acupuncture can be applied *along pathways known as meridians* to unblock these channels. *One commonly cited source describes meridians as 14 main channels* that are part of "a weblike interconnecting matrix" *of at least 2,000 acupuncture points*.

You can see that a number of phrases have been borrowed with almost the exact language from the original source. Additionally, although the example uses quotations, it does not properly cite materials borrowed from the source. This distillation would fall into the category of plagiarism rather than functioning as a proper summary or paraphrase.

Using Quotations

VIDEO
46. Using Quotations

There are several instances when it makes good sense to use quotations. Sometimes a research source is particularly clear or is rich with details. If the source has already succinctly spelled out something, you may want to borrow a portion of the material to provide that distillation for your readers. You can also use quotations to give your writing a stronger sense of authority; for example, a well-placed observation by an expert adds credibility and can broaden the appeal of your work. And sometimes something is just particularly well said; a powerful statement with insightful phrasing may be so compelling that you want to bring it to your readers.

In general, you should aim to use precisely the amount of source text required to meet your purpose. Often a sentence or even a phrase delivers the right idea. There may also be times when a larger block of source text is needed. Shorter pieces of text will be woven into the sentences of your paragraphs. If you quote a passage that requires more than five lines of text in your composition, you should set that larger excerpt off as a block quotation. Below is a good example of a block quotation that makes use of well-stated text.

> The subtle game of "Us versus Them" often has a scalar component. Recently, an author claimed that Chinese Medicine has little to offer because "the five elements and *yin–yang* theory are as nothing compared to the richness of biomedicine." Had an author remarked that biomedicine had little to offer besides "the idea of infection and the idea of metabolic abnormality," any Western reader would have objected, because we are aware of how much these few words hide in the way of knowledge and complexity. *The same level of complexity* lies behind the ideas of Chinese Medicine, and this point applies equally to any World Medicine. Authors need to take care to *know their subject* and *avoid making statements that belittle.* (Cassidy 615, emphasis in the original)

However, your general approach should strive to use smaller pieces of your sources, taking them apart and fitting the ideas into your own compositions. Consider this example, which makes use of the same source but with a shorter quotation embedded in the text:

> Using a term like *complementary* when talking about traditional and alternative medicine challenges the perception that these practices are competing against each other. As Claire M. Cassidy puts it, "while it's commonplace to represent biomedicine as standing apart on its own small island, contrasting it with a continent containing all other ways of practicing medicine, we are factually and philosophically more correct to draw a single circle encompassing all" (613).

In this example, the author is better able to control the way the source supports her ideas by picking a quotation that finishes and strengthens a point she wishes to make.

Related to thinking about the amount of text you will quote is the idea that you can edit and interact with quoted material to work it more seamlessly into your writing. You might ask, *How can I judiciously edit someone else's words to further my own ideas?* The primary means of doing this kind of modified quoting are through the use of ellipses to remove part of a quotation, the use of brackets to add clarifications, and the use of italics to create emphasis. The examples below follow Modern Language Association, or MLA, style guidelines. (You can find out more about MLA style and about American Psychological Association (APA) style in Chapter 17.) Consider this adjustment to the quotation above:

> Using a term like *complementary* when talking about traditional and alternative medicine challenges the perception that these practices are competing against each other. As Claire M. Cassidy puts it, "while it's commonplace to represent biomedicine as standing apart on its own small island . . . we are factually and philosophically more correct to draw a single circle encompassing *all* [kinds of healing practices]" (613, emphasis added).

The adjustments to the quotation emphasize the most important points and help the author bring the focus back to a more open-ended idea of medicine as including a range of healing practices. As you make these adjustments to quotations, follow these two rules.

Rule 1 for modifying quotations. To offer explanations or make adjustments in meaning so that quotations fit the flow of your text, use brackets with clarifying text inside, as in this example:

> Even alternative medicine proponents are calling on science, "claim[ing] such proofs [gathered from empirical studies] are increasingly available" (Goode).

Rule 2 for modifying quotations. To remove some material from a quotation, use ellipses points. For text removed in the middle of a sentence, use three points separated by spaces. For text removed at the end of a sentence, use four points with the first point next to the last word of the sentence and spaces between the other points. Examples of these two different approaches to editing a quotation are shown in relation to the original quotation:

> *Original quotation:* "One of the most common misperceptions—unfortunately common—is to conflate bioscience and biomedicine, typically claiming that 'only' biomedicine is 'scientific.'"
>
>   *Modified quotation:* "One of the most common misperceptions . . . [is] that 'only' biomedicine is 'scientific.'"
>
>   *Modified quotation with different emphasis:* "One of the most common misperceptions . . . is to conflate bioscience and biomedicine. . . ."

You will also need to know something about how to format and punctuate quotations. Remember these two rules:

Rule 1 for punctuating quotations. Set off a quotation that appears within a quotation with single quotation marks:

> Robert Park complains that an NIH report "discusses various magical cures, ranging from 'Lakota medicine wheels' to 'mental healing at a distance,' as though they deserve serious attention" (Park 49).

Rule 2 for punctuating quotations. Place punctuation marks within quotation marks for sentences without parenthetical citation and place punctuation outside of parentheses for quotations with citations:

> Cassidy contends that all kinds of medical practices "could function as complements to one another." She explains that, "a patient with cancer might seek acupuncture as a complement to chemotherapy" (613).

Although you will need to learn to follow the requirements for formatting quotations, remember also to keep the big picture in mind; that is, using the words of others is part of the conversational nature of research and one of the social dimensions of writing. Use the opportunity to better understand the thoughts of others and more effectively present your own ideas.

Finally, a good strategy for becoming more adept at weaving the words of others into your compositions, at least in your written work, is to learn something about attributive tags (sometimes called signal phrases), which are the terms you use to introduce a quotation and associate it with its author. You could use a standard way of introducing some quotations:

> According to Claire M. Cassidy, "authors need to take care to *know their subject* and *avoid making statements that belittle* [Complementary Alternative Medicine]" (615, emphasis in the original). According to Robert Park, we need to ask "Why [have scientists been] timid about condemning this sort of pseudo-scientific nincompoopery? [associated with Complementary Alternative Medicine]" (Park 50).

Or you can refine your message by adjusting the way you attribute quotations to sources:

> Claire M. Cassidy warns that "authors need to take care to *know their subject* and *avoid making statements that belittle* [Complementary Alternative Medicine]" (615, emphasis in the original); however, Robert Park seems to ignore Cassidy's concern by asking "Why [have scientists been] timid about condemning this sort of pseudo-scientific nincompoopery?" (Park 50).

Again, it's up to you to compose text that effectively leads up to and then transitions out of citations, making choices about what you want to say and about how to weave the pieces of text together to say it. The list (on page 380) of attributive tags (or signal phrases) can be of help. As you incorporate source material using tags and phrases like these, think also about how to adjust your language and punctuation to weave quotations smoothly into your text.

TABLE 16.1. Attributive tags, or signal phrases.

according to	acknowledges	adds
admits	affirms	agrees
alludes	argues	asserts
attests	believes	challenges
characterizes	chronicles	claims
comments	compares	concludes
concurs	confirms	contends
contrasts	counters	declares
delineates	demonstrates	demurs
denies	discloses	discounts
disputes	documents	emphasizes
endorses	explains	expresses
extrapolates	grants	highlights
hypothesizes	illustrates	implies
indicates	insists	maintains
narrates	notes	objects
observes	opines	points out
posits	presents	proposes
purports	reasons	recounts
refers	reflects	refutes
reiterates	rejects	relates
remarks	replies	reports
responds	reveals	shows
states	submits	suggests
supports	theorizes	thinks
understands	underscores	verifies
wonders	worries	writes

Know It   **Strategies for Summarizing, Paraphrasing, and Using Quotations**

LO

Learning
Objective 16.4

- Summarize with the aim of capturing the gist of a source, focusing on the main points and striving for objectivity. Summaries can use brief quotations.
- Use paraphrasing to translate the ideas in a source into your own words. Paraphrasing gives you more control as you adapt materials to your topic, but you must still maintain the intent of the original.
- Watch out for plagiarism. Some terminology in a source can also appear in a summary or paraphrase, but any specific borrowed phrases or terms coined by the author must be cited.
- Learn the ins and outs of incorporating the words of others into your work. Quotations are crucial for effective research projects. You can use the words of others when they provide the right information or phrasing. You need to use quotations as evidence to give your writing authority.
- Choose the right attributive tags, or signal phrases, to ensure that quotations accurately express your meaning, reference their sources, and help create good transitional flow. Modifying and correctly punctuating quotations helps clarify your meaning.

Ask
Questions
& Make
Decisions   **Exercises for Summarizing, Paraphrasing, and Using Quotations**

LO

Learning
Objective 16.5

1. Locate an article at least three pages long that is related to a topic of interest. Read the article carefully, and then distill the piece into a summary of no more than eight sentences. Revise the summary to just five sentences, and then to just three. Is there a point at which the summary no longer does justice to the piece?
2. Pursuing a topic of interest, find a resource that you might not normally associate with research—perhaps a film, song, painting, photograph, TV advertisement, city park, etc. Write a paraphrase that translates the item into words, capturing its substance and relationship to your topic.
3. Look over the list of attributive tags, or signal phrases, on page 380. Think about situations in which you would use several of the less familiar tags or

signals. How would these choices influence the points you might make? Think of one or two additional tags or signal phrases that might be added to the list and what they might accomplish in an essay.

Zoom **Out**   Reflecting on Evaluating and Composing with Sources

- **Evaluating and composing with sources is just one element of a larger research process.** Researchers ask questions, find information, and process materials. All of these activities play out in varying degrees as you read and write using research.

- **For researchers, evaluating sources is like breathing: you just need to do it all the time.** Use the rhetorical situation to guide you, asking questions about author(s), audience, purpose, context, genre, and medium. Also look at the construction of sources themselves. Researching is nothing without evaluation.

- **Begin to see research as *interacting* with sources, not just reading them.** Annotate materials and take notes. Expand the reading process to ask questions, discover insights, and sketch out ideas.

- **Writing is also directly connected to research and is actually an important part of the research process.** Write summaries and paraphrases to synthesize your research and begin composing. Learn to use quotations to explain your research and express your ideas.

For additional information and practice with the learning objectives in this chapter, go to www.mycomplab.com, Resources > Research > The Research Assignment > Evaluating Sources.

CHAPTER 17

Documenting Sources in MLA and APA Style

Zoom In Key Concepts and Learning Objectives

After studying this chapter, you should be able to:

17.1 Incorporate quoted sources accurately into your paper to build credibility with your readers.

17.2 Cite sources in the body of your paper so your readers can follow your reasoning and recognize where you found your sources.

17.3 Provide complete and accurate citations for your sources at the end of your paper, using the conventions of MLA or APA style.

Anumber of academic disciplines have developed their own citation styles for research. Some of the most frequently used styles are those of the American Psychological Association (APA), the Council of Science Editors (CSE), and the Modern Language Association (MLA). For work in the humanities, the MLA style is the standard. You can get complete MLA style information in the *MLA Handbook for Writers of Research Papers*, 7th edition (2009). APA style is commonly used in the social sciences. For APA style information you can refer to the *Publication Manual of the American Psychological Association*, 6th edition (2010). We provide detailed information on MLA and APA styles in this chapter.

MLA Style

MLA citation style generally consists of an in-text or parenthetical citation and a list of works cited. The in-text citations alert readers to the use of materials from a source and provide a reference to that source. The works cited page contains the bibliographic information for each reference.

Learning
Objective 17.1

Creating In-Text or Parenthetical Citations

There are several ways of adding references to sources in the body of your projects. One method is to reference the source as you introduce a quotation, usually using an attributive tag (see pages 379–80). The very first time you cite a source, you should provide the full name of the author and, ideally, provide the reader with some idea of who the person is. Once you have introduced the source, you can use the last name and, if materials are understood to be from the same source, you can provide just the page number. In most instances, you will use only part of a source and will use page numbers to indicate the portions you have used. The following excerpt shows this approach:

> Claire M. Cassidy, editor of *The Journal of Alternative and Complementary Medicine*, suggests that the terms we use to describe healing practices "are not mere labels, but carry weight—the weight of history, social convention, perceptual habit, plus economic and political clout" (613). The names we assign to medical practices color our perceptions of them. We can see this by thinking about the replacement of the term *unorthodox* with the term *alternative*, a change that "represented an improvement because it is socially easier to choose an 'alternative' than something unorthodox"

(Cassidy 613). But even this change was inadequate because "all medicines are alternative to one another" (613).

LO

Learning
Objective 17.2

Citing an entire source or a source with no page numbers

If you are summarizing the overall argument of a source or referencing key ideas that appear frequently, you can indicate this approach by providing the source information in parentheses. You can also cite the entire source for materials that lack page numbers (Web pages, films, television broadcasts, etc.). (You may also prefer to integrate information for these sources into attributive tags as you introduce a source.) If a source indicates its paragraph numbers, then you can refer to the appropriate paragraph (e.g., par. 4).

> While some argue alternative medicine diverts attention from what they see as more effective biomedical treatments (Park), others accept practices like touch therapy since "despite a lack of data on its effectiveness, many doctors are willing to give such treatments a shot, because gentle touching does no harm" (Bhanoo par. 4).
>
> Despite potential benefits, alternative treatments for pain raise a number of concerns when applied to children (*Nightline*).

Citing sources with no author listed

As you cite sources, especially online sources, you will encounter some that are harder to attribute because they don't list an author. When information comes from unnamed sources, of course, assess it carefully. If the materials are credible, you can attribute the citation using either an entity (such as an organization) or the title of the source:

> Because of the public's demand and the popularity of CAM, in 2000, the United States government released a report from the White House Commission on Complementary and Alternative Medicine Policy in order to regulate and "address issues related to access and delivery of CAM, priorities for research, and the need for better education of consumers and health care professionals about CAM" (White House 1). The National Institutes of Health invested some $300 million in CAM research in 2008 (Bhanoo).
>
> Similarly, the Mayo clinic suggests that "what's considered alternative medicine changes constantly as more and more treatments undergo rigorous study" (Mayo), as evidenced by the increased use of alternative pain treatments that corresponds with recent "extensive research to advance scientific understanding of acupuncture" ("Introduction to Acupuncture").

Citing more than one source in the same sentence

Sometimes you need to cite multiple sources to support the same idea in your paper. To cite more than one source in a single parenthetical reference, separate the sources with a semicolon:

> Most holistic clinics employ medical doctors, registered nurses, counselors, and physiotherapists together to promote a strong emphasis on prevention (Walton 412; Bhanoo par. 4).

You will need to focus on the specifics of how you introduce and acknowledge sources as you weave them into your text. Remember that you need to provide the citations that will help readers connect all the quotations and ideas you have borrowed to the original sources. You also want to decide how to weave into your writing quotations and citations in ways that will best express your ideas and engage your readers.

Creating a List of Works Cited

The second step in documenting your research is to provide detailed information that will help readers understand the nature of your sources and track down the materials.

Basic entry

Each type of source may have specific requirements for citation, but there are also some general rules that determine the format for basic entries and guide the citation of more specific sources. Lists of works cited are ordered alphabetically using the last name of the first author. (If no authors are listed, then the title is used.) MLA style also abbreviates elements like months, places, reference words, and publishers. Also include an indication of the medium of the source. The entries are listed on a separate page from the rest of the essay using double-spaced text and a hanging indent (which indents by five spaces all but the first line of any entry).

Books   The names of the author (or authors) begin an entry. The first (or a single) author is stated with last name first, a comma, and the first name (Smith, Joe). Additional authors are stated in normal order, with first name coming first. All authors are separated by commas, and a period comes at the end of all the authors—Smith, Joe, Mary Jones, and Jane Doe. The title follows the author information. Book titles are set in italics. Capitalize all words except articles and prepositions of any length, and capitalize any first word after a colon and any word (or words) in a hyphenated compound. The entry concludes with publication information that includes the city (followed by a colon), publisher, and date. End the entry by listing the medium of the source.

WN

VIDEO
31. Bibliographic Software

LO

Learning Objective 17.3

A book by a single author

Perko, Sandra J. *The Homeopathic Therapeutic Subject Reference: A Homeopathic Practice Guidebook for Physicians and Health Care Practitioners*. San Antonio: Benchmark Homeopathic Publications, 2005. Print.

Two or more books by same author

Notice that for the second book, the author's name (which would have been repeated) is replaced by three hyphens and a period.

Northrup, Christiane. *Women's Bodies, Women's Wisdom*. New York: Bantam Books, 1998. Print.

---. *Wisdom of Menopause*. New York: Bantam, 2001. Print.

A book by two or more authors

Frahm, Anne E., and David J. Frahm. *Cancer Battle Plan: Six Strategies for Beating Cancer from a Recovered "Hopeless Case."* New York: Penguin Putnam, 1992. Print.

A book by more than three authors

Lewis, Parker, et al. *Women in Eastern Culture: The Right to Education*. New York: Putnam, 2002. Print.

A book by a corporate or government author or entity

Committee on Identifying and Preventing Medication Errors, Board on Health Care Services. *Preventing Medication Errors*. Washington: Nat. Acad. P, 2007. Print.

A book by an unknown or unidentified author

The Family Circle Encyclopedia of Cooking. Danbury: Lexicon Publications, 1990. Print.

An edited collection

Ryan, Alan, ed. *The Penguin Book of Vampire Stories: Two Centuries of Great Stories with a Bite*. New York: Penguin, 1998. Print.

A book with an author and editor

Jacobs, Harriet A. *Incidents in the Life of a Slave Girl*. Ed. Jean Fagan Yellin. Cambridge: Harvard UP, 1987. Print.

A work in an anthology or collection

Crane, Stephen. "The Open Boat." *Literature: An Introduction to Fiction, Poetry, and Drama*. 9th ed. Ed. X. J. Kennedy and Dana Gioia. New York: Pearson, 2005. 215–33. Print.

A dictionary and entry

"Mecamylamine." *Webster's New Collegiate Dictionary*. 9th ed. 1986. Print.

A reference book and entry

Alston, Garvis D. "Coleopteran." *The Encyclopedia Britannica*. 2002 ed. Print.

Articles   The names of the author (or authors) begin an entry and are stated the same way as for a book (see examples above). The title follows the author information in quotation marks. Publication information varies depending on the frequency and format of the publication. For articles retrieved using a database, retrieval information is added.

An article in a scholarly journal

Trainor, Jennifer Seibel. "The Emotioned Power of Racism: An Ethnographic Portrait of an

      All-White High School." *College Composition and Communication* 60.1 (2008):

      82–110. Print.

An article in a scholarly journal numbered by issue

Fredrickson, Kathy. "Is There a Clock in This Sabbatical?" *Teaching English in the Two-Year*

      College 3 (2003): 277–80. Print.

An article from an online journal

Anderson, Daniel. "Prosumer Approaches to New Media Composition: Production and

      Consumption in Continuum." *Kairos: A Journal of Rhetoric, Technology, and Pedagogy*

      8.1 (2003): n. pag. Web. 1 Feb. 2009.

An article from a newspaper

Hilmantel, Robin. "Poor Pluto: Everyone's Favorite Dwarf Planet." *The Chapel Hill News* 4 Feb.

      2009: A1+. Print.

An article in a magazine

Barry, John, and Evan Thomas. "Obama's Vietnam." *Newsweek* 9 Feb. 2009: 30–35. Print.

A magazine article with an unlisted author

"Taking Time with Your Kids." *Parent's Choice* 5 Aug. 2005: 23. Print.

An editorial

"Our Future Is Now." Editorial. *The Progressive Farmer* Feb. 2009: 6. Print.

A letter to the editor

Wilkinson, Francis. Letter. *The Week*. 6 Feb. 2009: 1–2. Print.

FIGURE 17.1

Citing an article retrieved from a library database.

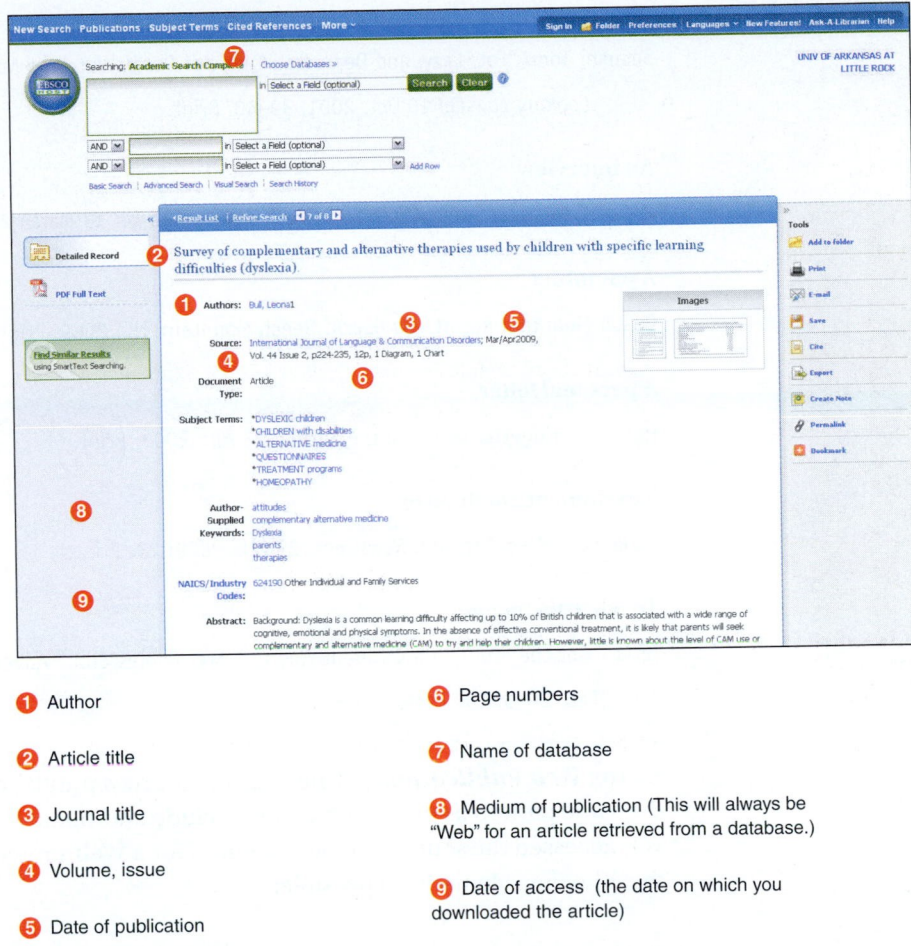

1. Author
2. Article title
3. Journal title
4. Volume, issue
5. Date of publication
6. Page numbers
7. Name of database
8. Medium of publication (This will always be "Web" for an article retrieved from a database.)
9. Date of access (the date on which you downloaded the article)

Format for citing an article retrieved from a library database

Author. "Article Title." *Journal Title*. Volume.Issue (Date): page numbers. *Name of Database*. Medium of publication. Date of access.

Bull, Leona. "Survey of Complementary and Alternative Therapies Used by Children with Specific Learning Difficulties (Dyslexia)." *International Journal of Language & Communication Disorders* 44.2 (2009): 224–35. *Academic Search Complete*. Web. 1 March 2009.

A review of a film, book, or performance

Smarsh, Tom. "Fat, Lazy, and Depressed." Rev. of *Better Nutrition Now*, by Henri Levinson.

   Cooking Low-Cal 10 Oct. 2001: 39–40. Print.

An interview

Meyer, George. Interview by David Owen. *The New Yorker* 13 March 2000. 25–28. Print.

A pamphlet

Beech Mountain Resort. *Ski Beech*. Beech Mountain, NC, 2009. Print.

A personal letter

Hobson, Bridgette. Letter to the author. 23 Apr. 2003. Print.

A cartoon or comic strip

Luckovich, Mike. Cartoon. *Newsweek*. 23 Feb. 2009: 23. Print.

An advertisement

Zetia. "Get the Story on a Different Way to Lower Cholesterol." Advertisement. *Newsweek* 23

   Feb. 2009: 15. Print.

Citing Web Publications   Citations for sources published on the Web follow the same pattern as print sources, but include additional information about how you accessed the source. A typical citation for a Web source includes as many of the following elements as possible:

1. Name of the author
2. Title of the work
3. Title of the Web site (italicized)
4. Publisher or sponsor of the site (or use *N.p.* for "no publisher listed")
5. Date of publication (or use *n.d.* for "no date listed")
6. Medium of publication (Web)
7. Date of access (day, month, year)

   Include the URL (Web address) for a source only if you cannot find the information listed above or if there is no other way in which to reference the source.

FIGURE 17.2
Citing a source published on the Web.

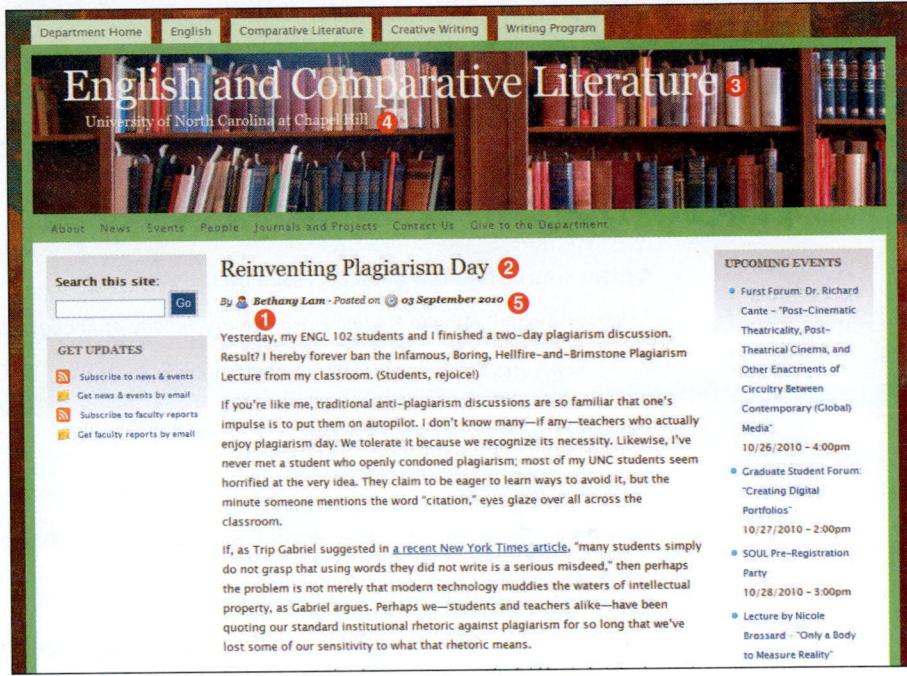

1 Name of the author

2 Title of the article

3 Title of the Web site

4 Publisher of the site

5 Date of publication

Format for citing a source published on the Web

Author. "Article Title." *Title of the Web Site*. Publisher of the Web Site, or N.p., date of
publication, or n.d. Medium of publication. Date of access.

Lam, Bethany. "Reinventing Plagiarism Day." *English and Comparative Literature*. U of North
Carolina, 3 Sept. 2010. Web. 14 Oct. 2010.

A Web page with a known author

Keim, Brandon. "Could Alternative Medicine Hurt Women's Fertility?" *Wired*. Condé Nast
Digital, 5 July 2007. Web. 23 Aug. 2010.

A Web page with an organization as the author

United States. Natl. Park Service. "NPS Oil Spill Response." *National Park Service*. Dept. of
the Interior, 28 July 2010. Web. 23 Aug. 2010.

A Web page, author's name unknown

The Living Prophecy. 13 Moon, 2005. Web. 26 July 2008.

A print source that has been accessed on the Web

Csikszentmihalyi, Mihaly. *Finding Flow: The Psychology of Engagement with Everyday Life*.
New York: Basic Books, 1997. Google Book Search. Web. 16 Oct. 2010.

Citing Other Non-Print Sources

An e-mail message

Graft, Terry. "Re: Insomnia." Message to the author. 6 Dec. 2008. E-mail.

A posting to an online discussion group or blog

Drew, Jan. "Alternative Medicine Goes Mainstream." 23 Aug. 2003. Online posting. Web. 1
Mar. 2009. <news:misc.health.alternative>.

SunProf [Thomas Sol]. "Re: All Education is DIY." *Digital Digs*. Alex-Reid.Net. 9 May 2010.
Web. 17 May 2010.

A film

Capote. Dir. Bennett Miller. Perf. Philip Seymour Hoffman, Chris Cooper, and Catherine
Keener. United Artists and Sony Pictures Classics, 2005. Film.

A television or radio broadcast

"Liberty! The American Revolution." *American Experience*. Narr. Edward Herrmann. Writ. and
Prod. Michael Hutchinson. PBS. Twin Cities Public Television. 23–25 Nov. 1997.
Television.

A performance

Altar Boyz. By Kevin Del Aguila. Dir. Stafford Arima. Perf. Michael Kadin Craig, Neil Haskell,
and Travis Nesbitt. Schubert Theater, New York. 1 Mar. 2005. Performance.

A work of art

Whistler, James McNeill. *Whistler's Mother*. 1871. Oil on canvas. Musée d'Orsay, Paris.

A photograph

Anderson, Daniel. *Gila Wilderness, New Mexico.* Personal photograph by author. 8 Aug. 2005.

A music recording

U2. "Angel of Harlem." *Rattle and Hum.* Sun Studio, 1988. CD.

Sample Paper in MLA Format

As you wrap up work on an essay, you can also rely on the MLA style guidelines to assist with the formatting and ensure that the paper is ready to be read. (Be sure to check with your instructor about any specific formatting requirements for your assignment.) Double space your entire paper. Use a standard font and size (e.g., Times, 12 point). Set your margins at 1 inch all around. Add a heading that lists your name, your instructor, your course, and the date. Add a descriptive title to the essay. Add a header at the top of all pages that includes your last name and the page number. Label any figures or tables used in the essay using an abbreviation for the word figure (Fig.), a number, a title, and source information (see page 396). Ensure that your citations and entries for works cited are complete and correct. You can look at Allison Johns's essay "Both/And: Complementary and Alternative Medicine" below to see all of these elements.

Focus on
Student
Writing

1"

Double-spaced text

Allison Johns

Professor Dan Anderson

English 101

6 Feb. 2009

Both/And: Complementary Alternative Medicine

Indent 1/2" → There always seems to be some sort of controversy or skepticism when a newcomer pops up in

the medical field, especially if that newcomer offers methods that differ from conventional practice.

1" → Over the past three decades, complementary and alternative medicine (CAM) has made a name for it-

self. This non-Western or unconventional approach is steadily becoming more popular and widespread

in the United States. Perhaps this trend is happening largely because CAM is said to not only treat the

illness or problem but also support whole body health with the intention of providing prevention of

future health problems. However, as the movement continues to grow, some conventional health care

professionals are increasingly questioning the effectiveness of CAM; a few even go so far as to call

this movement a fraud and a voodoo moneymaker. Is CAM a cash scheme or a helpful new approach?

Perhaps one of the biggest challenges in exploring this question has to do with the terms used

to discuss the issue. Claire M. Cassidy traces some of the difficulties, showing that there has been an

evolution of terms used to describe nontraditional medicine. In 1992 at a meeting of the National In-

stitutes of Health, the term *unorthodox* was replaced by the term *alternative*. Cassidy sees this evolu-

tion as an improvement, but also as only a partial measure because the term *alternative* suggests that

its opposite, conventional medicine, is the norm. To address some of the problems of terminology,

Cassidy proposes that we use *biomedicine* rather than *traditional medicine* or *conventional medicine* to   1"

describe approaches that emphasize medical doctors, pharmacists, drugs, or surgery (Cassidy 613).

Cassidy suggests that these debates over terms reflect an "Us versus Them" (615) relation-

ship between CAM and biomedicine. This mentality associates biomedicine with technology,

1"

science, and complexity while complementary approaches are often reduced to simple alternative practices. A closer look at CAM, however, reveals a range of skill sets, practices, therapies, and techniques that are often overlooked:

> The subtle game of "Us versus Them" often has a scalar component. Recently, an author claimed that Chinese Medicine has little to offer because "the five elements and *yin–yang* theory are as nothing compared to the richness of biomedicine." Had an author remarked that biomedicine had little to offer besides "the idea of infection and the idea of metabolic abnormality," any Western reader would have objected, because we are aware of how much these few words hide in the way of knowledge and complexity. *The same level of complexity* lies behind the ideas of Chinese Medicine, and this point applies equally to any World Medicine. Authors need to take care to *know their subject and avoid making statements that belittle* (Cassidy 615, emphasis in the original).

Cassidy's main point is that we need to use more care in labeling all kinds of healing practices and that doing so will help us appreciate the complexity of CAM. The most common practices of CAM include applied kinesiology, homeopathy, naturopathy, acupuncture, chiropractic, and herbal treatments. There is more complexity here than first appears.

Unfortunately, with complexity come other questions. Because complementary and alternative medicine encompasses a vast array of practices to treat health issues, it tends to get a bad rap by association with a few questionable practices that are grouped under its umbrella. As long as CAM is associated with the catch-all term *alternative*, there will always be easy targets that can bring its effectiveness into doubt. The key to exploring the value of CAM more deeply, then, is to focus on the complementary elements of its name. Using a term like *complementary* when talking about traditional and alternative medicine challenges the perception that these practices are competing against each other. As Cassidy puts it, "while it's commonplace to represent biomedicine as standing apart on its own small island . . . we are factually and philosophically more correct to draw a single circle encompassing *all* [kinds of healing practices]" (613, emphasis added). CAM does not propose an either/or approach. Instead, it offers a both/and conception of medicine. The easiest way to see this approach and the definition of CAM that offers the most promise is to think about holistic medicine. The true benefits of CAM come from

Double-spaced text

1"

Johns 3

understanding that medicine can complement treating symptoms with drugs or surgery by adding approaches that treat the whole body.

Many CAM followers complain that biomedical care is "fragmented and too narrowly focused on physical factors" (Walton 411). Some believers say that modern medicine lost concern for the "whole" patient, or even the patient as a person, in order to concentrate on the business aspect of cutting patient-doctor time and promoting the newest medicines for pharmaceutical companies (Goode). We might see CAM as a helpful correction to biomedicine's emphasis on drugs and the treatment of symptoms. Instead, CAM offers advice one might hope to receive in any doctor's office—eat well, exercise, avoid stress, take care of yourself. In this light, it's not surprising that CAM enjoys a good deal of popularity. According to the White House Commission on CAM policy, throughout the past thirty years, as much as 43 percent of the American population has used some form of a complementary and alternative medicine approach or product (White House Commission on CAM). You can see the appeal of CAM in the array of treatment areas represented in figure 1.

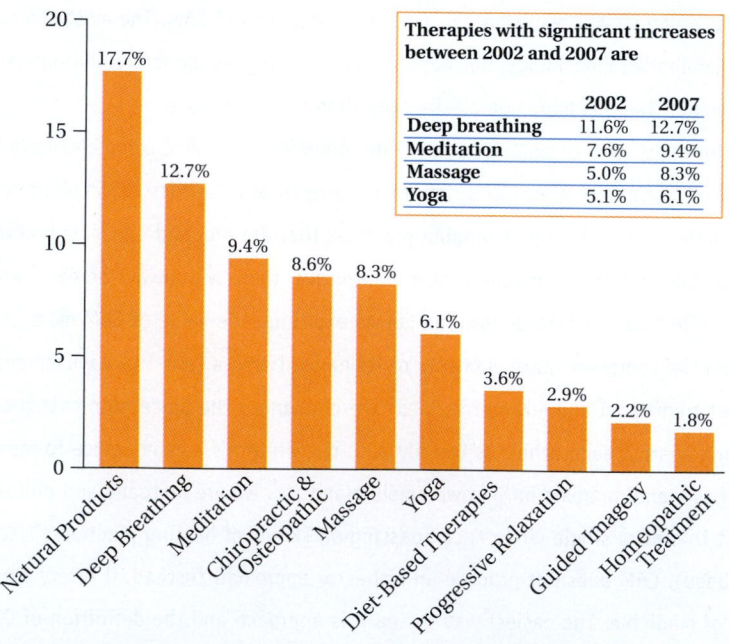

FIG. 1. Most common CAM therapies (National Center for Complementary and Alternative Medicine).

Figure label with source information

Johns 4

Figure 1 demonstrates that looking at CAM as simply good advice about staying healthy reveals only half the picture. What holistic medicine comes down to is the treatment of the entire body, which includes the mind, body, and soul (Goode). Norman Shealy, the president of the American Holistic Medical Association, explains:

> Holistic medicine uses seven basic therapies to guide practice. The first three are good nutrition, physical exercise and self regulation. . . . The remaining four: acupuncture, neuro-muscular integration, environmental medicine and spiritual awareness (defined as living according to your ideals) are also important, but either are used very specifically or involve factors less under our control (Quoted in Walton 411).

The first three of Shealy's therapies represent basic fundamentals of a healthy lifestyle. But it's when we move into the realms of the last four therapies he mentions, particularly acupuncture or spiritual awareness, that more questions arise. CAM proponents claim that these last four approaches are responsible for the many accounts of complementary therapies stepping in and fixing a health problem where biomedicine could not, accounts such as those reported by rheumatoid arthritis sufferers and chronic-fatigue patients who have been helped by acupuncture (Goode).

Opponents of CAM argue that the effectiveness of holistic medicine is made up in the patient's head. These nonbiomedical dimensions of CAM open the door for quackery and misdiagnoses, according to CAM critics. There is a fear that diseases that could have been cured by a simple conventional diagnosis will be uncared for or misdiagnosed until it is too late. To nonbelievers, complementary and alternative medicine is unscientific nonsense. University of Maryland Physics Professor Robert Park has said that the public should be "protected from fraudulent or misguided mental 'healers'" and asks, "Where is the outcry? Why . . . [have scientists been] timid about condemning this sort of pseudo-scientific nincompoopery?" (Park 50). A 1992 a report by the American Medical Association details a study that "looked at faith healing, acupuncture and naturopathy and concluded curtly that none of them makes any scientific sense at all" (Goode).

A huge problem with CAM centers on the fact that it is very difficult to find scientific accounts of successful use and that it lacks the power of the scientific terminology associated with biomedicine. The problem lies in what qualifies as proof or evidence. Consider the case of acupuncture. The traditional Chinese medicine concept of balance between yin and yang informs the practice of acupuncture. Yin (cold or passive energy) and yang (hot or active energy) must be in balance, and blockages of crucial meridian points can inhibit the flow of qi, jeopardizing the health of the patient. Using more than 2,000 points on the body, acupuncture targets between fourteen and twenty meridian channels to help restore the balance between yin and yang (National Center for CAM, *Introduction to Acupuncture*). We can see the complexity that Cassidy points toward beneath the terms *yin* and *yang*. But how are we to measure balance between yin and yang? As Paul T. Holland puts it, "clinical studies have documented acupuncture's effects, but they have not been able to fully explain how acupuncture works within the framework of the Western system. . . ." (Holland). But these questions regarding CAM research are not insurmountable. The first priority is to systemize research efforts. Much of this work is already under way. Because of the public's demand and the popularity of CAM, in 2000, the United States government released a report from the White House Commission on Complementary and Alternative Medicine Policy in order to regulate and "address issues related to access and delivery of CAM, priorities for research, and the need for better education of consumers and health care professionals about CAM" (White House 1). The National Institutes of Health invested some $300 million in CAM research in 2008 (Bhanoo).

The benefits of CAM lie in the fact that it does not try to choose between either one approach or the other. This blending of approaches can be seen in the number of holistic or integrative clinics opening up across the country. The Johns Hopkins University operates one such clinic, its Integrative Medicine & Digestive Center. Sindya N. Bhanoo explains that "the center's link with Hopkins is part of a trend toward integrating CAM with conventional medicine" (Bhanoo HE01). The number of hospitals offering some form of CAM treatment has risen from just 8 percent in 1998 to 27 percent in 2006 (Bhanoo). Most holistic clinics employ medical doctors, registered nurses, counselors, and physiotherapists together to promote a strong emphasis on prevention (Walton 412). Clinics and researchers are beginning to acknowledge the importance of treating the whole patient. It's clear that a holistic approach to health care, an approach that recognizes that the mind, body, and spirit need not be in competition, is not a quack scheme or a threat but rather a healthy complement to biomedicine.

Johns 6

Works Cited

Bhanoo, Sindya N. "Alternatives Enter the Mainstream: Unconventional Care Wins Some Converts." *Washington Post* 16 Sep. 2008, HE01+. Print.

Cassidy, Claire M. "Some Terminology Needs for Writers, Researchers, Practitioners, and Editors as We Move toward Integrating Medicines." Editorial. *The Journal of Alternative and Complementary Medicine* 14.6 (2008): 613–15. Print.

Goode, Stephen. "Whole Bodies, Divided Minds." *Insight on the News.* 15 July 1996. Web.

Holland, Paul T. "Re: Acupuncture: It's as Good as Drugs for Treating Pain." 2 May 2005. Online Posting Web. 3 Feb. 2009.

National Center for Complementary and Alternative Medicine. "An Introduction to Acupuncture." 11 Jan. 2009. Web.

—. "The Use of Complementary and Alternative Medicine in the United States." 11 Jan. 2009. Web. 3 Feb. 2009.

Park, Robert L. "Is There a Rebellion against Scientific Knowledge?" *USA Today Magazine* July 1996: 48–51. Print.

Walton, Susan. "Holistic Medicine." *Science News* 116.24 (2008): 410–12. *Academic Search Elite.* Web. 3 Feb. 2009.

United States. White House Commission on Complementary and Alternative Medicine Policy. *Final Report.* Mar. 2002. Web. 3 Feb. 2009.

Works Cited begins on a new page

1/2" hanging indent

Double-spaced text

WN

VIDEO
47. Formatting an Essay

APA Style

APA style relies on references to sources made in the body of a project and then a reference list at the end of a project that provides complete citation information for each source.

Creating In-Text or Parenthetical References

References in the body of the project follow an author-date-page number model that lists the author's last name, the date of publication, and the page(s) where the information can be found. You will include these citations both for quotations inserted in the text and for summaries and paraphrases. When it comes to electronic sources, APA style calls for following the same author, date, page number format. In instances where no date is available, you can substitute the phrase "n.d." for the date. In instances where no page numbers are available, you can use the phrase "para." to indicate the paragraph number where the information occurs or list headings in a document where information can be found.

The basic APA in-text citation can be handled in two ways. You can provide author information in a signal phrase, and then include date and page information in parentheses. Or you can include all of the information in parentheses after the citation:

Author Indicated in Signal Phrase

Das (2009) introduces the fact that white wine contains "cardioprotective antioxidants," similar to red wines (p. 3).

Author Indicated in Parentheses

In researching healthy compounds in white wine it is found that, "although white wines do not contain resveratrol in any appreciable amount, they contain other cardioprotective antioxidants" (Das, 2009, p. 3).

Additional types of works can be incorporated into the text following the basic signal phrase or parenthesis models. Here are some common examples:

Source with Two Authors

Ernest and Resch (1993) report that "fibrinogen can be a determiner of heart attacks" (p. 960).

"Fibrinogen can be a determiner of heart attacks" (Ernest & Resch, 1993, p. 960).

Source with More Than Two Authors

Antonini, Ferracuti, and Pennisi (1989) identify wine poisoning as a source of "lead intoxication" (pp. 283–289).

Lead intoxication "is a direct result of wine poisoning" (Antonini, Ferracuti, & Pennisi, 1989, pp. 283–289).

Note: after the first in-text reference to a work by more than two authors you can use the phrase "et al." after listing the first author: Antonini et al. (1989) also suggest that wine poisoning can be difficult to detect.

Source with More Than Six Authors

List the first author's name, and then use the phrase "et al." To indicate additional authors: (Hendricks et al., 1994) demonstrate that moderate amounts of wine reduce blood clotting (p. 1004).

Moderate amounts of wine taken with dinner yield reduced clotting the following morning (Hendricks et al., 1994, p. 1004).

Two or More Works by the Same Author Published in the Same Year

List the source, and then add a lower case letter for each source published in the same year:

Since ischaemic strokes are by far the more common, one might conclude "that the net effect of drinking, especially of moderate drinking, would be to reduce overall stroke risk" (Gill et al., 1991b, p. 9).

Works by an Unknown Author

List the title of the work, using italics for books or quotation marks for articles:

Additional reports argue that the potential benefits of wine consumption are outweighed by the dangers of birth defects for pregnant mothers ("Drinking Alcohol While Pregnant," 2008).

Works by an Organization or Agency

Use the name of the organization or agency as the author:

Although many women are aware that heavy drinking during pregnancy can cause birth defects, many do not realize that moderate or even light drinking also may harm the fetus" (March of Dimes, 2008, para. 2).

A Work by a Secondary Source

Bryan Walsh voiced his opinion when he stated "Americans can no longer afford to eat cheap food" (as cited in *Time Magazine,* 2009, p. 47).

VIDEO
31. Bibliographic
Software

Creating a List of References

The reference list will provide the bibliographic information for the sources referenced in the in-text citations within the body of the project. The basic format is to provide authors' names (last name first), dates, titles, and publication source information. Alphabetize the list of entries, setting the first line of each entry flush left on the page and the indenting each subsequent line five spaces.

Basic entry

Here are some of the standard expectations for APA reference listings:

- **Authors.** APA lists of references include the last name of authors, but only use their initials for first names. Authors' names are listed in inverse order (last name first).
- **Titles.** Capitalize the first word and all proper nouns in titles. For titles of books or longer works, use italicized text. Do not put article titles in quotation marks.
- **Publication source information.** Publication information lists the city in which the publisher is located. For lesser-known cities, include state or country information. Information also includes the name of the publisher. You can shorten lengthier publisher's names (e.g., "Summit Educational Press" becomes "Summit").
- **Interviews, e-mails, and personal communications.** No citation information is given in the reference list for these items; instead, include an in-text, parenthetical reference citing an instance of personal communication and including the source's name and the date of the exchange.

Books

A book by a single author

Lanham, R. (2006). *The economics of attention: style and substance in the age of information*. Chicago: University of Chicago Press.

A book by more than one author

Bolter, J. D. & Grusin, R. (2002). *Remediation: Understanding new media*. Cambridge: MIT Press.

A book in electronic form

Butler, J. M. (2005). *Forensic DNA typing: Biology, technology, and genetics of STR markers* (2nd ed.) [Kindle edition]. Retrieved from http://www.amazon.com/dp/B001UN2WHA

Book Chapters, Journal and Magazine Articles, and Other Publications

In addition to the standard expectations for APA format, you will need to pay attention to a few details related to articles. Include issue and volume information. For dates, include the month and day when citing an article in a newspaper or magazine. Here are some examples:

A book, chapter in an edited collection

Feagin, J. & Vera, H. (2002). Confronting one's own racism. In P. S. Rothenberg (Ed.), *White privilege: Essential readings on the other side of racism* (3rd ed., pp. 153–157). New York: Worth.

An article in a reference book

Reinka, W. E. (2008). For the self-published author the low down on dealing with agents. In *The guide to literary agents* (Vol. 18, p. 80). Cincinnati, OH: Writer's Digest Books.

An article in journal with continuous pagination (used when the journal continues pagination from issue to issue within a year)

Keiswetter, A. (2008). Political Islam: A primer for the perplexed. *Foreign Service Journal, 85,* 16–22.

An article in a journal without continuous pagination (used when the journal restarts page numbering with each issue)

Ginsburg, G. S., Grover, R. L., & Ialongo, N. (2005). Parenting behaviors among anxious and non-anxious mothers: Relation with concurrent and long-term child outcomes. *Child and Family Behavior Therapy, 26*(4), 23–41.

An article in a magazine with no issue numbers

Foroohar, R., & Margolis, M. (2010, March 15). The other middle class. *Newsweek,* 42–44.

An article in a magazine with numbered issues

Viadero, D. (2009, October 14). Scholars spar over research methods used to evaluate charters. *Education Week, 29*(7), 6–7.

An article in a newspaper
Online newspaper article:

Cone, M. (2005). Federal study finds human bodies loaded with toxic compounds. *Los Angeles Times,* July 22, 2005. Retrieved from http://articles.latimes.com/2005/jul/22/nation/na-chemicals22?pg=3

Print newspaper article:

Anderson, N. (2010, March 14). Obama calls for "No Child" remake. *The Washington Post,*
        pp. A1, A5.

An article with an unknown author

Marketing your private practice. (2009). *Private Practice: Section Connection* (Issue 2),
        pp. 1, 3–5.

Online Journals, Web Sites and Non-Print Materials

A Web page with a corporate author

Sportsmedicine.com. (2010). *Physical therapy organizations.* Retrieved from http://www.
        sportsmedicine.com/node/33

A Web page with an unknown author

The Indian refugees of Southern Kansas. (2000). Retrieved from http://www.nanations.com
        /civilwar/indian-refugees.htm

An article from an online journal, no digital object identifier (DOI)

Caruso, C. (2006). Possible broad impacts of long work hours. *Industrial Health, 44,*
        531–536. Retrieved from http://www.jniosh.go.jp/old/niih/en/indu_hel/2006/pdf
        /indhealth_44_4_531.pdf

An article from an online journal with a DOI

Barregard, L., Holmberg, E., & Sallsten, G. (2009). Leukaemia incidence in people living
        close to an oil refinery. *Environmental Research, 109,* 985–990. doi:
        10.1016/envres.2009.09.001

A podcast

White House. (Producer). (2009, December 5). *President Obama's weekly radio address (12.5.09).*
        Podcast retrieved from http://www.podcastdirectory.com/podswhos/6718388

A film or video recording

Zadan, C., Meron, N., Knox, T., & Zackman, J. (Producers), & Reiner, R. (Director). (2007).
        The bucket list [motion picture]. United States: Warner Brothers.

A television or radio program

ABC News. (2005, October 3), Eating dirt: It might be good for you. [Television broadcast].

New York: ABC.

A song or audio recording

Jones, N. (2002). Nightingale. On *Come away with me* [CD]. New York, NY: Blue

Note Records.

An online forum or discussion board posting

Muir, M. (2009, November 19). Re: Travel with cat or not [msg 4]. Message posted to

http://pets.groups.yahoo.com/group/domoreforcats/

A blog posting

Anderson, D. (2009, November 5). Colleges to try crowdsourcing their IT help. Message

posted to http://thoughtpress.org/daniel/node/15

An online video posting

Anderson, D. (2008, November 24). Is he bona fide? [video file]. Video posted to http://

www.vimeo.com/2336841

Other Publications

A document, government publication

Myers, D., Olsen, R., Seftor, N., Young, J., & Tuttle, C. (2004, April). *The impacts of regular*

Upward Bound: Results from the third follow-up data collection. Washington, D.C.: U.S.

Department of Education, Policy and Program Studies Service.

Sample Paper in APA Format

WINE CONSUMPTION AND HEALTH   1

A running header with title and page numbers

WINE CONSUMPTION AND HEALTH

FRANCIS ROTHEMEL

UNIVERSITY OF NORTH CAROLINA

Title, author's name, and institution, double-spaced and centered

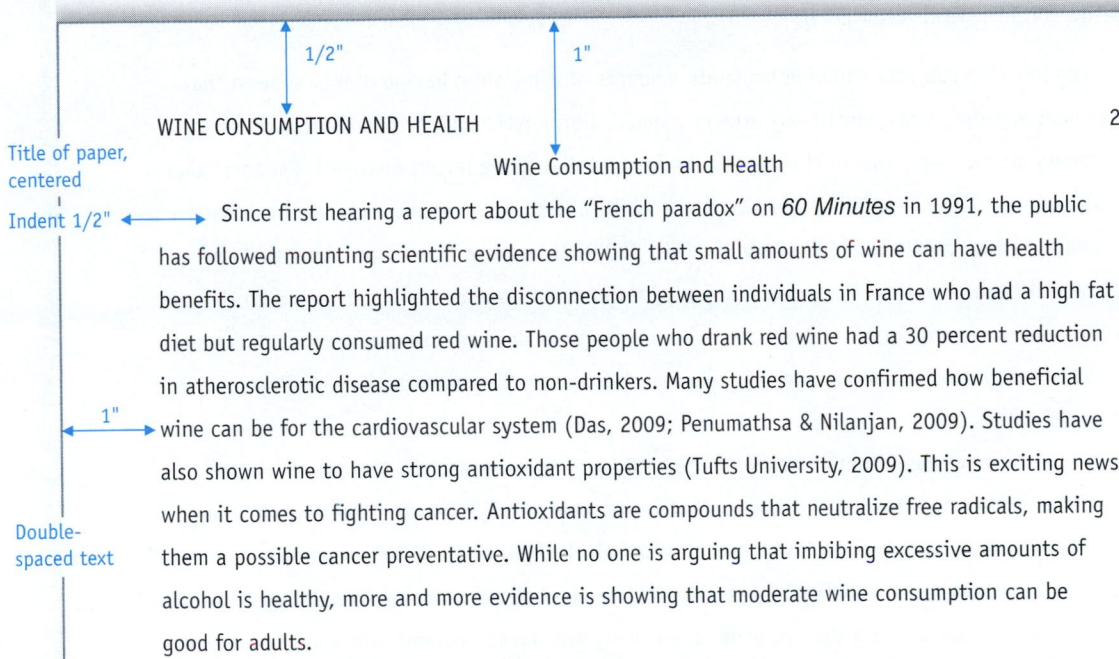

WINE CONSUMPTION AND HEALTH   2

Wine Consumption and Health

Since first hearing a report about the "French paradox" on *60 Minutes* in 1991, the public has followed mounting scientific evidence showing that small amounts of wine can have health benefits. The report highlighted the disconnection between individuals in France who had a high fat diet but regularly consumed red wine. Those people who drank red wine had a 30 percent reduction in atherosclerotic disease compared to non-drinkers. Many studies have confirmed how beneficial wine can be for the cardiovascular system (Das, 2009; Penumathsa & Nilanjan, 2009). Studies have also shown wine to have strong antioxidant properties (Tufts University, 2009). This is exciting news when it comes to fighting cancer. Antioxidants are compounds that neutralize free radicals, making them a possible cancer preventative. While no one is arguing that imbibing excessive amounts of alcohol is healthy, more and more evidence is showing that moderate wine consumption can be good for adults.

The key to many of the health benefits may be in phenols. Phenols are compounds found in the skins of grapes. Because red wines are fermented in the skins, they contain more phenols than white wines. White wine is fermented out of the skins. Many other fruits and vegetables such as broccoli and garlic contain phenols but the vinification process of winemaking unleashes the compounds and makes them active. Possible links have been established between the phenol hydroxytyrosol found in wine and improved health. Hydroxytyrosol is found in red wine in higher amounts than in other elements of a Mediterranean diet. Studies have found the presence of hydroxytyrosol to be five times as high in wine drinkers, and these amounts may synthesize with other chemicals in the body to create health benefits.

Another beneficial aspect of wine when it comes to cardiovascular disease is the role wine may play in reducing the risk of blood clotting and heart attacks. When a diseased blood vessel is at risk of blood coagulation, then retarding the clotting is of utmost importance. Fibrinogen, an important protein in coagulation, can be a determiner in heart attacks (Ernst & Resch, 1993). Alcohol reduces fibrinogen and plasma viscosity, while improving blood flow. Studies conducted with subjects imbibing moderate amounts of wine while having dinner showed that the next morning, when most heart attacks happen, fibrinolytic activity was reduced and coronary arteries were free of clots (Hendriks et al., 1994). More recent discoveries suggest that white wines could have similar benefits. Some white wines from Germany and Italy have been found to reduce oxidative stress (Bertelli et al., 2002). It has now been determined that the skins and flesh of both white and red grapes contain cardioprotective components. Even though white wine does not contain resveratrol in high amounts it does contain cinnamic acid, tyrosol, and hydroxytyrosol, which are phenolic compounds found in olives and produce cardioprotective properties.

Since most wines contain anywhere from 10 to 15 percent alcohol, the question often arises: is it the wine itself or the alcohol that imparts benefits? Research suggests that wine in particular can be more healthy than other forms of alcohol (Stockley, 1997). When wine is diluted, it still contains beneficial properties. And de-alcoholized wine improves artery flow. The concern is that when one consumes wine, one usually also takes in significant amounts of alcohol. We cannot consider the health dimensions of wine without questioning the impact of this alcohol consumption on the body. While moderate amounts of wine can be beneficial to the heart, abusing alcohol can cause blood to be too thin, and may cause high blood pressure, in turn making individuals more prone to stroke. Consuming two four-ounce glasses of red wine with the alcohol content of 10–12 percent is considered light drinking for men and one four ounce glass of red wine is light for women. Two to three glasses of wine would be considered moderate. Heavy drinking would be more than three glasses of wine each day (American Heart Association, 2009).

In every study, a common thread has been found. Light to moderate consumption of red or white wine can impart cardioprotective benefits. Studies also suggest a possible link between moderate wine consumption and cancer preventions. More recent studies connect moderate consumption with reduced risk of disabilities (Tufts University, 2009). The French paradox shows us that moderate wine consumption can stave off high blood pressure and clotting of blood vessels, protect against free radicals, and give an overall quality to one's life because of the natural health benefits. It is no wonder that in ancient medicine wine was used with a variety of other ingredients to treat ailments. In the *Talmud*, it is written that "Only where there is no wine are drugs required." And for moderate drinkers this is good news.

References

American Heart Association. (2010). Alcohol, wine and cardiovascular disease. Retrieved from
    http://www.americanheart.org/presenter.jhtml?identifier=4422

Bertelli, A. A., Migliori, M., Panichi, V., Longoni, B., Origlia, N., Ferretti, A., . . . Giovannini, L.
    (2002). Oxidative stress and inflammatory reaction modulation by white wine. *Annals of
    New York Academy of Science,* 957, 295–301. doi: 0.1111/j.1749-6632.2002.tb02929.x

Das, D. (2009). Wine and heart health. *Current Medical Literature: Cardiology,* 28(1), 1–5.

Ernst, E. & Resch, K. L. (1993). Fibrinogen as a cardiovascular risk factor: a meta-analysis and
    review of the literature. *Annals of Internal Medicine,* 118: 957–963.

Hendriks, H. F., Veenstra, J. Velthuis-Te Wierik, E. J., Shaafsma, G., & Kluft, C. (1994). Effect of
    moderate dose of alcohol with evening meal on fibrinolytic factors. *British Medical Journal,*
    308: 1003–1006.

Penumathsa, S. & Maulik, N. (2009). Resveratrol: a promising agent in promoting cardioprotection
    against coronary heart disease. *Canadian Journal of Physiology & Pharmacology,* 87(4), 275–286.

Stockley, C. (1997). Conference report: Wolf Blass Foundation International Wine and Health Con-
    ference. *Journal of Wine Research,* 8(1), 55.

Tufts University. (2009). Wine could help maximize healthy omega-3s. *Tufts University Health &
    Nutrition Letter,* 27(2), 1–2.

1/2" hanging
indent ⟵⟶

References
centered on a
new page

Double-
spaced text

For support in learning this chapter's content, follow this path in MyCompLab:
Resources › Research › Citing Sources.

Composing Strategies

The origins of hip hop reveal how artists adapt traditions.

Grandmaster Flash

Funk

1st place

Competition

Jazz

Urban Culture

Focus on Associations with Hip Hop

A Thesis Statement

Thesis Statements and Topic Sentences

Zoom In   Key Concepts and Learning Objectives

After studying this chapter, you should be able to:

18.1 Explore ideas to discover potential topics for writing projects.

18.2 Create a thesis that represents the main focus of a project.

18.3 Develop a complex thesis that does more than offer a broad statement about a topic.

18.4 Create topic sentences that articulate the focuses of paragraphs or sections of a project.

There is a lot of talk in this book about zooming in and out, about lenses for viewing a topic, and about angles of approach. These metaphors all speak to the need for writers to develop a focus as they work. For writing tasks, this area of focus is often termed a thesis. Developing a thesis is necessary in part because you simply have to scale a project into something manageable. You can't cover a topic like environmental sustainability in a five-page essay; however, you might be able to talk about a program offering tax rebates for homeowners who install wood stoves. A thesis allows you to zoom in, to narrow your focus enough so that you can cover a topic. A topic sentence performs a similar type of focusing for sections within a writing project.

WN

VIDEO
48. Narrowing
a Thesis

Developing a Thesis Statement

If you are like most writers, you sometimes struggle to get started with a project. The problem is often that the topic is not fully focused when you begin working. The good news is that your own thought processes can provide the energy for refining your approach, and this process can begin with something as unfocused as an interest in a person, thing, or idea. You might start with a broad interest in an area like hip hop music, for instance. You could identify a concern related to hip hop—perhaps artistic innovation. You could then look for connections with your idea, perhaps considering the relationship between hip hop and elements of mainstream culture. You could arrive at an initial focus that looks at the ways in which hip hop innovation is adopted by mainstream culture. Figure 18.1 illustrates this process of discovering connections.

You can see how refining the focus on innovation in hip hop music, surprisingly, requires making the topic more complex by connecting the idea with elements of mainstream culture. The resulting initial focus can be thought of as a potential thesis for a project on hip hop music.

FIGURE 18.1
An initial connection
related to a topic.

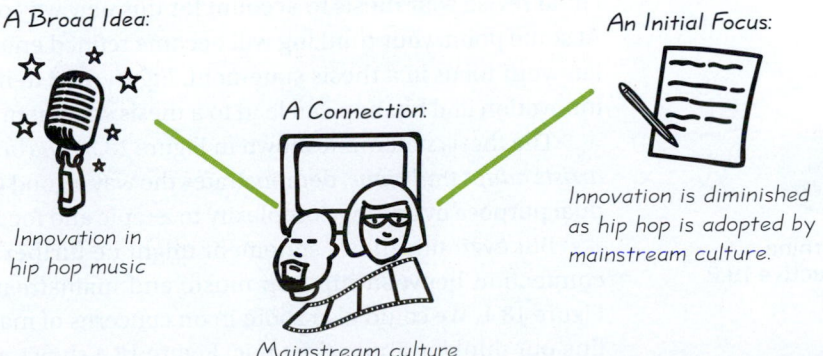

A Broad Idea:

Innovation in
hip hop music

A Connection:

Mainstream culture

An Initial Focus:

Innovation is diminished
as hip hop is adopted by
mainstream culture.

FIGURE 18.2
Zooming in to focus on
associations with hip hop.

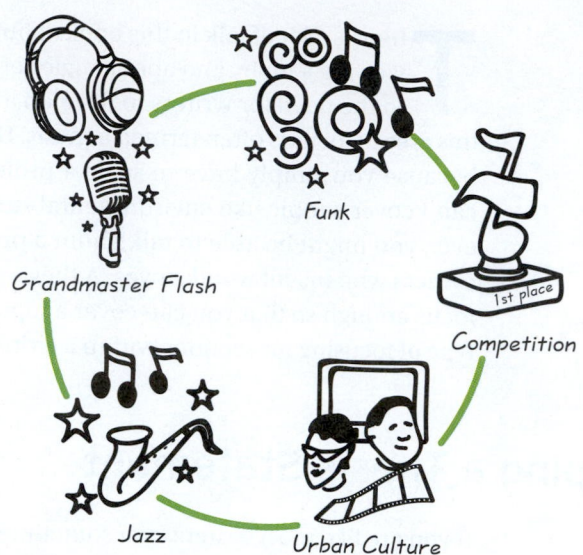

Focus on Associations with Hip Hop

LO

Learning
Objective 18.1

Recognizing a connection between hip hop and mainstream culture is really just a starting point. Figure 18.2 shows how zooming in on one aspect of a thesis idea reveals additional connections and complexities.

You could explore innovation by identifying a figure on which to focus—perhaps zooming in to consider Grandmaster Flash and the origins of hip hop. You might look at other elements of culture connected to hip hop innovation—perhaps considering musical connections in jazz or funk, the influence of urban culture, or the concern with competition found in hip hop.

After looking at the origins of hip hop and zooming in on a particular artist, you might realize that the idea of innovation is more complicated than you first supposed. You could discover that innovation does not occur in isolation but involves adapting and responding to musical influences and cultural contexts. You could revise your thesis to account for this new way of thinking about the topic. At some point, your thinking will become refined enough to allow you to articulate your focus in a thesis statement. Figure 18.3 demonstrates how a focus on innovation and hip hop can lead to a thesis statement.

LO

Learning
Objective 18.2

The thesis statement shown in Figure 18.3, *The origins of hip hop reveal how artists adapt traditions*, demonstrates the way a good thesis statement takes on a dual purpose by adding complexity to a topic and focusing that topic.

But even this thesis statement might be further refined. Recall the initial connection between hip hop music and mainstream culture represented in Figure 18.1. We could also zoom in on concerns of mainstream culture as we refine our thinking about the topic. Figure 18.4 shows a thesis statement that has been developed about hip hop artists and mainstream culture.

FIGURE 18.3
A thesis statement focusing on hip hop artists and innovation.

The origins of hip hop reveal how artists adapt traditions.

Grandmaster Flash

Funk

1st place

Competition

Jazz

Urban Culture

Focus on Associations with Hip Hop

A Thesis Statement

FIGURE 18.4
A thesis statement concerning hip hop artists and mainstream culture.

Artists assert themselves to bring social commentary to mainstream culture.

NWA

Competition

1st place

Videos

Social Commentary

Straight Outta Compton

Magazines

Focus on Mainstream Culture

A Thesis Statement

A final element of complexity can be developed by drawing a connection between both areas of focus. It may be true that artists adapt traditions (as in the first thesis statement), but it is also true that they can create change as they extend innovations into mainstream culture (as in the second thesis statement). Figure 18.5 demonstrates how a complex thesis can be developed by connecting the focus on hip hop innovation with the focus on the ways in which artists influence mainstream culture.

You can see that Figure 18.5 resonates with the initial idea concerning innovation in hip hop and the influence of hip hop on mainstream culture. The thesis statement is complex for several reasons. First, each of the initial elements has been more specifically stated. Innovation has been refined in terms of adapting cultural traditions; influencing mainstream culture has been focused on artists making social commentary. The thesis is also complex in that it articulates a statement about the relationship between the two areas of focus; artists are connected to tradition, but they are also capable of creating change.

Developing a complex thesis statement requires critical thinking and refines your understanding of your topic. The key, though it may seem incongruous, is that even while the scope of the project may be expanding, the focus is becoming tighter. A paper claiming that there are innovations in hip hop doesn't

LO

Learning
Objective 18.3

FIGURE 18.5
A complex thesis
statement.

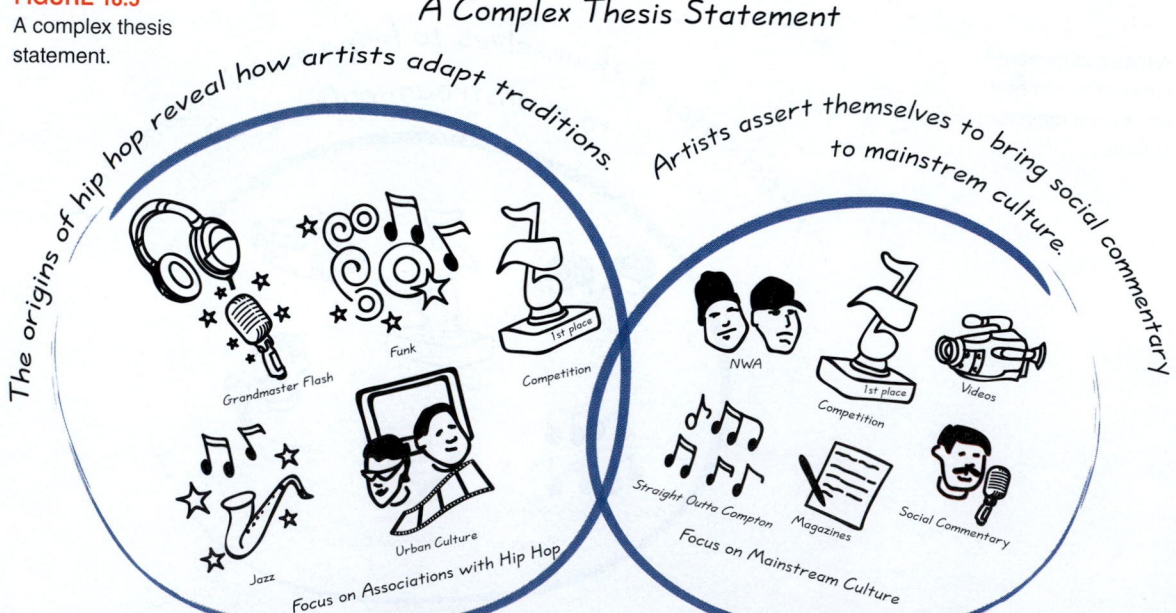

A Complex Thesis Statement

The origins of hip hop reveal how artists adapt traditions.

Artists assert themselves to bring social commentary to mainstrem culture.

Grandmaster Flash   Funk   Competition   1st place   NWA   Competition   1st place   Videos

Jazz   Urban Culture   Straight Outta Compton   Magazines   Social Commentary

Focus on Associations with Hip Hop   Focus on Mainstream Culture

The origins of hip hop reveal how artists adapt shared traditions and assert themselves to bring social commentary to mainstream culture.

say much. Connecting those innovations to changes in mainstream culture says more. Arguing that those innovations develop from cultural traditions and showing how the innovations can translate into social commentary that enters mainstream culture says even more. Having a thesis statement that casts the project in a complex light will allow you to develop a composition that says something meaningful while remaining focused.

Topic Sentences

Topic sentences perform for smaller segments of a project the same kind of work you might expect from a thesis statement. Often, topic sentences are associated with paragraphs. They act as a lens that focuses the discussion in the paragraph. Figure 18.6 shows a topic sentence related to one dimension of the larger topic of hip hop artists adapting traditions.

Learning Objective 18.4

You can see from Figure 18.6 that topic sentences can organize a discussion of related elements—in this case, the relationship between Grandmaster Flash and several local groups associated with the origins of hip hop. From the topic sentence, *Grandmaster Flash shows how an artist can emerge in the context of troubled yet creative communities,* you could develop a discussion either of the DJ scene in the late '70s, of the Bronx community where hip hop emerged, or of Fever Records and its role in bringing together early hip hop artists. Again, the key is zooming in and out, drawing connections, and then articulating what you discover in a clear statement.

FIGURE 18.6
A topic sentence focusing on artists and communities.

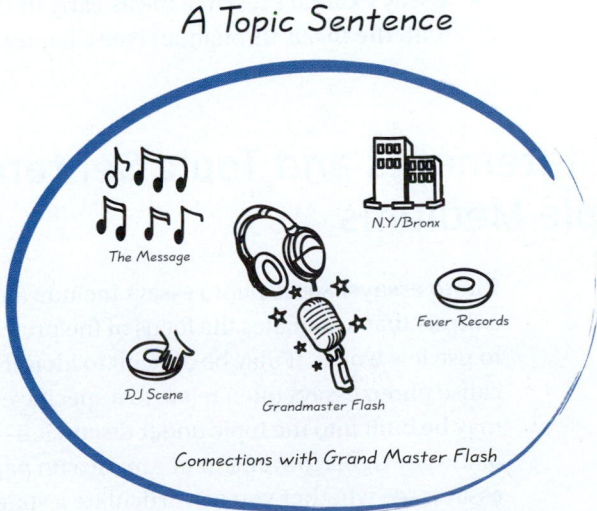

CONNECT IT Theses Statements and Topic Sentences in Multiple Genres

As you compose with various genres, you will have a number of opportunities to focus your work. Learn to create and revise statements about your projects, and then ask questions and make decisions as you explore those angles in your compositions.

- **Memoirs:** Consider a thesis that uses a key episode to make a statement about the person discussed in the memoir (see Chapter 5).
- **Profiles:** Use a thesis to capture core elements of the identity of the profile subject (see Chapter 6).
- **Position arguments:** Provide a clear thesis (often early in the argument) that stakes out your position (see Chapter 8).
- **Proposals:** Consider the idea or action being proposed as the thesis of the essay. Compose other sections to support the main proposal (see Chapter 9).
- **Explanatory research essays:** Use a thesis to forecast the key dimensions of the topic you will cover (see Chapter 10).
- **Book, music, or film reviews:** Use a thesis to provide your final recommendation about the work to readers (see Chapter 11).
- **Composition portfolios:** Consider a thesis that provides a takeaway message for the reader of the profile (see Chapter E2).
- **Essay exams:** Present a thesis early in the response and connect discussion with the thesis throughout (see Chapter E9).

Thesis Statements and Topic Sentences in Multiple Mediums

Photo essays. Some photo essays include an opening screen. If so, look there for a thesis that articulates the focus of the project. Because some photo essays tend to use few words, it may be difficult to identify a specific thesis statement. But because photo essays often relate to a specific event or concern, some of their focus may be built into the topic under discussion—as in the photo essay on the history of the gay rights movement in America on pages 316–21. As you encounter photo essays, see whether you can articulate a statement about the piece based on the collection of images and their relationship with the broad topic. If you are composing a photo essay, develop a thesis statement to guide your work, and then select images and compose captions that help further your thesis. Include an introductory screen where you can help viewers understand your focus.

Audio essays. Audio essays can take multiple forms. One constant, though, is the challenge of delivering information through the spoken word. Visual cues like paragraph breaks or headings are absent, so speakers must find alternative ways in which to announce key points and communicate how they fit within the overall focus of the project. If you are listening to an audio essay, consider taking notes, and be deliberate about translating into your notes what you take to be the key topics covered. If you are creating an audio essay, incorporate references to topic sentences and thesis statements. Reiterate the main focus of the essay, be sure to indicate who is speaking, and repeat statements to keep listeners oriented as they take in your key points.

Ask Questions & Make Decisions

Exercises for Understanding Thesis Statements and Topic Sentences

1. Working with a group of peers, brainstorm about the following list of connections. Zoom in to think about each aspect of the connection, and then develop a complex thesis statement that could be used to focus a project.

   The telephone ← → Attitudes about community

   Genetic research ← → Politics

   Ultimate fighting ← → American culture

   Sports blogging ← → Journalism

   Welfare reform ← → Attitudes about race

2. Think about some items that do not come with traditional thesis statements—product packages, a season-long TV drama, the playlist for a local radio station, a new car, etc. Select an item, and then think about the strategies it uses to focus attention. Consider any overarching messages presented by the item. Write a paragraph or two discussing the item in terms of thesis statements.

3. Revisit one of the readings in this book. Think about the way the piece uses (or avoids using) thesis statements and topic sentences. Consider how the use of focusing strategies relates to the piece's rhetorical situation as well as to its genre and medium. Write up your findings in one or two paragraphs.

4. Select an essay that you have previously written. Review the piece, taking note of its thesis statement and topic sentences. Identify as many topic

sentences as you can—highlighting them or jotting them in the margins if possible. Look for instances where paragraphs drift from the focus of their topic sentences. Look for instances where topic sentences can be reconnected with the thesis. Revise the piece, with the goal of demonstrating connections between the topic sentences and the thesis.

Zoom **Out**   **Reflecting on Thesis Statements and Topic Sentences**

- **Focusing a project is an ongoing activity, and it is closely linked with critical thinking.** Most topics evolve as writers explore, narrowing in focus, but also gaining in complexity.

- **Zooming in and out is crucial for understanding thesis statements and topic sentences.** Develop a thesis statement by using both zoom in and zoom out strategies. Think of the thesis statement as providing a focus for the overall project and the topic sentence as zooming in to focus on an aspect of the project.

- **Rhetorical situations shape the ways in which writers use thesis statements and topic sentences.** Some genres don't use concrete statements to articulate their theses, but all tend to use some strategies to focus their topics and organize their presentation.

- **Exploring cultural networks can help you develop theses as you take on a topic.** Think of collections of people, ideas, and things. Consider their associations to help you explain their relationships and develop a complex focus for a project.

For additional information and practice with the learning objectives in this chapter, go to www.mycomplab.com, Resources > Writing > The Writing Process > Planning.

CHAPTER 19

Organization

Zoom **In**   **Key Concepts and Learning Objectives**

After studying this chapter, you should be able to:

19.1   Understand how rhetorical situations can help shape the organization of projects.

19.2   Develop plans for successfully organizing compositions.

19.3   Use transitions to help readers and writers make sense of compositions.

19.4   Develop introductions that help readers see the organization of a composition.

19.5   Compose conclusions that balance the need to revisit what has been covered with the dangers of simply repeating key points.

f you have ever been taught to put together a large jigsaw puzzle, you probably have followed the advice to start with the corners, connect the edges, and then fill in the middle. This makes sense, because the framing structure helps you visualize where the other sections will fit in. The same holds true for your writing. Developing the underlying structure and organization of a project can go a long way toward creating a solid composition. You can ensure that you have a strong structure by checking that the main sections are sequenced well and that they create a flow of ideas that readers can understand. You can make sure that transitions between sections are clear and smooth. And you can craft introductions and conclusions that help orient readers to the organization of the piece.

Sequence and Flow

VIDEO
5. Graphic Maps

As you think about how best to organize your projects, you will want to get comfortable with some system of mapping the structure of a composition. Often, writers use an outline or a graphic map to represent the organization of a project. Chapter 2 discusses the writing process and ways in which you can use lists, outlines, maps, or flowcharts to help you plan the potential sections of a project. You should make deliberate use of these tools as you begin thinking about organization.

You can also use these tools to help you assess the organizational structure of your projects. Consider the outlines shown in Figure 19.1 representing two organizational options for an essay on film adaptations written by Trevor Jackson:

```
Adapting Books into Films

1. Introduction: The "I liked the book better"
   syndrome
      a. The big challenges for film
         adaptations
      b. Forecast essay
      c. Thesis—intertextuality is the best
         approach
2. Transcription versus interpretation (the
   fidelity question)
3. Adaptation versus appropriation (Sanders)
4. Three levels of adaptation
      a. Literal (close)—e.g., Harry Potter
         films
      b. Traditional (intermediate)—e.g.,
         Bridget Jones's Diary
      c. Radical (loose)—e.g., O' Brother Where
         Art Thou?
5. Intertextual Approaches
      a. Adaptations show Multiple influences
      b. Dudley Andrew and others—theories of
         intertextuality
6. Conclusion: The difficulty tracking down
   influences
      a. Even source texts can be viewed as
         adaptations
      b. What biases does the "I liked the book
         better" syndrome reveal?
      c. What does the future hold?
```

Starting Zoomed Out

A general problem
A forecast of the essay
The thesis of the essay

Zooming In

A comparison
A section on one view
Examples
A section on another view
Examples
A section on another view
Examples
Support of thesis

```
Adapting Books into Films

1. Introduction: The "I liked the book better"
   syndrome
      a. Two major approaches—transcription
         versus interpretation
2. Literal Transcription
3. Adaptation (Sanders)
4. The fidelity question
5. Interpretation
      a. Traditional (intermediate)—e.g.,
         Bridget Jones's Diary
      b. Appropriation (Sanders)
6. Intertextuality
      a. Thesis—intertextuality is the best
         approach
      b. Radical (loose)—e.g., O' Brother Where
         Art Thou?
      c. Dudley Andrew and others—theories of
         intertextuality
7. Conclusion: What biases does the "I liked
   the book better" syndrome reveal?
      a. Even source texts can be viewed as
         adaptations
      b. What does the future hold?
```

Starting Zoomed Out

A Comparison
A section on one view
Examples
A section on another view
Examples

Zooming In

The thesis of the essay
A section on another view
Examples
Support of thesis

FIGURE 19.1
Two organizational approaches to an essay.

LO

Learning
Objective 19.1

You can see from the figure that there are a number of ways to sequence the sections of a project. The version on the left takes an approach that might be described as starting broadly, then zooming in. This organization has the advantage of providing readers with an orientation to the project as a whole. Of note is the early announcement of the thesis. Writers can use this format to help add coherency to their essay, harkening back to the thesis as the piece moves from section to section. The organization suggested in the outline on the right in Figure 19.1 begins with a tighter focus on one of the key concerns of the project. The essay takes readers through some detailed points before broadening its focus with a delayed thesis. The advantage of this format is that you are more likely to engage readers with specific information right from the start so that readers will arrive at your thesis as a logical conclusion built from points made along the way.

Transitions

LO

Learning
Objective 19.3

Regardless of how you decide to sequence the sections of your projects, you need to provide readers with clues that can help them move through the structure smoothly. Transitions can work at zoomed-in levels, helping readers move from word to word or from sentence to sentence. Or they can work with a larger focus, helping readers move from paragraph to paragraph or among sections of a project. To think about transitions, let's look at a few paragraphs from Trevor Jackson's essay that we saw outlined in Figure 19.1:

> The paragraph uses a transition to set up a contrast with earlier points in the essay.

Although debates continue about the level of fidelity films should maintain with their book sources, the more examples of film adaptations we study, the more we realize that an approach based on intertextuality may be best. Intertextuality borrows much of its approach from theorists who have studied the relationships between works of literature and other aspects of culture. Roland Barthes, in particular, offers an approach that is based on the premise that readers create meaning by interpreting texts in terms of one another. In fact, for Barthes, the best texts are those that open themselves up for reader involvement (*S/Z*). Ideally, neither a book nor a film adaptation would allow for a simple correspondence or for fidelity because each would be understood only after multiple influences and connections are untangled by a reader. Film theorists also frequently cite the work of Michael Bakhtin, who similarly suggests that all texts emerge from multiple sources. Film scholar Thomas Leitch explains that the current goals of adaptation studies include moving away from discussions of fidelity "to a focus on Bakhtinian intertextuality—with each text, avowed adaptation or not, afloat upon a sea of countless earlier texts from which it could not help borrowing" (Leitch 63).

> Essay-level transitions and signal phrases create flow.

This process of borrowing from earlier texts can be seen clearly in the example of *O' Brother Where Art Thou?* This 1999 work by the Coen brothers announces with its opening credits that the film is based on *The Odyssey*. ==Recalling our discussion of traditional adaptations,== we might recognize in the film a number of direct allusions that could be considered close if not literal transcriptions. The siren scene provides a vivid example of borrowings from *The Odyssey*; the travelers are lured to a rocky setting by haunting voices heard from a distance and then seduced to the point of unconsciousness by the singing of the women. The film ==similarly== provides an evil Cyclops in the figure of Dan Teague, a violent bible salesman and KKK member. ==Further,== the film borrows one of the key motifs of *The Odyssey*, the mechanism of disguise. This motif emerges toward the end of the film when Everett and his band sneak into a political rally disguised as the Soggy Bottom Boys—complete with clip-on beards. The scene parallels Odysseus's disguising himself as a beggar to learn the true intentions of his wife.

==However,== these elements of overlap between the film and *The Odyssey* tell only half the story. For every example that suggests fidelity between the source and the film, there are multiple examples that show alternate influences informing the film. The title, for instance, is taken from a 1941 film entitled *Sullivan's Travels*. *Sullivan's Travels* depicts a Hollywood director. . . .

> Sentence-level transitions give a tight focus as the paper zooms in to discuss elements that have been borrowed from *The Odyssey*.

> A transition here signals a shift in direction for the essay.

You can see in the excerpt that Trevor makes use of transition devices to situate ideas and large movements within the paper as a whole. The sample also shows how transitions can work at the sentence or word level. You can see how weaving these short phrases into passages can help you zoom in to keep readers focused on the nuances of the details you discuss. And placing transitions strategically at the opening or closing of your paragraphs can help you zoom out to help readers see how each fits within the larger framework of your project.

Introductions and Conclusions

Learning Objective 19.4

Introductions and conclusions can be frustrating to write. Introductions can be challenging because you need to both engage readers and orient them to the organization of the project. Conclusions can be difficult because, although you don't want to simply repeat what you've already said, you have to be careful about introducing new information at the end of an essay. As you begin or end a project, you can benefit from zooming out to consider how to present readers with information that helps them understand your work as a whole.

For introductions, you will work with several overlapping goals. You need to engage readers. You need to articulate your thesis (or at least outline the angle of approach you will be taking to your topic). You will want to forecast the direction of your essay. You may need to define key terms or provide background information. And you may need to zoom out, showing readers how your topic is connected to related cultural concerns, why it matters. Your rhetorical situation will determine which of these goals drives the composition of your introduction, but you will want to be aware of all of the possibilities and make decisions accordingly. Consider Trevor's introduction to his essay on film adaptation:

> We're all familiar with the sensation of finishing a film and musing, "Hmm, I think I liked the book better." In some ways the reaction is a natural result of the strengths and weaknesses of the two forms. Books can use hundreds of pages to show the motivation of characters and discuss themes like love, courage, or adolescence. A film might have two hours to tell the entire story, so, naturally, some details get left out. But sometimes fans of books can take things to the extreme. When the first Harry Potter film came out, many readers complained about small changes in the phrasing of the dialog between characters or about details described in the text but left out in the sets recreating Hogwarts. These fans demonstrate the confusion that arises when it comes to film adaptations. Some expect exact fidelity between films and their book sources. Others, however, view films as an opportunity to interpret the source text, allowing for looser adaptations that capture the essence of the story without replicating every detail. Others, still, suggest that films owe no particular allegiance to texts that may have inspired them. Instead, they see a film as just another example of a work that is shaped by the ideas and texts that have come before it. By surveying the major approaches to adaptations—approaches that include literal or close adaptations, traditional or intermediate interpretations, and radical or loose appropriations—we can discover that an intertextual theory offers the most promise when it comes to interpreting films based on books.

Trevor's introduction accomplishes a number of goals. It begins with a hook to engage readers. Trevor uses an anecdote with a brief quotation that allows him to transition into talking about one of the key elements of the essay. The introduction also includes a forecast statement. Sometimes authors will explicitly tag such a statement, using language like "In this essay, I will discuss three approaches to film adaptations." Trevor does not tag his forecast in this way, but the sentences in the middle of the introduction all lay out the key concerns that will be taken up in the piece.

The introduction also closes with a thesis statement. It's possible to place a thesis elsewhere in an essay, but it's a good strategy to clearly state the thesis as you introduce things. The main benefit is that you (and your readers) can rely on a clear statement that articulates the angle you are taking. Trevor's introduction also does well at laying out the main points of the essay. You may want to draft a temporary introduction that lays a foundation for the piece, and then go back and fine-tune the section after the specifics of the project have been fleshed out.

For conclusions, you will again need to zoom out. In some ways, you will be resituating what you have discussed for readers, helping them to see the whole essay and how it fits within a bigger picture. Of course, your rhetorical situation will shape your conclusions; a proposal essay, for instance, will likely close with

LO

Learning
Objective 19.5

a call for action. You can also experiment with some particular strategies to help you bring your piece to a close. You might review what you have covered, though you need to be careful not to simply repeat yourself. Sometimes a bit of rein-forcement is fine, especially if you have taken readers through a complicated set of ideas. In most cases, though, even if you are reviewing points, you will want to reveal them in a new light, striking a balance between restating things and help-ing readers to consider your points within a larger context. You can also use strategies of engaging readers as you conclude a project, perhaps by sharing an anecdote or quotation that can help readers connect personally with the points you have just covered. Take a look at Trevor's conclusion to get some ideas:

> Regardless of your beliefs regarding different approaches to adaptation, one thing is clear: it can be difficult to determine the many streams of influence flowing into any text, be it a film version of a work of fiction or even the original book on which a film is based. Think about our Harry Potter example. No doubt many book fans complained that the film did not mirror its source in numerous examples. However, might we make the same complaint about the source itself? We could look at a book like *Harry Potter and the Sorcerer's Stone* and discover influences ranging from J.R. Tolkien's *Lord of the Rings* trilogy to C.S. Lewis's Narnia stories to the Bible. Would it be fair to say that Dumbledore drifts too far from Gandalf because he is portrayed more often with a wand than with a staff? Both wizards are, in fact, de-scended from the influential archetype of the wise old man. It is impossible to tell where the influence of one text begins and another ends. The complaint that the book is better, then, reveals a bias toward wanting to see works of art as discrete en-tities, as original creations that spring from the heads of their authors like mush-rooms spring from the soil, seemingly by magic. If we look more closely, we see that even mushrooms sprout from spores. Similarly, if we retrain our thinking about adaptations toward an intertextual approach, we may discover intriguing influences that help us understand the magical ways that texts adapt, appropriate, recreate, and refresh one another.

The biggest concern you will encounter when writing conclusions is making decisions about including new information. Trevor's conclusion really just ex-pands on an earlier point he has made about intertextuality. He reiterates the point with some new perspectives, however, demonstrating the ways that even what we think of as an original text might be viewed as an adaptation.

CONNECT IT Organization in Multiple Genres

Each situation offers opportunities to develop frameworks for your projects. Learn to create plans, and then consider genres and other concerns in terms of organization as you compose.

- **Memoirs:** Use the episodes in the memoir subject's life to organize a project; extend episodes with discussions of insights (see Chapter 5).
- **Profiles:** Consider a chronological organization that emphasizes key episodes to detail the profile subject (see Chapter 6).
- **Rhetorical analyses:** Let the close reading of the item under analysis guide your organizing structure, helping readers consider big picture elements like rhetorical situations as well as the details (see Chapter 7).
- **Position arguments:** Outline claims and provide reasons and evidence for support; develop sections that acknowledge and respond to opposing points of view (see Chapter 8).
- **Proposals:** Begin by detailing the problem, and then propose a solution; extend your proposal by justifying the solution and considering objections and alternatives (see Chapter 9).
- **Book, music, or film reviews:** Provide background, discuss related examples, and evaluate the item (see Chapter 11).
- **Photo essays:** Either sequence slides or pages chronologically or use themes to organize the project (see Chapter 13).
- **Résumés and business letters:** Use chronological and thematic entries in a resume and follow the formal structures expected of business letters (see Chapter E6).
- **Essay exams:** Forecast discussion, detail examples, and connect with the exam prompt (see Chapter E9).

Organization in Multiple Mediums

Digital videos. As you encounter or compose digital videos, you can benefit from the use of transitions to help organize the composition. Most films use transitions to suggest changes in setting or time. In digital videos, you can similarly insert transitions between segments of a video to help viewers move through the piece. A fade into a solid color might indicate the closing of an idea. A dissolve from one segment to the next might indicate more similarity between ideas. You can also consider the ways in which most digital videos use sound or text. An audio track can reinforce points and guide readers by explicitly making connections and transitions in its narration. Titles and other elements of text can be repeated or placed strategically to highlight the movement from idea to idea.

Images. A number of strategies can be used to organize images. The movie poster in Figure 19.2, for instance, makes careful use of organizational techniques. The poster uses a framing device in the shape of the circular window. Placing Harry, Hermione, and Ron within the circle of the frame organizes them. Pushing Harry toward the front of the image demonstrates the relative importance of each character to the story. Harry's gaze establishes contact with the viewer—a sort of introduction. The gazes of the other characters resonate with this initial contact. Setting Sirius Black behind a structure in the background creates intrigue as to his purpose and his relationship to the others. In addition to framing and gaze, images might use arrangement of elements, contrast, focal points, lines, colors, lighting, or repetition to help organize their messages (see Chapter 25).

FIGURE 19.2
Movie poster for *Harry Potter and the Prisoner of Azkaban*.

Ask Questions & Make Decisions

LO

Learning
Objective 19.2

Exercises for Understanding Organization

1. Choose a well-known speech or text—e.g., Martin Luther King Jr.'s "Letter from Birmingham Jail," Lincoln's "The Gettysburg Address," or Jonathon Swift's "A Modest Proposal." Read through the text, marking the main points in the margin and creating an outline or map of the organizational structure. Think about the way the organization of the piece relates to its longevity or popularity. Write up your thoughts in a paragraph.

2. Find a short essay that you judge to be well written. Read through the piece, highlighting all of the words, phrases, or sentences that create transitions. Write a few sentences discussing the strengths of the piece in terms of transitions.

3. Choose an essay that you have previously written but about which you are not completely satisfied. Rewrite the introduction to be more engaging and to forecast a new direction for the piece. Consider revising the essay to fit with your proposed new structure.

4. Identify a photograph or a poster that seems particularly well organized. Analyze the image with an eye toward discovering its organizational features. Write up your findings in a paragraph.

Zoom Out   Reflecting on Organization

- **Organizing your compositions requires that you revisit the writing process.** Strong planning is needed to create a clear structure. That structure should be sorted out before attempting any revisions to surface-level details.

- **Transitions can help you adjust the focus of your work.** Zooming in, you can use transitions to create flow within or among sentences. Zooming out, you can use transitions to show readers connections between ideas and to reiterate the larger focus of your projects.

- **Introductions prompt you to zoom out to check the overall structure of your composition.** At the same time, they prepare readers to take in the details as well as the main points of your piece. In addition, introductions serve to engage readers and demonstrate the relevance of a project.

- **Conclusions help you to tie together the major points of a project.** They also allow you to extend your thinking, perhaps situating a project or discussion within a larger cultural network.

For additional information and practice with the learning objectives in this chapter, go to www.mycomplab.com, Resources > Writing > The Writing Process > Revising.

Narration

Zoom **In**   **Key Concepts and Learning Objectives**

After studying this chapter, you should be able to:

20.1   Sequence events to organize the structure of a narration.

20.2   Use description to help bring your writing to life.

20.3   Compose dialog that sheds light on characters and helps move a narrative along.

20.4   Identify ways in which narration can be used in a variety of genres.

Most works of fiction and many films have a narrator, a voice that describes the events that take place in the story. But narration isn't important only in novels or movies. Essays that you write might describe and offer perspectives on people and events. For example, in Chapter 5, Annie Dillard relates a series of episodes that shed light on her family and childhood. You can use narration in all kinds of writing projects—arguments, reports, photo essays, memoirs, profiles, almost any genre.

Thinking about narration as you read or write requires that you pay attention to sequencing. You can ask questions and make decisions about the order in which information is organized, especially for episodes that tell a story. You will also need to understand the role of details and dialog in narration. Providing detailed descriptions enables you to bring ideas to life for readers. Using dialog can allow you to shed light on the characteristics of people about whom you are writing. Both sequencing and using details and dialog open a range of possibilities for writing projects.

Sequencing

Learning
Objective 20.1

Narration involves arranging episodes so that readers can take in a story. One of the most direct ways to sequence events is to use chronological order. In a profile essay on the Dixie Chicks, for instance, Susan Ramos uses chronology to provide background and trace the controversies that have developed for the group:

> The Dixie Chicks are perhaps the best-known female country group. The three members, Natalie Maines, Martie Maguire, and Emily Robison, formed in the mid '90s and first found fame with their albums *Wide Open Spaces* in 1998 and *Fly* in 1999. From the beginning, the group has challenged the values of country music. Their song "Goodbye Earl," released in 2000 as a single from the album *Fly*, offers a depiction of a woman in an abusive relationship who teams up with another woman to murder her husband. "Goodbye Earl" trades the traditional good old boy persona associated with country music, for a darker, even violent vision of working class life.

Susan's profile uses chronology to trace the rise of the group, using the release dates of their music to organize her discussion.

In most instances, however, you can use sequencing and dates as needed without having to organize an entire project chronologically. In a position argument, for instance, you might outline the development of mechanized agriculture to provide background for an essay opposing factory farming. In a review, you might trace the artistic ancestry of the latest gangster movie, before evaluating the film on its own terms. As with all writing tasks, know the benefits of sequencing events, and then make decisions about when and how to employ the strategy as you compose.

As you work with sequencing while composing, you will need to pay attention to transitions and to signaling devices that can help readers keep track of the movement of time in your projects (see pages 423–24). Some projects might use timestamps or markers to indicate movements through time—markers like Monday, 1998, or 8:15 A.M. For most projects, simple phrases like *looking back, historically, initially, first, next, second, over time,* or *subsequently* can organize episodes in a narration. You will need to weave these phrases into your writing, keeping the reader in mind as you make choices.

WN

VIDEO
49. Chronology
and Narrative

Showing Through Details

LO

Learning
Objective 20.2

If you have ever participated in a fiction writing workshop, you have probably heard the phrase "show, don't tell." It's a helpful formulation that reminds writers not to make flat statements about themes or characters. Instead you can use details to suggest thoughts, emotions, or key concerns. Consider this statement telling readers something about a character:

> Allison began to worry about Kylie.

Now compare the statement with a detailed description:

> Allison pulled her cell phone from her purse and checked for missed calls. She scrolled through the entries looking for Kylie's number, then tossed the phone back into her bag. A moment later she brought the phone back out and checked the time.

The second version of the episode uses details to show Allison's nervousness.

Using Dialog and the Words of Others

LO

Learning
Objective 20.3

Dialog can help bring the out key ideas in a narration. For memoirs, profiles, and other narratives focusing on people, dialog can also help bring figures to life. Consider an excerpt from Annie Dillard's memoir (pages 124–25):

> One Sunday afternoon Mother wandered through our kitchen, where Father was making a sandwich and listening to the ball game. The Pirates were playing the New York Giants at Forbes Field. In those days, the Giants had a utility infielder named Wayne Terwilliger. Just as Mother passed through, the radio announcer cried—with undue drama—"Terwilliger bunts one!"
>
> "Terwilliger bunts one?" Mother cried back, stopped short. She turned. "Is that English?"

"The player's name is Terwilliger," Father said. "He bunted."

"That's marvelous," Mother said. "'Terwilliger bunts one.' No wonder you listen to baseball. 'Terwilliger bunts one.'"

The dialog provides insights into the figure of Dillard's mother—"That's marvelous." We learn about the matter-of-fact demeanor of the father—"He bunted." And we move forward in the narration of the memoir as the dialog plays out.

To compose successful dialog, you need to learn to a few formatting rules:

- Every time a new person speaks, begin a new paragraph, indenting the first line. You'll need to think about the pacing of conversation and how to break up longer blocks of speech. Most dialog creates a back-and-forth exchange between characters.
- Place quotation marks around the words that are spoken by any of the figures, placing punctuation marks inside of the closing quotation marks. If a speaker utters a quoted phrase, use single quotation marks to indicate the quotation within a quotation (e.g., "'Terwilliger bunts one.' No wonder you listen to baseball.").
- Use signals to attribute the spoken words with their speaker. Often you can use a comma to connect the speaker and the spoken words (e.g., "That's marvelous," Mother said.). You can also use standalone quoted phrases within a paragraph if their relationship with the speaker is clear (e.g., She turned. "Is that English?").

You will also need to develop an ear for creating realistic and compelling exchanges. In general, shorter phrasings that mimic the ways people talk in conversation create more authentic dialog. You can try reading your dialog aloud to refine your exchanges. You should also learn to weave segments of dialog together with narration that describes and explains. Dialog, details, and described events can all be integrated into your narrative writing.

CONNECT IT   Narration in Multiple Genres

Narration can take different forms, depending on your situation. Learn to sequence events, use description, and perhaps dialog, and then adapt what you know to meet the needs of the genre and the project.

- **Memoirs:** Use narration, description, and dialog to relate episodes and to bring a figure to life (see Chapter 5).
- **Profiles:** Identify events in the life of the profile subject and use narration to explain them for readers (see Chapter 6).

- **Position arguments:** Consider using narration in the opening or closing of an essay to engage readers and emphasize key conclusions (see Chapter 8).
- **Explanatory research essays:** Think of narration as a framework for explaining concepts or processes (see Chapter 10).
- **Book, music, or film reviews:** Use narration to help readers understand what takes place in a work or to get the gist of the piece (see Chapter 11).
- **Photo essays:** For essays detailing events, think of the sequencing of the images themselves as helping to deliver the narration; use description to bring out the details of the images (see Chapter 13).

Narration in Multiple Mediums

LO

Learning
Objective 20.4

Digital videos. Think of the timeline used to compose the video in terms of narration: how can you sequence elements in the video to deliver your message? As you weigh the sequencing of materials, consider the modes through which you can express yourself—images, text, and sounds. The screen shot in Figure 20.1, for instance, shows a sequencing of still images and text screens. Don't forego the use of text simply because you are working with videos. Use titles or textual overlays to make important points. Be careful to maintain text on screen long enough for readers to take it in. Ask questions and make decisions as you adjust the sequencing of images or video samples. Are you creating a video profile or memoir? How can you order materials to emphasize points about a person's life? Are you creating an argument? How can you order visual components to make key points and

FIGURE 20.1
Still images from a student video on the history of fish management.

help move viewers toward your position? Also think about the vocal narration you can include in the video. You can use voiceover narration to analyze and explain visual materials in the piece. You can also script your narration to emphasize points you want to make and lead readers through your materials.

Audio essays. With audio essays, sequencing materials will be a key concern. Think of narration strategies as you imagine the kinds of materials you will weave together. Consider how you can integrate sound samples or ambient noise to create flow within the essay. You may also include interview clips. Here, you will need to think of narrative strategies as you write into and out of the interview clips. Don't repeat something that has been said in an interview or give away an interesting interview point ahead of time. Instead, adjust your statements to complement and situate the interview samples. Also think about the key role that voice plays in audio essays. Become adept at recording your voice with good sound quality. Experiment with tone, tempo, and enunciation as you record your voice. Learn to strike a balance between the formal and informal as you record. Make choices about when to be conversational, when to be carefully scripted, and how best to engage listeners with your voice.

Ask Questions & Make Decisions

Exercises for Understanding Narration

1. Working with a group of peers, select an essay from Chapter 5 (Memoirs) or Chapter 6 (Profiles). Examine the essay to identify its narrative strategies. What strikes you about the sequencing and the use of strategies that move the plot along? What can you say about the description or instances of dialog? Do you believe that the essay succeeds in terms of narration? Choose a member of the group to report your findings to the class.

2. On television or online, watch an advertisement for a product or service. Create a storyboard detailing the narrative sequence of the ad. For each of the major elements in the storyboard, add notations that explore the element in terms of the ad's message.

3. Select an essay that you have recently completed and evaluate its use of descriptive language. Revise the piece using strategies of description (see Chapter 21) to bring out details that further your points.

4. Choose an issue related either to a project you are working on or to one of your interests. Use dialog to create a brief exchange between two characters that brings out key concerns related to the topic.

Zoom Out   Reflecting on Narration

- **Some genres call for writers to use specific narrative strategies.** Memoirs and profiles benefit from carefully arranged episodes. Dialog can provide insights into figures discussed in memoirs, profiles, and other projects touching on people.

- **Composing descriptions can improve your ability to provide details about key facets of your topic.** Detailed descriptions can also help engage your readers.

- **Understanding the role of sequencing benefits a range of projects.** From arguments to flyers to research essays, the order in which you present information influences your message. Compositions like videos or audio essays also rely heavily on the sequencing of materials.

- **Narratives play important roles in cultural networks.** Our relationships with others and their stories help reinforce our status as people connected with one another.

For additional information and practice with the learning objectives in this chapter, go to www.mycomplab.com, Resources > Writing > Writing Purposes > Writing to Reflect.

armstrongplaylist.html   Q- Google

Neil Armstrong: One Giant Leap for Mankind Represented through Music

"The important achievement of Apollo was demonstrating that humanity is not forever chained to this planet and our visions go rather further than that and our opportunities are unlimited."
— Neil Armstrong

One of my favorite historical figures is perhaps most famous for being the first person to set foot on the moon. In order to show my respect and admiration for this astounding human being, I dedicate my playlist to Neil Alden Armstrong (born August 5, 1930). Neil is a former American astronaut, test pilot, university professor, and United States Naval Aviator. His first spaceflight was aboard *Gemini 8* in 1966, for which he was the command pilot. The topic of this playlist, Armstrong's second and last spaceflight was as commander of the *Apollo 11* moon landing mission on July 20, 1969. On this mission, Armstrong and Buzz Aldrin descended to the lunar surface and spent 2.5 hours exploring while Michael Collins remained in orbit in the command module. The intent of this Playlist is to transmit through music some of the physical and emotional experiences that Neil encountered up to and during the Apollo 11 mission.

Rolling Stones — "Start Me Up"

"Start Me Up" exemplifies how exhilarated and excited Neil must have felt during the liftoff of the Apollo 11 Lunar Landing Mission as the 363 ft. tall space vehicle was launched from Kennedy Space Center at 9:37 a.m. The energetic rock n' roll beat and heavy instrumentation by the guitars and drums reflect the rumble of the space ship firing on all cylinders as it tries to break out of the earth's atmosphere. The explosions generated from the craft in the music video for the song parallel the smoke and flames from the five engines of the Saturn V rocket which generate 7.5 million pounds of thrust. The fast tempo reflects the speed of the rocket after liftoff. It only takes twelve minutes for the astronauts to reach an orbital altitude of 120 miles above the Earth and reach 17,400 mph, then begin their four day journey to the moon, nearly a quarter of a million miles away; the amount of force required to escape the Earth's atmosphere is enough to *make a grown man cry*. The lyrics themselves — "Start Me Up" — are appropriate for the take-off because in one sense they suggest starting up the space ship. Moreover, the lyrics suggest that there is no turning back once the mission has begun.

CHAPTER 21

Description

Zoom In   Key Concepts and Learning Objectives

After studying this chapter, you should be able to:

21.1 Use details to create compelling descriptions.

21.2 Use descriptions to create a dominant impression.

21.3 Compose descriptions that appeal to the senses.

21.4 Develop step-by-step explanations to describe a process.

21.5 Identify strategies for using descriptions in multiple genres or mediums.

I magine sitting across a bistro table from someone who hands you an orange. You might raise an eyebrow and wonder about the offering, but you would have little trouble identifying the object that had been placed in your hands. Now imagine wearing a blindfold in the same situation. (Or imagine someone who is visually disabled in the same situation.) It might take a minute, but by considering the shape, weight, or texture of the item, you could probably also identify the fruit. If your sense of touch didn't provide enough information, you could use your nose to determine that you had been handed a piece of citrus.

Writers face similar difficulties when they communicate with readers. You must, in a sense, help readers see, hold, touch, smell, taste, hear, and understand the nature of things, ideas, and people. To engage readers and convey these details, you can rely on description. You can use descriptive language in reports, position essays, memoirs, profiles, explanatory essays, recipes, and any piece that calls for readers to identify with a subject or to understand a process. In genres like brochures, audio essays, playlists, or photo essays (to name a few possibilities), description similarly helps readers grasp ideas and get the gist of a message.

Describing Details That Appeal to the Senses

Learning Objective 21.1

Learning Objective 21.3

Suppose that you just witnessed an accident. You might be asked by a police officer to report what you saw. You might relate the accident to friends. You might later record the experience in your journal. In each of these situations, you would respond differently, and you would use varying strategies of descriptive writing (perhaps offering facts to the officer and capturing sensations for friends or in your journal). Descriptive writing both captures the informational essence of objects and events and brings those objects and events to life.

In the 1960s police show, *Dragnet*, officer Friday uses the phrase "Just the facts" to exhort witnesses to recount a crime. This famous phrase represents the way descriptive writing focuses on details. In our accident example, you might report the make and model of the car, its estimated speed, the time of day, the road conditions, and so on—the more details, the better. For descriptive writing, then, your powers of observation will generate a good deal of the information, allowing you to discuss the particulars of objects and situations and capture these items for your readers. Use accurate terms to identify items and discuss specific characteristics with as much detail as possible.

But descriptions don't merely record information. Often you will also need to bring these details to life. Even the police report might ask you to try to capture the intensity of a situation, and your descriptions to friends or in your journal might emphasize your emotional response to the accident. In your descriptions, then, you may often use language to create an impression for readers. You might experiment with diction (the choice of words that you use) to achieve some of this effect—compare "the car *ran* into the tree" with "the car *slammed* into the tree." You might also use similes or metaphors to add life to your descriptions— "the fog hung over the road like a soap-stained shower curtain." Use language to create impressions for your readers. Of course, you will make decisions based on your rhetorical situation, avoiding lyrical language in the police report, but perhaps using it in your journal.

You can think of descriptive writing as an opportunity to serve as a witness. But instead of simply acting as the eyes of your readers, consider how you can provide the eyes, ears, nose, taste, and touch—even sensations within your body—to bring information to life. Include information that creates a sensory scene: "The fog hung over the road like a soap-stained shower curtain, and even the car coming up the hill sounded muffled." Complement these details to create impressions: "The motor had a throaty sound, not high-pitched or even that loud, but I could hear the tires rolling fast over the asphalt. I knew the car was speeding, and my knees weakened; my neighbor's dog lurched through the mist and into the road." Use adjectives, diction, and figurative language to appeal to all of the senses of readers.

VIDEO
50. Using Sensory
Details

Establishing a Dominant Impression

Learning Objective 21.2

All of the details and sensory elements that go into a description can add up to an overall impression that sets a mood or conveys a broad message to readers. Consider this excerpt from Jimmy Santiago Baca's "Coming Into Language" (pages 136–41):

> On weekend graveyard shifts at St. Joseph's Hospital I worked the emergency room, mopping up pools of blood and carting plastic bags stuffed with arms, legs, and hands to the outdoor incinerator. I enjoyed the quiet, away from the screams of shotgunned, knifed, and mangled kids writhing on gurneys outside the operating rooms. Ambulance sirens shrieked and squad car lights reddened the cool nights, flashing against the hospital walls: gray—red, gray—red. On slow nights I would lock the door of the administration office, search the reference library for a book on female anatomy and, with my feet propped on the desk, leaf through the illustrations, smoking my cigarette. I was seventeen.

The details in the passage help readers grasp the scene. Sounds, sights, and sensations describe the hospital setting. Details such as the topic of the reference book and the "feet propped on the desk" show rather than tell the reader what is taking place. But if the description succeeds, these details will add up to a larger message about the nature of the character described in the passage. The description evokes the sensory chaos of the emergency room. But the details later in the passage bring into focus a picture of a young man finding solace in the sanctuary of the office and (as will be borne out later in the essay) the life of the mind.

Describing a Process

LO

Learning Objective 21.4

Description can also be helpful when you need to demonstrate for readers the way something is done. When you describe a process, you generally relate in detail the stages required to complete a task. (Because processes are described in a step-by-step fashion, they also call for you to think about strategies of narration—Chapter 20.) The kinds of tasks you describe are likely to be either personal—"how I learned to like my sister"—or technical—"how I created my own Web domain."

Most process descriptions are organized chronologically. The main techniques you will use when you describe a process will involve guiding readers through the use of transitions such as *first, next, then, later, finally,* etc. Consider this example:

> When I came home after my first year in college and my parents told me that I had to spend time with my sister or lose my driving privileges, I was furious at first. There was no way I was going to spend time surrounded by the grating sounds of her screamo music or her mop-haired friends in their black T-shirts. But later, when I began driving her to the pool, my thinking changed. I watched every day as she talked with her friends about music or movies, and I saw that she was not so different from me at that age—although my friends wore Polo shirts and khaki pants. I finally realized that I was still judging people by their appearances, and that I had not changed as much as I had thought since high school.

You can see how the excerpt combines strategies of description—lots of details and an overall impression—with a step-by-step discussion to provide insights into a process of personal discovery.

CONNECT IT   Description in Multiple Genres

Each situation offers opportunities to develop descriptions. Learn to use details, engage the senses of readers, and describe scenes and events, and then ask questions and make decisions about incorporating these elements into multiple genres.

- **Memoirs:** Use description to bring out the character of the subject of the memoir and the details of settings and episodes (see Chapter 5).
- **Profiles:** Describe events in the profile subject's life and use details to bring the subject into focus (see Chapter 6).
- **Rhetorical analyses:** Describe the ways in which the item under analysis appeals to its audience, using details to support points you make about the message (see Chapter 7).
- **Explanatory research essays:** Use description to help explain processes or to show the significance of key pieces of research (see Chapter 10).
- **Book, music, or film reviews:** Use description to serve as the ears, eyes, and touch of your readers, allowing them to share your engagement with the work (see Chapter 11).
- **Literary analyses:** Discuss details of the work as you make points about characters, settings, and motifs (see Chapter 12).
- **Photo essays:** Use description to provide analysis of images you include in the essay (see Chapter 13).
- **Annotated bibliography:** Capture the gist of a source in your annotation by describing its focus and relationship to your topic (see Chapter 30).
- **Résumés and business letters:** Use keywords in résumés to describe your abilities, and use details in business letters to support points you wish to make (see Chapter 34).

Description in Multiple Mediums

Learning
Objective 21.5

Annotated playlists. Composing an annotated playlist will provide a great opportunity to practice description. Putting together such a playlist requires that you first select and sequence songs that will help you convey your thoughts. However, you must also annotate those selections, as does the author of the Neil Armstrong playlist shown in Figure 21.1. Here, you will use description to develop your annotations. If you select a song based on its tempo or instrumentation, you will need to provide a description that helps readers hear those elements of the song. Similarly, you can describe the significance of any lyrics you include your annotations. When you do so, you can also use the descriptions to flesh out the connections between the lyrics and the points you wish to make about the songs or your topic. As you develop annotations for playlist songs, use detailed descriptions to analyze the materials and to further the message of the playlist as a whole. (See Chapter E5 for more on playlists.)

FIGURE 21.1
A screenshot depicting descriptions in a playlist.

Photo essays. The description in a photo essay will depend on the role that images play in the project. A photo essay documenting an event might use images that provide visual evidence of what took place. In that case, your descriptions will spend more time connecting this evidence to points you want to make about the event. A photo essay exploring the ways in which graffiti represents urban culture would require description that focuses more on the details of the images. You might discuss any symbols that occur in the images and assess messages put forth by the graffiti examples, and then draw connections with points about your topic. Description could zoom in even further in a photo essay exploring the visual arts or offering rhetorical analyses of advertisements. You might describe artistic techniques, discuss the ways in which the ads create visual appeals, and develop a close reading of the images. To think more about how you can describe visual elements in photo essays, refer to the advice on reading images in Chapter 25.

Ask Questions & Make Decisions

Exercises for Understanding Description

1. Identify a person or thing that you might want to write about. Brainstorm about elements that make your selection complex or interesting. What specific traits stand out? Write a paragraph describing the person or thing, focusing on bringing out important details and connecting them with key traits.

2. Find a place you believe to be rich with sensory activity—a street corner, food court, city bus, etc. Use your ears, eyes, nose, and touch to take in the surroundings, and then write a page or so that captures the sensory elements of the place.

3. Working with a group of peers, search online to find a striking image rich with details. Think about some of the ways in which images convey information (see Chapter 25), and then make a list of elements in the image that you could describe in an analysis. Show your image and report your findings to your classmates.

4. Explore one of the readings in Chapter 5 (Memoirs) or Chapter 6 (Profiles). Find a reading that you like, and then consider how its use of description contributes to a dominant impression that you take away from the piece. Write up your findings in a paragraph or two.

5. Identify a technical task with which you are well acquainted (building a Web site, baking brownies, painting a portrait, etc.). Compose a description of the process, striving to capture as much information as needed to explain the steps to readers. Add illustrations if possible to further your description.

Zoom Out   Reflecting on Description

- **Description can provide a sense of sight, sound, and touch.** These sensory impressions help readers identify with a topic.

- **Description requires writers and readers to zoom in.** Concentrating on details through careful descriptions can help bring ideas and elements into focus.

- **Strong descriptions also contribute to larger messages.** Zooming out, we can recognize a dominant impression or key concern that is brought to light through description.

- **Genres and mediums influence the ways in which we describe people, ideas, and things.** Images and sounds can act as descriptive evidence in projects, but authors still must discuss and draw connections from that evidence.

For additional information and practice with the learning objectives in this chapter, go to www.mycomplab.com, Resources > Writing > Writing Purposes > Writing to Describe.

CHAPTER 22

Research Question: Should new media composing be required in college writing classes?

1. What is new media composing?
    a. Digital—easy to reproduce and manipulate
    b. Social—easy to share and relevant to readers
    c. Multimedia—texts, images, sounds
2. Is new media a valuable form of writing instruction?
    a. Criteria/Match
        i.   Promotes critical thinking
        ii. Develops awareness of rhetorical situations
        iii. Offers opportunities to engage readers/the public
        iv. Allows writers to explore and understand topics
3. How can new media composing help revise our understanding of college writing?
    a. A new definition of composing—mixing and putting together
    b. More overlap and movement among areas of study—language, art, culture
    c. New methods of teaching—collaboration, workshops, online sharing and review

Definitions

Zoom In   Key Concepts and Learning Objectives

After studying this chapter, you should be able to:

22.1 Understand how definitions can work at multiple levels.

22.2 Emphasize your own ideas by developing definitions.

22.3 Extend definitions by using additional writing strategies.

You can understand how to use defining strategies in your writing by thinking about zooming in and out. Writers often zoom in to focus on the meaning of words and sentences. Often, writers need to clarify the meaning of a specific term, and a definition allows them to explain what they mean. At the same time, definitions can be developed on a larger scale. A writer could compose a paragraph discussing the nature of an idea like free trade. And an author might compose a whole project defining or explaining a concept like Internet neutrality.

Defining Words and Sentences

LO

Learning
Objective 22.1

Definitions at the level of words and sentences range from formal, dictionary-style descriptions to short explanations where you spell out the meanings for words and ideas as they relate to your particular project. You can think of a spectrum for these kinds of definitions. On one end of the spectrum, dictionary definitions clarify the formal meaning of a term (sometimes called the denotative meaning). Pencil: a wood-encased piece of graphite used for marking. On the other end of the spectrum, definitions enable you to articulate your own perspective and move your ideas forward. As the terms you define become more abstract, dictionary definitions become less helpful.

> Recent studies show that new media instruction benefits from broadening what we normally think of as the act of writing by applying a substitute term, *composing*. To understand this substitution, we need to consider the definition of composing as that of "to make something by merging parts."

Here, the definition is really an extension of the ideas that the author lays out. In most cases, you will be served well by developing your own definition that remains true to the accepted meanings of terms, but that clarifies your own use and furthers your larger message:

> When we think of composing in terms of new media writing, it's helpful to consider the act as bringing together the constituent parts of a project; much as a musical composer combines the tones of various instruments or as a painter arranges elements on a canvas, a new media writer mixes and arranges text, images, and sounds to create a message.

Taking ownership of terms and ideas helps both authors and readers. Readers get clear indications of the ways in which writers are using terms, and writers are better able to articulate their thoughts by using definitions to show how meanings connect with the ideas woven through their texts.

Definitions at the Paragraph Level

You can also use definitions as you create paragraphs or longer sections of projects. When it comes to these extended discussions, you will find that definitions are especially helpful with the development of paragraphs and sections. Consider this paragraph offering an extended discussion of new media:

> One difficulty with assessing the potential for new media composing is defining exactly what we mean by new media. Initial confusion arises over the status of emerging modes of communication. A new communication technology may have arrived on the scene in the last several years, but that does not necessarily qualify that form as new media. Consider the status of the lapel pin ribbon. Often worn by groups of people at public functions, these pins in pink, yellow, or other colors provide a message of support for an organization. But most people would not categorize them as a new media communications technology. For contrast, consider cell phone text messages. Imagine that someone stumbles across free bagels at the coffee shop or witnesses an abuse of authority at the courthouse and then sends off a dozen text messages to friends (who might each send off a dozen more messages). Within fifteen minutes, a flash mob of more than a hundred people might appear on the scene. In this case, the group is also using messages to solidify the connection among a group of people. But the development of the group is made possible by the near instant and endless duplication of text messages. As soon as someone gets a text, she can forward it, and so can the next recipient, and so on. The digital nature of text messages combined with their transmission through an electronic network allows this kind of spontaneous and almost limitless reproduction. The lapel pin, by contrast, would need to be reproduced in a factory, shipped by train or truck, and hand-delivered to group members. If a member snapped a photo of the pin with her cell phone, she would create a new media message that could be shared instantly.

WN

VIDEO
51. Extended
Definitions

Of note here is the way the paragraph sustains a definition of a term as a way of exploring connections and allowing the author to make larger points about her topic. Notice also how the section focuses primarily on defining an aspect of new media but incorporates additional writing strategies (such as comparison and contrast) to help develop ideas.

Definitions at the Project Level

LO

Learning
Objective 22.2

You can see how definitions can extend beyond simply explaining the meaning of a term to a way of making sense of topics and ideas. This zoomed out conception of definitions becomes most apparent as you organize entire projects. Even at the project level, work with definitions can range from the formal and concrete to the more abstract. Some writers use an organizational strategy known as "arguing by definition" to explore a topic. This strategy relies on a criteria-match format that outlines the nature of a category or classification and then considers an item in terms of that category.

Criteria-match definitions provide a helpful way of considering an item in detail. The basic format involves listing and justifying criteria for the category into which something falls and then discussing whether the item meets those criteria. If you wanted to propose that the local disc golf club on campus be granted status as a sport to receive intramural funding, you might use a criteria-match approach. You could begin by detailing the criteria that might qualify any item as a sport—competition, spectators, teamwork, scoring, physical exertion, training, etc. You would need to distinguish between criteria that are necessary and those that are incidental to the definition of a sport; for example, scoring and training might be needed to qualify anything as a sport, but teamwork and spectators might not be necessary.

As you develop these definitions, use writing strategies that help make your points. Examples are particularly helpful. To illustrate that scoring is more important than spectators in defining a sport, you could consider instances like target shooting or cross-country running. Providing relevant examples will help you support your criteria and refine your thinking. In addition, use descriptions, comparisons, discussions of research, or any means that will help justify your criteria. Once you have explored in detail the necessary criteria related to your broad category, you can discuss the item in question to complete the examination. If you had explained that competition, scoring, and training are key elements of any sport, you could then show how disc golf meets (or does not meet) those requirements. In this effort, you could use examples and other writing strategies to bolster your points about the item.

A criteria-match essay represents a formal structure, and you can use this formula to develop an entire project depending on your rhetorical situation. In many cases, though, you will find that you can use this strategy on a smaller scale, as needed in various writing projects. (In an evaluation of a book, you might outline criteria for a hero and then discuss a character; in an explanatory essay on college admissions processes, you might consider criteria for success in college and then discuss SAT scores, etc.)

You will also find that you can organize an entire essay around the process of defining something without having to follow an exact formula. Consider the outline for an essay on new media composing shown in Figure 22.1.

The outline demonstrates the ways in which strategies of defining can be combined. It also reveals how projects evolve organically in response to their rhetorical situations. The essay itself is guided by a research question. The plan for developing the essay includes sections that discuss the definition of new media as well as a section with a focused criteria-match exploration. The plan concludes with a discussion of what a revised definition of writing instruction might look like.

Research Question: Should new media composing be required in college writing classes?

    1. What is new media composing?
        a. Digital—easy to reproduce and manipulate
        b. Social—easy to share and relevant to readers
        c. Multimedia—texts, images, sounds
    2. Is new media a valuable form of writing instruction?
        a. Criteria/Match
            i. Promotes critical thinking
            ii. Develops awareness of rhetorical situations
            iii. Offers opportunities to engage readers/the public
            iv. Allows writers to explore and understand topics
    3. How can new media composing help revise our understanding of college writing?
        a. A new definition of composing—mixing and putting together
        b. More overlap and movement among areas of study—language, art, culture
        c. New methods of teaching—collaboration, workshops, online sharing and review

FIGURE 22.1
An outline for an essay that uses definition strategies.

CONNECT IT   Definitions in Multiple Genres

Definitions can be used in a number of genres. Learn how definitions work at multiple levels and how to use definitions to develop your ideas, and then consider how you can compose using definitions based on your situation.

- **Position arguments:** Use definitions to organize sections of projects, concentrating on making meanings clear as a way of persuading readers (see Chapter 8).
- **Explanatory research essays:** Define terms and concepts as a way of making your topic clear for readers (see Chapter 10).
- **Book, music, or film reviews:** Help readers understand the category of the item under review by using definitions (see Chapter 11).

- **Literary analyses:** Explore the range of meanings available for words or for a sentence to develop an interpretation (see Chapter 12).
- **Portfolios:** Stop to clarify the goals and parameters of assignments as you discuss materials included in the portfolio (see Chapter E2).
- **Résumés and business letters:** Provide descriptions of duties to help readers understand the definitions of job titles (see Chapter E6).

Definitions in Multiple Mediums

Audio essays. As you compose audio essays, you will need to be keenly aware of the auditory needs of readers. Unlike taking in a print essay, where readers move at their own pace, listening to an audio essay can become difficult if terms roll by without clarification. Listeners can pause an audio essay to look up meanings, but they will be better served by authors who make deliberate efforts to spell out the ways in which they are using key terms. You can provide definitions as asides to your narration to help listeners stay on track.

Oral presentations and slide shows. Oral presentations can also be a challenge for listeners because the information can come quickly. Further, in an oral presentation, you often will be presenting from your expertise to a group who is less familiar with your topic. You can plan segments of your presentation for defining terms and concepts. However, you have an opportunity to use the format of the oral presentation to your advantage by providing visuals that help readers make sense of your key concerns. The image in Figure 22.2, for instance, uses a visual representation to make the definitions of obesity easier to understand. Use images as needed to clarify your presentations. Additionally, rely on the format to allow your audience to express any confusion and ask for clarification. You can pause, asking audience members about their familiarity with your terms and concerns, and then adjust your presentation as needed.

Ask Questions & Make Decisions

Exercises for Understanding Definitions

1. Identify a word that you feel to be rich in meaning (e.g., *composing, modeling, nurturing*). Look up the term in a dictionary, considering all of the variant meanings listed. How well do all of the entries capture the mean-

LO

Learning
Objective 22.3

ing of the term? What senses of the word have been left out? Choose one or two of the entries that could be clarified and then edit them so that they further define the meaning of the term.

2. Think of a word that people generally take for granted (e.g., *cat, house, jump, sing*). Without looking in a dictionary, compose a definition capturing the denotative meaning of the term. Compose as many entries as needed to capture all the meanings of the word.

3. Identify a complex concept (e.g., *freedom of speech, capitalism, peer pressure*). Create a paragraph explaining the concept, using strategies of definition to develop ideas. Provide examples, make comparisons, and use additional writing strategies as you compose your paragraph.

4. Think about an item and category that would lend themselves to an argument by definition (graffiti and art, archery and sports, *CSI* and educational television). Develop an outline in which you list necessary criteria related to the category and sketch out ideas for matching (or not matching) the item with those criteria.

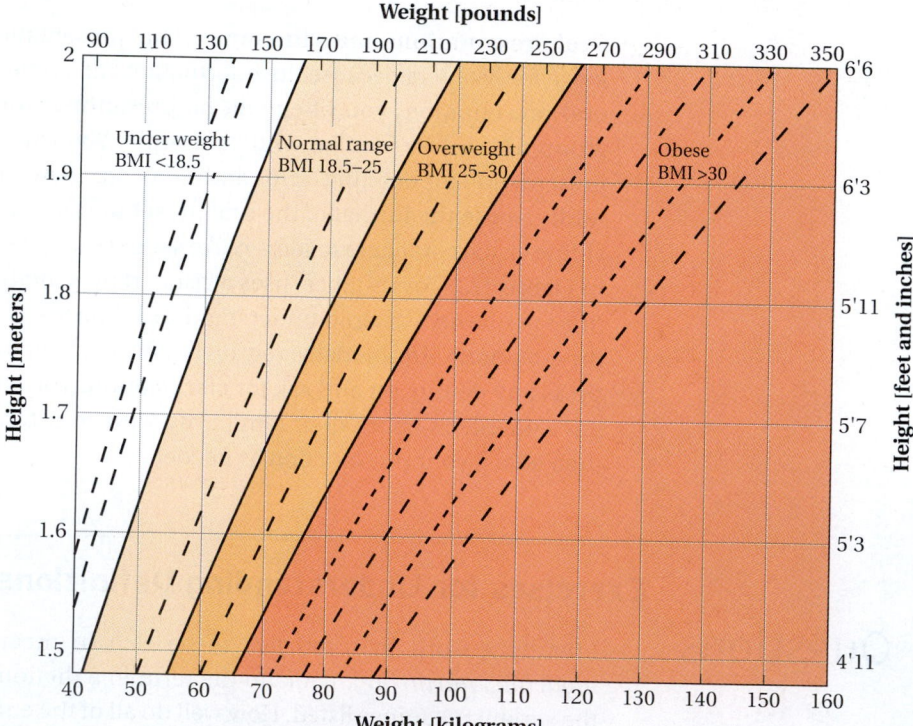

FIGURE 22.2

An information graphic representing definitions of obesity.

Zoom **Out**   Reflecting on Definitions

- **Definitions operate at multiple levels.** At the word and sentence level, definitions help clarify terms; at the paragraph and project level, definitions help explain the meaning of concepts.

- **Definition is one among many strategies for composing.** Use definitions as needed in whatever genre you happen to be working with. Use examples, description, comparison, and other strategies to strengthen your definitions.

- **As you move from the word to the project level, your thinking about definitions will evolve from the concrete to the abstract.** Zoom in and out as needed conceptually to understand how definitions can work in your writing as a whole.

For additional information and practice with the learning objectives in this chapter, go to www.mycomplab.com, Resources > Writing > Writing Samples: Technical and Workplace Writing > Writing Samples: Descriptions and Definitions.

Comparisons and Contrasts

Zoom In Key Concepts and Learning Objectives

After studying this chapter, you should be able to:

23.1 Develop point-by-point comparisons and contrasts that weave together discussion of several items.

23.2 Use chunk (block) comparisons and contrasts to discuss items, one after another.

23.3 Use transitions and tags to introduce and clarify comparisons and contrasts.

23.4 Understand how comparisons and contrasts can be made in many genres.

23.5 Develop comparisons and contrasts in a range of mediums.

Have you ever had to think twice at the checkout counter when responding to the question, "Paper or plastic?" We sometimes have trouble deciding; one might rip, the other might break. What to do? Well, we might start by using some comparison and contrast strategies. Comparisons focus on similarities while contrasts focus on differences. We could consider something that is important to us—say, the environment—and compare or contrast the two choices based on their environmental impact: paper uses trees, but degrades faster; plastic uses oil, but takes fewer resources to transport. When we make comparisons and contrasts like this we consider items in terms of each other. Sometimes we will notice patterns and related traits. Sometimes we will recognize distinctions. In practice, we move back and forth between comparing and contrasting as we relate items, and often the term "comparison" is used to represent this process of considering similarities and differences.

Of course, for writers, comparing and contrasting can be more challenging than determining which bag to use at the grocery store. It's possible to compose entire essays using comparison and contrast formats. Just as likely, however, you will need to bring comparisons and contrasts into a number of genres that you create. Comparisons and contrasts can be deliberately developed using either point-by-point or chunk (sometimes called block) strategies. Point-by-point comparisons/contrasts weave together observations about items, while chunk comparisons/contrasts separate discussion of items so each is considered in turn.

Point-By-Point Comparisons and Contrasts

Point-by-point comparisons and contrasts weave together observations about items being compared, as in this excerpt from a review of the album, *Mermaid Avenue*, which was put out by musical artists Billy Bragg and Wilco.

Learning
Objective 23.1

Hearing Billy Bragg and Wilco together, listeners will quickly realize this is not a dust bowl rerelease. Billy Bragg, who has been a stalwart on the music scene for nearly two decades and was politically born out of the ideological 1980s British left, has given his voice to tell of working-class hardships, growing economic disparity, labor unions, and social injustices. He comes at Guthrie's lyrics with a similar political stance, but with a different musical approach. The result gives Bragg's songs a greater sense of urgency—and a more raucous sound—than listeners of Guthrie's music will be used to. Wilco, on the other hand, came into this project a commercially successful American band with deep roots in folk and country music. Front-man Jeff Tweedy has emerged as one of the more important voices of the alternative country scene, first by forming the influential band Uncle Tupelo, and then by

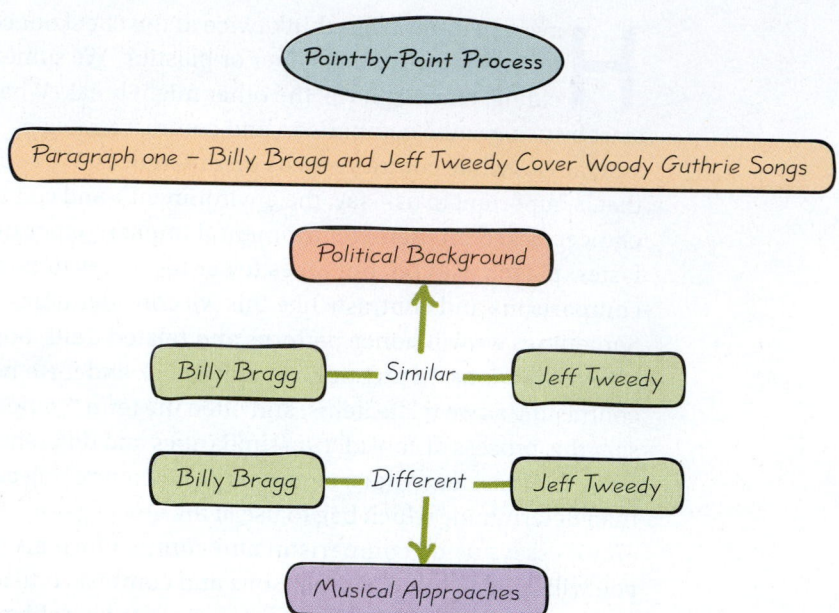

FIGURE 23.1
The point-by-point model of comparison and contrast.

assembling Wilco in 1995. On *Mermaid Avenue*, Tweedy's songs are simple yet powerful invocations of working people, lost love, and hope. Together, Billy Bragg and Wilco have created two unique albums with a singularity of purpose, deconstructing an icon into a man who stood at odds with his social and political surroundings, but whose passion for social justice remained resolute.

In this point-by-point process, the author moves back and forth, making points about musicians Billy Bragg and Jeff Tweedy in their coverage of folk songs by Woody Guthrie. The point-by-point discussion brings out comparisons and contrasts as it highlights distinctions and similarities in the backgrounds and approaches of both artists.

Chunked Comparisons and Contrasts

LO

Learning Objective 23.2

Chunked (or block) comparisons and contrasts separate discussion of items being compared into distinct blocks or sections, as in the excerpt below.

Knocked Up jumps out at the viewer. Typical of Judd Apatow's films, it skewers most every convention. Many of the film's scenes offer little new on the crude formula of potty humor and gross out visuals, as when Ben fails repeatedly at putting on a condom or later tries to have sex with a pregnant Alison. The pregnant sex scene shows the couple, contorting, adjusting, and discussing the anatomical details of the process until Ben loses his ability to perform. The scene is juvenile, and, depending on your sensibilities, reasonably funny. But the film does vary from other Apatow offerings in its subject matter. The decision Alison makes to keep her baby is not simple. Nor are the changes Ben must make to evolve from slacker slob to potential father. Unfortunately, the seriousness of the subject matter is watered down by the over-the-top efforts to generate laughs at any cost.

Juno, on the other hand, builds its humor more subtly on the foundation of the tough choices made by its sixteen-year-old protagonist. *Juno* is funny, very funny, but more serious about its subject matter. The key scene in this regard places Juno at an abortion clinic. Condoms appear here as well, but they add levity to an encounter that sees Juno accosted by a pro-life classmate who tries to sway Juno with information about fetal development and the assertion that her pregnancy is a miracle. The film does not offer simplistic treatments of abortion. Like the confrontations that play out daily in the lives of teens and their families, the film doesn't shy away from themes of sex and pregnancy—in fact, it looks them in the eye and sees there not only human drama, but also humor and possibility.

In this chunked approach, *Knocked Up* is discussed first, allowing the author to make key points about the movie before moving on to a similar discussion about the film *Juno*. The discussion uses examples to provide details about the films and looks at both similarities and differences.

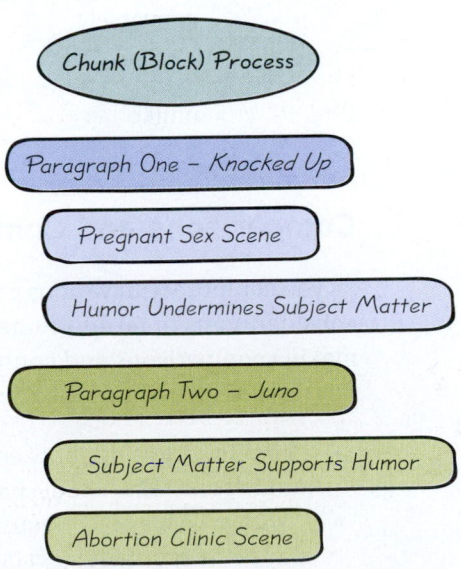

FIGURE 23.2
The chunk (block) model of comparison and contrast.

Transitions and Tags for Comparisons and Contrasts

Learning
Objective 23.3

To help readers follow comparisons and contrasts and to bring out points of similarity or difference, authors use transitions and comparison/contrast tags. In the point-by-point approach above, for instance, the author writes, "Wilco, *on the other hand*, came into this project a commercially successful American band. . . ." The contrast tag, "on the other hand," emphasizes the differences between Wilco and Billy Bragg.

Helpful Transitions and Tags for Contrasts and Comparisons

Contrast Tags	Comparison Tags
but	like
however	likewise
in contrast	much like
on the other hand	equally
on the contrary	similarly
while	comparably
yet	correspondingly
despite	analogously
still	just as
conversely	as well
otherwise	too
unlike	also

VIDEO
52. Comparisons
and Contrasts

CONNECT IT

Comparisons and Contrasts in Multiple Genres

Learning
Objective 23.4

As you compose with various genres, you will have a number of opportunities to consider items in terms of one another. Learn structures and approaches for making comparisons and contrasts (e.g., point-by-point or chunk/block), and then ask questions and make decisions as you relate items in your compositions.

- **Memoirs:** Consider how episodes can be compared and contrasted to one another and think about changes in the memoir subject's life (see Chapter 5).
- **Profiles:** Focus on comparing and contrasting developments in the personality of the profile subject (see Chapter 6).

- **Position arguments:** Focus on responding to opposing points of view by comparing and contrasting them (see Chapter 8).
- **Proposals:** Use comparisons and contrasts when responding to alternative proposals and demonstrating feasibility (see Chapter 9).
- **Explanatory research essays:** Concentrate on using comparisons when analyzing and synthesizing information for your readers (see Chapter 10).
- **Book, music, and film reviews:** When discussing a work, focus on relating the item to its genre and on noting similarities and differences with previous works (see Chapter 11).
- **Visuals:** Focus on using similar or contrasting elements to convey information about concepts (see Chapter 25).
- **Essay exams:** Focus on using comparisons to demonstrate knowledge and apply concepts (see Chapter E9).

Comparisons and Contrasts in Multiple Mediums

LO

Learning
Objective 23.5

Photographs. Consider the well-known photograph of the Louvre Museum in Figure 23.3. No doubt the decision to commission such a modern structure when building an addition to the museum was deliberate. Because the Louvre represents longstanding traditions of fine art, the glass pyramid that marks its entrance recasts the message offered by the formalized architecture of the original building. The Louvre is presented as both familiar and new, traditional and cutting edge. When composing photographs, consider how the objects you include in the frame can be used to create comparisons and contrasts.

FIGURE 23.3
The entry to the Louvre Museum.

FIGURE 23.4
Slave trade history
collage.

Visual collages. Collages similarly rely on strategies of comparison and contrast, but generally create more subtle relationships between multiple elements. Consider the collage in Figure 23.4. The message offered in the collage must be inferred by interpreting the multiple elements present in the image. The continent of Africa, the profile, and the cutaway slave ship all speak to the history of the slave trade. The segments of red, white, and blue in the bottom right, however, refine the message by recalling the American flag. When composing collages, think about how you can combine elements to create patterns and contrasts that convey meaning. Use cropping and layering tools to combine elements, and then use strategies of arrangement to create juxtapositions.

Ask Questions & Make Decisions

Exercises for Understanding Comparisons and Contrasts

1. Working with a group of peers, compose two paragraphs. In each paragraph, relate the most important details of your first semester in college. As you compose the first paragraph, imagine your audience to be your parents. For

the second paragraph, imagine your audience to be your best friends from childhood. Once finished, write a third paragraph comparing and contrasting the first two.

2. Examine the essay "Where Are My Beats?" on pages 37–40. Highlight all the instances where you find comparison and contrast strategies used to further the writing. Write a two- or three-sentence assessment, analyzing the strengths and weaknesses of the essay in terms of comparisons.

3. Develop a two- or three-paragraph comparison/contrast based on one of the following topics. Use an outline or graphic map to get started.
   - Your experiences traveling
   - A book that has been made into a movie
   - Two or more musical artists or genres
   - Two or more positions on a political issue

4. To learn more about using strategies of juxtaposition, create a video mashup in which you contrast the message of a visual composition with audio that presents an alternative message. To compose the mashup, you will use a video editor, most likely Windows Movie Maker or iMovie. You will need to import the images, video, or audio into the video editing program and then edit the materials, adjusting their sequencing and integrating additional items to create the message. (Find more information in Chapter E7.)

Zoom **Out**   Reflecting on Comparisons and Contrasts

- **Comparing and contrasting is an ongoing process that plays out as you read and write.** Asking questions and making decisions about similarities and differences is a key activity of critical thinking.

- **Authors can provide clues to readers about comparisons and contrasts.** By adjusting the organization of compositions, authors can integrate both point-by-point and block comparisons. Transitions and tags can alert readers to comparisons and contrasts.

- **Comparisons and contrasts can be understood in terms of genres and mediums.** Some genres—like film reviews—lend themselves well to comparisons. Changes in mediums enable different kinds of comparisons and contrasts—for instance, through the use of juxtaposition in images or videos.

- **Comparing and contrasting can help you make better sense of cultural networks.** Considering the relationships between people, ideas, and things reveals similarities and differences that can lead to understanding.

 For additional information and practice with the learning objectives in this chapter, go to www.mycomplab.com, Resources > Writing > Writing Purposes > Writing to Compare or Contrast.

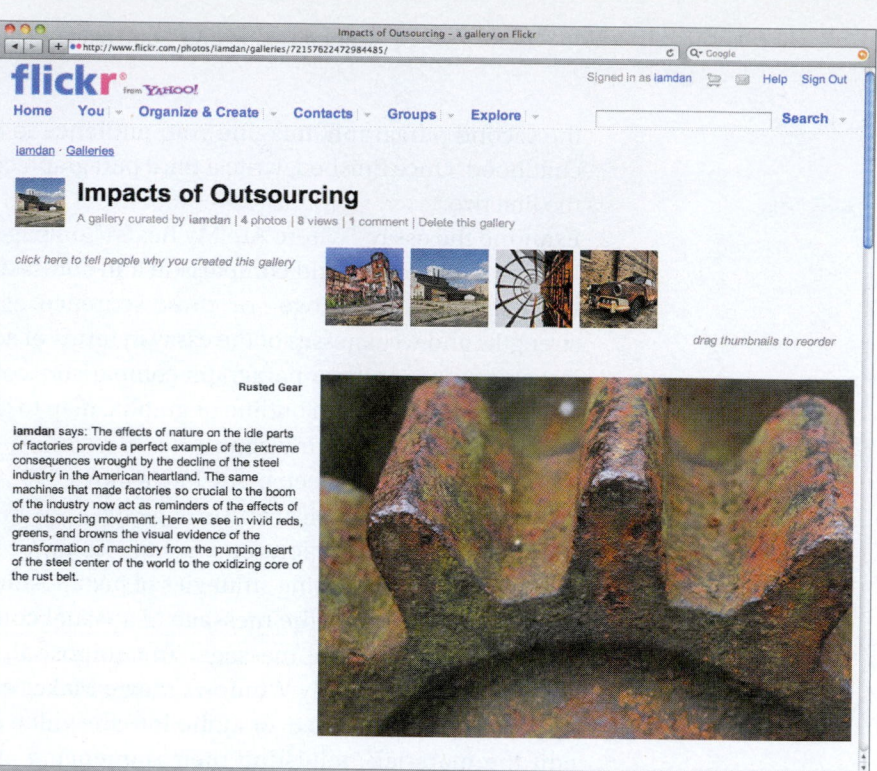

Rusted Gear

iamdan says: The effects of nature on the idle parts of factories provide a perfect example of the extreme consequences wrought by the decline of the steel industry in the American heartland. The same machines that made factories so crucial to the boom of the industry now act as reminders of the effects of the outsourcing movement. Here we see in vivid reds, greens, and browns the visual evidence of the transformation of machinery from the pumping heart of the steel center of the world to the oxidizing core of the rust belt.

Causes and Effects

Zoom **In**   **Key Concepts and Learning Objectives**

After studying this chapter, you should be able to:

24.1 Examine causes and effects to look forward and backward.

24.2 Use critical thinking to make sense of causes and effects.

24.3 Understand the role of speculation when discussing causes and effects.

24.4 Discuss causes and effects to create compelling compositions.

When it comes to writing, looking backward and forward can often be a good strategy for exploring ideas and developing a project. As you examine an event, for instance, you might be able to trace some of its precursors and discuss the consequences of the episode. (This kind of reflection might be a good way to explore a topic like the desegregation of the University of Alabama in 1963.) You can also project forward using cause and effect strategies, speculating about the potential outcome of an event or course of action. (Examining potential effects might be a good way to discuss a topic like sin taxes on sugary drinks and fast food.)

These strategies will be particularly helpful as you explore complex questions or think about trends or phenomena. You would necessarily examine potential causes if you wanted to investigate a question such as, *Why have childhood obesity rates in America risen dramatically in the last several decades?* As you did so, you would move forward to trace their effects, likely developing an argument that some causes are more significant than others. You could use a similar strategy to persuade readers about a possible course of action, perhaps tracing potential effects of a tax on fast food and sugary drinks as part of a proposal. Again, you would be looking backward and forward, pinpointing causes and effects, to organize and deliver ideas.

Analyzing Causes and Effects

Learning
Objective 24.1

Although you will be identifying one or more possible sources of a phenomenon as you explore causes, keep in mind that much of your work will be speculative. You could likely draw a connection between television watching and childhood obesity, but suggesting that too much TV is the definitive cause of overweight children would be nearly impossible. First, such direct causality would be hard to prove. And second, the suggestion would overlook the complexity of the issue. Instead, your analysis will focus on identifying plausible associations between causes and effects, and then supporting assertions about the validity of the connections you have found. To develop this analytical support, look for evidence that supports your conclusions (see pages 81–82) and weigh potential objections to your conjectures.

You will also need to practice analysis that considers multiple possibilities and that examines the ways in which several causes and various potential effects can be bound together and influence one another. Alongside television, you would need to consider evolving eating trends in America, changing family structures and routines, and attitudes toward exercise (to name a few possibilities) as you examine potential causes of childhood obesity. Your analysis would require assessing these potential causes in concert with one another. Ultimately, you will need to balance this need to remain open to complexity with the demands of offering tangible conclusions about causes. Through critical thinking, you can identify key causes, explore connections among them, and offer readers evaluations about their relative role in producing the effects you are considering.

Arguing About Causes and Effects

Learning Objective 24.2

Although identifying the relationship between an effect and its potential causes relies on some speculation, your writing projects require that you convincingly argue about the connections you believe to be behind a trend.

Evidence will be key to bolstering your argument. The more hard information you can provide about a connection between a cause and effect, the less speculative your conclusions become. The best evidence will come from facts and statistics drawn from research. If you can find studies with survey results showing a correlation between more time in front of the TV and childhood obesity, you can quickly solidify the link between the two for your readers. Reports, statistics, and the conclusions of experts all make solid sources of evidence for your speculations about causes.

You can also develop arguments about causes and effects by examining patterns or discussing chains of events. You can identify patterns as a way of demonstrating a correlation between a cause and effect. To explore one of the potential sources of childhood obesity, for instance, you could consider changing patterns in the home—the shift from one to two parents in the workforce, the "McMansioning" of America and resulting isolation of family members within the home, and the decreasing number of hours spent at family meals. Chains of events similarly allow you to explore patterns and connections—suburbanization in the 1950s leading to diminished opportunities for walking leading to dependence on cars leading to more time spent driving leading to more fast-food meals, with the end result being an unhealthy diet lifestyle for many Americans.

Learning Objective 24.3

You can use all of these strategies for arguing about causes and effects as part of an essay or larger project. An exploration of the future of climate change might examine key effects. You can develop the project by showing the connection between the causes and the effects and by solidifying that connection through the use of evidence. You will want to anticipate and respond to potential objections and consider possible alternatives to the correlations you identify.

VIDEO
53. Causes and Effects

CONNECT IT   Causes and Effects in Multiple Genres

Learning
Objective 24.4

Depending on your situation, you can use thinking about causes and effects to develop your compositions. Learn to identify causes and effects, and then ask questions and make decisions as you look backward or project forward in your projects.

- **Memoirs:** Focus on episodes in the past and the ways in which they have shaped the identity of the memoir writer (see Chapter 5).
- **Profiles:** Use episodes to show how the identity of the profile subject has evolved over time (see Chapter 6).
- **Rhetorical analyses:** Consider the ways in which rhetorical strategies in a work affect a reader (see Chapter 7).
- **Position arguments:** Examine the roots of a phenomenon and forecast the consequences of actions to persuade readers to support your points (see Chapter 8).
- **Proposals:** Concentrate on the effects the proposal will have in addressing a problem (see Chapter 9).
- **Book, music, or film reviews:** Trace the artistic genealogy of a work to provide context for your assessments (see Chapter 11).
- **Literary analyses:** Consider how plot elements and character development can be treated in terms of causes and effects (see Chapter 12).
- **Oral presentations:** Use cause and effect strategies to make persuasive points for your audience (see Chapter E1).
- **Composition portfolios:** Demonstrate learning, growth, and effort that result from your responses to assignments (see Chapter E2).
- **Résumés and business letters:** Use cause and effect strategies in business letters to convince readers to consider your requests (see Chapter E6).

Causes and Effects in Multiple Mediums

Photo essays. You can use images to bring to life points you wish to make about root causes. A series of photographs might depict historical precedents for an essay discussing the Title IX ruling that equalized opportunities in college sports for men and women. You can also use images to demonstrate the potential consequences of human actions and decisions. A photo essay arguing for the introduction of tariffs to reduce outsourcing could provide images depicting abandoned factories in the American rust belt. As you work with images to trace causes and demonstrate effects, be sure to

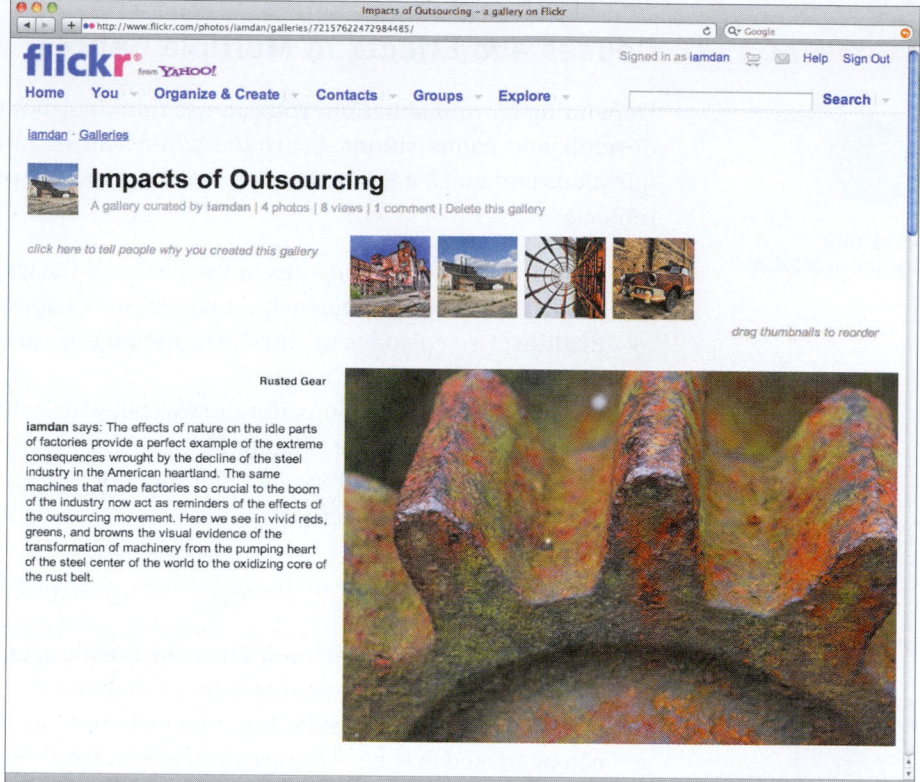

FIGURE 24.1
A flickr photo gallery showing the effects of outsourcing.

balance the emotional power of the visual medium with the need to justify the correlation of any causes you assign to an effect. Similarly, don't forget to provide evidence in other forms to bolster your points. Use titles and captions with detailed text to complement the images that you select.

Online postings and blogs. If you have a strong investment in a concern or a longstanding interest in a trend or phenomenon, you can engage others over time regarding causes and effects through online postings or blogs. Initially, your postings online might resemble what you could compose in an essay—looking backward at causes or conjecturing forward about consequences. Over time, however, you can explore the topic as developments occur. You can also engage other members of online forums about effects that play out under the watch of the group; groups concerned with copyright issues, education, the environment, journalism, etc. have new developments to discuss almost daily. For a concern about which you are significantly invested, consider creating your own blog where you can post your thoughts regularly and put your stamp on an approach to an evolving topic.

Ask Questions & Make Decisions

Exercises for Understanding Causes and Effects

1. Working with a group of peers, identify a contemporary trend or problem—trends in green architecture, reality television, teen pregnancy, credit card debt, etc. Make a list of possible causes for the concern you select. Narrow the list to two or three key causes, keeping in mind justifications for your selections. Report your findings to your classmates.

2. Think of a social concern about which you feel strongly—cruelty-free products, pre-K education, tax relief, etc. Develop a list of potential effects that you could cite in an argument in support of your cause. Think about evidence and examples you could use to support items in your list, then develop an outline for a causal argument related to your topic.

3. Search online for images related to a concern or trend. Identify one image that could help you talk about causes and one that could support discussion of effects related to the topic. Write captions for each, explaining how they speak to your concern.

4. Revisit Bill McKibben's essay on climate change (pages 92–95). Read the essay again, looking at ways in which it uses cause and effect strategies to make its points. Compose a paragraph analyzing the piece in terms of these strategies.

Zoom Out

Reflecting on Causes and Effects

- **Thinking and writing about causes and effects enables you to reflect on the past or project into the future.** Remain flexible; you might develop a project by examining historical causes, or you could speculate about consequences, or you could combine these approaches.

- **Critical thinking is crucial to understanding causes and effects.** Thinking about causes and effects requires analysis, comparison, and evaluation.

- **Conclusions drawn regarding causes and effects contain a speculative element.** Provide additional support through evidence and careful argumentation to help readers see why your conclusions warrant consideration.

For additional information and practice with the learning objectives in this chapter, go to www.mycomplab.com, Resources > Writing > Writing Purposes > Writing to Analyze.

PART 5

Visual and Design Strategies

25

Visual Rhetoric Strategies

Zoom In   Key Concepts and Learning Objectives

After studying this chapter, you should be able to:

25.1 Identify basic visual elements to understand how images work.

25.2 Use visual strategies to analyze and compose with the basic elements of images.

25.3 Understand how images provide information.

25.4 Understand visual strategies in conjunction with larger rhetorical concerns.

Visual reading and composing skills are more crucial than ever in a networked world. The Internet, for instance, makes little distinction between text or image files—both can be easily transmitted and displayed for readers. And people are taking advantage of these opportunities. In early 2009, the photo sharing site flickr.com had more than 35 million members and hosted more than 3.5 billion photos. Even documents created with a word processor can now be easily modified to include images, charts, and graphs. Whether you are building a Web page, locating a folder on your desktop, browsing through a magazine, taking in an exhibit, or shopping, situations continuously call for you to use and be aware of visual reading and writing strategies.

KEY TERMS

Dots: points in a visual composition. Dots convey meaning based on their placement or their combinations with other visual elements.

Lines: visual elements that create connections and provide a sense of movement. The direction and orientation of lines expresses different messages.

Shapes: two- or three-dimensional forms in visual compositions. Shapes include circles, squares, etc., as well as asymmetrical forms in a visual space.

Scale: The relative size of elements in visual compositions. Scale can suggest the importance of elements and convey relationships.

Tonal value: The relative intensity of a color. Values range from low, dark, and heavy tones to high, light tones.

Lighting: The effects developed by varying uses of light in a visual composition. Lighting can alter the mood of an image, create areas of emphasis, and also create shading in an image.

Textures: The qualities of the surfaces of visual elements. Textures can range from smooth to rough.

Arrangement: The placement of elements in a visual composition. Arrangements can create patterns, contrasts, balance, and emphasis.

Proximity: The relative distances involved in the placement of objects in a visual composition. Proximity can be both close (with objects near one another) or distant.

Patterns: Repetitions in visual compositions. Patterns can suggest motifs, create motion, and emphasize elements.

Balance: A state achieved through similarites in visual compositions. Balance can be achieved through the use of visual elements, such as shapes, scale, colors, tonal values, and arrangement.

Contrast: A state achieved through differences in visual compositions. Contrasts can be developed using visual elements and strategies like shapes, colors, scale, arrangement, and emphasis.

Framing: The bounding of elements in a visual image. Framing can be achieved through the cropping of the image itself, or through the use of elements within an image such as lines, colors, or shapes.

Emphasis: A strategy for highlighting an aspect of a visual image. Sometimes emphasis is achieved by highlighting a particular element of an image—a focal point. Emphasis can also be achieved by creating a dominant impression through the use of elements and strategies like lines, shapes, scale, lighting, and contrast.

WN

VIDEO
54. Visual
Elements

Thinking Conceptually About Visual Communication

A good way to understand visual communication is to start at a fundamental level that considers basics like shapes, lines, and colors. You might not think that something as elemental as a dot could have meaning, but consider the different messages that can pulled out of Figure 25.1.

You can see from Figure 25.1 that even basic visual elements like dots and framing boxes can deliver messages. A dot by itself means very little. Combine that dot with many others or strategically place that dot somewhere and you have created a message. The same holds true for basic concepts like lines, shapes, and scale (relative size), as seen in Figure 25.2.

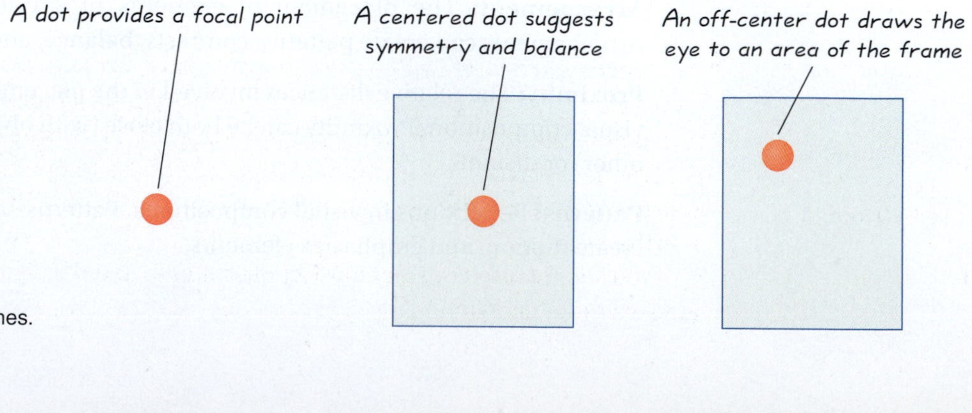

A dot provides a focal point

A centered dot suggests symmetry and balance

An off-center dot draws the eye to an area of the frame

FIGURE 25.1
Focal points and frames.

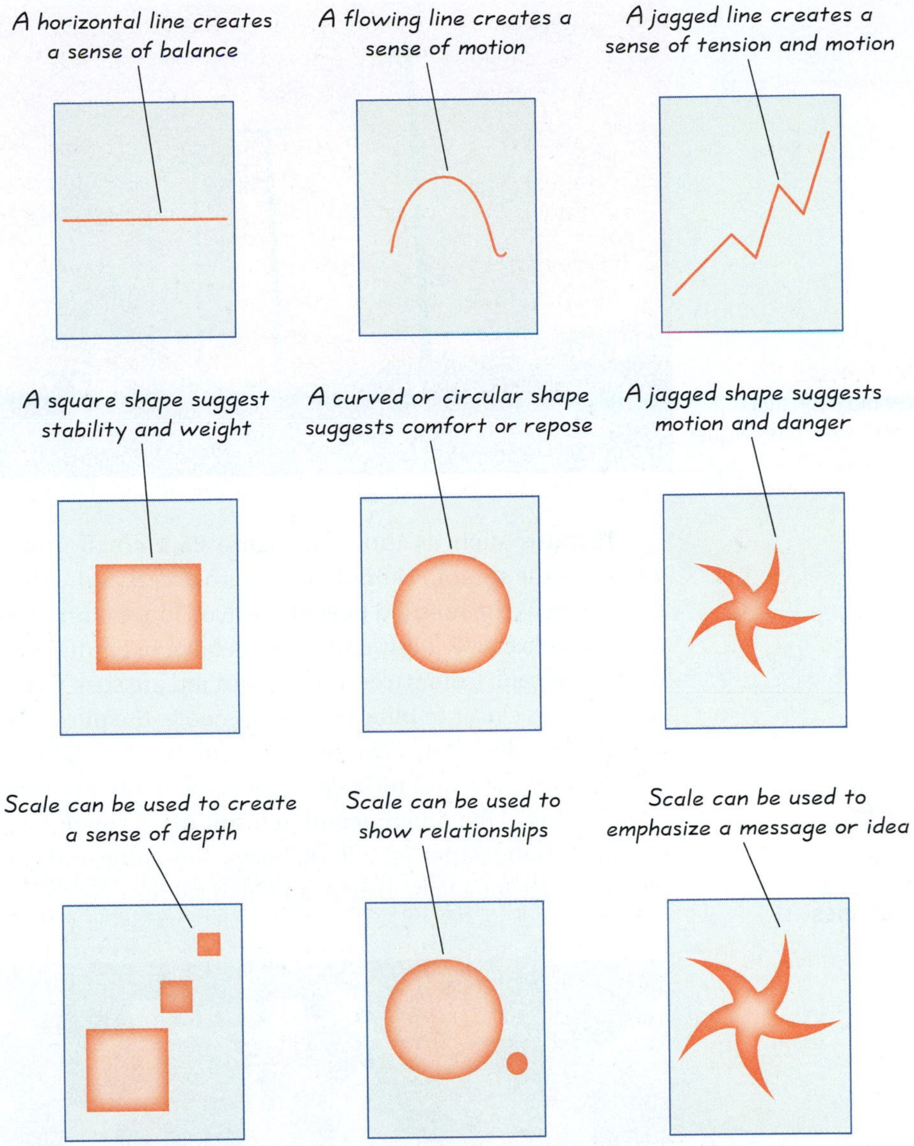

A horizontal line creates a sense of balance

A flowing line creates a sense of motion

A jagged line creates a sense of tension and motion

A square shape suggest stability and weight

A curved or circular shape suggests comfort or repose

A jagged shape suggests motion and danger

Scale can be used to create a sense of depth

Scale can be used to show relationships

Scale can be used to emphasize a message or idea

FIGURE 25.2
Lines, shapes, and scale.

Learning Objective 25.1

You can see how understanding something about basic visual elements could help you make sense of the composition of Figure 25.3. The varied horizontal line created by the landscape suggests a soft sense of motion across the frame as a whole. The diminishing scale of the telephone poles creates a sense of depth. The two points of light created by the headlights draw the eye into the distance.

You should also consider basic concerns associated with texture, colors, and tonal value, as seen in Figure 25.4.

FIGURE 25.3
A photograph that emphasizes basic visual elements.

Textures such as those in Figure 25.4 create different impressions on viewers—the smooth skin of the tomatoes versus the thorny leaves of the artichoke versus the mottled peel of the avocado. Colors similarly affect the emotions of viewers. Traditionally, colors have been divided into two categories, warm and cool. Colors trending toward red are seen as warm—the tomatoes—while colors closer to blue are seen as cool—the purple base of the artichokes. Tonal value designates the relative amount or weight of a color. Darker and heavier areas are said to have a low value while brighter areas have a higher value. Think of the differences that result when you draw with crayon; grind the crayon into the paper for a dark, heavy, low value and gently brush the crayon atop the page for a light, bright, and high value.

WN

VIDEO
55. Visual
Strategies

FIGURE 25.4
Textures, colors, and tonal value.

Visual Strategies

LO

Learning
Objective 25.2

You can discuss elements such as dots, lines, shapes, and color to zoom in on the characteristics of visual messages. Eventually, though, you will want to zoom out to draw broader conclusions. You can build on your understanding of the basics as you do so. Figure 25.5 demonstrates how looking at visual elements like shapes and colors can lead to conclusions about broader rhetorical strategies.

An initial reading of Figure 25.5 might prompt you to comment on the presence of the two colors—blue-green and red—in the uniforms of the two cashiers. A sketch of the shapes in the image would highlight the rectangular signboards or the horizontal block shapes of the cash registers. But progressing to a more extensive reading, you would look at the way these elements lend themselves to broader rhetorical strategies. The first step might be to think about the arrangement of these elements. Note the symmetry created by centering both cashiers in the frame. There is also a sense of balance created through the patterns that are established by the shapes—burger boards and cash registers arranged symmetrically. These elements are also placed in close proximity, highlighting their relationship. In addition, the cool blue-green color of one woman's uniform differs from the warm red of the other, creating a sense of contrast or relationship. The next step is to think about arrangement, patterns, proximity, and balance as you draw conclusions about representations of McDonald's in India or about the relationship between the Maharaja Mac (a chicken or lamb burger) and the vegetable burger.

In Figure 25.6, the arrangement of shapes and use of colors, light, and values create a sense of contrast between the strawberry soda bottle and the rest of the image. The vertical arrangement of the bottle atop the flat plane of the car hood

FIGURE 25.5
Arrangement, patterns, proximity, and balance in visuals.

FIGURE 25.6
Framing, contrast, and emphasis in a photograph (William Eggleston, "Untitled (Nehi bottle on car hood)". From the Los Alamos Portfolio. 1965–74. © 2009 Eggleston Artistic Trust, courtesy Cheim & Read, New York. Used with permission. All rights reserved).

creates a sense of juxtaposition. The bright red color and its placement in the sunlight draw the viewer's eye to the bottle. The use of framing (most of the car cropped out of the picture) further focuses our attention on the bottle in the center of the image. All of these strategies combine to create a sense of emphasis.

A reading of Figure 25.6 would likely start by considering the soda bottle and its placement atop the car hood. You might then ask questions: Who drinks strawberry soda? Why might someone place the bottle on the car? Why have details about the setting or the human actors in the image been left out? As with most reading and writing, you will need to zoom in and out to make sense of these kinds of questions. Learn to focus on basic visual elements (dots, lines, shapes, colors, light, value). Identify visual strategies (arrangement, proximity, patterns, balance, contrast, framing, emphasis). And zoom out to ask broader questions and to connect what you discover with larger cultural concerns.

Using Visuals to Provide Information

The Importance of Using Mobile Connections to Stay in Touch Easily with Other People

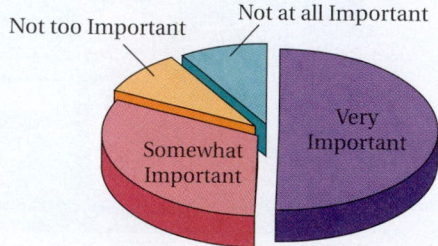

FIGURE 25.7
A pie chart listing the importance of using mobile devices to stay in touch with people.

LO

Learning
Objective 25.3

One of the primary ways in which visuals work within broader communication situations is by providing information. Informational graphics include pie charts, bar graphs, line graphs, tables, and charts. Again, you can think about basic elements of visual communication as you consider informational graphics. Consider the pie chart shown in Figure 25.7.

The pie chart is based on a recent study conducted by the Pew Internet & American Life Project. The study looks at people who regularly use Twitter or a status update Web site. As you think about some of the information in the chart, recall how the basic elements of lines, shapes, scale, and color can communicate meaning. Color is used to differentiate between categories. Scale is used to demonstrate relative amounts—here we can see that more than half of people who use mobile devices cited staying in touch with friends as very important.

Because lines, scale, shape, and color can be so suggestive, it's crucial that readers of informational graphics understand the data that visuals represent. Consider the two graphs representing change in Figure 25.8.

The number of Twitter users more than doubled from February to March 2009. The bar graph on the left more accurately represents that growth because it is presented on a scale that is appropriate for the data. The chart on the right uses a scale that is so large it tends to distort the presentation of the data. The growth figures are actually the same in both graphs, but their significance is diminished in the graph on the right by the contextual framework of the visual. As a reader you will need to pay attention to visuals to ensure that they accurately represent data. As an author, you will need to operate in good faith, using visuals to help readers make sense of your information, but not distorting facts through visual manipulation.

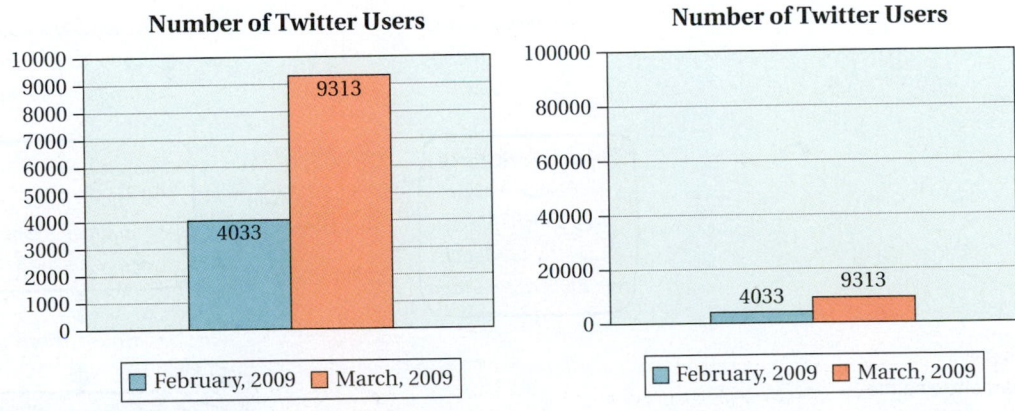

FIGURE 25.8
Two graphs demonstrating the growth of Twitter users (Comscore Media).

Flow charts and other visual maps work well to demonstrate relationships among items. Figure 25.9 shows a flow chart developed to help explain the publishing process of an online journal.

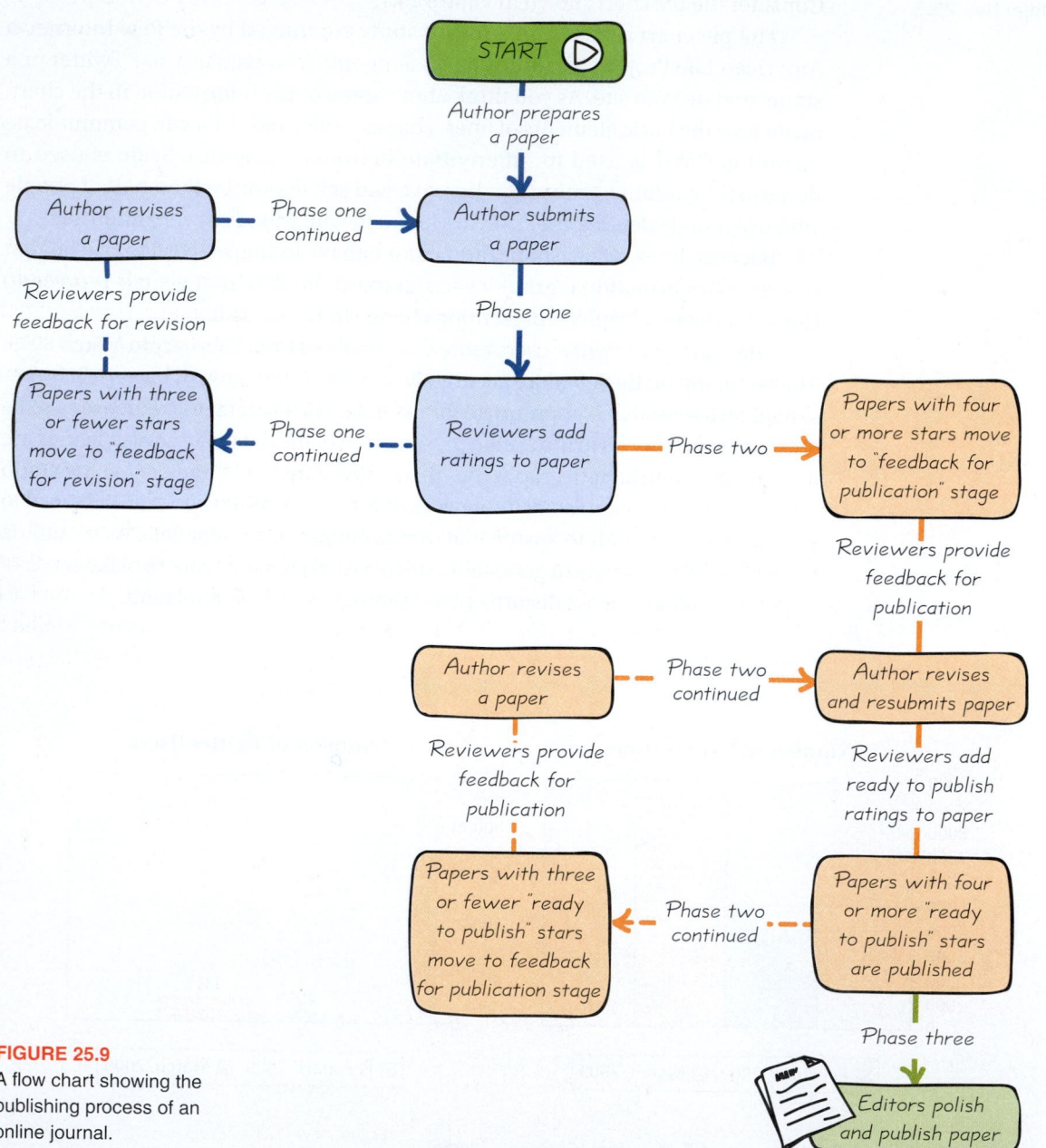

FIGURE 25.9

A flow chart showing the publishing process of an online journal.

The flow chart visually represents the process that plays out when authors submit papers to the online journal. The chart demonstrates the activities of authors, reviewers, and editors. It also shows how the papers can move through various stages of the publishing process. Flow charts and diagrams can be helpful for explaining complex processes. You can also use the act of developing charts like the one in Figure 25.9 to brainstorm about organizational schemes or processes.

WN

VIDEO
56. Visuals and
Invention

Connecting Visuals to Other Writing Strategies

LO

Learning
Objective 25.4

As you become adept at reading and creating visual forms of communication, you will discover connections with other writing strategies. Just as you should remain flexible as you consider how writing strategies complement one another, you should be ready to recognize the ways in which visual images can offer descriptions, narrate events, create comparisons, or persuade viewers (to name some possibilities). Consider the painting *Christina's World* by Andrew Wyeth shown in Figure 25.10.

You could begin examining *Christina's World* by zooming in to think about visual elements. What can be said about the texture of the field or about the shapes of the buildings in the distance? How does the arrangement of the elements affect a viewer? Or you could zoom out to begin your engagement with the image. What can you say about the figure in the image? In what way does the painting provide a description of the girl or of her life? What kind of story might the image be telling? These questions might lead you back into the image—perhaps to discuss the proximity (here a distant proximity) of the girl with the buildings.

FIGURE 25.10
Christina's World, by
Andrew Wyeth (Wyeth,
Andrew (1917–2009),
"Christina's World".
1948. Tempera on
gessoed panel, 32 1/4
× 47 3/4". Purchase.
The Museum of
Modern Art, New York,
NY, U.S.A. Digital
Image © The Museum
of Modern Art/Licensed
by SCALA/Art
Resource, NY).

CONNECT IT Visual Rhetoric Strategies in Multiple Genres

As you compose with other genres, you will have a number of opportunities to use visual rhetoric strategies. Learn about the basic visual elements and to use strategies like arrangement, emphasis, balance, etc., and then make decisions about visuals depending on your situation.

- **Memoirs:** Use photographs to demonstrate stages in a memoir subject's life or people, places, and things of importance (see Chapter 5).
- **Profiles:** Use photographs to help discuss the identity of your profile subject or to demonstrate people, places, and things (see Chapter 6).
- **Rhetorical analyses:** Include visuals that reproduce items under analysis; be sure to discuss the images you include (see Chapter 7).
- **Position arguments:** Use images to create visual appeals that complement the logic of your argument; use informational images to provide evidence for your points (see Chapter 8).
- **Proposals:** Use informational images to demonstrate the extent of a problem or the feasibility of a solution (see Chapter 9).
- **Explanatory research essays:** Include informational graphics to help readers make sense of the topic (see Chapter 10).
- **Book, music, or film reviews:** Use screen shots to create still images from key scenes in films; include images that illuminate people or ideas related to music or books (see Chapter 11).
- **Photo essays:** Call on visual elements and strategies to discuss the images included in your projects (see Chapter 13).
- **Oral presentations:** Use informational images to support points; use images for analysis and discussion (see Chapter E1).
- **Composition portfolios:** Take screen shots of writing projects to show their development or to represent online work in a portfolio (see Chapter E2).
- **Brochures and flyers:** Use images to create flow and emphasis within the brochure and to provide visual examples as needed (see Chapter E7).

Visual Rhetoric Strategies in Multiple Mediums

Videos. The area of film studies has some specific terminology for talking about the look of what goes into a movie frame, but generally you can read elements in a video much as you would those in a photograph or other image. You can discuss rhetorical strategies like framing, balance, contrast, arrangement, and patterns. You can also consider the ways in which objects or figures communicate meaning as part of a film image. If you are composing a video and wish to discuss visual elements, consider using voiceovers to add explanations about what appears on the screen.

Web pages. If you are creating a Web page, the visual strategies you use will relate not only to the design of the page but also to how you will integrate images into your pages and discuss them. (For concerns of design, consider the advice in Chapter 26.) If you are using the Web page to display and discuss images, you will need to think about when and how you can use the materials. (See the information concerning intellectual property and fair use on pages 345–47.) Be sure to attribute your use of the image to its owner. As you integrate the image into your own Web page, think about the usability of your site for readers.

WN

VIDEO
40. Fair Use
and Intellectual
Property

Ask Questions & Make Decisions

Exercises for Understanding Visual Rhetoric Strategies

1. Working with a group of peers, look over the images in this book. Identify an image that conveys a particularly strong message. Use the basic visual elements and visual strategies discussed in this chapter to develop an analysis of how the image delivers its message. Report your findings to the rest of the class.

2. Conduct some research online into well-known photographs. Identify a photograph that you feel deserves to be included in a list of great images. Examine the image with an eye toward spotting the visual strategies that make it stand out. Write up your findings in a paragraph or two.

3. Go to an online photo sharing site like flickr.com or photobucket.com. Explore some of the collections of photographs, paying particular attention to images that have a number of comments associated with them and then choosing one image to examine. Look over the commentary of viewers, considering how they debate the merits of the image and how your assessment relates to the reactions of others. Write up your experience in a page or so.

4. Conduct research into the phenomena related to doctoring photographs. Consider earlier, pre-digital instances of photographic manipulation. Explore contemporary debates related to the "photoshopping" of images. Think about subtle manipulations related to photography—posing, removal of red eye, cropping, etc. Hold a discussion with classmates about the relationships between photographs and truth.

5. Explore videos online, identifying several that make striking use of visuals. Consider the ways in which the composition of the videos shapes their visual

messages. Are certain visual elements repeated in the videos? How does the sequencing of elements influence your reading? What affect does motion have on the visual messages? Write up your thoughts in a paragraph or so.

Zoom **Out**   Reflecting on Visual Rhetoric Strategies

- **Basic visual elements make a good starting place for understanding images.** Elements like dots, lines, shapes, scale, value, and color all create impressions on viewers.

- **Visual strategies make use of elements like shape or color to create meaning.** Strategies include arrangement, framing, emphasis, and creating balance, patterns, and contrasts.

- **Understanding visual rhetoric calls for strategies similar to those required in all communication.** Think about mediums, genres, and rhetorical situations as you make sense of images.

- **Zooming in and out is key to working with images.** Much of the work of examining images relies on focusing on details. These details must be connected to larger concerns like visual strategies, writing strategies, and elements of culture.

For additional information and practice with the learning objectives in this chapter, go to www.mycomplab.com, Resources > Writing > Writing and Visuals.

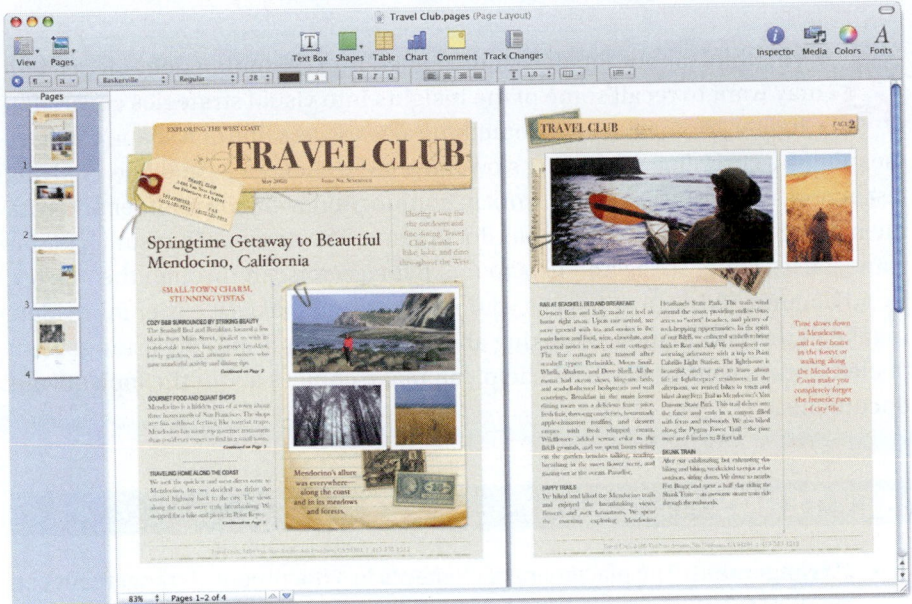

Document Design

Zoom In   Key Concepts and Learning Objectives

After studying this chapter, you should be able to:

26.1 Understand how the look of a text influences its message.

26.2 Use design principles to guide your work with documents.

26.3 Make decisions about how to display text, including fonts, headings, pull-out elements, boxes, sidebars, and visuals.

26.4 Identify design strategies for multiple genres and mediums.

As you think about the decisions that go into designing documents, you may want to recall some of the insights into visual strategies covered in Chapter 25. For instance, something as basic as a line or a shape can have meaning—a curvy line suggesting slow movement versus a jagged line implying fast action. And visual elements work in conjunction with one another and with the messages you put across in your documents. The design of a résumé, for instance, uses white space and lists to make it easy to scan through the entries. Good document design enhances your message and makes it easier for readers to take in the information. Thinking about visual details and the arrangement of elements in your projects will help you make choices about the look of your documents.

KEY TERMS

- **Arrangement:** The placement of elements in a document. Arrangement can be used to help readers move through information or to create emphasis.

- **Emphasis:** A strategy for highlighting information in a document. Emphasis can be achieved through the use of colors, headings, fonts and strategies like arrangement or the use of white space.

- **Flow:** Qualities associated with the way readers move through a document. Flow can be achieved by using strategies of design like arrangement, the use of white space, and emphasis.

- **Fonts:** The type styles used for text in a document. Fonts fall into two broad categores: serif fonts with small tails attached to characters and sans-serif fonts without tails.

- **Grouping:** A strategy of organizing similar elements together. When grouping elements, authors also strive to standardize their presentation.

- **Headings:** Phrases that organize information in a document. Headings are often set off with bold text and increased font sizes.

- **Lists:** Collections of items in a document. Lists are used to group similar items and are often set off with bullets or numbers.

- **Pull boxes:** Boxed elements used to highlight information in a document. The most common of these elements are pull quotes, which reproduce a snippet of text from a larger reading.

- **White space:** Open areas in a document. These spaces don't have to be white, instead they are empty areas that help control the flow of information.

Flow and Space

LO

Learning
Objective 26.1

At one point in the past, the people who made significant document design decisions were mostly a select group who worked for large magazines or newspapers. But the advent of desktop publishing in the 1980s brought design power into the hands of every writer. Decisions about the layout of materials in a document, about the choices of fonts, or about colors are now part of the composing process. Consider the document shown in Figure 26.1.

Looking at Figure 26.1 can reveal a good deal about the spatial elements of documents and about how readers move through a text. Visual elements like the colored swatch and the tag icon at the top of the first page catch the reader's eye. The use of images and columns creates a movement that pulls the eye down the page. On the second page, a visual emphasis continues at the top, then translates into a focus on the text of the article. If you look away and then turn back to the document, you will likely become aware of the way the arrangement of these elements creates a pattern of flow through the document.

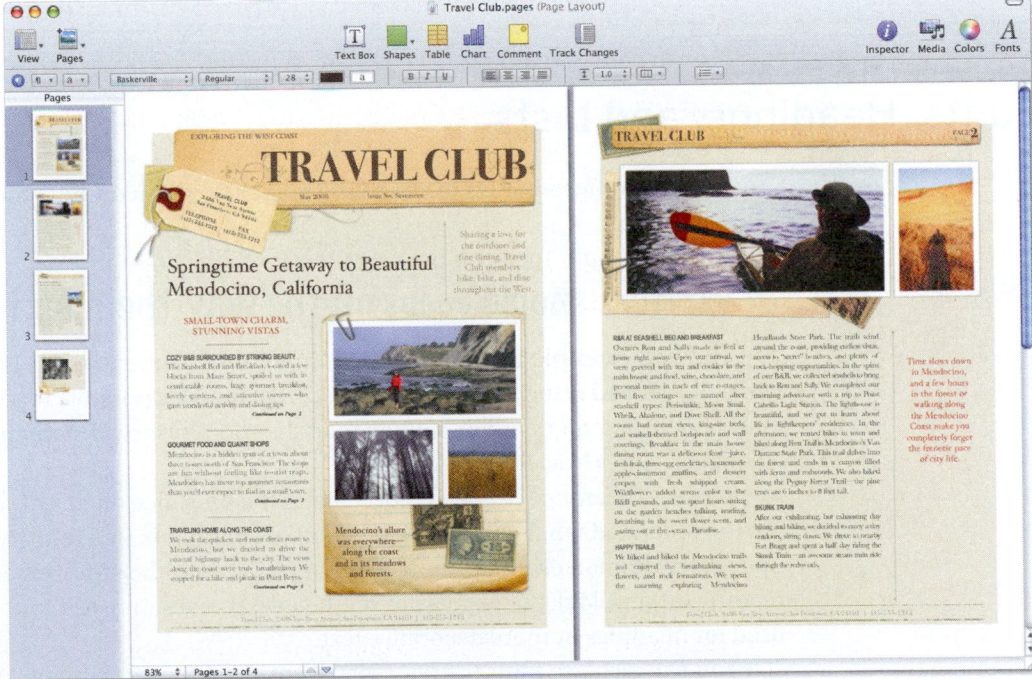

FIGURE 26.1

A page design program and a document.

LO

Learning
Objective 26.2

In addition to the selection and arrangement of these elements, the document creates emphasis and movement through the use of space. Sometimes designers call the unused space "white space," areas of emptiness that are important to help set off elements in the document. Notice the spacing around the large heading "Springtime Getaway to Beautiful Mendocino, California." Placing the heading amid an uncrowded space helps the text pop from the page, giving it emphasis. The pull quote (a short excerpt from the text displayed in a box) in the third panel on the second page similarly benefits from a large block of empty space that helps readers quickly focus on the selected bit of text.

The text itself also contributes to the flow of the document. Notice how the large heading in the banner on the opening page grabs the eye of the reader and states the title of the newsletter. The smaller "Springtime Getaway" heading that comes next announces the topic of the feature article. Smaller headings within the article break up the text, organizing its information for readers. The combination of headings, white space, and emphasis on visual elements creates a sense of flow. You can begin designing documents by making choices about these elements and thinking about how you want readers to move through your information.

WN

VIDEO
57. Flow and Space

Fonts, Headings, and Lists

Consider the different ways in which the reader's eye encounters the following two sentences:

Writers should focus on the way their text looks.

Writers should focus on the way their text looks.

The first example is set in the font Times New Roman at an 11-point size, while the second is the Marker Felt font at 16 points. It's possible to see the large Marker Felt statement as less refined than the more reserved statement offered in smaller Times New Roman.

The key difference between most fonts is the presence or lack of serifs. Serifs are the small tails that appear on the ends of characters in a font style like the Times New Roman example above. In general, fonts with serifs are said to make reading larger blocks of text easier on the eye, while sans-serif fonts are often used for headings or more decorative text.

You can also use fonts to create visual emphasis in a document. Most commonly, authors and designers accomplish this emphasis by using boldfaced or italicized (and sometimes underlined) text. Boldfaced text can be used for headings or to emphasize initial words or phrases in a list of items. Italicized text is often used for the titles of books, films, or other publications as well as for referring to words as words.

You will also need to make choices about the use of headings. A number of documents won't require headings—short essays, letters, e-mail messages, etc. Headings sometimes are used to create flow, but they really become important when readers must make sense of larger amounts of information. In these cases, your use of headings should correspond to the information you hope to communicate. In general, you will need to make choices about the number of levels to use when you create headings and subheadings. You will want to use font variations and adjustments to indentation to indicate the relationships among the levels of headings, as in the examples below:

LEVEL ONE HEADING

(centered, all capitals, boldface, and increase in point size to 2 points larger than what is used for the body text)

Level Two Heading

(flush left, boldface and increase in point size to 2 points larger than what is used for the body text)

Level Three Heading

(flush left, boldface and italics, and font size equal to the body text)

Methods of formatting headings vary from situation to situation. The objective of headings is not to insert overly flashy fonts but to represent the organization of your information. If you choose to use a font for your headings that is different from your body text, you should limit yourself to only one other font and reserve that font only for the headings or other visual labels. Ideally, a second font should create contrast with the main font; that is, if you are using a serif font in your body text, then your second font would be a sans-serif font, or vice versa. Designing with too many fonts can produce a cluttered and confusing piece. You should check on any specifications that might accompany your rhetorical situation, and then make choices about the look of your headings accordingly.

You will also want to the think about the ways in which you can group or arrange pieces of text. Lists represent the key strategy for arranging short bits of text. Most lists operate on a principle of grouping. Grouping assumes that a collection of items shares some kind of relationship. Use lists when you need to explain the steps in a process or highlight related aspects of a topic. But be careful not to overuse lists. Otherwise, your piece will become choppy, and readers might have a more difficult time making connections to your broader points. When you create a list, use parallel construction for your statements. You can also use spacing and visual elements like bullets to set off items in a list.

LO

Learning
Objective 26.3

Essay Design

It might seem a bit jarring to suggest that you have to design an essay; however, the features of most essays have been developed over time to make reading easier. For instance, the margin requirements (usually one inch) ensure an optimal amount of text on a given line. The white space of margins sets off the text, making it easier for the eyes to track from line to line. There are also a number of specific expectations associated with essays written in academic situations:

- Double space lines of text. The added space makes it easier for readers to take in larger blocks of text and to mark up documents. (The convention for business documents is single spaced.)
- Indent the first line of every paragraph five spaces. The white space gives readers a clue that a new idea or chunk of information is coming.
- Include at the top of the first page or on a separate page your name, the instructor's name, the date, and a title for the essay.
- Include your last name and page numbers in (usually) a header at the top of each page.
- Use a documentation system to cite information in the text. Include a bibliography or works cited page. Use endnotes or footnotes for any notes created in the text.
- Include figure numbers and titles for any images, charts, graphs, or tables in the text. Reference the figure by its number before its placement in the text.

WN

VIDEO
58. Essay Design

Check the expectations for your own projects, and then follow conventions like those above, knowing that they make it easier for readers to take in your thoughts. Of course, following the conventions has the added benefit of bolstering your credibility. (You can see model papers following MLA conventions on pages 393–99 and APA conventions on pages 407–10.)

CONNECT IT   Design in Multiple Genres

Design decisions differ from genre to genre. Learn to ask questions about layout, the use of text, and elements like headings, pull-out boxes, visuals, etc., and then use design strategies appropriate for your situation.

- **Memoirs:** Use images to illustrate episodes; use pull quotes to highlight key points about your subject (see Chapter 5).
- **Profiles:** Use images to bring the profile subject to life; use pull quotes to highlight key points or offer statements from your profile subject (see Chapter 6).

- **Rhetorical analyses:** Include images, pull quotes, annotations, or boxed elements to emphasize aspects of the item under analysis (see Chapter 7).
- **Position arguments:** Use headings to guide readers through your main ideas. Include lists and figures as needed to present evidence (see Chapter 8).
- **Proposals:** Use headings to demarcate the main sections of the proposal. Use charts, graphs, or tables to present information (see Chapter 9).
- **Explanatory research essays**: Use headings to organize information; pay attention to design as you integrate any figures, charts, or tables (see Chapter 10).
- **Book, music, or film reviews:** Consider ways of integrating media into your project—perhaps screen shots or links to samples; be sure to discuss the materials in detail (see Chapter 11).
- **Photo essays:** Use design to develop a template for your photo essay slides; think about navigation through the essay as you design the project (see Chapter 13).
- **Oral presentations:** Use design strategies to create your slides; select and group information using lists (see Chapter E1).
- **Composition portfolios:** Use headings in a print portfolio to demarcate projects; consider creating an electronic portfolio using Web tools (see Chapter E2).
- **Résumés and business letters:** Follow the formal expectations for business documents. Learn to translate resumes and business letters into electronic formats (see Chapter E6).

Design in Multiple Mediums

Learning
Objective 26.4

Blog design. If you have a personal blog, you can likely adjust its theme, changing colors, headers, and fonts. Learn to use the settings to adjust the look and feel of your blog. Most blogs come with a few standard themes (or skins); if possible, learn to install additional themes. You can also push further by learning how to edit a theme's style sheets and other codes to further refine the design of your page. Also think about blog design in terms of the way users will interact with your page as a whole. Investigate the options for integrating blocks with links to Web sites, archives of postings, lists of topic categories, blog subscription feeds, and other elements into the layout of your blog space.

Flyers and posters. For highly visible documents like flyers and posters, think first about grabbing your audience's attention. Figure 26.2 shows a

FIGURE 26.2
A teen pregnancy PSA poster.

PSA poster that uses a number of visual communication strategies like the use of lines, contrast, and emphasis. The poster creates a sense of flow that helps the reader move through the list of myths associated with pregnancy. As you compose documents designed to quickly engage an audience, use strategies of emphasis, relying on elements of visual rhetoric like scale, shape, color, or value (Chapter 25) to catch a viewer's eye. You will also need to communicate essential information. Use strategies of grouping, creating lists or arranging key materials in patterns that can be scanned quickly by readers. You won't be able to deliver large blocks of information; instead, use design to pull readers toward a concise message.

Ask Questions & Make Decisions

Exercises for Understanding Design

1. Think about the contrast between the Marker Felt and Times New Roman fonts in the earlier example (page 484). Do fonts really influence readers? Conduct research into concerns related to fonts and then hold a discussion with classmates about the significance of fonts and their relationships to rhetorical situations.

2. Identify a document you have created recently. Think about the rhetorical situation of the document and then choose an alternative genre and medium. Create a new version of the project, thinking about design decisions as you translate the piece into the new form.

3. Think about the Web sites where you spend a lot of time. What strategies of design do they use to influence your behavior? Identify a site and then log on; instead of going about your usual routine, spend fifteen minutes or so "reading" the design of the site. Keep the perspective of a design archeologist in mind as you explore. Write up your findings in a page or so.

4. Find a computer that has basic publishing software. (If you can't locate a copy of a publishing program, you can use a word processor.) Explore the templates to create a rough design of a newsletter. Experiment with the program to see how easily you can modify the design to your liking. Mock up a layout and some sections of a newsletter related to an interest—your family, a hobby, a band, your major. Once you have a mockup ready, write up your thoughts about the process or recruit partners to further develop and publish the newsletter.

Zoom Out   Reflecting on Design

- **Thinking about design requires zooming in and out.** Large strategies like using emphasis, white space, and grouping to create flow can guide you. You can also zoom in to make decisions focused on elements like fonts, headings, and lists.

- **Design conventions help organize and express ideas.** Design should guide readers through the information.

- **Every kind of document participates in design expectations.** Essays use standards for margins, fonts, spacing, and other features.

For additional information and practice with the learning objectives in this chapter, go to www.mycomplab.com, Resources > Writing > Writing and Visuals.

Handbook

The chapters in Part 4 of *Write Now* provide you with strategies you can use during the prewriting, drafting, and revising stages of your composing process. In this part of the book, the focus is on strategies and tools you can use in the later stages, as you edit, proofread, and polish your project for final delivery and presentation.

The polishing process begins after the substantive changes you have made while revising (see Chapter 2). You then tighten and refine your writing through editing. Papers and compositions must be combed through carefully for stylistic and mechanical problems that can be corrected through proofreading. At this late stage of the process, you also need to check the formatting of your final project to be sure it meets the expectations of your readers and the conventions of the genre in which you are working. (See Chapter 26 on document design, and Chapter 17 for a sample research paper in MLA format.)

H1 EDITING AND PROOFREADING

When drafting or revising, we write to explain and organize ideas. When editing, we examine how clearly and economically our writing expresses those ideas. Even after it has gone through a draft and revision, most writing can be improved by revising flat and passive sentences and combining sentences for concision and clarity.

1A Editing Sentences for Concision and Clarity

Begin sharpening your writing by replacing flat and passive sentences with active language that demonstrates your points powerfully. Consider this paragraph:

> One way the story shows the way that the structures of society can mask human cruelty is through the depiction of military roles. In the story, military roles allow individuals to avoid responsibility for the atrocities of death and war. In the opening passages we are presented with a description of the scene of the hanging. This depiction, however, focuses primarily on the roles of the members of the military.

You can edit the first sentence to make it more compelling and concise by replacing the "is through" verb construction with a stronger verb.

> Original sentence
>
> One way the story shows the way that the structures of society can mask human cruelty is through the depiction of military roles.

> Revised sentence
>
> Military roles illustrate how the structures of society can mask human cruelty.

Similarly, you can eliminate the passive language from the third sentence.

> Original sentence
>
> In the opening passages we are presented with a description of the scene of the hanging.

> Revised sentence
>
> The opening passages present a description of the hanging.

When editing, look for opportunities to eliminate passive baggage attached to the core of your sentences. Look for phrases like "it is. . . ." or "there are. . . ." When you find passive sentences, revise them to emphasize a concrete subject and a strong verb that demonstrate your meaning concisely.

You can also combine sentences and delete unnecessary language to make your writing more powerful. In the sample, the first two sentences discuss military roles. Even without editing the passive language, the writing can benefit from consolidating the ideas.

Original sentences

One way the story shows the way that the structures of society can mask human cruelty is through the depiction of military roles. In the story, military roles allow individuals to avoid responsibility for the atrocities of death and war.

Revised sentence

Military roles illustrate how the structures of society can mask human cruelty and allow individuals to avoid responsibilities for the atrocities of death and war.

We can also combine the last two sentences:

Original sentences

In the opening passages we are presented with a description of the scene of the hanging. This depiction, however, focuses primarily on the roles of the members of the military.

Revised sentence

The description of the hanging in the opening scene focuses primarily on the roles of the members of the military.

When combining sentences, first distill them into their core meanings, eliminating unnecessary language. Then look for opportunities to combine sentences to make your writing more powerful and concise.

Our revised passage expresses the same ideas with clarity and concision:

Military roles illustrate how the structures of society can mask human cruelty and allow individuals to avoid responsibilities for the atrocities of death and war. The description of the hanging in the opening scene focuses primarily on the roles of the members of the military.

1B Proofreading

At this stage of the writing process, you may feel like you know every detail of your essay. That level of familiarity, unfortunately, can prevent you from seeing problems at all. Figure 1 shows some proofreading that has been performed on a few sentences from a sample essay. In the second line, the writer has deleted a repetition of the word *that*. These kinds of errors result directly from our familiarity with our work. We may have read the sentence fifteen times and we know what it says, so we overlook details like repeated words.

The techniques used by the filmmaker to represent this scene suggest

that ~~that~~ the realities of war are painful. In the *scene* seen, slow motion is

used; so that the actions of the soldiers on the bridge seem inhuman.

The technique makes the soldiers appear brutal an*d* monstrous.

Their speech is hard to recognize. But eventually the effect is lessened

until the captain is heard to say *you're* your trapped like a rat in a trap. . . ."

This bit of dialog has been added ~~by the filmmaker~~ to suggest that war

dehumanizes individuals.

Figure 1
Proofreading Marks.

In the second line, we see a common problem that results from relying on spell check. The word *seen* is spelled correctly, but it is a homonym (a word that sounds exactly like another word) that is used incorrectly here. In line four, the spell checker fails to recognize *an* as a problem because it is spelled correctly; however, the sentence requires the word *and*. To catch problems with homonyms or words spelled correctly but used incorrectly, you must rely on your own proofreading skills rather than your spell checker.

The other corrections in Figure 1 demonstrate the careful attention necessary for proofreading. Catching the comma splice at the end of line two demands that you see and hear your writing objectively. A good strategy is to work sentence by sentence through your essay. You can use a ruler or folded sheet of paper to "block out" each section as you read. When you stumble over a confusing phrase, consult your own knowledge and the grammar and style resources in the following sections to make things clear.

See Chapter 2 for additional samples of edited and proofread drafts.

H2 SENTENCES

To write a good sentence, it is not enough to have a good idea. You have to express your idea in a form that your readers will understand. The form of a sentence has to follow certain conventions, traditional guidelines that are generally understood and accepted.

The conventions of written English are much like rules of etiquette; they are essential for helping people to communicate clearly and effectively with one another. In fact, you know most of these conventions so well that you follow them without even thinking about them. Some, however, you might need to review.

2A Fragments

A **sentence fragment** is an incomplete sentence punctuated as if it were a complete sentence. A sentence fragment lacks a subject, a predicate, or both or is a subordinate clause presented as if it were a sentence.

Fragments Lacking a Subject

Avoid punctuating as a sentence a group of words that lacks a subject.

To eliminate a sentence fragment lacking a subject, simply add a subject to this group of words or connect it to another sentence containing its subject.

> Fragment:
>
> Most Americans had considered World War II a just war. Were willing to give their lives for their country. But many came to think Vietnam was an unjust war. And were repelled by the slaughter of their sons.

> Sentence:
>
> Most Americans had considered World War II a just war and were willing to give their lives for their country. But many came to think Vietnam was an unjust war and were repelled by the slaughter of their sons.

Fragments Lacking a Predicate

Avoid punctuating as a sentence a group of words that lacks a predicate.

A predicate connects with the subject of the sentence and contains a verb. To eliminate a sentence fragment that lacks a predicate, add a finite verb, or connect the fragment to another sentence that contains its verb.

> Fragment:
>
> People of many different nationalities together on the same block.

> Sentence:
>
> People of many different nationalities live together on the same block.

> Fragment:
>
> In the back of the theater were standing-room-only ticket holders. And latecomers impatient for their seats.

Sentence:

In the back of the theater were standing-room-only ticket holders and latecomers impatient for their seats.

Phrase Fragments

Avoid punctuating a phrase as a sentence.

To eliminate a phrase fragment, simply make it part of an independent clause.

Fragment:

We swerved when we saw the deer. Running across the highway.

Sentence:

We swerved when we saw the deer running across the highway.

Fragment:

Because of public opposition. The city refused to grant permission. For a skyscraper to be built on the site of the church.

Sentence:

Because of public opposition, the city refused to grant permission for a skyscraper to be built on the site of the church.

Dependent Clause Fragments

Avoid punctuating a dependent clause as a sentence.

A dependent clause usually begins with a subordinating word, which may be a subordinating conjunction or a relative pronoun. One way in which to eliminate a dependent clause fragment is to remove the subordinating word. Another way is to connect the dependent clause to an independent clause.

Fragment:

Before Harrison wrote his term paper. He prepared an outline.

Sentence:

Before Harrison wrote his term paper, he prepared an outline.

Fragment:

Although John Muir is often pictured as a genial and perhaps somewhat innocent nature guide. He was actually a shrewd, strong-willed, thoughtful man. Who was an effective political lobbyist for conservation.

Sentence:

Although John Muir is often pictured as a genial and perhaps somewhat innocent nature guide, he was actually a shrewd, strong-willed, thoughtful man who was an effective political lobbyist for conservation.

2B Comma Splices

Avoid separating two independent clauses with only a comma, unless the clauses are very short and closely related.

A comma is sometimes used between clauses of two or three words, especially if the clauses are in parallel grammatical form.

One sings, the other dances.
The grass withers, the flowers fade.

In general, however, using only a comma between two independent clauses is considered a grammatical error called a **comma splice.**

Comma Splice:

Researchers are attempting to program robots to see, this procedure is much more complicated than you might expect.

Revised:

Researchers are attempting to program robots to see. This procedure is much more complicated than you might expect.

Or:

Researchers are attempting to program robots to see, but this procedure is much more complicated than you might expect.

A comma splice also occurs when a comma (instead of a semi-colon) is used between two independent clauses joined by a transitional phrase or conjunctive adverb (in **boldface**).

Comma Splice:

The exhibit at the museum was well reviewed and well promoted, **consequently,** there were long lines for tickets.

Revised:

The exhibit at the museum was well reviewed and well promoted; **consequently,** there were long lines for tickets.

2C Fused Sentences

Avoid writing two independent clauses without any punctuation between them.

This error is called a **fused sentence.**

Fused Sentence:

The school was closed because of the snowstorm not knowing this, some students
   showed up for classes.

Revised:

The school was closed because of the snowstorm. Not knowing this, some students
   showed up for classes.

Or:

Not knowing that the school was closed because of the snowstorm, some students
   showed up for classes.

Although there are many ways of correcting fused sentences, these are the four most
common:

   1. Make two sentences by adding a period at the end of the first clause and capitalizing
      the first word of the second clause.

   Fused Sentence:

   Doctors are again using leeches these creatures can prevent the problem of clotting
      that occurs after reattachment surgery.

   Revised:

   Doctors are again using leeches. These creatures can prevent the problem of clotting
      that occurs after reattachment surgery.

   2. Add a coordinating conjunction between the two clauses. Place a comma before the
      coordinating conjunction unless the two clauses are very short.

   Fused Sentence:

   Maria washed the car Carlos mowed the lawn.

   Revised:

   Maria washed the car **and** Carlos mowed the lawn.

   3. Rewrite one of the independent clauses as a dependent clause.

   Fused Sentence:

   The cat wanted her breakfast she mewed loudly at the foot of the bed.

   Revised:

   When the cat wanted her breakfast, she mewed loudly at the foot of the bed.

   4. If the two clauses are closely related, place a semicolon between them.

   Fused Sentence:

   Cindy found the movie disappointing Lee thought it was wonderful.

Revised:
Cindy found the movie disappointing; Lee thought it was wonderful.

2D Parallelism

Use the same grammatical form for elements that are part of a series or a compound construction.

Sentence elements that have the same grammatical structure are said to be *parallel*.

The speech was **concise, witty,** and **effective.**
He tried to be honest **with himself** as well as **with others.**

When elements that are part of a series or a compound construction do not have the same form, a sentence is said to have **faulty parallelism.**

Repeat articles, prepositions, and the word *to* before the infinitive to make the meaning of a sentence clear.

The audience applauded the composer and lyricist.

The preceding sentence is clear if the composer and the lyricist are the same person. It is misleading if they are not the same person. Repeat the article *the* to indicate two people.

The audience applauded **the** composer and **the** lyricist.

Unclear: She was a prominent critic and patron of young poets.
Clear: She was **a** prominent critic and **a** patron of young poets.
Unclear: His father had taught him to shoot and ride a horse.
Clear: His father had taught him **to** shoot and **to** ride a horse.

Place elements joined by a coordinating conjunction in the same grammatical form. Balance a noun with a noun, an adjective with an adjective, a prepositional phrase with a prepositional phrase, and so on.

NOT PARALLEL: The scientific community in general regarded him

adjective   adjective   noun
↓   ↓   ↓

as **outspoken, eccentric,** and a **rebel.**

PARALLEL: The scientific community in general regarded him

adjective   adjective   adjective
↓   ↓   ↓

as **outspoken, eccentric,** and **rebellious.**

prepositional phrase
↓

NOT PARALLEL: A hobbit is a creature **with a hearty appetite** and

adjective clause
↓

who loves home.

verb
↓

PARALLEL: A hobbit is a creature who **has** a hearty appetite

verb
↓

and **loves** home.

2E Coordination and Subordination

Coordination

Use coordination in a balanced structure to link two independent clauses together with a coordinating conjunction to form a compound sentence.

Independent clauses that are joined in coordination are considered to be of approximately equal weight or importance. In effect, in such a sentence, two or more equally important statements are linked as if by a "plus" sign. The following example shows two independent clauses stated separately and then paired in coordination, joined by punctuation and a coordinating conjunction (shown in **boldface**):

Separate:
The football game ended at dusk. For three hours afterward all the local restaurants were crowded.

Coordinated:
The football game ended at dusk, **and** for three hours afterward all the local restaurants were crowded.

Words and phrases, as well as clauses, can be linked by using the basic **coordinating conjunctions** preceded by a comma to show specific balanced relationships between elements: *and* shows a simple addition (I jumped, *and* I gasped.); *or/nor* is used to show choice (You go *or* I go.); *but/yet* is used to show contrast (I am close, *yet* I'm not ready.).

While coordination can be used to create a number of interesting balanced relationships between independent clauses, some writers may get carried away with a repetitive accumulation of clauses glued together with the conjunctions *and* or *but*. As you rewrite a paragraph, think about the kinds of relationships and links you want:

Misused:

We finally located a big car lot and we looked around for quite a while, but I didn't see much of interest, and it seemed I didn't know a good-looking car from a lemon. My friend and I kicked about forty tires and we opened lots of doors, and then a salesperson started talking fast about convertibles, but we didn't trust anything we saw, so we left.

Revised:

We finally located a big car lot; afterward we looked around for quite a while. I didn't see much of interest; furthermore, I didn't seem to know a good-looking car from a lemon. My friend and I kicked about forty tires, and we opened lots of doors. A salesperson started talking fast about convertibles; consequently, we really didn't trust anything we saw. We left.

Subordination

Use subordination to form sentences with two or more closely linked statements involving a dependent clause.

Subordination occurs when a dependent clause (one that cannot stand alone) is intimately linked with an independent clause using a subordinating conjunction or a relative pronoun. In the following sentence, the dependent clause appears in *italics* and the subordinating conjunction in **boldface:**

Subordinated:

Because *the football game ended at dusk,* all the local restaurants were crowded for three hours.

An **adjective clause** is a group of words with a subject and a predicate that modifies a noun or a pronoun. Usually, an adjective clause begins with a relative pronoun. Notice how the choppy sentences in the following examples can be combined through the use of adjective clauses:

Separate:

William W. Warner described blue crabs as "beautiful swimmers." He wrote a study of the Chesapeake Bay. The book won a Pulitzer Prize.

Combined:

William W. Warner, whose study of the Chesapeake Bay won a Pulitzer Prize, described blue crabs as "beautiful swimmers."

An **adverb clause** is a group of words with a subject and a predicate that functions as an adverb in a sentence. Usually, an adverb clause begins with a subordinating conjunction (such as *because, after,* or *so that*) that shows the relation of the adverb clause to the word or words it modifies. Notice how the choppy sentences in the following examples can be combined through the use of adverb clauses:

Separate:
He was never in a battle. Nevertheless, he wrote movingly about war.

Combined:
Although he was never in a battle, he wrote movingly about war.

2F Mixed Sentences

Maintain a consistent sentence structure. Do not start a sentence with one type of structure and end it with another type.

Inconsistent:
First rub olive oil over the outside of the chicken; then salt the chicken lightly, but no pepper.

The writer of the preceding sentence begins with an independent clause, continues with another independent clause, and then concludes beginning with the conjunction *but,* indicating that another independent clause will follow. However, the writer then ends the sentence with a phrase rather than a clause. The problem can be eliminated by turning the phrase into a clause.

Consistent:
First rub olive oil over the outside of the chicken; then salt the chicken lightly, but do not pepper it.
Another kind of mixed sentence structure is created by clauses that are not clearly related to one another.

Inconsistent:
When your parents were poorly educated and you yourself have attended substandard schools, what kind of odds for success are those?

In this sentence, the writer begins with an adverb clause that should modify a word in an independent clause. However, the independent clause that follows does not contain any word for the adverb clause to modify. To correct the problem, simply provide such a word.

Consistent:
What kind of odds for success do you have when your parents were poorly educated and you yourself have attended substandard schools?

2G Shifts

Shifts occur when writers lose track of their sentence elements. Shifts occur in a variety of ways:

In person

In music, where left-handed people seem to be talented, the right-handed world puts *you* at a disadvantage. Shift from *people,* third person, to *you,* second person

In tense

Even though many musicians *are* left-handed, instruments *had been designed for right-handers*. Shift from present tense to past perfect

In number

A left-handed *violinist* has to pay extra to buy *their* left-handed violin. Shift from singular to plural

In mood

Every time the *violinist played, she could always know* when her instrument was out of tune. Shift from the indicative mood, *violinist played,* to the subjunctive mood, *she could always know*

In voice

The sonata *was being practiced* by the violinists in one room while the cellists *played* the concerto in the other room. Shift from the passive voice, *was being practiced,* to active voice, *played*

In discourse type

She said, "*Your violin is out of tune,*" and that *I was playing the wrong note*. Shift from the direct quotation, *Your violin is out of tune,* to indirect quotation, that *I was playing the wrong note*

Once you recognize shifts, revise them by ensuring that the same grammatical structures are used consistently throughout the sentence:

In music, where left-handed *people* seem talented, the right-handed world puts *them* at a disadvantage.

Even though many musicians *are* left-handed, instruments *have been designed* for right-handers.

Left-handed *violinists* have to pay extra to buy *their* left-handed violins.

Every time the violinist *played,* she *knew* when her instrument was out of tune.

The violinists *practiced* the sonata in one room while the cellists *played* the concerto in the other room.

She said, "*Your violin is out of tune and you are playing the wrong note.*"

2H Dangling and Misplaced Modifiers

Dangling and misplaced modifiers are words and word groups that, because of their position or the way in which they are phrased, make the meaning of a sentence unclear and sometimes even ludicrous. These troublesome modifiers are most commonly verbal phrases, prepositional phrases, and adverbs. Here are examples:

Reaching to pick up the saddle, the obnoxious horse may shake off the blanket. The dangling verbal phrase appears to relate to *horse.*

To extend lead out of the eversharp pencil, the eraser cap is depressed. The dangling verbal phrase implies that *the eraser cap* does something.

The eversharp pencil is designed to be used permanently, *only periodically replacing the lead.* The dangling verbal phrase implies that the pencil replaces the lead.

Dick *only* had to pay ten dollars for his parking ticket. The misplaced adverb should immediately precede *ten.*

Theodore caught a giant fish in the very same spot where he had lost the ring *two years later.* The misplaced adverb phrase confusingly appears to modify the last part of the sentence instead of, correctly, the first part.

To recognize your own dangling verbal modifiers, make sure that the implied subject of the verbal phrase is the same as the subject of the sentence. In the first example above, the implied subject of *Reaching* is not *the horse.* In the second example, the implied subject of *To extend* is not *the eraser cap.* And in the third example, the implied subject of *replacing* is not *the pencil.* Also check passive voice, because in a passive sentence the subject is not the doer of the action. In the second example, the dangling modifier can be corrected when the verb, changed from passive to active voice, tells who should depress the eraser (see correction that follows).

Correcting dangling and misplaced modifiers depends on the type of error. Misplaced modifiers can often be moved to a more appropriate position:

Dick had to pay *only* ten dollars for his parking ticket.
Two years later, Theodore caught a giant fish in the very same spot where he had lost the ring.

Dangling modifiers usually require some rewording:

As you reach to pick up the saddle, the obnoxious horse may shake off the blanket. The dangling verbal phrase is converted to a clause.

To extend lead out of the eversharp pencil, *depress the eraser cap.* The main clause is revised so that *you* is the implied subject of *depress* (as it is for *To extend*).

The eversharp pencil is designed to be used permanently, *only periodically needing the lead replaced.* The dangling verbal phrase is revised so that implied subject of *needing* is *pencil.*

21 Restrictive and Non-Restrictive Modifiers

Some modifiers are essential to a sentence because they *restrict,* or limit, the meaning of the words they modify; others, while adding important information, are not essential to the meaning of a sentence. The first type is called restrictive and the second non-restrictive. The terms usually refer to subordinate clauses and phrases. Here are examples of restrictive and non-restrictive modifiers:

Restrictive

People *who plan to visit Europe* should take time to see Belgium. Relative clause modifying and identifying *People.*

The industrialized country *between the Netherlands and France on the North Sea* is constitutionally a kingdom. Prepositional phrases modifying and identifying *country.*

The Kempenland was thinly populated *before coal was discovered there.* Subordinate clause modifying *was populated* and giving meaning to the sentence.

Non-Restrictive

Belgium has two major populations: the Flemings, *who live in the north and speak Flemish,* and the Walloons, *who live in the south and speak French.* Two relative clauses, the first modifying *Flemings* and the second modifying *Walloons.*

With Brussels in the middle of the country, both groups inhabit the city. Prepositional phrases, together modifying *inhabit.*

Covering southeastern Belgium, the sandstone Ardennes Mountains follow the Sambre and Meuse Rivers. Participial (verbal) phrase modifying *mountains.*

These examples illustrate several aspects of restrictive and non-restrictive modifiers:

1. They *modify* a word in the clause or sentence; they therefore function as adjectives or adverbs.

2. They can appear at the beginning, somewhere in the middle, or at the end of a sentence or clause.

3. Most types of subordinate elements can be restrictive and non-restrictive.

4. Whether a clause or phrase is restrictive or non-restrictive depends on its function in the sentence.

5. Restrictive elements are not set off with punctuation; non-restrictive elements are set off with commas (and sometimes dashes).

To get a feel for the distinction between restriction and non-restriction, consider the following sentences, the first restrictive and the second non-restrictive:

People who wear braces on their teeth should not eat caramel apples.

People, who wear braces on their teeth, should not eat caramel apples.

Set off with commas, the non-restrictive *who* clause implies that all people wear braces on their teeth and should not eat caramel apples, which is clearly not the case. It does not *restrict,* or limit, the meaning of *people*. In the first sentence, however, the *who* clause does restrict, or limit, the meaning of *people* to only those who wear braces on their teeth. Often only the writer knows the intended meaning and therefore needs to make the distinction by setting off, or not setting off, the modifier.

2J Adjectives and Adverbs

Misused Adjective Forms

Avoid using an adjective to modify a verb, an adjective, or an adverb. Use an adverb or qualifier instead.

> not: The lawyer answered very **quick.**
> but: The lawyer *answered* very **quickly.**
> not: The group performing at the club plays **real** well.
> but: The group performing at the club plays **really** *well.*

Do not be confused by words separating the adverb from the word it modifies. For example:

> The lawyer *answered* each of her client's questions very **quickly.**

Avoid using an adjective ending in *-ly* in place of an adverb or an adverb phrase.

Although the suffix *-ly* usually signals an adverb, a few adjectives end in *-ly* too. For example:

earthly	ghostly	holy	lovely
friendly	heavenly	homely	manly

Do not mistake these adjectives for adverbs or try to use them as adverbs. Either use another word or express your idea as a phrase.

> NOT: A figure was moving **ghostly** through the darkened room.
> BUT: A figure was moving **like a ghost** through the darkened room.
> OR: A figure was moving **ghostlike** through the darkened room.

Misused Adverb Forms

Avoid using an adverb to modify a direct object. Use an adjective as an object complement instead.

Think about the difference in meaning between the following two sentences:

The instructor considered the student's paper intelligent.

The instructor considered the student's paper intelligently.

In the first sentence, the adjective *intelligent* modifies the direct object *paper*. It tells what opinion the instructor held of the paper. In the second sentence, the adverb *intelligently* modifies the verb *considered*. It tells in what manner the instructor considered the paper.

NOT: The jury found the defendant **guiltily.**
BUT: The jury found the *defendant* **guilty.**
Avoid using an adverb after a linking verb. Use the corresponding adjective instead as a predicate adjective.

NOT: After he took that cooking course, his meals tasted **differently.**
BUT: After he took that cooking course, his *meals* tasted **different.**

Two words that are especially confusing are *good* and *well*. *Good* is always used as an adjective. *Well* is usually used as an adverb, but it can also be used as an adjective that means "healthy" or "satisfactory."

The preliminary *findings* look **good.** (*adjective*)
Janet *dances* **well.** (*adverb*)
The town crier shouted, "*All* is **well!**" (*adjective*)

H3 VERBS

Verbs are the central core of a sentence; together with subjects, they make statements. Verbs often tell what the subject is doing:

The company *agreed* to plead guilty to criminal charges.

Nearly every miner *can name* a casualty of black lung disease.

Another common function of verbs is to link subjects to complements:

Logan *is* an isolated county in the corner of the state.

Sometimes the verb tells something about the subject, as the following passive verb does:

Casualties of mining *cannot be measured* only by injuries.

Through changes in form, verbs can tell the time of the action (past, present, future), the number of the subject (singular or plural), and the person of the subject (first person, *I, we;* second person, *you;* third person, *he, she, it, they*).

3A Tense

The problems that writers sometimes encounter when using verbs in writing result from the fact that verbs, unlike most other words in English, have many forms, and a slight shift in form can alter meaning. Notice how the meanings of the following pairs of sentences change as the verbs change:

> The fish *has jumped* into the boat.
> The fish *have jumped* into the boat.
> The concert *starts* at 8:15 p.m.
> The concert *started* at 8:15 p.m.

In the first pair, the meaning changes from one fish to more than one fish jumping into the boat. In the second pair, the first verb implies that the concert has not yet begun; in the second, that it had already begun. It is important, therefore, to use the verb form that conveys the intended meaning. Observe how the verb *vanish* changes in the following sentences to indicate differences in time, or *tense:*

Present:	Many agricultural jobs *vanish.*
Past:	Many agricultural jobs *vanished.*
Future:	Many agricultural jobs *will vanish.*
Perfect:	Many agricultural jobs *have vanished.*
Past Perfect:	Many agricultural jobs *had vanished.*
Future Perfect:	Many agricultural jobs *will have vanished.*

To omit an *-ed* ending or use the wrong helping verb gives readers a false message.

Helping (Auxiliary) Verbs. Sometimes helping verbs are required to complete the meaning of a verb form, as in the following example:

> The fish *jumping* into the boat.

The word *jumping* does not have one of the primary functions of verbs—telling time of the action, called *tense.* The time of the occurrence could have been the past (*the fish were jumping*), present (*the fish are jumping*), or the future (*the fish will be jumping*). We also don't know whether the writer meant one fish or many. The *-ing* form is a *verbal* and requires a helping, or auxiliary, verb to make it finite, or able to tell time: words such as *am, is, are, was, were* (forms of *be*). Other helping verbs are *do* (*Do* you *want* the paper? She *doesn't want* the paper) and *have* (I *haven't seen* the paper; *has* she *seen* it?).

Irregular Verbs. Most verbs change forms in a regular way: *want* in the present becomes *wanted* in the past, *wanting* with the auxiliary *be* (i.e., *is wanting*), and *wanted* with the auxiliary *have* (i.e., *have wanted*). Many verbs change irregularly, however—internally rather than at the ending. Here are a few of the most common irregular verbs:

Base form	Past tense	Present participle	Past participle
be (is, am, are)	was, were	being	been
come	came	coming	come
do	did	doing	done
drink	drank	drinking	drunk
give	gave	giving	given
go	went	going	gone
grow	grew	growing	grown
lie	laid	lying	lain
see	saw	seeing	seen
take	took	taking	taken
teach	taught	teaching	taught
throw	threw	throwing	thrown
wear	wore	wearing	worn
write	wrote	writing	written

Check your dictionary for the forms of other verbs you suspect may be irregular.

3B Voice

English sentences are usually written in the active voice, in which the subject of the sentence is the doer of the action of the verb:

> Scott misplaced the file folder. *Scott,* the subject of the sentence, performed the action, *misplaced.*

With the passive voice, the doer of the action is the object of a preposition or is omitted entirely:

> The file folder was misplaced by Scott. *File folder* is now the subject of the sentence.

> The file folder was misplaced. The person doing the action is not named.

At best, the passive voice is wordier than the active voice; at worst, it fails to acknowledge who performs the action of the verb. Use the passive voice when you do not know or want to name the doer or when you want to keep the subjects consistent within a paragraph.

To avoid the passive voice, look for *by* phrases near the ends of your sentences; if you find any, see if the subject of your sentence performs the action of your verb. If not, revise the sentence so that it does. Another way in which to find occurrences of the passive voice is to look for forms of *be: am, is, are, was, were, been, being.* Not all these verbs will be passive, but if they function as part of an action verb, see if the subject performs the action. If it does not, and if your sentence would be clearer with the subject performing the action, revise to the active voice.

3C Mood

Mood refers to the writer's attitude toward the action of the verb. Mood has three forms: indicative, imperative, and subjunctive. Verbs in the *indicative mood* are used to make statements, to ask questions, and to declare opinions. For example:

Not many people today *think* the world *is* flat. Makes a statement.

Does anybody today *think* the world is flat? Asks a question.

Members of the Flat Earth Society *should reevaluate* their thinking. Declares an opinion.

Verbs in the *imperative mood* issue commands, requests, or directions. Imperative verbs never change form. When the subject of an imperative verb is not explicitly identified it is understood to be *you*.

Julia, *stop* teasing your baby brother. Issues command.

Please *complete* this report by tomorrow morning. Issues request.

Turn right at the light and *drive* for another two blocks. Issues directions.

Verbs in the *subjunctive mood* communicate wishes, make statements contrary to fact, list requirements and demands, and imply skepticism or doubt. They usually appear in clauses introduced by *if, that, as if,* and *as though.* Use the base form of the verb for the present tense subjunctive. For the past tense subjunctive of the verb *be,* use *were* for all subjects.

She wishes that her son's best friend *were* more responsible. Communicates wish.

If the world *were* to end tomorrow, we would not have to pay taxes anymore. Makes statement contrary to fact.

The jury summons requires that your cousin *arrive* punctually at 8:00 a.m. and *sign* in with the court clerk. Lists requirements.

His girlfriend talks as if she *were* a pop music diva. Implies skepticism.

Be sure to select the correct verb forms to express indicative, imperative, and subjunctive moods.

3D Subject-Verb Agreement

Clauses are made of subjects and verbs plus their modifiers and other related words. A fundamental principle of usage is that verbs agree with their subjects. In most cases, this principle presents no problem: You say "Birds *have* feathers," not "Birds *has* feathers." But not all sentences are this simple. Here are some situations that may cause problems.

When a subject and a verb are side by side, they usually do not present a problem. Often, however, writers separate them with subordinate elements, such as clauses, prepositional or verbal phrases, and other elements. The result may be a verb error. The following sentence illustrates this problem:

The realization that life is a series of compromises never occur to some people. The subject is *realization*, a singular noun, and should be followed by the singular verb *occurs*. The corrected sentence would read "The realization that life is a series of compromises never occurs to some people."

Subject complements follow some verbs and rename the subject, although they are not always in the same number as the subject. Because a singular subject may have a plural complement, and vice versa, confused writers might make the verb agree with the complement instead of the subject. Here's an example:

The result of this mistake are guilt, low self-esteem, and depression. The subject is *result*, not *guilt, low self-esteem*, and *depression*; the singular subject should be followed by the singular verb *is*. The corrected sentence would read "The result of this mistake is guilt, low self-esteem, and depression."

Two or more words may be compounded to make a subject. Whether they are singular or plural depends on their connector. Subjects connected by *and* and *but* are plural, but those connected by *or* and *nor* are singular or plural depending on whether the item closer to the verb is singular or plural. Here are examples:

The young mother and the superior student *are* both candidates for compulsive perfectionism. Two subjects, *mother* and *student*, are joined by *and* and take a plural verb.

Promotions or an employee award *tells* the perfectionist he or she is achieving personal goals. When two subjects, *promotions* and *award*, are joined by *or*, the verb agrees with the nearer one; in this sentence a singular verb is required.

An employee award or promotions *tell* the perfectionist he or she is achieving personal goals. Here the plural verb, *tell*, agrees with *promotions*, the closer of the two subjects.

Indefinite pronouns are defined and listed under 5C Pronoun Agreement. Although these words often seem plural in meaning, most of them are singular grammatically. When indefinite pronouns are the subjects of sentences or clauses, their verbs are usually singular. Here are examples:

Everyone *has* at some time worried about achieving goals. The singular indefinite pronoun *everyone* takes a singular verb, *has*.

Each car and truck on the highway *was* creeping along on the icy pavement. The singular indefinite, *each*, requires a singular verb, *was*.

Neither of us *is* going to worry about being late. The singular indefinite, *neither*, takes a singular verb, *is.*

Nevertheless, some of us *are* going to be very late. The indefinite *some* (like *all, any,* and *none*) is singular or plural depending on context; compare "Some of the book *is* boring."

Inverted sentence order can confuse your natural inclination to subject–verb agreement. Examples of inverted order are questions, plus sentences beginning with *there.* Sentences like these demand closer attention to agreement.

Have the results of the test come back yet? The plural subject, *results,* takes a plural verb, *have.*

There *are* many special services provided just for kids at hotels, ski lodges, and restaurants. The plural subject, *services,* takes a plural verb, *are. There* is never a subject; it only holds the place for the subject in an inverted sentence.

Subordinate clauses that begin with the relative pronouns *who, which,* or *that* present special problems in subject–verb agreement. Their verbs must agree with their own subjects, not with a word in another clause. These subordinate clauses demand special attention because whether the pronouns are singular or plural depends on their antecedents. These sentences illustrate agreement within relative clauses:

Every person who *attends* the baseball game will receive a free cap. *Who,* the subject of *attends,* means "person," a singular noun.

John is one of the few people I know who *care* about frogs. *Who,* the subject of *care,* means "people," a plural noun.

John is the only one of all the people I know who *cares* about frogs. *Who* in this sentence means "one."

H4 PRONOUNS

Pronouns can have all the same sentence functions as nouns; the difference is that pronouns do not have the meaning that nouns have. Nouns name things; a noun stands for the thing itself. Pronouns, however, refer only to nouns. Whenever that reference is ambiguous or inconsistent, there is a problem in clarity.

4A Pronoun Case

Case is a grammatical term for the way in which nouns and pronouns show their relationships to other parts of a sentence. In English, nouns have only two case forms: the regular form (the one listed in a dictionary, such as *year*) and the possessive form (used to show ownership or connection, such as *year's*).

Pronouns, however, have retained their case forms. Here are the forms for personal and relative pronouns:

	Subjective	Objective	Possessive
Personal	I	me	my, mine
	you	you	your, yours
	he	him	his
	she	her	her, hers
	it	it	its
	we	us	our, ours
	they	them	their, theirs
Relative	who	whom	whose
	whoever	whomever	whosever

Notice, first, that possessive pronouns, unlike possessive nouns, do not take apostrophes—none of them. Sometimes writers confuse possessive pronouns with contractions, which do have apostrophes (such as *it's,* meaning *it is* or *it has;* and *who's,* meaning *who is*).

Another problem writers sometimes have with pronoun case is using a subjective form when they need the objective or using an objective form when they need the subjective.

Subjective Case. Use the subjective forms for subjects and for words referring to subjects, as in these examples:

Among the patients a nutritionist sees are the grossly overweight people *who* have tried all kinds of diets. *Who* is subject of the verb *have tried* in its own clause.

He and the patient work out a plan for permanent weight control. *He* and *patient* are the compound subjects of *work.*

Notice that pronoun case is determined by the function of the pronoun in its own clause and that compounding (*he and the patient*) has no effect on case.

Objective Case. Use the *objective* forms for objects of all kinds:

"Between *you* and *me*," said the patient to his nutritionist, "I'm ready for something that works." *You* and *me* are objects of the preposition *between.*

An exercise program is usually assigned the patient for *whom* diet is prescribed. *Whom* is the object of the preposition *for.*

Notice again that the case of a pronoun is determined by its function in its own clause and is not affected by compounding (*you and me*).

Possessive Case. Use the possessive forms to indicate ownership. Possessive pronouns have two forms: adjective forms (*my, your, his, her, its, our, their*) and possessive forms (*mine,* *yours, his, hers, its, ours, theirs*). The adjective forms appear before nouns or gerunds; the possessive forms replace possessive nouns.

> The patient purchased *his* supplements from the drug store *his* nutritionist recommended. Adjective form before nouns.

4B Pronoun Reference

Personal and relative pronouns (see list under 4A Pronoun Case) must refer to specific nouns or antecedents. By themselves they have no meaning. As a result, they can cause problems in clarity for writers. If you were to read "She teaches technical writing at her local technical college," you would know only that *someone,* a woman, teaches technical writing at the college. But if the sentence were preceded by one like this, "After getting her master's degree, my mother has achieved one of her life goals," the pronoun *she* would have meaning. In this case, *mother* is the antecedent of *she*. The antecedent gives meaning to the pronoun. For this reason, it is essential that pronouns refer unambiguously to their antecedents and that pronouns and antecedents agree. Here are sentences in which the pronouns do not clearly refer to their antecedents:

> The immunologist refused to admit fraudulence of the data reported by a former colleague in a paper *he* had cosigned. More than one possible antecedent. *He* could refer to *immunologist* or to *colleague.*

> *It* says in the newspaper that the economy will not improve soon. Implied antecedent. There is no antecedent for it.

> *This* only reinforces the public skepticism about the credibility of scientists. Implied antecedent. There is no antecedent for *This.*

Faulty pronoun reference is corrected by clarifying the relationship between the pronoun and its intended antecedent. Observe how the example sentences have been revised:

> The immunologist refused to admit fraudulence of the data reported by a former colleague in a paper *the immunologist* had cosigned. *The immunologist* replaces the unclear pronoun *he.*

> *The newspaper* reports that the economy will not improve soon. The unclear pronoun *it* is replaced by its implied antecedent, *newspaper.*

> This *kind of waffling* only reinforces public skepticism about the credibility of scientists. The unclear pronoun *this* is replaced by the adjective *this* modifying the intended antecedent *kind of waffling.*

Revising an unclear pronoun reference is sometimes like working a jigsaw puzzle: finding and adding a missing piece or moving parts around to achieve the best fit. Often only the writer can make the right connections.

4C Pronoun Agreement

Some pronoun errors result because the pronoun and its antecedent do not agree. In the sentence, "When a student is late for this class, they find the door locked," the plural pronoun *they* refers to a singular antecedent, *a student*. There is no agreement in *number*. In this sentence, "When a student is late for this class, you find the door locked," again the pronoun, this time *you,* does not agree with the antecedent. This time the problem is *person*. Pronouns must agree with their antecedents in number, person, and gender.

Compound Antecedents

Problems sometimes occur with compound antecedents. If the antecedents are joined by *and,* the pronoun is plural; if joined by *or,* the pronoun agrees with the nearer antecedent. Here are examples of correct usage:

> In the pediatric trauma center, the head doctor and head nurse direct *their* medical team. The pronoun *their* refers to both *doctor* and *nurse.*

Indefinite Pronouns as Antecedents

Indefinite pronouns can sometime cause particular problems with agreement. As their name implies, indefinite pronouns do not refer to particular people or things; grammatically they are usually singular but are often intended as plural. Here are the common indefinite pronouns:

all	every	none
any	everybody	nothing
anybody	everyone	one
anyone	everything	some
anything	neither	somebody
each	no one	someone
either	nobody	something

Like nouns, these pronouns can serve as antecedents of personal and relative pronouns. But because most of them are grammatically singular, they can be troublesome in sentences. Here are examples of correct usage:

> Everyone in the trauma center has *his or her* specific job to do. **or** All the personnel in the trauma center have *their* specific jobs to do. The neutral, though wordy, alternative *his or her* agrees with the singular indefinite *everyone*. The second sentence illustrates the use of plural when gender is unknown.

Shifts in Person

Agreement errors in *person* are shifts between *I* or *we* (first person), *you* (second person), and *he, she, it,* and *they* (third person). These errors are probably more often a result of carelessness than of imperfect knowledge. Being more familiar with casual speech than formal writing, writers sometimes shift from *I* to *you,* for example, when only one of them is meant, as in these sentences:

> Last summer *I* went on a canoeing trip to northern Manitoba. It was *my* first trip that far north, and it was so peaceful *you* could forget all the problems back home. The person represented by *you* was not present. The writer means *I.*

4D Relative Pronouns

Use relative pronouns to introduce clauses that modify nouns or pronouns. Personal relative pronouns refer to people. They include *who, whom, whoever, whomever,* and *whose.* Non-personal relative pronouns refer to things. They include *which, whichever, whatever,* and *whose.*

Most college writers know to use *who* when referring to people and *which* or *that* when referring to things, but sometimes carelessness or confusion can lead to errors. Many writers assume that *which* and *that* are interchangeable when they are not. Use *which* to introduce non-restrictive clauses and *that* to introduce restrictive clauses (see 3B Restrictive and Non-Restrictive Modifiers). Another problem area concerns the correct use of *who* and *whom.* Use *who* to refer to the subject of the sentence and *whom* to refer to an object of the verb or preposition. Following are examples of common errors:

> The lawyer *that* lost the case today went to law school with my sister. Uses impersonal relative pronoun *that.*

> Later, the lawyer *whom* lost the case spoke with the jurors *who* we had interviewed. The first relative pronoun *whom* refers to the subject *lawyer* while the second relative pronoun *who* refers to the object of the verb *had interviewed.*

Once you recognize relative pronoun errors it is usually easy to fix them:

> The lawyer *who* lost the case today went to law school with my sister.

> Later, the lawyer *who* lost the case spoke with the jurors *whom* we had interviewed.

H5   STYLE

Style in writing, like style in clothes, art, or anything else, is individual and develops with use and awareness. But even individual writers vary their style, depending on the situation. At school and work, the preferred style tends to be more formal and objective. The readings in this book provide abundant examples of this style. It is not stuffy, patronizing, or coldly analytical. It is simply clean, direct, and clear. This handbook section treats a few of the obstacles to a good writing style.

5A Conciseness

Nobody wants to read more words than necessary. When you write concisely, therefore, you are considerate of your readers. To achieve conciseness you do not need to eliminate details and other content; rather, you cut empty words, repetition, and unnecessary details.

In the following passage, all the italicized words could be omitted without altering the meaning:

> *In the final analysis, I feel that* the United States should have converted to the *use of the* metric system *of measurement* a long time ago. *In the present day and age,* the United States, except for Borneo and Liberia, is the *one and* only country in the *entire* world that has not yet adopted this measurement system.

Repetition of key words is an effective technique for achieving emphasis and coherence, but pointless repetition serves only to bore the reader. See Section 1 for more advice about editing sentences for conciseness.

5B Appropriate Language

Effective writers communicate using appropriate language; that is, language that:

1. Suits its subject and audience.
2. Avoids sexist usage.
3. Avoids bias and stereotype.

Suitability

The style and tone of your writing should be suitable to your subject and audience. Most academic and business contexts require the use of *formal language*. Formal language communicates clearly and directly with a minimum of stylistic flourish. *Informal language,* on the other hand, is particular to the writer's personality and also assumes a closer and more familiar relationship between the writer and the reader. Its tone is casual, subjective, and intimate.

As informal language is rarely used within an academic setting, the following examples show errors in the use of formal language:

> Professor Oyo *dissed* Marta when she arrived late to his class for the third time in a row. Uses slang.

The *aromatic essence* of the gardenia was intoxicating. Uses pretentious words.

The doctor told him to take *salicylate* to ease the symptoms of *viral rhinorrhea*. Uses unnecessary jargon.

Sexist Usage

Terms such as *policeman* and *chairman* are gender biased. Replace them with expressions such as *police officer* and *chairperson* or *chair*. Most sexist usage in language involves masculine nouns, masculine pronouns, and patronizing terms.

Masculine Nouns. Do not use *man* and its compounds generically. Here are some examples of masculine nouns and appropriate gender neutral substitutions:

Masculine Noun	Gender-Neutral Substitution
businessman	businessperson, executive, manager
fireman	firefighter
man hours	work hours
mankind	humanity, people
manmade	manufactured, synthetic
salesman	salesperson, sales representative, sales agent

Using gender-neutral substitutions often entails using a more specific word for a generalized term, which adds more precision to writing.

Masculine Pronouns. Avoid using the masculine pronouns *he, him,* and *his* in a generic sense, meaning both male and female. This can pose some challenges, however, because English does not have a generic singul]ar pronoun that can be used instead. Consider the following options:

1. Eliminate the pronoun.

   Every writer has an individual style. Instead of Every writer has his own style.

2. Use plural forms.

   Writers have their own styles. Instead of A writer has his own style.

3. Use *he or she, one,* or *you* as alternates only sparingly.

   Each writer has his or her own style. Instead of Each writer has his own style.

   One has an individual writing style. Instead of He has his own individual writing style.

4. Alternate between the use of she and he.

   Every writer has her own style. When a reader encounters this style, he gets to know the writer.

Biases and Stereotypes

Most writers are sensitive to racial and ethnic biases or stereotypes, but writers should also avoid language that shows insensitivity to age, class, religion, and sexual orientation. The accepted terms for identifying groups and group members have changed over the years and continue to change today. Avoid using terms that might be derogatory, outdated, inflammatory, or otherwise offensive.

H6 PUNCTUATION

Punctuation is a system of signals telling readers how the parts of written discourse relate to one another. They are similar to road signs that tell the driver what to expect: A sign with an arrow curving left means that the road makes a left curve, a "stop ahead" sign that a stop sign is imminent, a speed limit sign what the legal speed is. Drivers trust that the signs mean what they say. Readers, too, expect punctuation marks to mean what they say: A period means the end of a sentence, a colon that an explanation will follow, and a comma that the sentence is not finished. Punctuation helps writers and readers understand the meanings of words, sentences, and messages.

6A End Punctuation

A period is the normal mark for ending sentences. A question mark ends a sentence that asks a direct question, and an exclamation point ends forceful assertions.

Period

Sentences normally end with a period:

> Studies suggest that eating fish two or three times a week may reduce the risk of heart attack. Statement.

> The patient asked whether eating fish would reduce risk of heart attack. Indirect question.

Question Mark

A sentence that asks a direct question ends in a question mark:

> How does decaffeinated coffee differ from regular coffee?

Do not use a question mark to end an indirect question:

> The customer asked how decaffeinated coffee differs from regular coffee.

With quoted questions, place the question mark inside the final quotation marks:

> The customer asked, "How does decaffeinated coffee differ from regular coffee?"

Exclamation Point

The exclamation point ends forceful assertions:

> Fire!
>
> Shut that door immediately!

Because they give the impression of shouting, exclamation points are rarely needed in formal business and academic writing.

6B Semicolon

The main use for a semicolon is to connect two closely related independent clauses:

> Dengue hemorrhagic fever is a viral infection common to Southeast Asia; it kills about 5,000 children a year.

Sometimes the second clause contains a transitional adverb:

> Dengue has existed in Asia for centuries; *however,* it grew more virulent in the 1950s.

Do not use a comma where a semicolon or period is required; the result is a comma splice. In contrast, a semicolon used in place of a comma may result in a type of fragment:

> In populations where people have been stricken by an infectious virus, survivors have antibodies in their bloodstreams; *which prevent or reduce the severity of subsequent infections.* The semicolon makes a fragment of the *which* clause.

6C Comma

The comma is probably the most troublesome mark of punctuation because it has so many uses. Its main uses are explained here.

Compound Sentences. A comma joins two independent clauses connected with a coordinating conjunction:

> Martinique is a tropical island in the West Indies, *and* it attracts flocks of tourists annually.

Do not use the comma between independent clauses without the conjunction, even if the second clause begins with a transitional adverb:

> Faulty: Martinique is a tropical island in the West Indies, it attracts flocks of tourists annually. Two independent clauses with no conjunction; use a semicolon or create two sentences.

Introductory Sentence Elements. Commas set off a variety of introductory sentence elements, as illustrated here:

> *When the French colonized Martinique in 1635,* they eliminated the native Caribs. Introductory subordinate clause.

Short prepositional phrases sometimes are not set off:

> *In 1658* the Caribs leaped to their death.

Sometimes, however, a comma must be used after a short prepositional phrase to prevent misreading:

> *Before,* they had predicted retribution. Comma is required to prevent misreading.

Non-Restrictive and Parenthetical Elements. Words that interrupt the flow of a sentence are set off with commas before and after. If they come at the end of a sentence, they are set off with one comma.

In this class are non-restrictive modifiers (see 3B Restrictive and Non-Restrictive Modifiers), transitional adverbs (see 1B Comma Splices), and a few other types of interrupters. Here are examples:

> This rugged island, *which Columbus discovered in 1502,* exports sugar and rum. Non-restrictive *which* clause; commas before and after.

> A major part of the economy, *however,* is tourism. Interrupting transitional adverb; commas before and after.

Series

Commas separate items in a series:

> Martiniquans dance to *steel drums, clarinets, empty bottles, and banjos.* Four nouns.

> *Dressing in colorful costumes, dancing through the streets, and thoroughly enjoying the celebration,* Martiniquans celebrate Carnival with enthusiasm. Three participial (verbal) phrases.

Quotations

Commas set off quoted sentences from the words that introduce them:

> "A wise man," says David Hume, "proportions his belief to the evidence."

> According to Plato, "Writing will produce forgetfulness" in writers because "they will not need to exercise their memories." The second clause is not set off with a comma.

Coordinate Adjectives

Commas separate adjectives that equally modify a noun:

> The "food pyramid" was designed as a *meaningful, memorable* way in which to represent the ideal daily diet. Two adjectives modify the noun *way* equally.

Addresses and Dates

Use a comma to separate city and state in an address, but do not set off the zip code:

> Glen Ridge, New Jersey 07028 *or* Glen Ridge, NJ 07028

In a sentence, a state name is enclosed in commas:

> The letter from Glen Ridge, New Jersey, arrived by express mail.

Dates are treated similarly:

> January 5, 1886 *but* 5 January 1886
>
> The events of January 5, 1886, are no longer remembered. When other punctuation is not required, the year is followed by a comma.

When Not to Use a Comma

Some people mistakenly believe that commas should be used wherever they might pause in speech. A comma does mean pause, but not all pauses are marked by commas. Use a comma only when you know you need one. Avoid the following comma uses:

1. To set off restrictive sentence elements:

    > People, *who want a balanced diet,* can use the food pyramid as a guide. The restrictive *who* clause is necessary to identify *people* and should not be set off with commas.

2. To separate a subject from its verb and a preposition from its object:

    > People who want a balanced diet, can use the food pyramid as a guide. The comma following the *who* clause separates the subject, *people*, from its verb, *can use*.

3. To follow a coordinating conjunction (see 1B Comma Splices):

    > The food pyramid describes a new approach to a balanced diet. But, the meat and dairy industries opposed it. The coordinating conjunction *but* should not be set off with a comma.

4. To separate two independent clauses (see 1B Comma Splices) not joined with a coordinating conjunction:

    > The pyramid shows fewer servings of dairy and meat products, therefore, consumers would buy less of these higher-priced foods. The comma should be replaced with a semicolon (7B).

5. To set off coordinate elements joined with a coordinating conjunction:

    > Vegetables and fruits are near the bottom of the pyramid, *and should be eaten several times a day.* The coordinating conjunction *and* joins a second verb, *should be eaten*, not a second independent clause; therefore no comma is needed.

6D Colon

The colon is used most often to introduce an explanatory element, often in the form of a list:

The space shuttle *Challenger* lifted off on January 28, 1986, with a seven-member crew: Francis R. Scobee, Michael J. Smith, Ronald E. McNair, Ellison S. Onizuka, Judith A. Resnik, Gregory B. Jarvis, and Christa McAuliffe. The list explains *crew*.

A twelve-member investigating team discovered the cause of the disaster: a leak in one of the shuttle's two solid-fuel booster rockets. The phrase explains the *cause of the disaster*.

Colons have a few other set uses:

Time: 10:15 a.m.

Salutation in a business letter: Dear Patricia Morton:

Biblical reference: Genesis 2:3

6E Dash

The dash separates sentence elements with greater emphasis than a comma:

In *The War of the Worlds* (1898), science fiction writer H. G. Wells described an intense beam of light that destroyed objects on contact—the laser.

It is also used to set off a non-restrictive sentence element (see 3B Restrictive and Non-Restrictive Modifiers) that might be confusing if set off with commas:

A number of medical uses—performing eye surgery, removing tumors, and unclogging coronary arteries—make the laser more than a destructive weapon. The three explanatory items separated by commas are set off from the rest of the sentence with dashes.

Be careful not to use a hyphen when you intend to add a dash to a sentence; the dash is generally the length of two hyphens.

6F Quotation Marks

The main use for quotation marks is to set off direct quotations:

Professor Charlotte Johnson announced, "Interdisciplinary science is combining fields of scientific knowledge to make up new disciplines."

"Biochemistry," she went on to say, "combines biology and chemistry."

Quotations within quotations are marked with single quotation marks:

> "The term 'interdisciplinary science' thus describes a change in how processes are investigated," she concluded.

Use quotation marks correctly with other punctuation marks. Periods and commas always go inside the end quotation marks; colons and semicolons almost always go outside the quotation. Dashes, question marks, and exclamation points go inside or outside depending on meaning—inside if the mark applies to the quotation and outside if it applies to the surrounding sentence.

Do not use quotation marks to set off indirect quotations:

> The professor said that histology and cytology are different branches of study.

6G Other Marks

Parentheses

Parentheses enclose interrupting elements, setting them off from the rest of the sentence or discourse with a greater separation than other enclosing marks such as commas and dashes. They usually add explanatory information that might seem digressive to the topic:

> The Particle Beam Fusion Accelerator *(PBFA II)* is a device designed to produce energy by fusion. Parentheses set off an abbreviation that will henceforth be used in place of the full term.

Parentheses are always used in pairs. They might have internal punctuation (as in the second example), but marks related to the sentence as a whole go outside the parentheses. Parentheses are almost never preceded by a comma. Note the following example:

> During fusion *(joining of two atomic nuclei to form a larger nucleus),* mass is converted to energy. Parenthetical element is followed by a comma, showing that it relates to *fusion*. If it had been preceded by a comma, it would appear, illogically, to relate to *mass*.

Brackets

Square brackets have limited uses and are not interchangeable with parentheses. Their most common use is to mark insertions in quoted material:

> Describing the Great Depression, Frederick Lewis Allen says, "The total amount of money paid out in wages *[in 1932]* was 60 percent less than in 1929." The words *in 1932* were not part of the original text.

Ellipsis Dots

Ellipsis dots (spaced periods) are used in quotations to indicate where words have been omitted. Three spaced dots mark omissions within a sentence. If the omission comes at the end of your sentence but not at the end of the original sentence, use four spaced periods:

> One of the legacies of the Great Depression, says Frederick Lewis Allen, is that "if in- dividual Americans are in deep trouble, . . . their government [should] come to their aid." Words following a comma in the original sentence are omitted within the sentence. The brackets enclose an inserted word.

> This idea, adds Allen, "was fiercely contested for years. . . ." Allen's sentence did not end at *years*, where the quoted sentence ends.

When using ellipsis dots, be careful not to distort the meaning of the original by your se- lection of what to include and what to omit.

Credits

Text Credits

"Don't Believe the Hypermarket" by Sarah Irving from "New Internationalist," November 2006. Used by permission.

"Genre Jumping Pays Off" by Jon Weisman from "Daily Variety," January 24, 2006. Copyright © 2010 Reed Business Information, a division of Reed Elsevier, Inc. Used by permission.

"The Whole Damn Bus Is Cheering" by Michael Bierut in DesignObserver.com, 2004. Used by permission of the author.

"Writing with Pictures" an excerpt from UNDERSTANDING COMICS by Scott McCloud, pages 8-13. Copyright © 1993, 1994 by Scott McCloud. Reprinted by permission of HarperCollins Publishers.

"Pollock Paints a Picture" by Robert Goodnough from "ARTnews," November 2007. Copyright © 1951, ARTnews, LLC, May.

"What Boy Crisis?" by Judith Warner from "The New York Times," July 3, 2006. Copyright © 2006 The New York Times. All rights reserved. Used by permission and protected by the Copyright Laws of the United States. The printing, copying, redistribution, or retransmission of the Material without express written permission is prohibited.

"Re-Examining the 'Boy Crisis'" by Kathleen Parker, first appeared in The Lowell Sun, July 9, 2006. Used by permission.

"Students Set Rules at New York School" by Nahal Toosi, Associated Press, November 21, 2006. Used with permission of The Associated Press. Copyright © 2010. All rights reserved.

"Take the Debate Over Degrading Rap Videos Off Mute" by Michele Goodwin from "The Christian Science Monitor," August 11, 2006. Used by permission of the author.

"Where Did That Video Spoofing Gore's Film Come From?" by Antonio Regalado and Dionne Searcey from The Wall Street Journal, August 3, 2006. Copyright © 2006 by Dow Jones and Company, Inc. Reproduced with permission of Dow Jones and Company, Inc. in the format Textbook via Copyright Clearance Center.

"Meltdown: Running Out of Time on Global Warming" by Bill McKibben from "The Christian Century," February 2007. Copyright © 2007 by the Christian Century. Reproduced by permission.

"Unboxed: Yes, People Still Read, but Now It's Social" by Steven Johnson from The New York Times, © June 20, 2010 The New York Times. All rights reserved. Used by permission and protected by the Copyright Laws of the United States. The printing, copying, redistribution, or retransmission of the Material without express written permission is prohibited.

From AN AMERICAN CHILDHOOD by Annie Dillard. Copyright © 1987 by Annie Dillard. Reproduced by permission of HarperCollins Publishers.

From "The Veil", from PERSEPHOLIS: THE STORY OF A CHILDHOOD by Marjane Satrapi, translated by Mattias Ripa and Blake Ferris, translation copyright © 2003 by L'Association, Paris, France. Used by permission of Pantheon Books, a division of Random House, Inc.

"Coming Into Language" by Jimmy Santiago Baca. Copyright Jimmy Santiago Baca. Used by permission.

"A Hero's Journey" by Neil Broverman from "The Advocate," February 2007. Used by permission.

"Raw Nerve: The Political Art of Steve Brodner" reprinted with permission from USA Today Magazine, September 2008. Copyright © 2008 by the Society for the Advancement of Education, Inc. All rights reserved.

"Soulful Survivor Sewing" by Tara Cady Sartorius from "Arts & Activities," February 2009. Reproduced with permission of Arts & Activities magazine, www.artsandactivities.com.

"Reading the Speeches of McCain and Obama Has Made Me Ashamed of Our Political Class" by Matthew Paris from The Times, March 29, 2008. Copyright © 2008 The Times, nisyndication.com. Used by permission.

"A Word from Our Sponsor" by Jennie Yabroff (with Susan Elgin) from Newsweek, August 4, 2008. Copyright © 2008 Newsweek, Inc. All rights reserved. Used by permission and protected by the Copyright Laws of the United States. The printing, copying, redistribution, or retransmission of the Material without express written permission is prohibited.

"Auto Erotic: Jacqueline Hassink's Car Girls" by Francine Prose. Copyright © 1997 by Francine Prose. First appeared in the journal APERTURE. Reprinted with permission of the Denise Shannon Literary Agency, Inc. All rights reserved.

"Let's Talk About Sex" by Anna Quindlen from Newsweek, March 7, 2009. Copyright © 2009 by Anna Quindlen. Reproduced by permission of International Creative Management, Inc.

"Seeking a Drinking Age Debate: Perspectives from an Amethyst Initiative Signatory About Moving the Dialog Forward" by Elisabeth Muhlenfeld. Used with permission, University Business Magazine, Vol. 11, No. 10, October 2008.

"Drinking Age Paradox" by George Will from The Washington Post, April 2007. Copyright © 2007 The Washington Post. All rights reserved. Used by permission and protected by the Copyright Laws of the United States. The printing, copying, redistribution, or retransmission of the Material without express written permission is prohibited."

Music administered by Sony/ATV Publishing LLC, 8 Music Square West, Nashville, TN 37203. All rights reserved. Used by permission. "Close My Eyes" Words and Music by Mariah Carey and Walter Afanasieff. Copyright © 1997 SONGS OF UNIVERSAL, INC., RYE SONGS, SONY/ATV MUSIC PUBLISHING LLC and WALLY WORLD MUSIC. All Rights for RYE SONGS Controlled and Administered by SONGS OF UNIVERSAL, INC. All Rights for WALLY WORLD MUSIC Controlled and Administered by SONY/ATV MUSIC PUBLISHING LLC, 8 Music Square West, Nashville, TN 3720.

"Watch Me Shine" Words and Music by Dino Esposito. © 2001 EMI BLACKWOOD MUSIC INC. and ONID MUSIC. All Rights Controlled and Administered by EMI BLACKWOOD MUSIC INC. All Rights Reserved. International Copyright Secured. Used by permission. Reprinted by permission of Hal Leonard Corporation.

From The New York Times. © March 22, 2009, The New York Times. All rights reserved. Used by permission and protected by the Copyright Laws of the United States. The printing, copying, redistribution or retransmission of the Material without express written permission is prohibited.

"Keep Your Resume Honest" by Martha Fay Africa and Deborah Ben-Canaan in "The Recorder," copyright 2009. Reprinted by permission of ALM.

Photo Credits

Page 1: © Clearview/Alamy; **p. 2 (top left):** Peter Barritt/Alamy Images; (top right): Peter Barritt/Alamy Images; (bottom): © Brendan McDermid/CORBIS All Rights Reserved; **p. 20:** NBC-TV/Picture Desk, Inc./Kobal Collection; **p. 25:** Sonny Boyden/PhotoEdit Inc.; **pp. 34, 54 (top):** Hans Namuth. Photograph of Jackson Pollock Painting, The Springs, New York, 1950. National Portrait Gallery/Smithsonian Institution, Washington DC. © 1991 Hans Namuth Estate/ARS Artists Rights Society; **p. 54 (bottom):** Hans Namuth Ltd.; **p. 55:** © Pollock-Krasner Foundation/Artists Rights Society (ARS), New York/Carnegie Museum of Art, Pittsburgh; Gift of Frank R. S. Kaplan; **p. 58:** Tom Carter/PhotoEdit Inc.; **p. 63:** Courtesy Daniel Anderson; **p. 85 (top):** Phyllis Leibowitz/Stone/Getty Images; **p. 85 (bottom):** Gilbert Carrasquillo/Getty Images-WireImage.com; **pp. 89, 117:** Lawrence Bender Prods./The Kobal Collection/Lee, Eric/Picture Desk, Inc./Kobal Collection; **p. 110:** Image courtesy of The Advertising Archives/The Advertising Archives; **p. 119:** Courtesy Daniel Anderson; **p. 121:** Patrick J. Lynch/Photo Researchers, Inc.; **pp. 122, 129–135:** From "The Veil," from PERSEPOLIS: THE STORY OF A CHILDHOOD by Marjane Satrapi, translated by Mattias Ripa and Blake Ferris, translation copyright © 2003 by L'Association, Paris, France. Used by permission of Pantheon Books, a division of Random House, Inc. For online information about other Random House, Inc. books and authors, see the Internet web site at http://www.randomhouse.com. **pp. 152, 159, 160, 161:** Copyright © Steve Brodner. Used by permission. **p. 165:** Montgomery Museum of Fine Arts, Montgomery, Alabama, Gift of Kempf Hogan. **pp. 177, 185:** Courtesy of the Library of Congress; **p. 189:** Jacqueline Hassink; **pp. 201 211 (top):** Natacha Pisarenko/AP Wide World Photos; **p. 211 (bottom):** PETA/People for the Ethical Treatment of Animals; **p. 222:** Syracuse Newspaper/The Image Works; **p. 248:** Stuwdamdorp/Alamy Images; **p. 265:** Courtesy of adbusters.org; **p. 273:** © Warner Bros./Courtesy Everett Collection; **p. 291:** CHOCKSTONE PICTURES/THE KOBAL COLLECTION; **p. 314 (left):** CORBIS-NY; **p. 314 (center):** © Marc Asnin/CORBIS SABA All Rights Reserved; **p. 314 (right):** Joseph Sohm/CORBIS- NY; **p. 317:** Fred W. McDarrah/Getty Images; **p. 318 (top):** Fred W. McDarrah/Getty Images; **p. 318 (bottom):** © Bettmann/CORBIS All Rights Reserved; **p. 319 (top):** © Terry Schmitt/San Francisco Chronicle/Corbis All Rights Reserved; **p. 319 (bottom):** © John Storey/San Francisco Chronicle/Corbis All Rights Reserved; **p. 320:** Sara Krulwich/New York Times Co./Getty Images; **pp. 323, 324, 325:** W. Eugene Smith//Time Life Pictures/Getty Images; **p. 331 (top and bottom):** Courtesy of the Library of Congress; **pp. 332, 333:** National Archives and Records Administration; **p. 334:** Bonnie Kamin/PhotoEdit Inc.; **p. 337:** Getty Images Inc.-Stone Allstock; **p. 383:** Courtesy Michael Greer; **p. 411:** © Allstar Picture Library/Alamy; **pp. 421, 428:** © Warner Brothers Enterprises/Topham/The Image Works; **pp. 430, 434:** Courtesy of the Library of Congress; **pp. 437, 442:** Photos courtesy of NASA/JPL. Screenshot created by Daniel Anderson. **pp. 452, 458:** Art © Romare Bearden Foundation/Licensed by VAGA, New York, NY/Courtesy of the Library of Congress; **p. 457:** Catherine Ursillo/Photo Researchers, Inc.; **pp. 460, 464:** Photos courtesy Daniel Anderson; screenshot courtesy of Flickr; **p. 467:** Britta Jaschinski © Dorling Kindersley; **pp. 468, 474:** William Eggleston, "Untitled (Nehi bottle on car hood)". From the Los Alamos Portfolio. 1965-74. © 2009 Eggleston Artistic Trust, courtesy Cheim & Read, New York. Used with permission. All rights reserved. **p. 472 (top):** Copyright © John Greim/Mira.com; **p. 472 (bottom):** Eric Meacher © Dorling Kindersley; **p. 473:** Douglas E. Curran/Getty Images, Inc.-Agence France Presse; **p. 477:** Wyeth, Andrew (1917–2009), "Christina's World". 1948. Tempera on gessoed panel, 32 1/4 X 47 3/4". Purchase. The Museum of Modern Art, New York, NY, U.S.A. Digital Image © The Museum of Modern Art/Licensed by SCALA/Art Resource, NY; **pp. 481, 483:** Apple Computer, Inc.; **p. 488:** Bill Aron/PhotoEdit Inc.; **p. 491:** Getty Images-Stockbyte, Royalty Free

E-Book Photo Credits

Index

Note: Page numbers followed by f refer to Figures